# I to Myself

'Say's I to myself' should be the motto of my journal.

—Thoreau in his Journal, 11 November 1851

# I to Myself

AN ANNOTATED SELECTION FROM THE JOURNAL OF HENRY D. THOREAU

Edited by Jeffrey S. Cramer

Yale University Press   New Haven and London

Designed by Sonia Shannon.
Set in Adobe Garamond Pro by Tseng Information
Systems, Inc.
Printed in the United States of America.

*Library of Congress Cataloging-in-Publication Data*
Thoreau, Henry David, 1817–1862.
[Journal. Selections]
I to myself : an annotated selection from the journal
of Henry D. Thoreau / edited by Jeffrey S. Cramer.
    p.    cm.
Includes bibliographical references and index.
ISBN 978-0-300-11172-9 (alk. paper)
1. Thoreau, Henry David, 1817–1862—Diaries.
2. Authors, American—19th century—Diaries.
I. Cramer, Jeffrey S., 1955– II. Title.
PS3053.A2 2007
818′.303—dc22
[B]
                                    2007014317

A catalogue record for this book is available from the
British Library.

♾ The paper in this book meets the guidelines for
permanence and durability of the Committee on
Production Guidelines for Book Longevity of the
Council on Library Resources.

10  9  8  7  6  5  4  3  2  1

*To Lee and Cerf Berkley*

THANK YOU

A man does best when he is most himself.

—21 January 1852

# Contents

# Preface

In a letter to the secretary of his Harvard class Thoreau wrote, "I am a Schoolmaster—a Private Tutor, a Surveyor—a Gardener, a Farmer—a Painter, I mean a House Painter, a Carpenter, a Mason, a Day-Laborer, a Pencil-Maker, a Glass-paper Maker, a Writer, and sometimes a Poetaster." When he received a request from the Association for the Advancement of Science on his particular branch of study, Thoreau declared in his journal: "The fact is I am a mystic, a transcendentalist, and a natural philosopher to boot. Now I think of it, I should have told them at once that I was a transcendentalist."

A reader of *Walden* knows one Thoreau; a reader of his natural history essays may know another; and a reader of his social reform writings still another. Some know of a curmudgeon and egoist; others of a devoted friend. Some recognize a man who relishes solitude; others a neighbor recording the latest news and gossip. Some see a paragon of self-sufficiency; others a man who ate dinner with the Emersons. Some know of a deeply spiritual person; others of an irreverent and irreligious individual.

Thoreau wrote of Sir Walter Raleigh that it was not "of so much importance to inquire of a man what actions he performed at one and what at another period, as what manner of man he was at all periods." The purpose of this collection is to answer that question—what manner of man?—as it pertains to one Henry D. Thoreau, of Concord, Massachusetts, in all his manifestations: the natural historian, the chronicler of local history; the social reformer, the Transcendentalist, the environmentalist; the disciple, the mentor; the friend, the brother, the son; the writer, the man.

# Acknowledgments

A work like this could not have been made without the help of literally hundreds of people, known and unknown. Many are acknowledged below, but there are many who, I regret, have become anonymous and for these omissions of credit I apologize. There is generosity and enthusiasm in the world for which I am appreciative, and it is rewarding to know that such dedication and passion exists.

I would like to thank Robert M. Peck, of the Academy of Natural Sciences, Philadelphia; Thomas Knoles, American Antiquarian Society; Jeanne Bracken, Lincoln Public Library; Janice Chadbourne and Diane Ota of the Boston Public Library, who helped with questions about art and music; Denis Lien of the University of Minnesota Libraries; Lee Townsend, Extension Entomologist, Department of Entomology, University of Kentucky, for his help with oak galls; J. Walter Brain with help locating the Depot Field; David Wood of the Concord Museum; Nancy Browne for resurrecting her understanding of the German language; Edmund A. Schofield; Edward J. Renehan, Jr.; Ray Angelo, of the Department of Organismic and Evolutionary Biology at Harvard University, for his help with several botanical questions; Graeme Rymill of the University of Western Australia Library; Josephine Crawley Quinn of Worcester College, Oxford; and my colleagues on Project Wombat.

Bob Maker was more than generous in sharing his unpublished research about Thoreau's visits to New Bedford.

For sharing their thoughts with me about Thoreau, I would

like to thank: Annie Dillard, Robert Finch, and Scott Russell Sanders.

I have also been a beneficiary of the assistance of librarians at Houghton Library at Harvard University and the Berg Collection of the New York Public Library; Sue Hodson of the Henry E. Huntington Library in San Marino, California; and Christine Nelson of the Pierpont Morgan Library.

Greg Joly meticulously read portions of this text, and for his unflagging encouragement, perspective, and enthusiasm I am indebted beyond words. Helen Bowdoin has been a true support in innumerable ways. I feel fortunate to be able to call them both friends.

I am indebted to the various Thoreau scholars who have donated their research to the collections of the Walden Woods Project, the Thoreau Society, and the Ralph Waldo Emerson Society. These collections, housed at the Thoreau Institute at Walden Woods, Lincoln, Massachusetts, and managed by Walden Woods Project, are an invaluable and unparalleled resource, without which this book could not have been completed. And to Don Henley, Founder and President of the Walden Woods Project, and to Kathi Anderson, its Executive Director, for their vision of a center for Thoreau studies, and for the opportunities it has offered, and the doors it has opened, thank you.

I especially want to thank John Kulka of Yale University Press, for whom *Walden* was only the beginning. His support and enthusiasm for this project have been invaluable. Through my association with John I have learned the difference between having an editor and having a *great* editor.

And my family—my daughters, Kazia and Zoë, and my wife, Julia Berkley—because Henry has become a much more permanent guest in our home than they ever could have anticipated.

Grateful acknowledgement is made to the following institutions to quote from the following manuscript material:

- Diaries of William Ellery Channing, Houghton MS Am 800.6, and Thoreau's manuscript journal passages for 1843, Houghton MS Am 278.5, by permission of the Houghton Library, Harvard University.
- Daniel Ricketson's sketch of Martha Simons's house, and Thoreau's sketch of the *Phallus impudicus,* courtesy of the Morgan Library and Museum.
- Journal passages for 1848 through 28 February 1850 from Huntington HM13182, courtesy of the Henry E. Huntington Library in San Marino, California.
- Letter from Thoreau to George Thatcher, 9 February 1849, courtesy of the Thoreau Society (Raymond Adams Collection) and the Thoreau Institute at Walden Woods.

# Introduction

"My Journal is that of me which would else spill over and run to waste," Thoreau wrote in 1841. At Walden a few years later he wrote this about the purpose of his journal:

> From all points of the compass, from the earth beneath and the heavens above, have come these inspirations and been entered duly in the order of their arrival in the journal. Thereafter, when the time arrived, they are winnowed into lectures, and again, in due time, from lectures into essays. And at last they stand, like the cubes of Pythagoras, firmly on either basis; like statues on their pedestals, but the statues rarely take hold of hands. There is only such connection and series as is attainable in the galleries. And this affects their immediate practical and popular influence.

Nearly two million words written over twenty-five years, Thoreau's journal is in itself a greater literary production than most authors create in a lifetime. Sheer magnitude in words cannot, however, account for the journal's longevity and attraction. That comes from the force of Thoreau's consideration and reflection in it. It is the record of a lifetime of thought as were the writings of Montaigne, Rousseau, and Pepys.

Henry David Thoreau, from a daguerreotype by Benjamin D. Maxham, 18 June 1856, as published in *The Writings of Henry D. Thoreau* by Houghton Mifflin in 1906

Thoreau wrote in his journal that autobiography is preferred over biography: "If I am not I, who will be?" Or again: "Is not the poet bound to write his own biography? Is there any other work for him but a good journal? We do not wish to know how his imaginary hero, but how he, the actual hero, lived from day to day."

In Thoreau's completed essays and books, the works he saw through or readied for publication, the personal pronoun is not strictly Henry D. Thoreau. The "I" found within those pages is as much a persona as Mark Twain or the narrator of *Remembrance of Things Past* whom we call Marcel Proust. In those works, as he wrote of Thomas Carlyle, "We do not want a Daguerreotype likeness." The individual balances between Thoreau and not-Thoreau.

In the journal, however, we come closer to Thoreau, to the Thoreau who traveled around Concord, spending four or more hours a day in nature; who dined with friends, went to the lyceum, visited the libraries of Cambridge and Boston, helped fugitive slaves, led huckleberrying parties, and played his flute. We come a little closer to the man of whom Emerson wrote, "It was a pleasure and a privilege to walk with him," and of whom Mrs. Minot Pratt said, "I loved to hear him talk, but I did not like his books so well. . . . They did not do him justice. I liked to see Thoreau rather in his life."

It is a mistake to think of the objective of a journal as being synonymous with that of a diary, which is in many ways a private work, and yet the differences between such genres as diary, journal, autobiography, and memoir are subtle at best, and may be more a matter of literary analysis than artistic choice. "Of all strange and unaccountable things," Thoreau admitted in 1841, "this journalizing is the strangest." The private practice of writing a journal was, in Thoreau's circle and elsewhere, made public through sharing with friends and family. The raw and unpolished text was often returned to and corrected or revised. Emerson even went so far as to publish excerpts from his late brother's journal as "Notes from the Journal of a Scholar" in the *Dial,* and Bronson Alcott published selections from his own journals as "Days from a Diary."

The artlessness of these spontaneous outpourings was in itself an art. A reader was often present to the writer. Although he wrote in 1851 that "'Say's I to myself' should be the motto of my journal," Thoreau was no longer writing simply to, or about, himself. As he noted about Menu, the legendary author of the Hindu code of religious law, Thoreau, too, was writing "from the loftiest plateau of the soul," and, like Menu, what he wrote "does not imply any contemporaneous speaker." His writing became imbued with universality.

The very nature of a journal gives the effect of being a record of immediate responses, of having been written extemporaneously. In Thoreau's instance, however, this was not always the case, and often the impression had a small window of time in which to germinate. "I find some advantage in describing the experience of a day on the day following," he wrote on 20 April 1853. "At this distance it is more ideal, like the landscape seen with the head inverted, or reflections in water." When Thoreau wrote that he was a clerk who at evening transferred "the account from day-book to ledger," he was being literal as well as figurative. He wrote minutes in a field notebook and afterward, usually the same evening when he got home, but sometimes slightly later, he transcribed those entries into his journal. Looking back over twenty years of journaling, Thoreau wrote in 1857: "I would fain make two reports in my Journal, first the incidents and observations of to-day; and by to-morrow I review the same and record what was omitted before, which will often be the most significant and poetic part. I do not know at first what it is that charms me. The men and things of to-day are wont to lie fairer and truer in to-morrow's memory."

It was the poet's business, he wrote, to be "continually watching the moods of his mind, as the astronomer watches the aspects of the heavens. What might we not expect from a long life faithfully spent in this wise? . . . As travellers go around the world and report natural objects and phenomena, so faithfully let another stay at home and report the phenomena of his own life." But for a Harvard graduate to stay at home, watching the moods of his mind rather than venturing forth to a more culturally honorable and productive profession, in the clergy, law, teaching, or even business, was an act of rebelliousness and defiance against his neighbors. The task he set himself was not one easily appreciated. As he lamented, thinking about the ancient Scandinavian poets, "Surely the scald's office was a significant and an honorable one then."

Thoreau's business was to explore the fundamental facts of existence in order to be able to recognize the real, the eternal truth and substance underlying all existence, as distinct from the actual, the distracting and sometimes misdirecting commotion that prevents our paying attention. The task he set himself was to find the reality that transcended his day-to-day experiences. It was a sacred quest for the miracle that daily fronted him: life; nature; spirit. "There is no interpreter," he wrote in 1850, "between us and our consciousness."

Thoreau was aware that there were, as he wrote in *A Week on the Concord and Merrimack Rivers,* "manifold visions in the direction of every object." To appreciate this complexity may take several readings of that book. As he wrote to the Emersons, "It is the height of art that on the first perusal plain common sense should appear—on the second severe truth—and on a third beauty—and having these warrants for its depth and reality, we may then enjoy the beauty forever more." It is not always possible to immediately appreciate the correspondence between things seen and things unseen. "Poetry," Thoreau wrote in 1851, "puts an interval between the impression and the expression,—waits till the seed germinates naturally."

By 1851 his journal had become a work in its own right, regardless of its use as a storehouse or testing ground. Thoreau no longer cut up pages, as he did earlier, to be arranged to create a draft of an essay or lecture, or simply excised. That actual pages from the journal found their way into the *Walden* manuscript, for instance, shows that before this time Thoreau did not yet think of his journal as having a purpose independent of its function as a notebook of draft material. After about 1850 the journal began to have an integrity that would no longer be compromised. Thoreau wrote in the journal nearly every day for the next ten years, from mid-1851 (previously his journaling was not as consistent) until his final illness prevented him from doing so in late 1861.

Critical assessment of the journal over the past quarter century has shown that many consider it Thoreau's greatest achievement as a writer, no small claim for the author of *Walden*. By 1851 the journal had become what could only be considered a life-work, that by which his life could be defined, and the creation of which was central to his existence.

As he wrote in "Walking," "I think that I cannot preserve my health and spirits unless I spend four hours a day at least—and it is commonly more than that—sauntering through the woods and over the hills and fields absolutely free from all worldly engagements." But this was only part of the story. He also preserved his health and spirits by writing, by deliberate contemplation of the day's events, the day's thoughts and moods and conversations, with himself, his neighbors, and nature.

Although a few excerpts from the journal were made public at Thoreau's funeral in 1862, and were first published as part of Emerson's funeral oration in the *Atlantic Monthly*, interest had surfaced many years before. As early as 1843 John L. O'Sullivan, founder and editor of the *United States Magazine and Democratic Review*, wrote Thoreau asking for "some of those extracts from your Journal, reporting some of your private interviews with nature, with which I have before been so much pleased." Ten years later, in 1853, Thoreau's friend Ellery Channing was beginning to prepare a book of passages from the journals of Emerson and Thoreau as well as from his own. Channing made transcriptions from Thoreau's journal that he incorporated into *Thoreau: The Poet-Naturalist* (1873) and used as the basis for his "Days and Nights in Concord," published in *Scribner's Monthly* (1878), but the earlier volume was never finished.

As the posthumous significance of Thoreau's journal grew, there were still roadblocks. Thoreau's sister Sophia, who acted as his literary executor, was reluctant to see them published. When Thomas Wentworth Higginson was unable to secure permission from Sophia and tried to engage the help of the respected Concord citizen Judge Rockwood Hoar, he was told by Hoar, "Who would ever bother to read Thoreau's journals if published?" The Emerson and Channing pieces provided the only extracts published during Sophia's life. It wasn't until her death in 1876, when the journals passed to Harrison Gray Otis Blake, a friend and disciple of Thoreau, that their long publishing history truly began.

The journals and other papers were entrusted to Bronson Alcott when Sophia moved from Concord to Maine in 1873. She instructed Alcott that the journals were "not to be public, nor copied for publication by anyone." He kept them under lock and key in his attic, writing, "I am to hold them sacred from all but Thoreau's friends, allow none to take them away for perusal. . . . Many volumes may be compiled from them, and will be when his editor appears." Alcott, on hearing that Blake had inherited the journals, wrote in his own journal: "He, or some one interested in Thoreau's genius, should edit selections at least from these papers. Volumes as unique and instructive may be compiled from them as those already published; and Thoreau's fame is sure to increase with years."

Following the suggestion of Alcott that he publish Thoreau's journals in seasonal excerpts, somewhat like Alcott's own *Concord Days,* Blake selected and arranged journal passages that were published in the *Atlantic Monthly* beginning in 1878 and collected into four seasonal volumes published between 1881 and 1892: *Early Spring in Massachusetts, Summer, Winter,* and *Autumn.* Although some reviews of these selections from Thoreau's journals argued that such arrangements were "unfortunate for his reputation" (the *Nation,* 26 January 1893) and showed only a "narrow range" (the *Nation,* 31 July 1884), the volumes were critically successful and popular, and they were included in Houghton Mifflin's 1894 Riverside Edition of Thoreau's works.

*Daniel Ricketson and His Friends* (1902), a memorial volume edited by Ricketson's children, contained many passages from Thoreau's journals pertaining to his visits with Ricketson in New Bedford and Ricketson's visits to Concord. These excerpts were more whole, although episodic, and gave a fuller view of Thoreau's range than did the seasonal excerpts, but they centered on the Ricketson-Thoreau friendship, and the book had a very limited circulation.

Blake bequeathed Thoreau's manuscripts to E. Harlow Russell. This was an attempt to keep them away from Franklin Sanborn, who, many believed, would use the manuscripts for his own personal advancement and fame. Although Sanborn may well have used his friendship and knowledge of Thoreau to his personal benefit, he was nevertheless instrumental, along with Blake, in popularizing Thoreau and advancing his reputation. Ironically, Russell proved far more self-interested. Appreciating the monetary value of Thoreau's manuscripts more than any other quality in them, he sold the publication rights to Houghton Mifflin and the journals—thirty-nine manuscript volumes held in a pine box possibly of Thoreau's fashioning—to Stephen Wakeman, which led to their being placed in the Pierpont Morgan Library in New York in 1909.

The success of Blake's published excerpts led Bliss Perry to advocate publication of the journals in full: the contents of the then thirty-eight manuscript volumes. One volume, the third, had apparently been lost by Blake. In 1906, in an unprecedented publishing venture, Houghton Mifflin published what was considered Thoreau's entire extant journal. It was edited over three years by Francis Allen, an editor at Houghton Mifflin and amateur ornithologist, and the writer and naturalist Bradford Torrey. Although this was purportedly Thoreau's complete journal, sections from the early journals were missing, as well as what is referred to as the "lost" journal—the third manuscript volume once in Blake's possession, which did not resurface until 1912 and would not be edited for publication until Perry Miller's *Consciousness in Concord* (1958). Editorial decisions were made to exclude certain material—sentence fragments, long quotations befitting a commonplace book, lengthy lists of plants or other natural phenomena, and the material printed "*in extenso* in the volume entitled 'The Maine Woods.'"

The 1906 edition of the journals has been reprinted in full four times: in 1949 by Houghton Mifflin; in 1962 by Dover in two folio volumes with four of the 1906 pages printed on each large-format page; in 1969 by AMS Press in a facsimile reprint of the entire 1906 edition; and in 1984 by Peregrine Smith in a boxed fourteen-volume paperback edition, with the text of the "lost" journal appended, creating the most complete edition to date. The Peregrine Smith edition is the only paperback release of the journals to date.

In the century since the 1906 edition of the journals, more than twenty volumes of selections from Thoreau's journals have been published. Most had a very specific subject as the focus of their selection process. These include Thoreau on birds (*Notes on New England Birds,* 1910); Thoreau as a naturalist (*In Wildness Is the Preservation of the World,* 1962, *The River,* 1963, *Thoreau Revisited: Diary of a Country Year,* 1973, *Thoreau's Country,* 1999); Thoreau on his neighbors (*Men of Concord,* 1936); Thoreau as night-walker (*The Moon,* 1927); Thoreau as a writer (*H. D. Thoreau: A Writer's Journal,* 1961); and Thoreau as belle-lettrist (*Thoreau's World: Miniatures from His Journal,* 1971). Some told only one story, such as *A Pig Tale* (1947) and *What Befell at Mrs. Brooks* (1974); another arranged journal passages as poetry, in *All Nature Is My Bride* (1975). One covered a single year in its entirety, *A Year in Thoreau's Journal, 1851* (1993), while another arranged passages into a year's worth of selections: *Daily Observations* (2005).

Only two books attempted to present a more complete picture of Thoreau. Odell Shepard's *The Heart of Thoreau's Journals* (1927) focused on Thoreau as "a man of letters," with the editor selecting passages from the 1906 edition that seemed to him "particularly memorable either for their thought, for their beauty, or for their revelation of the man who wrote them and of the times in which he lived." Carl Bode did not describe the selection process used in his *Selected Journals of Henry David Thoreau* (1967), although he noted that he did supplement it with brief excerpts from Sanborn's *The First and Last Journeys of Thoreau.*

In 1981, as part of *The Writings of Henry D. Thoreau,* Princeton University Press published the first of a projected sixteen-volume edition of the journals. The Princeton edition of the journals is a masterful and painstaking attempt to reproduce Thoreau's text as accurately as possible. As such, it is a work of unparalleled scholarly achievement. However, the length of time between published volumes, as well as the size and cost of such a multivolume edition, places these books out of reach for most general readers and students.

When a line was omitted from his essay "Chesuncook" during periodical publication, Thoreau wrote, "I hardly need to say that this is a liberty which I will not permit to be taken with my MS. The editor has, in this case, no more right to omit a sentiment than to insert one, or put words into my mouth." This is too often taken as Thoreau's final word on editors and the editorial process. As he wrote: "I do not ask anybody to adopt my opinions, but I do expect that when they ask for them to print, they will print them, or obtain my consent to their alteration or omission. I should not read many books if I thought that they had been thus *expurgated.*"

Thoreau is clear that his thought and opinion must not be altered. He has considerably less concern for other corrections, what he called "other cases of comparatively little importance to me." Although Thoreau suggested that "thoughts written down thus in a journal might be printed in the same form," this policy did not necessarily extend to spelling errors, punctuation, or slips of the pen as he hurriedly made his entries, and should not be adopted as editorial policy. In reviewing the first volume of the Princeton journals for the *New York Times* (20 December 1981) Leon Edel wrote: "For some time it has been clear that many editors have the strange notion that a manuscript book must be treated in print as if it still had its written features."

The journal is neither cohesive nor a finished product. The act of publishing the journal creates an impression of a more finished work than it is. This in itself presents the editor with a difficult choice, whether publishing the journal whole or through selected passages, because ultimately it is the editor's job to remain faithful to the author's intentions and the nature of the journal while fulfilling an obligation to the intended reader. It always comes down to an editorial decision whether a passage is punctuated one way or another, or whether one word is chosen over another, or whether in our arrogance we lay claim to knowing Thoreau's intentions.

Although Thoreau's original notebook jottings—the field notes on which he based the journal—do not exist, the journal was a fluid production. What we read as immediate had already been consciously edited when transcribed from notebook to journal. Over time passages would continue to be corrected, changed, and revised, queries answered, and marginal notations added; the published journal, regardless of the edition, is merely a snapshot of the journal as it existed at one particular moment in time, and always subject to the editorial discipline.

The copy text for *I to Myself,* except where noted in the end matter, is the standard fourteen-volume edition, *The Journal of Henry D. Thoreau,* edited by Bradford Torrey and Francis H. Allen (Boston: Houghton Mifflin, 1906). The purpose of *I to Myself* is to provide a reading text of selections from Thoreau's journals. It is, therefore, not encumbered with elaborate scholarly apparatus.

Readability was a primary determining factor in choosing the copy text. Anticipating a possible need for a more literal transcrip-

Almshouse: G7 (#2)
Annursnack Hill: D3
Back Road: G6–H7
Barrett's Saw & Grist Mill: E5 (#8)
Bateman's Pond: B6–C6
Bear Garden Hill: H6
Bear Hill: J9
Beck Stow's Swamp: E8–E9
Bedford Road: F7–E9
Bedford Road, Old: E9–F9
Bittern Cliff: J6
Blood, Perez: B8 (#11)
Boulder Field: C7
Brown, James Potter: H4 (#18)
Channing, Ellery: F6 (#21)
Clamshell Hill: G5 (#23)
Cliffs, The: J7 (#26)
Conantum: J6–K6
Corner Road: G6–K6
Corner Spring: H5 (#31)
Deep Cut: H7
Dennis, S.: F5
Dodge's or Dakin's Brook: D6–E6
Dove Rock: E6 (#38)
Everett, George: G9 (#43)
Fair Haven Bay, or Pond: J7
Fair Haven Hill: H7
Fair Haven Pond Island: J7 (#44)
Flint's Pond: J10
Goodwin, John: G6 (#50)
Goose Pond: H8
Goose Pond, Little: H9
Gowing Swamp: F9
Great Fields: F8
Great Meadows: D8
Hayden, E. G.: G6
Hayward's Mill Pond: G2
Heywood's Brook: J7 (#55)
Heywood's Meadow: J7 (#56)
Heywood's Peak: H8 (#57)
Heywood's Wood-lot: H8 (#58)
Holbrook's Coffee-House: F7 (#62)

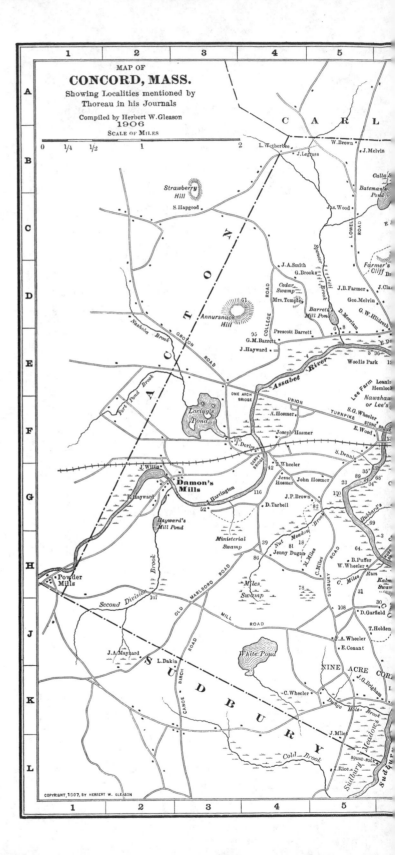

MAP OF
**CONCORD, MASS.**
Showing Localities mentioned by
Thoreau in his Journals
Compiled by Herbert W. Gleason
1906
SCALE OF MILES

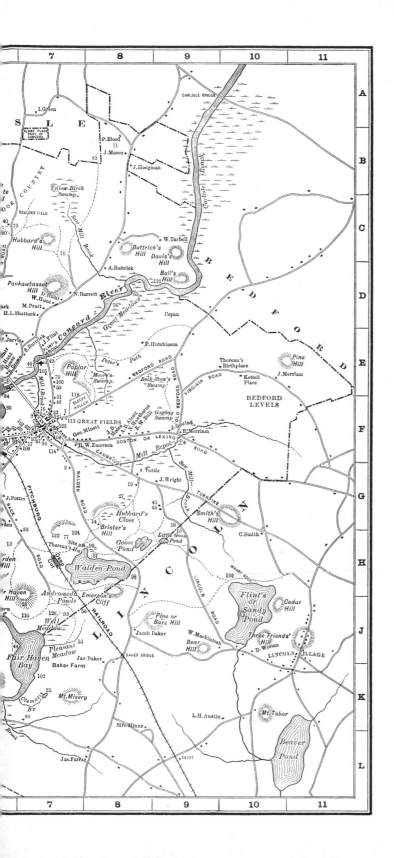

tion of the manuscript journal, Torrey wrote in 1906 that it "may some day be of interest to antiquaries and special students; but such an edition could never be adapted, more than the literal reproduction of Milton's manuscripts, to the needs of those who read for pleasure and general profit." Walter Harding, the first editor-in-chief for *The Writings of Henry D. Thoreau,* agreed. He wrote in his introduction to the 1984 paperback reprint of the journals: "The 1906 edition is not without its advantages. Because it is not encumbered by the Greg-Bowers charts and tables and because Allen did not hesitate to round off some of the rough edges of the manuscript readings, the 1906 edition is in some respects more readable for the layman than is the Princeton Edition." Harding also extolled Francis Allen's accomplishment: "Using principles well in advance of his time, he did a masterly job of editing the entire text."

In their general introduction to the first volume of the Princeton edition, the editors cite as the "most serious limitation" of the 1906 edition its "incompleteness." This has been remedied in *I to Myself* with the addition of excerpted passages from the "lost" journal and new transcriptions from the manuscript journals that were unavailable to Torrey and Allen (see the end matter for further discussion). These transcriptions have been minimally edited in a way stylistically consistent with the 1906 edition. Editorial deletions from the 1906 edition—such as proper names that were replaced by dashes, or Thoreau's expurgated sketch of the *Phallus impudicus*—have also been restored. Thus *I to Myself* presents the first and only annotated selection of Thoreau's journals culled from all available manuscripts and printed editions.

Selectively presenting a work of two million words in one volume is a challenge, and one that no two editors would meet in the same way. The earlier journals, prior to 1851, are sparingly represented here, with some years having no entries at all. This is due to several factors. The journal at this point was more clearly a storehouse for ideas and drafts of material that would find its way into lectures and essays. Many of the best passages from those years are found in *A Week on the Concord and Merrimack Rivers* and *Walden.*

This volume portrays a man of contrary thoughts, wrestling and contradicting himself, arguing with himself and his neighbors, and ultimately observing and questioning. It was my intention in this volume to representatively portray a Thoreau who was neither a naturalist, philosopher, environmentalist, social reformer, nor Transcendentalist, but all of these at all times. Passages that tell us something about Thoreau personally—his love for Ellen Sewall, his setting fire to the woods, his friendships with Emerson, Alcott, and Channing, the death of his father, playing with the family cat—and those that embody his aspirations, his fears, his prejudices, his social quirks and behaviors, his humor, his joy of life, have been given preference, while allowing for a fair representation of passages that offer the familiar Thoreauvian themes found in his other works. Although passages that have found their way into Thoreau's published works are not routinely included here, there is a reasonable sampling of them, to give the reader an understanding of how Thoreau used his journals as a sourcebook for his lectures, essays, and books.

The journal is the record of a journey. In fact, one meaning of journal, albeit now obsolete, is just that: a journey or day's travel. Thoreau once wrote that he yearned "for one of those old, meandering, dry, uninhabited roads, which lead away from towns, which lead us away from temptation, which conduct to the outside of earth, over its uppermost crust; where you may forget in what country you are traveling . . . along which you may travel like a pilgrim . . . where my spirit is free." The journal is just such a road.

I anticipate that the reader of *I to Myself* will find this Thoreau different from the man who sojourned at Walden Pond or who spent a night in jail, and will read or reread Thoreau's other works with a different sensibility and a new appreciation. It is my hope that he or she will be intrigued enough by what is presented here to consider these selections as an introduction to the complete journal.

A note on journal passages quoted in the annotations: those with a date only are found in the text of this book; those referenced by a bracketed journal volume and page number are not.

C       *The Correspondence of Henry David Thoreau.* Edited by Walter Harding and Carl Bode. New York: New York University Press, 1958.

H       *Huckleberries.* Edited, with an introduction, by Leo Stoller. Iowa City: Windhover Press of the University of Iowa, 1970.

J       *The Journal of Henry Thoreau.* Edited by Bradford Torrey and Francis H. Allen. Boston: Houghton Mifflin, 1906.

PJ      *Journal.* Edited by John C. Broderick et al. Princeton: Princeton University Press, 1981–.

W       *The Writings of Henry D. Thoreau.* Walden edition. Boston: Houghton Mifflin, 1906.

Wa      *Walden: A Fully Annotated Edition.* Edited by Jeffrey S. Cramer. New Haven: Yale University Press, 2004.

# The Journal

## 1830s

AGE 20-22

### 1837

AGE 20

*October 22.* "What are you doing now?" he asked.[1] "Do you keep a journal?" So I make my first entry to-day.

To be alone I find it necessary to escape the present, — I avoid myself. How could I be alone in the Roman emperor's chamber of mirrors?[2] I seek a garret. The spiders must not be disturbed, nor the floor swept, nor the lumber[3] arranged.

The Germans say, "Es ist alles wahr wodurch du besser wirst."[4]

*November 3.* If one would reflect, let him embark on some placid stream, and float with the current. He cannot resist the Muse.[5] As we ascend the stream, plying the paddle with might and main, snatched and impetuous thoughts course through the brain. We dream of conflict, power, and grandeur. But turn the prow down stream, and rock, tree, kine, knoll, assuming new and varying positions, as wind and water shift the scene, favor the liquid lapse[6] of thought, far-reaching and sublime, but ever calm and gently undulating.

*November 12.* I yet lack discernment to distinguish the whole lesson of to-day; but it is not lost, — it will come to me at last. My desire is to know *what* I have lived, that I may know *how* to live henceforth.

1 Ralph Waldo Emerson (1803–1882), who wrote in his journal of 23 October 1837, perhaps thinking of this encounter, that the French essayist Michel de Montaigne (1533–1592), Amos Bronson Alcott (cf. 1851 note 157), his aunt, Mary Moody Emerson (cf. 1851 note 174), "and I, have written Journals; beside these, I did not last night think of another."
2 Titus Flavius Domitian (51–96 C.E.) who, according to Suetonius's (75–160) *The Lives of the Twelve Caesars* ("The Life of Domitian" 14:4), "lined the walls of the colonnades in which he used to walked with phengite stone, to be able to see in its brilliant surface the reflection of all that went on behind his back."
3 Anything useless and cumbersome, or bulky and thrown aside as of no use.
4 German: Everything through which you are bettered is true. Thoreau apparently learned this phrase through Emerson, in whose 1837 journal it is also found. Emerson's source was Henry Fothergill Chorley's (1808–1872) *Memorials of Mrs. Hemans.*
5 The nine muses of Greek mythology were responsible for, respectively, music, epic poetry, history, lyric poetry, tragedy, sacred poetry, dancing, comedy, and astronomy.
6 Echo of John Milton's (1608–1674) *Paradise Lost* 8:263: "liquid lapse of murmuring streams."

7 During another autumnal period of mild, sunny weather, on 31 October 1850, Thoreau called Indian summer "the finest season of the year" [J 2:76].

8 Hill in Concord, west of where the Sudbury and Assabet Rivers meet, also known as Lee's Hill.

9 Variantly in *A Week on the Concord and Merrimack Rivers*: "Upon an isolated hilltop, in an open country, we seem to ourselves to be standing on the boss of an immense shield, the immediate landscape being apparently depressed below the more remote, and rising gradually to the horizon, which is the rim of the shield,—villas, steeples, forests, mountains, one above another, till they are swallowed up in the heavens" [W 1:373].

10 Emerson wrote in his journal on 10 December 1836: "At Walden Pond I found a new musical instrument which I call the ice-harp. A thin coat of ice covered a part of the pond, but melted around the edge of the shore. I threw a stone upon the ice which rebounded with a shrill sound, and falling again and again, repeated the note with pleasing modulation. I thought at first it was the 'peep, peep' of a bird I had scared. I was so taken with the music that I threw down my stick and spent twenty minutes in throwing stones single or in handfuls on this crystal drum."

11 Thoreau used a similar phrase to describe the telegraph-harp: cf. 22 September 1851.

12 Romulus and Remus were the legendary founders of Rome; Hengist and Horsa were, according to tradition, two brothers who led the 5th-century Jutish invasion of Britain and founded the kingdom of Kent.

*November 17.* The smothered breathings of awakening day strike the ear with an undulating motion; over hill and dale, pasture and woodland, come they to me, and I am at home in the world.

*November 21.* One must needs climb a hill to know what a world he inhabits. In the midst of this Indian summer[7] I am perched on the topmost rock of Nawshawtuct,[8] a velvet wind blowing from the southwest. I seem to feel the atoms as they strike my cheek. Hills, mountains, steeples stand out in bold relief in the horizon, while I am resting on the rounded boss of an enormous shield, the river like a vein of silver encircling its edge, and thence the shield gradually rises to its rim, the horizon. Not a cloud is to be seen, but villages, villas, forests, mountains, one above another, till they are swallowed up in the heavens.[9]

*December 5.* My friend tells me he has discovered a new note in nature, which he calls the Ice-Harp.[10] Chancing to throw a handful of pebbles upon the pond where there was an air chamber under the ice, it discoursed a pleasant music to him.

Herein resides a tenth muse,[11] and as he was the man to discover it probably the extra melody is in him.

*December 27.* Revolutions are never sudden. Not one man, nor many men, in a few years or generations, suffice to regulate events and dispose mankind for the revolutionary movement. The hero is but the crowning stone of the pyramid,—the keystone of the arch. Who was Romulus or Remus, Hengist or Horsa,[12] that we should attribute to them Rome or England? They are famous or infamous because the progress of events has chosen to make them its stepping-stones. But we would know where the avalanche commenced, or the hollow in the rock whence springs the Amazon. The most important is apt to be some silent and unobtrusive fact in history. In 449 three Saxon cyules[13] arrived on the British coast,— "Three scipen gode comen mid than flode, three hundred cnihten."[14]

**December 31.** As the least drop of wine tinges the whole goblet, so the least particle of truth colors our whole life. It is never isolated, or simply added as treasures to our stock. When any real progress is made, we unlearn and learn anew what we thought we knew before. We go picking up from year to year and laying side by side the *disjecta membra*[15] of truth, as he who picked up one by one a row of a hundred stones, and returned with each separately to his basket.[16]

### 1838
#### AGE 20–21

**After January 21.** Every leaf and twig was this morning covered with a sparkling ice armor; even the grasses in exposed fields were hung with innumerable diamond pendants, which jingled merrily when brushed by the foot of the traveller. It was literally the wreck of jewels and the crash of gems.[17]

**March 5.** But what does all this scribbling amount to? What is now scribbled in the heat of the moment one can contemplate with somewhat of satisfaction, but alas! to-morrow—aye, to-night—it is stale, flat, and unprofitable,—in fine, is not, only its shell remains, like some red parboiled lobster-shell which, kicked aside never so often, still stares at you in the path.

What may a man do and not be ashamed of it? He may not do nothing surely, for straightway he is dubbed Dolittle[18]—aye! christens himself first—and reasonably, for he was first to duck. But let him do something, is

13  Middle English, from the Anglo-Saxon, cēol: keel, or longboat.
14  Translation: "Three good ships came with the flood, with three hundred knights." From Layamon (fl. 13th century) as quoted (with variant: *three* for *threo*) from Sharon Turner's (1768–1847) *History of the Anglo-Saxons* (1:90). This marked the Anglo-Saxon invasion of Britain and the end of Roman rule. Thoreau also quoted these lines in a letter to Lucy Brown, Lidian Emerson's sister, of 8 September 1841 [C 47].
15  Latin: disjointed members or parts, usually applied to fragments of poetry or disjointed quotations.
16  Allusion to the person in the algebraic problem found in Leonard Euler's (1707–1783) *Elements of Algebra,* which Thoreau owned: "One hundred stones being placed on the ground, in a straight line, at the distance of a yard from each other, how far will a person travel who shall bring them one by one to a basket, which is placed one yard from the first stone? Ans. 5 *miles* and 1300 *yards.*"
17  Echo of phrase found in Thomas Carlyle's (1795–1881) *Sartor Resartus*—"the wreck of matter and the crash of worlds"—an allusion to Joseph Addison's (1672–1719) *Cato* (5.1.31): "The wrecks of matter, and the crush of worlds."
18  Common epithet for a lazy person.

**19** Thoreau wrote the comment "Carlyleish" in the margin against this passage, referring to Thomas Carlyle, Scottish writer and historian, and friend of Emerson. Thoreau described Carlyle's style as "eminently colloquial, and no wonder it is strange to meet with in a book. It is not literary or classical; it has not the music of poetry, nor the pomp of philosophy, but the rhythms and cadences of conversation endlessly repeated. It resounds with emphatic, natural, lively, stirring tones, muttering, rattling, exploding, like shells and shot, and with like execution" [W 4:323].

**20** Allusion to the concept of Pythagoras (ca. 582–500 B.C.E.) who, having ascertained that pitch is dependent on the rapidity of vibrations and that planets move at different rates, concluded that the sound of the planets or spheres must vary accordingly, and, since all things in nature are harmoniously made, the music of the spheres must also be harmonious. Sir Thomas Browne (1605–1682) wrote in *Religio Medici*: "There is music wherever there is harmony, order, or proportion; and thus far we may maintain the music of the Spheres; for those well-ordered motions and regular paces, though they give no sound to the ear, yet to the understanding they strike a note most full of harmony." On 8 August 1838 Thoreau described "the true sphere music" as "pure, unmixed music" [J 1:53] and on 5 February 1841 he wrote: "If the law of the universe were to be audibly promulgated, no mortal lawgiver would suspect it, for it would be a finer melody than his ears ever attended to. It would be sphere music" [J 1:195].

**21** Variant of randan: a loud noise or uproar.

**22** Allusion to Milton's *Paradise Lost* (2:995–996): "With ruin upon ruin, rout on rout, / Confusion worse confounded."

**23** Unidentified allusion. In *A Week on the Concord and Merrimack Rivers* Thoreau similarly wrote: "Silence is audible to all men, at all times, and in all places" [W 1:418].

**24** Phrase found as early as Edmund Burke (1729–1797) describing his first impressions of

he the less a Dolittle? Is it actually something done, or not rather something undone; or, if done, is it not badly done, or at most well done comparatively?

Such is man,—toiling, heaving, struggling ant-like to shoulder some stray unappropriated crumb and deposit it in his granary; then runs out, complacent, gazes heavenward, earthward (for even pismires can look down), heaven and earth meanwhile looking downward, upward; there seen of men, world-seen, deed-delivered, vanishes into all-grasping night. And is he doomed ever to run the same course? Can he not, wriggling, screwing, self-exhorting, self-constraining, wriggle or screw out something that shall live,—respected, intact, intangible, not to be sneezed at?[19]

**March 6.** How can a man sit down and quietly pare his nails, while the earth goes gyrating ahead amid such a din of sphere music,[20] whirling him along about her axis some twenty-four thousand miles between sun and sun, but mainly in a circle some two millions of miles actual progress? And then such a hurly-burly on the surface—wind always blowing—now a zephyr, now a hurricane—tides never idle, ever fluctuating—no rest for Niagara, but perpetual ran-tan[21] on those limestone rocks—and then that summer simmering which our ears are used to, which would otherwise be christened confusion worse confounded,[22] but is now ironically called "silence audible,"[23] and above all the incessant tinkering named "hum of industry,"[24] the hurrying to and fro and confused jabbering of men. Can man do less than get up and shake himself?

**March 7.** We should not endeavor coolly to analyze our thoughts, but, keeping the pen even and parallel with the current, make an accurate transcript of them. Impulse is, after all, the best linguist, and for his logic, if not conformable to Aristotle,[25] it cannot fail to be most convincing. The nearer we approach to a complete but simple transcript of our thought the more tolerable will be the piece, for we can endure to consider ourselves in a state of passivity or in involuntary action, but rarely our efforts, and least of all our rare efforts.

*March 14.*[26] Every proverb in the newspapers originally stood for a truth. Thus the proverb that man was made for society,[27] so long as it was not allowed to conflict with another important truth, deceived no one; but, now that the same words have come to stand for another thing, it may be for a lie, we are obliged, in order to preserve its significance, to write it anew, so that properly it will read, Society was made for man.

The mass never comes up to the standard of its best member, but on the contrary degrades itself to a level with the lowest.

One goes to a cattle-show[28] expecting to find many men and women assembled, and beholds only working oxen and neat[29] cattle. He goes to a commencement thinking that there at least he may find the men of the country; but such, if there were any, are completely merged in the day, and have become so many walking commencements, so that he is fain to take himself out of sight and hearing of the orator, lest he lose his own identity in the nonentities around him.[30]

But you are getting all the while further and further from true society. Your silence was an approach to it, but your conversation is only a refuge from the encounter of men; as though men were to be satisfied with a meeting of heels, and not heads.

Nor is it better with private assemblies, or meetings

London in 1750: "every village as neat and compact as a bee-hive, resounding with the busy hum of industry."

**25** Aristotle (384–322 B.C.E.), Greek philosopher, pupil of Plato (428–347 B.C.E.), and author of works on logic, metaphysics, ethics, natural sciences, politics, and poetics. For Aristotle, contrary to what he considered Plato's metaphysical excesses, theory follows empirical observation, and logic based on deductive reasoning is the essential method of rational inquiry.

**26** The selections under this date are from Thoreau's entry "Scraps from a lecture on 'Society' written March 14th, 1838, delivered before our lyceum, April 11th." In 1826 Josiah Holbrook (1788–1854) started the first lyceum in the United States as a local association for the discussion of topics of current interest. The Concord Lyceum began in 1829. Thoreau's lecture was given at Masonic Hall, Concord. This was his first public lecture, excluding college exercises at Harvard, and the first of twenty-one lectures he delivered at the Concord Lyceum, the last of which, "Wild Apples," was given on 8 February 1860.

**27** Axiom found in many sources—such as John Wesley's (1703–1791) "The Doctrine of Original Sin" (1757): "Consider the necessity of human laws, fenced with terrors and severities. Man was made for society, and God himself said, when he created him, it was not good for him to be alone." This was based on Genesis 2:18: "And the LORD God said, It is not good that the man should be alone; I will make him an help meet for him." All biblical references are to the Authorized (King James) Version unless otherwise noted.

**28** The Middlesex Agricultural Society's annual agricultural fair, the Middlesex Cattle Show and Ploughing Match, later the Annual Exhibition of the Middlesex Agricultural Society, was held in Concord each September or October. The society was incorporated in 1824 as the Society of Middlesex Husbandmen and Manufacturers.

**29** From the Anglo-Saxon *neat*, from the verb *neotan*, to use or possess. On 23 June 1852

Thoreau wrote that cattle make "such an impression of neatness (I think of a white cow, spotted with red, and her two sizeable calves of like color, which I saw this afternoon) that one who was unacquainted with etymology might be excused if he gave a new signification to the word neat as applied to cattle" [J 4:134].

**30** Although Thoreau participated in certain Commencement Day exercises at Harvard in August 1837, he left as precipitously as possible and may not have stayed to hear Emerson give the address, "The American Scholar." One classmate wrote to him: "After you had finished your part in the Performances of Commencement . . . I hardly saw you again at all. Neither at Mr. [Josiah] Quincy's levee, neither at any of our Classmates' evening entertainments, did I find you" [C 11].

**31** In Greek mythology, drink and food of the gods.

**32** An inferior, low-priced black tea from China.

**33** Gingerbread is made short (brittle or inclined to flake) with butter or lard.

**34** Allusion to Job 4:19: "them that dwell in houses of clay, whose foundation is in the dust."

**35** Possible allusion to the Yankee farmer in Washington Irving's (1783–1859) *A History of New York, from the Beginning of the World to the End of the Dutch Dynasty* who "sells his farm, air castle, petticoat windows and all, reloads his cart, shoulders his axe, puts himself at the head of his family, and wanders away in search of new lands—again to fell trees—again to clear cornfields—again to build a shingle palace, and again to sell off, and wander."

together, with a sociable design, of acquaintances so called,—that is to say of men and women who are familiar with the lineaments of each other's countenances, who eat, drink, sleep, and transact the business of living within the circuit of a mile.

With a beating heart he fares him forth, by the light of the stars, to this meeting of gods. But the illusion speedily vanishes; what at first seemed to him nectar and ambrosia,[31] is discovered to be plain bohea[32] and short gingerbread.[33]

It is provoking, when one sits waiting the assembling together of his neighbors around his hearth, to behold merely their clay houses,[34] for the most part newly shingled and clapboarded, and not unfrequently with a fresh coat of paint, trundled to his door. He has but to knock slightly at the outer gate of one of these shingle palaces,[35] to be assured that the master or mistress is not at home.

After all, the field of battle possesses many advantages over the drawing-room. There at least is no room for pretension or excessive ceremony, no shaking of hands or rubbing of noses, which make one doubt your sincerity, but hearty as well as hard hand-play. It at least exhibits one of the faces of humanity, the former only a mask.

The utmost nearness to which men approach each other amounts barely to a mechanical contact. As when you rub two stones together, though they emit an audible sound, yet do they not actually touch each other.

In obedience to an instinct of their nature men have pitched their cabins and planted corn and potatoes within speaking distance of one another, and so formed towns and villages, but they have not associated, they have only assembled, and society has signified only a *convention* of men.

॰⁓

Let ours be like the meeting of two planets, not hastening to confound their jarring spheres, but drawn together by the influence of a subtile attraction, soon to roll diverse in their respective orbits, from this their perigee, or point of nearest approach.

If thy neighbor hail thee to inquire how goes the world, feel thyself put to thy trumps[36] to return a true and explicit answer. Plant the feet firmly, and, will he nill he, dole out to him with strict and conscientious impartiality his modicum of a response.

Let not society be the element in which you swim, or are tossed about at the mercy of the waves, but be rather a strip of firm land running out into the sea, whose base is daily washed by the tide, but whose summit only the spring tide can reach.

But after all, such a morsel of society as this will not satisfy a man. But like those women of Malamocco and Pelestrina, who when their husbands are fishing at sea, repair to the shore and sing their shrill songs at evening, till they hear the voices of their husbands in reply borne to them over the water,[37] so go we about indefatigably, chanting our stanza of the lay, and awaiting the response of a kindred soul out of the distance.

*May 10.* The railroad from Bangor to Oldtown[38] is civilization shooting off in a tangent into the forest. I had much conversation with an old Indian at the latter place, who sat dreaming upon a scow at the waterside and striking his deer-skin moccasins against the planks, while his arms hung listlessly by his side. He was the most communicative man I had met. Talked of hunting and fishing, old times and new times. Pointing up the

**36** Forced to the last expedient or to the utmost.
**37** Allusion to Johann Wolfgang von Goethe's (1749–1832) *Italiänische Reise,* which Thoreau read in German. On 6 October 1786 Goethe wrote: "He wished that I might hear the women of the Lido, especially those of Malamocco and Pelestrina, who also sang Tasso to the same and similar melodies. He said further: 'It is their custom, when their husbands are off in the sea, fishing, to sit down at the shore and let those songs rise out in the evening with penetrating voices, until from afar they hear the voices of their men and thus converse with them.' Is not that very lovely?"
**38** In Maine, where Thoreau made an excursion on 3 May, returning to Concord on 17 May.

**39** River in central Maine.
**40** On the southern side of Fair Haven Hill on the shore of the Sudbury River, about half a mile southwest of Walden. This was one of Thoreau's favorite spots: cf. 12 May 1850.
**41** Allusion to the mythical heroes of the Trojan War, as told in Homer's *Iliad*.
**42** Epithet for the Trojan War, as told in Homer's *Odyssey*, book 16, translated by Alexander Pope (1688–1744) as:

> but should I lose my life,
> Oppress'd by numbers in the glorious strife,
> I choose the nobler part, and yield my breath,
> Rather than bear dishonor, worse than death.

**43** This sentence was adapted for use in the following context in *A Week on the Concord and Merrimack Rivers:* "Now that we are casting away these melon seeds, how can we help feeling reproach? He who eats the fruit should at least plant the seed; ay, if possible, a better seed than that whose fruit he has enjoyed. Seeds, there are seeds enough which need only to be stirred in with the soil where they lie, by an inspired voice or pen, to bear fruit of a divine flavor. O thou spendthrift! Defray thy debt to the world; eat not the seed of institutions, as the luxurious do, but plant it rather, while thou devourest the pulp and tuber for thy subsistence; that so, perchance, one variety may at last be found worthy of preservation" [W 1:129–130].

Penobscot,[39] he observed, "Two or three miles up the river one beautiful country!" and then, as if he would come as far to meet me as I had gone to meet him, he exclaimed, "Ugh! one very hard time!" But he had mistaken his man.

*July 8.*

### Cliffs[40]

The loudest sound that burdens here the breeze
Is the wood's whisper; 't is, when we choose to list,
Audible sound, and when we list not,
It is calm profound. Tongues were provided
But to vex the ear with superficial thoughts.
When deeper thoughts upswell, the jarring
   discord
Of harsh speech is hushed, and senses seem
As little as may be to share the ecstasy.

*July 13.* What a hero one can be without moving a finger! The world is not a field worthy of us, nor can we be satisfied with the plains of Troy.[41] A glorious strife[42] seems waging within us, yet so noiselessly that we but just catch the sound of the clarion ringing of victory, borne to us on the breeze. There are in each the seeds of a heroic ardor, which need only to be stirred in with the *soil where they lie,* by an inspired voice or pen, to bear fruit of a divine flavor.[43]

*August 13.* If with closed ears and eyes I consult consciousness for a moment, immediately are all walls and barriers dissipated, earth rolls from under me, and I float, by the impetus derived from the earth and the system, a subjective, heavily laden thought, in the midst of an unknown and infinite sea, or else heave and swell like a vast ocean of thought, without rock or headland, where are all riddles solved, all straight lines making there their two ends to meet, eternity and space gambolling familiarly through my depths. I am from the beginning, knowing no end, no aim. No sun illumines me, for I dissolve all lesser lights in my own intenser and steadier light. I am a restful kernel in the magazine of the universe.

*August 27.* Verily I am the creature of circumstances. Here I have swallowed an indispensable tooth, and so am no whole man, but a lame and halting piece of manhood. I am conscious of no gap in my soul, but it would seem that, now the entrance to the oracle has been enlarged, the more rare and commonplace the responses that issue from it. I have felt cheap, and hardly dared hold up my head among men, ever since this accident happened. Nothing can I do as well and freely as before; nothing do I undertake but I am hindered and balked by this circumstance. What a great matter a little spark kindleth![44] I believe if I were called at this moment to rush into the thickest of the fight, I should halt for lack of so insignificant a piece of armor as a tooth. Virtue and Truth go undefended, and Falsehood and Affectation are thrown in my teeth,—though I am toothless. One does not need that the earth quake for the sake of excitement, when so slight a crack proves such an impassable moat. But let the lame man shake his leg, and match himself with the fleetest in the race. So shall he do what is in him to do. But let him who has lost a tooth open his mouth wide and gabble, lisp, and sputter never so resolutely.

*September 20.* It is a luxury to muse by a wall-side in the sunshine of a September afternoon,—to cuddle down under a gray stone, and hearken to the siren song[45] of the cricket. Day and night seem henceforth but accidents, and the time is always a still eventide, and as the close

44 Allusion to James 3:5: "Behold, how great a matter a little fire kindleth!"
45 In Greek mythology, the song of a sea nymph, supposed to lure sailors to their destruction by their seductive singing.

**46** Latin: nourishing nature.

**47** Compensation in this sense encompassed balance, unity, and an ability to accept and move beyond apparent tragedies. Emerson wrote in his journal in 1841 that he told Thoreau: "I only know three persons who seem to me fully to see this law of reciprocity or compensation—himself, Alcott, and myself: and 't is odd that we should all be neighbors, for in the wide land or the wide earth I do not know another who seems to have it as deeply and originally as these three Gotham-ites." Emerson expressed the compensatory idea succinctly in his poem "Give All to Love," which ends, "When half-gods go, / The gods arrive," and in his essay "Compensation": "For every thing you have missed, you have gained something else; and for every thing you gain, you lose something."

**48** This was incorporated in *A Week on the Concord and Merrimack Rivers:* "'Nothing that naturally happens to man can *hurt* him, earthquakes and thunder-storms not excepted,' said a man of genius, who at this time lived a few miles farther on our road. When compelled by a shower to take shelter under a tree, we may improve that opportunity for a more minute inspection of some of Nature's works. I have stood under a tree in the woods half a day at a time, during a heavy rain in the summer, and yet employed myself happily and profitably there prying with microscopic eye into the crevices of the bark or the leaves [or] the fungi at my feet" [W 1:319].

**49** Lines 3–6 of Thoreau's poem "The Thaw."

of a happy day. Parched fields and mulleins gilded with the slanting rays are my diet. I know of no word so fit to express this disposition of Nature as Alma Natura.[46]

*September 23.* If we will be quiet and ready enough, we shall find compensation in every disappointment.[47] If a shower drives us for shelter to the maple grove or the trailing branches of the pine, yet in their recesses with microscopic eye we discover some new wonder in the bark, or the leaves, or the fungi at our feet. We are interested by some new resource of insect economy, or the chickadee is more than usually familiar. We can study Nature's nooks and corners then.[48]

## 1839
### AGE 21–22

*January 11.*

> Fain would I stretch me by the highway-side,
> To thaw and trickle with the melting snow,
> That, mingled soul and body with the tide,
> I too may through the pores of nature flow.[49]

*After January 20.*

> Love
> We two that planets erst had been
> Are now a double star,
> And in the heavens may be seen,
> Where that we fixèd are.
>
> Yet, whirled with subtle power along,
> Into new space we enter,
> And evermore with spheral song
> Revolve about one centre.

*February 9.* It takes a man to make a room silent.

*March 3.* The Poet.

He must be something more than natural, — even supernatural. Nature will not speak through but along with him. His voice will not proceed from her midst, but, breathing on her, will make her the expression of his thought. He then poetizes when he takes a fact out of nature into spirit. He speaks without reference to time or place. His thought is one world, hers another. He is another Nature, — Nature's brother. Kindly offices do they perform for one another. Each publishes the other's truth.

*April 24.* Why should we concern ourselves with what has happened to us, and the unaccountable fickleness of events, and not rather with how we have happened to the universe, and it has demeaned itself in consequence? Let us record in each case the judgment we have awarded to circumstances.

*June 4.* My Attic.[50]

I sit here this fourth of June, looking out on men and nature from this that I call my perspective window,[51] through which all things are seen in their true relations. This is my upper empire, bounded by four walls, viz., three of boards yellow-washed, facing the north, west, and south, respectively, and the fourth of plaster, like- wise yellow-washed, fronting the sunrise, — to say noth- ing of the purlieus and outlying provinces, unexplored as yet but by rats.

*After June 4.* The words of some men are thrown forcibly against you and adhere like burs.

**50** At this time the Thoreau family home was at 63 Main Street (the Parkman house) in Concord.
**51** In art, a frame or window (sometimes called a "perspectival window") creating a perspective grid, probably from the work of Leon Battista Alberti (1404–1474), who described in his *Della Pittura* how an artist could get a correct perspec- tive by observing a scene through a thin veil or window.

**52** Ellen Sewall (1822–1892), whose aunt Prudence Ward boarded in the Thoreau family home, visited Concord for two weeks starting on 20 July. During this period Thoreau fell in love with Ellen, as did his brother, John (1815–1842). Thoreau had been in her company the three previous days: seeing a giraffe on display in Concord, rowing on the Assabet River, and walking to the Cliffs. Cf. 19 June, 19 July, and 1 November 1840.

**53** This sentence and one several lines later were incorporated into *A Week on the Concord and Merrimack Rivers*: "Yet, after all, the truly efficient laborer will not crowd his day with work, but will saunter to his task surrounded by a wide halo of ease and leisure, and then do but what he loves best. He is anxious only about the fruitful kernels of time. Though the hen should sit all day, she could lay only one egg, and, besides, would not have picked up materials for another. Let a man take time enough for the most trivial deed, though it be but the paring of his nails. The buds swell imperceptibly, without hurry or confusion, as if the short spring days were an eternity" [W 1:110–111].

**54** Greek tragic poet (525–456 B.C.E.) and author of more than 70 plays, of which only seven are extant.

**55** Reference to Attica, a region of ancient Greece, in the dialect of which is written the bulk of classical Greek literature, but also with a possible pun on his living in an attic, above at 4 June 1839.

*July 25.* There is no remedy for love but to love more.[52]

*September 17.* Nature never makes haste; her systems revolve at an even pace. The bud swells imperceptibly, without hurry or confusion, as though the short spring days were an eternity.[53] All her operations seem separately, for the time, the single object for which all things tarry. Why, then, should man hasten as if anything less than eternity were allotted for the least deed? Let him consume never so many æons, so that he go about the meanest task well, though it be but the paring of his nails. If the setting sun seems to hurry him to improve the day while it lasts, the chant of the crickets fails not to reassure him, even-measured as of old, teaching him to take his own time henceforth forever. The wise man is restful, never restless or impatient. He each moment abides there where he is, as some walkers actually rest the whole body at each step, while others never relax the muscles of the leg till the accumulated fatigue obliges them to stop short.

As the wise is not anxious that time wait for him, neither does he wait for it.

*November 5.* Æschylus.[54]

There was one man lived his own healthy Attic[55] life in those days. The words that have come down to us evidence that their speaker was a seer in his day and generation. At this day they owe nothing to their dramatic form, nothing to stage machinery, and the fact that they were spoken under these or those circumstances. All display of art for the gratification of a factitious taste is silently passed by to come at the least particle of absolute and genuine thought they contain. The reader will be disappointed, however, who looks for traits of a rare wisdom or eloquence, and will have to solace himself, for the most part, with the poet's humanity and what it was in him to say. He will discover that, like every genius, he was a solitary liver and worker in his day.[56]

We are accustomed to say that the common sense[57] of this age belonged to the seer of the last,—as if time gave him any vantage ground. But not so: I see not but Genius[58] must ever take an equal start, and all the generations of men are virtually at a standstill for it to come and consider of them. Common sense is not so familiar with any truth but Genius will represent it in a strange light to it. Let the seer bring down his broad eye to the most stale and trivial fact, and he will make you believe it a new planet in the sky.

As to criticism, man has never to make allowance to man; there is naught to excuse, naught to bear in mind.

All the past is here present to be tried; let it approve itself if it can.

*November 14.* There is nowhere any apology for despondency. Always there is life which, rightly lived, implies a divine satisfaction. I am soothed by the rain-drops on the door-sill; every globule that pitches thus confidently from the eaves to the ground is my life insurance. Disease and a rain-drop cannot coexist.[59]

**56** Thoreau wrote similarly about Aeschylus in early 1840: "The social condition of genius is the same in all ages. Æschylus was undoubtedly alone and without sympathy in his simple reverence for the mystery of the universe" [J 1:117].

**57** On common sense as practical sense, Thoreau wrote in *A Week on the Concord and Merrimack Rivers* that "common sense always takes a hasty and superficial view" [W 1:347]. Thoreau does not disparage common sense, however. He praised John Brown for his "rare common sense and directness of speech" [W 4:413] and Chaucer for his "rare common sense and proverbial wisdom" [W 1:397]. He takes issue with its confinement and unexpansiveness: as when he compared "a comparatively narrow and partial, what is called common-sense view of things, to an infinitely expanded and liberating one, from seeing things as men describe them, to seeing them as men cannot describe them. This implies a sense which is not common, but rare in the wisest man's experience; which is sensible or sentient of more than common" [W 1:413]. "What is called common sense is excellent in its department, and as invaluable as the virtue of conformity in the army and navy,—for there must be subordination,—but uncommon sense, that sense which is common only to the wisest, is as much more excellent as it is more rare" [W 1:414].

For Thoreau, however, common sense also carried with it the meaning that came out of the Scottish common sense school of philosophy, in particular, Thomas Reid's (1710–1796) *An Inquiry into the Human Mind, on the Principles of Common Sense*, which emphasized common sense as natural judgment from a set of innate principles of conception and belief implanted in the human mind by God. This is the antecedent of the concept of inspiration, of which Emerson wrote in "Self-Reliance": "the essence of genius, of virtue, and of life, which we call Spontaneity or Instinct. We denote this primary wisdom as Intuition. . . . In that deep force, the last fact behind which analysis cannot go, all things find their common origin."

"The wildest dreams of wild men, even," Thoreau wrote in "Walking," "are not the less true, though they may not recommend themselves to the sense which is most common among Englishmen and Americans to-day. It is not every truth that recommends itself to the common sense" [W 5:233]. And more concretely in "Ktaadn" from *The Maine Woods,* where three words—solid, actual, common—share the emphasis: "Talk of mysteries! Think of our life in nature,—daily to be shown matter, to come in contact with it,—rocks, trees, wind on our cheeks! the *solid* earth! the *actual* world! the *common sense!*" [W 3:79].

**58**  From the Latin, meaning "begetter," it referred originally to an attendant spirit, and later to a personification of an individual's natural desires and appetites, although now more commonly used to mean a person of extraordinary mental perception, comprehension, discrimination, and expression. Sampson Reed (1800–1880) in his "Oration on Genius" (1821) wrote about its relation to "divine truth" and related the term to its original meaning: "Men say there is an inspiration in genius. The genius of the ancients was the good or evil spirit that attended the man." Emerson, in his early lecture "Genius," defined the term as: "1. Genius, a man's natural bias or turn of mind. . . . 2. The second and popular sense of Genius is the intellect's spontaneous perception and exhibition of truth."

**59**  Cf. 17 June 1857.

## 1840s

AGE 22–32

**1** Unidentified, although Thoreau may have been speaking generally.
**2** This was written during the Seminole Indian War (1836–1842).
**3** In Nova Scotia.
**4** Cf. 1857 note 102.
**5** The melancholy, brooding, and vacillating hero of William Shakespeare's (1564–1616) *Hamlet.*
**6** The poll tax was levied on each adult male who was between 20 and 70, rather than on goods or property. Thoreau stopped paying his poll tax probably in 1842. His justification for not paying the tax was initially to protest Massachusetts's involvement with the institution of slavery and later the war with Mexico, which began in 1845. This led to his brief arrest in July 1846 recounted in "Resistance to Civil Government."

### 1840
AGE 22–23

*January 27.* What a tame life we are living! How little heroic it is!

*February 28.* On the death of a friend,[1] we should consider that the fates through confidence have devolved on us the task of a double living, that we have henceforth to fulfill the promise of our friend's life also, in our own, to the world.

*March 21.* The world is a fit theater to-day in which any part may be acted. There is this moment proposed to me every kind of life that men lead anywhere, or that imagination can paint. By another spring I may be a mail-carrier in Peru, or a South African planter, or a Siberian exile, or a Greenland whaler, or a settler on the Columbia River, or a Canton merchant, or a soldier in Florida,[2] or a mackerel-fisher off Cape Sable,[3] or a Robinson Crusoe in the Pacific,[4] or a silent navigator of any sea. So wide is the choice of parts, what a pity if the part of Hamlet[5] be left out!

I am freer than any planet; no complaint reaches round the world. I can move away from public opinion, from government, from religion, from education, from society. Shall I be reckoned a ratable poll in the county of Middlesex,[6] or be rated at one spear under

**7** On the east coast of Africa, and the principal source of slaves from the 16th to the 18th centuries.

**8** Financial and mercantile district of Boston representative of business and material wealth.

**9** A vast region of eastern Europe and northern Asia controlled by the Mongols in the 13th and 14th centuries.

**10** In Jonathan Swift's (1667–1745) *Gulliver's Travels,* Brobdingnag was a land of giants, Lilliput a land of very small people. Patagonia, in South America, and Lapland, in northern Europe, represent distant lands.

**11** Also known as *The Thousand and One Nights,* the 10th-century collection of ancient Persian, Indian, and Arabian tales, which include the famous stories of Aladdin, Sinbad, and Ali Baba.

**12** Pun on sounding, not only as resonance but as the act of measuring the depth of water.

**13** In Greek mythology, sea gods.

**14** Allusion to Captain James Cook (1728–1779), British explorer who visited Nootka Sound on the west coast of Vancouver, British Columbia, in 1778, from where he carried sea otter furs to China to trade. Publication of his journals in 1784 sparked an expansive fur trade.

**15** In Greek mythology, Jason sailed the *Argo* in search of the Golden Fleece.

**16** Allusion to the expedition led by Lieutenant Charles Wilkes (1798–1877) of the U.S. Navy to explore the South Pacific and Antarctic Oceans. It began in 1838 and continued until 1842, and was known as the South Sea Exploring Expedition, the Wilkes Expedition, or the United States Exploring Expedition.

**17** Carthaginian explorer (ca. 500 B.C.E.) who sailed around the west coast of Africa; his account of the journey became known as "The Periplus of Hanno."

**18** Marco Polo (1254–1324), Venetian trader and explorer in China, and Sir John Mandeville, pseudonym for the unknown compiler of the 14th-century travel romance *The Voyage and Travels of Sir John Mandeville, Knight.*

the palm trees of Guinea?[7] Shall I raise corn and potatoes in Massachusetts, or figs and olives in Asia Minor? sit out the day in my office in State Street,[8] or ride it out on the steppes of Tartary?[9] For my Brobdingnag I may sail to Patagonia; for my Lilliput, to Lapland.[10] In Arabia and Persia, my day's adventures will surpass the Arabian Nights' Entertainments.[11] I may be a logger on the head waters of the Penobscot, to be recorded in fable hereafter as an amphibious river-god, by as sounding[12] a name as Triton or Proteus;[13] carry furs from Nootka to China,[14] and so be more renowned than Jason and his golden fleece;[15] or go on a South Sea exploring expedition,[16] to be hereafter recounted along with the periplus of Hanno.[17] I may repeat the adventures of Marco Polo or Mandeville.[18]

These are but few of my chances, and how many more things may I do with which there are none to be compared!

*April 20.* An early morning walk is a blessing for the whole day. To my neighbors who have risen in mist and rain I tell of a clear sunrise and the singing of birds as some traditionary mythus. I look back to those fresh but now remote hours as to the old dawn of time, when a solid and blooming health reigned and every deed was simple and heroic.

*June 16.* Would it not be a luxury to stand up to one's chin in some retired swamp for a whole summer's day, scenting the sweet-fern and bilberry blows, and lulled by the minstrelsy of gnats and mosquitoes?

*June 18.* I am startled when I consider how little I am *actually* concerned about the things I write in my journal.

*June 19.* The other day I rowed in my boat a free, even lovely young lady,[19] and, as I plied the oars, she sat in the stern, and there was nothing but she between me and the sky.[20] So might all our lives be picturesque if they were free enough, but mean relations and prejudices intervene to shut out the sky, and we never see a man as simple and distinct as the man-weathercock on a steeple.

*June 30.* A man's life should be a stately march to a sweet but unheard music, and when to his fellows it shall seem irregular and inharmonious, he will only be stepping to a livelier measure,[21] or his nicer ear hurry him into a thousand symphonies and concordant variations. There will be no halt ever, but at most a marching on his post, or such a pause as is richer than any sound, when the melody runs into such depth and wildness as to be no longer heard, but implicitly consented to with the whole life and being. He will take a false step never, even in the most arduous times, for then the music will not fail to swell into greater sweetness and volume, and itself rule the movement it inspired.[22]

*July 10.* We know men through their eyes. You might say that the eye was always original and unlike another. It is the feature of the individual, and not of the family, — in twins still different. All a man's privacy is in his eye, and its expression he cannot alter more than he can alter his character. So long as we look a man in the eye, it seems to rule the other features, and make them, too, original. When I have mistaken one person for another, observing only his form, and carriage, and inferior features, the unlikeness seemed of the least consequence; but when I caught his eye, and my doubts were removed, it seemed to pervade every feature.

The eye revolves on an independent pivot which we

**19** Ellen Sewall (cf. 1830s note 52), who was visiting Concord at this time and with whom both the Thoreau brothers fell in love: cf. 1840s notes 23 and 26.
**20** This was integrated into *A Week on the Concord and Merrimack Rivers*: "Why should not our whole life and its scenery be actually thus fair and distinct? All our lives want a suitable background. They should at least, like the life of the anchorite, be as impressive to behold as objects in the desert, a broken shaft or crumbling mound against a limitless horizon. Character always secures for itself this advantage, and is thus distinct and unrelated to near or trivial objects, whether things or persons. On this same stream a maiden once sailed in my boat, thus unattended but by invisible guardians, and as she sat in the prow there was nothing but herself between the steersman and the sky" [W 1:45].
**21** Thoreau's oft-quoted phrase found in *Walden*—"If a man does not keep pace with his companions, perhaps it is because he hears a different drummer. Let him step to the music which he hears, however measured or far away" [Wa 317]—can be traced to its earliest form here. For further variants of this phrase, cf. *A Week on the Concord and Merrimack Rivers*: "Marching is when the pulse of the hero beats in unison with the pulse of Nature, and he steps to the measure of the universe; then there is true courage and invincible strength" [W 1:183], and Thoreau's journal of 19 and 25 July 1851.
**22** This appeared in "The Service" with minor variants.

**23** Thoreau's brother John had gone to Scituate, Massachusetts, to propose to Ellen Sewall. Although Ellen briefly accepted, her mother insisted that the engagement be broken off.

**24** The ancient land of Syria in southwest Asia was settled ca. 2100 B.C.E. by Amorites and was conquered several times, by Hittites, Assyrians, Babylonians, Persians, Greeks, and Romans, until it became part of the Ottoman Empire in 1516.

**25** Reference to a series of Persian empires in southwest Asia that had various permutations and each of which had its own rise and fall.

**26** Around this time Thoreau wrote to Ellen Sewall proposing marriage. At her father's insistence Ellen wrote to Thoreau on 10 November rejecting his proposal. The following week she wrote to her aunt, Prudence Ward: "I never felt so badly at sending a letter in all my life. I could not bear to think that both those friends whom I have enjoyed so much with would now no longer be able to have the free pleasant intercourse with us as formerly."

**27** Hannibal (247–182 B.C.E.), the Carthaginian military commander, defeated the Romans in several battles during the Second Punic War (218–202 B.C.E.).

can no more control than our own will. Its axle is the axle of the soul, as the axis of the earth is coincident with the axis of the heavens.

*July 19.* These two days[23] that I have not written in my Journal, set down in the calendar as the 17th and 18th of July, have been really an æon in which a Syrian empire[24] might rise and fall. How many Persias[25] have been won and lost in the interim. Night is spangled with fresh stars.

*November 1.* The day is won by the blushes of the dawn.[26]

## 1841
### AGE 23–24

*January 20.* Disappointment will make us conversant with the nobler part of our nature, it will chasten us, and prepare us to meet accident on higher ground the next time, as Hannibal taught the Romans the art of war.[27] So is all misfortune only our stepping-stone to fortune.

The desultory moments, which are the grimmest features of misfortune, are a step before me on which I should set foot, and not stumbling blocks in the path. To extract its whole good I must be disappointed with the best fortune, and not be bribed by sunshine nor health.

*January 24.* I almost shrink from the arduousness of meeting men erectly day by day.

Be resolutely and faithfully what you are; be humbly what you aspire to be. Be sure you give men the best of your wares, though they be poor enough, and the gods will help you to lay up a better store for the future. Man's noblest gift to man is his sincerity, for it embraces his integrity also. Let him not dole out of himself anxiously, to suit their weaker or stronger stomachs, but make a clean gift of himself, and empty his coffers at once. I would be in society as in the landscape; in the presence of nature there is no reserve, nor effrontery.

*January 26.* I have as much property as I can command and use. If by a fault in my character I do not derive my just revenues, there is virtually a mortgage on my inheritance. A man's wealth is never entered in the registrar's office. Wealth does not come in along the great thoroughfares, it does not float on the Erie or Pennsylvania canal,[28] but is imported by a solitary track without bustle or competition, from a brave industry to a quiet mind.

I had a dream last night which had reference to an act in my life in which I had been most disinterested and true to my highest instinct but completely failed in realizing my hopes; and now, after so many months, in the stillness of sleep, complete justice was rendered me. It was a divine remuneration. In my waking hours I could not have conceived of such retribution; the presumption of desert would have damned the whole. But now I was permitted to be not so much a subject as a partner to that retribution. It was the award of divine justice, which will at length be and is even now accomplished.[29]

*January 28.* No innocence can quite stand up under suspicion, if it is conscious of being suspected. In the company of one who puts a wrong construction upon your actions, they are apt really to deserve a mean construction. While in that society I can never retrieve myself. Attribute to me a great motive, and I shall not fail to have one; but a mean one, and the fountain of virtue will be poisoned by the suspicion. Show men unlimited faith as the coin with which you will deal with them, and they will invariably exhibit the best wares they have.

28 Canals that opened in 1825 and 1834, respectively.

29 The following day Thoreau wrote in his journal: "In the compensation of the dream, there was no implied loss to any, but immeasurable advantage to all" [J 1:177]. In *A Week on the Concord and Merrimack Rivers* this appeared variantly as: "I dreamed this night of an event which had occurred long before. It was a difference with a Friend, which had not ceased to give me pain, though I had no cause to blame myself. But in my dream ideal justice was at length done me for his suspicions, and I received that compensation which I had never obtained in my waking hours. I was unspeakably soothed and rejoiced, even after I awoke, because in dreams we never deceive ourselves, nor are deceived, and this seemed to have the authority of a final judgment" [W 1:315]. Cf. after 19 July 1850 and 23 November 1852.

30 Allusion to Miguel de Cervantes' (1547–1616) *Don Quixote:* "Just then they came in sight of thirty or forty windmills that rise from that plain. And no sooner did Don Quixote see them that he said to his squire, 'Fortune is guiding our affairs better than we ourselves could have wished. Do you see over yonder, friend Sancho, thirty or forty hulking giants? I intend to do battle with them and slay them. With their spoils we shall begin to be rich for this is a righteous war and the removal of so foul a brood from off the face of the earth is a service God will bless.'"

31 On the alert, from the sentinel's challenge in French, meaning literally: Long live who?

32 Allusion to the debate—"Is it ever proper to offer forcible resistance"—held before the Concord Lyceum on 27 January 1841 in which Thoreau and his brother John took the affirmative side against Alcott.

I would meet men as the friends of all their virtue, and the foes of all their vice, for no man is the partner of his guilt. If you suspect me you will never see me, but all our intercourse will be the politest leave-taking; I shall constantly defer and apologize, and postpone myself in your presence. The self-defender is accursed in the sight of gods and men; he is a superfluous knight, who serves no lady in the land. He will find in the end that he has been fighting windmills,[30] and battered his mace to no purpose. The injured man with querulous tone resisting his fate is like a tree struck by lightning, which rustles its sere leaves the winter through, not having vigor enough to cast them off.

*February 4.* When you are once comfortably seated at a public meeting, there is something unmanly in the sitting on tiptoe and *qui vive* attitude,[31]—the involuntarily rising into your throat, as if gravity had ceased to operate,—when a lady approaches, with quite godlike presumption, to elicit the miracle of a seat where none is.

When presumptuous womanhood demands to surrender my position, I bide my time,—though it be with misgiving,—and yield to no mortal shove, but expect a divine impulse. Produce your warrant, and I will retire; for not now can I give you a clear seat, but must leave part of my manhood behind and wander a diminished man, who at length will not have length and breadth enough to fill any seat at all.

*February 6.* One may discover a new side to his most intimate friend when for the first time he hears him speak in public.[32] He will be stranger to him as he is more familiar to the audience. The longest intimacy could not foretell how he would behave then. When I observe my friend's conduct toward others, then chiefly

I learn the traits in his character, and in each case I am unprepared for the issue.

When one gets up to address briefly a strange audience, in that little he may have opportunity to say he will not quite do himself injustice. For he will instantly and instinctively average himself to his audience, and while he is true to his own character still, he will in a few moments make that impression which a series of months and years would but expand. Before he answers, his thought like lightning runs round the whole compass of his experiences, and he is scrupulous to speak from that which he is and with a more entire truthfulness than usual. How little do we know each other then! Who can tell how his friend would behave on any occasion?

The value of the recess in any public entertainment consists in the opportunity for self-recovery which it offers.[33] We who have been swayed as one heart, expanding and contracting with the common pulse, find ourselves in the interim, and set us up again, and feel our own hearts beating in our breasts. We are always a little astonished to see a man walking across the room, through an attentive audience, with any degree of self-possession. He makes himself strange to us. He is a little stubborn withal, and seems to say, "I am self-sustained and independent as well as the performer, and am not to be swallowed up in the common enthusiasm. No, no, there are two of us, and John's as good as Thomas." In the recess the audience is cut up into a hundred little coteries, and as soon as each individual life has recovered its tone and the purposes of health have been answered, it is time for the performances to commence again.

In a public performer, the simplest actions, which at other times are left to unconscious nature, as the ascend-

**33** On 3 February Thoreau heard a performance by the Rainers at the courthouse in Concord. The Rainers were a Tyrolese minstrel family forming a quartet of, at this time, three males and one female.

34  Allusion to Matthew 19:6, used as part of the Christian marriage ceremony: "What therefore God hath joined together, let not man put asunder."
35  The evening primrose (*Oeonothera parviflora*) and, probably, the bird's-eye primrose (*Primula mistassinica*).
36  For further comments on his journal, cf. 16 November 1850; after 10 January 1851; 22 January 1852.
37  Common practice of any counting-room clerk or merchant, but also an allusion to Thoreau's notebook, in which he wrote his field notes prior to inscribing them into his journal.

ing a few steps in front of an audience, acquire a fatal importance and become arduous deeds.

When I select one here and another there, and strive to join sundered thoughts, I make but a partial heap after all. Nature strews her nuts and flowers broadcast, and never collects them into heaps. A man does not tell us all he has thought upon truth or beauty at a sitting, but, from his last thought on the subject, wanders through a varied scenery of upland, meadow, and woodland to his next. Sometimes a single and casual thought rises naturally and inevitably with a queenly majesty and escort, like the stars in the east. Fate has surely enshrined it in this hour and circumstances for some purpose. What she has joined together, let not man put asunder.[34] Shall I transplant the primrose by the river's brim, to set it beside its sister on the mountain?[35] *This* was the soil it grew in, *this* the hour it bloomed in. If sun, wind, and rain came *here* to cherish and expand it, shall not we come here to pluck it? Shall we require it to grow in a conservatory for our convenience?

*February 8.* My Journal is that of me which would else spill over and run to waste, gleanings from the field which in action I reap.[36] I must not live for it, but in it for the gods. They are my correspondent, to whom daily I send off this sheet postpaid. I am clerk in their counting-room, and at evening transfer the account from day-book to ledger.[37] It is as a leaf which hangs over my head in the path. I bend the twig and write my prayers on it; then letting it go, the bough springs up and shows the scrawl to heaven. As if it were not kept shut in my desk, but were as public a leaf as any in nature. It is papyrus by the riverside; it is vellum in the pastures; it is parchment on the hills. I find it everywhere as free as the leaves which troop along the lanes in autumn. The crow, the goose, the eagle carry my quill, and the wind blows the leaves as far as I go. Or, if my imagination does not soar, but gropes in slime and mud, then I write with a reed.

*February 11.* True help, for the most part, implies a greatness in him who is to be helped as well as in the helper. It takes a god to be helped even. A great person, though unconsciously, will constantly give you great opportunities to serve him, but a mean one will quite preclude all active benevolence. It needs but simply and *greatly* to want it for once, that all true men may contend who shall be foremost to render aid. My neighbor's state must pray to heaven so devoutly yet disinterestedly as he never prayed in words, before my ears can hear. It must ask divinely. But men so cobble and botch their request, that you must stoop as low as they to give them aid. Their meanness would drag down your deed to be a compromise with conscience, and not leave it to be done on the high table-land of the benevolent soul. They would have you doff your bright and knightly armor and drudge for them,—serve *them* and not God. But if I am to serve them I must not serve the devil.

What is called charity is no charity, but the interference of a third person.[38] Shall I interfere with fate? Shall I defraud man of the opportunities which God gave him, and so take away his life? Beggars and silent poor[39] cry—how often!—"Get between me and my god." I will not stay to cobble and patch God's rents, but do clean, new work when he has given me my hands full. This almshouse charity is like putting new wine into old bottles,[40] when so many tuns in God's cellars stand empty. We go about mending the times, when we should be building the eternity.[41]

*February 14.* I am confined to the house by bronchitis,[42] and so seek to content myself with that quiet and serene

**38** In *Walden* Thoreau wrote: "There are those who have used all their arts to persuade me to undertake the support of some poor family in the town; and if I had nothing to do,—for the devil finds employment for the idle,—I might try my hand at some such pastime as that. However, when I have thought to indulge myself in this respect, and lay their Heaven under an obligation by maintaining certain poor persons in all respects as comfortably as I maintain myself, and have even ventured so far as to make them the offer, they have one and all unhesitatingly preferred to remain poor. While my townsmen and women are devoted in so many ways to the good of their fellows, I trust that one at least may be spared to other and less humane pursuits. You must have a genius for charity as well as for any thing else. As for Doing-good, that is one of the professions which are full. Moreover, I have tried it fairly, and, strange as it may seem, am satisfied that it does not agree with my constitution. Probably I should not consciously and deliberately forsake my particular calling to do the good which society demands of me, to save the universe from annihilation" [Wa 69–70].

**39** Lemuel Shattuck (1793–1859) defined the silent poor in *A History of the Town of Concord* as "those individuals who are needy, but do not wish to throw themselves on the town for support." The *Reports of the Selectmen of Concord* for 1844–1845 showed that the town had money for the support of the poor, but kept a separate accounting for the silent poor, with the "income of the several donations" which were then "paid out to sundry persons."

**40** Allusion to Matthew 9:17: "Neither do men put new wine into old bottles, else the bottles break, and the wine runneth out . . . but they put new wine into new bottles, and both are preserved." Thoreau also used it in "Economy" in *Walden:* "Perhaps we should never procure a new suit, however ragged or dirty the old, until we have so conducted, so enterprised or sailed in some way, that we feel like new men in the old, and that to retain it would be like keeping new wine in old bottles" [Wa 22].

**41** In "Life Without Principle" Thoreau punned: "Read not the Times. Read the Eternities" [W 4:475].

**42** Bronchitis plagued Thoreau throughout his life. On 22 March 1861 he wrote to Daniel Ricketson (cf. 1854 note 72): "I took a severe cold about the 3 of Dec. which at length resulted in a kind of bronchitis" [C 609].

**43** Cf. 5 November 1857: "The important fact is its effect on me."

**44** "Say the thing with which you labor. It is a waste of time for the writer to use his talents merely. Be faithful to your genius," Thoreau wrote on 20 December 1851 [J 3:144].

**45** Any of various plants that can be dried without loss of form or color.

**46** Emerson wrote in 1837 in his essay "The American Scholar": "Books are the best of things, well used; abused, among the worst. What is the right use? What is the one end, which all means go to effect? They are for nothing but to inspire. I had better never see a book, than to be warped by its attraction clean out of my own orbit, and made a satellite instead of a system."

**47** In ancient times, the northern entrance into Greece, where in 480 B.C.E. the outnumbered Greek army temporarily and heroically resisted an attacking Persian army.

life there is in a warm corner by the fireside, and see the sky through the chimney-top. Sickness should not be allowed to extend further than the body. We need only to retreat further within us to preserve uninterrupted the continuity of serene hours to the end of our lives.

As soon as I find my chest is not of tempered steel, and heart of adamant, I bid good-by to these and look out a new nature. I will be liable to no accidents.

*February 15.* There is elevation in every hour.

*February 18.* I do not judge men by anything they can do. Their greatest deed is the impression they make on me.[43] Some serene, inactive men can do everything. Talent only indicates a depth of character in some direction.[44] We do not acquire the ability to do new deeds, but a new capacity for all deeds. My recent growth does not appear in any visible new talent, but its deed will enter into my gaze when I look into the sky, or vacancy. It will help me to consider ferns and everlasting.[45]

*February 19.* A truly good book attracts very little favor to itself. It is so true that it teaches me better than to read it. I must soon lay it down and commence living on its hint.[46] I do not see how any can be written more, but this is the last effusion of genius. When I read an indifferent book, it seems the best thing I can do, but the inspiring volume hardly leaves me leisure to finish its latter pages. It is slipping out of my fingers while I read. It creates no atmosphere in which it may be perused, but one in which its teachings may be practiced. It confers on me such wealth that I lay it down with regret. What I began by reading I must finish by acting. So I cannot stay to hear a *good* sermon and applaud at the conclusion, but shall be half-way to Thermopylæ[47] before that.

*February 23.* The care of the body is the highest exercise of prudence. If I have brought this weakness on my lungs, I will consider calmly and disinterestedly how the thing came about, that I may find out the truth and render justice. Then, after patience, I shall be a wiser man than before.

Let us apply all our wit to the repair of our bodies, as we would mend a harrow, for the body will be dealt plainly and implicitly with. We want no moonshine nor surmises about it. This matter of health and sickness has no fatality in it, but is a subject for the merest prudence. If I know not what ails me, I may resort to amulets and charms and, moonstruck, die of dysentery.

We do wrong to slight our sickness and feel so ready to desert our posts when we are harassed. So much the more should we rise above our condition, and make the most of it, for the fruit of disease may be as good as that of health.

*February 28.* Nothing goes by luck in composition. It allows of no tricks. The best you can write will be the best you are. Every sentence is the result of a long probation.[48] The author's character is read from title-page to end. Of this he never corrects the proofs. We read it as the essential character of a handwriting without regard to the flourishes. And so of the rest of our actions; it runs as straight as a ruled line through them all, no matter how many curvets about it. Our whole life is taxed for the least thing well done; it is its net result. How we eat, drink, sleep, and use our desultory hours, now in these indifferent days, with no eye to observe and no occasion to excite us, determines our authority and capacity for the time to come.

*March 13.* How alone must our life be lived! We dwell on the seashore, and none between us and the sea. Men are

**48** Cf. Thoreau's letter to Harrison Gray Otis Blake (1818–1876) on 16 November 1857: "Not that the story need be long, but it will take a long while to make it short" [C 498].

**49** In Greek mythology, goddess of divine retribution and vengeance.

**50** Possible allusion to the Native American name for the Concord River: Musketaquid, or Grass-ground River, a fifteen-mile tributary of the Merrimack River, which it meets in Lowell. In *A Week on the Concord and Merrimack Rivers* Thoreau wrote: "The Musketaquid, or Grass-ground River, though probably as old as the Nile or Euphrates, did not begin to have a place in civilized history until the fame of its grassy meadows and its fish attracted settlers out of England in 1635, when it received the other but kindred name of CONCORD from the first plantation on its banks, which appears to have been commenced in a spirit of peace and harmony. It will be Grass-ground River as long as grass grows and water runs here; it will be Concord River only while men lead peaceable lives on its banks. To an extinct race it was grass-ground, where they hunted and fished; and it is still perennial grass-ground to Concord farmers, who own the Great Meadows, and get the hay from year to year" [W 1:3].

my merry companions, my fellow-pilgrims, who beguile the way but leave me at the first turn in the road, for none are travelling *one* road so far as myself.

*March 15.* When I have access to a man's barrel of sermons, which were written from week to week, as his life lapsed, though I now know him to live cheerfully and bravely enough, still I cannot conceive what interval there was for laughter and smiles in the midst of so much sadness. Almost in proportion to the sincerity and earnestness of the life will be the sadness of the record. When I reflect that twice a week for so many years he pondered and preached such a sermon, I think he must have been a splenetic and melancholy man, and wonder if his food digested well. It seems as if the fruit of virtue was never a careless happiness.

A great cheerfulness have all great wits possessed, almost a prophane levity to such as understood them not, but their religion had the broader basis in proportion as it was less prominent. The religion I love is very laic. The clergy are as diseased, and as much possessed with a devil, as the reformers. They make their topic as offensive as the politician, for our religion is as unpublic and incommunicable as our poetical vein, and to be approached with as much love and tenderness.

*March 27.* I must not lose any of my freedom by being a farmer and landholder. Most who enter on any profession are doomed men. The world might as well sing a dirge over them forthwith. The farmer's muscles are rigid. He can do one thing long, not many well. His pace seems determined henceforth; he never quickens it. A very rigid Nemesis[49] is his fate. When the right wind blows or a star calls, I can leave this arable and grass ground,[50] without making a will or settling my estate. I would buy a farm as freely as a silken streamer. Let me not think my front windows must face east henceforth because a particular hill slopes that way. My life must undulate still. I will not feel that my wings are clipped when once I have settled on ground which the law calls my own, but find new pinions grown to the old, and talaria[51] to my feet beside.

**April 22.** There are two classes of authors: the one write the history of their times, the other their biography.[52]

**April 26.** The charm of the Indian to me is that he stands free and unconstrained in Nature, is her inhabitant and not her guest, and wears her easily and gracefully. But the civilized man has the habits of the house.[53] His house is a prison, in which he finds himself oppressed and confined, not sheltered and protected. He walks as if he sustained the roof; he carries his arms as if the walls would fall in and crush him, and his feet remember the cellar beneath. His muscles are never relaxed. It is rare that he overcomes the house, and learns to sit at home in it, and roof and floor and walls support themselves, as the sky and trees and earth.

It is a great art to saunter.[54]

**May 2.**

Wachusett[55]
Especial I remember thee,
Wachusett, who like me
Standest alone without society.
Thy far blue eye,
A remnant of the sky,
Seen through the clearing or the gorge,
Or from the windows of the forge,
Doth leaven all it passes by.
Nothing is true

51 Winged sandals worn by, or wings growing directly from the ankles of, several minor Greek gods, giving them swift and unimpeded flight.
52 Cf. 21 October 1857.
53 Thoreau spent part of this day at the Emerson house.
54 Cf. "Walking" in which Thoreau wrote: "I have met with but one or two persons in the course of my life who understood the art of Walking, that is, of taking walks,—who had a genius, so to speak, for *sauntering*, which word is beautifully derived 'from idle people who roved about the country, in the Middle Ages, and asked charity, under pretence of going *à la Sainte Terre,*' to the Holy Land, till the children exclaimed, 'There goes a *Sainte-Terrer,*' a Saunterer, a Holy-Lander. They who never go to the Holy Land in their walks, as they pretend, are indeed mere idlers and vagabonds; but they who do go there are saunterers in the good sense, such as I mean. Some, however, would derive the word from *sans terre,* without land or a home, which, therefore, in the good sense, will mean, having no particular home, but equally at home everywhere. For this is the secret of successful sauntering. He who sits still in a house all the time may be the greatest vagrant of all; but the saunterer, in the good sense, is no more vagrant than the meandering river, which is all the while sedulously seeking the shortest course to the sea. But I prefer the first, which, indeed is the most probable derivation. For every walk is a sort of crusade, preached by some Peter the Hermit in us, to go forth and reconquer this Holy Land from the hands of the Infidels" [W 5:205–206].
55 Mountain north of Worcester, Massachusetts, twenty-six miles west of Concord, the peak of which is visible from Concord. In "A Walk to Wachusett" these lines appear as part of a longer poem, beginning "With frontier strength ye stand your ground" [W 5:135], and variantly in *A Week on the Concord and Merrimack Rivers* [W 1:172–173].

**56** Franklin Benjamin Sanborn (1831–1917), abolitionist, journalist, and unofficial memorialist of the Transcendental circle, wrote: "Henry's favorite instrument was the flute, which his father had played before him; he was accompanied on the piano sometimes by one of his sisters; but the best place for hearing its pastoral note was on some hillside, or the edge of the wood or stream; and Emerson took pleasure in its strains upon those excursions to the Cliffs, or Walden, which were so frequent in the youth of the musician." Thoreau often would bring his flute to entertain the Alcott girls. After Thoreau's death, Louisa May Alcott (1832–1888) published "Thoreau's Flute" in the *Atlantic Monthly* of September 1863, in which she wrote:

> Then from the flute, untouched by hands,
>   There came a low, harmonious breath:
>   "For such as he there is no death;—
> His life the eternal life commands;
> Above man's aims his nature rose:
>   The wisdom of a just content
>   Made one small spot a continent,
> And tuned to poetry Life's prose. . . ."

Thoreau's brother also played the flute. Cf. Thoreau's reminiscence in May 1850: "I have heard my brother playing on his flute at evening half a mile off through the houses of the village" [J 2:12].

**57** Cf. 1840s note 11.

**58** Regarding his Walden house Thoreau wrote: "I had three chairs in my house; one for solitude, two for friendship, three for society. When visitors came in larger and unexpected numbers there was but the third chair for them all, but they generally economized the room by standing up" [Wa 135].

**59** The Assabet River.

But stands 'tween me and you,
Thou western pioneer,
Who know'st not shame nor fear,
By venturous spirit driven
Under the eaves of heaven;
And canst expand thee there,
And breathe enough of air?
Upholding heaven, holding down earth,
Thy pastime from thy birth,
Not steadied by the one, nor leaning on the
    other;
May I approve myself thy worthy brother!

*May 27.* I sit in my boat on Walden, playing the flute this evening,[56] and see the perch, which I seem to have charmed, hovering around me, and the moon travelling over the bottom, which is strewn with the wrecks of the forest, and feel that nothing but the wildest imagination can conceive of the manner of life we are living. Nature is a wizard. The Concord nights are stranger than the Arabian nights.[57]

We not only want elbow-room, but eye-room in this gray air which shrouds all the fields. Sometimes my eyes see over the county road by daylight to the tops of yonder birches on the hill, as at others by moonlight.

*June 8.* Having but one chair, I am obliged to receive my visitors standing, and, now I think of it, those old sages and heroes must always have met erectly.[58]

*August 18.* I sailed on the North River[59] last night with my flute, and my music was a tinkling stream which meandered with the river, and fell from note to note as a brook from rock to rock. I did not hear the strains after they had issued from the flute, but before they were breathed into it, for the original strain precedes the sound by as much as the echo follows after, and the rest is the perquisite of the rocks and trees and beasts.[60] Unpremeditated music is the true gauge which measures the current of our thoughts, the very undertow of our life's stream.

*September 2.* There is but one obligation, and that is the obligation to obey the highest dictate.[61] None can lay me under another which will supersede this. The gods have given me these years without any incumbrance; society has no mortgage on them. If any man assist me in the way of the world, let him derive satisfaction from the deed itself, for I think I never shall have dissolved my prior obligations to God. Kindness repaid is thereby annulled. I would let his deed lie as fair and generous as it was intended. The truly beneficent never relapses into a creditor; his great kindness is still extended to me and is never done. Of those noble deeds which have me for their object I am only the most fortunate spectator, and would rather be the abettor of their nobleness than stay their tide with the obstructions of impatient gratitude. As true as action and reaction are equal, that nobleness which was as wide as the universe will rebound not on him the individual, but on the world. If any have been kind to me, what more do they want? I cannot make them richer than they are. If they have not been kind, they cannot take from me the privilege which they have not improved. My obligations will be my lightest load, for that gratitude which is of kindred stuff in me, expanding every pore, will easily sustain the pressure. We walk the freest through the air we breathe.

*September 4.* I think I could write a poem to be called "Concord." For argument[62] I should have the River, the Woods, the Ponds, the Hills, the Fields, the Swamps and Meadows, the Streets and Buildings, and the Villagers.

**60** Used apropos of Orpheus in *A Week on the Concord and Merrimack Rivers*: "Orpheus does not hear the strains which issue from his lyre, but only those which are breathed into it; for the original strain precedes the sound, by as much as the echo follows after. The rest is the perquisite of the rocks and trees and beasts" [W 1:363].

**61** Moral principles or laws of conscience that take precedence over the constitutions or statutes of society. The concept of higher law can be found in the Judeo-Christian belief in moral law, as well as in the idea of natural law formulated by Plato and Cicero. In "On the Republic" Cicero wrote: "There is in fact a true law—namely, right reason—which is in accordance with nature, applies to all men, and is unchangeable and eternal. By its commands it summons men to the performance of their duties; by its prohibitions it restrains them from doing wrong. To invalidate this law by human legislation is never morally right, nor is it permissible ever to restrict its operation; and to annul it wholly is impossible."

In 19th-century New England, as debates about the legality and morality of slavery raged, the call to a higher law became paramount. "They only can force me who obey a higher law than I," Thoreau wrote in "Resistance to Civil Government": "Seen from a lower point of view, the Constitution, with all its faults, is very good; the law and the courts are very respectable; even this State and this American government are, in many respects, very admirable, and rare things, to be thankful for, such as a great many have described them; but seen from a point of view a little higher, they are what I have described them; seen from a higher still, and the highest, who shall say what they are, or that they are worth looking at or thinking of at all?" [W 4:376, 383]. Cf. "Slavery in Massachusetts": "What is wanted is men, not of policy, but of probity,—who recognize a higher law than the Constitution, or the decision of the majority" [W 4:403].

**62** An abstract or summary of the chief points in a written work or a section of a written work.

**63** In *A Week on the Concord and Merrimack Rivers* Thoreau wrote: "It is remarkable that almost all speakers and writers feel it to be incumbent on them, sooner or later, to prove or to acknowledge the personality of God. . . . In reading a work on agriculture, we have to skip the author's moral reflections, and the words 'Providence' and 'He' scattered along the page, to come at the profitable level of what he has to say. What he calls his religion is for the most part offensive to the nostrils. He should know better than expose himself, and keep his foul sores covered till they are quite healed" [W 1:79].

**64** Thoreau experienced two deaths in the previous month and for over a month wrote neither in his journal nor in correspondence. On 11 January 1842 his brother John died of lockjaw. As he wrote on 21 February 1842: "I feel as if years had been crowded into the last month" [J 1:321]. Ralph Waldo Emerson's wife, Lidian Emerson (1802–1892), wrote to her sister on 11–12 January:

> I begin my letter with the strange sad news that John Thoreau has this afternoon left this world. He died of lockjaw occasioned by a slight cut on his thumb. Henry mentioned on Sunday morning that he had been at home helping the family who were all ailing; and that John was disabled from his usual work by having cut his finger. In the evening Mr. [Nathan?] Brooks came for him to go home again, and said they were alarmed by symptoms of the lockjaw in John. Monday John was given over by the physicians—and to-day he died—retaining his senses and some power of speech to the last. . . . Henry has been here this evening and seen Mr Emerson but no one else. He says John took leave of all the family on Monday with perfect calmness and more than resignation. . . . Henry has just been here—(it is now Wednesday noon) I love him for the feeling he showed and the effort he made to be cheerful. He did not give way in the least but his whole de-

Then Morning, Noon, and Evening, Spring, Summer, Autumn, and Winter, Night, Indian Summer, and the Mountains in the Horizon.

## 1842
### AGE 24–25

*January 8.* What offends me most in my compositions is the moral element in them.[63] The repentant say never a brave word. Their resolves should be mumbled in silence. Strictly speaking, morality is not healthy. Those undeserved joys which come uncalled and make us more pleased than grateful are they that sing.

*February 20.* The death of friends should inspire us as much as their lives.[64] If they are great and rich enough, they will leave consolation to the mourners before the expenses of the funerals.[65] It will not be hard to part with any worth, because it is worthy. How can any good depart? It does not go and come, but we. Shall we wait for it? Is it slower than we?

*February 21.* I must confess there is nothing so strange to me as my own body.[66] I love any other piece of nature, almost, better.

*March 11.* We can only live healthily the life the gods assign us. I must receive my life as passively as the willow leaf that flutters over the brook. I must not be for myself, but God's work, and that is always good. I will wait the breezes patiently, and grow as Nature shall determine. My fate cannot but be grand so. We may live the life of a plant or an animal, without living an animal life. This constant and universal content of the animal comes of resting quietly in God's palm. I feel as if I could at any time resign my life and the responsibility of living into

meanour was that of one struggling with sickness of heart. He came to take his clothes—and says he does not know when he shall return to us. We are wholly indebted to John for Waldo's picture. Henry and myself each carried him to a sitting but did not succeed in keeping him in the right attitude—and still enough. But John by his faculty of interesting children succeeded in keeping him looking as he should while the impression was making.

On 27 January Emerson's son Waldo (1836–1842) died from scarlatina. Thoreau wrote of him: "As for Waldo, he died as the mist rises from the brook, which the sun will soon dart his rays through. Do not the flowers die every autumn? He had not even taken root here. I was not startled to hear that he was dead;—it seemed the most natural event that could happen. His fine organization demanded it, and nature gently yielded its request. It would have been strange if he had lived" [C 63]. On 11 March he wrote to Emerson:

Nature is not ruffled by the rudest blast—The hurricane only snaps a few twigs in some nook of the forest. . . .
    Every blade in the field—every leaf in the forest—lays down its life in its season as beautifully as it was taken up. It is the pastime of a full quarter of the year. Dead trees—sere leaves—dried grass and herbs—are not these a good part of our life? And what is that pride of our autumnal scenery but the hectic flush—the sallow and cadaverous countenance of vegetation—Its painted throes—with the November air for canvass—
    When we look over the fields we are not saddened because the particular flowers or grasses will wither—for the law of their death is the law of new life[.] Will not the land be in good heart *because* the crops die down from year to year? The herbage cheerfully consents to bloom, and wither, and give place to a new.

So is it with the human plant. We are partial and selfish when we lament the death of the individual, unless our plaint be a paean to the departed soul, and a sigh as the wind sighs over the fields, which no shrub interprets into its private grief.
    One might as well go into mourning for every sere leaf—but the more innocent and wiser soul will snuff a fragrance in the gales of autumn, and congratulate Nature upon her health. [C 64–65]

**65**  This was reworked into the section on friendship in *A Week on the Concord and Merrimack Rivers:* "Even the death of Friends will inspire us as much as their lives. They will leave consolation to the mourners, as the rich leave money to defray the expenses of their funerals, and their memories will be incrusted over with sublime and pleasing thoughts, as monuments of other men are overgrown with moss; for our Friends have no place in the graveyard" [W 1:303].

**66**  Possible reference to Thoreau's sympathetic lockjaw following the death of John. Emerson wrote to his brother William (1801–1868) on 24 January 1842: "My pleasure at getting home on Saturday night at the end of my task was somewhat checked by finding that Henry Thoreau who has been at his fathers since the death of his brother was ill & threatened with *lockjaw!* his brother's disease. It is strange—unaccountable—yet the symptoms seems precise & on the increase. You may judge we were all alarmed & I not the least who have the highest hopes for this youth. This morning his affection be it what it may, is relieved essentially, & what is best, his own feeling of better health established."

67 Possible allusion to Luke 23:46: "And when Jesus had cried with a loud voice, he said, Father, into thy hands I commend my spirit."

68 Cf. 1840s note 65.

69 With the close of his school in 1841, Thoreau helped out in the family plumbago and pencil business. In his correspondence Thoreau wrote on 8 September 1841: "I, who am going to be a pencil-maker to-morrow, can sympathize with God Apollo, who served King Admetus for a while on earth" [C 47].

70 The First Welland Canal, between Lake Ontario and Lake Erie, was completed in 1829. Thoreau's unidentified schoolmate worked on the Second Welland Canal, which was begun in 1842 to accommodate the passage of larger ships.

God's hands,[67] and become as innocent, free from care, as a plant or stone.

*March 12.* Consider what a difference there is between living and dying. To die is not to *begin* to die, and *continue;* it is not a state of continuance, but of transientness; but to live is a condition of continuance, and does not mean to be born merely. There is no continuance of death. It is a transient phenomenon. Nature presents nothing in a state of death.

*March 13.* The sad memory of departed friends is soon incrusted over with sublime and pleasing thoughts, as their monuments are overgrown with moss.[68] Nature doth thus kindly heal every wound. By the mediation of a thousand little mosses and fungi, the most unsightly objects become radiant of beauty. There seem to be two sides to this world, presented us at different times, as we see things in growth or dissolution, in life or death. For seen with the eye of a poet, as God sees them, all are alive and beautiful; but seen with the historical eye, or the eye of the memory, they are dead and offensive. If we see Nature as pausing, immediately all mortifies and decays; but seen as progressing, she is beautiful.

*March 17.* I have been making pencils all day,[69] and then at evening walked to see an old schoolmate who is going to help make the Welland Canal navigable for ships round Niagara.[70] He cannot see any such motives and modes of living as I; professes not to look beyond the securing of certain "creature comforts." And so we go silently different ways, with all serenity, I in the still moonlight through the village this fair evening to write these thoughts in my journal, and he, forsooth, to mature his schemes to ends as good, maybe, but different. So are we two made, while the same stars shine quietly over us. If I or he be wrong, Nature yet consents placidly. She bites her lip and smiles to see how her children will agree. So does the Welland Canal get built, and other conveniences, while I live. Well and good, I must confess. Fast sailing ships are hence not detained.

*March 18.* Whatever book or sentence will bear to be read twice, we may be sure was thought twice.[71]

*March 21.* Who is old enough to have learned from experience?

*March 24.* Those authors are successful who do not *write down* to others, but make their own taste and judgment their audience. By some strange infatuation we forget that we do not approve what yet we recommend to others. It is enough if I please myself with writing; I am then sure of an audience.

*April 3.* On one side of man is the actual, and on the other the ideal.[72] The former is the province of the reason; it is even a divine light when directed upon it, but it cannot reach forward into the ideal without blindness.[73] The moon was made to rule by night, but the sun to rule by day. Reason will be but a pale cloud, like the moon, when one ray of divine light comes to illumine the soul.[74]

## 1843

### AGE 25–26

*April 19.* I should prefer that my farm be bounded by a river. It is to live on the outside of the world and to be well flanked on one side. It would increase my sense of

71 Thoreau was thinking about Carlyle, "who writes pictures or first impressions merely, which consequently will only bear a first reading" [J 1:336].

72 Thoreau differentiated between his actual— the life he experienced on a day-to-day basis— and his ideal, or real, life. He wrote to his friend H. G. O. Blake: "My actual life is a fact in view of which I have no occasion to congratulate myself, but for my faith and aspiration I have respect. It is from these that I speak" [C 216].

73 The Transcendentalists made a distinction between reason and understanding. The understanding examines that which can be proved; reason intuits what is beyond proof. Emerson explained it this way in a letter to his brother Edward (1805–1834) on 31 May 1834: "Reason is the highest faculty of the soul—what we mean often by the soul itself; it never *reasons,* never proves, it simply perceives; it is vision. The Understanding toils all the time, compares, contrives, adds, argues, near sighted but strong-sighted, dwelling in the present the expedient the customary. . . . Reason is potentially perfect in every man."

74 Cf. Thoreau's May 1851 translation from the French edition of the *Harivansa, ou Histoire de la Famille de Hari,* translated from Sanskrit into French by Simon Alexandre Langlois (1788–1854): "They are not ordinary practices which can bring light into the soul" [J 2:191].

**75** Geometrician: arithmetician specializing in geometry.

**76** Variantly in *A Week on the Concord and Merrimack Rivers:* "Men nowhere, east or west, live yet a *natural* life, round which the vine clings, and which the elm willingly shadows" [W 1:405].

**77** Latin: no more beyond, i.e., the pinnacle or highest point of excellence or achievement.

**78** Thoreau went to Staten Island on 6 May to tutor the sons of Emerson's brother William. Homesick, Thoreau returned to Concord sometime in November, and then went back to Staten Island briefly on 3 December to wind up his affairs.

security and my energy and boyancy when I would take any step, as the Geometer[75] cannot proceed without his base line is given.

*After June 19?* Men no where live as yet a natural life.[76] The poets even have not described it. Man's life must be of equal simplicity and sincerity with nature, and his actions harmonize with her grandeur and beauty. I do not know of any reformer who is *ultra plus ne,*[77] one unworthy to speak with critical reserve on this subject.

Shall we suffer a single action to be mean? We have now our Sabbaths and our moments of inspiration, as if these could be too protracted or constant. I see plainly that my own meanness is that which robs me of my birthright and shuts me out from the society of the gods.

The life of men will ere long be of such purity and innocence, that it will deserve to have the sun to light it by day and the moon by night, to be ushered in by the freshness and melody of spring, to be entertained by the luxuriance and vigor of summer, and matured and solaced by the hues and dignity of Autumn.

*August 26.* The future will no doubt be a more natural life than this. We shall be acquainted and shall use flowers and stars, and sun and moon, and occupy this nature which now stands over and around us. We shall reach up to the stars and pluck fruit from many parts of the universe. We shall purely use the earth and not abuse it. God is in the breeze and whispering leaves and we shall then hear him. We live in the midst of all the beauty and grandeur that was ever described or conceived.

*September 24.* Staten Island.[78]

The poet is he that hath fat enough like bears and marmots to suck his claws o' winters. He feeds on his own marrow. He hibernates in this world, till spring breaks. He records a moment of pure life. Who can see these cities and say that there is any life in them? I walked through New York yesterday, and met no real and living person. I love to think of dormice and all that tribe of dormant creatures, who have such a superfluity of life while man is pining, enveloped in thick folds of life, impervious to winter. I love to think as I walk over the snowy plain of those happy dreamers that lie in the sod. The poet is a sort of dormouse, early in the autumn he goes in to winter quarters till the sun shall fetch the year about. But most men lead a starved existence, like hawks that would fain keep on the wing, and catch but a sparrow now and then.

*September 29.* I am winding up my music-box;[79] and, as I pause meanwhile, the strains burst forth like a pent-up fountain of the middle ages. Music is strangely allied to the past. Every era has its strain. It awakens and colors my memories.

The first sparrow of spring! The year beginning with younger hope than ever. The first silvery warblings heard over the bare dank fields, as if the last flakes of winter tinkled as they fell. What, then, are histories, chronologies, and all written revelations? Flakes of warm sunlight fall on the congealed fields. The brooks and rills sing carols and glees for the spring. The marsh hawk already seeks the first slimy life that awakes. The sough of melting snow is heard in all dells, and on all hillsides, and by the sunny river-banks; and the ice dissolves in the ponds. The earth sends forth, as it were, an inward heat; and not yellow like the sun, but green is the color of *her* flames; and the grass flames up on the warm hillsides as her spring fire. Methinks the sight of the first sod of fresh grass in the spring would make the reformer reconsider his schemes; the faithless and despairing man revive. Grass is a symbol of perpetual growth—its blades

**79** Richard Fuller (1824–1869), who had come to Concord in September 1841 and been tutored there by Thoreau, gave him this music box in the winter of 1842 as a memento of their excursion to Mount Wachusett (cf. "A Walk to Wachusett") and as thanks for his tutoring. (Thoreau "furnished me with a good deal of companionship," Fuller wrote in his *Recollections.* "He was thoroughly unselfish, truly refined, sincere, and of a true spirit.") Lidian Emerson wrote to her husband on 15 January 1843: "I never saw any one made so happy by a new possession. He said nothing could have been so acceptable. After we had heard its performance he said he must hasten to exhibit it to his sisters & mother. My heart really warmed with sympathy, and admiration at his whole demeanour on the occasion—and I like human nature better than I did. Richard's note was very good, I thought. It ended with saying that in presenting the box he was but an interested capitalist—and should look for its harmonies to re-appear in the poet's senses."

Thoreau left his music box with Nathaniel Hawthorne (1804–1864) for a short period before going to Staten Island. In his *American Notebooks* Hawthorne wrote on 8 April 1843 that he was "occasionally refreshing myself with a tune from Mr. Thoreau's musical-box, which he had left in my keeping." The next day, however, he noted: "Many times I wound and re-wound Mr. Thoreau's little musical-box; but certainly its peculiar sweetness had evaporated, and I am pretty sure that I should throw it out the window were I doomed to hear it long and often." The music box was returned to Thoreau on 11 April when he visited Hawthorne before departing for New York.

**80** Various plants of the genus *Uvularia* having yellowish drooping bell-shaped flowers.

**81** Also known as sweet everlasting (*Gnaphalium obtusifolium*).

**82** On 17 December 1859 Thoreau described nature's beneficence: "By the side of the Pout's Nest, I see on the pure white snow what looks like dust for half a dozen inches under a twig. Looking closely, I find that the twig is hardhack and the dust its slender, light-brown, chaffy-looking seed, which falls still in copious showers, dusting the snow, when I jar it; and here are the tracks of a sparrow which has jarred the twig and picked the minute seeds a long time, making quite a hole in the snow. The seeds are so fine that it must have got more snow than seed at each peck. But they probably look large to its microscopic eyes. I see, when I jar it, that a meadow-sweet close by has quite similar, but larger, seeds. This the reason, then, that these plants rise so high above the snow and retain their seed, dispersing it on the least jar over each successive layer of snow beneath them; or it is carried to a distance by the wind. What abundance and what variety in the diet of these small granivorous birds, while I find only a few nuts still! These stiff weeds which no snow can break down hold their provender. What the cereals are to men, these are to the sparrows. The only threshing they require is that the birds fly against their spikes or stalks" [J 13:30–31].

**83** From medieval times when bakers were required to place a unique registered mark on their breads.

like a long green ribbon, streaming from the sod into the summer, checked indeed by the frost, but anon pushing on again, lifting its last year's spear of withered hay with the fresh life below. I have seen where early in spring the clumps of grass stood with their three inches of new green upholding their withered spears of the last autumn. It is as steady a growth as the rill which leaps out of the ground—indeed it is almost identical with that; for in the vigorous fertile days of June when the rills are dry, the grass-blades are their only channels. And from year to year, the herds drink this green stream, and the mower cuts from the out-welling supply—what their needs require.

So the human life but dies down to the surface of Nature, but puts forth a green blade to eternity. When the ground is completely bare of snow, and a few warm days have dried its surface, it is pleasant to compare the faint tender signs of the infant year, just peeping forth, with the stately beauty of the withered vegetation which has withstood the winter,—the various thistles which have not yet sown their seeds; the graceful reeds and rushes, whose winter is more gay and stately than their summer, as if not till then was their beauty ripe. I never tire of admiring their arching, drooping sheaflike tops. It is like summer to our winter memories, and one of the forms which art loves to perpetuate—wild oats[80] perchance, and Life Everlasting,[81] whose autumn has now arrived. These unexhausted granaries of the winter with their seeds entertain the earliest birds.[82]

We are obliged to respect that custom which stamps the loaf of bread with the sheaf of wheat and the sickle.[83] Men have come at length after so many centuries to regard these gifts properly. The gift of bread even to the poor is perhaps better received than any other—more religiously given and taken, and is not liable to be a stone. The manner in which men consider husbandry is marked and worthy of the race. They have slowly learned thus much. Let the despairing race of men know that there is in Nature no sign of decay, but universal uninterrupted vigor. All waste and ruin has a speedy period. Who ever detected a wrinkle on her brow, or a weather seam, or a gray hair on her crown, or a rent in her garment? No one sees Nature who sees her not as young and fresh, without history. We may have such intercourse to-day, as we imagine to constitute the employment of gods. We live here to have intercourse with rivers, forests, mountains—beasts and men. How few do we see conversing with these things!

We think the ancients were foolish who worshipped the sun. I would worship it forever if I had grace to do so. Observe how a New England farmer moves in the midst of Nature, his potato and grain fields, and consider how poets have dreamed that the more religious shepherd lived, and ask which is the wiser, which made the highest use of Nature? As if the Earth were made to yield pumpkins mainly! Did you never observe that the seasons were ripening another kind of fruit?

*October 12.* It is hard to read a contemporary poet critically, for we go within the shallowest verse and inform it with all the life and promise of this day. We are such a near and kind and knowing audience as he will never have again. We go within the fane[84] of the temple and hear the faint[85] music of the worshippers, but posterity will have to stand without and consider the vast proportions and grandeur of the building. It will be solidly and conspicuously great and beautiful, for the multitudes who pass at a distance, as well as for the few pilgrims who enter in to its shrine.

The Poet will prevail and be popular in spite of his faults, and in spite of his beauties too. He will be careful only that you feel the hammer hit, without regarding the

84 Archaic, primarily a poetic term: temple or place consecrated to religion.
85 Not only in its common meaning as indistinct or quiet, but in its earlier meaning as feigned.

87 Probable allusion to Shakespeare's *Richard III:* cf. 1851 note 152.

88 In Greek mythology, the final resting place of the souls of the virtuous, and thus a place or condition of ideal happiness.

form of its head. No man is enough his own overseer to take cognizance of *all* the particulars which impress men in his actions. The impression will always proceed from a more general influence than he can ever dream of. We may count our steps, but we must not count our breaths. We must be careful not to mix consciousness with the vital functions.

May the gods deliver us from too critical an age—when cross-eyed, near-sighted men are born, who, instead of looking out and bathing their eyes in the deep heaven, introvert them, and think to walk erect and not to stumble by watching their feet, and not by preserving pure hearts.

*November 2.* I believe that there is an ideal or real Nature, infinitely more perfect than the actual, as there is an ideal life of man;[86] else where are the glorious summers[87] which in vision sometimes visit my brain? When Nature ceases to be supernatural to a man, what will he do then? Of what worth is human life if its actions are no longer to have this sublime and unexplored scenery? Who will build a cottage and dwell in it with enthusiasm if not in the Elysian fields?[88]

*November 7.* Let two stand on the highway, and it shall be known that the sun belongs to one rather than the other; the one will be found to claim, while the other simply retains possession. The winds blow for one more than another, and on numerous occasions the uncertain or unworthy possessors silently relinquish their right in them. The most doubtful claimants have paid their money and taken a deed of their birthright, but the real owner is forever known to all men wherever he goes, and no one disputes his claim. For he cannot help using and deriving the profit, while to the dishonest possessor an estate is as idle as his parchment deed of it, and that is all he has purchased. Wherever the owner goes, inanimate things will fly to him and adhere.

## 1845
### AGE 27–28

*July 5. Saturday.* Walden.—Yesterday I came here to live.[89]

*July 6.* I wish to meet the facts of life—the vital facts, which are the phenomena or actuality the gods meant to show us—face to face, and so I came down here.[90] Life! who knows what it is, what it does? If I am not quite right here, I am less wrong than before.

*After July 14.* And earlier to-day came five Lestrigones,[91] railroad men[92] who take care of the road, some of them at least. They still represent the bodies of men, transmitting arms and legs and bowels downward from those remote days to more remote. They have some got a rude wisdom withal, thanks to their dear experience. And one with them, a handsome younger man, a sailor-like, Greek-like man, says: "Sir, I like your notions. I think I shall live so myself. Only I should like the wilder country, where is more game. I have been among the Indians near Appalachicola.[93] I have lived with them. I like your kind of life. Good day. I wish you success and happiness."

*After August 23.* Why not live a hard and emphatic life, not to be avoided, full of adventures and work, learn much in it, travel much, though it be only in these woods?[94] I sometimes walk across a field with unexpected expansion and long-missed content, as if there were a field worthy of me. The usual daily boundaries of life are dispersed, and I see in what field I stand.

89 In a journal entry on 17 January 1852, Thoreau noted: "It was on the 4th of July that I put a few things into a hay-rigging some of which I had made myself, & commenced housekeeping" [PJ 4:263]. Friday, 4 July 1845, was a day of fair weather. The sun rose at 4:29 A.M. and set at 8 P.M. Although Thoreau stated in *Walden*, "When first I took up my abode in the woods, that is, began to spend my nights as well as days there, which, by accident, was on Independence Day, or the fourth of July, 1845" [Wa 81], it is likely that his move on that date was a purposeful and deliberate act to establish a connection with national independence.

90 In *Walden* this became: "I went to the woods because I wished to live deliberately, to front only the essential facts of life, and see if I could not learn what it had to teach, and not, when I came to die, discover that I had not lived" [Wa 88].

91 Laestrygones, which, according to John Lemprière's (1765?–1824) *Bibliotheca Classica*, Thoreau's primary classical dictionary, were "the most ancient inhabitants of Sicily. . . . They fed on human flesh, and when Ulysses came on their coasts, they sunk his ships and devoured his companions. . . . They were of gigantic stature, according to Homer."

92 Working for the Boston and Fitchburg Railroad, laying the tracks for which began in 1843 and reached Concord in 1844.

93 The Appalachicola, or Apalachicola, part of the Creek Nation, who lived by the river of the same name in northwest Florida.

94 Cf. 6 August 1851.

95 Cf. 8 July 1852. As Thoreau wrote in *Walden:* "I got up early and bathed in the pond; that was a religious exercise, and one of the best things which I did" [Wa 86].

96 Brahme, or Brahma, is the essence of spiritual being in Hindu philosophy. Cf. 1850 note 9.

97 Allusion to Matthew 14:25: "And in the fourth watch of the night Jesus went unto them, walking on the sea."

## 1848
### AGE 30–31

*After July 30.* I find that I conciliate the gods by some sacrament as bathing,[95] or abstemiousness in diet, or rising early, and directly they smile on me. These are my sacraments.

Considering how few poetical friendships there are, it is astonishing that so many men and women are married. It would seem as if men were too ready to be married, as they are to choose their profession in life. As if they yielded a too easy obedience to nature without consulting their genius. But one may be drunk with love without being any nearer to finding his mate. If common sense had been consulted, how many marriages would never have taken place? If uncommon or divine sense were consulted, how few such as any that we witness would ever take place?

## 1849
### AGE 31–32

*After May 26.* The fragments of fables handed down to us from the remotest antiquity in the mythologies and traditions of all nations would seem to indicate that the life of Christ, his divine preeminence and his miracles, are not without a precedent in the history of mankind. Brahma.[96]

I learned this by my experiments in the woods, of more value perhaps than all the rest—that if one will advance confidently in the direction of his dreams, and live that life which he has imagined,—if he will walk the water,[97] if he will step forth on to the clouds, if he will heartily embrace the true, if in his life he will transcend the temporal,—he shall walk securely, perfect success shall attend him, there shall be the *terra firma*[98] or the *coelum firmior.*[99] If he will do that in which alone he has faith, if he will yield to love and go whither it leads him, he shall be translated,[100] he shall know no interval, he shall be surrounded by new environments, new and more universal and liberal laws shall establish themselves around and within.[101]

It is not enough that my friend[102] is good, he must be wise. Our intercourse is likely to be a tragedy with that one who cannot measure us. Where there is not discernment the behavior even of a pure soul may in effect amount to coarseness. In a difference with a friend I have felt that our intercourse was prophaned when that friend made haste come to speech about it. I am more grieved that my friend can so easily give utterance to his wounded feelings—than by what he says. Such a wound cannot be permanently healed. There is a certain vulgarity and coarseness in that sentiment that is liable to a common difference, such wordy reproaches as are heard in street and the kitchen.

*After September 11.* To have a brother or a sister,[103] to have a gold mine on your farm, to find diamonds in the gravel heaps before your door,—how rare these things are.

What a difference whether you have a brother on earth or not, whether in all your walks you meet only strangers, or in one house is one who knows you, and whom you know.[104]

We never have the benefit of our friend's criticism, and none is so severe and searching, until he is estranged from us.

No one appreciates our virtues like our friend, yet methinks that I do not receive from my friend that criti-

98  Latin: solid ground.
99  Latin: firmer heaven.
100  Removed to a higher plane, as in Enoch's translation to Heaven in Hebrews 11:5: "By faith Enoch was translated that he should not see death; and was not found, because God had translated him."
101  In *Walden* this became: "I learned this, at least, by my experiment; that if one advances confidently in the direction of his dreams, and endeavors to live the life which he has imagined, he will meet with a success unexpected in common hours. He will put some things behind, will pass an invisible boundary; new, universal, and more liberal laws will begin to establish themselves around and within him; or the old laws be expanded, and interpreted in his favor in a more liberal sense, and he will live with the license of a higher order of beings. In proportion as he simplifies his life, the laws of the universe will appear less complex, and solitude will not be solitude, nor poverty poverty, nor weakness weakness. If you have built castles in the air, your work need not be lost; that is where they should be. Now put the foundations under them" [Wa 313–314].
102  Throughout the journal, the epithet "my friend" is commonly used for Emerson. At various times, such as here, each felt disillusionment and disappointment with the other. Emerson, aware of the difficulties of sustaining the heights of friendship, wrote in "Society and Solitude": "We begin with friendships, and all our youth is a reconnoitring and recruiting of the holy fraternity they shall combine for the salvation of men. But so the remoter stars seem a nebula of united light, yet there is no group which a telescope will not resolve; and the dearest friends are separated by impassable gulfs. . . . Though the stuff of tragedy and of romances is in a moral union of two superior persons whose confidence in each other for long years, out of sight and in sight, and against all appearances, is at last justified by victorious proof of probity to gods and men, causing joyful emotions, tears and glory,—though there be for

heroes this *moral union*, yet they too are as far off as ever from an intellectual union, and the moral union is for comparatively low and external purposes, like the coöperation of a ship's company or of a fire-club. But how insular and pathetically solitary are all the people we know!" Edward Waldo Emerson (1844–1930) summed up his father's relationship with Thoreau as a "friendship which, in spite of the difference of fourteen years in their ages, and of temperamental impediments to its fullest enjoyment, was deep and lasting. . . . Although their personal relations could not be close, each held the other in highest honor."
**103** Probable reference to his brother John (cf. 1840s note 64) and his sister Helen, who had died on 14 June, although Thoreau may be writing in general terms here.
**104** This, and the previous entry, became part of Thoreau's brief essay on "Love" sent to Blake in September 1852: "What a difference, whether, in all your walks, you meet only strangers, or in one house is one who knows you, and whom you know. To have a brother or a sister! To have a gold mine on your farm! To find diamonds in the gravel heaps before your door! How rare these things are! To share the day with you,—to people the earth. Whether to have a god or a goddess for companion in your walks, or to walk alone with hinds and villains and carles" [W 6:203].
**105** Emerson was encouraging and full of praise for *A Week on the Concord and Merrimack Rivers*, urging Thoreau toward publication. Emerson wrote to Evert Duyckinck (1816–1878) at Wiley and Putnam on Thoreau's behalf on 12 March 1847 that Thoreau's book "has many merits. It will be attractive to *lovers of nature*, in every sense, that is, to naturalists, and to poets, as Isaak Walton. It will be attractive to scholars for its excellent literature, & to all thoughtful persons for its originality & profoundness." Despite various rejections, and offers to print at Thoreau's own risk, Emerson continued to urge Thoreau: "I am not of the opinion that your book should be delayed a month. I should print it at once, nor do I think that you would incur any risk in doing so that you cannot

cism which is most valuable and indispensable to me until he is estranged from me. He who knows best what we are, knows what we are not. He will never tell me the fatal truth which it concerns me most to know until he is estranged from—and then the harmless truth will be shot with a poisoned arrow will have a poisoned barb.

When we are such friends, and have such for our friends, that our love is not partiality, that truth is not crowded out or postponed, or delayed, there will be Friendship.

Now first we are dealt with absolutely. This truth without that poison and we were friends still and indeed.

The fruit of partiality is enmity.

I had a friend, I wrote a book, I asked my friend's criticism, I never got but praise for what was good in it. My friend became estranged from me and then I got blame for all that was bad, and so I got at last the criticism which I wanted.[105]

While my friend was my friend he flattered me, and I never heard the truth from him, but when he became my enemy he shot it to me on a poisoned arrow.

There is as much hatred as love in the world. Hate is a good critic.

When two can treat each other with absolute truth, then there will be but those two in the world. Then men will no longer be divided but be one as God is.


How near to good is what is wild.[106] There is the marrow of nature, there her divine liquors, that is the wine I love. A man's health requires as many acres of meadow as his farm does loads of muck. They are indispensable both to men and corn. There are the only strong meats.[107] We pine and starve and lose spirit on the thin gruel of society.

A town is saved not by any righteous men in it[108] but by the woods and swamps that surround it.

*After October 15.* Why should we be related as mortals merely, as limited to one state of existence? Our lives are immortal, our transmigrations are infinite. The virtue that we are lives ever, the vice dieth ever. Shall I exhibit to my friend a human narrowness? To what purpose mythology? The petty tragedy or comedy of our human life—we can sit spectators of it—let it pass. I would meet my friend not in the light or shadow of our human life alone—but as daimons.[109] We should not be less tender and human sympathizing for this because we should meet intimately as essences.

I should consider this friend of mine is a *great* fellow. My knowledge of him, our intercourse, is not to be limited to a few of nature's revolutions, a few paltry summers and winters. No! no! We are great fellows. We shall be a long time together. I do not despair of knowing him better. Ours is a tragedy of more than five acts. This is not the fifth act in our tragedy. No, no! Blow high, blow low,[110] I will come upon my feet, and holding my friend by the hand. The undertaker will have a dusty time that undertakes to bury me. I go with the party of the gods. What falsehoods men do tell. They say that life's a fallacy. They are benighted, they are ineffectual men who walk in the valley of the shadow of Death.[111] I am not a-going to be a man merely,—I will be Hari.[112]

What sort of fruit comes of living as if you were a-going to die? Live rather as if you were coming to life. How can the end of living be death? The end of living is life. Living is an active transitive state to life. Life in the green state.

well afford" [C 195]. Following publication in 1849, however, Emerson refused to review it for the *Massachusetts Quarterly Review* when requested by Theodore Parker.

**106** Allusion to Ben Jonson's (1572–1637) masque *Love Freed from Ignorance and Folly* (l. 296): "How near to good is what is fair!" On the wild, cf. 27 January 1853 and "Walking": "Life consists with wildness. The most alive is the wildest. Not yet subdued to man, its presence refreshes him. One who pressed forward incessantly and never rested from his labors, who grew fast and made infinite demands on life, would always find himself in a new country or wilderness, and surrounded by the raw material of life. He would be climbing over the prostrate stems of primitive forest-trees" [W 5:226].

**107** Profound or philosophical thought, or higher doctrine, from Hebrews 5:12–14: "For when for the time ye ought to be teachers, ye have need that one teach you again which be the first principles of the oracles of God; and are become such as have need of milk, and not of strong meat. For every one that useth milk is unskillful in the word of righteousness: for he is a babe. But strong meat belongeth to them that are of full age, even those who by reason of use have their senses exercised to discern both good and evil."

**108** Allusion to Genesis 18, in which Abraham attempts to save Sodom if he can find ten righteous people.

**109** In Greek mythology, an attendant spirit or genius (cf. 1830s note 58), not to be confused with the malignant Judeo-Christian demon.

**110** Allusion to Charles Dibdin's (1745–1814) nautical song "Blow High, Blow Low." Dibdin also composed Thoreau's favorite song, "Poor Tom Bowling": cf. 1857 note 48.

**111** Allusion to Psalm 23:4: "Yea, though I walk through the valley of the shadow of death, I will fear no evil: for thou art with me; thy rod and thy staff they comfort me."

**112** Shapeless omnipresent form of Vishnu, a four-armed, blue-skinned, humanoid-shaped Hindu god.

1 Sir Richard Arkwright (1732–1792), who established cotton mills that were among the first to
utilize machinery on a large scale.
2 John Rennie (1761–1821), Scottish engineer and
bridge-builder, who started out as a millwright.
3 Mill towns in New Hampshire and Massachusetts, respectively.

## 1850

AGE 32–33

*After January 5.* There is no interpreter between us and
our consciousness.

We lose our friends when we cease to be friends, not
when they die. Then they depart; then we are sad and go
into mourning for them. Death is no separation compared with that which takes place when we cease to have
confidence in one with whom we have walked in confidence, when we cease to love one whom we had loved,
when we know him no more. When we look for him and
cannot find him, how completely is he departed!

*February 28.* I sometimes discovered a miniature water-
wheel, a saw or grist mill, where the whole volume of
water in some tiny rill was conducted through a junk
bottle in at the open bottom and out at the nose, where
some county boy whose house was not easy to be seen,
some Arkwright[1] or Rennie[2] was making his first essay
in mechanics,—some little trip-hammer in operation
mimicking the regular din of a factory,—where the wild
weeds and huckleberry bushes hang unmolested over the
stream as the pines still do at Manchester and Lawrence.[3]
It was the work of a fabulous, farmer boy such as I never
saw. To come upon such unquestionable traces of a boy
when I doubted if any were lingering still in this vicinity,
as when you discover the trail of an otter.

One Sunday afternoon in March when the earth
which had once been bared was again covered with a few

inches of snow rapidly melting in the sun, as I was walking in a retired cross road away from the town, at a distance from any farmhouse, I heard suddenly wafted over the meadow a faint tink-tink, tink-tink, as of a cow-bell amidst the birches and huckleberry bushes, but I considered that it was quite too early in the season for cows to be turned out to pasture, the ground being covered with snow and it was not time to think of new-butter, and the cow-bells were all safely put away in the cupboard or the till of a chest in the farm chamber. It made me think of the days when I went huckleberrying a long time ago and heard the distant tinkling of some cow's bell who was not yet mired in the swamp. From association I know of no more sweet and wild sound than this piece of copper yields, though it may not be compounded with much art. Well, still the sound came over the meadow louder and louder as I walked on,—tink tink tink, too regular for a cow-bell—and I conjectured that it was a man drilling a hole in a rock, and this was the sound of his sledge on the drill, but it was Sunday and what Concord farmer could be drilling stone! I referred the mystery to the woods beyond the meadow where alone, as I thought, it could be concealed, and began to think it was produced by some owl or other bird under peculiar circumstances. So getting over the fence I directed my steps through the meadow toward the wood.

But as I advanced the sound seemed gradually to sink into the earth while it grew louder and louder, till finally it proceeded from the open meadow ground itself, and I thought of muskrats, minks and otters, and expected to make a discovery in natural history. I stepped eagerly over the quaking ground,[4] a peeping hyla,[5] and then in a little rill not more than a foot wide but as deep as wide, and swollen by the melting snows, was a small water-mill, and at each revolution the wheel, its crank, raised a small hammer which as often fell on a tongueless cow-

4 Literal translation for quagmire, from quake and mire: soft wet land with a surface firm enough to bear a person but which shakes or yields under the feet.
5 The piping frog (*Hyla pickeringii*), a small American tree frog that sings with high, shrill, but musical notes in early spring while breeding in swamps and ditches.

6 Colloquial or Thoreauvian name for an unidentified plant, but possibly the skunk cabbage
(*Symplocarpus foetidus*), which Thoreau described
on 23 June 1853: "A skunk-cabbage leaf makes
the best vessel to drink out of at a spring, it is so
large, already somewhat dishing, oftenest entire,
and grows near at hand, and, though its odor
when the stem is cut off is offensive, it does not
flavor the water and is not perceived in drinking"
[J 5:296]. In "Natural History of Massachusetts"
Thoreau wrote: "Nature is mythical and mystical always, and works with the license and ex-
travagance of genius. She has her luxurious and
florid style as well as art. Having a pilgrim's cup
to make, she gives to the whole—stem, bowl,
handle, and nose—some fantastic shape, as if it
were to be the car of some fabulous marine deity,
a Nereus or Triton" [W 5:125–126].

7 Two miles west of Walden Pond, extending
west from the Sudbury River to Miles' Swamp.

8 Cf. 1851 note 39.

bell which was nailed down on a board, a loud tinkling gurgle as of water leaking out of the meadow. The little rill itself seemed delighted with the din and rushed over the miniature dam and fell on the water-wheel eagerly as if delighted at and proud of this loud tinkling, fast by a pilgrim's cup,[6] the bell all spattered with mist from the fall above, and when I had walked half a mile away a favorable wind wafted to me in a hollow among the hills, its faint tink-tink-tink-tink. Just a fortnight after, when a new snow had fallen, I walked near enough to this meadow to hear the steady tink tink from the water-wheel away there in the out-skirts of the town, and what is stranger than all, that very evening when I came home from a neighbor's through the village far in the night, to my astonishment I heard from far over the meadows toward the woods more than a mile off in a direct line the distinct tink tink tink of that hammer. As I called the family to the window in the village to hear the sound of the boy's trip-hammer in Nut Meadow Brook,[7] a distant and solitary place which most of them had never seen,— and they all heard it distinctly, even some old ears which ordinarily could not hear the birds sing and were greatly astonished,—which I had told them of a fortnight be-fore as of a thing far away, the sound was wafted over the water, for the meadows were flooded, a peculiar state or atmosphere.

Before I had thought how unlike this to all the village sounds, how remote from them as the tinkling of the rill itself, as the golden age,[8] the village boys know not of it. It lies far back in the out-skirting meadows as the first in-vention of the water mill in history, and now this evening it was the one sound which possessed all the village street, and no doubt many a villager heard it but knew not from what remoteness as of antiquity it proceeded, borne on the breeze gale of time from a simpler age when the sound of every artisan was hushed,—no flail, no tinkling anvil was heard,—there was the still spring night, the slumbering village, and for all sound the boy's water-wheel.

The next day I went out and listened in broad daylight, but no sound of the water-wheel in Nut Meadow Brook could be heard more than the domestic sounds of the early ages. You could not hear it,—you could not remember it,—and yet the fit ear could hear it ever, the ear of the boy who made it. The busy and bustling village heard it not, yet the sound of the boy's water-wheel mingled with the din of its streets and at night was heard above the slumberous breathing when other sounds were hushed, where the skunk-cabbage grew, making music for the meadow mice and I could not believe that it still agitated with its waves of sound the atmosphere of the village, that it was still echoing through the streets.

*After April 26.* The Hindoos are more serenely and thoughtfully religious than the Hebrews.[9] They have perhaps a purer, more independent and impersonal knowledge of God. Their religious books[10] describe the first inquisitive and contemplative access to God; the Hebrew bible a conscientious return, a grosser and more personal repentance. Repentance is not a free and fair highway to God. A wise man will dispense with repentance. It is shocking and passionate. God prefers that you approach him thoughtful, not penitent, though you are the chief of sinners.[11] It is only by forgetting yourself that you draw near to him.

What extracts from the Vedas I have read[12] fall on me like the light of a higher and purer luminary, which describes a loftier course through a purer stratum,—free from particulars, simple, universal. It rises on me like the full moon after the stars have come out, wading through some far summer stratum of the sky.

9  In *A Week on the Concord and Merrimack Rivers* Thoreau described the Hindu religion as: "a sublime conservatism; as wide as the world, and as unwearied as time; preserving the universe with Asiatic anxiety, in that state in which it appeared to their minds. These philosophers dwell on the inevitability and unchangeableness of laws, on the power of temperament and constitution, the three *goon,* or qualities, and the circumstances [of] birth and affinity. The end is an immense consolation; eternal absorption in Brahma. Their speculations never venture beyond their own table-lands, though they are high and vast as they. Buoyancy, freedom, flexibility, variety, possibility, which also are qualities of the Unnamed, they deal not with. The undeserved reward is to be earned by an everlasting moral drudgery; the incalculable promise of the morrow is, as it were, weighed. And who will say that their conservatism has not been effectual?" [W 1:140–141].

10  The most ancient and sacred literature of the Hindus, the product of divine revelation, and handed down in four collections: the *Rigveda* ("The Veda of Verses"); the *Yajurveda* ("The Veda of Sacrificial Texts"); the *Samaveda* ("The Veda of Chants"); and the *Atharvaveda* ("The Veda of the Fire-Priest"). In its wider sense, it also includes the *Brahmanas,* the mystical *Aranyakas,* and the *Upanishads.* The impact of Thoreau's reading the Vedas is apparent by his several references to these texts throughout his journals and other writings.

11  Thoreau did not believe in the sacrament of penance in the Catholic Church: contrition, confession, penance, and absolution. In *Walden* Thoreau wrote that his neighbors in Concord "appeared to me to be doing penance in a thousand remarkable ways" [Wa 2]. Emerson wrote in "Self-Reliance" that man's "virtues are penances. I do not wish to expiate, but to live."

12  Rajah Rammohun Roy's (ca. 1772–1833) *Translation of Several Principal Books, Passages, and Texts of the Veds and of Some Controversial Works of Brahmunical Theology.*

13  Names for the principal deities in, respectively, Hinduism, Buddhism, and many Native American religions.

14  For Thoreau, all religion and scripture were given the same status. In the "Sunday" chapter of *A Week on the Concord and Merrimack Rivers* he wrote: "The reading which I love best is the scriptures of the several nations, though it happens that I am better acquainted with those of the Hindoos, the Chinese, and the Persians, than of the Hebrews, which I have come to last. Give me one of these bibles, and you have silenced me for a while" [W 1:72]. Cf. After 26 May 1849.

15  The Chinese custom of foot-binding began in the Song Dynasty (960–976) as a practice to produce aesthetically pleasing small feet in women. The Chinook tribe was noted for artificial flattening of the head. Washington Irving wrote in *Astoria*: "A singular custom prevails not merely among the Chinooks, but among most of the tribes about this part of the coast, which is the flattening of the forehead. . . . It must be noted, however, that this flattening of the head has something in it of aristocratical significancy, like the crippling of the feet among the Chinese ladies of quality," and commenting later, "It is one of those instances of human caprice, like the crippling of the feet in China, which are quite incomprehensible."

16  On the west side of Sawmill River, in Haverhill, Massachusetts. In *A Week on the Concord and Merrimack Rivers* Thoreau told the story of Hannah Dustin, sometimes Dustan (b. 1657):

> On the thirty-first day of March, one hundred and forty-two years before this, probably about this time in the afternoon, there were hurriedly paddling down this part of the river, between the pine woods which then fringed these banks, two white women and a boy, who had left an island at the mouth of the Contoocook before daybreak. They were slightly clad for the season, in the English fashion, and handled their paddles unskillfully, but with nervous energy and determination, and at the bottom

❧

I do not prefer one religion or philosophy to another. I have no sympathy with the bigotry and ignorance which make transient and partial and puerile distinctions between one man's faith or form of faith and another's, — as Christian and heathen. I pray to be delivered from narrowness, partiality, exaggeration, bigotry. To the philosopher all sects, all nations, are alike. I like Brahma, Hari, Buddha, the Great Spirit,[13] as well as God.[14]

Shoes are commonly too narrow. If you should take off a gentleman's shoes, you would find that his foot was wider than his shoe. Think of his wearing such an engine! walking in it many miles year after year! A shoe which presses against the sides of the foot is to be condemned. To compress the foot like the Chinese is as bad as to compress the head like the Flatheads,[15] for the head and the foot are one body. The narrow feet, — they greet each other on the two sides of the Pacific. A sensible man will not follow fashion in this respect, but reason. Better moccasins, or sandals, or even bare feet, than a tight shoe. A wise man will wear a shoe wide and large enough, shaped somewhat like the foot, and tied with a leather string, and so go his way in peace, letting his foot fall at every step.

*May 12.* Sunday, May 12, 1850, visited the site of the Dustin house in the northwest part of Haverhill,[16] now but a slight indentation in a corn-field, three or four feet deep, with an occasional brick and cellar-stone turned up in plowing. The owner, Dick Kimball,[17] made much of the corn grown in this hole, some ears of which were sent to Philadelphia.[18] The apple tree which is said to have stood north from the house at a considerable distance is gone. A brick house occupied by a descendant is visible from the spot, and there are old cellar-holes in the neighborhood, probably the sites of some of the other eight houses which were burned on that day. It is a question with some which is the site of the true Dustin house.

In all my rambles I have seen no landscape which can make me forget Fair Haven. I still sit on its Cliff in a new spring day, and look over the awakening woods and the river, and hear the new birds sing, with the same delight as ever. It is as sweet a mystery to me as ever, what this world is. Fair Haven Lake[19] in the south, with its pine-covered island and its meadows, the hickories putting out fresh young yellowish leaves, and the oaks light-grayish ones, while the oven-bird thrums his sawyer-like strain, and the chewink[20] rustles through the dry leaves or repeats his jingle on a tree-top, and the wood thrush, the genius of the wood, whistles for the first time his clear and thrilling strain,—it sounds as it did the first time I heard it. The sight of these budding woods intoxicates me,—this diet drink.[21]

I have been surprised to discover the amount and the various kinds of life which a single shallow swamp will sustain. On the south side of the pond,[22] not more than a quarter of a mile from it, is a small meadow of ten or a dozen acres in the woods,[23] considerably lower than Walden, and which by some is thought to be fed by the former by a subterranean outlet,—which is very likely, for its shores are quite springy and its supply of water is abundant and unfailing,—indeed tradition says that a sawmill once stood over its outlet,[24] though its whole extent, including its sources, is not more than I have mentioned,—a meadow through which the Fitchburg Railroad passes by a very high causeway, which required many a carload of sand, where the laborers for a long time seemed to make no progress, for the sand settled so much in the night that by morning they were where they were

of their canoe lay the still bleeding scalps of ten of the aborigines. They were Hannah Dustan, and her nurse, Mary Neff, both of Haverhill, eighteen miles from the mouth of this river, and an English boy, named Samuel Lennardson, escaping from captivity among the Indians. On the 15th of March previous, Hannah Dustan had been compelled to rise from childbed, and half dressed, with one foot bare, accompanied by her nurse, commence an uncertain march, in still inclement weather, through the snow and the wilderness. She had seen her seven elder children flee with their father, but knew not of their fate. She had seen her infant's brains dashed out against an apple tree, and had left her own and her neighbors' dwellings in ashes. . . . The family of Hannah Dustan all assembled alive once more, except the infant whose brains were dashed out against the apple tree, and there have been many who in later times have lived to say that they had eaten of the fruit of that apple tree. [W 1:341–345]

Thoreau visited Haverhill again in April 1853, and while walking along Creek Pond, on the east side of which "the Indians are said to have taken their way with Hannah Dustin and her nurse . . . I walked along it and thought how they might have been ambuscaded" [J 5:113].
17 Richard Kimball (1788–1856).
18 To the American Association for the Advancement of Science, which was founded in 1848, or its precursor, the Association of American Geologists and Naturalists, founded in 1842.
19 Usually called Fair Haven Pond, or Bay, a natural widening of the Sudbury River.
20 Rufous-sided towhee (*Pipilo erythrophthlamus*), which Thoreau also called the ground-robin. On 19 September 1858 Thoreau wrote of the "chewink's *chewink*" [J 9:169].
21 A decoction, often of guaiacum, sarsaparilla, or sassafras, taken either singly or in combination as normal drink throughout the day, usually for

months, to change the habit of the body. Thoreau wrote in his journal: "Live in each season as it passes; breathe the air, drink the drink, taste the fruit, and resign yourself to the influences of each. Let these be your only diet drink and botanical medicines" [J 5:394].

**22** Walden Pond.

**23** Heywood's Meadow.

**24** No source for this tradition has been found, nor does Thoreau refer to it in *Walden*.

**25** Rod: a linear measurement equal to 16½ feet, used especially in surveying.

**26** His companion is unidentified but was probably William Ellery Channing (1817–1901), poet, Thoreau's first biographer, and brother-in-law of Margaret Fuller. Channing, nephew of the Unitarian minister of the same name (cf. 1851 note 181), moved to Concord in 1843 and was a frequent companion of Thoreau on his walks.

the day before, and finally the weight of the sand forced upward the adjacent crust of the meadow with the trees on it many feet, and cracked it for some rods[25] around. It is a wet and springy place throughout the summer, with a ditch-like channel, and in one part water stands the year round, with cat-o'-nine-tails and tussocks and muskrats' cabins rising above it, where good cranberries may be raked if you are careful to anticipate the frost which visits this cool hollow unexpectedly early. Well, as I was saying, I heard a splashing in the shallow and muddy water and stood awhile to observe the cause of it. Again and again I heard and saw the commotion, but could not guess the cause of it,—what kind of life had its residence in that insignificant pool. We[26] sat down on the hillside. Ere long a muskrat came swimming by as if attracted by the same disturbance, and then another and another, till three had passed, and I began to suspect that they were at the bottom of it. Still ever and anon I observed the same commotion in the waters over the same spot, and at length I observed the snout of some creature slyly raised above the surface after each commotion, as if to see if it were observed by foes, and then but a few rods distant I saw another snout above the water and began to divine the cause of the disturbance. Putting off my shoes and stockings, I crept stealthily down the hill and waded out slowly and noiselessly about a rod from the firm land, keeping behind the tussocks, till I stood behind the tussock near which I had observed the splashing. Then, suddenly stooping over it, I saw through the shallow but muddy water that there was a mud turtle there, and thrusting in my hand at once caught him by the claw, and, quicker than I can tell it, heaved him high and dry ashore; and there came out with him a large pout just dead and partly devoured, which he held in his jaws. It was the pout in his flurry and the turtle in his struggles to hold him fast which had created the commotion. There he had lain, probably buried in the mud at the bottom up to his eyes, till the pout came sailing over, and then this musky lagune[27] had put forth in the direction of his ventral fins, expanding suddenly under the influence of a more than vernal heat,—there are sermons in stones,[28] aye and mud turtles at the bottoms of the pools,—in the direction of his ventral fins, his tender white belly, where he kept no eye; and the minister[29] squeaked his last. Oh, what an eye was there, my countrymen![30] buried in mud up to the lids, meditating on what? sleepless at the bottom of the pool, at the top of the bottom, directed heavenward, in no danger from motes. Pouts expect their foes not from below. Suddenly a mud volcano swallowed him up, seized his midriff; he fell into those relentless jaws from which there is no escape, which relax not their hold even in death. There the pout might calculate on remaining until nine days after the head was cut off. Sculled through Heywood's shallow meadow, not thinking of foes, looking through the water up into the sky. I saw his[31] brother sunning and airing his broad back like a ship bottom up which had been scuttled,—foundered at sea. I had no idea that there was so much going on in Heywood's meadow.

*May 31.* The year has many seasons more than are recognized in the almanac. There is that time about the first of June, the beginning of summer, when the buttercups blossom in the now luxuriant grass and I am first reminded of mowing and of the dairy. Every one will have observed different epochs. There is the time when they begin to drive cows to pasture,—about the 20th of May,—observed by the farmer, but a little arbitrary year by year. Cows spend their winters in barns and cowyards, their summers in pastures. In summer, therefore, they may low with emphasis, "To-morrow to fresh woods and pastures new."[32] I sometimes see a neighbor or two

27 Lagoon.
28 Allusion to Shakespeare's *As You Like It* (2.1.15–17): "And this our life, exempt from public haunt, / Finds tongues in trees, books in the running brooks, / Sermons in stones, and good in everything."
29 Horned pout (*Pimelodus nebulosus*), which, Thoreau wrote in *A Week on the Concord and Merrimack Rivers,* is "sometimes called Minister, from the peculiar squeaking noise it makes when drawn out of the water" [W 1:29–30].
30 Allusion to Shakespeare's *Julius Caesar* (3.2.184): "O, what a fall was there, my countrymen!"
31 The turtle's.
32 Quoted from John Milton's poem "Lycidas" (l. 193). This was also used in *Walden.*

**33** Allusion to Psalms 50:10: "For every beast of the forest is mine, and the cattle upon a thousand hills."

**34** Thoreau accidentally set the woods on fire on 30 April 1844 with his companion Edward Hoar (1823–1893). A spark from their fire caught on the extremely dry grass nearby. More than 300 acres burned, causing over $2,000 in damage. The *Concord Freeman* reported on 3 May 1844:

> The fire, we understand, was communicated to the woods through the thoughtlessness of two of our citizens, who kindled it in a *pine stump*, near the Pond, for the purpose of making a chowder. As every thing around them was as combustible almost as a fireship, the flames spread with rapidity, and hours elapsed before it could be subdued. It is to be hoped that this unfortunate result of sheer carelessness, will be borne in mind by those who may visit the woods in future for recreation.

For years Thoreau had to endure being called "woods-burner" in whispers behind his back. His prolonged feelings of guilt caused him to write this lengthy journal account of the incident six years later.

**35** Unidentified. There were several shoemakers in Concord. As Emerson wrote in "The Fortunes of the Republic": "In Massachusetts, every twelfth man is a shoemaker."

united with their boys and hired men to drive their cattle to some far-off country pasture, fifty or sixty miles distant in New Hampshire, early in the morning, with their sticks and dogs. It is a memorable time with the farmers' boys, and frequently their first journey from home. The herdsman in some mountain pasture is expecting them. And then in the fall, when they go up to drive them back, they speculate as to whether Janet or Brindle will know them. I heard such a boy exclaim on such an occasion, when the calf of the spring returned a heifer, as he stroked her side, "She knows me, father; she knows me." Driven up to be the cattle on a thousand hills.[33]

I once set fire to the woods.[34] Having set out, one April day, to go to the sources of Concord River in a boat with a single companion, meaning to camp on the bank at night or seek a lodging in some neighboring country inn or farmhouse, we took fishing tackle with us that we might fitly procure our food from the stream, Indian-like. At the shoemaker's near the river,[35] we obtained a match, which we had forgotten. Though it was thus early in the spring, the river was low, for there had not been much rain, and we succeeded in catching a mess of fish sufficient for our dinner before we had left the town, and by the shores of Fair Haven Pond we proceeded to cook them. The earth was uncommonly dry, and our fire, kindled far from the woods in a sunny recess in the hillside on the east of the pond, suddenly caught the dry grass of the previous year which grew about the stump on which it was kindled. We sprang to extinguish it at first with our hands and feet, and then we fought it with a board obtained from the boat, but in a few minutes it was beyond our reach; being on the side of a hill, it spread rapidly upward, through the long, dry, wiry grass interspersed with bushes.

"Well, where will this end?" asked my companion. I saw that it might be bounded by Well Meadow Brook on one side, but would, perchance, go to the village side of the brook. "It will go to town," I answered. While my companion took the boat back down the river, I set out through the woods to inform the owners and to raise the town. The fire had already spread a dozen rods on every side and went leaping and crackling wildly and irreclaimably toward the wood. That way went the flames with wild delight, and we felt that we had no control over the demonic creature to which we had given birth. We had kindled many fires in the woods before, burning a clear space in the grass, without ever kindling such a fire as this.

As I ran toward the town through the woods, I could see the smoke over the woods behind me marking the spot and the progress of the flames. The first farmer whom I met driving a team, after leaving the woods, inquired the cause of the smoke. I told him. "Well," said he, "it is none of my stuff," and drove along. The next I met was the owner in his field, with whom I returned at once to the woods, running all the way. I had already run two miles. When at length we got into the neighborhood of the flames, we met a carpenter who had been hewing timber, an infirm man who had been driven off by the fire, fleeing with his axe. The farmer returned to hasten more assistance. I, who was spent with running, remained. What could I do alone against a front of flame half a mile wide?

I walked slowly through the wood to Fair Haven Cliff, climbed to the highest rock, and sat down upon it to observe the progress of the flames, which were rapidly approaching me, now about a mile distant from the spot where the fire was kindled. Presently I heard the sound of the distant bell giving the alarm, and I knew that the town was on its way to the scene. Hitherto I had felt like a guilty person,—nothing but shame and regret. But now I settled the matter with myself shortly. I said

**36** After 21 June 1850 Thoreau wrote: "When the lightning burns the forest its Director makes no apology to man, and I was but His agent" [J 2:40].
**37** Cf. 5 June 1850.

to myself: "Who are these men who are said to be the owners of these woods, and how am I related to them? I have set fire to the forest, but I have done no wrong therein, and now it is as if the lightning had done it. These flames are but consuming their natural food." (It has never troubled me from that day to this more than if the lightning had done it.[36] The trivial fishing was all that disturbed me and disturbs me still.) So shortly I settled it with myself and stood to watch the approaching flames. It was a glorious spectacle, and I was the only one there to enjoy it.[37] The fire now reached the base of the cliff and then rushed up its sides. The squirrels ran before it in blind haste, and three pigeons dashed into the midst of the smoke. The flames flashed up the pines to their tops, as if they were powder.

When I found I was about to be surrounded by the fire, I retreated and joined the forces now arriving from the town. It took us several hours to surround the flames with our hoes and shovels and by back fires subdue them. In the midst of all I saw the farmer whom I first met, who had turned indifferently away saying it was none of his stuff, striving earnestly to save his corded wood, his stuff, which the fire had already seized and which it after all consumed.

It burned over a hundred acres or more and destroyed much young wood. When I returned home late in the day, with others of my townsmen, I could not help noticing that the crowd who were so ready to condemn the individual who had kindled the fire did not sympathize with the owners of the wood, but were in fact highly elated and as it were thankful for the opportunity which had afforded them so much sport; and it was only half a dozen owners, so called, though not all of them, who looked sour or grieved, and I felt that I had a deeper interest in the woods, knew them better and should feel their loss more, than any or all of them. The farmer whom I had first conducted to the woods was obliged to ask me the shortest way back, through his own lot. Why, then, should the half-dozen owners and the individuals who set the fire alone feel sorrow for the loss of the wood, while the rest of the town have their spirits raised? Some of the owners, however, bore their loss like men, but other some declared behind my back that I was a "damned rascal;"[38] and a flibbertigibbet[39] or two, who crowed like the old cock,[40] shouted some reminiscences of "burnt woods" from safe recesses for some years after. I have had nothing to say to any of them. The locomotive engine has since burned over nearly all the same ground and more, and in some measure blotted out the memory of the previous fire. For a long time after I had learned this lesson I marvelled that while matches and tinder were contemporaries the world was not consumed; why the houses that have hearths were not burned before another day; if the flames were not as hungry now as when I waked them. I at once ceased to regard the owners and my own fault,—if fault there was any in the matter,— and attended to the phenomenon before me, determined to make the most of it. To be sure, I felt a little ashamed when I reflected on what a trivial occasion this had happened, that at the time I was no better employed than my townsmen.

That night I watched the fire, where some stumps still flamed at midnight in the midst of the blackened waste, wandering through the woods by myself; and far in the night I threaded my way to the spot where the fire had taken, and discovered the now broiled fish,—which had been dressed,—scattered over the burnt grass.

*June 4.* Today, June 4th, I have been tending a burning in the woods. Ray[41] was there. It is a pleasant fact that you will know no man long, however low in the social scale, however poor, miserable, intemperate, and worthless he

**38** This was probably John L. Tuttle, of whom Emerson wrote in "Montaigne, or The Skeptic": "I knew a philosopher of this kidney who was accustomed briefly to sum up his experience of human nature in saying, 'Mankind is a damned rascal.'"
**39** A frivolous, garrulous, and restless person, but Thoreau may have had in mind specifically the "foul fiend Flibbertigibbet" in Shakespeare's *King Lear* (3.4.106). In the 1833 Andrus and Judd edition of Shakespeare, which Thoreau sometimes used, is the further description of Flibbertigibbet as the fiend "of mopping and mowing" (4.1.63), that is, of grimacing or making faces.
**40** Probable reference to Gonzalo, in Shakespeare's *The Tempest* (2.1.30), referred to as "the old cock" of whom it was said (2.1.23–24): "Fie, what a spendthrift is he of his tongue!"
**41** Probably Heman Ray (1783–1868).

may appear to be, a mere burden to society, but you will find at last that there is something which he understands and can do better than any other. I was pleased to hear that one man had sent Ray as the one who had had the most experience in setting fires of any man in Lincoln. He had experience and skill as a burner of brush.

You must burn against the wind always, and burn slowly. When the fire breaks over the hoed line, a little system and perseverance will accomplish more toward quelling it than any man would believe. It fortunately happens that the experience acquired is oftentimes worth more than the wages. When a fire breaks out in the woods, and a man fights it too near and on the side, in the heat of the moment, without the systematic coöperation of others, he is disposed to think it a desperate case, and that this relentless fiend will run through the forests till it is glutted with food; but let the company rest from their labors a moment, and then proceed more deliberately and systematically, giving the fire a wider berth, and the company will be astonished to find how soon and easily they will subdue it. The woods themselves furnish one of the best weapons with which to contend with the fires that destroy them,—a pitch pine bough. It is the best instrument to thrash it with. There are few men who do not love better to give advice than to give assistance.

However large the fire, let a few men go to work deliberately but perseveringly to rake away the leaves and hoe off the surface of the ground at a convenient distance from the fire, while others follow with pine boughs to thrash it with when it reaches the line, and they will finally get round it and subdue it, and will be astonished at their own success.

A man who is about to burn his field in the midst of woods should rake off the leaves and twigs for the breadth of a rod at least, making no large heaps near the outside, and then plow around it several furrows and break them up with hoes, and set his fire early in the morning, before the wind rises.

As I was fighting the fire to-day, in the midst of the roaring and crackling,—for the fire seems to snort like a wild horse,—I heard from time to time the dying strain, the last sigh, the fine, clear, shrill scream of agony, as it were, of the trees breathing their last, probably the heated air or steam escaping from some chink. At first I thought it was some bird, or a dying squirrel's note of anguish, or steam escaping from the tree. You sometimes hear it on a small scale in the log on the hearth. When a field is burned over, the squirrels probably go into the ground. How foreign is the yellow pine[42] to the green woods—and what business has it here?

The fire stopped within a few inches of a partridge's nest to-day, June 4th, whom we took off in our hands and found thirteen creamy-colored eggs. I started up a woodcock when I went to a rill to drink, at the western-most angle of Emerson's wood-lot.

*June 5.* Men go to a fire for entertainment. When I see how eagerly men will run to a fire, whether in warm or in cold weather, by day or by night, dragging an engine at their heels, I am astonished to perceive how good a purpose the love of excitement is made to serve. What other force, pray, what offered pay, what disinterested neighborliness could ever effect so much? No, these are boys who are to be dealt with, and these are the motives that prevail. There is no old man or woman dropping into the grave but covets excitement.[43]

*After July 19.* I find the actual to be far less real to me than the imagined.[44] Why this singular prominence and importance is given to the former, I do not know. In proportion as that which possesses my thoughts is re-moved from the actual, it impresses me. I have never

**42** Cf. 1853 note 67.
**43** Although in "Life Without Principle" he wrote, "We do not live for idle amusement. I would not run round a corner to see the world blow up" [W 4:472], Thoreau could sometimes appreciate the entertainment value of such events. Going to Cape Cod on 9 October 1849, Thoreau decided to travel by way of Cohasset to view a shipwreck after reading handbills in Boston advertising, "Death! one hundred and forty-five lives lost at Cohasset" [W 4:5].
**44** Cf. 1840s note 72.

**45** In *A Week on the Concord and Merrimack Rivers* Thoreau wrote: "We are scarcely less afflicted when we remember some unworthiness in our conduct in a dream, than if it had been actual, and the intensity of our grief, which is our atonement, measures the degree by which this is separated from an actual unworthiness" [W 1:315]. Cf. 23 November 1852.

**46** On 19 July 1850 Sarah Margaret Fuller (1810–1850)—author, Transcendentalist, friend of Emerson, editor of the *Dial,* author of *Summer on the Lakes in 1843* and *Women in the Nineteenth Century,* and foreign correspondent for the *New York Tribune*—together with her husband, Giovanni Angelo, Marchese d'Ossoli (ca. 1820–1850), and their son, Angelo Eugenio Filippo Ossoli (1848–1850), drowned off Fire Island, New York, when the ship *Elizabeth,* on which they were returning to America, wrecked. Emerson sent Thoreau to recover what he could of their remains and any personal belongings, particularly Fuller's papers, that he could locate. In *Cape Cod* Thoreau wrote:

> Once also it was my business to go in search of the relics of a human body, mangled by sharks, which had just been cast up, a week after a wreck, having got the direction from a light-house: I should find it a mile or two distant over the sand, a dozen rods from the water, covered with a cloth, by a stick stuck up. I expected that I must look very narrowly to find so small an object, but the sandy beach, half a mile wide, and stretching farther than the eye could reach, was so perfectly smooth and bare, and the mirage toward the sea so magnifying, that when I was half a mile distant the insignificant sliver which marked the spot looked like a bleached spar, and the relics were as conspicuous as if they lay in state on that sandy plain, or a generation had labored to pile up their cairn there. Close at hand they were simply some bones with a little flesh adhering to them, in fact only a slight inequality in the sweep of the shore. There was nothing

met with anything so truly visionary and accidental as some actual events. They have affected me less than my dreams.[45] Whatever actually happens to a man is wonderfully trivial and insignificant,—even to death itself, I imagine. He complains of the fates who drown him, that they do not touch *him.* They do not deal directly with him. I have in my pocket a button which I ripped off the coat of the Marquis of Ossoli on the sea shore the other day.[46] Held up, it intercepts the light and casts a shadow,—an *actual* button so called,—and yet all the life it is connected with is less substantial to me than my faintest dreams. This stream of events which we consent to call actual, and that other mightier stream which alone carries us with it,—what makes the difference? On the one our bodies float, and we have sympathy with it through them; on the other, our spirits. We are ever dying to one world and being born into another, and possibly no man knows whether he is at any time dead in the sense in which he affirms that phenomenon of another, or not. Our thoughts are the epochs of our life: all else is but as a journal of the winds that blew while we were here.[47]

*After July 29.* Would it not be worth the while to discover Nature in Milton?[48] Be native to the universe. I, too, love Concord best, but I am glad when I discover, in oceans and wildernesses far away,[49] the materials out of which a million Concords can be made,—indeed, unless I discover them, I am lost myself,—that there too I am at home. Nature is as far from me as God, and sometimes I have thought to go West after her.[50] Though the city is no more attractive to me than ever, yet I see less difference between a city and some dismallest swamp[51] than formerly. It is a swamp too dismal and dreary, however, for me. I would as lief[52] find a few owls and frogs and mosquitoes less. I prefer even a more cultivated place, free from miasma and crocodiles, and I will take my choice.

From time to time I overlook the promised land,[53] but I do not feel that I am travelling toward it. The moment I begin to look there, men and institutions get out of the way that I may see. I see nothing permanent in the society around me, and am not quite committed to any of its ways.

*After August 31.* My friends wonder that I love to walk alone in solitary fields and woods by night. Sometimes in my loneliest and wildest midnight walk I hear the sound of the whistle and the rattle of the cars, where perchance some of those very friends are being whirled by night over, as they think, a well-known, safe, and public road. I see that men do not make or choose their own paths, whether they are railroads or trackless through the wilds, but what the powers permit each one enjoys. My solitary course has the same sanction that the Fitchburg Railroad has. If they have a charter from Massachusetts and—what is of much more importance—from Heaven, to travel the course and in the fashion they do, I have a charter, though it be from Heaven alone, to travel the course I do,—to take the necessary lands and pay the damages. It is by the grace of God in both cases.

*After October 31.* What does education often do? It makes a straight-cut ditch of a free, meandering brook.

*After November 11.* Some circumstantial evidence is very strong, as when you find a trout in the milk.[54]

*November 16.* I found three good arrowheads to-day behind Dennis's.[55] The season for them began some time

at all remarkable about them, and they were singularly inoffensive both to the senses and the imagination. But as I stood there they grew more and more imposing. They were alone with the beach and the sea, whose hollow roar seemed addressed to them, and I was impressed as if there was an understanding between them and the ocean which necessarily left me out, with my snivelling sympathies. That dead body had taken possession of the shore, and reigned over it as no living one could, in the name of a certain majesty which belonged to it. [W 4:107–108]

**47** Parts of this and the following entry formed part of Thoreau's letter of 9 August 1850 to H. G. O. Blake.

**48** Milton, Massachusetts, where Blake was then living.

**49** Reference to Thoreau's excursions to the Maine woods in 1846 and Cape Cod in October 1849 and June 1850, as well as his lengthy stay in New York on Staten Island in 1843.

**50** Cf. "Walking": "Eastward I go only by force; but westward I go free. Thither no business leads me. It is hard for me to believe that I shall find fair landscapes, or sufficient wildness and freedom behind the eastern horizon. I am not excited by the prospect of a walk thither; but I believe that the forest which I see in the western horizon stretches uninterruptedly towards the setting sun, and there are no towns nor cities in it of enough consequence to disturb me. Let me live where I will, on this side is the city, on that the wilderness, and ever I am leaving the city more and more, and withdrawing into the wilderness. I should not lay so much stress on this fact, if I did not believe that something like this is the prevailing tendency of my countrymen. I must walk toward Oregon, and not toward Europe. And that way the nation is moving, and I may say that mankind progress from east to west" [W 5:217–218].

**51** Allusion to the Dismal Swamp in southeastern Virginia and northeastern North Carolina. It figured in William Byrd's (1674–1744) *History of the Dividing Line Betwixt Virginia and North Carolina,* Thomas Moore's (1779–1852) "The Lake of the Dismal Swamp," and Henry Wadsworth Longfellow's (1807–1882) "The Slave in the Dismal Swamp."

**52** Gladly, willingly.

**53** Specifically an allusion to the land of Canaan, promised to Abraham and his descendants in Genesis 12, but also any place believed to promise ultimate fulfillment or realization of hopes.

**54** Allusion to the practice of some dairymen of watering down milk.

**55** On the Lupine Hill or Promontory, on the west bank of the Sudbury River, behind S. Dennis who lived on the Sudbury Road, one-quarter mile south of the railroad tracks.

**56** Cf. 28 March 1859.

**57** Cf. 8 February 1841.

**58** Quickly cooked pudding made by stirring corn meal in boiling water or hot milk, sweetened with brown sugar or maple syrup.

ago, as soon as the farmers had sown their winter rye, but the spring, after the melting of the snow, is still better.[56]

I love my friends very much, but I find that it is of no use to go to see them. I hate them commonly when I am near them. They belie themselves and deny me continually.

What shall we do with a man who is afraid of the woods, their solitude and darkness? What salvation is there for him? God is silent and mysterious.

Some of our richest days are those in which no sun shines outwardly, but so much the more a sun shines inwardly.

My Journal should be the record of my love.[57] I would write in it only of the things I love, my affection for any aspect of the world, what I love to think of. I have no more distinctness or pointedness in my yearnings than an expanding bud, which does indeed point to flower and fruit, to summer and autumn, but is aware of the warm sun and spring influence only. I feel ripe for something, yet do nothing, can't discover what that thing is. I feel fertile merely. It is seedtime with me. I have lain fallow long enough.

Notwithstanding a sense of unworthiness which possesses me, not without reason, notwithstanding that I regard myself as a good deal of a scamp, yet for the most part the spirit of the universe is unaccountably kind to me, and I enjoy perhaps an unusual share of happiness. Yet I question sometimes if there is not some settlement to come.

*November 20.* It is a common saying among country people that if you eat much fried hasty pudding[58] it will make your hair curl. My experience, which was considerable, did not confirm this assertion.

*November 24.* I have certain friends whom I visit occasionally, but I commonly part from them early with a certain bitter-sweet sentiment. That which we love is so mixed and entangled with that we hate in one another that we are more grieved and disappointed, aye, and estranged from one another, by meeting than by absence. Some men may be my acquaintances merely, but one whom I have been accustomed to regard, to idealize, to have dreams about as a friend, and mix up intimately with myself, can never degenerate into an acquaintance. I must know him on that higher ground or not know him at all. We do not confess and explain, because we would fain be so intimately related as to understand each other without speech. Our friend must be broad. His must be an atmosphere coextensive with the universe, in which we can expand and breathe. For the most part we are smothered and stifled by one another. I go and see my friend and try his atmosphere. If our atmospheres do not mingle, if we repel each other strongly, it is of no use to stay.

# 1851

AGE 33–34

*January 7.* I must live above all in the present.

I felt my spirits rise when I had got off the road into the open fields, and the sky had a new appearance. I stepped along more buoyantly. There was a warm sunset over the wooded valleys, a yellowish tinge on the pines. Reddish dun-colored clouds like dusky flames stood over it. And then streaks of blue sky were seen here and there. The life, the joy, that is in blue sky after a storm! There is no account of the blue sky in history. Before I walked in the ruts of travel; now I adventured.

*After January 10.* It is something to know when you are addressed by Divinity and not by a common traveller. I went down cellar just now to get an armful of wood and, passing the brick piers with my wood and candle, I heard, methought, a commonplace suggestion, but when, as it were by accident, I reverently attended to the hint, I found that it was the voice of a god who had followed me down cellar to speak to me. How many communications may we not lose through inattention!

I would fain keep a journal which should contain those thoughts and impressions which I am most liable to forget that I have had; which would have in one sense the greatest remoteness, in another, the greatest nearness to me.

*February 12.* I find that it is an excellent walk for variety and novelty and wildness, to keep round the edge of the meadow,—the ice not being strong enough to bear and transparent as water,—on the bare ground or snow, just between the highest water mark and the present water line,—a narrow, meandering walk, rich in unexpected views and objects.

*February 15.* Fatal is the discovery that our friend is fallible, that he has prejudices. He is, then, only prejudiced in our favor. What is the value of his esteem who does not justly esteem another?

Alas! Alas! when my friend begins to deal in confessions, breaks silence, makes a theme of friendship (which then is always something past), and descends to merely human relations! As long as there is a spark of love remaining, cherish that alone. Only *that* can be kindled into a flame. I thought that friendship, that love was still possible between us. I thought that we had not withdrawn very far asunder. But now that my friend rashly, thoughtlessly, profanely speaks, *recognizing* the distance between us, that distance seems infinitely increased.

Of our friends we do not incline to speak, to complain, to others; we would not disturb the foundations of confidence that may still be.

*February 18.* If it were not that I desire to do something here,—accomplish some work,—I should certainly prefer to suffer and die rather than be at the pains to get a living by the modes men propose.

*After March 30.* Much as has been said about American slavery, I think that commonly we do not yet realize what slavery is. If I were seriously to propose to Congress to make mankind into sausages,[1] I have no doubt that most would smile at my proposition and, if any believed me to be in earnest, they would think that I proposed something much worse than Congress had ever done.

1 Echo of Jonathan Swift's "A Modest Proposal," which satirically suggested the eating of Irish children, "for preventing the children of poor people in Ireland from being a burden to their parents or country, and for making them beneficial to the public."

But, gentlemen, if any of you will tell me that to make a man into a sausage would be much worse—would be any worse—than to make him into a slave,—than it was then to enact the fugitive slave law,[2]—I shall here accuse him of foolishness, of intellectual incapacity, of making a distinction without a difference.[3] The one is just as sensible a proposition as the other.[4]

*April 29.* Every man, perhaps, is inclined to think his own situation singular in relation to friendship. Our thoughts would imply that other men *have* friends, though we have not. But I do not know of two whom I can speak of as standing in this relation to one another. Each one makes a standing offer to mankind, "On such and such terms I will give myself to you"; but it is only by a miracle that his terms are ever accepted.

We have to defend ourselves even against those who are nearest to friendship with us.

What a difference it is!—to perform the pilgrimage of life in the society of a mate, and not to have an acquaintance among all the tribes of men![5]

What signifies the census—this periodical numbering of men—to one who has no friend?

I distinguish between my *actual* and my *real* communication with individuals. I *really* communicate with my friends and congratulate myself and them on our relation and rejoice in their presence and society oftenest when they are personally absent. I remember that not long ago, as I laid my head on my pillow for the night, I was visited by an inexpressible joy that I was permitted to know and be related to such mortals as I was then actually related to; and yet no special event that I could think of had occurred to remind me of any with whom I was connected, and by the next noon, perchance, those essences that had caused me joy would have receded somewhat. I experienced a remarkable gladness in the thought that

**2** The Fugitive Slave Act of 1850, passed as part of the Compromise of 1850, required the return of runaway slaves to their owners and provided severe penalties for helping fugitive slaves escape. Thoreau wrote in "Slavery in Massachusetts": "I hear a good deal said about trampling this law under foot. Why, one need not go out of his way to do that. This law rises not to the level of the head or the reason; its natural habitat is in the dirt. It was born and bred, and has its life, only in the dust and mire, on a level with the feet; and he who walks with freedom, and does not with Hindoo mercy avoid treading on every venomous reptile, will inevitably tread on it, and so trample it under foot,—and Webster, its maker, with it, like the dirt-bug and its ball" [W 4:394–395]. Daniel Webster (1782–1852), senator from Massachusetts, was not the author of the bill, but he became associated with it through his support for its enforcement. Emerson wrote several diatribes against Webster in his journal, such as, "The word *liberty* in the mouth of Mr Webster sounds like the word *love* in the mouth of a courtesan."
**3** Allusion to Royall Tyler's (1757–1826) *The Contrast*, in which the character of Jonathan, in differentiating between a servant and a waiter, is said to have made a "true Yankee distinction, egad, without a difference." Thoreau also used the phrase in "Ktaadn," "Paradise (to be) Regained," and "Slavery in Massachusetts."
**4** With minor variants this appeared in "Slavery in Massachusetts" [W 4:394].
**5** Cf. 1840s note 104.

they existed. Their existence was then blessed to me. Yet such has never been my actual waking relation to any.

*April 30.* Does not the history of chivalry and knight-errantry suggest or point to another relation to woman than leads to marriage, yet an elevating and all-absorbing one, perchance transcending marriage? As yet men know not one another, nor does man know woman.

I am sure that the design of my maker when he has brought me nearest to woman was not the propagation, but rather the maturation, of the species. Man is capable of a love of woman quite transcending marriage.[6]

*May 1.* In regard to purity, I do not know whether I am much worse or better than my acquaintances. If I confine my thought to myself, I appear, whether by constitution or by education, irrevocably impure, as if I should be shunned by my fellow-men if they knew me better, as if I were of two inconsistent natures;[7] but again, when I observe how the mass of men speak of woman and of chastity, —with how little love and reverence,[8]—I feel that so far I am unaccountably better than they. I think that none of my acquaintances has a greater love and admiration for chastity than I have.[9] Perhaps it is necessary that one should actually stand low himself in order to reverence what is high in others.

All distant landscapes seen from hilltops are veritable pictures, which will be found to have no actual existence to him who travels to them. "'T is distance lends enchantment to the view."[10] It is the bare landscape without this depth of atmosphere to glass it. The distant river-reach seen in the north from the Lincoln Hill,[11] high in the horizon, like the ocean stream flowing round Homer's shield,[12] the rippling waves reflecting the light, is unlike the same seen near at hand. Heaven intervenes between me and the object. By what license do I call it

6  Cf. 11 August 1853: "The marriage which the mass of men comprehend is but little better than the marriage of beasts."

7  In September 1852 Thoreau sent Blake his thoughts on "Chastity and Sensuality," in which he wrote: "The intercourse of the sexes, I have dreamed, is incredibly beautiful, too fair to be remembered. I have had thoughts about it, but they are among the most fleeting and irrecoverable in my experience" [W 6:208]. Calvin Greene (1817–1898) recalled an anecdote that Sophia Thoreau told him in which Thoreau purportedly said: "I never had any trouble in my life, or only when I was about fourteen; then I felt pretty bad a little while on account of my sins, but no trouble since that I know of. That must be the reason why my hair doesn't turn gray faster. But there is Blake; he is as gray as a rat."

8  Cf. 12 April 1852.

9  In "Chastity and Sensuality" Thoreau wrote: "Chastity is something positive, not negative. It is the virtue of the married especially. All lusts or base pleasures must give place to loftier delights. They who meet as superior beings cannot perform the deeds of inferior ones. The deeds of love are less questionable than any action of an individual can be, for, it being founded on the rarest mutual respect, the parties incessantly stimulate each other to a loftier and purer life, and the act in which they are associated must be pure and noble indeed, for innocence and purity can have no equal" [W 6:205].

10  Quoted from Thomas Campbell's (1777–1844) "Pleasures of Hope" (1.7).

11  On which the town of Lincoln's first meeting-house was built and from which the Concord River is seen approximately two miles to the north. Thoreau described Lincoln as "lying high up in among the hills. You see that it is the highest town hereabouts" [J 2:26].

12  The shield of Achilles in the *Iliad*, book 18, with its description translated by Pope as:

Thus the broad shield complete the artist
crown'd
With his last hand, and pour'd the ocean
round:
In living silver seem'd the waves to roll,
And beat the buckler's verge, and bound the
whole.

13 Before the advent of modern science, one who
studied nature and the physical universe.
14 Cf. 26 January 1856.

Concord River. It redeems the character of rivers to see them thus. They were worthy then of a place on Homer's shield.

*May 6.* How important is a constant intercourse with nature and the contemplation of natural phenomenon to the preservation of moral and intellectual health! The discipline of the schools or of business can never impart such serenity to the mind. The philosopher contemplates human affairs as calmly and from as great a remoteness as he does natural phenomena. The ethical philosopher needs the discipline of the natural philosopher.[13] He approaches the study of mankind with great advantages who is accustomed to the study of nature.

*May 12.* If I have got false teeth, I trust that I have not got a false conscience. It is safer to employ the dentist than the priest to repair the deficiencies of nature.

By taking the ether the other day I was convinced how far asunder a man could be separated from his senses.[14] You are told that it will make you unconscious, but no one can imagine what it is to be unconscious—how far removed from the state of consciousness and all that we call "this world"—until he has experienced it. The value of the experiment is that it does give you experience of an interval as between one life and another,—a greater space than you ever travelled. You are a sane mind without organs,—groping for organs,—which if it did not soon recover its old senses would get new ones. You expand like a seed in the ground. You exist in your roots, like a tree in the winter. If you have an inclination to travel, take the ether; you go beyond the furthest star.

It is not necessary for them to take ether, who in their sane and waking hours are ever translated by a thought; nor for them to see with their hindheads, who sometimes see from their foreheads; nor listen to the spiritual knockings,[15] who attend to the intimations of reason and conscience.

**May 21.** I think that we are not commonly aware that man is our contemporary,—that in this strange, outlandish world, so barren, so prosaic, fit not to live in but merely to pass through, that even here so divine a creature as man does actually live. Man, the crowning fact, the god we know. While the earth supports so rare an inhabitant, there is somewhat to cheer us. Who shall say that there is no God, if there is a *just* man. It is only within a year that it has occurred to me that there is such a being actually existing on the globe.[16] Now that I perceive that it is so, many questions assume a new aspect. We have not only the idea and vision of the divine ourselves, but we have brothers, it seems, who have this idea also. Methinks my neighbor is better than I, and his thought is better than mine. There is a representative of the divinity on earth,[17] of whom all things fair and noble are to be expected. We have the material of heaven here. I think that the standing miracle[18] to man is man. Behind the paling yonder, come rain or shine, hope or doubt, there dwells a man, an actual being who can sympathize with our sublimest thoughts.[19]

I think that the existence of man in nature is the divinest and most startling of all facts. It is a fact which few have realized.

**June 7.** We believe that the possibility of the future far exceeds the accomplishment of the past. We review the past with the common sense, but we anticipate the future with transcendental senses.

**June 11.** No one, to my knowledge, has observed the minute differences in the seasons. Hardly two nights

**15** Spiritualism, sometimes called spiritism: belief in contact with the spirit world. Thoreau wrote on 13 July 1852: "Concord is just as idiotic as ever in relation to the spirits and their knockings. . . . If I could be brought to believe in the things in which they believe—I should make haste to get rid of my certificate of stock in this & the next world's enterprises, and buy a share in the first Immediate Annihilation Company that offered—I would exchange my immortality for a glass of small beer this hot weather. . . . See—smell—taste—feel—hear—anything—& then hear these idiots inspired by the cracking of a restless board—humbly asking 'Please spirit, if you cannot answer by knocks, answer by tips of the table.'!!!!!!" [C 283–284].

**16** It is unknown if Thoreau was referring to anyone specifically, but the thought was probably related to someone speaking or acting against the Fugitive Slave Act (cf. 1851 note 2), as in the rescue of Shadrach (cf. 1851 note 137).

**17** Cf. the divinity within, 1851 note 181.

**18** A perpetual or continuing miracle rather than a singular miracle from the biblical past.

**19** On the idea of sympathy Thoreau wrote: "The more complete our sympathy, the more our senses are struck dumb, and we are repressed by a delicate respect, so that to indifferent eyes we are least his friend, because no vulgar symbols pass between us" [J 1:108]. As he wrote on 24 November 1858: "I love that one with whom I sympathize" [J 11:342].

20 An allusion to William Howitt's (1792–1879) *The Book of the Seasons, or the Calendar of Nature*, although Thoreau was writing here of a more extensive work, such as he would undertake in his calendar of nature: cf. 1859 note 87.

21 Possible echo of Proverbs 2:20: "That thou mayest walk in the way of good men, and keep the paths of the righteous."

22 Probable allusion to the Delectable Mountains, in John Bunyan's (1628–1688) *The Pilgrim's Progress*, which Pilgrim must pass on his way to the Celestial City.

are alike. The rocks do not feel warm to-night, for the air is warmest; nor does the sand particularly. A book of the seasons,[20] each page of which should be written in its own season and out-of-doors, or in its own locality wherever it may be.

When you get into the road, though far from the town, and feel the sand under your feet, it is as if you had reached your own gravel walk. You no longer hear the whip-poor-will, nor regard your shadow, for here you expect a fellow-traveller. You catch yourself walking merely. The road leads your steps and thoughts alike to the town. You see only the path, and your thoughts wander from the objects which are presented to your senses. You are no longer in place. It is like conformity,—walking in the ways of men.[21]

*June 13.* I noticed night before night before last from Fair Haven how valuable was some water by moonlight, like the river and Fair Haven Pond, though far away, reflecting the light with a faint glimmering sheen, as in the spring of the year. The water shines with an inward light like a heaven on earth. The silent depth and serenity and majesty of water! Strange that men should distinguish gold and diamonds, when these precious elements are so common. I saw a distant river by moonlight, making no noise, yet flowing, as by day, still to the sea, like melted silver reflecting the moonlight. Far away it lay encircling the earth. How far away it may look in the night, and even from a low hill how miles away down in the valley! As far off as paradise and the delectable country![22] There is a certain glory attends on water by night. By it the heavens are related to the earth, undistinguishable from a sky beneath you.

We do not commonly live our life out and full; we do not fill all our pores with our blood; we do not inspire and expire fully and entirely enough, so that the wave, the comber,[23] of each inspiration shall break upon our extremest shores, rolling till it meets the sand which bounds us, and the sound of the surf come back to us. Might not a bellows assist us to breathe? That our breathing should create a wind in a calm day! We live but a fraction of our life. Why do we not let on the flood, raise the gates, and set all our wheels in motion? He that hath ears to hear, let him hear.[24] Employ your senses.

As I approached the pond down Hubbard's Path,[25] after coming out of the woods into a warmer air, I saw the shimmering of the moon on its surface, and, in the near, now flooded cove, the water-bugs, darting, circling about, made streaks or curves of light. The moon's inverted pyramid of shimmering light commenced about twenty rods off, like so much micaceous sand. But I was startled to see midway in the dark water a bright flame-like, more than phosphorescent light crowning the crests of the wavelets, which at first I mistook for fireflies, and thought even of cucullos.[26] It had the appearance of a pure, smokeless flame a half-dozen inches long, issuing from the water and bending flickeringly along its surface. I thought of St. Elmo's lights[27] and the like. But, coming near to the shore of the pond itself, these flames increased, and I saw that even this was so many broken reflections of the moon's disk, though one would have said they were of an intenser light than the moon herself; from contrast with the surrounding water they were. Standing up close to the shore and nearer the rippled surface, I saw the reflections of the moon sliding down the watery concave like so many lustrous burnished coins poured from a bag with inexhaustible lavishness, and the lambent flames on the surface were much multiplied, seeming to slide along a few inches with each wave before they were extinguished; and I saw how farther and

23 A long wave that has reached its peak; a breaker.
24 Quoted from Mark 4:9 and Luke 8:8, and used again in Thoreau's entry for 31 December 1853.
25 Walden Pond, by way of Hubbard's Close.
26 Cucujos: *Pyrophorus noctilucus*, fire beetles found in Central and South America.
27 A corposant: a visible flamelike electrical discharge on a pointed object, such as a mast.

**28** Thoreau used the word dreaming in the archaic sense of making noise, jubilation, or music. He discovered on 6 May 1852: "My dream frog turns out to be a toad. . . . One, which I brought home, answers well enough to the description of the common toad (*Bufo Americanus*), though it is hardly so gray" [J 4:24–25].

**29** Belch.

**30** The location of the bean field, east of Thoreau's Walden house site, was described by Emerson's son Edward as being "in the square between the Lincoln Road and the wood roads," now routes 126 and 2, respectively.

farther off they gradually merged in the general sheen, which, in fact, was made up of a myriad little mirrors reflecting the disk of the moon with equal brightness to an eye rightly placed. The pyramid or sheaf of light which we see springing from near where we stand only, in fact, is the outline of that portion of the shimmering surface which an eye takes in. To myriad eyes suitably placed, the whole surface of the pond would be seen to shimmer, or rather it would be seen, as the waves turned up their mirrors, to be covered with those bright flame-like reflections of the moon's disk, like a myriad candles everywhere issuing from the waves; *i. e.* if there were as many eyes as angles presented by the waves, the whole surface would appear as bright as the moon; and these reflections are dispersed in all directions into the atmosphere, flooding it with light. No wonder that water reveals itself so far by night; even further in many states of the atmosphere than by day. I thought at first it was some unusual phosphorescence. In some positions these flames were star-like points, brighter than the brightest stars. Suddenly a flame would show itself in a near and dark space, precisely like some inflammable gas on the surface,—as if an inflammable gas made its way up from the bottom.

I heard my old musical, simple-noted owl. The sound of the *dreaming* frogs[28] prevails over the others. Occasionally a bullfrog near me made an obscene noise, a sound like an eructation,[29] near me. I think they must be imbodied eructations. They suggest flatulency.

As I climbed the hill again toward my old bean-field,[30] I listened to the ancient, familiar, immortal, dear cricket sound under all others, hearing at first some distinct chirps; but when these ceased I was aware of the general earth-song, which my hearing had not heard, amid which these were only taller flowers in a bed, and I wondered if behind or beneath this there was not some other chant yet more universal.

*June 14.* How moderate, deliberate, is Nature! How gradually the shades of night gather and deepen, giving man ample leisure to bid farewell to day, conclude his day's affairs, and prepare for slumber! The twilight seems out of proportion to the length of the day. Perchance it saves our eyes. Now for some hours the farmers have been getting home.

Since the alarm about mad dogs a couple of years ago[31] there are comparatively few left to bark at the traveller and bay the moon. All nature is abandoned to me.

*June 22.* We are enabled to criticise others only when we are different from, and in a given particular superior to, them ourselves. By our aloofness from men and their affairs we are enabled to overlook and criticise them. There are but few men who stand on the hills by the roadside. I am sane only when I have risen above my common sense, when I do not take the foolish view of things which is commonly taken, when I do not live for the low ends for which men commonly live. Wisdom is not common. To what purpose have I senses, if I am thus absorbed in affairs? My pulse must beat with Nature. After a hard day's work without a thought, turning my very brain into a mere tool, only in the quiet of evening do I so far recover my senses as to hear the cricket, which in fact has been chirping all day. In my better hours I am conscious of the influx of a serene and unquestionable wisdom which partly unfits, and if I yielded to it more rememberingly would wholly unfit me, for what is called the active business of life, for that furnishes nothing on which the eye of reason can rest. What is that other kind of life to which I am thus continually allured? which alone I love? Is it a life for this world? Can a man feed

31  Thoreau introduced the days' news to his cousin, George Thatcher, on 9 February 1849 as: "California, mad dogs, and rail-roads are still the great topics here as everywhere."

**32**  *A Week on the Concord and Merrimack Rivers,* published in 1849 by James Munroe and Company, Boston.

**33**  Probable allusion to David Roberts's (1796–1864) "The Hypaethral Temple at Philae, Called the Bed of Pharaoh," from his *Egypt and Nubia from Drawings Made on the Spot* (London: Moon, 1846–1849).

**34**  Element believed in ancient and medieval civilizations to fill all space above the sphere of the moon and to compose the stars and planets.

**35**  Thoreau composed a first draft of *A Week on the Concord and Merrimack Rivers* in the autumn of 1845 while living at Walden Pond, and began a second draft in early 1846 while still living there.

**36**  It was in March 1848, while living at the Emerson home, that his book was "swelling again" [C 225] and probably began to take on signs of a domestic life.

and clothe himself gloriously who keeps only the truth steadily before him? who calls in no evil to his aid? Are there duties which necessarily interfere with the serene perception of truth? Are our serene moments mere foretastes of heaven,—joys gratuitously vouchsafed to us as a consolation,—or simply a transient realization of what might be the whole tenor of our lives?

To be calm, to be serene! There is the calmness of the lake when there is not a breath of wind; there is the calmness of a stagnant ditch. So is it with us. Sometimes we are clarified and calmed healthily, as we never were before in our lives, not by an opiate, but by some unconscious obedience to the all-just laws, so that we become like a still lake of purest crystal and without an effort our depths are revealed to ourselves. All the world goes by us and is reflected in our deeps. Such clarity! obtained by such pure means! by simple living, by honesty of purpose. We live and rejoice. I awoke into a music which no one about me heard. Whom shall I thank for it? The luxury of wisdom! the luxury of virtue! Are there any intemperate in these things? I feel my Maker blessing me. To the sane man the world is a musical instrument. The very touch affords an exquisite pleasure.

*June 29.* I thought that one peculiarity of my "Week"[32] was its *hypæthral* character, to use an epithet applied to those Egyptian temples which are open to the heavens above,[33] *under the ether.*[34] I thought that it had little of the atmosphere of the house about it, but might wholly have been written, as in fact it was to a considerable extent, out-of-doors.[35] It was only at a late period in writing it, as it happened, that I used any phrases implying that I lived in a house or lead a *domestic* life.[36] I trust it does not smell so much of the study and library, even of the poet's attic, as of the fields and woods; that it is a hypæthral or unroofed book, lying open under the ether and permeated by it, open to all weathers, not easy to be kept on a shelf.

*July 2.* A traveller! I love his title. A traveller is to be reverenced as such. His profession is the best symbol of our life. Going from —— toward ——; it is the history of every one of us. I am interested in those that travel in the night.

*July 6.* Sunday. I walked by night last moon, and saw its disk reflected in Walden Pond, the broken disk, now here, now there, a pure and memorable flame unearthly bright, like a cucullo[37] of a water-bug. Ah! but that first faint tinge of moonlight on the gap! (seen some time ago),[38] — a silvery light from the east before day had departed in the west. What an immeasurable interval there is between the first tinge of moonlight which we detect, lighting with mysterious, silvery, poetic light the western slopes, like a paler grass, and the last wave of daylight on the eastern slopes! It is wonderful how our senses ever span so vast an interval, how from being aware of the one we become aware of the other. And now the night wind blows, — from where? What gave it birth? It suggests an interval equal to that between the most distant periods recorded in history. The silver age is not more distant from the golden[39] than moonlight is from sunlight. I am looking into the west, where the red clouds still indicate the course of departing day. I turn and see the silent, spiritual, contemplative moonlight shedding the softest imaginable light on the western slopes of the hills, as if, after a thousand years of polishing, their surfaces were just beginning to be bright, — a pale whitish lustre. Already the crickets chirp to the moon a different strain, and the night wind rustles the leaves of the wood. A different dynasty has commenced. Yet moonlight, like daylight, is more valuable for what it suggests than for what

**37** Thoreau may have intended to write cucullus: a formation or coloration of the head like or likened to a hood.

**38** On the night of 12 June 1851, about which Thoreau wrote in his journal the next day: "As I entered the Deep Cut, I was affected by beholding the first faint reflection of genuine and unmixed moonlight on the eastern sand-bank while the horizon, yet red with day, was tingeing the western side. What an interval between those two lights! The light of the moon, — in what age of the world does that fall upon the earth? The moonlight was as the earliest and dewy morning light, and the daylight tinge reminded me much more of the night. There were the old and new dynasties opposed, contrasted, and an interval between, which time could not span. Then is night, when the daylight yields to the nightlight" [J 2:249–250].

**39** Ancient Greek and Roman writers, including the Greek poet Hesiod (8th century B.C.E.), spoke of the Golden Age as a time of perfection. It was followed by the Silver Age, a period of relative decline characterized by a refusal to serve the gods and a love of luxury.

**40** Ancient capital of the Assyrian Empire, on the Tigris River, captured and destroyed by Babylonia and its allies in 612 B.C.E. Thoreau read and made several references to Austen Henry Layard's (1817–1894) *Nineveh and Its Remains* (New York: G. P. Putnam, 1849) and *Discoveries Among the Ruins of Nineveh and Babylon* (New York: Harper and Brothers, 1853) in his journals.

**41** In Greek mythology, a river in Hades that induces forgetfulness.

**42** Anthony Wright (b. ca. 1796), local sexton and laborer.

**43** Perez Blood (1785–1856), farmer, laborer, and amateur astronomer who lived in the northern part of Concord. Thoreau described him on 13 December 1851 as "a stuttering, sure, unpretending man, who does not speak without thinking, does not guess" [J 3:137]. Thoreau and Emerson attended the auction of Blood's effects on 2 June 1856, at which his telescope "sold for fifty-five dollars; cost ninety-five plus ten" [J 8:362].

**44** Of his first experience looking through Blood's telescope, Thoreau wrote to his sister Sophia on 24 October 1847: "I went to see Perez Blood's, some time ago, with Mr. Emerson. He had not gone to bed, but was sitting in the woodshed, in the dark, alone, in his astronomical chair, which is all legs and rounds, with a seat which can be inserted at any height. We saw Saturn's rings, and the mountains in the moon, and the shadows in their craters, and the sunlight on the spurs of the mountains in the dark portion, etc., etc." [C 187]. Cf. 29 September 1854.

**45** Towns 10 and 14 miles northeast, and 15 miles east, respectively, from Concord.

it actually is. It is a long past season of which I dream. And the reason is perchance because it is a more sacred and glorious season, to which I instantly refer all glorious actions in past time. Let a nobler landscape present itself, let a purer air blow, and I locate all the worthies of the world. Ah, there is the mysterious light which for some hours has illustrated Asia and the scene of Alexander's victories, now at length, after two or three hours spent in surmounting the billows of the Atlantic, come to shine on America. There, on that illustrated sand-bank, was revealed an antiquity beside which Nineveh[40] is young. Such a light as sufficed for the earliest ages. From what star has it arrived on this planet? Yet even at midday I see the full moon shining in the sky. What if, in some vales, only its light is reflected? What if there are some spirits which walk in its light alone still? who separate the moonlight from the sunlight, and are shined on by the former only? I passed from dynasty to dynasty, from one age of the world to another age of the world, from Jove perchance back to Saturn. What river of Lethe[41] was there to run between? I bade farewell to that light sitting in the west and turned to salute the new light rising in the east.

*July 7.* I have been to-night with Anthony Wright[42] to look through Perez Blood's[43] telescope a second time.[44] A dozen of Blood's neighbors were swept along in the stream of our curiosity. One who lived half a mile this side said that Blood had been down that way within a day or two with his terrestrial, or day, glass looking into the eastern horizon at the hills of Billerica, Burlington, and Woburn.[45] I was amused to see what sort of respect this man with a telescope had obtained from his neighbors, something akin to that which savages award to civilized men, though in this case the interval between the parties was very slight. Mr. Blood, with his skull-cap on, his short figure, his north European figure, made me think of Tycho Brahe.[46] He did not invite us into his house this cool evening, — men nor women, — nor did he ever before to my knowledge. I am still contented to see the stars with my naked eye.[47]

The writer expressing his thought must be as well seated as the astronomer contemplating the heavens; he must not occupy a constrained position.

Be ever so little distracted, your thoughts so little confused, your engagements so few, your attention so free, your existence so mundane, that in all places and in all hours you can hear the sound of crickets in those seasons when they are to be heard. It is a mark of serenity and health of mind when a person hears this sound much, — in streets of cities as well as in fields. Some ears never hear this sound; are called deaf. Is it not because they have so long attended to other sounds?

*July 11.* I hear the sound of Heywood's Brook[48] falling into Fair Haven Pond, inexpressibly refreshing to my senses. It seems to flow through my very bones.[49] I hear it with insatiable thirst. It allays some sandy heat in me. It affects my circulations; methinks my arteries have sympathy with it. What is it I hear but the pure waterfalls within me, in the circulation of my blood, the streams that fall into my heart? What mists do I ever see but such as hang over and rise from my blood? The sound of this gurgling water, running thus by night as by day, falls on all my dashes,[50] fills all my buckets, overflows my floatboards,[51] turns all the machinery of my nature, makes me a flume, a sluice-way, to the springs of nature. Thus I am washed; thus I drink and quench my thirst. Where the streams fall into the lake, if they are only a few inches more elevated, all walkers may hear.

46  Danish astronomer (1546–1601) whose accurate astronomical observations formed the basis for the laws of planetary motion by the German astronomer Johannes Kepler (1571–1630), which accurately describe the revolutions of the planets around the sun.

47  On 9 July 1851 Thoreau wrote: "Visited the Observatory. Bond said they were cataloguing the stars at Washington (?), or trying to. They do not at Cambridge; of no use with their force. Have not force enough now to make mag[netic] obs[ervations]. When I asked if an observer with the small telescope could find employment, he said, Oh yes, there was employment enough for observation with the naked eye, observing the changes in the brilliancy of stars, etc., etc., if they could only get some good observers. One is glad to hear that the naked eye still retains some importance in the estimation of astronomers" [J 2:294].

48  On the east side of Fair Haven.

49  Cf. 12 February 1851: "There is something more than association at the bottom of the excitement which the roar of a cataract produces. It is allied to the circulation in our veins. We have a waterfall which corresponds even to Niagara somewhere within us" [J 2:155].

50  Boards placed on the front of a carriage or sleigh to block water, mud, and snow thrown up by the horses; also known as a dashboard or splashboard.

51  Boards of an undershot waterwheel (where the water passes under the wheel).

52 At the Deep Cut and home to the Patrick Riordan family: Patrick, his wife, an older woman, and two children, Julia and Johnny (cf. Thoreau's poem "The Little Irish Boy" and his entry at 28 January 1852).
53 Allusion to William Wordsworth's (1770–1850) "Ode: Intimations of Immortality from Recollections of Early Childhood" (l. 58): "Our birth is but a sleep and a forgetting."

❧

Going by the shanty,[52] I smell the excrements of its inhabitants, which I had never smelt before.

*July 16.* Methinks my present experience is nothing; my past experience is all in all. I think that no experience which I have to-day comes up to, or is comparable with, the experiences of my boyhood. And not only this is true, but as far back as I can remember I have unconsciously referred to the experiences of a previous state of existence. "For life is a forgetting,"[53] etc. Formerly, methought, nature developed as I developed, and grew up with me. My life was ecstasy. In youth, before I lost any of my senses, I can remember that I was all alive, and inhabited my body with inexpressible satisfaction; both its weariness and its refreshment were sweet to me. This earth was the most glorious musical instrument, and I was audience to its strains. To have such sweet impressions made on us, such ecstasies begotten of the breezes! I can remember how I was astonished. I said to myself,—I said to others,—"There comes into my mind such an indescribable, infinite, all-absorbing, divine, heavenly pleasure, a sense of elevation and expansion, and I have had nought to do with it. I perceive that I am dealt with by superior powers. This is a pleasure, a joy, an existence which I have not procured myself. I speak as a witness on the stand, and tell what I have perceived." The morning and the evening were sweet to me, and I led a life aloof from society of men. I wondered if a mortal had ever known what I knew. I looked in books for some recognition of a kindred experience, but, strange to say, I found none. Indeed, I was slow to discover that other men had had this experience, for it had been possible to read books and to associate with men on other grounds. The maker of me was improving me. When I detected this interference I was profoundly moved. For years I marched as to a music in comparison with which the military music of the streets is noise and discord. I was daily intoxicated, and yet no man could call me intemperate. With all your science can you tell how it is, and whence it is, that light comes into the soul?

Berries are just beginning to ripen, and children are planning expeditions after them. They are important as introducing children to the fields and woods, and as wild fruits of which much account is made.[54] During the berry season the schools have a vacation, and many little fingers are busy picking these small fruits. It is ever a pastime, not a drudgery. I remember how glad I was when I was kept from school a half a day to pick huckleberries on a neighboring hill all by myself to make a pudding for the family dinner. Ah, they got nothing but the pudding, but I got invaluable experience beside! A half a day of liberty like that was like the promise of life eternal. It was emancipation in New England. O, what a day was there, my countrymen![55]

May I go to my slumbers as expecting to arise to a new and more perfect day. May I so live and refine my life as fitting myself for a society ever higher than I actually enjoy. May I treat myself tenderly as I would treat the most innocent child whom I love; may I treat children and my friends as my newly discovered self. Let me forever go in search of myself; never for a moment think that I have found myself; be as a stranger to myself, never a familiar, seeking acquaintance still.[56]

*July 18.* It is a test question affecting the youth of a person,—Have you knowledge of the morning? Do you sympathize with that season of nature? Are you abroad early, brushing the dews aside? If the sun rises on you slumbering, if you do not hear the morning cock-crow,

**54** In his unfinished essay "Huckleberries," Thoreau mentioned the accounts of such writers as, among others, John Lawson (d. 1711), John Lindley (1799–1865), Asa Gray (1818–1888), John Claudius Loudon (1783–1843), and William Stephen Coleman (1829–1904).
**55** Cf. 1850 note 29.
**56** For a similar personal prayer, see 15 March 1852.

57 In Roman mythology, goddess of the dawn.
58 The planet Venus is sometimes called the morning star, used as a symbol of the dawn and renewal.
59 Allusion to Ecclesiastes 12:1: "Remember now thy Creator in the days of thy youth."
60 In *Walden* Thoreau wrote: "think of dashing the hopes of a morning with a cup of warm coffee, or of an evening with a dish of tea!" [Wa 208].
61 His birthday was one week before, on 12 July.
62 Cf. 1840s note 21.

if you do not witness the blushes of Aurora,[57] if you are not acquainted with Venus as the morning star,[58] what relation have you to wisdom and purity? You have then forgotten your Creator in the days of your youth![59] Your shutters were darkened till noon! You rose with a sick headache! In the morning sing, as do the birds. What of those birds which should slumber on their perches till the sun was an hour high? What kind of fowl would they be and new kind of bats and owls,—hedge sparrows or larks? then took a dish of tea or hot coffee before they began to sing?[60]

*July 19.* Here I am thirty-four years old,[61] and yet my life is almost wholly unexpanded. How much is in the germ! There is such an interval between my ideal and the actual in many instances that I may say I am unborn. There is the instinct for society, but no society. Life is not long enough for one success. Within another thirty-four years that miracle can hardly take place. Methinks my seasons revolve more slowly than those of nature; I am differently timed. I am contented. This rapid revolution of nature, even of nature in me, why should it hurry me? Let a man step to the music which he hears, however measured.[62] Is it important that I should mature as soon as an apple tree? aye, as soon as an oak? May not my life in nature, in proportion as it is supernatural, be only the spring and infantile portion of my spirit's life? Shall I turn my spring to summer? May I not sacrifice a hasty and petty completeness here to entireness there? If my curve is large, why bend it to a smaller circle? My spirit's unfolding observes not the pace of nature. The society which I was made for is not here. Shall I, then, substitute for the anticipation of that this poor reality? I would rather have the unmixed expectation of that than this reality. If life is a waiting, so be it. I will not be shipwrecked on a vain reality. What were any reality which I can substitute? Shall I with pains erect a heaven of blue glass over myself, though when it is done I shall be sure to gaze still on the true ethereal heaven far above, as if the former were not,—that still distant sky o'er-arching that blue expressive eye of heaven?[63] I am enamored of the blue-eyed arch of heaven.

*July 21.* Now I yearn for one of those old, meandering, dry, uninhabited roads, which lead away from towns, which lead us away from temptation,[64] which conduct to the outside of earth, over its uppermost crust; where you may forget in what country you are travelling; where no farmer can complain that you are treading down his grass, no gentleman who has recently constructed a seat in the country that you are trespassing; on which you can go off at half-cock and wave adieu to the village; along which you may travel like a pilgrim, going nowhither; where travellers are not too often to be met; where my spirit is free; where the walls and fences are not cared for; where your head is more in heaven than your feet are on earth; which have long reaches where you can see the approaching traveller half a mile off and be prepared for him; not so luxuriant a soil as to attract men; some root and stump fences which do not need attention; where travellers have no occasion to stop, but pass along and leave you to your thoughts; where it makes no odds which way you face, whether you are going or coming, whether it is morning or evening, mid-noon or midnight; where earth is cheap enough by being public; where you can walk and think with least obstruction, there being nothing to measure progress by; where you can pace when your breast is full, and cherish your moodiness; where you are not in false relations with men, are not dining nor conversing with them; by which you may go

**63** Many of the ideas expressed in this entry became central in the "Conclusion" chapter of *Walden:* "Why should we be in such desperate haste to succeed, and in such desperate enterprises? If a man does not keep pace with his companions, perhaps it is because he hears a different drummer. Let him step to the music which he hears, however measured or far away. It is not important that he should mature as soon as an apple-tree or an oak. Shall he turn his spring into summer? If the condition of things which we were made for is not yet, what were any reality which we can substitute? We will not be shipwrecked on a vain reality. Shall we with pains erect a heaven of blue glass over ourselves, though when it is done we shall be sure to gaze still at the true ethereal heaven far above, as if the former were not?" [Wa 317].

**64** Possibly referring to the phrase "And lead us not into temptation" from Matthew 6:13 and Luke 11:4.

65 Allusion to John 14:6: "Jesus saith unto him,
I am the way, the truth, and the life."
66 Jonas Potter (b. 1784).

to the uttermost parts of the earth. It is wide enough, wide as the thoughts it allows to visit you. Sometimes it is some particular half-dozen rods which I wish to find myself pacing over, as where certain airs blow; then my life will come to me, methinks; like a hunter I walk in wait for it. When I am against this bare promontory of a huckleberry hill, then forsooth my thoughts will expand. Is it some influence, as a vapor which exhales from the ground, or something in the gales which blow there, or in all things there brought together agreeably to my spirit? The walls must not be too high, imprisoning me, but low, with numerous gaps. The trees must not be too numerous, nor the hills too near, bounding the view, nor the soil too rich, attracting the attention to the earth. It must simply be the way and the life,[65]—a way that was never known to be repaired, nor to need repair, within the memory of the oldest inhabitant. I cannot walk habitually in those ways that are liable to be mended; for sure it was the devil only that wore them. Never by the heel of thinkers (of thought) were they worn; the zephyrs could repair that damage. The saunterer wears out no road, even though he travel on it, and therefore should pay no highway, or rather *low* way, tax. He may be taxed to construct a higher way than men travel. A way which no geese defile, nor hiss along it, but only sometimes their wild brethren fly far overhead; which the kingbird and the swallow twitter over, and the song sparrow sings on its rails; where the small red butterfly is at home on the yarrow, and no boys threaten it with imprisoning hat. There I can walk and stalk and pace and plod. Which nobody but Jonas Potter[66] travels beside me; where no cow but his is tempted to linger for the herbage by its side; where the guide-board is fallen, and now the hand points to heaven significantly,—to a Sudbury and Marlborough in the skies. That's a road I can travel, that's the particular Sudbury I am bound for, six miles an hour, or two, as you please; and few there be that enter thereon. There I can walk, and recover the lost child that I am without any ringing of a bell; where there was nothing ever discovered to detain a traveller, but all went through about their business; where I never passed the time of day with any,—indifferent to me were the arbitrary divisions of time; where Tullus Hostilius might have disappeared,[67]—at any rate has never been seen. The road to the Corner! the ninety and nine acres that you go through to get there![68] I would rather see it again, though I saw it this morning, than Gray's church-yard.[69] The road whence you may hear a stake-driver,[70] a whip-poor-will, a quail in a midsummer day, a—yes, a quail comes nearest to the *gum*-c bird[71] heard there; where it would not be sport for a sportsman to go. And the mayweed looks up in my face,—not there; the pale lobelia, the Canada snapdragon, rather. A little hardhack and meadowsweet peep over the fence,—nothing more serious to obstruct the view,—and thimble-berries are the food of thought, before the drought, along by the walls.[72]

It is they who go to Brighton[73] and to market that wear out the roads, and they should pay all the tax. The deliberate pace of a thinker never made a road the worse for travelling on.

There I have freedom in my thought, and in my soul am free.[74]

I thought to walk this forenoon instead of this afternoon, for I have not been in the fields and woods much of late except when surveying, but the least affair of that kind is as if you had a black veil drawn over your face which shut out nature, as that eccentric and melancholy minister whom I have heard of.[75] It may be the fairest

67 Tullus Hostilius (673–641 B.C.E.), third legendary king of Rome, disappeared during a storm. Some legends have it that he was struck by lightning for his pride.
68 Allusion to Nine-Acre Corner, in the south corner of Concord.
69 Reference to Thomas Gray's (1716–1771) "Elegy in a Country Churchyard."
70 American bittern (*Botaurus lentiginous*), so named because the male's booming call in spring resembles the sound of a stake being driven into the ground.
71 Unidentified bird of which Channing wrote: "One of Thoreau's names for some bird, so named by the farmers."
72 Thoreau later inserted a note here referring to another passage in his journal, written on 5 August 1851: "A road (the Corner road) that passes over the height of land between earth and heaven, separating those streams which flow earthward from those which flow heavenward" [J 2:372–373].
73 A town in Massachusetts, now a section of Boston, and home to slaughterhouses and farmers' markets. "Bright" was a common name for an ox, thus "Cattle-town."
74 Allusion to Richard Lovelace's (1618–1657) "To Althea in Prison" (ll.29–30):

Stone walls do not a prison make,
Nor iron bars a cage;
Minds innocent and quiet take
    That for an hermitage;
If I have freedom in my love,
    And in my soul am free,
Angels alone that soar above
    Enjoy such liberty.

Thoreau quoted this phrase again in his journal on 28 January 1852 [J 3:241] in a passage repeated in *Walden* [Wa 28].
75 Allusion to Reverend Hooper, in Hawthorne's "The Minister's Black Veil" collected in *Twice-Told Tales* (1837), who is described as both eccentric

and melancholy. He wore a veil of "two folds of crepe, which entirely concealed his features, except the mouth and chin, but probably did not intercept his sight, further than to give a darkened aspect to all living and inanimate things."

**76** Cf. 1851 note 59.

**77** Allusion to the continuation of Ecclesiastes 12:1: "while the evil days come not."

**78** Cf. 1851 note 24.

**79** An instrument consisting of an open sound box over which strings are stretched that sound when the wind passes over them, named after Aeolus, god of the winds. Thoreau had made one. Cf. "Rumors from an Æolian Harp" [W 1:184].

**80** Allusion to Plato's "Ion": "For the authors of those great poems which we admire, do not attain to excellence through the rules of any art, but they utter their beautiful melodies of verse in a state of inspiration, and, as it were, possessed by a spirit not their own. Thus the composers of lyrical poetry create those admired songs of theirs in a state of divine insanity. . . . For a poet is indeed a thing ethereally light, winged, and sacred, nor can he compose anything worth calling poetry until he becomes inspired, and, as it were, mad, or whilst any reason remains in him."

**81** Biblically, the harp is an instrument of cheerfulness, which can heal and remove the evil spirit, and is also used to accompany songs of praise of God.

**82** On 12 September 1851 Thoreau similarly wrote: "I had already bathed in Walden as I passed, but now I forgot that I had been wetted, and wanted to embrace and mingle myself with the water of Flint's Pond this warm afternoon, to get wet inwardly and deeply" [J 2:501].

day in all the year and you shall not know it. One little chore to do, one little commission to fulfill, one message to carry, would spoil heaven itself.

Remember thy Creator in the days of thy youth;[76] *i. e.,* lay up a store of natural influences. Sing while you may, before the evil days come.[77] He that hath ears, let him hear.[78] See, hear, smell, taste, etc., while these senses are fresh and pure.

There is always a kind of fine æolian harp[79] music to be heard in the air. I hear now, as it were, the mellow sound of distant horns in the hollow mansions of the upper air, a sound to make all men divinely insane[80] that hear it, far away overhead, subsiding into my ear. To ears that are expanded what a harp[81] this world is! The occupied ear thinks that beyond the cricket no sound can be heard, but there is an immortal melody that may be heard morning, noon, and night, by ears that can attend, and from time to time this man or that hears it, having ears that were made for music.

8:30 P.M. — The streets of the village are much more interesting to me at this hour of a summer evening than by day. Neighbors, and also farmers, come a-shopping after their day's haying, are chatting in the streets, and I hear the sound of many musical instruments and of singing from various houses. For a short hour or two the inhabitants are sensibly employed. The evening is devoted to poetry, such as the villagers can appreciate.

*July 22.* I bathe me in the river. I lie down where it is shallow, amid the weeds over its sandy bottom; but it seems shrunken and parched; I find it difficult to get *wet* through. I would fain be the channel of a mountain brook. I bathe, and in a few hours I bathe again, not remembering that I was wetted before.[82] When I come to the river, I take off my clothes and carry them over, then bathe and wash off the mud and continue my walk.

*July 23.* 8 A.M. — A comfortable breeze blowing. Methinks I can write better in the afternoon, for the novelty of it, if I should go abroad this morning. My genius makes distinctions which my understanding cannot, and which my senses do not report. If I should reverse the usual, — go forth and saunter in the fields all the forenoon, then sit down in my chamber in the afternoon, which it is so unusual for me to do, — it would be like a new season to me, and the novelty of it would inspire me. The wind has fairly blown me outdoors; the elements were so lively and active, and I so sympathized with them, that I could not sit while the wind went by. And I am reminded that we should especially improve the summer to live out-of-doors. When we may so easily, it behooves us to break up this custom of sitting in the house, for it is but a custom, and I am not sure that it has the sanction of common sense. A man no sooner gets up than he sits down again. Fowls leave their perch in the morning, and beasts their lairs, unless they are such as go abroad only by night. The cockerel does not take up a new perch *in the barn,* and he is the embodiment of health and common sense. Is the literary man to live always or chiefly sitting in a chamber through which nature enters by a window only? What is the use of the summer?

You must walk so gently as to hear the finest sounds, the faculties being in repose. Your mind must not perspire. True, out of doors my thought is commonly drowned, as it were, and shrunken, pressed down by stupendous piles of light ethereal influences, for the pressure of the atmosphere is still fifteen pounds to a square inch. I can do little more than preserve the equilibrium and resist the pressure of the atmosphere. I can only nod like the rye-heads in the breeze. I expand more surely in

83 Thoreau made an excursion on foot from Hull to Plymouth, leaving Plymouth on 1 August.
84 Of Boston.

my chamber, as far as expression goes, as if that pressure were taken off; but here outdoors is the place to store up influences.

The influences which make for one walk more than another, and one day more than another, are much more ethereal than terrestrial. It is the quality of the air much more than the quality of the ground that concerns the walker, — cheers or depresses him. What he may find in the air, not what he may find on the ground.

I was too discursive and rambling in my thought for the chamber, and must go where the wind blows on me walking.

The mind is subject to moods, as the shadows of clouds pass over the earth. Pay not too much heed to them. Let not the traveller stop for them. They consist with the fairest weather. By the mood of my mind, I suddenly felt dissuaded from continuing my walk, but I observed at the same instant that the shadow of a cloud was passing over the spot on which I stood, though it was of small extent, which, if it had no connection with my mood, at any rate suggested how transient and little to be regarded that mood was. I kept on, and in a moment the sun shone on my walk within and without.

Poetry puts an interval between the impression and the expression, — waits till the seed germinates naturally.

*July 25.* At 9 A.M. took the Hingham boat and was landed at Hull.[83] There was a pleasure party on board, apparently boys and girls belonging to the South End,[84] going to Hingham. There was a large proportion of ill-dressed and ill-mannered boys of Irish extraction. A sad sight to behold! Little boys of twelve years, prematurely old, sucking cigars! I felt that if I were their mothers I should whip them and send them to bed. Such children should be dealt with as for stealing or impurity. The opening of this valve for the safety of the city! Oh, what a wretched resource! What right have parents to beget, to bring up, and attempt to *educate* children in a city. I thought of infanticide among the Orientals[85] with complacency. I seemed to hear infant voices lisp, "Give us a fair chance, parents." There is no such squalidness in the country. You would have said that they must all have come from the house of correction and the farm-school,[86] but such a company do the boys in Boston streets make. The birds have more care for their young,—where they place their nests. What are a city's charities? She cannot be charitable any more than the old philosopher could move the earth, unless she had a resting place without herself.[87] A true culture is more possible to the savage than to the boy of average intellect, born of average parents, in a great city. I believe that they perish miserably. How can they be kept clean, physically or morally? It is folly to attempt to educate children within a city; the first step must be to remove them out of it.

I am bothered to walk with those who wish to keep step with me.[88] It is not necessary to keep step with your companion, as some endeavor to do.[89]

*August 5.* Ah, what a poor, dry compilation is the "Annual of Scientific Discovery"![90] I trust that observations are made during the year which are not chronicled there,—that some mortal may have caught a glimpse of Nature in some corner of the earth during the year 1851. One sentence of perennial poetry would make me forget, would atone for, volumes of mere science. The astronomer is as blind to the significant phenomena, or the significance of phenomena, as the wood-sawyer who wears

85 There were numerous reports on infanticide in China, such as "China," reprinted from the *North British Review* in *Littell's Living Age* (October 1847): "With regard to the truth of the commonly received reports of infanticide among the Chinese, there can be no doubt. Mr. Smith took special care personally to inquire into this fact. It is practised chiefly among the poorer classes, and it is the female infants who suffer; a poor man in his old age usually receiving support and assistance from his sons, whereas his daughters are generally married early, and are then no longer considered as part of the family. On repeated occasions, and before a numerous assemblage, fathers, when questioned by Mr. Smith regarding this subject, seemed to have no hesitation in openly and simply avowing the fact."
86 The Boston Asylum and Farm School for Indigent Boys, or the Boston Farm School, on Thompson Island in Boston Harbor, was formed by the merger of the Boston Farm School Society and the Boston Asylum for Indigent Boys to care for poor boys and teach them agricultural skills.
87 Allusion to Archimedes (287–212 B.C.E.), Greek mathematician, physicist, engineer, astronomer, and philosopher who is reported to have said regarding the use of the lever: "Give me a place to stand, and I will move the world."
88 Probable reference to Channing, often his walking companion: cf. 7 and 9 November 1851 and 31 August 1856.
89 Cf. 1840s note 21.
90 *The Annual of Scientific Discovery; or, Year-book of Facts in Science and Art, For Exhibiting the Most Important Discoveries and Improvements,* which began publication in 1850 in Boston.

**91** Cf. 21 January 1853.

**92** Similarly, after feeling elevated from hearing a few strains of music from his neighbor who was learning to play accordion, Thoreau wrote: "The question is not whether you drink, but what liquor" [J 2:72].

**93** Probable reference to Emerson's 1847 tour of England, about which he began lecturing in 1849.

**94** Possible reference to Charles Dickens (1812–1870), who published his *American Notes for General Circulation* in 1842, or to Harriet Martineau (1802–1876), who made a tour of America in 1834–1835, which led her to become an abolitionist and write two highly critical books: *Society in America* (1837) and *A Retrospect of Western Travel* (1838).

**95** John Ledyard (1751–1789), American traveler who visited the Barbary Coast, the West Indies, New Zealand, Europe, Asia, and the west coast of North America.

**96** First chapter heading of William Bartram's (1739–1823) *Travels Through North and South Carolina*.

glasses to defend his eyes from sawdust.[91] The question is not what you look at, but what you see.[92]

***August 6.*** A man must generally get away some hundreds or thousands of miles from home before he can be said to begin his travels. Why not begin his travels at home? Would he have to go far or look very closely to discover novelties? The traveller who, in this sense, pursues his travels at home, has the advantage at any rate of a long residence in the country to make his observations correct and profitable. Now the American goes to England,[93] while the Englishman comes to America,[94] in order to describe the country. No doubt there are some advantages in this kind of mutual criticism. But might there not be invented a better way of coming at the truth than this scratch-my-back-and-I-'ll-scratch-yours method? Would not the American, for instance, who had himself, perchance, travelled in England and elsewhere make the most profitable and accurate traveller in his own country? How often it happens that the traveller's principal distinction is that he is one who knows less about a country than a native! Now if he should begin with all the knowledge of a native, and add thereto the knowledge of a traveller, both natives and foreigners would be obliged to read his book; and the world would be absolutely benefited. It takes a man of genius to travel in his own country, in his native village; to make any progress between his door and his gate. But such a traveller will make the distances which Hanno and Marco Polo and Cook and Ledyard[95] went over ridiculous. So worthy a traveller as William Bartram heads his first chapter with the words, "The author sets sail from Philadelphia, and arrives at Charleston, from whence he begins his travels."[96]

I am, perchance, most and most profitably interested in the things which I already know a little about;

a mere and utter novelty is a mere monstrosity to me. I am interested to see the yellow pine, which we have not in Concord, though Michaux says it grows in Massachusetts;[97] or the Oriental plane,[98] having often heard of it and being well acquainted with its sister, the Occidental plane;[99] or the English oak, having heard of the royal oak and having oaks ourselves; but the new Chinese flower, whose cousin I do not happen to know, I pass by with indifference. I do not know that I am very fond of novelty. I wish to get a clearer notion of what I have already some inkling.

*August 17.* For a day or two it has been quite cool, a coolness that was felt even when sitting by an open window in a thin coat on the west side of the house in the morning, and you naturally sought the sun at that hour. The coolness concentrated your thought, however. As I could not command a sunny window, I went abroad on the morning of the 15th and lay in the sun in the fields in my thin coat, though it was rather cool even there. I feel as if this coolness would do me good. If it only makes my life more pensive! Why should pensiveness be akin to sadness? There is a certain fertile sadness which I would not avoid, but rather earnestly seek. It is positively joyful to me. It saves my life from being trivial. My life flows with a deeper current, no longer as a shallow and brawling stream, parched and shrunken by the summer heats. This coolness comes to condense the dews and clear the atmosphere. The stillness seems more deep and significant. Each sound seems to come from out a greater thoughtfulness in nature, as if nature had acquired some character and mind. The cricket, the gurgling stream, the rushing wind amid the trees, all speak to me soberly yet encouragingly of the steady onward progress of the universe. My heart leaps into my mouth

**97** Not what is colloquially called the yellow, or pumpkin, pine (cf. 1853 note 67) but a distinct species of pine (*Pinus mitis*), which François André Michaux (1770–1855) wrote about in *The North American Sylva, or a Description of the Forest Trees of the United States, Canada, and Nova Scotia*. Thoreau noted in his journal on 18 May 1851, from his reading in Michaux: "The *Pinus mitis*, yellow pine, or spruce pine, or short-leaved pine. A two-leaved pine widely diffused, but not found northward beyond certain districts of Connecticut and Massachusetts" [J 2:198].

**98** *Platanus orientalis.*

**99** *Platanus occidentalis*, also known as western plane, sycamore, and buttonwood.

100 Blue-curls, in the mint family.

at the sound of the wind in the woods. I, whose life was but yesterday so desultory and shallow, suddenly recover my spirits, my spirituality, through my hearing. I see a goldfinch go twittering through the still, louring day, and am reminded of the peeping flocks which will soon herald the thoughtful season. Ah! if I could so live that there should be no desultory moment in all my life! that in the trivial season, when small fruits are ripe, my fruits might be ripe also! that I could match nature always with my moods! that in each season when some part of nature especially flourishes, then a corresponding part of me may not fail to flourish! Ah, I would walk, I would sit and sleep, with natural piety! What if I could pray aloud or to myself as I went along by the brooksides a cheerful prayer like the birds! For joy I could embrace the earth; I shall delight to be buried in it. And then to think of those I love among men, who will know that I love them though I tell them not! I sometimes feel as if I were rewarded merely for expecting better hours. I did not despair of worthier moods, and now I have occasion to be grateful for the flood of life that is flowing over me. I am not so poor; I can smell the ripening apples; the very rills are deep; the autumnal flowers, the *Trichostema dichotomum*,[100] — not only its bright blue flower above the sand, but its strong wormwood scent which belongs to the season, — feed my spirit, endear the earth to me, make me value myself and rejoice; the quivering of pigeons' wings reminds me of the tough fibre of the air which they rend. I thank you, God. I do not deserve anything, I am unworthy of the least regard; and yet I am made to rejoice. I am impure and worthless, and yet the world is gilded for my delight and holidays are prepared for me, and my path is strewn with flowers. But I cannot thank the Giver; I cannot even whisper my thanks to those human friends I have. It seems to me that I am more rewarded for my expectations than for anything I do or can do. Ah, I would not tread on a cricket in whose song is such a revelation, so soothing and cheering to my ear! Oh, keep my senses pure! And why should I speak to my friends? for how rarely is it that I am I; and are they, then, they? We will meet, then, far away. The seeds of the summer are getting dry and falling from a thousand nodding heads. If I did not know you through thick and thin, how should I know you at all? Ah, the very brooks seem fuller of reflections than they were! Ah, such provoking sibylline sentences they are! The shallowest is all at once unfathomable. How can that depth be fathomed where a man may see himself reflected? The rill I stopped to drink at I drink in more than I expected. I satisfy and still provoke the thirst of thirsts.

*August 19.* The poet must be continually watching the moods of his mind, as the astronomer watches the aspects of the heavens. What might we not expect from a long life faithfully spent in this wise? The humblest observer would see some stars shoot. A faithful description as by a disinterested person of the thoughts which visited a certain mind in threescore years and ten, as when one reports the number and character of the vehicles which pass a particular point. As travellers go round the world and report natural objects and phenomena, so faithfully let another stay at home and report the phenomena of his own life,—catalogue stars, those thoughts whose orbits are as rarely calculated as comets. It matters not whether they visit my mind or yours,—whether the meteor falls in my field or in yours,—only that it came from heaven. (I am not concerned to express that kind of truth which Nature has expressed. Who knows but I may suggest some things to her? Time was when she was indebted to such suggestions from another quarter, as her present advancement shows. I deal with the truths that recommend themselves to me,—please me,—not those merely which any system has voted to accept.) A meteorological journal of the mind. You shall observe what occurs in your latitude, I in mine.

Some institutions—most institutions, indeed,—have had a divine origin. But of most that we see prevailing in society nothing but the form, the shell, is left; the life is extinct, and there is nothing divine in them. Then the reformer arises inspired to reinstitute life, and whatever he does or causes to be done is a reëstablishment of that same or a similar divineness. But some, who never knew the significance of these instincts, are, by a sort of false instinct, found clinging to the shells. Those who have no knowledge of the divine appoint themselves defenders of the divine, as champions of the church, etc. I have been astonished to observe how long some audiences can endure to hear a man speak on a subject which he knows nothing about, as religion for instance, when one who has no ear for music might with the same propriety take up the time of a musical assembly with putting through his opinions on music. This young man who is the main pillar of some divine institution,—does he know what he has undertaken? If the saints were to come again on earth, would they be likely to stay at his house? would they meet with his approbation even? *Ne sutor ultra crepidam.*[101] They who merely have a talent for affairs are forward to express their opinions. A Roman soldier sits there to decide upon the righteousness of Christ.[102] The world does not long endure such blunders, though they are made every day. The weak-brained and pusillanimous farmers would fain abide by the institutions of their fathers. Their argument is they have not long to live, and for that little space let them not be disturbed in their slumbers; blessed are the peacemakers;[103] let this cup pass from me,[104] etc.

101 Latin: "Shoemaker, not beyond the sandal," a rebuke attributed to the Greek painter Apelles (4th century B.C.E.) to a shoemaker who criticized his art, meaning: do not venture beyond what you know.

102 Allusion to Pontius Pilate (1st century C.E.), Roman prefect of Judea who ordered the crucifixion of Jesus.

103 Quoted from Matthew 5:9: "Blessed are the peacemakers: for they shall be called the children of God."

104 Quoted from Matthew 26:39: "And he went a little further, and fell on his face, and prayed, saying, O my Father, if it be possible, let this cup pass from me: nevertheless not as I will, but as thou wilt."

How vain it is to sit down to write when you have not stood up to live! Methinks that the moment my legs begin to move, my thoughts begin to flow, as if I had given vent to the stream at the lower end and consequently new fountains flowed into it at the upper. A thousand rills which have their rise in the sources of thought burst forth and fertilize my brain. You need to increase the draught below, as the owners of meadows on Concord River say of the Billerica Dam.[105] Only while we are in action is the circulation perfect. The writing which consists with habitual sitting is mechanical, wooden, dull to read.

*August 21.* What a faculty must that be which can paint the most barren landscape and humblest life in glorious colors! It is pure and invigorated senses reacting on a sound and strong imagination. Is not that the poet's case? The intellect of most men is barren. They neither fertilize nor are fertilized. It is the marriage of the soul with Nature that makes the intellect fruitful, that gives birth to the imagination.

*August 23.* Resolve to read no book, to take no walk, to undertake no enterprise, but such as you can endure to give an account of to yourself.[106] Live thus deliberately for the most part.

*August 28.* I omit the unusual—the hurricanes and earthquakes—and describe the common. This has the greatest charm and is the true theme of poetry. You may have the extraordinary for your province, if you will let me have the ordinary. Give me the obscure life, the cottage of the poor and humble, the workdays of the world, the barren fields, the smallest share of all things but poetic perception. Give me but the eyes to see the things which you possess.

**105** The Billerica Dam had far-reaching repercussions on the river. Thoreau further wrote on 22 June 1859: "The testimony of the farmers, etc., is that the river thirty to fifty years ago was much lower in the summer than now" [J 12:211]. It also had impact on the shad of the river: "Shad are still taken in the basin of Concord River, at Lowell, where they are said to be a month earlier than the Merrimack shad, on account of the warmth of the water. Still patiently, almost pathetically, with instinct not to be discouraged, not to be *reasoned* with, revisiting their old haunts, as if their stern fates would relent, and still met by the Corporation with its dam. . . . I for one am with thee, and who knows what may avail a crowbar against that Billerica dam?" [W 1:35–36].

**106** As he wrote in *Walden*: "Moreover, I, on my side, require of every writer, first or last, a simple and sincere account of his own life, and not merely what he has heard of other men's lives; some such account as he would send to his kindred from a distant land; for if he has lived sincerely, it must have been in a distant land to me" [Wa 2].

**107** On the southern end of Conantum.

**108** Although native to North America, the horse died out approximately ten thousand years ago, and was reintroduced by the Spanish in the 16th century, so Thoreau is correct in regard to the horse on this continent.

*September 2.* We cannot write well or truly but what we write with gusto. The body, the senses, must conspire with the mind. Expression is the act of the whole man, that our speech may be vascular. The intellect is powerless to express thought without the aid of the heart and liver and of every member. Often I feel that my head stands out too dry, when it should be immersed. A writer, a man writing, is the scribe of all nature; he is the corn and the grass and the atmosphere writing. It is always essential that we love to do what we are doing, do it with a heart.

*September 3.* Why was there never a poem on the cricket? Its creak seems to me to be one of the most prominent and obvious facts in the world, and the least heeded. In the report of a man's contemplations I look to see somewhat answering to this sound. When I sat on Lee's Cliff[107] the other day (August 29th), I saw a man working with a horse in a field by the river, carting dirt; and the horse and his relation to him struck me as very remarkable. There was the horse, a mere animated machine, — though his tail was brushing off the flies, — his whole existence subordinated to the man's, with no tradition, perhaps no instinct, in him of independence and freedom, of a time when he was wild and free, — completely humanized. No compact made with him that he should have the Saturday afternoons, or the Sundays, or any holidays. His independence never recognized, it being now quite forgotten both by men and by horses that the horse was ever free. For I am not aware that there are any wild horses known surely not descended from tame ones.[108] Assisting that man to pull down that bank and spread it over the meadow; only keeping off the flies with his tail, and stamping, and catching a mouthful of grass or leaves from time to time on his own account, — all the rest for man. It seemed hardly worth while that he should be *animated* for this. It was plain that the man was not educating the horse; not trying to develop his nature, but merely getting work out of him. That mass of animated matter seemed more completely the servant of man than any inanimate. For slaves have their holidays; a heaven is conceded to them, but to the horse none.[109] Now and forever he is man's slave. The more I considered, the more the man seemed akin to the horse; only his was the stronger will of the two. For a little further on I saw an Irishman shovelling, who evidently was as much tamed as the horse. He had stipulated that to a certain extent his independence be recognized, and yet really he was but little more independent. I had always instinctively regarded the horse as a free people somewhere, living wild. Whatever has not come under the sway of man is wild. In this sense original and independent men are wild, — not tamed and broken by society. Now for my part I have such a respect for the horse's nature as would tempt me to let him alone; not to interfere with him, — his walks, his diet, his loves. But by mankind he is treated simply as if he were an engine which must have rest and is sensible of pain. Suppose that every squirrel were made to turn a coffee-mill! Suppose that the gazelles were made to draw milk-carts!

There he was with his tail cut off, because it was in the way, or to suit the taste of his owner; his mane trimmed, and his feet shod with iron that he might wear longer. What is a horse but an animal that has lost its liberty? What is it but a system of slavery? and do you not thus by *insensible* and unimportant degrees come to human slavery? Has lost its liberty! — and has man got any more liberty himself for having robbed the horse, or has he lost just as much of his own, and become more like the horse he has robbed? Is not the other end of the bridle in this case, too, coiled round his own neck? Hence stable-boys, jockeys, all that class that is daily transported by

[109] As Thoreau suggests, biblical authority makes no provision for the ascent of an animal's soul or spirit to heaven; for example, Ecclesiastes 3:21: "Who knoweth the spirit of man that goeth upward, and the spirit of the beast that goeth downward to the earth?"

110 Achilles in Greek mythology was the hero of Homer's *Iliad* and the slayer of Hector, and Nestor was the elderly and wise counselor to the Greeks at Troy.

111 Second Division Brook, which extends south of the Assabet River from Damon's Mills through Hayward's Mill Pond and ends in Sudbury.

fast horses. There he stood with his oblong square figure (his tailed being cut off) seen against the water, brushing off the flies with his tail and stamping, braced back while the man was filling the cart.

It is a very remarkable and significant fact that, though no man is quite well or healthy, yet every one believes practically that health is the rule and disease the exception, and each invalid is wont to think himself in a minority, and to postpone somewhat of endeavor to another state of existence. But it may be some encouragement to men to know that in this respect they stand on the same platform, that disease is, in fact, the *rule* of our terrestrial life and the prophecy of a *celestial* life. Where is the coward who despairs because he is sick? Every one may live either the life of Achilles or of Nestor.[110] Seen in this light, our life with all its diseases will look healthy, and in one sense the more healthy as it is the more diseased. Disease is not the accident of the individual, nor even of the generation, but of life itself. In some form, and to some degree or other, it is one of the permanent conditions of life. It is, nevertheless, a cheering fact that men affirm health unanimously, and esteem themselves miserable failures. Here was no blunder. They gave us life on exactly these conditions, and methinks we shall live it with more heart when we perceive clearly that these are the terms on which we have it. Life is a warfare, a struggle, and the diseases of the body answer to the troubles and defeats of the spirit. Man begins by quarrelling with the animal in him, and the result is immediate disease. In proportion as the spirit is the more ambitious and persevering, the more obstacles it will meet with. It is as a seer that man asserts his disease to be exceptional.

*September 4.* To have a hut here, and a footpath to the brook![111] For roads, I think that a poet cannot tolerate more than a footpath through the fields; that is wide enough, and for purposes of winged poesy suffices. It is not for the muse to speak of cart-paths. I would fain travel by a footpath round the world. I do not ask the railroads of commerce, not even the cart-paths of the farmer. Pray, what other path would you have than a footpath? What else should wear a path? This is the track of man alone. What more suggestive to the pensive walker?[112] One walks in a wheel-track with less emotion; he is at a greater distance from man; but this footpath was, perchance, worn by the bare feet of human beings, and he cannot but think with interest of them.

It is wise to write on many subjects, to try many themes, that so you may find the right and inspiring one. Be greedy of occasions to express your thought. Improve the opportunity to draw analogies. There are innumerable avenues to a perception of the truth. Improve the suggestion of each object however humble, however slight and transient the provocation. What else is there to be improved? Who knows what opportunities he may neglect? It is not in vain that the mind turns aside this way or that: follow its leading; apply it whither it inclines to go. Probe the universe in a myriad points. Be avaricious of these impulses. You must try a thousand themes before you find the right one, as nature makes a thousand acorns to get one oak. He is a wise man and experienced who has taken many views; to whom stones and plants and animals and a myriad objects have each suggested something, contributed something.

And now, methinks, this wider wood-path[113] is not bad, for it admits of society more conveniently. Two can walk side by side in it in the ruts, aye, and one more in the horse-track. The Indian walked in single file, more solitary,—not side by side, chatting as he went. The woodman's cart and sled make just the path two walkers want through the wood.

112  Thoreau's note: "*Vide* last journal for bare foot track in Corner road." Cf. 21 July 1851.
113  Near Second Division Brook.

114 James John Garth Wilkinson's (1812–1899) *The Human Body and Its Connexion with Man* (1851). Thoreau was also familiar with Wilkinson's essay "Correspondence," published in *Aesthetic Papers* (1849).

115 Small nipplelike projection or protuberance on the skin, such as at the base of a hair.

116 Quoted from Wilkinson's *The Human Body and Its Connexion with Man*.

117 Martineau's *Letters on the Laws of Man's Nature and Development*, published in 1851.

*September 5.* Wilkinson's book[114] to some extent realizes what I have dreamed of,—a return to the primitive analogical and derivative senses of words. His ability to trace analogies often leads him to a truer word than more remarkable writers have found; as when, in his chapter on the human skin, he describes the papillary cutis[115] as "an encampment of small conical tents coextensive with the surface of the body."[116] The faith he puts in old and current expressions as having sprung from an instinct wiser than science, and safely to be trusted if they can be interpreted. The man of science discovers no world for the mind of man with all its faculties to inhabit. Wilkinson finds a *home* for the imagination, and it is no longer outcast and homeless. All perception of truth is the detection of an analogy; we reason from our hands to our head.

*September 7.* We sometimes experience a mere fullness of life, which does not find any channels to flow into. We are stimulated, but to no obvious purpose. I feel myself uncommonly prepared for *some* literary work, but I can select no work. I am prepared not so much for contemplation, as for forceful expression. I am braced both physically and intellectually. It is not so much the music as the marching to the music that I feel. I feel that the juices of the fruits which I have eaten, the melons and apples, have ascended to my brain and are stimulating it. They give me a heady force. Now I can write nervously. Carlyle's writing is for the most part of this character.

Miss Martineau's last book[117] is not so bad as the timidity which fears its influence. As if the popularity of this or that book would be so fatal, and man would not still be man in the world. Nothing is so much to be feared as fear. Atheism may be popular with God himself.

What shall we say of these timid folk who carry the

principle of thinking nothing and doing nothing and being nothing to such an extreme? As if, in the absence of thought, that vast yearning of their natures for something to fill the vacuum made the least traditional expression and shadow of a thought to be clung to with instinctive tenacity. They atone for their producing nothing by a brutish respect for something. They are as simple as oxen, and as guiltless of thought and reflection. Their reflections are reflected from other minds. The creature of institutions, bigoted and a conservatist, can say nothing hearty. He cannot meet life with life, but only with words. He rebuts you by avoiding you. He is shocked like a woman.

Our ecstatic states, which appear to yield so little fruit, have this value at least; though in the seasons when our genius reigns we may be powerless for expression, yet, in calmer seasons, when our talent is active, the memory of those rarer moods comes to color our picture and is the permanent paint-pot, as it were, into which we dip our brush. Thus no life or experience goes unreported at last; but if it be not solid gold it is gold-leaf, which gilds the furniture of the mind. It is an experience of infinite beauty on which we unfailingly draw, which enables us to exaggerate ever truly. Our moments of inspiration are not lost though we have no particular poem to show for them; for those experiences have left an indelible impression, and we are ever and anon reminded of them. Their truth subsides, and in cooler moments we can use them as paint to gild and adorn our prose. When I despair to sing them, I will remember that they will furnish me with paint with which to adorn and preserve the works of talent one day. They are like a pot of pure ether. They lend the writer when the moment comes a certain superfluity of wealth, making his expression to overrun and float itself. It is the difference between our river, now parched and dried up, exposing its unsightly and weedy

118 Allusion to I Thessalonians 5:17: "Pray without ceasing."
119 A phrase found in several places in the Bible, as in Matthew 14:27, John 16:33, and Acts 27:22.
120 The mountain from which Moses saw the Promised Land, in Deuteronomy 3:27: "Get thee up into the top of Pisgah, and lift up thine eyes westward, and northward, and southward, and eastward, and behold it with thine eyes: for thou shalt not go over this Jordan."

bottom, and the same when, in the spring, it covers all the meads with a chain of placid lakes, reflecting the forests and the skies.

We are receiving our portion of the infinite. The art of life! Was there ever anything memorable written upon it? By what disciplines to secure the most life, with what care to watch our thoughts. To observe what transpires, not in the street, but in the mind and heart of me! I do not remember any page which will tell me how to spend this afternoon. I do not so much wish to know how to economize time as how to spend it, by what means to grow rich, that the day may not have been in vain.

The art of spending a day. If it is possible that we may be addressed, it behooves us to be attentive. If by watching all day and all night I may detect some trace of the Ineffable, then will it not be worth the while to watch? Watch and pray without ceasing,[118] but not necessarily in sadness. Be of good cheer.[119] Those Jews were too sad: to another people a still deeper revelation may suggest only joy. Don't I know what gladness is? Is it but the reflex of sadness, its back side? In the Hebrew gladness, I hear but too distinctly still the sound of sadness retreating. Give me a gladness which has never given place to sadness.

I am convinced that men are not well employed, that this is not the way to spend a day. If by patience, if by watching, I can secure one new ray of light, can feel myself elevated for an instant upon Pisgah,[120] the world which was dead prose to me become living and divine, shall I not watch ever? shall I not be a watchman henceforth? If by watching a whole year on the city's walls I may obtain a communication from heaven, shall I not do well to shut up my shop and turn a watchman? Can a youth, a man, do more wisely than to go where his life is to be found? As if I had suffered that to be rumor which may be verified. We are surrounded by a rich and fertile mystery. May we not probe it, pry into it, employ ourselves about it, a little? To devote your life to the discovery of the divinity in nature or to the eating of oysters, would they not be attended with very different results?

My profession is to be always on the alert to find God in nature, to know his lurking-places, to attend all the oratorios, the operas, in nature.

*September 12.* I go to Flint's Pond[121] for the sake of the mountain view from the hill beyond, looking over Concord. I have thought it the best, especially in the winter, which I can get in this neighborhood. It is worth the while to see the mountains in the horizon once a day. I have thus seen some earth which corresponds to my least earthly and trivial, to my most heavenward-looking, thoughts. The earth seen through an azure, an ethereal, veil. They are the natural *temples,* elevated brows, of the earth, looking at which, the thoughts of the beholder are naturally elevated and sublimed,—etherealized. I wish to see the earth through the medium of much air or heaven, for there is no paint like the air. Mountains thus seen are worthy of worship.

At the entrance to the Deep Cut,[122] I heard the telegraph-wire vibrating like an æolian harp. It reminded me suddenly,—reservedly, with a beautiful paucity of communication, even silently, such was its effect on my thoughts,—it reminded me, I say, with a certain pathetic moderation, of what finer and deeper stirrings I was susceptible, which grandly set all argument and dispute aside, a triumphant though transient exhibition of the truth. It told me by the faintest imaginable strain, it told me by the finest strain that a human ear can hear, yet conclusively and past all refutation, that there were

121  Flint's Pond in Lincoln, approximately one mile southeast of Walden Pond, was named after the original owner of the land, Thomas Flint (1603–1653). It was also known as Mr. Flint's Pond, Mrs. Flint's Pond, and Great Pond in the 17th century and Sandy Pond since the beginning of the 18th century. In *Walden* Thoreau wrote: "Flint's, or Sandy Pond, in Lincoln, our greatest lake and inland sea, lies about a mile east of Walden. It is much larger, being said to contain one hundred and ninety-seven acres, and is more fertile in fish; but it is comparatively shallow, and not remarkably pure. A walk through the woods thither was often my recreation. It was worth the while, if only to feel the wind blow on your cheek freely, and see the waves run, and remember the life of mariners" [Wa 188].
122  Spot west of Walden Pond where the earth had been excavated to level the tracks for the railroad.

higher, infinitely higher, plains of life, which it behooved me never to forget. As I was entering the Deep Cut, the wind, which was conveying a message to me from heaven, dropped it on the wire of the telegraph which it vibrated as it past. I instantly sat down on a stone at the foot of the telegraph-pole, and attended to the communication. It merely said: "Bear in mind, Child, and never for an instant forget, that there are higher plains, infinitely higher plains, of life than this thou art now travelling on. Know that the goal is distant, and is upward, and is worthy all your life's efforts to attain to." And then it ceased, and though I sat some minutes longer I heard nothing more.

There is every variety and degree of inspiration from mere fullness of life to the most rapt mood. A human soul is played on even as this wire, which now vibrates slowly and gently so that the passer can hardly hear it, and anon the sound swells and vibrates with such intensity as if it would rend the wire, as far as the elasticity and tension of the wire permits, and now it dies away and is silent, and though the breeze continues to sweep over it, no strain comes from it, and the traveller harkens in vain. It is no small gain to have this wire stretched through Concord, though there may be no office here. Thus I make my own use of the telegraph, without consulting the directors, like the sparrows, which I perceive use it extensively for a perch. Shall I not go to this office to hear if there is any communication for me, as steadily as to the post-office in the village?[123]

*September 20.* 3 P.M. — To Cliffs *via* Bear Hill.[124]

As I go through the fields, endeavoring to recover my tone and sanity and to perceive things truly and simply again, after having been perambulating the bounds of the town all the week,[125] and dealing with the most com-

**123** Although Thoreau wrote in *Walden* that he "could easily do without the post-office" [Wa 91], according to Sanborn, "few residents of Concord frequented the Post Office more punctually." Nevertheless, Thoreau wrote in "Life Without Principle": "In proportion as our inward life fails, we go more constantly and desperately to the post-office. You may depend on it, that the poor fellow who walks away with the greatest number of letters, proud of his extensive correspondence, has not heard from himself this long while" [W 4:471]. In his journal, Thoreau differentiated between "two worlds, the post-office and nature" [J 4:446].
**124** In Lincoln, a half mile southwest of Flint's Pond.
**125** Thoreau was making an official inspection of the town of Concord's boundaries: on the 15th, the Concord-Acton line; on the 16th, the Concord-Sudbury line; on the 17th, the Concord-Lincoln line; on the 18th, the Concord-Bedford line; and on the 20th the Concord-Carlisle line.

monplace and worldly-minded men and emphatically *trivial* things, I feel as if I had committed suicide in a sense. I am again forcibly struck with the truth of the fable of Apollo serving King Admetus,[126] its universal applicability. A fatal coarseness is the result of mixing in the trivial affairs of men. Though I have been associating even with the *select* men of this and the surrounding towns, I feel inexpressibly begrimed. My Pegasus[127] has lost his wings; he has turned a reptile and gone on his belly.[128] Such things are compatible only with a cheap and superficial life.

The poet must keep himself unstained and aloof. Let him perambulate the bounds of Imagination's provinces, the realms of faery, and not the insignificant boundaries of towns. The excursions of the imagination are so boundless, the limits of towns are so petty.

*September 22.* Yesterday and to-day the stronger winds of autumn have begun to blow, and the telegraph harp has sounded loudly. I heard it especially in the Deep Cut this afternoon, the tone varying with the tension of different parts of the wire. The sound proceeds from near the posts, where the vibration is apparently more rapid. I put my ear to one of the posts, and it seemed to me as if every pore of the wood was filled with music, labored with the strain, — as if every fibre was affected and being seasoned or tuned, rearranged according to a new and more harmonious law. Every swell and change or inflection of tone pervaded and seemed to proceed from the wood, the divine tree or wood, as if its very substance was transmuted. What a recipe for preserving wood perchance, — to keep it from rotting, — to fill its pores with music! How this wild tree from the forest, stripped of its bark and set up here, rejoices to transmit this music! When no music proceeds from the wire, on

**126** In Greek mythology Apollo, the god of music and poetry, was banished from heaven and forced to tend the flocks of the Pheraean king, Admetus. Thoreau had several times identified himself with a god fallen, what Emerson called a "god in ruins." Thoreau made many references to this myth in his correspondence (cf. 1840s note 69 for one example) and his journals: cf. 22 June 1853 and 5 April 1854.

**127** Winged horse of Greek mythology, a favorite of the muses and so associated with poetic inspiration.

**128** Allusion to Genesis 3:14: "And the LORD God said unto the serpent, Because thou hast done this, thou art cursed above all cattle, and above every beast of the field; upon thy belly shalt thou go, and dust shalt thou eat all the days of thy life."

**129** Allusion to Shakespeare's *Othello* (3.4.68–70): "A sybil that had numbered in the world / The sun to coarse two hundred compasses / In her prophetic fury sewed the work."

**130** Thoreau used a similar trope in describing the ice-harp: cf. 5 December 1837.

**131** In Roman mythology, god of commerce, travel, and thievery, and messenger to the other gods; but also the metal, liquid at room temperature and also known as quicksilver.

**132** Finished six days earlier: cf. 1851 note 125.

applying my ear I hear the hum within the entrails of the wood,—the oracular tree acquiring, accumulating, the prophetic fury.[129]

The resounding wood! how much the ancients would have made of it! To have a harp on so great a scale, girdling the very earth, and played on by the winds of every latitude and longitude, and that harp were, as it were, the manifest blessing of heaven on a work of man's! Shall we not add a tenth Muse to the immortal Nine?[130] And that the invention thus divinely honored and distinguished— on which the Muse has condescended to smile—is this magic medium of communication for mankind!

To read that the ancients stretched a wire round the earth, attaching it to the trees of the forest, by which they sent messages by one named Electricity, father of Lightning and Magnetism, swifter far than Mercury,[131] the stern commands of war and news of peace, and that the winds caused this wire to vibrate so that it emitted a harp-like and æolian music in all the lands through which it passed, as if to express the satisfaction of the gods in this invention. Yet this is fact, and we have yet attributed the invention to no god.

*September 23.* Notwithstanding the fog, the fences this morning are covered with so thick a frost that you can write your name anywhere with your nail.

*September 25.* That nation is not Christian where the principles of humanity do not prevail, but the prejudices of race. I expect the Christian not to be superstitious, but to be distinguished by the clearness of his knowledge, the strength of his faith, the breadth of his humanity.

*September 26.* Since I perambulated the bounds of the town,[132] I find that I have in some degree confined myself,—my vision and my walks. On whatever side I look off I am reminded of the mean and narrow-minded men whom I have lately met there. What can be uglier than a country occupied by grovelling, coarse, and low-lived men? No scenery will redeem it. What can be more beautiful than any scenery inhabited by heroes? Any landscape would be glorious to me, if I were assured that its sky was arched over a single hero.

*September 28.* The railroads as much as anything appear to have unsettled the farmers. Our young Concord farmers and their young wives, hearing this bustle about them, seeing the world all going by as it were,—some daily to the cities about their business, some to California,—plainly cannot make up their minds to live the quiet, retired, old-fashioned, country-farmer's life. They are impatient if they live more than a mile from a railroad. While all their neighbors are rushing to the road, there are few who have character or bravery enough to live off the road. He is too well aware what is going on in the world not to wish to take some part in it.

*September 29.* Walden plainly can never be spoiled by the wood-chopper,[133] for, do what you will to the shore, there will still remain this crystal well.[134]

*October 1.* 5 P.M.—Just put a fugitive slave, who has taken the name of Henry Williams,[135] into the cars for Canada.[136] He escaped from Stafford County, Virginia, to Boston last October; has been in Shadrach's place at the Cornhill Coffee-House;[137] had been corresponding through an agent with his master, who is his father, about buying himself, his master asking $600, but he having been able to raise only $500. Heard that there were writs out for two Williamses, fugitives, and was informed by his fellow-servants and employer that Augerhole Burns[138] and others of the police had called for him

**133** Much of Concord's forest was being cut to meet the demand for wood. Thoreau noted on 21 January 1852: "This winter they are cutting down our woods more seriously then ever,—Fair Haven Hill, Walden, Linnæa Borealis Wood, etc., etc. Thank God, they cannot cut down the clouds!" [J 3:212–213].

**134** In *Walden* Thoreau described Walden and White Pond as "great crystals on the surface of the earth, Lakes of Light" [Wa 192].

**135** Williams's real name was Seth Botts.

**136** Moncure Daniel Conway (1832–1907), in his *Autobiography*, described a similar incident that took place in July 1853: "When I went to the house next morning, I found them all (Thoreau was then living in his father's house) in a state of excitement by reason of the arrival of a fugitive negro from the South, who had come fainting to their door about daybreak and thrown himself on their mercy. . . . I sat and watched the singularly tender and lowly devotion of the scholar to the slave. He must be fed, his swollen feet bathed, and he must think of nothing but rest. Again and again this coolest and calmest of men drew near to the trembling negro, and bade him feel at home, and have no fear that any power should again wrong him. He could not walk that day, but must mount guard over the fugitive, for slavehunters were not extinct in those days; and so I went away after a while much impressed by many little traits that I had seen as they appeared in this emergency, and not much disposed to cavil at their sources, whether Bible or Bhaghavat."

**137** Shadrach was the name used by Frederick Minkins (d. 1875), a slave from Virginia who escaped to Boston in May 1850 but was caught in February 1851. While he was being held at the Boston Court House, a mob of approximately twenty black men stormed the building and freed Minkins; they then hid him, and transported him safely to Concord, where abolitionists helped him to Canada. There he married, raised a family, and worked as a barber. Taft's Cornhill Coffee House was where Shadrach had lodged and worked as a waiter while in Boston, and Henry Williams had also been working at the same place.

**138** U.S. Deputy Marshal Frederic D. Byrnes, who was one of the officers who had arrested Shadrach. Thoreau may have christened him with the nickname Augerhole, meaning in ambush or in a cranny.

**139** Probably Joseph Cammett Lovejoy (1805–1871), abolitionist and minister of the Second Evangelical Congregational Church in Cambridgeport.

**140** William Lloyd Garrison (1805–1879), abolitionist leader and publisher of the *Liberator* (1831–1865). Thoreau's letter "Wendell Phillips before the Concord Lyceum" was published in the *Liberator* on 28 March 1845.

**141** In Vermont.

**142** George Minott, sometimes Minot (1783–1861), Emerson's neighbor. Thoreau described many encounters with Minott in his journal.

**143** Corruption of lean-to: a shelter or shed having a roof with a single slope or pitch, often attached to the side of a building as a wing or an extension.

when he was out. Accordingly fled to Concord last night on foot, bringing a letter to our family from Mr. Lovejoy of Cambridge[139] and another which Garrison[140] had formerly given him on another occasion. He lodged with us, and waited in the house till funds were collected with which to forward him. Intended to dispatch him at noon through to Burlington,[141] but when I went to buy his ticket, saw one at the depot who looked and behaved so much like a Boston policeman that I did not venture that time. An intelligent and very well-behaved man, a mulatto.

*October 4.* Minott[142] is, perhaps, the most poetical farmer—who most realizes to me the poetry of the farmer's life—that I know. He does nothing with haste and drudgery, but as if he loved it. He makes the most of his labor, and takes infinite satisfaction in every part of it. He is not looking forward to the sale of his crops or any pecuniary profit, but he is paid by the constant satisfaction which his labor yields him. He has not too much land to trouble him,—too much work to do,—no hired man nor boy,—but simply to amuse himself and live. He cares not so much to raise a large crop as to do his work well. He knows every pin and nail in his barn. If another linter[143] is to be floored, he lets no hired man rob him of that amusement, but he goes slowly to the woods and, at his leisure, selects a pitch pine tree, cuts it, and hauls it or gets it hauled to the mill; and so he knows the history of his barn-floor.

Farming is an amusement which has lasted him longer than gunning or fishing. He is never in a hurry to get his garden planted and yet it is always planted soon enough, and none in the town is kept so beautifully clean.

He always prophecies a failure of the crops, and yet is satisfied with what he gets. His barn floor is fastened down with oak pins, and he prefers them to iron spikes, which he says will rust and give way. He handles and amuses himself with every ear of his corn crop as much as a child with its playthings, and so his small crop goes a great way. He might well cry if it were carried to market. The seed of weeds is no longer in his soil.

He loves to walk in a swamp in windy weather and hear the wind groan through the pines. He keeps a cat in his barn to catch the mice. He indulges in no luxury of food or dress or furniture, yet he is not penurious but merely simple. If his sister[144] dies before him, he may have to go to the almshouse in his old age; yet he is not poor, for he does not want riches. He gets out of each manipulation in the farmers' operations a fund of entertainment which the speculating drudge hardly knows. With never-failing rheumatism and trembling hands, he seems yet to enjoy perennial health. Though he never reads a book,—since he has finished the "Naval Monument,"[145]—he speaks the best of English.

*October 6.* I shout like a farmer to his oxen,—a short barking shout,—and instantly the woods on the eastern shore take it up, and the western hills a little up the stream; and so it appears to rebound from one side the river valley to the other, till at length I hear a farmer call to his team far up as Fair Haven Bay,[146] whither we are bound.

We[147] pass through reaches where there is no fog, perhaps where a little air is stirring. Our clothes are almost wet through with the mist, as if we sat in water. Some portions of the river are much warmer than others. In one instance it was warmer in the midst of the fog than in a clear reach.

In the middle of the pond we tried the echo again. First the hill on the right took it up; then further up the stream on the left; and then after a long pause, when we had almost given it up,—and the longer expected, the

144 Mary Minott (1781–1861).
145 Abel Bowen's (1790–1850) *The Naval Monument, containing official and other accounts of all battles fought between the United States and Great Britain during the late war, and an account of the war with Algiers*, originally published in 1816.
146 Previously referred to as Fair Haven Pond.
147 Probably Channing.

148 Also known as the angle of reflection: cf.
1859 note 15.
149 Square, from the Vulgar Latin, *exquadra*.

more in one sense unexpected and surprising it was,—we heard a farmer shout to his team in a distant valley, far up on the opposite side of the stream, much louder than the previous echo; and even after this we heard one shout faintly in some neighboring town. The third echo seemed more loud and distinct than the second. But why, I asked, do the echoes always travel up the stream? I turned about and shouted again, and then I found that they all appeared equally to travel down the stream, or perchance I heard only those that did so.

As we rowed to Fair Haven's eastern shore, a moonlit hill covered with shrub oaks, we could form no opinion of our progress toward it,—not seeing the water-line where it met the hill,—until we saw the weeds and sandy shore and the tall bulrushes rising above the shallow water like the masts of large vessels in a haven. The moon was so high that the angle of excidence[148] did not permit of our seeing her reflection in the pond.

As we paddled down the stream with our backs to the moon, we saw the reflection of every wood and hill on both sides distinctly. These answering reflections—shadow to substance—impress the voyager with a sense of harmony and symmetry, as when you fold a blotted paper and produce a regular figure,—a dualism which nature loves. What you commonly see is but half. Where the shore is very low the actual and reflected trees appear to stand foot to foot, and it is but a line that separates them, and the water and the sky almost flow into one another, and the shore seems to float. As we paddle up or down, we see the cabins of muskrats faintly rising from amid the weeds, and the strong odor of musk is borne to us from particular parts of the shore. Also the odor of a skunk is wafted from over the meadows or fields. The fog appears in some places gathered into a little pyramid or squad[149] by itself, on the surface of the water. Home at ten.

*October 10.* Ah, I yearn toward thee, my friend, but I have not confidence in thee. We do not believe in the same God. I am not thou; thou art not I. We trust each other to-day, but we distrust to-morrow. Even when I meet thee unexpectedly, I part from thee with disappointment. Though I enjoy thee more than other men, yet I am more disappointed with thee than with others. I know a noble man; what is it hinders me from knowing him better? I know not how it is that our distrust, our hate, is stronger than our love. Here I have been on what the world would call friendly terms with one fourteen years,[150] have pleased my imagination sometimes with loving him; and yet our hate is stronger than our love. Why are we related, yet thus unsatisfactorily? We almost are a sore to one another. Ah, I am afraid because thy relations are not my relations. Because I have experienced that in some respects we are strange to one another, strange as some wild creature. Ever and anon there will come the consciousness to mar our love that, change the theme but a hair's breadth, and we are tragically strange to one another. We do not know what hinders us from coming together. But when I consider what my friend's relations and acquaintances are, what his tastes and habits, then the difference between us gets named. I see that all these friends and acquaintances and tastes and habits are indeed my friend's self. In the first place, my friend is prouder than I am,—and I am very proud, perchance.

*October 12.* I love very well this cloudy afternoon, so sober and favorable to reflection after so many bright ones. What if the clouds shut out the heavens, provided they concentrate my thoughts and make a more celestial heaven below! I hear the crickets plainer; I wander less in my thoughts, am less dissipated; am aware how shallow was the current of my thoughts before. Deep streams

**150** Thoreau and Emerson met in 1837. "My first intimacy with Henry began after his graduation in 1837," Emerson told Sanborn. "Mrs. Brown, Mrs. Emerson's sister from Plymouth, then boarded with Mrs. Thoreau and her children in the Parkman house, where the Library now stands, and saw the young people every day. She would bring me verses of Henry's,—the 'Sic Vita,' for instance, which he had thrown into Mrs. Brown's window, tied around a bunch of violets gathered in his walk,—and once a passage out of his Journal, which he had read to Sophia, who spoke of it to Mrs. Brown as resembling a passage in one of my Concord lectures. He always looked forward to authorship as his work in life, and fitted himself for that. Finding he could write prose so well,— and he talked equally well,—he soon gave up much verse-writing, in which he was not patient enough to make his lines smooth and flowing."

**151** In his journal of 23 March 1856 Thoreau defined these as "the cougar, panther, lynx, wolverene, wolf, bear, moose, deer, the beaver, the turkey, etc., etc." [J 8:220].

**152** Allusion to the opening of Shakespeare's *Richard III* (1.1.1–2): "Now is the winter of our discontent / Made glorious summer by this son of York." It was a line Thoreau liked, as evidenced by his use of it in *Walden* [Wa 40], "Natural History of Massachusetts" [W 5:125], and his journal again at 31 October 1857 [J 10:150].

**153** Possible allusion to the ships in the "Saga of King Olaf Haraldsson the Saint" as described in Samuel Laing's note to his translation of *The Heimskringla* (cf. 1851 note 160): "The ships appear to have been decked fore and aft only; and in the middle, where the rowers sat, to have tilts or tents set up at night to sleep under."

**154** Large inlet of the Atlantic Ocean between New Brunswick and southwestern Nova Scotia.

**155** Miramichi Bay, an inlet of the Gulf of the Saint Lawrence, in New Brunswick.

are dark, as if there were a cloud in their sky; shallow ones are bright and sparkling, reflecting the sun from their bottoms. The very wind on my cheek seems more fraught with meaning.

*October 13.* The alert and energetic man leads a more intellectual life in winter than in summer. In summer the animal and vegetable in him are perfected as in a torrid zone; he lives in his senses mainly. In winter cold reason and not warm passion has her sway; he lives in thought and reflection; he lives a more spiritual, a less sensual, life. If he has passed a merely sensual summer, he passes his winter in a torpid state like some reptiles and other animals.

The mind of man in the two seasons is like the atmosphere of summer compared with the atmosphere of winter. He depends more on himself in winter, — on his own resources, — less on outward aid. Insects, it is true, disappear for the most part, and those animals which depend upon them; but the nobler animals[151] abide with man the severity of winter. He migrates into his mind, to perpetual summer. And to the healthy man the winter of his discontent[152] never comes.

*October 26.* I awoke this morning to infinite regret. In my dream I had been riding, but the horses bit each other and occasioned endless trouble and anxiety, and it was my employment to hold their heads apart. Next I sailed over the sea in a small vessel such as the Northmen used,[153] as it were to the Bay of Fundy,[154] and thence overland I sailed, still over the shallows about the sources of rivers toward the deeper *channel* of a stream, which emptied into the Gulf beyond, — the Miramichi,[155] was it? Again I was in my own small pleasure-boat, learning to sail on the sea, and I raised my sail before my anchor, which I dragged far into the sea. I saw the buttons which had come off the coats of drowned men,[156] and suddenly I saw my dog—when I knew not that I had one—standing in the sea up to his chin, to warm his legs, which had been wet, which the cool wind numbed. And then I was walking in a meadow, where the dry season permitted me to walk further than usual, and there I met Mr. Alcott,[157] and we fell to quoting and referring to grand and pleasing couplets and single lines which we had read in times past; and I quoted one which in my waking hours I have no knowledge of, but in my dream it was familiar enough. I only know that those which I quoted expressed regret, and were like the following, though they were not these, *viz.:*—

"The short parenthesis of life was sweet,"[158]
"The remembrance of youth is a sigh,"[159] etc.

It had the word "memory" in it!! And then again the instant that I awoke, methought I was a musical instrument from which I heard a strain die out,—a bugle, or a clarionet, or a flute. My body was the organ and channel of melody, as a flute is of the music that is breathed through it. My flesh sounded and vibrated still to the strain, and my nerves were the chords of the lyre. I awoke, therefore, to an infinite regret,—to find myself, not the thoroughfare of glorious and world-stirring inspirations, but a scuttle full of dirt, such a thoroughfare only as the street and the kennel, where, perchance, the wind may sometimes draw forth a strain of music from a straw.

I can partly account for this. Last evening I was reading Laing's account of the Northmen,[160] and though I did not write in my Journal, I remember feeling a fertile regret, and deriving even an inexpressible satisfaction, as it were, from my ability to feel regret, which made that evening richer than those which had preceded it. I heard

**156** Cf. 1850 note 46.
**157** Amos Bronson Alcott (1799–1888), educator and philosopher, author of *Conversations with Children on the Gospels*, and subject of Elizabeth Peabody's (1804–1894) *Record of a School*. Cf. 9 May 1853.
**158** Quoted from Thomas Storer's (1571–1604) "The Life and Death of Thomas Wolsey, Cardinal."
**159** Quoted from the epigraph, attributed to "Ali," from Robert Southey's (1774–1843) "Remembrance."
**160** Samuel Laing's (1780–1868) translation of Snorri Sturluson's (ca. 1179–1241) *The Heimskringla; or, the Chronicle of the Kings of Norway*.

161 On 26 October 1851 Emerson and Thoreau discussed, according to Emerson's journal, "the eternal loneliness. . . . how insular and pathetically solitary are all the people we know!"
162 Unidentified, but possibly Lidian Emerson.
163 The Greek astronomer and geographer Hipparchus (ca. 170–120 B.C.E.) introduced the practice of dividing the stars into different classes of magnitude based on their apparent brightness. The brightest stars he classed as first magnitude and those just visible to the naked eye as sixth magnitude.

the last strain or flourish, as I woke, played on my body as the instrument. Such I knew I had been and might be again, and my regret arose from the consciousness how little like a musical instrument my body was now.

*October 27.* The obstacles which the heart meets with are like granite blocks which one alone cannot move.[161] She who was as the morning light to me[162] is now neither the morning star nor the evening star. We meet but to find each other further asunder, and the oftener we meet the more rapid our divergence. So a star of the first magnitude[163] pales in the heavens, not from any fault in the observer's eye nor from any fault in itself, perchance, but because its progress in its own system has put a greater distance between.

*November 1.* It is a rare qualification to be able to state a fact simply and adequately, to digest some experience cleanly, to say "yes" and "no" with authority, to make a square edge, to conceive and suffer the truth to pass through us living and intact, even as a waterfowl an eel, as it flies over the meadow, thus stocking new waters. First of all a man must see, before he can say. Statements are made but partially. Things are said with reference to certain conventions or existing institutions, not absolutely. A fact truly and absolutely stated is taken out of the region of common sense and acquires a mythologic or universal significance. Say it and have done with it. Express it without expressing yourself. See not with the eye of science, which is barren, nor of youthful poetry, which is impotent. But taste the world and digest it. It would seem as if things got said but rarely and by chance. As you *see,* so at length will you *say.* When facts are seen superficially, they are seen as they lie in relation to certain institutions, perchance. But I would have them expressed as more deeply seen, with deeper references; so that the hearer or reader cannot recognize them or apprehend their significance from the platform of common life, but it will be necessary that he be in a sense translated in order to understand them; when the truth respecting his things shall naturally exhale from a man like the odor of the muskrat from the coat of the trapper. At first blush a man is not capable of reporting truth; he must be drenched and saturated with it first. What was *enthusiasm* in the young man must become *temperament* in the mature man. Without excitement, heat, or passion, he will survey the world which excited the youth and threw him off his balance. As all things are significant, so all words should be significant. It is a fault which attaches to the speaker, to speak flippantly or superficially of anything. Of what use are words which do not move the hearer,—are not oracular and fateful? A style in which the matter is all in all, and the manner nothing at all.

*November 7.* Channing[164] kept up an incessant strain of wit, banter, about my legs, which were so springy and unweariable, declared I had got my double legs on, that they were not cork but steel, that I should let myself to Van Amburgh,[165] should have sent them to the World's Fair,[166] etc., etc.; wanted to know if I could not carry my father Anchises.[167]

*November 9.* In our walks Channing takes out his notebook sometimes and tries to write as I do, but all in vain. He soon puts it up again, or contents himself with scrawling some sketch of the landscape.[168] Observing me still scribbling, he will say that he confines himself to the ideal, purely ideal remarks; he leaves the facts to me. Sometimes, too, he will say a little petulantly, "*I* am universal; I have nothing to do with the particular and definite." He is the moodiest person, perhaps, that I ever

164 With whom Thoreau had made an excursion to Cochituate Pond, also known as Long Pond, a large lake in Wayland, Framingham, and Natick, Massachusetts.
165 Isaac Van Amburgh (ca. 1808–1865), renowned American lion-tamer and menagerie manager.
166 The Great Exhibition of 1851 at the Crystal Palace in Hyde Park, London.
167 In Virgil's *Aeneid*, book 1, when Troy fell, Aeneas carried his father, Anchises, out of the city on his back. In the poem's translation by John Dryden (1631–1700), Aeneas tells his father: "Haste, my dear father, ('t is no time to wait,) / And load my shoulders with a willing freight."
168 Channing's notebooks for 1851 are not extant. On 20 April 1852, his first extant notebook entry, Channing wrote: "I see nothing today of very great acct." Emerson commented in his journal on 12 June 1852: "Since he knew Thoreau, he carries a little pocket-book, in which he affects to write down the name of each new plant or the first day on which he finds the flower."

**169** In *Thoreau, the Poet-Naturalist* Channing characterized the objective of his walks: "As I walk for recreation and variety, after reading, these walks of Thoreau were something aside from my local habits; and, unlike my own, had a local aim."
**170** Cf. 10 May 1853.
**171** Cf. 1851 note 53.

saw. As naturally whimsical as a cow is brindled, both in his tenderness and his roughness he belies himself. He can be incredibly selfish and unexpectedly generous. He is conceited, and yet there is in him far more than usual to ground conceit upon.[169]

I, too, would fain set down something beside facts. Facts should only be as the frame to my pictures; they should be material to the mythology which I am writing; not facts to assist men to make money, farmers to farm profitably, in any common sense; facts to tell who I am, and where I have been or what I have thought: as now the bell rings for evening meeting, and its volumes of sound, like smoke which rises from where a cannon is fired, make the tent in which I dwell. My facts shall be falsehoods to the common sense. I would so state facts that they shall be significant, shall be myths or mythologic.[170]

*November 10.* Our life is not altogether a forgetting[171] but also, alas, to a great extent a remembering, of that which perchance we should never have been conscious of,—the consciousness of what should not be permitted to disturb a man's waking hours.

*November 11.* When I have been confined to my chamber for the greater part of several days by some employment, or perchance by the ague, till I felt weary and house-worn, I have been conscious of a certain softness to which I am otherwise and commonly a stranger, in which the gates were loosened to some emotions; and if I were to become a confirmed invalid, I see how some sympathy with mankind and society might spring up. Yet what is my softness good for, even to tears. It is not I, but nature in me. I laughed at myself the other day to think that I cried while reading a pathetic story. I was no more affected in spirit than I frequently am, methinks. The tears were merely a phenomenon of the bowels,[172] and I felt that that expression of my sympathy, so unusual with me, was something mean, and such as I should be ashamed to have the subject of it understand. I had a cold in my head withal, about those days. I found that I had some bowels, but then it was because my bowels were out of order.

"Say's I to myself" should be the motto of my journal.

It is fatal to the writer to be too much possessed by his thought. Things must lie a little remote to be described.[173]

*November 13.* Just spent a couple of hours (eight to ten) with Miss Mary Emerson[174] at Holbrook's.[175] The wittiest and most vivacious woman that I know, certainly that woman among my acquaintance whom it is most profitable to meet, the least frivolous, who will most surely provoke to good conversation and the expression of what is in you. She is singular, among women at least, in being really and perseveringly interested to know what thinkers think. She relates herself surely to the intellectual where she goes. It is perhaps her greatest praise and peculiarity that she, more surely than any other woman, gives her companion occasion to utter his best thought. In spite of her own biases, she can entertain a large thought with hospitality, and is not prevented by any intellectuality in it, as women commonly are. In short, she is a genius, as woman seldom is, reminding you less often of her sex than any woman whom I know. In that sense she is capable of a masculine appreciation of poetry and philosophy. I never talked with any other woman who I thought accompanied me so far in describing a poetic experience. Miss Fuller is the only woman I think of in this connection, and of her rather from her fame than

172 Seat or root of emotions, as in Isaiah 57:18: "As he has bowels to pity."
173 Cf. 28 March 1857: "Often I can give the truest and most interesting account of any adventure I have had after years have elapsed, for then I am not confused, only the most significant facts surviving in my memory."
174 Mary Moody Emerson (1774–1862), Emerson's aunt, of whom he wrote in his biographical sketch of her: "She delighted in success, in youth, in beauty, in genius, in manners. When she met a young person who interested her, she made herself acquainted and intimate with him or her at once, by sympathy, by flattery, by raillery, by anecdotes, by wit, by rebuke, and stormed the castle. . . . She surprised, attracted, chided and denounced her companion by turns, and pretty rapid turns. But no intelligent youth or maiden could have once met her without remembering her with interest, and learning something of value. Scorn trifles, lift your aims: do what you are afraid to do: sublimity of character must come from sublimity of motive: these were the lessons which were urged with vivacity, in ever new language."

Thoreau described her as "the youngest person in Concord, though about eighty,—and the most apprehensive of a genuine thought; earnest to know of your inner life; most stimulating society; and exceedingly witty withal. She says they called her old when she was young, and she has never grown any older. I wish you could see her" [C 401–402].
175 Inn and coffee-house run by Colonel Joseph Holbrook (b. 1797).

176 Margaret Fuller: cf. 1850 note 46.
177 Allusion to I Peter 3:7: "Likewise, ye husbands, dwell with them according to knowledge, giving honor unto the wife, as unto the weaker vessel."
178 A countryman or rustic.
179 There is no record of who hosted the party.
180 Joseph Hosmer, Sr. (1783–1854), farmer who lived east of the Assabet River and north of the railroad.

from any knowledge of her.[176] Miss Emerson expressed to-night a singular want of respect for her own sex, saying that they were frivolous almost without exception, that woman was the weaker vessel,[177] etc.; that into whatever family she might go, she depended more upon the "clown"[178] for society than upon the lady of the house. Men are more likely to have opinions of their own.

*November 14.* In the evening went to a party.[179] It is a bad place to go to,—thirty or forty persons, mostly young women, in a small room, warm and noisy. Was introduced to two young women. The first one was as lively and loquacious as a chickadee; had been accustomed to the society of watering-places, and therefore could get no refreshment out of such a dry fellow as I. The other was said to be pretty-looking, but I rarely look people in their faces, and, moreover, I could not hear what she said, there was such a clacking,—could only see the motion of her lips when I looked that way. I could imagine better places for conversation, where there should be a certain degree of silence surrounding you, and less than forty talking at once. Why, this afternoon, even, I did better. There was old Mr. Joseph Hosmer[180] and I ate our luncheon of cracker and cheese together in the woods. I heard all he said, though it was not much, to be sure, and he could hear me. And then he talked out of such a glorious repose, taking a leisurely bite at the cracker and cheese between his words; and so some of him was communicated to me, and some of me to him, I trust.

These parties, I think, are a part of the machinery of modern society, that young people may be brought together to form marriage connections.

What is the use of going to see people whom yet you never see, and who never see you? I begin to suspect that it is not necessary that we should see one another.

Some of my friends make singular blunders. They go

out of their way to talk with certain young women of whom they think, or have heard, that they are pretty, and take pains to introduce me to them. That may be a reason why they should look at them, but it is not a reason why they should talk with them. I confess that I am lacking a sense, perchance, in this respect, and I derive no pleasure from talking with a young woman half an hour simply because she has regular features. The society of young women is the most unprofitable I have ever tried. They are so light and flighty that you can never be sure whether they are there or not there. I prefer to talk with the more staid and settled, *settled for life,* in every sense.

*November 16.* It is remarkable that the highest intellectual mood which the world tolerates is the perception of the truth of the most ancient revelations, now in some respects out of date; but any direct revelation, any original thoughts, it hates like virtue. The fathers and the mothers of the town would rather hear the young man or young woman at their tables express reverence for some old statement of the truth than utter a direct revelation themselves. They don't want to have any prophets born into their families,—damn them! So far as thinking is concerned, surely original thinking is the divinest thing. Rather we should reverently watch for the least motions, the least scintillations, of thought in this sluggish world, and men should run to and fro on the occasion more than at an earthquake. We check and repress the divinity that stirs within us,[181] to fall down and worship the divinity that is dead without us. I go to see many a good man or good woman, so called, and utter freely that thought which alone it was given to me to utter; but there was a man who lived a long, long time ago, and his name was Moses, and another whose name was Christ, and if your thought does not, or does not appear

**181** The "divinity within" is an idea prevalent in such writers as Sir Thomas Browne in *Religio Medici*—"There is surely a peece of Divinity in us; something that was before the Elements, and owes no homage unto the Sun"—and John Milton's *Paradise Lost* 9:1009–1011: "they feel / Divinity within them breeding wings / Wherewith to scorn the earth." It was this idea that allowed for a personal innate relationship with God and separated the Transcendentalists from the Unitarians, who were grounded in historical Christianity. In "The Service" Thoreau wrote: "The divinity in man is the true vestal fire of the temple which is never permitted to go out" [W 4:278]. William Ellery Channing (1780–1842), Unitarian minister and uncle of Thoreau's friend of the same name, wrote in his sermon "Likeness to God": "Men, as by a natural inspiration, have agreed to speak of conscience as the voice of God, as the Divinity within us. This principle, reverently obeyed, makes us more and more partakers of the moral perfection of the Supreme Being, of that very excellence, which constitutes the rightfulness of his sceptre, and enthrones him over the universe. Without this inward law, we should be as incapable of receiving a law from Heaven, as the brute. Without this, the thunders of Sinai might startle the outward ear, but would have no meaning, no authority to the mind. I have expressed here a great truth. Nothing teaches so encouragingly our relation and resemblance to God." In *Nature* Emerson wrote simply: "I am part or particle of God."

**182** Carolus Linnaeus (Carl von Linné, 1707–1778), Swedish naturalist who established the classification of plants in terms of genus and species, using a Latin binomial nomenclature.

**183** Dietrich Johann Heinrich Stöver (1767–1822) wrote in *The Life of Sir Charles Linnaeus:* "The attacks of the whole phalanx of his foreign opponents could not induce him to accept a challenge. The method of his vengeance was equally original and piquant. He sat enthroned above the whole reign of vegetation. With the plants he transmitted honour and disgrace to posterity. To beautiful plants he assigned the names of his friends, and to the pernicious and inferior ones he gave the names of his enemies."

**184** During this period Thoreau surveyed the Ministerial Lot in the southwest of Concord, 14–25 November; ran a line for the Town of Concord between Concord and Carlisle on 2–5, 10, and 13 December; surveyed Samuel Barrett's woodlot on 6 December; and lotted off part of the 40-acre Ministerial Lot in the southeast of Concord on 8–9 December. There are no entries in his journal between 30 November and 12 December.

**185** Cf. 22 December 1853.

to, coincide with what they said, the good man or the good woman has no ears to hear you. They think they love God! It is only his old clothes, of which they make scarecrows for the children. Where will they come nearer to God than in those very children?

What more fatal vengeance could Linnæus[182] have taken than to give the names of his enemies to pernicious and unsightly plants, thus simply putting upon record for as long as the Linnæan system shall prevail who were his friends and foes? It was enough to record the fact that they were opposed to him. To this they could not themselves have objected, nor could he have taken a more fatal vengeance.[183]

***December 12.*** I have been surveying for twenty or thirty days,[184] living coarsely, even as respects my diet,—for I find that that will always alter to suit my employment,[185]—indeed, leading a quite trivial life;—and tonight, for the first time, had made a fire in my chamber and endeavored to return to myself. I wished to ally myself to the powers that rule the universe. I wished to dive into some deep stream of thoughtful and devoted life, which meandered through retired and fertile meadows far from towns. I wished to do again, or for once, things quite congenial to my highest inmost and most sacred nature, to lurk in crystalline thought like the trout under verdurous banks, where stray mankind should only see my bubble come to the surface. I wished to live, ah! as far away as a man can think. I wished for leisure and quiet to let my life flow in its proper channels, with its proper currents; when I might not waste the days, might establish daily prayer and thanksgiving in my family; might do my own work and not the work of Concord and Carlisle, which would yield me better than money. (How much forbearance, aye, sacrifice and loss, goes to every accomplishment! I am thinking by what long discipline and at what cost a man learns to speak simply at last.) I bethought myself, while my fire was kindling, to open one of Emerson's books, which it happens that I rarely look at, to try what a chance sentence out of that could do for me; thinking, at the same time, of a conversation I had with him the other night, I finding fault with him for the stress he had laid on some of Margaret Fuller's whims and superstitions, but he declaring gravely that she was one of those persons whose experience warranted her attaching importance to such things,[186]—as the *Sortes Virgilianae*,[187] for instance, of which her numerous friends could tell remarkable instances. At any rate, I saw that he was disposed to regard such things more seriously than I. The first sentence which I opened upon in his book was this: "If, with a high trust, he can thus submit himself, he will find that ample returns are poured into his bosom out of what seemed hours of obstruction and loss. Let him not grieve too much on account of unfit associates. . . . In a society of perfect sympathy, no word, no act, no record, would be. He will learn that it is not much matter what he reads, what he does. Be a scholar, and he shall have the scholar's part of everything," etc., etc.[188]

Most of this responded well enough to my mood, and this would be as good an instance of the *Sortes Virgilianae* as most to quote. But what makes this coincidence very little if at all remarkable to me is the fact of the obviousness of the moral, so that I had, perhaps, *thought* the same thing myself twenty times during the day, and yet had not been *contented* with that account of it, leaving me thus to be amused by the coincidence, rather than impressed as by an intimation out of the deeps.

***December 17.*** Improve every opportunity to express yourself in writing, as if it were your last.

**186** Emerson wrote in *Memoirs of Margaret Fuller:* "It was soon evident that there was somewhat a little pagan about her; that she had some faith more or less distinct in a fate, and in a guardian genius; that her fancy, or her pride, had played with her religion. She had a taste for gems, ciphers, talismans, omens, coincidences, and birth-days. . . . She tried *sortes biblicæ*, and her hits were memorable. I think each new book which interested her, she was disposed to put to this test, and know if it had somewhat personal to say to her."

**187** Divination, or fortune telling, through Virgil's *Aeneid*, in which the book is opened at random and the passage touched with a finger is the oracular response.

**188** Quoted from Emerson's "Literary Ethics" in *Nature; Addresses and Lectures* (1849): "If, with a high trust, he can thus submit himself, he will find that ample returns are poured into his bosom, out of what seemed hours of obstruction and loss. Let him not grieve too much on account of unfit associates. When he sees how much thought he owes to the disagreeable antagonism of various persons who pass and cross him, he can easily think that in a society of perfect sympathy, no word, no act, no record, would be. He will learn, that it is not much matter what he reads, what he does. Be a scholar, and he shall have the scholar's part of every thing."

**189** In "Chesuncook" Thoreau wrote of the pine tree: "It is as immortal as I am, and perchance will go to as high a heaven, there to tower above me still" [W 3:135].

I do not know but a pine wood is as substantial and as memorable a fact as a friend. I am more sure to come away from it cheered, than from those who come nearest to being my friends. It is unfortunate for the chopper and the walker when the cold wind comes from the same side with the sun, for then he cannot find a warm recess in which to sit. It is pleasant to walk now through open and stately white pine woods. Their plumes do not hold so much snow commonly, unless where their limbs rest or are weighed down onto a neighboring tree. It is cold but still in their midst, where the snow is untracked by man, and ever and anon you see the snow-dust, shone on by the sun, falling from their tops and, as it strikes the lower limbs, producing innumerable new showers. For, as after a rain there is a second rain in the woods, so after a light snow there is a second snow in the woods, when the wind rises. The branches of the white pine are more horizontal than those of the pitch, and the white streaks of snow on them look accordingly. I perceive that the young black oaks and the red oaks, too, methinks, still keep their leaves as well as the white. This piercing wind is so nearly from the west this afternoon that, to stand at once in a sheltered and a sunny place, you must seek the south-southeast side of the woods.

*December 20.* Nothing stands up more free from blame in this world than a pine tree.[189]

*December 25.* It would be a truer discipline for the writer to take the least film of thought that floats in the twilight sky of his mind for his theme, about which he has scarcely one idea (that would be teaching his ideas how to shoot), faintest intimations, shadowiest subjects, make a lecture on this, by assiduity and attention get perchance two views of the same, increase a little the stock of knowledge, clear a new field instead of manuring the old; instead of making a lecture out of such obvious truths, hackneyed to the minds of all thinkers. We seek too soon to ally the perceptions of the mind to the experience of the hand, to prove our gossamer truths practical, to show their connection with our every-day life (better show their distance from our every-day life), to relate them to the cider-mill and the banking institution. Ah, give me pure mind, pure thought! Let me not be in haste to detect the *universal law;* let me see more clearly a particular instance of it! Much finer themes I aspire to, which will yield no satisfaction to the vulgar mind, not one sentence for them. Perchance it may convince such that there are more things in heaven and earth than are dreamed of in their philosophy.[190] Dissolve one nebula, and so destroy the nebular system and hypothesis. Do not seek expressions, seek thoughts to be expressed. By perseverance you get two views of the same rare truth.

That way of viewing things you know of, least insisted on by you, however, least remembered, — take that view, adhere to that, insist on that, see all things from that point of view. Will you let these intimations go unattended to and watch the door-bell or knocker? That is your text. Do not speak for other men; speak for yourself. They show you as in a vision the kingdoms of this world, and of all the worlds, but you prefer to look in upon a puppet-show. Though you should only speak to one kindred mind in all time, though you should not speak to one, but only utter aloud, that you may the more completely realize and live in the idea which contains the reason of your life, that you may build yourself up to the height of your conceptions, that you may remember your Creator in the days of your youth[191] and justify His ways to man,[192] that the end of life may not be its amusement, speak — though your thought presup-

190 Allusion to Shakespeare's *Hamlet* (1.5.168–169): "There are more things in heaven and earth, Horatio, / Than are dreamt of in your philosophy."
191 Cf. 1851 note 59.
192 Allusion to the Shorter Catechism, religious doctrine in the form of questions and answers, which states that the chief end of man is to glorify God and enjoy him forever.

poses the non-existence of your hearers—thoughts that transcend life and death. What though mortal ears are not fitted to hear absolute truth! Thoughts that blot out the earth are best conceived in the night, when darkness has already blotted it out from sight.

We look upward for inspiration.

**1852**

AGE 34–35

1 Cf. 28 March 1857: "Often I can give the truest and most interesting account of any adventure I have had after years have elapsed, for then I am not confused, only the most significant facts surviving in my memory."

2 Easternmost portion of mainland Canada.

3 Channing.

4 Dr. Edward Augustus Kittredge (ca. 1810–1869), who lectured and wrote on many subjects, including hydrotherapy, under the name "Noggs." Kittredge had a water cure spa in Boston and was a frequent contributor to the *Water Cure Journal.*

*January 11.* What need to travel? There are no sierras equal to the clouds in the sunset sky. And are not these substantial enough?

The question is not where did the traveller go? what places did he see?—it would be difficult to choose between places—but who was the traveller? how did he travel? how genuine an experience did he get?[1] For travelling is, in the main, like as if you stayed at home, and then the question is how do you live and conduct yourself at home? What I mean is that it might be hard to decide whether I would travel to Lake Superior, or Labrador,[2] or Florida. Perhaps none would be worth the while, if I went by the usual mode. But if I travel in a simple, primitive, original manner, standing in a truer relation to men and nature, travel away from the old and commonplace, get some honest experience of life, if only out of my feet and homesickness, then it becomes less important whither I go or how far. I so see the world from a new and more commanding point of view. Perhaps it is easier to live a true and natural life while travelling,—as one can move about less awkwardly than he can stand still.

*January 12.* He[3] went to hear Noggs[4] the other night. It was the poorest lecture he ever heard. Did n't know why he did n't come out. But then he found himself in a handsome hall well lighted and warmed, and thought it would be cheaper to spend the evening there than to go home.

I sometimes think that I may go forth and walk hard and earnestly, and live a more substantial life and get a glorious experience; be much abroad in heat and cold, day and night; live more, expend more atmosphere, be weary often, etc., etc. But then swiftly the thought comes to me, Go not so far out of your way for a truer life; keep strictly onward in that path alone which your genius points out. Do the things which lie nearest to you, but which are difficult to do. Live a purer, a more thoughtful and laborious life, more true to your friends and neighbors, more noble and magnanimous, and that will be better than a wild walk. To live in relations of truth and sincerity with men is to dwell in a frontier country. What a wild and unfrequented wilderness that would be! What Saguenays[5] of magnanimity that might be explored! Men talk about travelling this way or that, as if seeing were all in the eyes, and a man could sufficiently report what he stood bodily before, when the seeing depends ever on the being. All report of travel is the report of victory or defeat, of a contest with every event and phenomenon and how you came out of it. A blind man who possesses inward truth and consistency will see more than one who has faultless eyes but no serious and laborious astronomer to look through them. As if the eyes were the only part of a man that travelled! Men convert their property into cash, ministers fall sick to obtain the assistance of their parishes, all chaffer with sea-captains, etc., as if the whole object were to get conveyed to some part of the world a pair of eyes merely. A telescope conveyed to and set up at the Cape of Good Hope at great expense,[6] and only a Bushman to look through it. Nothing like a little internal activity called life—if it were only walking much in a day—to keep the eyes in good order; no such collyrium.[7]

5 River in southern Quebec, first explored by Jacques Cartier (1491–1557) in 1535, and a major route for exploration, missionary work, and fur trading.
6 The Royal Observatory at the Cape of Good Hope, also known as the Royal Cape Observatory, established in 1820 by the Royal Astronomical Society of England. The original telescope there was a 14-foot wooden-tube instrument made by Sir William Herschel (1738–1822) and was first set up by Thomas Maclear (1794–1879) in 1835.
7 Eyewash or medicinal lotion applied to the eye.

*January 15.* I do not know but the poet is he who generates poems.[8]

*January 16.* Bill Wheeler[9] had two clumps for feet and progressed slowly, by short steps, having frozen his feet once, as I understood. Him I have been sure to meet once in five years, progressing into the town on his stubs, holding the middle of the road as if he drove an invisible load before him, especially on a military day,[10] — out of what confines, whose hired man having been, I never knew, — in what remote barn having quartered all these years. He seemed to belong to a different caste from other men, and reminded me of both the Indian Pariah[11] and martyr. I understood that somebody was found to give him his drink for the few chores he could do. His meat was never referred to, he had so sublimed his life. One day since this, not long ago, I saw in my walk a kind of shelter such as woodmen might use, in the woods by the Great Meadows,[12] made of meadow-hay cast over a rude frame. Thrusting my head in at a hole, as I am wont to do in such cases, I found Bill Wheeler there curled up asleep on the hay, who, being suddenly wakened from a sound sleep, rubbed his eyes and inquired if I found any game, thinking I was sporting. I came away reflecting much on that man's life, — how he communicated with none; how now, perchance, he did chores for none; how low he lived, perhaps from a deep principle, that he might be some mighty philosopher, greater than Socrates or Diogenes,[13] simplifying life, returning to nature, having turned his back on towns; how many things he had put off, — luxuries, comforts, human society, even his feet, — wrestling with his thoughts. I felt even as Diogenes when he saw the boy drinking out of his hands, and threw away his cup.[14] Here was one who went alone, did no work, and had no relatives that I knew of, was not ambitious that I could see, did not depend on the good opinion of men. Must he not see things with an im-

**8** Cf. 3 March 1839, and Emerson's essay "The Poet": "The poet is the sayer, the namer, and represents beauty. . . . The poet does not wait for the hero or the sage, but, as they act and think primarily, so he writes primarily what will and must be spoken," and "For it is not metres, but a metre-making argument that makes a poem."
**9** Unidentified, although probably the William Wheeler listed in the 1850 census as thirty-nine years old and with no occupation given.
**10** Days of militia training or muster, as in May Training on the first Tuesday in May.
**11** In India, the pariah, or untouchable, was considered on the bottom, or outside, of the caste system.
**12** The largest of Concord's meadows.
**13** Socrates (ca. 470–399 B.C.E.), Greek philosopher known for his view that philosophy is a proper and necessary pursuit for all intelligent men and who lived and died as an exemplar of a life of principle, and Diogenes (ca. 412–323 B.C.E.), Greek Cynic philosopher who advocated simple living.
**14** According to Diogenes Laërtius's (3rd century C.E.) *Lives of the Eminent Philosophers* ("The Life of Diogenes"): "On one occasion he saw a child drinking out of its hands, and so he threw away the cup which belonged to his wallet, saying, 'That child has beaten me in simplicity.'"

partial eye, disinterested, as a toad observes the gardener? Perchance here is one of a sect of philosophers, the only one, so simple, so abstracted in thought and life from his contemporaries, that his wisdom is indeed foolishness to them. Who knows but in his solitary meadow-hay bunk he indulges, in thought, only in triumphant satires[15] on men? Who knows but here is a superiority to literature and such things, unexpressed and inexpressible? Who has resolved to humble and mortify himself as never man was humbled and mortified. Whose very vividness of perception, clear knowledge, and insight have made him dumb, leaving no common consciousness and ground of parlance with his kind,—or, rather, his unlike kindred! Whose news plainly is not my news nor yours. I was not sure for a moment but here was a philosopher who had left far behind him the philosophers of Greece and India, and I envied him his advantageous point of view. I was not to be deceived by a few stupid words, of course, and apparent besottedness. It was his position and career that I contemplated.

I would have liked to know what view he took of life. A month or two after this, as I heard, he was found dead among the brush over back of the hill,—so far decomposed that his coffin was carried to his body and it was put into it with pitchforks. I have my misgivings still that he may have died a Brahmin's death, dwelling at the roots of trees at last, and been absorbed into the spirit of Brahm;[16] though I have since been assured that he suffered from disappointed love,—was what is called love-cracked,—than which can there be any nobler suffering, any fairer death,[17] for a human creature?—that that made him to drink, froze his feet, and did all the rest for him. Why have not the world the benefit of his long trial?

---

**15** Possible reference to Aulus Persius Flaccus (34–62 C.E.) or Juvenal (ca. 60–140 C.E.), Roman poets known for their satires.

**16** In his selection from "The Laws of Menu," published in the *Dial,* Thoreau had the following: "Not solicitous for the means of gratification, chaste as a student, sleeping on the bare earth, in the haunts of pious hermits, without one selfish affection, dwelling at the roots of trees; for the purpose of uniting his soul with the divine spirit."

**17** Possible allusion to Shakespeare's *Macbeth* (5.11.14–16): "Had I as many sons as I have hairs / I would not wish them to a fairer death; / And so his knell is knolled."

*January 17.* One day two young women—a Sunday—stopped at the door of my hut and asked for some water. I answered that I had no cold water but I would lend them a dipper.[18] They never returned the dipper, and I had a right to suppose that they came to steal. They were a disgrace to their sex and to humanity. Pariahs of the moral world. Evil spirits that thirsted not for water but threw the dipper into the lake. Such as Dante saw.[19] What the lake to them but liquid fire and brimstone?[20] They will never know peace till they have returned the dipper. In all the worlds this is decreed.

*January 20.* The farmers nowadays can cart out peat and muck over the frozen meadows. Somewhat analogous, methinks, the scholar does; drives in with tight-braced energy and winter cheer onto his now firm meadowy grounds, and carts, hauls off, the virgin loads of fertilizing soil which he threw up in the warm, soft summer. We now bring our muck out of the meadows, but it was thrown up first in summer. The scholar's and the farmer's work are strictly analogous. Easily he now conveys, sliding over the snow-clad ground, great loads of fuel and of lumber which have grown in many summers, from the forest to the town. *He* deals with the dry hay and cows, the spoils of summer meads and fields, stored in his barns, doling it out from day to day, and manufactures milk for men. When I see the farmer driving into his barn-yard with a load of muck, whose blackness contrasts strangely with the white snow, I have the thought which I have described. He is doing like myself. My barn-yard is my journal.

*January 21.* A man does best when he is most himself.[21]

I never realized so distinctly as this moment that I am peacefully parting company with the best friend I ever

18  In *Walden* Thoreau wrote: "Many a traveller came out of his way to see me and the inside of my house, and, as an excuse for calling, asked for a glass of water. I told them that I drank at the pond, and pointed thither, offering to lend them a dipper" [Wa 145].

19  Allusion to Dante Alighieri's (1265–1321) *Inferno.*

20  Allusion to Revelation 21:8: "But the fearful, and unbelieving, and the abominable, and murderers, and whoremongers, and sorcerers, and idolaters, and all liars, shall have their part in the lake which burneth with fire and brimstone."

21  Thoreau had gone to a lecture on Muhammad by Thomas Wentworth Higginson (1823–1911), Unitarian minister and a prominent figure in the abolitionist movement, and described the talk as "not simple enough. For the most part the manner overbore, choked off, and stifled, put out of sight and hearing, the matter. . . . It is as if a man whose mind was at ease should supply the tones and gestures for a man in distress who found only the words; as when one makes a speech and another behind him makes gestures" [J 3:213].

**23** The immediate reason for leaving the woods was Lidian Emerson's request that Thoreau care for her family and household while her husband was away on a lecture tour abroad. Emerson wrote to his brother William on 30 August 1847: "Lidian has invited Henry Thoreau to spend the winter here," although the day before, in writing Margaret Fuller, this plan had not yet been adopted: "In my absence Mamma will go to Staten Island for the winter, & Lidian probably continue to board with Mrs Goodwin till my return." Although Emerson did not leave for Europe until the first week in October, Thoreau left the woods on 6 September 1847, a week after being invited, and moved directly into the Emerson household. He had also completed one of his primary tasks in moving to Walden, to write what became *A Week on the Concord and Merrimack Rivers*. During his stay he completed two drafts, the second of which Emerson described as "quite ready" for publication.

**24** Even though Thoreau was still occasionally lecturing about his Walden experience at this time, here he was working toward a conclusion for *Walden, or Life in the Woods*.

**25** Large open farm wagon.

**26** Although Thoreau rarely used the word "cabin" to describe his house, it is likely that he was punning on the term "cabin passage," referring to both passage on a ship in a cabin as opposed to steerage or as a sailor, and his passage through life in his Walden cabin.

**27** Common sailors slept before the mast, that is, between the mast and the bow. Thoreau's Harvard classmate Richard Henry Dana wrote *Two Years Before the Mast* (1840) describing his experiences as a common sailor.

**28** Where the passenger cabins or berths were located.

**29** In *Walden* this and the previous paragraph became: "I left the woods for as good a reason as I went there. Perhaps it seemed to me that I had several more lives to live, and could not

had, by each pursuing his proper path.[22] I perceive that it is possible that we may have a better *understanding* now than when we were more at one. Not expecting such essential agreement as before. Simply our paths diverge.

*January 22.* But why I changed? why I left the woods?[23] I do not think that I can tell. I have often wished myself back. I do not know any better how I ever came to go there. Perhaps it is none of my business, even if it is yours.[24] Perhaps I wanted a change. There was a little stagnation, it may be. About 2 o'clock in the afternoon the world's axle creaked as if it needed greasing, as if the oxen labored with the wain[25] and could hardly get their load over the ridge of the day. Perhaps if I lived there much longer, I might live there forever. One would think twice before he accepted heaven on such terms. A ticket to Heaven must include tickets to Limbo, Purgatory, and Hell. Your ticket to the boxes admits you to the pit also. And if you take a cabin passage, you can smoke, at least forward of the engine,—you have the liberty of the whole boat. But no, I do not wish for a ticket to the boxes, nor to take a cabin passage.[26] I will rather go before the mast[27] and on the deck of the world. I have no desire to go "abaft the engine."[28]

I must say that I do not know what made me leave the pond. I left it as unaccountably as I went to it. To speak sincerely, I went there because I had got ready to go; I left for the same reason.[29]

The pleasures of the intellect are permanent, the pleasures of the heart are transitory.

My friend invites me to read my papers to him.[30] Gladly would I read, if he would hear. He must not hear coarsely but finely, suffering not the *least* to pass through the sieve of hearing. To associate with one for years with joy who never met your thought with thought! An over-flowing sympathy while yet there is no intellectual communion. Could we not meet on higher ground with the same heartiness? It is dull work reading to one who does not apprehend you. How can it go on? I will still abide by the truth in my converse and intercourse with my friends, whether I am so brought nearer to or removed further from them. I shall not be the less your friend for answering you truly though coldly. Even the estrangement of friends is a fact to be serenely contemplated, as in the course of nature. It is of no use to lie either by word or action. Is not the everlasting truth agreeable to you?

To set down such choice experiences that my own writings may inspire me and at last I may make wholes of parts. Certainly it is a distinct profession to rescue from oblivion and to fix the sentiments and thoughts which visit all men more or less generally, that the contemplation of the unfinished picture may suggest its harmonious completion. Associate reverently and as much as you can with your loftiest thoughts. Each thought that is welcomed and recorded is a nest egg, by the side of which more will be laid. Thoughts accidentally thrown together become a frame in which more may be developed and exhibited. Perhaps this is the main value of a habit of writing, of keeping a journal, — that so we remember our best hours and stimulate ourselves. My thoughts are my company. They have a certain individuality and separate existence, aye, personality. Having by chance recorded a few disconnected thoughts and then brought them into juxtaposition, they suggest a whole new field in which it was possible to labor and to think. Thought begat thought.

*January 24.* If thou art a writer, write as if thy time was short, for it is indeed short at the longest. Improve

spare any more time for that one. It is remarkable how easily and insensibly we fall into a particular route, and make a beaten track for ourselves. I had not lived there a week before my feet wore a path from my door to the pond-side; and though it is five or six years since I trod it, it is still quite distinct. It is true, I fear that others may have fallen into it, and so helped to keep it open. The surface of the earth is soft and impressible by the feet of men; and so with the paths which the mind travels. How worn and dusty, then, must be the highways of the world, how deep the ruts of tradition and conformity! I did not wish to take a cabin passage, but rather to go before the mast and on the deck of the world, for there I could best see the moonlight amid the mountains. I do not wish to go below now" [Wa 313].
**30** Emerson.

31 Cf. 1851 note 59.

32 Thoreau's younger sister, Sophia (1819–1876), who, after Thoreau's death, managed his literary estate.

each occasion when thy soul is reached. Drain the cup of inspiration to its last dregs. Fear no intemperance in that, for the years will come when otherwise thou wilt regret opportunities unimproved. The spring will not last forever. These fertile and expanding seasons of thy life, when the rain reaches thy root, when thy vigor shoots, when thy flower is budding, shall be fewer and farther between. Again I say, Remember thy creator in the days of thy youth.[31] Use and commit to life what you cannot commit to memory. I hear the tones of my sister's piano below.[32] It reminds me of strains which once I heard more frequently, when, possessed with the inaudible rhythm, I sought my chamber in the cold and communed with my own thoughts. I feel as if I then received the gifts of the gods with too much indifference. Why did I not cultivate those fields they introduced me to? Does nothing withstand the inevitable march of time? Why did I not use my eyes when I stood on Pisgah? Now I hear those strains but seldom. My rhythmical mood does not endure. I cannot draw from it and return to it in my thought as to a well all the evening or the morning. I cannot dip my pen in it. I cannot work the vein, it is so fine and volatile. Ah, sweet, ineffable reminiscences!

These woods! Why do I not feel their being cut more sorely? Does it not affect me nearly? The axe can deprive me of much. Concord is sheared of its pride. I am certainly the less attached to my native town in consequence. One, and a main, link is broken. I shall go to Walden less frequently.

*January 27.* I do not know but thoughts written down thus in a journal might be printed in the same form with greater advantage than if the related ones were brought together into separate essays. They are now allied to life, and are seen by the reader not to be far-fetched. It is more simple, less artful. I feel that in the other case I should have no proper frame for my sketches. Mere facts and names and dates communicate more than we suspect. Whether the flower looks better in the nosegay than in the meadow where it grew and we had to wet our feet to get it! Is the scholastic air any advantage?

*January 28.* Our life should be so active and progressive as to be a journey. Our meals should all be of journey-cake[33] and hasty pudding. We should be more alert, see the sun rise, not keep fashionable hours, enter a house, our own house, as a khan, a caravansary.[34] At noon I did not dine; I ate my journey-cake. I quenched my thirst at a spring or a brook. As I sat at the table, the hospitality was so perfect and the repast so sumptuous that I seemed to be breaking my fast upon a bank in the midst of an arduous journey, that the water seemed to be a living spring,[35] the napkins grass, the conversation free as the winds; and the servants that waited on us were our simple desires.

They showed me Johnny Riordan[36] to-day, with one thickness of ragged cloth over his little shirt for all this cold weather, with shoes with large holes in the toes, into which the snow got, as he said, without an outer garment, to walk a mile to school every day over the bleakest of causeways, — the clothes with countless patches, which hailed from, claimed descent from, were originally identical with, pantaloons of mine, which set as if his mother had fitted them to a tea-kettle first. This little mass of humanity, this tender gobbet for the fates, cast into a cold world with a torn lichen leaf wrapped about him, — Oh, I should rather hear that America's first-born were all slain than that his little fingers and toes should feel cold while I am warm. Is man so cheap that he cannot be clothed but with a mat, a rag, that we should

33 A flat cornbread made of cornmeal, salt, and either boiling water or cold milk; also called hoe-cake because they were sometimes baked on the iron blade of a hoe.
34 Both khan and caravansary are inns built around a large courtyard to accommodate caravans traveling the trade routes in central and western Asia.
35 Flowing or issuing continually from the earth as opposed to stagnant.
36 Cf. 1851 note 52.

37 Color of royalty or high office.

38 On 8 February 1852 Thoreau wrote: "Carried a new cloak to Johnny Riordan. I found that the shanty was warmed by the simple social relations of the Irish. On Sunday they come from the town and stand in the doorway and so keep out the cold. One is not cold among his brothers and sisters. What if there is less fire on the hearth, if there is more in the heart!" [J 3:289].

39 On 28 January, not 29 January, Channing lectured on "Society" for the Concord Lyceum.

40 Conundrums, from the early 18th century, as in: a hard, or tough, nut to crack.

41 Cf. 1830s note 58.

42 Originally, in the pulpit in a church, but by extension, at a reading table or lectern.

bestow on him our *cold* victuals? Are there any fellow-creatures to whom we abandon our rags, to whom we give our old clothes and shoes when they will not fend the weather from ourselves? Let the mature rich wear the rags and insufficient clothing; let the infant poor wear the purple[37] and fine linen. I shudder when I think of the fate of innocency. Our charitable institutions are an insult to humanity. A charity which dispenses the crumbs that fall from its overloaded tables, which are left after its feasts![38]

*January 29.* Heard Channing lecture to-night.[39] It was a bushel of nuts.[40] Perhaps the most original lecture I ever heard. Ever so unexpected, not to be foretold, and so sententious that you could not look at him and take his thought at the same time. You had to give your undivided attention to the thoughts, for you were not assisted by set phrases or modes of speech intervening. There was no sloping up or down to or from his points. It was all genius,[41] no talent. It required more close attention, more abstraction from surrounding circumstances, than any lecture I have heard. For, well as I know Channing, he more than any man disappoints my expectation. When I see him in the desk,[42] hear him, I cannot realize that I ever saw him before. He will be strange, unexpected, to his best acquaintance. I cannot associate the lecturer with the companion of my walks. It was from so original and peculiar a point of view, yet just to himself in the main, that I doubt if three in the audience apprehended a tithe that he said. It was so hard to hear that doubtless few made the exertion. A thick succession of mountain passes and no intermediate slopes and plains. Other lectures, even the best, in which so much space is given to the elaborate development of a few ideas, seemed somewhat meager in comparison. Yet it would be how much more glorious if talent were added to genius, if there were a just arrangement and development of the thoughts, and each step were not a leap, but he ran a space to take a yet higher leap![43]

*January 30.* I feel as if I were gradually parting company with certain friends, just as I perceive familiar objects successively disappear when I am leaving my native town in the cars.

I doubt if Emerson could trundle a wheelbarrow through the streets, because it would be out of character. One needs to have a comprehensive character.

Though they are cutting off the woods at Walden,[44] it is not all loss. It makes some new and unexpected prospects. We read books about logging in the Maine woods[45] as if it were wholly strange to these parts. But I here witness almost exactly the same things, scenes that might be witnessed in Maine or New Hampshire: the logger's team, his oxen on the ice chewing the cud, the long pine tree, stripped of its branches, chained upon his sled, resting on a stout cross-bar or log and trailing behind, the smoke of his fire curling up blue amid the trees, the sound of the axe and of the teamsters' voices. A pretty forest scene, seeing oxen, so patient and stationary, good for pictures, standing on the ice,—a piece of still life. Oh, it is refreshing to see, to think of, these things after hearing of the discussions and politics of the day! The smoke I saw was quite blue. As I stood on the partially cleared bank at the east end of the pond, I looked south over the side of the hill into a deep dell still wooded, and I saw, not more than thirty rods off, a chopper at his work. I was half a dozen rods distant from the standing wood, and I saw him through a vista between two trees (it was now mainly an oak wood, the pine having been cut), and he appeared to me apparently half a mile dis-

**43** On 30 January Thoreau added to his journal: "Channing's lecture was full of wise, acute, and witty observations, yet most of the audience did not know but it was mere incoherent and reckless verbiage and nonsense. I lose my respect for people who do not know what is good and true. I know full well that readers and hearers, with the fewest exceptions, ask me for my second best" [J 3:250].

**44** At this time the woods surrounding Walden were primarily used as and considered woodlots. By 6 March 1855 Thoreau would be lamenting: "Our woods are now so reduced that the chopping of this winter has been a cutting to the quick. At least we walkers feel it as such. There is hardly a woodlot of any consequence left but the chopper's axe has been heard in it this season. They have even infringed fatally on White Pond, on the south of Fair Haven Pond, shaved off the topknot of the Cliffs, the Colburn farm, Beck Stow's, etc., etc." [J 7:231].

**45** Thoreau had recently read John S. Springer's (1811–1852) *Forest Life and Forest Trees: Comprising Winter Camp-Life Among the Loggers, and Wild-Wood Adventure; with Descriptions of Lumbering Operations on the Various Rivers of Maine and New Brunswick* (New York: Harper and Brothers, 1851).

**46** Cf. 16 October 1856.

tant, yet charmingly distinct, as in a picture of which the two trees were the frame. He was seen against the snow on the hillside beyond. I could distinguish each part of his dress perfectly, and the axe with distinct outline as he raised it above his head, the black iron against the snow, and could hear every stroke distinctly. Yet I should have deemed it ridiculous to have called to him, he appeared so distant. He appeared with the same distinctness as objects seen through a pinhole in a card. This was the effect rather than by comparison of him, his size, with the nearer trees, between which I saw him and which made the canopied roof of the grove far above his head. It was, perhaps, one of those coincidences and effects which have made men painters. I could not behold him as an actual man; he was more ideal than in any picture I have seen. He refused to be seen as actual. Far in the hollow, yet somewhat enlightened, aisles of this wooded dell. Some scenes will thus present themselves as picture. Those scenes which are picture, subjects for the pencil, are distinctly marked; they do not require the aid of the genius to idealize them. They must be seen as ideal.

Nature allows of no universal secrets. The more carefully a secret is kept on one side of the globe, the larger the type it is printed in on the other. Nothing is too pointed, too personal, too immodest, for her to blazon. The relations of sex, transferred to flowers, become the study of ladies in the drawing-room. While men wear fig leaves, she grows the *Phallus impudicus* and *P. caninus* & other phallus-like fungi.[46]

The rhymes which I used to see on the walls of privies, scribbled by boys, I have lately seen, word for word the same; in spite of whitewash and brick walls and admonitions they survive. They are no doubt older than Orpheus, and have come down from an antiquity as remote as mythology or fable. So, too, no doubt corporations have ever struggled in vain to obtain cleanliness in those provinces. Filth and impurity are as old as cleanliness and purity. To correspond to man completely, Nature is even perhaps unchaste herself. Or perchance man's impurity begets a monster somewhere, to proclaim his sin. The poetry of the jakes,[47]—it flows as perennially as the gutter.

I am afraid to travel much or to famous places, lest it might completely dissipate the mind. Then I am sure that what we observe at home, if we observe anything, is of more importance than what we observe abroad. The far-fetched is of the least value. What we observe in travelling are to some extent the accidents of the body, but what we observe when sitting at home are, in the same proportion, phenomena of the mind itself. A wakeful night will yield as much thought as a long journey. If I try thoughts by their quality, not their quantity, I may find that a restless night will yield more than the longest journey.

*February 1.* When I hear that a friend on whom I relied has spoken of me, not with cold words perhaps, but even with a cold and indifferent tone, to another, ah! what treachery I feel it to be!—the sum of all crimes against humanity. My friend may cherish a thousand suspicions against me, and they may but represent his faith and expectations, till he cherishes them so heartlessly that he can speak of them.

If I have not succeeded in my friendships, it was because I demanded more of them and did not put up with what I could get; and I got no more partly because I gave so little.

*February 3.* I have been to the libraries (yesterday) at Cambridge and Boston.[48] It would seem as if all things compelled us to originality. How happens it that I find not in the country, in the field and woods, the *works* even

47 An Anglicization of the French term *jacques*, from which the English term for privy, john, probably derived.
48 At Harvard, where Thoreau retained borrowing privileges, and the Boston Athenaeum, a private membership library established in 1807.

49 Possible reference to such libraries as the Boston Athenaeum or to Stacy's Circulating Library (cf. 1853 note 31) in Concord.

50 Probable reference to Palenque, an ancient Mayan city of southern Mexico and the site of the Temple of Inscriptions, noted for its hieroglyphic tablets.

of like-minded naturalists and poets. Those who have expressed the purest and deepest love of nature have not recorded it on the bark of the trees with the lichens; they have left no memento of it there; but if I would read their books I must go to the city,—so strange and repulsive both to them and to me,—and deal with men and institutions with whom I have no sympathy. When I have just been there on this errand, it seems too great a price to pay for access even to the works of Homer, or Chaucer, or Linnæus. Greece and Asia Minor should henceforth bear Iliads and Odysseys as their trees lichens. But no! if the works of nature are in any sense collected in the forest, the works of man are to a still greater extent collected in the city. I have sometimes imagined a library, *i. e.* a collection of the works of true poets, philosophers, naturalists, etc., deposited not in a brick or marble edifice in a crowded and dusty city, guarded by cold-blooded and methodical officials and preyed on by bookworms, in which you own no share,[49] and are not likely to, but rather far away in the depths of a primitive forest, like the ruins of Central America,[50] where you can trace a series of crumbling alcoves, the older books protecting the more modern from the elements, partially buried by the luxuriance of nature, which the heroic student could reach only after adventures in the wilderness amid wild beasts and wild men. That, to my imagination, seems a fitter place for these interesting relics, which owe no small part of their interest to their antiquity, and whose occasion is nature, than the well-preserved edifice, with its well-preserved officials on the side of a city's square.

*February 10.* Now if there are any who think that I am vainglorious, that I set myself up above others and crow over their low estate, let me tell them that I could tell a pitiful story respecting myself as well as them, if my spirits held out to do it; I could encourage them with a sufficient list of failures, and could flow as humbly as the very gutters themselves; I could enumerate a list of as rank offences as ever reached the nostrils of heaven; that I think worse of myself than they can possibly think of me, being better acquainted with the man. I put the best face on the matter. I will tell them this secret, if they will not tell it to anybody else.

Write while the heat is in you. When the farmer burns a hole in his yoke, he carries the hot iron quickly from the fire to the wood, for every moment it is less effectual to penetrate (pierce) it. It must be used instantly, or it is useless. The writer who postpones the recording of his thoughts uses an iron which has cooled to burn a hole with. He cannot inflame the minds of his audience.

*February 14.* The traveller's is so apt to be a progress more or less rapid toward his home (I have read many a voyage round the world more than half of which, certainly, was taken up with the return voyage; he no sooner is out of sight of his native hills than he begins to tell us how he got home again) that I wonder he did not stay at home in the first place.

*February 18.* I have a common-place book for facts and another for poetry,[51] but I find it difficult always to preserve the vague distinction which I had in my mind, for the most interesting and beautiful facts are so much the more poetry and that is their success. They are *translated* from earth to heaven.[52] I see that if my facts were sufficiently vital and significant,—perhaps transmuted more into the substance of the human mind,—I should need but one book of poetry to contain them all.

It is impossible for the same person to see things from the poet's point of view and that of the man of science. The poet's second love may be science, not his first,—

51 Thoreau kept a "fact book" for excerpts from his natural history readings, and a separate commonplace book of poetry and prose.
52 Cf. 1840s note 100.

**53** Cf. 1854 note 73.
**54** Whalebone, which is both firm and elastic, was used in making fans, screens, and corsets.

when use has worn off the bloom. I realize that men may be born to a condition of mind at which others arrive in middle age by the decay of their poetic faculties.[53]

*February 24.* As we grow older, is it not ominous that we have more to write about evening, less about morning?

*March 4.* It is discouraging to talk with men who will recognize no principles. How little use is made of reason in this world! You argue with a man for an hour, he agrees with you step by step, you are approaching a triumphant conclusion, you think that you have converted him; but ah, no, he has a habit, he takes a pinch of snuff, he remembers that he entertained a different opinion at the commencement of the controversy, and his reverence for the past compels him to reiterate it now. You began at the butt of the pole to curve it, you gradually bent it round according to rule, and planted the other end in the ground, and already in imagination saw the vine curling round this segment of an arbor, under which a new generation was to recreate itself; but when you had done, just when the twig was bent, it sprang back to its former stubborn and unhandsome position like a bit of whalebone.[54]

*March 15.* I go forth to make new demands on life. I wish to begin this summer well; to do something in it worthy of it and of me; to transcend my daily routine and that of my townsmen; to have my immortality now, that it be in the *quality* of my daily life; to pay the greatest price, the greatest tax, of any man in Concord, and enjoy the most!! I will give all I am for *my* nobility. I will pay all my days for *my* success. I pray that the life of this spring and summer may ever lie fair in my memory. May I dare as I have never done! May I persevere as I have never done! May I purify myself anew as with fire and water, soul and body! May my melody not be wanting to the season! May I gird myself to be a hunter of the beautiful, that naught escape me! May I attain to a youth never attained! I am eager to report the glory of the universe; may I be worthy to do it; to have got through with regarding human values, so as not to be distracted from regarding divine values. It is reasonable that a man should be something worthier at the end of the year than he was at the beginning.

*March 17.* I catch myself philosophizing most abstractly when first returning to consciousness in the night or morning. I make the truest observations and distinctions then, when the will is yet wholly asleep and the mind works like a machine without friction. I am conscious of having, in my sleep, transcended the limits of the individual, and made observations and carried on conversations which in my waking hours I can neither recall nor appreciate. As if in sleep our individual fell into the infinite mind, and at the moment of awakening we found ourselves on the confines of the latter. On awakening we resume our enterprise, take up our bodies and become limited mind again. We meet and converse with those bodies which we have previously animated. There is a moment in the dawn, when the darkness of the night is dissipated and before the exhalations of the day commence to rise, when we see things more truly than at any other time. The light is more trustworthy, since our senses are purer and the atmosphere is less gross. By afternoon all objects are seen in mirage.

*April 3.* The bluebird carries the sky on his back.

*April 4.* I have got to that pass with my friend[55] that our words do not pass with each other for what they are worth. We speak in vain; there is none to hear. He finds

55 Emerson.

**56** Thoreau did many jobs for Emerson, such as carpentry, for which he was compensated: in October 1845 he built a fence; in September 1846 he was advanced money for work to be done adding a barn room; in the summer of 1847 he, with Bronson Alcott, worked at building a summerhouse for Emerson; in the fall of 1847 he put shelves in a closet. While Thoreau lived in the Emerson household from April 1841 to May 1843, he worked in the garden and around the house in exchange for room and board. In October 1845 Emerson paid Thoreau for building a drain and laying a cellar floor and in March 1850 he wanted Thoreau to "reestablish our fallen arbour in the great path and he may set new posts, if he will."
**57** Probably Channing, who was married to Margaret Fuller's sister, Ellen (1820–1856), in 1841. She would leave him in 1853 after bearing four children. On 4 March 1852 Thoreau wrote: "Each man's mode of speaking of the sexual relation proves how sacred his own relations of that kind are. We do not respect the mind that can jest on this subject" [J 3:335]. In his journal of 9 July 1853 Channing noted, after a walk with Emerson: "Sex goes into everything." Cf. 5 July 1852 and 4 March 1856.

fault with me that I walk alone, when I pine for want of a companion; that I commit my thoughts to a diary even on my walks, instead of seeking to share them generously with a friend; curses my practice even. Awful as it is to contemplate, I pray that, if I am the cold intellectual skeptic whom he rebukes, his curse may take effect, and wither and dry up those sources of my life, and my journal no longer yield me pleasure nor life.

*April 11.* If I am too cold for human friendship, I trust I shall not soon be too cold for natural influences. It appears to be a law that you cannot have a deep sympathy with both man and nature. Those qualities which bring you near to the one estrange you from the other.

It is hard for a man to take money from his friends, or any service.[56] This suggests how all men should be related.

*April 12.* I am made somewhat sad this afternoon by the coarseness and vulgarity of my companion,[57] because he is one with whom I have made myself intimate. He inclines latterly to speak with coarse jesting of facts which should always be treated with delicacy and reverence. I lose my respect for the man who can make the mystery of sex the subject of a coarse jest, yet, when you speak earnestly and seriously on the subject, is silent. I feel that this is to be truly irreligious. Whatever may befall me, I trust that I may never lose my respect for purity in others. The subject of sex is one on which I do not wish to meet a man at all unless I *can* meet him on the most inspiring ground,—if his view degrades, and does not elevate. I would preserve purity in act and thought, as I would cherish the memory of my mother. A companion can possess no worse quality than vulgarity. If I find that *he* is not habitually reverent of the fact of sex, I, even I, will not associate with him. I will cast this first stone.[58] What were life without some religion of this kind? Can I walk with one who by his jests and by his habitual tone reduces the life of men and women to a level with that of cats and dogs? The man who uses such a vulgar jest describes his relation to his dearest friend. Impure as I am, I could protect and worship purity. I can have no really serious conversation with my companion. He seems not capable of it. The men whom I most esteem, when they speak at all on this subject, do not speak with sufficient reverence. They speak to men with a coarseness which they would not use in the presence of women, and I think they would feel a slight shame if a woman coming in should hear their remarks. A man's speech on this subject should, of course, be ever as reverent and chaste and simple as if it were to be heard by the ears of maidens.

*April 15.* My face still burns with yesterday's sunning.

*April 16.* How many there are who advise you to print![59] How few who advise you to lead a more interior life! In the one case there is all the world to advise you, in the other there is none to advise you but yourself. Nobody ever advised me not to print but myself. The public persuade the author to print, as the meadow invites the brook to fall into it. Only he can be trusted with gifts who can present a face of bronze to expectations.

As I turned round the corner of Hubbard's Grove,[60] saw a woodchuck, the first of the season, in the middle of the field, six or seven rods from the fence which bounds the wood, and twenty rods distant. I ran along the fence and cut him off, or rather overtook him, though he started at the same time. When I was only a rod and a half off, he stopped, and I did the same; then he ran again, and I ran up within three feet of him, when he stopped again, the fence between us. I squatted down and sur-

58 Allusion to John 8:7: "He that is without sin among you, let him first cast a stone at her."
59 Although it is unknown who advised Thoreau to print at this time, shortly thereafter he published excerpts from his not yet completed *Walden* in *Sartain's Union Magazine:* "The Iron Horse" in July and "A Poet Buying a Farm" in August.
60 On the east bank of the Sudbury River.

**61** On 15 April 1858 Thoreau noted: "The naturalist accomplishes a great deal by patience, more perhaps than by activity. He must take his position, and then wait and watch. It is equally true of quadrupeds and reptiles. Sit still in the midst of their haunts" [J 10:369].

veyed him at my leisure.[61] [. . .] It appeared to tremble, or perchance shivered with cold. When I moved, it gritted its teeth quite loud, sometimes striking the under jaw against the other chatteringly, sometimes grinding one jaw on the other, yet as if more from instinct than anger. Whichever way I turned, that way it headed. I took a twig a foot long and touched its snout, at which it started forward and bit the stick, lessening the distance between us to two feet, and still it held all the ground it gained. I played with it tenderly awhile with the stick, trying to open its gritting jaws. Ever its long incisors, two above and two below, were presented. But I thought it would go to sleep if I stayed long enough. It did not sit upright as sometimes, but *standing* on its fore feet with its head down, *i. e.* half sitting, half standing. We sat looking at one another about half an hour, till we began to feel mesmeric influences. When I was tired, I moved away, wishing to see him run, but I could not start him. He would not stir as long as I was looking at him or could see him. I walked round him; he turned as fast and fronted me still. I sat down by his side within a foot. I talked to him *quasi* forest lingo, baby-talk, at any rate in a conciliatory tone, and thought that I had some influence on him. He gritted his teeth less. I chewed checkerberry leaves and presented them to his nose at last without a grit; though I saw that by so much gritting of the teeth he had worn them rapidly and they were covered with a fine white powder, which, if you measured it thus, would have made his anger terrible. He did not mind any noise I might make. With a little stick I lifted one of his paws to examine it, and held it up at pleasure. I turned him over to see what color he was beneath (darker or more purely brown), though he turned himself back again sooner than I could have wished. His tail was also all brown, though not very dark, rat-tail like, with loose hairs standing out on all sides like a caterpillar brush. He had a rather mild look. I spoke kindly to him. I reached checkerberry leaves to his mouth. I stretched my hands over him, though he turned up his head and still gritted a little. I laid my hand on him, but immediately took it off again, instinct not being wholly overcome. If I had had a few fresh bean leaves, thus in advance of the season, I am sure I should have tamed him completely. It was a frizzly tail. His is a humble, terrestrial color like the partridge's, well concealed where dead wiry grass rises above darker brown or chestnut dead leaves,—a modest color. If I had had some food, I should have ended with stroking him at my leisure. Could easily have wrapped him in my handkerchief. He was not fat nor particularly lean. I finally had to leave him without seeing him move from the place. A large, clumsy, burrowing squirrel. *Arctomys,*[62] bear-mouse.[63] I respect him as one of the natives. He lies there, by his color and habits so naturalized amid the dry leaves, the withered grass, and the bushes. A sound nap, too, he has enjoyed in his native fields, the past winter. I think I might learn some wisdom of him. His ancestors have lived here longer than mine. He is more thoroughly acclimated and naturalized than I. Bean leaves the red men raised for him, but he can do without them.

*April 18.* This is the spring of the year. Birds are migrating northward to their breeding-places; the melted snows are escaping to the sea. We have now the unspeakable rain of the Greek winter.[64] The element of water prevails. The river has far overflowed its channel. What a conspicuous place Nature has assigned to the skunk-cabbage, first flower to show itself above the bare ground! What occult[65] relation is implied between this plant and man?[66] Most buds have expanded perceptibly,—show some greenness or yellowness. Universally Nature relaxes somewhat of her rigidity, yields to the influence of heat.

62 *Arctomys monax:* woodchuck or groundhog.
63 Book name—a nontechnical name found only in scientific treatises and not in common use as a vernacular name, often an adaptation of the Latin or technical name—for the *Arctomys.*
64 Allusion to the opening to Homer's *Iliad,* book 3, which Thoreau translated in his journal of 17 April 1846 as:

> The Trojans rushed with a clang & a shout like birds;
> As when there is a clangor of cranes in the heavens
> Who avoid winter & unspeakable rain,
> They fly with clangor toward the streams of Ocean
> Bearing slaughter & Fate to Pygmaean men.
> [PJ 2:234]

65 Hidden, inscrutable.
66 Possible allusion to Emerson's *Nature:* "The greatest delight which the fields and woods minister is the suggestion of an occult relation between man and the vegetable."

Each day the grass springs and is greener. The skunk-cabbage is inclosed in its spathe, but the willow catkin expands its bright-yellow blossoms without fear at the end of its twigs, and the fertile flower of the hazel has elevated its almost invisible crimson star of stigmas above the sober and barren earth.

The sight of the sucker floating on the meadow at this season affects me singularly, as if it were a fabulous or mythological fish, realizing my *idea* of a fish. It reminds me of pictures of dolphins or of Proteus. I see it for what it is,—not an actual terrene fish, but the fair symbol of a divine idea, the design of an artist. Its color and form, its gills and fins and scales, are perfectly beautiful, because they completely express to my mind what they were intended to express. It is as little fishy as a fossil fish. Such a form as is sculptured on ancient monuments and will be to the end of time; made to point a moral. I am serene and satisfied when the birds fly and the fishes swim as in fable, for the moral is not far off; when the migration of the goose is significant and has a moral to it; when the events of the day have a mythological character, and the most trivial is symbolical.

For the first time I perceive this spring that the year is a circle. I see distinctly the spring arc thus far. It is drawn with a firm line. Every incident is a parable of the Great Teacher.

*April 24.* I know two species of men. The vast majority are men of society. They live on the surface; they are interested in the transient and fleeting; they are like driftwood on the flood. They ask forever and only the news, the froth and scum of the eternal sea. They use policy; they make up for want of matter with manner. Wealth and the approbation of men is to them success. The enterprises of society are something final and sufficing for them. The world advises them, and they listen to its advice. They live wholly an evanescent life, creatures of circumstance. It is of prime importance to them who is the president of the day.[67] They have no knowledge of truth, but by an exceedingly dim and transient instinct, which stereotypes the church and some other institutions. They dwell, they are ever, right in my face and eyes like gnats; they are like motes, so near the eyes that, looking beyond, they appear like blurs; they have their being between my eyes and the end of my nose. The *terra firma* of my existence lies far beyond, behind them and their improvements. If they write, the best of them deal in "elegant literature."[68] Society, man, has no prize to offer me that can tempt me; not one. That which interests a town or city or any large number of men is always something trivial, as politics. It is impossible for me to be interested in what interests men generally. Their pursuits and interests seem to me frivolous. When I am most myself and see the clearest, men are least to be seen; they are like *muscae volitantes*,[69] and that they are seen at all is the proof of imperfect vision. These affairs of men are so narrow as to afford no vista, no distance; it is a shallow foreground only, no large extended views to be taken. Men put to me frivolous questions: When did I come? where am I going? That was a more pertinent question, — what I lectured for? — which one auditor put once to another.[70] What an ordeal it were to make men pass through, to consider how many ever put to you a vital question! Their knowledge of something better gets no further than what is called religion and spiritual knockings.

*May 8.* No tarts that I ever tasted at any table possessed such a refreshing, cheering, encouraging acid that literally put the heart in you and set you on edge for this

67 Master of ceremonies.

68 Belles-lettres, represented by such journals as *Godey's Lady's Book* and *Arthur's Ladies Magazine of Elegant Literature and Fine Arts.*

69 Latin: flying flies, a term referring to spots before the eyes.

70 Probable reference to his 6 April lecture on "Life in the Woods" at Cochituate Hall, Phillips Palace, in Boston. Thomas Wentworth Higginson, who had arranged the lecture, later recalled "the disastrous entertainment" in which he and Thoreau "found a few young mechanics reading newspapers. . . . Some laid down their newspapers, more retained them; the lecture proved to be one of the most introspective chapters from 'Walden.' A few went to sleep, the rest rustled their papers." In "Life Without Principle" Thoreau recalled: "Ordinarily, the inquiry is, Where did you come from? or, Where are you going? That was a more pertinent question which I overheard one of my auditors put to another one, — 'What does he lecture for?' It made me quake in my shoes" [W 4:470].

world's experiences, bracing the spirit, as the cranberries I have plucked in the meadows in the spring. They cut the winter's phlegm, and now I can swallow another year of this world without other sauce. Even on the Thanksgiving table they are comparatively insipid, have lost as much flavor as beauty, are never so beautiful as in water.

*June 9.* For a week past we have had *washing* days.[71] The grass waving, and trees having leaved out, their boughs wave and feel the effect of the breeze. Thus new life and motion is imparted to the trees. The season of waving boughs; and the lighter under sides of the new leaves are exposed.

Evelyn well says "a *sobbing* rain."[72]

*June 12.* Boys are bathing at Hubbard's Bend,[73] playing with a boat (I at the willows).[74] The color of their bodies in the sun at a distance is pleasing, the not often seen flesh-color. I hear the sound of their sport borne over the water. As yet we have not man in nature. What a singular fact for an angel visitant to this earth to carry back in his note-book, that men were forbidden to expose their bodies under the severest penalties! A pale pink, which the sun would soon tan. White men! There are no white men to contrast with the red and the black; they are of such colors as the weaver gives them. I wonder that the dog knows his master when he goes in to bathe and does not stay by his clothes.

*June 19.* Facts collected by a poet are set down at last as winged seeds of truth, samaræ,[75] tinged with his expectation. Oh, may my words be verdurous and sempiternal as the hills! Facts fall from the poetic observer as ripe seeds.

**71**  Days on which laundry hung outdoors would dry quickly.

**72**  Quoted from John Evelyn's (1620–1706) *Sylva*, chapter 26: "Moss is to be rubb'd and scrap'd off with some fit instrument of Wood, which may not excorticate the Tree, or with a piece of Hair-cloth after a sobbing Rain."

**73**  Hubbard's Bath, also called the Hubbard Bathing-Place, on the Concord River.

**74**  Willow Bay: cf. 1859 note 85.

**75**  Latin: the winged, often one-seeded fruit of the elm, ash, or maple.

❧

It requires considerable skill in crossing a country to avoid the houses and too cultivated parts,—somewhat of the engineer's or gunner's skill,—so to pass a house, if you must go near it through high grass,—pass the enemy's lines where houses are thick,—as to make a hill or wood screen you,—to shut every window with an apple tree. For that route which most avoids the houses is not only the one in which you will be least molested, but it is by far the most agreeable.

*June 20.* Lying with my window open, these warm, even sultry nights, I hear the sonorously musical trump of the bullfrogs from time to time, from some distant shore of the river, as if the world were given up to them. By those villagers who live on the street they are never seen and rarely heard by day, but in the quiet sultry nights their notes ring from one end of the town to another. It is as if you had waked up in the infernal regions. I do not know for a time in what world I am. It affects my morals, and all questions take a new aspect from this sound.

*June 21.* Nature has looked uncommonly bare and dry to me for a day or two. With our senses applied to the surrounding world we are reading our own physical and corresponding moral revolutions. Nature was so shallow all at once I did not know what had attracted me all my life. I was therefore encouraged when, going through a field this evening, I was unexpectedly struck with the beauty of an apple tree. The perception of beauty is a moral test.

*June 23.* I am inclined to think that my hat, whose lining is gathered in midway so as to make a shelf,[76] is about as good a botany-box as I could have and far more conve-

**76** Cf. 4 December 1856.

**77** Thoreau had been walking in "pleasant rocky and bushy pastures" along the old Carlisle Road, sometimes called Boulder Field, approximately one mile northwest of Ponkawtasset.
**78** On 19 June Thoreau walked to Flag Hill, on which the towns of Stow, Acton, and Boxboro corner, accompanied by Channing.
**79** French: points of support.
**80** Near the Concord depot, southeast of the Thoreau family's Texas house (cf. 1859 note 36).
**81** In Kentucky, the longest recorded cave system in the world. It was visited by Emerson on 9 June 1850.

nient, and there is something in the darkness and the vapors that arise from the head—at least if you take a bath—which preserves flowers through a long walk. Flowers will frequently come fresh out of this botany-box at the end of the day, though they have had no sprinkling.

I sit on one of these boulders[77] and look south to Ponkawtasset. Looking west, whence the wind comes, you do not see the under sides of the leaves, but, looking east, every bough shows its under side; those of the maples are particularly white. All leaves tremble like aspen leaves. Perhaps on those westward hills where I walked last Saturday[78] the fields are somewhat larger than commonly with us, and I expand with a sense of freedom. The side of the hill commonly makes but one field. They begin to partake of the character of up-country pastures a little more. Two or three large boulders, fifteen or twenty feet square, make a good foreground in this landscape, for the gray color of the rock contrasts well with the green of the surrounding and more distant hills and woods and fields. They serve instead of cottages for a wild landscape as perches or *points d'appui*[79] for the eye.

*June 25.* 8.30 P.M.—To Conantum.

Moon half full. Fields dusky; the evening star and one other bright one near the moon. It is a cool but pretty still night. Methinks I am less thoughtful than I was last year at this time. The flute I now hear from the Depot Field[80] does not find such caverns to echo and resound in my mind,—no such answering depths. Our minds should echo at least as many times as a Mammoth Cave[81] to every musical sound. It should awaken reflections in us. I hear not many crickets. Some children calling their kitten home by some endearing name. Now his day's work is done, the laborer plays his flute,—only possible at this hour. Contrasted with his work, what an accomplishment! Some drink and gamble. He plays some well-known march. But the music is not in the tune; it is in the sound. It does not proceed from the trading nor political world. He practices this ancient art. There are light, vaporous clouds overhead; dark, fuscous ones in the north. The trees are turned black. As candles are lit on earth, stars are lit in the heavens. I hear the bullfrog's trump from afar.

Now I turn down the Corner road.[82] At this quiet hour the evening wind is heard to moan in the hollows of your face, mysterious, spirit-like, conversing with you. It can be heard now only. The whip-poor-will sings. I hear a laborer going home, coarsely singing to himself. Though he has scarcely had a thought all day, killing weeds, at this hour he sings or talks to himself. His humble, earthy contentment gets expression. It is kindred in its origin with the notes or music of many creatures. A more fit and natural expression of his mood, this humming, than conversation is wont to be. The fireflies appear to be flying, though they may be stationary on the grass stems, for their perch and the nearness of the ground are obscured by the darkness, and now you see one here and then another there, as if it were one in motion. Their light is singularly bright and glowing to proceed from a living creature. Nature loves variety in all things, and so she adds glow-worms to fireflies, though I have not noticed any this year The great story of the night is the moon's adventures with the clouds. What innumerable encounters she has had with them! When I enter on the moonlit causeway, where the light is reflected from the glistening alder leaves, and their deep, dark, liquid shade beneath strictly bounds the firm damp road and narrows it, it seems like autumn. The rows of willows completely fence the way and appear to converge in perspective, as I had not noticed by day. The bullfrogs are of various tones. Some horse in a distant

**82** From Back Road to Nine-Acre Corner.

83 Sound of ten-pound hammer hitting an anvil.

84 On 11 April 1858 Thoreau described this house, "of which only the chimney and frame now stand. . . . So this was an old rats' nest as well as human nest, and so it is with every old house. The rats' nest may have been a hundred and fifty years old. Wherever you see an old house, there look for an old rats' nest. . . . Conant says this house was built by Rufus Hosmer's great-grandfather" [J 10:364–365].

85 A mosslike cup lichen.

pasture whinnies; dogs bark; there is that dull, dumping sound of frogs, as if a bubble containing the lifeless sultry air of day burst on the surface, a belching sound. When two or more bullfrogs trump together, it is a ten-pound-ten note.[83] In Conant's meadow I hear the gurgling of unwearied water, the trill of a toad, and go through the cool, primordial liquid air that has settled there. As I sit on the great door-step, the loose clapboards on the old house rattle in the wind weirdly, and I seem to hear some wild mice running about on the floor, and sometimes a loud crack from some weary timber trying to change its position.[84]

On Conantum-top, all white objects like stones are observed, and dark masses of foliage, at a distance even. How distant is day and its associations! The light, dry cladonia lichens[85] on the brows of hills reflect the moonlight well, looking like rocks. The night wind comes cold and whispering, murmuring weirdly from distant mountain-tops. No need to climb the Andes or Himalayas, for brows of lowest hills are highest mountain-tops in cool moonlight nights. Is it a cuckoo's chuckling note I heard? Occasionally there is something enormous and monstrous in the size and distance of objects. A rock, is it? or an elephant asleep? Are these trees on an upland or a lowland? Or do they skirt the brink of a sea-beach? When I get there, shall I look off over the sea? The white-weed is the only obvious flower. I see the tops of the rye wave, and grain-fields are more interesting than by day. The water is dull-colored, hardly more light than a rye-field. There is dew only in the low grounds. What were the firefly's light, if it were not for darkness? The one implies the other.

What a mean and wretched creature is man! By and by some Dr. Morton may be filling your cranium with white mustard seed to learn its internal capacity.[86] Of all ways invented to come at a knowledge of a living man, this seems to me the worst, as it is the most belated. You would learn more by once paring the toe-nails of the living subject. There is nothing out of which the spirit has more completely departed, and in which it has left fewer significant traces.

*June 26.* I have a faint recollection of pleasure derived from smoking dried lily stems before I was a man. I had commonly a supply of these. I have never smoked anything more noxious.

*June 27.* Saw a very large white ash tree, three and a half feet in diameter, in front of the house which White formerly owned, under this hill,[87] which was struck by lightning the 22nd, about 4 P.M. The lightning apparently struck the top of the tree and scorched the bark and leaves for ten or fifteen feet downward, then began to strip off the bark and enter the wood, making a ragged narrow furrow or crack, till, reaching one of the upper limbs, it apparently divided, descending on both sides and entering deeper and deeper into the wood. At the first general branching, it had got full possession of the tree in its centre and tossed off the main limbs butt foremost, making holes in the ground where they struck; and so it went down in the midst of the trunk to the earth, where it apparently exploded, rending the trunk into six segments, whose tops, ten or twenty feet long, were rayed out on every side at an angle of about 30° from a perpendicular, leaving the ground bare directly under where the tree had stood, though they were still fastened to the earth by their roots. The lightning appeared to have gone off through the roots, furrowing them as the branches, and through the earth, making a

**86** Samuel George Morton (1799–1851) explained in his *Crania Americana:* "In order to measure the capacity of the cranium, the foramina was first stopped with cotton, and the cavity was then filled with *white pepper seed* poured into the foramen magnum until it reached the surface, and pressed down with the finger until the skull would receive no more."
**87** Bear Hill.

88 Jove was the Roman god of the earth, originally a sky god, also known as Jupiter, associated
with lightning and the thunderbolt and considered
the chief god; identified with the Greek god Zeus.
89 Related to the Titans, the primordial giant
gods of Greek mythology who ruled the earth
prior to Zeus and were symbolic of great power
and force.

furrow like a plow, four or five rods in one direction, and in another passing through the cellar of the neighboring house, about thirty feet distant, scorching the tin milk-pans and throwing dirt into the milk, and coming out the back side of the house in a furrow, splitting some planks there. The main body of the tree was completely stripped of bark, which was cast in every direction two hundred feet; and large pieces of the inside of the tree, fifteen feet long, were hurled with tremendous force in various directions, one into the side of a shed, smashing it, another burying itself in a wood-pile. The heart of the tree lay by itself. Probably a piece as large as a man's leg could not have been sawn out of the trunk which would not have had a crack in it, and much of it was very finely splintered. The windows in the house were broken and the inhabitants knocked down by the concussion. All this was accomplished in an instant by a kind of fire out of the heavens called lightning, or a thunderbolt, accompanied by a crashing sound. For what purpose? The ancients called it Jove's bolt,[88] with which he punished the guilty, and we moderns understand it no better. There was displayed a Titanic[89] force, some of that force which made and can unmake the world. The brute forces are not yet wholly tamed. Is this of the character of a wild beast, or is it guided by intelligence and mercy? If we trust our natural impressions, it is a manifestation of brutish force or vengeance, more or less tempered with justice. Yet it is our own consciousness of sin, probably, which suggests the idea of vengeance, and to a righteous man it would be merely sublime without being awful.

This is one of those instances in which a man hesitates to refer his safety to his prudence, as the putting up of a lightning-rod. There is no lightning-rod by which the sinner can finally avert the avenging Nemesis. Though I should put up a rod if its utility were satisfactorily demonstrated to me, yet, so mixed are we,

I should feel myself safe or in danger quite independently of the senseless rod. Yet there is a degree of faith and righteousness in putting up a rod, as well as trusting without one, though the latter, which is the rarest, I feel to be the most effectual rod of the two. It only suggests that impunity in respect to all forms of death or disease, whether sickness or casualty, is only to be attained by moral integrity. It is the faith with which we take medicine that cures us. Otherwise we may be cured into greater disease. In a violent tempest, we both fear and trust. We are ashamed of our fear, for we know that a righteous man would not suspect danger, nor incur any. Wherever a man feels fear, there is an avenger. The savage's and the civilized man's instincts are right. Science affirms too much. Science assumes to show *why* the lightning strikes a tree, but it does not show us the moral *why* any better than our instincts did. It is full of presumption. Why should trees be struck? It is not enough to say because they are in the way. Science answers, *Non scio,* I am ignorant.[90] All the phenomena of nature need to be seen from the point of view of wonder and awe, like lightning; and, on the other hand, the lightning itself needs to be regarded with serenity, as the most familiar and innocent phenomena are. There runs through the righteous man's moral spinal column a rod with burnished points to heaven,[91] which conducts safely away into the earth the flashing wrath of Nemesis, so that it merely clarifies the air. This moment the confidence of the righteous man erects a sure conductor within him; the next, perchance, a timid staple[92] diverts the fluid to his vitals. If a mortal be struck with a thunder bolt *coelo sereno,*[93] it is naturally felt to be more awful and vengeful. Men are probably nearer to the essential truth in their superstitions than in their science. Some places are thought to be particularly exposed to lightning, some oaks on hilltops, for instance.

**90** Thoreau's translation of the preceding Latin phrase, which literally means: I know not.
**91** Emerson commented in his July 1852 journal: "Henry T. rightly said, the other evening, talking of lightning-rods, that the only rod of safety was in the vertebrae of his own spine."
**92** Benjamin Franklin (1706–1790) in his treatise "Of Lightning, and the Method (Now Used in America) of Securing Buildings and Persons from Its Mischievous Effects" wrote that a lightning rod may be fastened to a building "with staples of iron."
**93** Latin: serene sky, here used to mean "out of a clear blue sky."

**94**  Thoreau camped on Wachusett, in New Hampshire, with Richard Fuller on 20 July 1841, about which he wrote in "A Walk to Wachusett" (*Boston Miscellany*, January 1843); Saddleback, or Mount Greylock, in Massachusetts, in July 1844, about which he wrote in the "Tuesday" chapter of *A Week on the Concord and Merrimack Rivers*; Ktaadn, in Maine, in September 1846, which he wrote about in "Ktaadn, and the Maine Woods: IV. The Ascent of Ktaadn" (*Sartain's Union Magazine*, October 1848); and Monadnock, in New Hampshire, in July 1844, and which he would visit again three more times.

**95**  Cf. 23 October 1855.

**96**  Channing: cf. 12 April 1852.

*June 28.* I have camped out all night on the tops of four mountains,—Wachusett, Saddle-back, Ktaadn, and Monadnock,[94]—and I usually took a ramble over the summit at midnight by moonlight. I remember the moaning of the wind on the rocks, and that you seemed much nearer to the moon than on the plains. The light is then in harmony with the scenery. Of what use the sunlight to the mountain-summits? From the cliffs you looked off into vast depths of illumined air.

*June 30.* Nature must be viewed humanly to be viewed at all;[95] that is, her scenes must be associated with humane affections, such as are associated with one's native place, for instance. She is most significant to a lover. A lover of Nature is preëminently a lover of man. If I have no friend, what is Nature to me? She ceases to be morally significant.

*July 5.* I know a man who never speaks of the sexual relation but jestingly,[96] though it is a subject to be approached only with reverence and affection. What can be the character of that man's love? It is ever the subject of a stale jest, though his health or his dinner can be seriously considered. The glory of the world is seen only by a chaste mind. To whomsoever this fact is not an awful but beautiful mystery, there are no flowers in nature.

How perfect an invention is glass! There is a fitness in glass windows which reflect the sun morning and evening, windows, the doorways of light, thus reflecting the rays of that luminary with a splendor only second to itself. This invention one would say was anticipated in the arrangement of things. The sun rises with a salute and leaves the world with a farewell to our windows. To have, instead of opaque shutters or dull horn or paper, a material like solidified air, which reflects the sun thus brightly! It is inseparable from our civilization and enlightenment. It is encouraging that this intelligence and brilliancy or splendor should belong to the dwellings of men, and not to the cliffs and micaceous rocks and lakes exclusively.

We are favored in having two rivers, flowing into one, whose banks afford different kinds of scenery, the streams being of different characters; one a dark, muddy, dead stream, full of animal and vegetable life, with broad meadows and black dwarf willows and weeds, the other *comparatively* pebbly and swift, with more abrupt banks and narrower meadows.[97] To the latter I go to see the ripple, and the varied bottom with its stones and sands and shadows; to the former for the influence of its dark water resting on invisible mud, and for its reflections. It is a factory of soil, depositing sediment.

The wood thrush's[98] is no opera music; it is not so much the composition as the strain, the tone,—cool bars of melody from the atmospheres of everlasting morning or evening. It is the quality of the sound, not the sequence. In the peawai's[99] note there is some sultriness, but in the thrush's, though heard at noon, there is the liquid coolness of things that are just drawn from the bottom of springs. The thrush alone declares the immortal wealth and vigor that is in the forest. Here is a bird in whose strain the story is told, though Nature waited for the science of æsthetics to discover it to man. Whenever a man hears it, he is young, and Nature is in her spring. Wherever he hears it, it is a new world and a free country, and the gates of heaven are not shut against him.[100] Most other birds sing from the level of my ordinary cheerful hours—a carol; but this bird never fails to speak to me out of an ether purer than that I breathe, of immortal beauty and vigor. He deepens the signifi-

**97** The "dark, muddy" Sudbury and the "pebbly and swift" Assabet meet at Egg Rock to form the Concord River.
**98** Thoreau used "wood thrush" to refer to any singing thrush, apparently not distinguishing between the different vocalizations of the wood thrush (*Hylocichla mustelina*) and the hermit thrush (*Hylocichla guttata*). On 21 July 1851 Thoreau called the wood thrush "the finest songster of the grove" [J 2:331].
**99** Eastern wood pewee (*Contopus virens*).
**100** Allusion to John Bunyan's *The Straight Gate; or, Great Difficulty of Going to Heaven:* "They will look for heaven, but the gate of heaven will be shut against them: what a disappointment here!"

101 His neighbors, of whom Thoreau wrote in *Walden:* "I sometimes wonder that we can be so frivolous, I may almost say, as to attend to the gross but somewhat foreign form of servitude called Negro Slavery, there are so many keen and subtle masters that enslave both north and south. It is hard to have a southern overseer; it is worse to have a northern one; but worst of all when you are the slave-driver of yourself" [Wa 6].

102 Edmund Hosmer (1798–1881), Concord farmer and friend of Thoreau. He helped Thoreau raise his house at Walden Pond. Sanborn identified Hosmer as "living on the Cambridge Turnpike, or a little off from that, along which his well-tilled farm extended. This made him one of Thoreau's nearest neighbors."

103 On 1 June 1853 Thoreau described a "farmer's horn calling his hands in from the field to an early tea. Heard afar by the walker, over the woods at this hour or at noon, bursting upon the stillness of the air, putting life into some portion of the horizon, this is one of the most suggestive and pleasing of the country sounds produced by man" [J 5:212–213].

104 Allusion to "A Lytell Gest of Robyn Hode" (Part I, Fourth Fytte, 102–103) — "Let blowe a horne, sayd Robyn, / That felaushyp may us knowe"—quoted from *Robin Hood: A Collection of All the Ancient Poems, Songs, and Ballads,* compiled by Joseph Ritson (1752–1803), several verses of which Thoreau copied into his literary notebook.

105 In phrenology, a popular pseudo-science in Thoreau's day first proposed by the Viennese doctor Franz Josef Gall (1758–1828), character was believed to be related to the shape of one's head. The shape of the skull was thought to reflect the development of the underlying parts of the brain, and therefore mental development. A long head was an indication of shrewdness and talent.

Phrenology was popularized in America with the publication in 1829 of George Combe's (1788–1858) *Constitution of Man,* which Emerson called "the best Sermon I have read for some time." It was given support by the writings of

cance of all things seen in the light of his strain. He sings to make men take higher and truer views of things. He sings to amend their institutions; to relieve the slave on the plantation and the prisoner in his dungeon, the slave in the house of luxury and the prisoner of his own low thoughts.[101]

*July 6.* Hosmer[102] is haying, but inclined to talk as usual. I blowed on his horn at supper-time.[103] I asked if I should do any harm if I sounded it. He said no, but I called Mrs. Hosmer back, who was on her way to the village, though I blowed it but poorly. I was surprised to find how much skill and breath it took, depending on the size of the throat. Let blow a horn, says Robin, that good fellowship may us know.[104] Where could a man go to practice on the horn, unless he went round to the farmer's at meal-time?

I am disappointed that Hosmer, the most intelligent farmer in Concord, and perchance in Middlesex, who admits that he has property enough for his use without accumulating more, and talks of leaving off hard work, letting his farm, and spending the rest of his days easier and better, cannot yet think of any method of employing himself but in work with his hands; only he would have a little less of it. Much as he is inclined to speculation in conversation — giving up any work to it for the time — and long-headed[105] as he is, he talks of working for a neighbor for a day now and then and taking his dollar. He "would not like to spend his time sitting on the mill-dam."[106] He has not even planned an essentially better life.

*July 8.* I am inclined to think bathing almost one of the necessaries of life, but it is surprising how indifferent some are to it. What a coarse, foul, busy life we lead, compared even with the South-Sea-Islanders, in some respects. Truant boys steal away to bathe, but the farmers, who most need it, rarely dip their bodies into the streams or ponds. Minot was telling me last night that he had thought of bathing when he had done his hoeing,—of taking some soap and going down to Walden and giving himself a good scrubbing,—but something had occurred to prevent it, and now he will go unwashed to the harvesting, aye, even till the next hoeing is over.[107]

*July 9.* Bathing is an undescribed luxury. To feel the wind blow on your body, the water flow on you and lave you, is a rare physical enjoyment this hot day. The water is remarkably warm here, especially in the shallows,—warm to the hand, like that which has stood long in a kettle over a fire. The pond water being so warm made the water of the brook feel very cold; and this kept close on the bottom of the pond for a good many rods about the mouth of the brook, as I could feel with my feet; and when I thrust my arm down where it was only two feet deep, my arm was in the warm water of the pond, but my hand in the cold water of the brook.

*July 10.* When I had left the river[108] and walked in the woods for some time, and jumped into the river again, I was surprised to find for the first time how warm it was,—as it seemed to me, almost warm enough to boil eggs,—like water that has stood a considerable while in a kettle over a fire. There are many interesting objects of study as you walk up and down a clear river like this in the water, where you can see every inequality in the bottom and every object on it. The breams' nests are interesting and even handsome, and the shallow water in them over the sand is so warm to my hand that I think their ova will soon be hatched. Also the numerous heaps of stones, made I know not certainly by what fish, many of them rising above the surface.[109] There are weeds on the bottom which remind you of the sea.

Johann Kaspar Spurzheim (1776–1832) and Orson (1809–1887) and Lorenzo (1811–1896) Fowler, and by Isaac Ray's (1807–1881) essay, "Moral Aspects of Phrenology," in the *Christian Examiner* (May 1834). Emerson was later more circumspect in his praise: "Gall and Spurzheim's Phrenology laid a rough hand on the mysteries of animal and spiritual nature, dragging down every sacred secret to a street show. The attempt was coarse and odious to scientific men, but had a certain truth in it; it felt connection where professors denied it, and was a leading to a truth which had not yet been announced."

106  Town center. Concord originated as a mill-dam site, a center of converging roads, from which a settlement grew.

107  Books on hygiene from the 19th century indicate that bathing for cleanliness had not yet become a regular practice. The Women's Christian Temperance Union recommended in 1836: "All should bathe at least twice a week." William Andrus Alcott's (1798–1859) *Young Man's Guide* urged: "Cleanliness of the body has, some how or other, such a connection with mental and moral purity, (whether cause or effect—or both—I will not undertake now to determine) that I am unwilling to omit the present opportunity of urging its importance. There are those who are so attentive to this subject as to wash their whole bodies in water, either cold or warm, every day, and never to wear the same clothes, during the day, that they have slept in the previous night. Now this habit may by some be called whimsical; but I think it deserves a better name. I consider this extreme, if it ought to be called an extreme, as vastly more safe than the common extreme of neglect."

108  The Assabet.

109  Made by the lamprey, an eel-like fish, many of which are parasitic, with a circular sucking mouth, of which Thoreau wrote in *A Week on the Concord and Merrimack Rivers:* "you may sometimes see the curious circular nests of the lamprey eel (*Petromyzon Americanus*), the American stone-sucker, as large as a cart-wheel, a foot or

two in height, and sometimes rising half a foot above the surface of the water. They collect these stones, of the size of a hen's egg, with their mouths, as their name implies, and are said to fashion them into circles with their tails" [W 1:31].

Two days later, on 12 July, Thoreau again noted: "The most striking phenomenon in this stream is the heaps of small stones about the size of a walnut, more or less, which line the shore, in shallow water, one every rod or two, the recent ones frequently rising by more than half their height above the water, at present, *i. e.* a foot or a foot and a half, and sharply conical, the older flattened by the elements and greened over with the thread like stem of *Ranunculus filiformis,* with its minute bright-yellow flower. Some of these heaps contain two cartloads of stones, and as probably the creature that raised them took up one at a time, it must have been a stupendous task" [J 4:221].

110 Allusion to the nursery rhyme, "There was an old woman who lived in a shoe. She had so many children she didn't know what to do."

111 Conflated allusion to John Fletcher's (1579–1625) *The Faithful Shepherdess* and John Milton's "L'Allegro," ll. 67–68: "And every Shepherd tells his tale / Under the Hawthorn in the dale."

❦

There are but few fishes to be seen. They have, no doubt, retreated to the deepest water. In one somewhat muddier place, close to the shore, I came upon an old pout cruising with her young. She dashed away at my approach, but the fry remained. They were of various sizes from a third of an inch to an inch and a half long, quite black and pout-shaped, except that the head was most developed in the smallest. They were constantly moving about in a somewhat circular, or rather lenticular, school, about fifteen or eighteen inches in diameter, and I estimated that there were at least a thousand of them. Presently the old pout came back and took the lead of her brood, which followed her, or rather gathered about her, like chickens about a hen; but this mother had so many children she did n't know what to do.[110] Her maternal yearnings must be on a great scale. When one half of the divided school found her out, they came down upon her and completely invested her like a small cloud. She was soon joined by another smaller pout, apparently her mate, and all, both old and young, began to be very familiar with me; they came round my legs and felt them with their feelers, and the old pouts nibbled my toes, while the fry half concealed my feet. Probably if I had been standing on the bank with my clothes on they would have been more shy. Ever and anon the old pouts dashed aside to drive away a passing bream or perch. The larger one kept circling about her charge, as if to keep them together within a certain compass. If any of her flock were lost or devoured she could hardly have missed them. I wondered if there was any calling of the roll at night,—whether she, like a faithful shepherdess, ever told her tale under some hawthorn in the river's dales.[111] Ever ready to do battle with the wolves that might break into her fold. The young pouts are protected then for a season by the old.

❧

I wonder if any Roman emperor ever indulged in such luxury as this,—of walking up and down a river in torrid weather with only a hat to shade the head. What were the baths of Caracalla[112] to this?

*July 12.* Now for another fluvial walk. There is always a current of air above the water, blowing up or down the course of the river, so that this is the coolest highway. Divesting yourself of all clothing but your shirt and hat, which are to protect your exposed parts from the sun, you are prepared for the fluvial excursion. You choose what depth you like, tucking your toga higher or lower, as you take the deep middle of the road or the shallow sidewalks.

*July 13.* A journal, a book that shall contain a record of all your joy, your ecstasy.

*July 14.* A writer who does not speak out of a full experience uses torpid words, wooden or lifeless words, such words as "humanitary,"[113] which have a paralysis in their tails.

Is it not more attractive to be a sailor than a farmer? The farmer's son is restless and wants to go to sea. Is it not better to plow the ocean than the land? In the former case the plow runs further in its furrow before it turns. You may go round the world before the mast,[114] but not behind the plow.

*July 22.* There men in the fields are at work thus indefatigably,[115] more or less honestly getting bread for men. The writer should be employed with at least equal industry to an analogous though higher end.

112  Roman public baths, built between 212 and 216 C.E., during the reign of Emperor Caracalla (Marcus Aurelius Antonius, 186–217 C.E.), although they may have been begun during the reign of his father, Septimius Severus (146–211 C.E.).

113  Rare variant of humanitarian. Probable reference to Arnold Henry Guyot's (1807–1884) *The Earth and Man: Lectures on Comparative Physical Geography, in Its Relation to the History of Mankind,* which Thoreau read in 1851, wherein Guyot described the "work to which Christian nations of modern Europe appear to be summoned. To this spread of the blessings of civilization abroad, ought to correspond, as we have said, a work of diffusion within civilized society itself; to the *humanitary* work, a social work."

114  Possible allusion to Dana's *Two Years Before the Mast:* cf. 1852 note 27.

115  During the day's excursion to Lee's Bridge by way of Conantum, returning by Clematis Brook, Thoreau observed farmers haying.

**116** In "Autumnal Tints" Thoreau wrote: "A man shall perhaps rush by and trample down plants as high as his head, and cannot be said to know that they exist, though he may have cut many tons of them, littered his stables with them, and fed them to his cattle for years. Yet, if he ever favorably attends to them, he may be overcome by their beauty. Each humblest plant, or weed, as we call it, stands there to express some thought or mood of ours; and yet how long it stands in vain! . . . Beauty and true wealth are always thus cheap and despised" [W 5:257]. "When the farmer cleans out his ditches," Thoreau wrote on 10 April 1853, "I mourn the loss of many a flower which he calls a weed" [W 5:108], and later defined weeds as "uncultivated herbaceous plants which do not bear handsome flowers" [J 9:59].

*July 23.* Every man says his dog will not touch you. Look out, nevertheless.

*July 24.* I sympathize with weeds[116] perhaps more than with the crop they choke, they express so much vigor. They are the truer crop which the earth more willingly bears.

*July 26.* By my intimacy with nature I find myself withdrawn from man. My interest in the sun and the moon, in the morning and the evening, compels me to solitude.

The grandest picture in the world is the sunset sky. In your higher moods what man is there to meet? You are of necessity isolated. The mind that perceives clearly any natural beauty is in that instant withdrawn from human society. My desire for society is infinitely increased; my fitness for any actual society is diminished.

*July 27.* It is pleasing to behold at this season contrasted shade and sunshine on the side of neighboring hills. They are not so attractive to the eye when all in the shadow of a cloud or wholly open to the sunshine. Each must enhance the other.

*August 2.* Wachusett from Fair Haven Hill looks like this: —

the dotted line being the top of the surrounding forest. Even on the low principle that misery loves company and is relieved by the consciousness that it is shared by many, and therefore is not so insignificant and trivial, after all, this blue mountain outline is valuable. In many moods it is cheering to look across hence to that blue rim of the earth, and be reminded of the invisible towns and communities, for the most part also unremembered, which lie in the further and deeper hollows between me and those hills. Towns of sturdy uplandish fame, where some of the morning and primal vigor still lingers, I trust. Ashburnham, Rindge, Jaffrey, etc.,—it is cheering to think that it is with such communities that we survive or perish. Yes, the mountains do thus impart, in the mere prospect of them, some of the New Hampshire vigor. The melancholy man who had come forth to commit suicide on this hill might be saved by being thus reminded how many brave and contented lives are lived between him and the horizon. Those hills extend our plot of earth; they make our native valley or indentation in the earth so much the larger. There is a whitish line along the base of Wachusett more particularly, as if the reflection of bare cliffs there in the sun. Undoubtedly it is the slight vaporous haze in the atmosphere seen edge-wise just above the top of the forest, though it is a clear day. It, this line, makes the mountains loom in fact, a faint whitish line separating the mountains from their bases and the rest of the globe.

*August 7.* We see the rainbow apparently when we are on the edge of the rain, just as the sun is setting. If we are too deep in the rain, then it will appear dim. Sometimes it is so near that I see a portion of its arch this side the woods in the horizon, tingeing them. Sometimes we are completely within it, enveloped by it, and experience the realization of the child's wish.[117] The obvious colors are red and green. Why green? It is astonishing how brilliant the red may be. What is the difference between that red and the ordinary red of the evening sky. Who does not feel that here is a phenomenon which natural philosophy[118] alone is inadequate to explain? The use of the rainbow, who has described it?

117 Thoreau repeated this claim in *Walden:* "Once it chanced that I stood in the very abutment of a rainbow's arch, which filled the lower stratum of the atmosphere, tinging the grass and leaves around, and dazzling me as if I looked through colored crystal. It was a lake of rainbow light, in which, for a short while, I lived like a dolphin" [Wa 195]. He had reported this phenomenon once before. On 9 August 1851 he wrote: "We were in the westernmost edge of the shower at the moment the sun was setting, and its rays shone through the cloud and the falling rain. We were, in fact, in a rainbow and it was here its arch rested on the earth" [J 2:382–383]. In spite of Thoreau's assertion, he could not have both stood where a rainbow meets the earth and seen it at the same time. Optical physics dictates that the rainbow must appear opposite the sun at 42 degrees from the observer, or the "rainbow angle," to be visible. It is unclear what natural phenomenon Thoreau experienced.

118 The study of nature and the physical universe before the advent of modern science.

119 Reference to the Freemasons, or order of Free and Accepted Masons, an international fraternal and charitable organization with secret rites and signs.

120 Sa'di (or Saadi), Persian poet born Sheikh Muslih Addin (1184–1291), from whose *The Gulistan, or Rose Garden*, a collection of poems, prose, and maxims concerning moral issues, Thoreau copied several extracts into his literary notebooks. Emerson, in his poem "Saadi" published in the *Dial* (October 1842), identified himself with the Persian poet.

*August 8.* Men have circumnavigated this globe of land and water, but how few have sailed out of sight of common sense over the ocean of knowledge!

The entertaining a single thought of a certain elevation makes all men of one religion. It is always some base alloy that creates the distinction of sects. Thought greets thought over the widest gulfs of time with unerring freemasonry.[119] I know, for instance, that Sadi[120] entertained once identically the same thought that I do, and thereafter I can find no essential difference between Sadi and myself. He is not Persian, he is not ancient, he is not strange to me. By the identity of his thought with mine he still survives. It makes no odds what atoms serve us. Sadi possessed no greater privacy or individuality than is thrown open to me. He had no more interior and essential and sacred self than can come naked into my thought this moment. Truth and a true man is something essentially public, not private. If Sadi were to come back to claim a *personal* identity with the historical Sadi, he would find there were too many of us; he could not get a skin that would contain us all. The symbol of a personal identity preserved in this sense is a mummy from the catacombs, — a whole skin, it may be, but no life within it. By living the life of a man is made common property. By sympathy with Sadi I have embowelled him. In his thoughts I have a sample of *him,* a slice from his core, which makes it unimportant where certain bones which the thinker once employed may lie; but I could not have got this without being equally entitled to it with himself. The difference between any man and that posterity amid whom he is famous is too insignificant to sanction that he should be set up again in any world as distinct from them. Methinks I can be as intimate with the essence of an ancient worthy as, so to speak, he was with himself.

I only know myself as a human entity, the scene, so to speak, of thoughts and affections, and am sensible of a certain doubleness by which I can stand as remote from myself as from another. However intense my experience, I am conscious of the presence and criticism of a part of me which, as it were, is not a part of me, but spectator, sharing no experience, but taking note of it, and that is no more I than it is you. When the play—it may be the tragedy of life—is over, the spectator goes his way. It was a kind of fiction, a work of the imagination only, so far as he was concerned. A man *may* be affected by a theatrical exhibition; on the other hand he *may not* be affected by an actual event which appears to concern him never so much.

*August 11.* Alcott here the 9th and 10th. He, the spiritual philosopher, is, and has been for some months, devoted to the study of his own genealogy,[121]—he whom only the genealogy of humanity, the descent of man from God, should concern! He has been to his native town of Wolcott, Connecticut, on this errand, has faithfully perused the records of some fifteen towns, has read the epitaphs in as many churchyards, and, wherever he found the name Alcock, excerpted it and all connected with it,—for he is delighted to discover that the original name was All-*cock* and meant something,[122] that some grandfather or great-grandfather bore it, Philip Alcock (though his son wisely enough changed it to Alcott).[123] He who wrote of Human Culture,[124] he who conducted the Conversations on the Gospels,[125] he who discoursed of Sleep, Health, Worship, Friendship, etc., last winter,[126] now reading the wills and the epitaphs of the Alcocks with the zeal of a professed antiquarian and genealogist!

*August 22.* The ways by which men express themselves are infinite,—the literary through their writings, and often they do not mind with what air they walk the streets, being sufficiently reported otherwise. But some

**121** As a teacher Alcott believed that inequalities in education accounted for inequalities in success, but he later questioned the influence of ancestry. "The child's body is a recollection of ancestral particles from seven generations preceding," he wrote in his journal on 11 March 1852. In June 1852 he began a five-month genealogical study.

**122** The name Alcock means "Little Hal." *Al* is a variant of Hal, a diminutive for Henry; *cock(e)* or *cox* means small or little.

**123** Philip Alcocke was Bronson Alcott's great-great-great-grandfather. Alcott's great-great-grandfather and great-grandfather were both named John Alcocke. His grandfather was John Alcox and his father was Joseph Chatfield Alcox. It was Bronson who ultimately changed the surname to Alcott.

**124** *The Doctrine and Discipline of Human Culture* (Boston: James Munroe, 1836).

**125** Conversations held at the Temple School, Boston—founded by Alcott in 1834—published as *Conversations with Children on the Gospels* (Boston: James Munroe, 1836–1837).

**126** Starting in 1849 Alcott held a series of "Conversations on Man—his History, Resources, and Expectations,—illustrated from the Experiences of the Company, and from the Text of the eminent Teachers of Mankind, ancient and modern."

127 Nobscot Hill, highest point in Sudbury, southwest of Concord.
128 Emerson.

express themselves chiefly by their gait and carriage, with swelling breasts or elephantine roll and elevated brows, making themselves moving and adequate signs of themselves, having no other outlet. If their greatness had signalized itself sufficiently in some other way, though it were only in picking locks, they could afford to dispense with the swagger.

*August 23.* Now I sit on the Cliffs, and look abroad over the river and Conantum hills. I live so much in my habitual thoughts, a routine of thought, that I forget there is any outside to the globe, and am surprised when I behold it as now,—yonder hills and river in the moonlight, the monsters. Yet it is salutary to deal with the surface of things. What are these rivers and hills, these hieroglyphics which my eyes behold? There is something invigorating in this air, which I am peculiarly sensible is a real wind, blowing from over the surface of a planet. I look out at my eyes, I come to my window, and I feel and breathe the fresh air. It is a fact equally glorious with the most inward experience. Why have we ever slandered the outward? The perception of surfaces will always have the effect of miracle to a sane sense. I can see Nobscot[127] faintly.

Descend the rocks and return through woods to railroad. How picturesque the moonlight on rocks in the woods! To-night there are no fireflies, no nighthawks nor whip-poor-wills.

*August 24.* How far we can be apart and yet attract each other! There is one who almost wholly misunderstands me and whom I too probably misunderstand,[128] toward whom, nevertheless, I am distinctly drawn. I have the utmost human good-will toward that one, and yet I know not what mistrust keeps us asunder. I am so much and so exclusively the friend of my friend's virtue that I am compelled to be silent for the most part, because his vice is present. I am made dumb by this third party. I only desire *sincere* relations with the worthiest of my acquaintance, that they may give me an opportunity once in a year to speak the truth. They invite me to see them, and do not show themselves. Who *are* they, pray? I pine and starve near them. The hospitable man will invite me to an atmosphere where truth can be spoken, where a man can live and breathe. Think what crumbs we offer each other,—and think to make up for the deficiency with our *roast meats!* Let us have a human creature's heart and let go the beeve's[129] heart. How happens it that I find myself making such an enormous demand on men and so constantly disappointed? Are my friends aware how disappointed I am? Is it all my fault?[130] Have I no heart? Am I incapable of expansion and generosity? I shall accuse myself of everything else sooner. I have never met with a friend who furnished me sea-room. I have only tacked a few times and come to anchor,—not sailed,— made no voyage, carried no venture. Do they think me eccentric because I refuse this chicken's meat, this babe's food? Would not men have something to communicate if they were sincere? Is not my silent expectation an invitation, an offer, an opportunity offered? My friend has complained of me, cursed me even, but it did not affect me; I did not know the persons he talked about. I have been disappointed from first to last in my friends, but I have never complained of them, nor to them. I would have them know me, guess at me. It is not petty and trivial relations that I seek to establish with them. A world in which there is a demand for ice-creams but not for truths! I leave my friends early; I go away to cherish my idea of friendship. Is not friendship a great relation? My friend so treats me that I feel a thousand miles off; like the greatest possible stranger, speaking a different language; as if it would be the fittest thing in the world for

129 Rare and erroneous singular form of beeves, the plural of beef.

130 Margaret Fuller went through a similar period with Emerson, which she noted in her journal: "After the first excitement of intimacy with him,—when I was made so happy by his high tendency, absolute purity, the freedom and infinite graces of an intellect cultivated much beyond any I had known,—came with me the questioning season. I was greatly disappointed in my relation to him. I was, indeed, always called on to be worthy,—this benefit was sure in our friendship. But I found no intelligence of my best self; far less was it revealed to me in new modes; for not only did he seem to want the living faith which enables one to discharge the holiest office of a friend, but he absolutely distrusted me in every region of my life with which he was unacquainted. The same trait I detected in his relations with others."

us to be introduced. Persists in thinking me the opposite to what I am, and so shuts my mouth. Intercourse with men! How little it amounts to! How rarely we love them! Do we not meet very much as Yankees meet Arabs? It is remarkable if a man gives us a civil answer about the road. And how far from love still are even pretty intimate friends! How little it is that we can trust each other! It is the bravest thing we do for one moment to put so much confidence in our companion as to treat him for what he aspires to be, a confidence which we retract instantly.

Like cuttlefish we conceal ourselves, we darken the atmosphere in which we move; we are not transparent. I pine for one to whom I can speak my *first thoughts;* thoughts which represent me truly, which are no better and no worse than I; thoughts which have the bloom on them, which alone can be sacred and divine. Our sin and shame prevent our expressing even the innocent thoughts we have. I know of no one to whom I can be transparent instinctively. I live the life of the cuttlefish; another appears, and the element in which I move is tinged and I am concealed. My first thoughts are azure; there is a bloom and a dew on them; they are papillary-feelers which I put out, tender, innocent. Only to a friend can I expose them. To all parties, though they be youth and maiden, if they are transparent to each other, and their thoughts can be expressed, there can be no further nakedness. I cannot be surprised by an intimacy which reveals the outside, when it has shown me the inside. The result of a full communication of our thoughts would be the immediate neglect of those coverings which a false modesty wears.

*August 31.* It is pleasant to embark on a voyage, if only for a short river excursion, the boat to be your home for the day, especially if it is neat and dry. A sort of moving studio it becomes, you can carry so many things with you. It is almost as if you put oars out at your windows and moved your house along. A sailor, I see, easily becomes attached to his vessel. How continually we are thankful to the boat if it does not leak! We move now with a certain pomp and circumstance, with planetary dignity. The pleasure of sailing is akin to that which a planet feels. It seems a more complete adventure than a walk. We make believe embark our all,—our house and furniture. We are further from the earth than the rider; we receive no jar from it. We can carry many things with us.

A few days ago some saw a circular rainbow about the sun at midday.[131] Singular phenomenon. Is not this the season when conventions are held? Or do they not appoint conventions, temperance or political, at such times as the farmers are most at leisure? There is a silvery light on the washed willows this morning, and the shadows under the wood-sides appear deeper, perchance by contrast, in the brilliant air. Is not the air a little more bracing than it was? Looking up the sparkling river, whose waves are flashing in the sun, it appears to be giving off its pure silver from the amalgam. The sky is more beautiful, a clearer blue, methinks, than for some time past, with light and downy clouds sailing all round a quarter of the way up it. The fields of bulrushes are now conspicuous, being left alone above the water. The balls of the button-bush have lost their bloom. From the shore I hear only the creak of crickets. The winds of autumn begin to blow. Now I can sail.

The very sounds made by moving the furniture of my boat are agreeable, echoing so distinctly and sweetly over the water; they give the sense of being aboard. I find myself *at home* in new scenery. I carry more of myself with me; I am more entirely abroad, as when a man takes his children into the fields with him. I carry so many

**131** A parhelion. Cf. 2 February 1860: "The sundogs, if that is their name, were not so distinctly bright as an ordinary rainbow, but were plainly orange-yellow and a peculiar light violet-blue, the last color looking like a hole in the cloud, or a thinness through which you saw the sky. . . . But higher up, so that its centre would have been in the zenith or apparently about in the zenith, was an arc of a distinct rainbow. A rainbow right overhead. Is this what is called a parhelion?" [J 13:121–122].

**132** In *A Yankee in Canada* Thoreau wrote: "We styled ourselves the Knights of the Umbrella and the Bundle; for, wherever we went . . . the umbrella and the bundle went with us; for we wished to be ready to digress at any moment. We made it our home nowhere in particular, but everywhere where our umbrella and bundle were" [W 5:33].
**133** Writing desk.

me's with me. This large basket of melons, umbrella,[132] flowers, hammer, etc., etc., all go with me to the end of the voyage without being the least incumbrance, and preserve their relative distances. Our capacity to carry our furniture with us is so much increased. There is little danger of overloading the steed. We can go completely equipped to fields a dozen miles off. The tent and the chest can be taken as easily as not. We embark; we go aboard a boat; we sit or we stand. If we sail, there is no exertion necessary. If we move in the opposite direction, we nevertheless progress. And if we row, we sit to an agreeable exercise, akin to flying. A student, of course, if it were perfectly convenient, would always move with his escritoire[133] and his library about him. If you have a cabin and can descend into that, the charm is double.

All the fields and meadows are shorn. I would like to go into perfectly new and wild country where the meadows are rich in decaying and rustling vegetation, present a wilder luxuriance. I wish to lose myself amid reeds and sedges and wild grasses that have not been touched. If haying were omitted for a season or two, a voyage up this river in the fall, methinks, would make a much wilder impression. I sail and paddle to find a place where the bank has a more neglected look. I wish to bury myself amid reeds. I pine for the luxuriant vegetation of the river-banks.

It is worth the while to have had a cloudy, even a stormy, day for an excursion, if only that you are out at the clearing up. The beauty of the landscape is the greater, not only by reason of the contrast with its recent lowering aspect, but because of the greater freshness and purity of the air and of vegetation, and of the repressed and so recruited spirits of the beholder. Sunshine is nothing to be observed or described, but when it is seen in patches on the hillsides, or suddenly bursts forth with splendor at the end of a storm. I derive pleasure now from the shadows of the clouds diversifying the sunshine on the hills, where lately all was shadow. The spirits of the cows at pasture on this very hillside appear excited. They are restless from a kind of joy, and are not content with feeding. The weedy shore is suddenly blotted out by this rise of waters.

*September 9.* There are enough who will flatter me with sweet words, and anon use bitter ones to balance them, but they are not my friends. Simple sincerity and truth are rare indeed. One acquaintance criticises me to my face, expecting every moment that I will become his friend to pay for it.[134] I hear my acquaintance thinking his criticism aloud. We love to talk with those who can make a good guess at us, not with those who talk to us as if we were somebody else all the while. Our neighbors invite us to be amiable toward their vices. How simple is the law of love! One who loves us acts accordingly, and anon we come together and succeed together without let or hindrance.

*September 13.* In my ride I experienced the pleasure of coming into a landscape where there was more distance and a bluish tinge in the horizon. I am not contented long with such narrow valleys that all is greenness in them. I wish to see the earth translated, the green passing into blue. How this heaven intervenes and tinges our more distant prospects! The farther off the mountain which is the goal of our enterprise, the more of heaven's tint it wears. This is the chief value of a distance in landscapes.

I must walk more with free senses. It is as bad to *study* stars and clouds as flowers and stones. I must let my senses wander as my thoughts, my eyes see without

134 Fuller wrote of Emerson: "He had faith in the Universal, not in the Individual Man; he met men, not as a brother, but as a critic."

135 Unidentified allusion.

136 In Lincoln, three-quarters of a mile north of Flint's Pond.

137 This, his second excursion to Monadnock, took place 6–7 September 1852. He was accompanied by Channing.

138 It was part of Thoreau's enjoyment of the natural world not to be controlled by fences and property lines. When visiting Canada in 1850 he went "across lots in spite of numerous signs threatening the severest penalties to trespassers" [W 5:98]. On this preferred method of travel Thoreau wrote: "At any rate, I might pursue some path, however solitary and narrow and crooked, in which I could walk with love and reverence. Wherever a man separates from the multitude, and goes his own way in this mood, there indeed is a fork in the road, though ordinary travelers may see only a gap in the paling. His solitary path across lots will turn out the *higher way* of the two" [W 4:466].

139 Joseph Eveleth's house stood near Thorndike Pond at the junction of Mountain and Dublin Roads.

looking. Carlyle said that how to observe was to look,[135] but I say that it is rather to see, and the more you look the less you will observe. I have the habit of attention to such excess that my senses get no rest, but suffer from a constant strain. Be not preoccupied with looking. Go not to the object; let it come to you. When I have found myself ever looking down and confining my gaze to the flowers, I have thought it might be well to get into the habit of observing the clouds as a corrective; but no! that study would be just as bad. What I need is not to look at all, but a true sauntering of the eye.

*September 27.* From Smith's Hill[136] I looked toward the mountain line. Who can believe that the mountain peak which he beholds fifty miles off in the horizon, rising far and faintly blue above an intermediate range, while he stands on his trivial native hills, or in the dusty highway, can be the same with that which he looked up at once near at hand from a gorge in the midst of primitive woods? For a part of two days[137] I travelled across lots[138] once, loitering by the way, through primitive wood and swamps over the highest peak of the Peterboro Hills to Monadnock, by ways from which all landlords and stage-drivers endeavored to dissuade us. It was not a month ago. But now that I look across the globe in an instant to the dim Monadnock peak, and these familiar fields and copsewoods appear to occupy the greater part of the interval, I cannot realize that Joe Eavely's house[139] still stands there at the base of the mountain, and all that long tramp through wild woods with invigorating scents before I got to it. I cannot realize that on the tops of those cool blue ridges are in abundance berries still, bluer than themselves, as if they borrowed their blueness from their locality. From the mountains we do not discern our native hills; but from our native hills we look out easily to the far blue mountains, which seem to preside over them. As I look northwestward to that summit from a Concord cornfield, how little can I realize all the life that is passing between me and it,—the retired up-country farmhouses, the lonely mills, wooded vales, wild rocky pastures, and new clearings on stark mountain-sides, and rivers murmuring through primitive woods! All these, and how much more, I *overlook*. I see the very peak,— there can be no mistake,—but how much I do not see that is between me and it![140] How much I overlook! In this way we see stars. What is it but a faint blue cloud, a mist that may vanish? But what is it, on the other hand, to one who has travelled to it day after day, has threaded the forest and climbed the hills that are between this and that, has tasted the raspberries or the blueberries that grow on it, and the springs that gush from it, has been wearied with climbing its rocky sides, felt the coolness of its summit, and been lost in the clouds there?

*October 20.* Many a man, when I tell him that I have been on to a mountain, asks if I took a glass with me. No doubt, I could have seen further with a glass, and particular objects more distinctly,—could have counted more meeting-houses; but this has nothing to do with the peculiar beauty and grandeur of the view which an elevated position affords. It was not to see a few particular objects, as if they were near at hand, as I had been accustomed to see them, that I ascended the mountain, but to see an infinite variety far and near in their relation to each other, thus reduced to a single picture. The facts of science, in comparison with poetry, are wont to be as vulgar as looking from the mountain with a telescope. It is a counting of meeting-houses. At the public house, the mountain-house, they keep a glass to let, and think the journey to the mountain-top is lost, that you have got but half the view, if you have not taken a glass with you.

**140** Cf. 5 November 1857.

**141** On 3 September 1851 Thoreau wrote of the lines that had been strung the previous month: "As I went under the new telegraph-wire, I heard it vibrating like a harp high overhead. It was as the sound of a far-off glorious life, a supernal life, which came down to us, and vibrated the lattice-work of this life of ours" [J 2:450].

**142** At the end of the "Wednesday" chapter in *A Week on the Concord and Merrimack Rivers,* Thoreau similarly wrote of dreams:

Dreams are the touchstones of our characters. We are scarcely less afflicted when we remember some unworthiness in our conduct in a dream, than if it had been actual, and the intensity of our grief, which is our atonement, measures the degree by which this is separated from an actual unworthiness. For in dreams we but act a part which must have been learned and rehearsed in our waking hours, and no doubt could discover some waking consent thereto. If this meanness had not its foundation in us, why are we grieved at it? In dreams we see ourselves naked and acting out our real characters, even more clearly than we see others awake. But an unwavering and commanding virtue would compel even its most fantastic and faintest dreams to respect its ever-wakeful authority; as we are accustomed to say carelessly, we should never have *dreamed* of such a thing. Our truest life is when we are in dreams awake. [W 1:315]

*October 23.* October has been the month of autumnal tints.

*October 28.* As I cross the railroad I hear the telegraph harp again,[141] the undecayed oracle. Its vibrations are communicated through the tall pole to the surrounding earth for a considerable distance, so that I feel them when I stand near. And when I put my ear to a fence-rail, it is all alive with them, though the post with which it is connected is planted two feet from the telegraph-post; yet the rail resounded with the harp music so that a deaf man might have heard it.

*November 23.* I had a thought in a dream last night which surprised me by its strangeness, as if it were based on an experience in a previous state of existence, and could not be entertained by my waking self. Both the thought and the language were equally novel to me, but I at once perceived it to be true and to coincide with my experience in this state.[142]

*December 2.* Men commonly talk as if genius were something proper to an individual. I esteem it but a common privilege, and if one does not enjoy it now, he may congratulate his neighbor that *he* does. There is no place for man-worship. We understand very well a man's relation, not to *his* genius, but to the genius.

*December 28.* Both for bodily and mental health, court the present. Embrace health wherever you find her.

## AGE 35–36

**1** Knots of the fat pine, which are full of pitch or resin. In *Walden* Thoreau wrote: "A few pieces of fat pine were a great treasure. It is interesting to remember how much of this food for fire is still concealed in the bowels of the earth. In previous years I had often gone 'prospecting' over some bare hill-side, where a pitch-pine wood had formerly stood, and got out the fat pine roots. They are almost indestructible. Stumps thirty or forty years old, at least, will still be sound at the core, though the sap-wood has all become vegetable mould, as appears by the scales of the thick bark forming a ring level with the earth four or five inches distant from the heart. With axe and shovel you explore this mine, and follow the marrowy store, yellow as beef tallow, or as if you had struck on a vein of gold, deep into the earth" [Wa 242].
**2** Potash: principally potassium carbonate, used in making soap.

*January 2.* We build a fire on the Cliffs. When kicking to pieces a pine stump for the fat knots[1] which alone would burn in this icy day, at the risk of spoiling my boots, having looked in vain for a stone, I thought how convenient would be an Indian stone axe to batter it with. The bark of white birch, though covered with ice, burned well. We soon had a roaring fire of fat pine on a shelf of rock, from which we overlooked the icy landscape. The sun, too, was melting the ice on the rocks, and the water was bubbling and pulsing downward in dark bubbles, exactly like pollywogs. What a good word is "flame," expressing the form and soul of fire, lambent with forked tongue! We lit a fire to see it rather than to feel it, it is so rare a sight these days. To have our eyes ache once more with smoke! What a peculiar, perhaps indescribable color has this flame!—a reddish or lurid yellow, not so splendid or full of light as of life and heat. These fat roots made much flame, and a very black smoke, commencing where the flame left off, which cast fine flickering shadows on the rocks. There was some bluish-white smoke from the rotten part of the wood. Then there was the fine white ashes, which farmers' wives sometimes use for pearlash.[2] Fire is the most tolerable third party.

*January 3.* I love Nature partly *because* she is not man, but a retreat from him. None of his institutions control or pervade her. There a different kind of right prevails. In her midst I can be glad with an entire gladness. If this

3 Echo of Charles Mackay's (1814–1899) sonnet "The True Companion," which has the lines: "And the o'erflowing joy which nature yields / To her true lovers"; in Mackay's *Voices from the Mountains and from the Crowd* (Boston, 1853), issued in December 1852.
4 Thoreau's couplet. That man is the source of evil is found in many religious texts, such as Mark 7:21–23: "For from within, out of the heart of men, proceed evil thoughts, adulteries, fornications, murders, thefts, covetousness, wickedness, deceit, lasciviousness, an evil eye, blasphemy, pride, foolishness: All these evil things come from within, and defile the man."
5 Tedious writer or talker.
6 Pratt's Powder Mills, also known as the Acton Powder Mills, on the Concord-Acton line.

world was all man, I could not stretch myself, I should lose all hope. He is constraint, she is freedom to me. He makes me wish for another world. She makes me content with this. None of the joys she supplies is subject to his rules and definitions. What he touches he taints. In thought he moralizes. One would think that no free, joyful labor was possible to him. How infinite and pure the least pleasure of which Nature is basis, compared with the congratulation of mankind! The joy which Nature yields is like that afforded by the frank words of one we love.[3]

> Man, man is the devil,
> The source of all evil.[4]

Methinks that these prosers,[5] with their saws and their laws, do not know how glad a man can be. What wisdom, what warning, can prevail against gladness? There is no law so strong which a little gladness may not transgress. I have a room all to myself; it is nature. It is a place beyond the jurisdiction of human governments. Pile up your books, the records of sadness, your saws and your laws. Nature is glad outside, and her merry worms within will erelong topple them down. There is a prairie beyond your laws. Nature is a prairie for outlaws. There are two worlds, the post-office and nature. I know them both.

*January 7.* About ten minutes before 10 A.M., I heard a very loud sound, and felt a violent jar, which made the house rock and the loose articles on my table rattle, which I knew must be either a powder-mill blown up[6] or an earthquake. Not knowing but another and more violent might take place, I immediately ran down-stairs, but I saw from the door a vast expanding column of whitish smoke rising in the west directly over the powder-mills four miles distant. It was unfolding its volumes above, which made it widest there. In three or four minutes it had all risen and spread it self into a lengthening, somewhat copper-colored cloud parallel with the horizon from north to south, and about ten minutes after the explosion it passed over my head, being several miles long from north to south and distinctly dark and smoky toward the north, not nearly so high as the few cirrhi[7] in the sky. I jumped into a man's wagon and rode toward the mills. In a few minutes more, I saw behind me, far in the east, a faint salmon-colored cloud carrying the news of the explosion to the sea, and perchance over the head of the absent proprietor.[8]

*January 9.* The telegraph harp again. Always the same unrememberable revelation it is to me. It is something as enduring as the worm that never dies.[9] Before thee it was, and will be after. I never hear it without thinking of Greece. How the Greeks *harped*[10] upon the words immortal, ambrosial! They are what it says. It stings my ear with everlasting truth. It allies Concord to Athens, and both to Elysium. It always intoxicates me, makes me sane, reverses my views of things. I am pledged to it. I get down the railroad till I hear that which makes all the world a lie. When the zephyr, or west wind, sweeps this wire, I rise to the height of my being. A period—a semicolon, at least—is put to my previous and habitual ways of viewing things. This wire is my redeemer.[11] It always brings a special and a general message to me from the Highest. Day before yesterday I looked at the mangled and blackened bodies of men which had been blown up by powder,[12] and felt that the lives of men were not innocent, and that there was an avenging power in nature. To-day I hear this immortal melody, while the west wind is blowing balmily on my cheek, and methinks a roseate sunset is preparing. Are there not two powers?

**7** Cirri: plural of cirrus.

**8** Nathan Pratt (b. 1795) started the powder mills in 1835.

**9** Allusion to Isaiah 66:24: "And they shall go forth, and look upon the carcasses of the men that have transgressed against me: for their worm shall not die, neither shall their fire be quenched," and to the torments of hell in Mark 9:44, 46, 48: "Where their worm dieth not, and the fire is not quenched."

**10** The Greek poets used a lyre, or harp, to accompany their recitations.

**11** Allusion to Psalms 19:14: "O LORD, my Rock and my Redeemer."

**12** Thoreau had described the men's clothes "in the tops of the trees, where undoubtedly their bodies had been and left them. The bodies were naked and black, some limbs and bowels here and there, and a head at a distance from its trunk. The feet were bare; the hair singed to a crisp" [J 4:455].

13  Richard Chenevix Trench (1807–1896) wrote in the "Introductory Lecture" of his *On the Study of Words:* "But it was said just now that words often contain a witness for great moral truths—God having impressed such a seal of truth upon language, that men are continually uttering deeper things than they know, asserting mighty principles, it may be asserting themselves against themselves, in words that to them may seem nothing more than the current coin of society. . . . Take three of four of these words—'transport,' 'rapture,' 'ravishment,' 'ecstasy,'—'transport,' that which *carries* us, as 'rapture,' or 'ravishment,' that which *snatches* us, out of and above ourselves; and 'ecstasy' is very nearly the same, only drawn from the Greek."

14  Trench wrote: "'Rivals' are properly those who dwell on the banks of the same river. But as all experience shows, there is no such fruitful source of contention as a water-right, and these would be often at strife with one another in regard of the periods during which they severally had a right to the use of the stream, turning it off into their own fields before the time, or leaving open the sluices beyond the time, or in other ways interfering, or being counted to interfere, with the rights of their neighbors. And in this way 'rivals' came to be applied to any who were on any grounds in un-friendly competition with one another."

15  Pun: roaring or flowing noisily, but also fight-ing over water rights.

16  Thoreau's note: "Bailey I find has it 'Rival (*Rivalis* L.q. d. qui juxta eundem rivum pascit).' My friends my rivals are." Thoreau's quotation is from Nathan Bailey's (d. 1742) *A New Universal Etymological English Dictionary* (1755).

*January 15.* True words are those, as Trench says,—trans-port, rapture, ravishment, ecstasy.[13] These are the words I want. This is the effect of music. I am rapt away by it, out of myself. These are truly poetical words. I am inspired, elevated, expanded. I am on the mount.

*January 16.* Trench says that "'rivals,' in the primary sense of the word, are those who dwell on the banks of the same stream" or "on opposite banks," but as he says, in many words, since the use of water-rights is a fruitful source of contention between such neighbors, the word has acquired this secondary sense.[14] My friends are my *rivals* on the Concord, in the primitive sense of the word. There is no strife between us respecting the use of the stream. The Concord offers many privileges, but none to quarrel about. It is a peaceful, not a brawling,[15] stream. It has not made *rivals* out of neighbors *that lived on its banks,* but friends. My friends are my *rivals;* we dwell on opposite banks of the stream, but that stream is the Con-cord, which flows without a ripple or a murmur, with-out a rapid or a brawl, and offers no petty privileges to quarrel about.[16]

*January 21.* A fine, still, warm moonlight evening. We have had one or two already. Moon not yet full.

To the woods by the Deep Cut at 9 o'clock.

The blueness of the sky at night—the color it wears by day—is an everlasting surprise to me, suggesting the constant presence and prevalence of light in the firma-ment, that we see through the veil of night to the con-stant blue, as by day. The night is not black when the air is clear, but blue still. The great ocean of light and ether is unaffected by our partial night. Night is not universal. At midnight I see into the universal day. Walking at that hour, unless it is cloudy, still the blue sky o'erarches me.

I am somewhat oppressed and saddened by the sameness and apparent poverty of the heavens, — that these irregular and few geometrical figures which the constellations make are no other than those seen by the Chaldean shepherds.[17] The same simplicity and unchangeableness which commonly impresses me by wealth sometimes affects me as barrenness. I pine for a new world in the heavens as well as on the earth, and though it is some consolation to hear of the wilderness of stars and systems invisible to the naked eye, yet the sky does not make that impression of variety and wildness that even the forest does, as it ought. It makes an impression, rather, of simplicity and unchangeableness, as of eternal laws; this being the same constellation which the shepherds saw, and obedient still to the same law. It does not affect me as that unhandselled[18] wilderness which the forest is. I seem to see it pierced with visual rays from a thousand observatories. It is more the domain of science than of poetry. But it is the stars as not known to science that I would know, the stars which the lonely traveller knows.

The Chaldean shepherds saw not the same stars which I see, and if I am elevated in the least toward the heavens, I do not accept their classification of them. I am not to be distracted by the names which they have imposed.[19] The sun which I know is not Apollo, nor is the evening star Venus.[20] The heavens should be as new, at least, as the world is new. This classification of the stars is old and musty; it is as if a mildew had taken place in the heavens, as if the stars so closely packed had heated and moulded there. If they appear fixed, it is because that hitherto men have been thus necessitated to see them. I see not merely old but new testaments in the skies. Do not I stand as near the stars as the Chaldean shepherds? The heavens commonly look as dry and meagre as our astronomies are, — mere troops, as the latter are catalogues, of stars.[21] The Milky Way[22] yields no milk.

A few good anecdotes is our science, with a few im-

17 Shepherds from the land of Chaldea, an ancient region of Mesopotamia, considered the originators of the science of astronomy.
18 Unused or untried, as in Emerson's "The American Scholar": "unhandselled savage nature," or Thoreau's "Ktaadn": "Here was no man's garden, but the unhandseled globe" [W 3:78].
19 Neither Apollo (Greek) nor Venus (Roman) in the next line is a Chaldean name.
20 Apollo is the Greek god of prophecy, music, medicine, and poetry, sometimes identified with the sun; Venus is the Roman goddess of love and beauty, but also the second nearest planet to the sun, visible as an early morning or evening star.
21 Cf. 5 August 1851.
22 Galaxy containing the solar system, visible as a broad band of faint, milky light in the night sky.

**23** Although here Thoreau wrote of the greater allegorical truth of astrology compared with the more factual science of astronomy, in *Walden* he complained that the works of the great poets "have only been read as the multitude read the stars, at most astrologically, not astronomically" [Wa 102].

**24** Allusion to Shakespeare's *A Midsummer Night's Dream* 5.1.12–13: "The poet's eye, in a fine frenzy rolling, / Doth glance from heaven to earth, from earth to heaven."

**25** Allusion to the "Comet Seeker" telescope designed by Henry Fritz (1808–1863) ca. 1850, offering a wide view of field at a low power, optimizing the ability to discover comets.

posing statements respecting distance and size, and little or nothing about the stars as they concern man; teaching how he may survey a country or sail a ship, and not how he may steer his life. Astrology contained the germ of a higher truth than this.[23] It may happen that the stars are more significant and truly celestial to the teamster than to the astronomer. Nobody sees the stars now. They study astronomy at the district school, and learn that the sun is ninety-five millions of miles distant, and the like,— a statement which never made any impression on me, because I never walked it, and which I cannot be said to believe. But the sun shines nevertheless. Though observatories are multiplied, the heavens receive very little attention. The naked eye may easily see farther than the armed. It depends on who looks through it. No superior telescope to this has been invented. In those big ones the recoil is equal to the force of the discharge. The poet's eye in a fine frenzy rolling ranges from earth to heaven,[24] but this the astronomer's does not often do. It does not see far beyond the dome of the observatory.

Compared with the visible phenomena of the heavens, the anecdotes of science affect me as trivial and petty. Man's eye is the true star-finder, the comet-seeker.[25] As I sat looking out the window the other evening just after dark, I saw the lamp of a freight-train, and, near by, just over the train, a bright star, which looked exactly like the former, as if it belonged to a different part of the same train. It was difficult to realize that the one was a feeble oil lamp, the other a world.

As I walk the railroad causeway I am, as the last two months, disturbed by the sound of my steps on the frozen ground. I wish to hear the silence of the night, for the silence is something positive and to be heard. I cannot walk with my ears covered. I must stand still and listen with open ears, far from the noises of the village, that the night may make its impression on me. A fertile and eloquent silence. Sometimes the silence is merely negative, an arid and barren waste in which I shudder, where no ambrosia grows. I must hear the whispering of a myriad voices. Silence alone is worthy to be heard. Silence is of various depth and fertility, like soil. Now it is a mere Sahara,[26] where men perish of hunger and thirst, now a fertile bottom, or prairie, of the West. As I leave the village, drawing nearer to the woods, I listen from time to time to hear the hounds of Silence baying the Moon,— to know if they are on the track of any game. If there 's no Diana[27] in the night, what is it worth? I hark the goddess Diana. The silence rings; it is musical and thrills me. A night in which the silence was audible.[28] I hear the unspeakable.

I easily read the moral of my dreams. Yesterday I was impressed with the rottenness of human relations. They appeared full of death and decay, and offended the nostrils. In the night I dreamed of delving amid the graves of the dead, and soiled my fingers with their rank mould. It was *sanitarily, morally,* and *physically* true.[29]

If night is the mere negation of day, I hear nothing but my own steps in it. Death is with me, and life far away. If the elements are not human, if the winds do not sing or sigh, as the stars twinkle, my life runs shallow. I measure the depth of my own being. I walk with vast alliances. I am the allied powers, the holy alliance, absorbing the European potentates.[30] I do not get much from the blue sky, these twinkling stars, and bright snow-fields reflecting an almost rosaceous light. But when I enter the woods I am fed by the variety,—the forms of the trees above against the blue, with the stars seen through the pines like the lamps hung on them in an illumination, the somewhat indistinct and misty fineness of the pine-tops, and the finely divided spray of the oaks, etc., and the shadows of all these on the snow. The first shadow I came to I thought was a black place where the wood-

26 In northern Africa, the world's largest desert.
27 In Roman mythology, goddess of the moon and the hunt.
28 Cf. 6 March 1838.
29 Cf. 1852 note 142.
30 An alliance of Russia, Prussia, and Austria in 1815 to regulate the affairs of Europe by advocating government according to Christian principles.

**31** The Concord Social Library was available for a subscription fee, and the Concord Town Library, beginning with the donated collections of the Concord Social Library, was established in 1851. The town's first librarian, Albert Stacy (1821–1868), also operated Stacy's Circulating Library, the books of which were available for a rental fee, or through the purchase of a share at an annual subscription rate. Stacy's library complemented, rather than duplicated, the holdings of the town library. He also had a shop where he offered "books, stationery and fancy goods" for sale.

**32** Lemuel Shattuck wrote in *A History of the Town of Concord* (1835), regarding fish in Walden Pond: "It is said no fish were caught in it, till they were transplanted there from other waters. Pickerel and other fish are now plenty there." In *Walden* Thoreau wrote: "Ah, the pickerel of Walden! when I see them lying on the ice, or in the well which the fisherman cuts in the ice, making a little hole to admit the water, I am always surprised by their rare beauty, as if they were fabulous fishes, they are so foreign to the streets, even to the woods, foreign as Arabia to our Concord life" [Wa 275].

**33** In *Walden* Thoreau wrote: "Yet notwithstanding the objection on the score of humanity, I am compelled to doubt if equally valuable sports are ever substituted for these; and when some of my friends have asked me anxiously about their boys, whether they should let them hunt, I have answered, yes,—remembering that it was one of the best parts of my education,—*make* them hunters, though sportsmen only at first, if possible, mighty hunters at last, so that they shall not find game large enough for them in this or any vegetable wilderness,—hunters as well as fishers of men" [Wa 204].

choppers had had a fire. These myriad shadows checker the white ground and enhance the brightness of the enlightened portions. See the shadows of these young oaks which have lost half their leaves, more beautiful than themselves, like the shadow of a chandelier, and motionless as if they were fallen leaves on the snow,—but shake the tree, and all is in motion.

*January 26.* It is surprising how much room there is in nature,—if a man will follow his proper path. In these broad fields, in these extensive woods, on this stretching river, I never meet a walker. Passing behind the farmhouses, I see no man out. Perhaps I do not meet so many men as I should have met three centuries ago, when the Indian hunter roamed these woods. I enjoy the retirement and solitude of an early settler. Men have cleared some of the earth, which no doubt is an advantage to the walker. I see a man sometimes chopping in the woods, or planting or hoeing in a field, at a distance; and yet there may be a lyceum in the evening, and there is a book-shop and library in the village,[31] and five times a day I can be whirled to Boston within an hour.

It is remarkable that many men will go with eagerness to Walden Pond in the winter to fish for pickerel[32] and yet not seem to care for the landscape. Of course it cannot be *merely* for the pickerel they may catch; there is some adventure in it; but any love of nature which they may feel is certainly very slight and indefinite. They call it going a-fishing, and so indeed it is, though, perchance, their natures know better. Now I go a-fishing and a-hunting every day, but omit the fish and the game, which are the least important part. I have learned to do without them. They were indispensable only as long as I was a boy.[33] I am encouraged when I see a dozen villagers drawn to Walden Pond to spend a day in fishing through the ice, and suspect that I have more fellows than I knew, but I am disappointed and surprised to find that they lay so much stress on the fish which they catch or fail to catch, and on nothing else, as if there were nothing else to be caught.

*January 27.* Trench says a wild man is a *willed* man.[34] Well, then, a man of will who does what he wills or wishes, a man of hope and of the future tense, for not only the obstinate is willed, but far more the constant and persevering. The obstinate man, properly speaking, is one who will not. The perseverance of the saints[35] is positive willedness, not a mere passive willingness. The fates are wild, for they *will;* and the Almighty is wild above all, as fate is.

*February 11.* While surveying on the Hunt farm the other day, behind Simon Brown's House[36] I heard a remarkable echo. In the course of surveying, being obliged to call aloud to my assistant[37] from every side and almost every part of a farm in succession, and at various hours of a day, I am pretty sure to discover an echo if any exists, and the other day it was encouraging and soothing to hear it. After so many days of comparatively insignificant drudgery with stupid companions, this leisure, this sportiveness, this generosity in nature, sympathizing with the better part of me; somebody I could talk with,—one degree, at least, better than talking with one's self. Ah! Simon Brown's premises harbor a hired man and a hired maid he wots not of.[38] Some voice of somebody I pined to hear, with whom I could form a community. I did wish, rather, to linger there and call all day to the air and hear my words repeated, but a vulgar necessity dragged me along round the bounds of the farm, to hear only the stale answers of my chain-man[39] shouted back to me.

I am surprised that we make no more ado about

**34** In Trench's *On the Study of Words* Thoreau found: "'Wild' is the participle past of 'to will;' a 'wild' horse is a 'willed' or self-willed horse, one that has never been tamed or taught to submit its will to the will of another; and so with a man."
**35** The doctrine of the Perseverance of the Saints is stated in the Westminster Confession of Faith, chapter 17, in the following words: "They whom God hath accepted in His Beloved, effectually called and sanctified by His Spirit, can neither totally nor finally fall away from the state of grace; but shall certainly persevere therein to the end, and be eternally saved."
**36** Thoreau was surveying the Hunt Farm, at the intersection of the Lowell Road and the Cambridge Turnpike, on 31 January and 1–3 February 1853. Simon Brown (1802–1873) was a farmer in Concord from 1848 to 1873, editor of the *New England Farmer,* publisher of the *Concord Freeman,* and founding member of the Concord Farmer's Club.
**37** Unidentified.
**38** Possible allusion to Echo, in Greek mythology, a nymph who pined away for love of the youth Narcissus, until nothing was left of her but her voice.
**39** A surveyor's assistant, responsible for moving the heavy metal surveying chain of 100 links used to measure property bounds.

**40** Thoreau was surveying John B. Moore's farm on Lexington Road on this day.

**41** Method of reasoning used by Socrates, who attempted to arrive at the truth through a process of questioning, answering, and criticizing the answer.

**42** Founded in 1848 to promote science and serve society. Spencer Fullerton Baird (1823–1887) was its secretary from 1851 to 1854.

**43** Thoreau returned the circular to Baird on 19 December 1853, completed as follows:

> *Occupation (Professional, or otherwise).* Literary and Scientific, combined with Land-surveying.
> *Post-office address* Henry D. Thoreau Concord Mass.
> *Branches of science in which especial interest is felt* The manners & Customs of the Indians of the Algonquin Group previous to contact with the civilized man.
> *Remarks* I may add that I am an observer of nature generally, and the character of my observations, so far as they are scientific, may be inferred from the fact that I am especially attracted by such books of science as White's Selborne and Humboldt's "Aspects of Nature." [C 310]

echoes. They are almost the only kindred voices that I hear. I wonder that the traveller does not oftener remark upon a remarkable echo,—he who observes so many things. There needs some actual doubleness like this in nature, for if the voices which we commonly hear were all that we ever heard, what then? Has it to do with the season of the year? I have since heard an echo on Moore's farm.[40]

It was the memorable event of the day, that echo I heard, not anything my companions said, or the travellers whom I met, or my thoughts, for they were all mere repetitions or echoes in the worst sense of what I had heard and thought before many times; but this echo was accompanied with novelty, and by its repetition of my voice it did more than double that. It was a profounder Socratic method[41] of suggesting thoughts unutterable to me the speaker. There was one I heartily loved to talk with. Under such favorable auspices I could converse with myself, could reflect; the hour, the atmosphere, and the conformation of the ground permitted it.

*March 5.* The secretary of the Association for the Advancement of Science[42] requests me, as he probably has thousands of others, by a printed circular letter from Washington the other day, to fill the blank against certain questions,[43] among which the most important one was what branch of science I was specially interested in, using the term science in the most comprehensive sense possible. Now, though I could state to a select few that department of human inquiry which engages me, and should be rejoiced at an opportunity to do so, I felt that it would be to make myself the laughing-stock of the scientific community to describe or attempt to describe to them that branch of science which specially interests me, inasmuch as they do not believe in a science which deals with the higher law. So I was obliged to speak to their condition and describe to them that poor part of me which alone they can understand. The fact is I am a mystic, a transcendentalist, and a natural philosopher to boot. Now I think of it, I should have told them at once that I was a transcendentalist. That would have been the shortest way of telling them that they would not understand my explanations.

How absurd that, though I probably stand as near to nature as any of them, and am by constitution as good an observer as most, yet a true account of my relation to nature should excite their ridicule only! If it had been the secretary of an association of which Plato or Aristotle was the president, I should not have hesitated to describe my studies at once and particularly.

*March 10.* This is the first really spring day. The sun is brightly reflected from all surfaces, and the north side of the street begins to be a little more passable to foot-travellers. You do not think it necessary to button up your coat.

*March 12.* It is essential that a man confine himself to pursuits—a scholar, for instance, to studies—which lie next to and conduce to his life, which do not go against the grain, either of his will or his imagination. The scholar finds in his experience some studies to be moist, fertile and radiant with light, others dry, barren, and dark. If he is wise, he will not persevere in the last, as a plant in a cellar will strive toward the light. He will confine the observations of his mind as closely as possible to the experience or life of his senses. His thought must live with and be inspired with the life of the body. The death-bed scenes and observations even of the best and wisest afford but a sorry picture of our humanity. Some men endeavor to live a constrained life, to subject their whole lives to their will, as he who said he would give a

44 Possible allusion to Pierre-François Lacenaire (1803–1836), a convicted murderer, who agreed to test consciousness after decapitation by closing one eye and leaving one eye open, or Antoine-Laurent de Lavoisier (1743–1794), French chemist and scientist, who said he would blink as many times as he could, and whose work on the circulation of blood Thoreau mentioned in *A Week on the Concord and Merrimack Rivers* [W 1:275].

45 Allusion to John 3:19: "And this is the condemnation, that light is come into the world, and men love darkness rather than the light, because their deeds were evil." In his journal of 15 September 1850 Thoreau used the same phrase regarding those who believed in bottomless ponds: "To name two ponds bottomless when both of them have a bottom! Verily men choose darkness rather than light" [J 2:68]. He mentioned the idea again when he wrote of people who would rather surmise the age of a tree than accept an accurate count of its rings [J 8:146], or who bowed to tradition: "It is the old error, which the church, the state, the school ever commit, choosing darkness rather than light, holding fast to the old and to tradition" [J 12:390].

46 Thoreau may have had in mind the curling stamens of the blue-curl plant (cf. 1853 note 113).

47 Possibly Julius Michael Smith (1823–1912), who was, among other occupations, a house painter, and whose general store was on Main Street in Concord.

48 Composition of beeswax, rosin, and tallow, used in binding up the cuts of newly grafted trees.

sign if he were conscious after his head was cut off, —but he gave no sign.[44] Dwell as near as possible to the channel in which your life flows. A man may associate with such companions, he may pursue such employments, as will darken the day for him. Men choose darkness rather than light.[45]

*March 18.* I no sooner step out of the house than I hear the bluebirds in the air, and far and near, everywhere except in the woods, throughout the town you may hear them, — the blue curls[46] of their warblings, —harbingers of serene and warm weather, little azure rills of melody trickling here and there from out the air, their short warble trilled in the air reminding me of so many corkscrews assaulting and thawing the torpid mass of winter, assisting the ice and snow to melt and the streams to flow.

*March 20.* Yesterday I forgot to say I painted my boat. Spanish brown and raw oil were the ingredients. I found the painter[47] had sold me the brown in hard lumps as big as peas, which I could not reduce with a stick; so I poured the whole when mixed through an old coffee-mill, which made a very good paint-mill, catching it in an old coffee-pot, whose holes I puttied up, there being a lack of vessels; and then I broke up the coffee-mill and nailed a part over the bows to protect them, the boat is made so flat. I had first filled the seams with some grafting-wax[48] I had, melted.

*March 21.* It is a genial and reassuring day; the mere warmth of the west wind amounts almost to balminess. The softness of the air mollifies our own dry and congealed substance. I sit down by a wall to see if I can muse again. We become, as it were, pliant and ductile again to strange but memorable influences; we are led a little way by our genius. We are affected like the earth, and yield to the elemental tenderness; winter breaks up within us; the frost is coming out of me, and I am heaved like the road; accumulated masses of ice and snow dissolve, and thoughts like a freshet pour down unwonted channels. A strain of music comes to solace the traveller over earth's downs and dignify his chagrins, the petty men whom he meets are the shadows of grander to come. Roads lead elsewhither than to Carlisle and Sudbury.[49] The earth is uninhabited but fair to inhabit, like the old Carlisle road.[50] Is then the road so rough that it should be neglected? Not only narrow but rough is the way that leadeth to life everlasting.[51] Our experience does not wear upon us. It is seen to be fabulous or symbolical, and the future is worth expecting. Encouraged, I set out once more to climb the mountains of the earth, for my steps are symbolical steps, and in all my walking I have not reached the top of the earth yet.

*March 22.* As soon as those spring mornings arrive in which the birds sing, I am sure to be an early riser. I am waked by my genius. I wake to inaudible melodies and am surprised to find myself expecting the dawn in so serene and joyful and expectant a mood.[52]

*March 23.* Man cannot afford to be a naturalist, to look at Nature directly, but only with the side of his eye. He must look through and beyond her. To look at her is fatal as to look at the head of Medusa.[53] It turns the man of science to stone. I feel that I am dissipated by so many observations. I should be the magnet in the midst of all this dust and filings. I knock the back of my hand against a rock, and as I smooth back the skin, I find myself prepared to study lichens there. I look upon man but as a fungus. I have almost a slight, dry headache as the result of all this observing. How to observe is how to behave. O for a little Lethe![54] To crown all, lichens, which are

**49** Towns bordering Concord on the north and southwest, respectively.
**50** Extending northward from Concord to Carlisle. Thoreau described it as "bordered on each side with wild apple pastures, where the trees stand without order, having, many if not most of them, sprung up by accident or from pomace sown at random, and are for the most part concealed by birches and pines. . . . It is a paradise for walkers in the fall" [J 5:239].
**51** Allusion to Matthew 7:14: "Because straight is the gate, and narrow is the way, which leadeth unto life, and few there be that find it."
**52** Cf. 2 September 1856, and *Walden:* "We must learn to reawaken and keep ourselves awake, not by mechanical aids, but by an infinite expectation of the dawn, which does not forsake us in our soundest sleep. I know of no more encouraging fact than the unquestionable ability of man to elevate his life by a conscious endeavor" [Wa 88].
**53** In Greek mythology, a Gorgon whose look could turn a person to stone.
**54** Symbol of forgetfulness: cf. 1851 note 41.

**55** Right belonging to a person by reason of citizenship.

**56** Allusion to Gilbert White's (1720–1793) *The Natural History of Selborne:* "Such forests . . . are of considerable service to neighbourhoods that verge upon them, by furnishing them with peat and turf for their firing; with fuel for the burning their lime; and with ashes for their grasses; and by maintaining their geese and their stock of young cattle at little or no expense."

**57** White's editor Edward Jesse (1780–1868) wrote: "This was the case when Mr. White wrote this passage; but alas, since then Parliamentary enactments have deprived the labourers of much of their rights of common, by enclosing them, and thus much of their means of subsistence, and consequently of their property, have disappeared. Whenever labour was slack, the common was always a reserve on which the labourer could employ himself, by cutting fuel, making brooms, &c."

**58** In the opening to "Resistance to Civil Government," Thoreau wrote: "I heartily accept the motto, 'That government is best which governs least;' and I should like to see it acted up to more rapidly and systematically. Carried out, it finally amounts to this, which also I believe,— 'That government is best which governs not at all;' and when men are prepared for it, that will be the kind of government which they will have" [W 4:356]. The phrase alludes to the motto found on the title page of the *United States Magazine, and Democratic Review.*

**59** Knot tied tight and fast.

**60** Cf. 25 July 1853.

**61** Maria Thoreau (1794–1881), whom Mabel Loomis Todd (1856–1932) remembered as "a sharp and brilliant soul, a great talker, with very decided opinions upon religion, politics, and the world in general."

**62** Thomas Chalmers (1780–1847), Scottish theologian. William Hanna's (1808–1882) four-volume *Memoirs of the Life and Writings of Thomas Chalmers* was published in 1850–1852 in New York by Harper and Brothers.

so thin, are described in the *dry* state, as they are most commonly, not most truly, seen. Truly, they are *dryly* described.

Without being the owner of any land, I find that I have a civil right[55] in the river,—that, if I am not a landowner I am a water-owner. It is fitting, therefore, that I should have a boat, a cart, for this my farm. Since it is almost wholly given up to a few of us, while the other highways are much travelled, no wonder that I improve it. Such a one as I will choose to dwell in a township where there are most ponds and rivers and our range is widest. In relation to the river, I find my natural rights least infringed on. It is an extensive "common" still left. Certain savage liberties still prevail in the oldest and most civilized countries. I am pleased to find that, in Gilbert White's day, at least, the laborers in that part of England enjoyed certain rights of common in the royal forests,[56]—so called, though no large wood,—where they cut their turf and other fuel, etc., etc., and obtained materials for broom-making, etc., when other labor failed. It is no longer so, according to his editor.[57] Nobody legislates for me, for the way would be not to legislate at all.[58]

*March 25.* I find that the shoemakers, to save a few iron heel-pegs, do not complete the rows on the inside by three or four,—the very place in the whole boot where they are most needed,—which has fatal consequences to the buyer. It is as if you were to put no under-pinning under one corner of your house. I have managed to cross very wet and miry places dry-shod by moving rapidly on my heels. I always use leather strings tied in a hard knot;[59] they untie but too easily even then.[60]

*March 28.* My Aunt Maria[61] asked me to read the life of Dr. Chalmers,[62] which however I did not promise to do.

Yesterday, Sunday, she was heard through the partition shouting to my Aunt Jane,[63] who is deaf, "Think of it! He stood half an hour to-day to hear the frogs croak, and he would n't read the life of Chalmers."

*April 3.* Nothing is more saddening than an ineffectual and proud intercourse with those of whom we expect sympathy and encouragement.[64] I repeatedly find myself drawn toward certain persons but to be disappointed.

*May 9.* I have devoted most of my day to Mr. Alcott.[65] He is broad and genial, but indefinite; some would say feeble; forever feeling about vainly in his speech and touching nothing. But this is a very negative account of him, for he thus suggests far more than the sharp and definite practical mind. The feelers of his thought diverge,—such is the breadth of their grasp,—not converge; and in his society almost alone I can express at my leisure, with more or less success, my vaguest but most cherished fancy or thought. There are never any obstacles in the way of our meeting. He has no creed. He is not pledged to any institution. The sanest man I ever knew; the fewest crotchets,[66] after all, has he.

It has occurred to me, while I am thinking with pleasure of our day's intercourse, "Why should I not think aloud to you?" Having each some shingles of thought well dried, we walk and whittle them, trying our knives, and admiring the clear yellowish grain of the pumpkin pine.[67] We wade so gently and reverently, or we pull together so smoothly, that the fishes of thought are not scared from the stream, but come and go grandly, like yonder clouds that float peacefully through the western sky. When we walk it seems as if the heavens—whose mother-o'-pearl and rainbow tints come and go, form and dissolve—and the earth had met together, and righteousness and peace had kissed each other.[68] I have

63 Jane Thoreau (1784–1864), whom Mabel Loomis Todd described as "a saintly character with a placid and lovable nature, most winning to a child."

64 Although Thoreau was with Channing the day before, this probably alludes to Emerson, who wrote in his journal in March 1853 that Thoreau "complained of Clough or somebody that he or they recited to every one at table the paragraph just read by him & by them in the last newspaper & studiously avoided every thing private. I should think he was complaining of one H.D.T."

65 The following paragraphs, with minor variants, form part of the "Former Inhabitants" chapter of *Walden*, which also contains this description of Alcott: "One of the last of the philosophers,—Connecticut gave him to the world,—he peddled first her wares, afterwards, as he declares, his brains. These he peddles still, prompting God and disgracing man, bearing for fruit his brain only, like the nut its kernel. I think that he must be the man of the most faith of any alive. His words and attitude always suppose a better state of things than other men are acquainted with, and he will be the last man to be disappointed as the ages revolve. . . . A true friend of man; almost the only friend of human progress. . . . With his hospitable intellect he embraces children, beggars, insane, and scholars, and entertains the thought of all, adding to it commonly some breadth and elegance. I think that he should keep a caravansary on the world's highway, where philosophers of all nations might put up, and on his sign should be printed, 'Entertainment for man, but not for his beast. Enter ye that have leisure and a quiet mind, who earnestly seek the right road'" [Wa 259–260].

66 Eccentric, highly individual opinions or preferences.

67 First-growth white pines have a yellowish color to their wood. George B. Emerson (1797–1881) wrote in *A Report on the Trees and Shrubs Growing Naturally in the Forests of Massachusetts* (1846): "The white pines receive different names, according to their mode of growth and the ap-

pearance of the wood. When growing densely in deep and damp old forests, with only a few branches near the top, the slowly-grown wood is perfectly clear and soft, destitute of resin, and almost without sap-wood, and has a yellowish color, like the flesh of a pumpkin. It is then called pumpkin pine. . . . [The name is] little used except in Maine, and by persons who import wood from that State." Thoreau also called such trees yellow pine.

**68** Allusion to Psalms 85:10: "Mercy and truth are met together; righteousness and peace have kissed each other."

**69** Satan, as referred to in Milton's *Paradise Lost* 1:81–82: "th' Arch-Enemy, / And thence in Heav'n call'd Satan."

**70** Symbol of faith and humility, from the Hebrew high priests who wore a long blue robe that was visible below the ephod. In Numbers 15:38 God commanded: "Speak unto the children of Israel, and bid them that they make them fringes in the borders of their garments throughout their generations, and that they put upon the fringe of the borders a ribband of blue." In *Walden* Thoreau also referred to Alcott as a "blue-robed man, whose fittest roof is the overarching sky which reflects his serenity" [Wa 260].

**71** Perennial herb (*Silene caroliniana*) with pink or white flowers, opposite leaves, and glandular, hairy flower clusters, which Thoreau described as "certainly one of the finest of our flowers" [J 6:317].

**72** A large table knife, often kept in a case or sheath.

**73** The final two lines of this paragraph appeared with minor variants in "Life Without Principle" [W 4:469].

**74** Cf. 9 November 1851.

an ally against the arch-enemy.[69] A blue-robed man[70] dwells under the blue concave. The blue sky is a distant reflection of the azure serenity that looks out from under a human brow. We walk together like the most innocent children, going after wild pinks[71] with case-knives.[72] Most with whom I endeavor to talk soon fetch up against some institution or particular way of viewing things, theirs not being a universal view. They will continually bring their own roofs or—what is not much better—their own narrow skylights between us and the sky, when it is the unobstructed heavens I would view.[73]

*May 10.* He is the richest who has most use for nature as raw material of tropes and symbols with which to describe his life. If these gates of golden willows affect me, they correspond to the beauty and promise of some experience on which I am entering. If I am overflowing with life, am rich in experience for which I lack expression, then nature will be my language full of poetry,—all nature will *fable,* and every natural phenomenon be a myth. The man of science, who is not seeking for expression but for a fact to be expressed merely, studies nature as a dead language. I pray for such inward experience as will make nature significant.[74]

*May 11.* I hear the distant drumming of a partridge. Its beat, however distant and low, falls still with a remarkably forcible, almost painful, impulse on the ear, like veritable little drumsticks on our tympanum, as if it were a throbbing or fluttering in our veins or brows or the chambers of the ears, and belonging to ourselves,—as if it were produced by some little insect which had made its way into the passages of the ear, so penetrating is it. It is as palpable to the ear as the sharpest note of a fife. Of course, that bird can drum with its wings on a log which can go off with such a powerful whir, beating the air. I have seen a thoroughly frightened hen and cockerel fly almost as powerfully, but neither can sustain it long. Beginning slowly and deliberately, the partridge's beat sounds faster and faster from far away under the boughs and through the aisles of the wood until it becomes a regular roll, but is speedily concluded. How many things shall we not see and be and do, when we walk there where the partridge drums!

*May 15.* I love to sit in the wind on this hill[75] and be blown on. We bathe thus first in the air; then, when the air has warmed it, in water.

*May 17.* He who cuts down woods beyond a certain limit exterminates birds.

The fragrance of the apple blossom reminds me of a pure and innocent and unsophisticated country girl bedecked for church.

*May 24.* Talked, or tried to talk, with Emerson. Lost my time—nay, almost my identity. He, assuming a false opposition where there was no difference of opinion, talked to the wind—told me what I knew—and I lost my time trying to imagine myself somebody else to oppose him.[76]

*May 25.* Two young men who borrowed my boat the other day returned from the riverside through Channing's yard,[77] quietly. It was almost the only way for them. But, as they passed out his gate, Channing boorishly walked out his house behind them in his shirt-sleeves, and shut his gate again behind them as if to shut them out. It was just that sort of behavior which, if he had met with it in Italy or France, he would have complained of, whose meanness he would have condemned.

**75** Annursnack Hill, on the west side of Concord.
**76** Emerson wrote similarly of Thoreau in his journal ca. 24 May 1853: "He seemed stubborn and implacable; always manly and wise, but rarely sweet. One would say that, as Webster could never speak without an antagonist, so Henry does not feel himself except in opposition. He wants a fallacy to expose, a blunder to pillory, requires a little sense of victory, a roll of the drums, to call his powers into full exercise."
**77** Channing lived on Main Street, across from the Thoreau family's Yellow house.

**78** Pink azalea (*Rhododendron periclymenoides*).

**79** Allusion to Hamlet: cf. 1851 note 190.

**80** Although Thoreau referred to finding the pincushion or crimson-tinged gall on the white oak, the pincushion gall is not an oak gall. It is likely that Thoreau confused the pincushion gall with the hedgehog gall, which does occur on the white oak and has a similar dark red or crimson appearance.

**81** Thoreau may have meant the pearl as "the hardened tear of a diseased clam," as he defined it on 10 August 1857, or the teardrop shape of certain pearls.

**82** Allusion to Isaiah 1:18: "Come now, and let us reason together, saith the Lord: though your sins be as scarlet, they shall be as white as snow; though they be red like crimson, they shall be as wool."

*May 31.* Some incidents in my life have seemed far more allegorical than actual; they were so significant that they plainly served no other use. That is, I have been more impressed by their allegorical significance and fitness; they have been like myths or passages in a myth, rather than mere incidents or history which have to wait to become significant. Quite in harmony with my subjective philosophy. This, for instance: that, when I thought I knew the flowers so well, the beautiful purple azalea or pinxter-flower[78] should be shown me by the hunter who found it. Such facts are lifted quite above the level of the actual. They are all just such events as my imagination prepares me for, no matter how incredible. Perfectly in keeping with my life and characteristic. Ever and anon something will occur which my philosophy has not dreamed of.[79] The limits of the actual are set some thoughts further off. That which had seemed a rigid wall of vast thickness unexpectedly proves a thin and undulating drapery. The boundaries of the actual are no more fixed and rigid than the elasticity of our imaginations. The fact that a rare and beautiful flower which we never saw, perhaps never heard of, for which therefore there was no place in our thoughts, may at length be found in our immediate neighborhood, is very suggestive.

*June 1.* The pincushion galls[80] on young white oaks are now among the most beautiful objects in the woods, coarse wooly white to appearance, spotted with bright red or crimson on the exposed side. It is remarkable that a mere gall, which at first we are inclined to regard as something abnormal, should be made so beautiful, as if it were the *flower* of the tree; that a disease, an excrescence, should prove, perchance, the greatest beauty,—as the tear of the pearl.[81] Beautiful scarlet sins[82] they may be. Through our temptations,—aye, and our falls,—our virtues appear. As in many a character,—many a poet,—

we see that beauty exhibited in a gall, which was meant to have bloomed in a flower, unchecked. Such, however, is the accomplishment of the world. The poet cherishes his chagrins and sets his sighs to music. This gall is the tree's "Ode to Dejection."[83] How oft it chances that the apparent fruit of a shrub, its apple, is merely a gall or blight! How many men meeting with some blast in the moist growing days of their youth, and what should have been a sweet and palatable fruit in them becomes a mere puff and excrescence, ripening no kernel, and they say that they have experienced religion! For the hardening of the seed is the crisis. Their fruit is a gall, a puff, an excrescence, for want of moderation and continence. So many plants never ripen their fruit.

*June 14.* Channing says he saw a "lurker" yesterday in the woods on the Marlboro road.[84] He heard a distressing noise like a man sneezing but long continued, but at length found it was a man wheezing. He was oldish and grizzled, the stumps of his grizzled beard about an inch long, and his clothes in the worst possible condition,—a wretched-looking creature, an escaped convict hiding in the woods, perhaps. He appeared holding on to his paunch, and wheezing as if it would kill him. He appeared to have come straight through the swamp, and—what was most interesting about him, and proved him to be a lurker of the first class,—one of our party, as Channing said,—he kept straight through a field of rye which was fully grown, not regarding it in the least; and, though Channing tried to conceal himself on the edge of the rye, fearing to hurt his feelings if the man should mistake him for the proprietor, yet they met, and the lurker, giving him a short bow, disappeared in the woods on the opposite side of the road. He went through everything.

83 Allusion to Samuel Taylor Coleridge's (1772–1834) "Ode to Dejection." As Thoreau added (ca. 1853–1854) to the not-yet-published *Walden:* "I do not propose to write an ode to dejection, but to brag as lustily as chanticleer in the morning, standing on his roost, if only to wake my neighbors up" [Wa 81]. Coleridge was a major influence on the Transcendentalists through such philosophical works as *The Friend* (1810) and *Aids to Reflection* (1825).

84 Having been recently reading *London Labour and the London Poor*, Thoreau may have had in mind Henry Mayhew's (1812–1887) differentiation between a beggar and a lurker: "a lurker being strictly one who loiters about for some dishonest purpose. Many modes of thieving as well as begging are termed 'lurking.' . . . The term 'lurk,' however, is mostly applied to the several modes of plundering by representations of sham distress."

85 In *Walden* Thoreau called such self-styled reformers "the greatest bores of all" [Wa 148].
86 Rev. Andrew T. Foss (1803–1875).
87 Loring Moody (ca. 1814–1883), author of *Facts for the People; Showing the Relations of the United States Government to Slavery, Embracing a History of the Mexican War, Its Origin and Objects* (1847).
88 Rev. H. C. Wright (1797–1870), author of *A Kiss for a Blow; or, A Collection of Stories for Children; Showing Them How to Prevent Quarrelling* (1842).
89 Jonah 1:17, in the Old Testament, records how Jonah was swallowed by a whale, or "a great fish": "Now the LORD had prepared a great fish to swallow up Jonah. And Jonah was in the belly of the fish three days and three nights."
90 Cf. 1851 note 172.

*June 17.* Here have been three ultra-reformers,[85] lecturers on Slavery, Temperance, the Church, etc., in and about our house and Mrs. Brooks's the last three or four days, — A. D. Foss,[86] once a Baptist minister in Hopkinton, N.H.; Loring Moody,[87] a sort of travelling pattern-working chaplain; and H. C. Wright,[88] who shocks all the old women with his infidel writings. Though Foss was a stranger to the others, you would have thought them old and familiar cronies. (They happened here together by accident.) They addressed each other constantly by their Christian names, and rubbed you continually with the greasy cheeks of their kindness. They would not keep their distance, but cuddle up and lie spoon-fashion with you, no matter how hot the weather nor how narrow the bed, — wholly Wright. I was awfully pestered with his benignity; feared I should get greased all over with it past restoration; tried to keep some starch in my clothes. He wrote a book called "A Kiss for a Blow," and he behaved as if there was no alternative between these, or as if I had given him a blow. I would have preferred the blow, but he was bent on giving me a kiss, when there was no quarrel and no agreement between us. I wanted that he should straighten his back, smooth out those ogling wrinkles of benignity about his eyes, and, with a healthy reserve, pronounce something in a downright manner. It was difficult to keep clear of his slimy benignity, with which he sought to cover you before he swallowed you and took you fairly into his bowels. It would have been far worse than the fate of Jonah.[89] I do not wish to get any nearer to a man's bowels[90] than usual. They lick you as a cow her calf. They would fain wrap you about with their bowels. Wright addressed me as "Henry" within one minute from the time I first laid eyes on him, and when I spoke, he said with drawling, sultry sympathy, "Henry, I know all you would say; I understand you perfectly; you need not explain anything to me;" and to an-

other, "I am going to dive into Henry's inmost depths."
I said "I trust you will not strike your head against the
bottom." He could tell in a dark room, with his eyes
blinded and in perfect stillness, if there was one there
whom he loved. One of the most attractive things about
the flowers is their beautiful reserve. The truly beautiful
and noble puts its lover, as it were, at an infinite distance,
while it attracts him more strongly than ever. I do not
like the men who come so near me with their bowels.
It is the most disagreeable kind of snare to be caught in.
Men's bowels are far more slimy than their brains. They
must be ascetics indeed who approach you from this
side. What a relief to have heard the ring of one healthy
reserved tone! With such a forgiving disposition, as if he
were all the while forgiving you for existing. Considering
our condition or *habit* of soul,—may be corpulent and
asthmatic,—maybe dying of atrophy, with all our bones
sticking out,—is it kindness to embrace a man? They
lay their sweaty hand on your shoulder, or your knee, to
magnetize you.

*June 20.* Saw a little skunk coming up the river-bank in
the woods at the White Oak,[91] a funny little fellow, about
six inches long and nearly as broad. It faced me and actually compelled me to retreat before it for five minutes.
Perhaps I was between it and its hole. Its broad black tail,
tipped with white, was erect like a kitten's. It had what
looked like a broad white band drawn tight across its
forehead or top-head, from which two lines of white ran
down, one on each side of its back, and there was a narrow white line down its snout. It raised its back, sometimes ran a few feet forward, sometimes backward, and
repeatedly turned its tail to me, prepared to discharge its
fluid like the old. Such was its instinct. And all the while
it kept up a fine grunting like a little pig or a squirrel. It
reminded me that the red squirrel, the woodchuck, and

**91**  Swamp white oak on Henry L. Shattuck's land.

**92** A dungeon, reportedly 14 by 18 feet, in which British soldiers were imprisoned after Indian troops captured Fort William in 1756. According to the account told by one survivor, John Zephaniah Holwell (1711–1798), in *A Genuine Narrative of the Deplorable Deaths of the English Gentlemen and Others Who Were Suffocated in the Black Hole,* 123 of the 146 prisoners died overnight.

**93** Allusion to 2 Kings 5:12: "Are not Abana and Pharpar, rivers of Damascus, better than all the waters of Israel? may I not wash in them, and be clean?"

**94** Reference to the rivers Scamander and Simois on the plain of Troy, which would be rivers of discord.

the skunk all make a similar sound. Now there are young rabbits, skunks, and probably woodchucks.

*June 22.* I do not remember a warmer night than the last. In my attic under the roof, with all windows and doors open, there was still not a puff of the usual coolness of the night. It seemed as if heat which the roof had absorbed during the day was being reflected down upon me. It was far more intolerable than by day. All windows being open, I heard the sounds made by pigs and horses in the neighborhood and of children who were partially suffocated with the heat. It seemed as if it would be something to tell of, the experience of that night, as of the Black Hole of Calcutta[92] in a degree, if one survived it.

The sun down, and I am crossing Fair Haven Hill, sky overcast, landscape dark and still. I see the smooth river in the north reflecting two shades of light, one from the water, another from the surface of the pads which broadly border it on both sides, and the very irregular waving or winding edge of the pads, especially perceptible in this light, makes a very agreeable border to distinguish,—the edge of the film which seeks to bridge over and inclose the river wholly. These pads are to the smooth water between like a calyx to its flower. The river at such an hour, seen half a mile away, perfectly smooth and lighter than the sky, reflecting the clouds, is a paradisaical scene. What are the rivers around Damascus[93] to this river sleeping around Concord? Are not the Musketaquid and the Assabet, rivers of Concord, fairer than the rivers of the plain?[94]

And then the rich warble of the blackbird may still occasionally even at this season be heard. As I come over the hill, I hear the wood thrush singing his evening lay. This is the only bird whose note affects me like music, affects the flow and tenor of my thought, my fancy and imagination. It lifts and exhilarates me. It is inspiring. It is a medicative draught to my soul. It is an elixir to my eyes and a fountain of youth to all my senses. It changes all hours to an eternal morning. It banishes all trivialness. It reinstates me in my dominion, makes me the lord of creation, is chief musician of my court. This minstrel sings in a time, a heroic age, with which no event in the village can be contemporary. How can they be contemporary when only the latter is *temporary* at all? How can the infinite and eternal be contemporary with the finite and temporal? So there is something in the music of the cow-bell, something sweeter and more nutritious, than in the milk which the farmers drink. This thrush's song is a *ranz des vaches* [95] to me. I long for wildness, a nature which I cannot put my foot through, woods where the wood thrush forever sings, where the hours are early morning ones, and there is dew on the grass, and the day is forever unproved, where I might have a fertile unknown for a soil about me. I would go after the cows, I would watch the flocks of Admetus there forever, only for my board and clothes. A New Hampshire everlasting and unfallen.

*July 1.* I am surveying the Bedford road these days, [96] and have no time for my Journal.

*July 21.* Went, in pursuit of boys who had stolen my boat-seat, to Fair Haven.

Nature is beautiful only as a place where a life is to be lived. It is not beautiful to him who has not resolved on a beautiful life.

*July 25.* I have for years had a great deal of trouble with my shoe-strings, because they get untied continually.

95 Swiss pastoral song for calling cows, with a probable reference specifically to Friedrich von Schiller's (1759–1805) "Ranz des Vaches" from *Wilhelm Tell* (1804), as found in Charles Timothy Brooks's (1813–1883) *Songs and Ballads: Translated from Uhland, Korner, and Other German Lyric Poets* (Boston: James Munroe, 1842), published as volume 14 of George Ripley's *Specimens of Foreign Standard Literature.*
96 Thoreau was surveying for the new road between Concord and Bedford to replace what became known as Old Bedford Road.

**97** Probably Channing.
**98** In 1851: cf. 1851 note 166.

They are leather, rolled and tied in a hard knot. But some days I could hardly go twenty rods before I was obliged to stop and stoop to tie my shoes. My companion[97] and I speculated on the distance to which one tying would carry you,—the length of a shoe-tie,—and we thought it nearly as appreciable and certainly a more simple and natural measure of distance than a stadium, or league, or mile. Ever and anon we raised our feet on to whatever fence or wall or rock or stump we chanced to be passing, and drew the strings once more, pulling as hard as we could. It was very vexatious, when passing through low scrubby bushes, to become conscious that the strings were already getting loose again before we had fairly started. What should we have done if pursued by a tribe of Indians? My companion sometimes went without strings altogether, but that loose way of proceeding was not to be thought of by me. One shoemaker sold us shoe-strings made of the hide of a South American jackass, which he recommended; or rather he gave them to us and added their price to that of the shoes we bought of him. But I could not see that these were any better than the old. I wondered if anybody had exhibited a better article at the World's Fair,[98] and whether England did not bear the palm from America in this respect. I thought of strings with recurved prickles and various other remedies myself. At last the other day it occurred to me that I would try an experiment, and, instead of tying two simple knots one over the other the same way, putting the end which fell to the right over each time, that I would reverse the process, and put it under the other. Greatly to my satisfaction, the experiment was perfectly successful, and from that time my shoe-strings have given me no trouble, except sometimes in untying them at night.

On telling this to others I learned that I had been all the while tying what is called a granny's knot, for I had never been taught to tie any other, as sailors' children are; but now I had blundered into a square knot, I think they called it, or two running slip-nooses. Should not all children be taught this accomplishment, and an hour, perchance, of their childhood be devoted to instruction in tying knots?

*August 7.* When, yesterday, a boy spilled his huckleberries in the pasture,[99] I saw that Nature was making use of him to disperse her berries, and I might have advised him to pick another dishful.

Is it not as language that all natural objects affect the poet? He sees a flower or other object, and it is beautiful or affecting to him because it is a symbol of his thought, and what he indistinctly feels or perceives is matured in some other organization. The objects I behold correspond to my mood.[100]

I was struck by the perfect neatness, as well as elaborateness and delicacy, of a lady's dress the other day. She wore some worked lace or gauze over her bosom, and I thought it was beautiful, if it indicated an equal inward purity and delicacy,—if it was the soul she dressed and treated thus delicately.

Here is the barber[101] sailing up the still, dark, cloud-reflecting river in the long boat which he built so elaborately himself, with two large sails set. He is quite alone thus far from town, and so quiet and so sensibly employed,—bound to Fair Haven Bay, instead of meeting comrades in a shop on the Mill-Dam or sleeping away his Sabbath in a chamber,—that I think of him as having experienced religion. I know so much good of him, at least, that one dark, still Sunday he sailed alone from the village to Fair Haven Bay. What chance was there to serve

**99** In his *Autobiography* Moncure Conway told of Thoreau's "huckleberrying parties. These were under the guidance of Thoreau, because he alone knew the precise locality of every variety of the berry. I recall an occasion when little Edward Emerson, carrying a basket of fine huckleberries, had a fall and spilt them all. But Thoreau came, put his arm around the troubled child, and explained to him that if the crop of huckleberries was to continue it was necessary that some should be scattered. Nature had provided that little boys should now and then stumble and sow the berries. We shall have a grand lot of bushes and berries in this spot, and we shall owe them to you. Edward began to smile."

**100** This echoes in part Emerson's *Nature:* "Every natural fact is a symbol of some spiritual fact. Every appearance in nature corresponds to some state of the mind, and that state of the mind can only be described by presenting that natural appearance as its picture."

**101** Unidentified.

**102** Emerson wrote in his Divinity School Address: "It is already beginning to indicate character and religion to withdraw from the religious meetings. I have heard a devout person, who prized the Sabbath, say in bitterness of heart, 'On Sundays, it seems wicked to go to church.'"

**103** According to Alcott's journal and correspondence, he spent 7 August with Emerson, not the following day, as Thoreau's journal implies.

**104** Term commonly used for dear meat but, as here, any wild game meat.

**105** In his journal Alcott wrote that he and Emerson walked to Walden "with discussions—not usual—on ways and means, the largest concernment being given to a purposed conversational tour for me along the great Canal towns, west: Syracuse, Rochester, Buffalo. . . . This jaunt to be undertaken some time during the current autumn, and to be so managed as to defray its expenses and more, if the same can be made feasible and continue to seem desirable to me." To help with this enterprise, Emerson pledged Alcott's ticket to Cincinnati.

**106** Cutting grain with a cradle scythe, a light scythe with a wood frame (cradle), which allowed the harvester, with a slight movement, to throw the grain into a swath.

**107** Probably the American Anti-Slavery Society, founded in 1833 by William Lloyd Garrison and Arthur Tappan (1786–1865), and preceded by the New England Anti-Slavery Society, which itself was preceded by what Alcott called the Preliminary Anti-Slavery Society, which he helped found in 1830.

**108** Reference to Alcott's height of six feet; the average height for a male in the 1850s was five and a half feet.

**109** Wendell Phillips (1811–1884), abolitionist and lecturer, of whom Thoreau wrote: "We would fain express our appreciation of the freedom and steady wisdom, so rare in the reformer, with which he declared that he was not born to abolish slavery, but to do right. . . . It is so rare and encouraging to listen to an orator . . . who is at the

the devil by that excursion? If he had had a companion I should have had some doubts,—but being alone, it seemed communion day with him.[102]

*August 10.* Alcott spent the day with me yesterday. He spent the day before with Emerson.[103] He observed that he had got his wine and now he had come after his venison.[104] Such was the compliment he paid me. The question of a livelihood was troubling him. He knew of nothing which he could do for which men would pay him.[105] He could not compete with the Irish in cradling grain.[106] His early education had not fitted him for a clerkship. He had offered his services to the Abolition Society,[107] to go about the country and speak for freedom as their agent, but they declined him. This is very much to their discredit; they should have been forward to secure him. Such a connection with him would confer unexpected dignity on their enterprise. But they cannot tolerate a man who stands by a head above them.[108] They are as bad—Garrison and Phillips,[109] etc.—as the overseers and faculty of Harvard College. They require a man who will train well *under* them. Consequently they have not in their employ any but small men,—trainers.[110]

*August 11.* Found Conant[111] rather garrulous (his breath smelled of rum). He was complaining that his sons did not get married (thirty-odd years ago), how his wife bore him eight children and then died, and in what respect she proved herself a true woman, etc., etc. I saw that it was as impossible to speak of marriage to such a man—to the mass of men—as of poetry. Its advantages and disadvantages are not such as they have dreamed of. Their marriage is prose or worse. To be married at least should be the one poetical act of a man's life. If you fail in this respect, in what respect will you succeed? The marriage which the mass of men comprehend is but little better than the marriage of the beasts. It would be just as fit for such a man to discourse to you on the love of flowers, thinking of them as hay for his oxen.

The difference between men affects every phase of their lives, so that at last they cannot communicate with each other. An old man of average worth, who spoke with the downrightness and frankness of age, not exaggerating aught, said he was troubled about his water, etc.,—altogether of the earth.

Evening draws on while I am gathering bundles of pennyroyal on the further Conantum height. I find it amid the stubble[112] mixed with blue-curls[113] and, as fast as I get my hand full, tie it into a fragrant bundle. Evening draws on, smoothing the waters and lengthening the shadows, now half an hour or more before sundown. What constitutes the charm of this hour of the day? Is it the condensing of dews in the air just beginning, or the grateful increase of shadows in the landscape? Some fiat has gone forth and stilled the ripples of the lake; each sound and sight has acquired ineffable beauty. How agreeable, when the sun shines at this angle, to stand on one side and look down on flourishing sprout-lands or copses, where the cool shade is mingled in greater proportion than before with the light! Broad, shallow lakes of shadow stretch over the lower portions of the top of the woods. A thousand little cavities are filling with coolness. Hills and the least inequalities in the ground begin to cast an obvious shadow. The shadow of an elm stretches quite across the meadow. I see pigeons (?) in numbers fly up from the stubble. I hear some young bluebird's plaintive warble near me and some young hawks uttering a puling[114] scream from time to time across the pond, to whom life is yet so novel. From far over the pond and woods I hear also a farmer calling loudly to his cows, in the clear still air, "Ker, ker, ker, ker."

What shall we name this season?—this very late after-

same time an eloquent speaker and a righteous man" [W 4:313–314].

**110** Members of a "train band" training for service in the militia.

**111** Ebenezer Conant (ca. 1778–1868), Concord farmer and owner of the large tract of land west of the Sudbury River that Thoreau named Conantum. On 31 August 1856 Thoreau wrote: "I am frequently amused when I come across the proprietor in my walks, and he asks me if I am not lost. I commonly approach his territory by the river, or some other back way, and rarely meet with him. The other day Conant observed to me, 'Well, you have to come out once in a while to take a survey.' He thinks that I do not visit his neighborhood more than once in a year, but I go there about once a week, and formerly much oftener; perhaps as often as he" [J 9:48–49].

**112** Stumps, or parts of stalk, left in a field after harvesting.

**113** Any of several North American plants (genus *Trichostema*) in the mint family, having clusters of blue or purple flowers with long curved or curled stamens.

**114** Weak or soft.

115 Allusion to William Collins's (1721–1759) "Ode to Evening" (l. 2).
116 Quoted from Collins's "Ode to Evening" (ll. 39–40): "Thy dewey fingers draw / The gradual dusky veil."
117 Quoted from Gray's "Elegy Written in a Country Churchyard" (l. 3).
118 Allusion to Gray's "Elegy Written in a Country Churchyard" (l. 9): "The moping owl does to the moon complain"; and (l. 7), "the beetle wheels his droning flight."
119 *Scientific American* (27 August 1853) reported: "During the three days previous to the 12th inst., the solar heat was so great in our city that no less than two hundred persons died from its effect."

noon, or very early evening, this serene and placid season of the day, most favorable for reflection, after the insufferable heats and the bustle of the day are over and before the dampness and twilight of evening! The serene hour, the Muses' hour, the season of reflection! It is commonly desecrated by being made tea-time. It begins perhaps with the very earliest condensation of moisture in the air, when the shadows of hills are first observed, and the breeze begins to go down, and birds begin again to sign. The pensive season. It is earlier than the "chaste Eve" of the poet.[115] Bats have not come forth. It is not twilight. There is no dew yet on the grass, and still less any early star in the heavens. It is the turning-point between afternoon and evening. The few sounds now heard, far or near, are delicious. It is not more dusky and obscure, but clearer than before. The clearing of the air by condensation of mists more than balances the increase of shadows. Chaste eve is merely *preparing* with "dewy fingers" to draw o'er all "the gradual dusky veil."[116] Not yet "the ploughman homeward plods his weary way,"[117] nor owls nor beetles are abroad.[118] It is a season somewhat earlier than is celebrated by the poets. There is not such a sense of lateness and approaching night as they describe. I mean when the first emissaries of Evening come to smooth the lakes and streams. The poet arouses himself and collects his thoughts. He postpones tea indefinitely. Thought has taken his siesta. Each sound has a broad and deep relief of silence.

*August 19.* Cooler weather. Last Sunday we were sweltering here and one hundred died of the heat in New York;[119] to-day they have fires in this village. After more rain, with wind in the night, it is now clearing up cool. There is a broad, clear crescent of blue in the west, slowly increasing, and an agreeable autumnal coolness, both under the high, withdrawn clouds and the edges of the woods, and a considerable wind wafts us along with our one sail and two umbrellas, sitting in thick coats.[120] I was going to sit and write or mope all day in the house, but it seems wise to cultivate animal spirits, to embark in enterprises which employ and recreate the whole body. Let the divine spirits like the huntsman with his bugle accompany the animal spirit that would fain range the forest and meadow. Even the gods and goddesses, Apollo and Diana, are found in the field, though they are superior to the dog and the deer.

It is a glorious and ever-memorable day. We observe attentively the first beautiful days in the spring, but not so much in the autumn. We might expect that the first fair days after so much rain would be remarkable. It is a day affecting the spirits of men, but there is nobody to enjoy it but ourselves. What do the laborer ox and the laborer man care for the beautiful days? Will the haymaker when he comes home to-night know that this has been such a beautiful day? This day itself has been the great phenomenon, but will it be reported in any journal, as the storm is, and the heat? It is like a great and beautiful flower unnamed. I see a man trimming willows on the Sudbury causeway[121] and others raking hay out of the water in the midst of all this clarity and brightness, but are they aware of the splendor of this day? The mass of mankind, who live in houses or shops, or are *bent* upon their labor out of doors, know nothing of the beautiful days which are passing above and around them. Is not such a day worthy of a hymn? It is such a day as mankind might spend in praising and glorifying nature. It might be spent as a natural sabbath, if only all men would accept the hint, devoted to unwordly thoughts. The first bright day of the fall, the earth reflector. The

120 Thoreau was on a river excursion to Sudbury with Channing.
121 Road (now River Road) that runs along the west side of the Sudbury River.

122 Dog-days: hottest days of summer, from the first week of July to the second week of August, so named for Sirius, the Dog Star, which rises with the sun at that time of year.

123 Thoreau had been reading Charles Pickering's (1805–1878) *The Races of Man; and Their Geographical Distribution*, noting that missionaries in the Hawaiian Islands, according to Pickering, "regarded as one main obstacle to improvement the extremely limited views of the natives in respect to style of living; 'a little fish and a little poi, and they were content'" [J 5:410].

dog-day[122] mists are gone; the washed earth shines; the cooler air braces man. No summer day is so beautiful as the fairest spring and fall days.

*August 23.* I am again struck by the perfect correspondence of a day—say an August day—and the year. I think that a perfect parallel may be drawn between the seasons of the day and of the year. Perhaps after middle age man ceases to be interested in the morning and in the spring.

Live in each season as it passes; breathe the air, drink the drink, taste the fruit, and resign yourself to the influences of each.

*September 1.* The savage lives simply through ignorance and idleness and laziness, but the philosopher lives simply through wisdom.[123] In the case of the savage, the accompaniment of simplicity is idleness with its attendant vices, but in the case of the philosopher, it is the highest employment and development. The fact for the savage, and for the mass of mankind, is that it is better to plant, weave, and build than do nothing or worse; but the fact for the philosopher, or a nation loving wisdom, is that it is most important to cultivate the highest faculties and spend as little time as possible in planting, weaving, building, etc. It depends upon the height of your standard, and no doubt through manual labor as a police men are educated up to a certain level. The simple style is bad for the savage because he does worse than to obtain the luxuries of life; it is good for the philosopher because he does better than to work for them. The question is whether you can bear freedom. At present the vast majority of men, whether black or white, require the discipline of labor which enslaves them for their good. If the Irishman did not shovel all day, he would get drunk and quarrel. But the philosopher does not require the same discipline; if he shovelled all day, we should receive no elevating suggestions from him.

There are two kinds of simplicity,—one that is akin to foolishness, the other to wisdom. The philosopher's style of living is only outwardly simple, but inwardly complex.[124] The savage's style is both outwardly and inwardly simple. A simpleton can perform many mechanical labors, but is not capable of profound thought. It was their limited view, not in respect to *style*, but to the *object* of living. A man who has equally limited views with respect to the end of living will not be helped by the most complex and refined style of living. It is not the tub that makes Diogenes, the Jove-born,[125] but Diogenes the tub.[126]

*September 3.* Now is the season for those comparatively rare but beautiful wild berries which are not food for man. If we so industriously collect those berries which are sweet to the palate, it is strange that we do not devote an hour in the year to gathering those which are beautiful to the eye. It behooves me to go a-berrying in this sense once a year at least.[127]

*September 12.* It occurred to me when I awoke this morning, feeling regret for intemperance of the day before in eating fruit,[128] which had dulled my sensibilities, that man was to be treated as a musical instrument, and if any viol was to be made of sound timber and kept well tuned always, it was he, so that when the bow of events is drawn across him he may vibrate and resound in perfect harmony. A sensitive soul will be continually trying its strings to see if they are in tune. A man's body must be rasped down exactly to a shaving. It is of far more importance than the wood of a Cremona violin.[129]

124 In a letter to H. G. O. Blake dated 27 March 1848, Thoreau explained his theory of simplicity: "I do believe in simplicity. It is astonishing as well as sad, how many trivial affairs even the wisest man thinks he must attend to in a day; how singular an affair he thinks he must omit. When the mathematician would solve a difficult problem, he first frees the equation of all incumbrances, and reduces it to its simplest terms. So simplify the problem of life, distinguish the necessary and the real. Probe the earth to see where your main roots run" [C 215].

125 The title *diogenes* in Greek means "sprung from Zeus" or, in the case of kings and princes, ordained and upheld by Zeus. Jove is the Roman counterpart of Zeus.

126 According to Lemprière, Diogenes was "a celebrated cynic philosopher" who "walked about the streets with a tub on his head, which served him as a house and a place of repose. Such singularity, joined to the greatest contempt for riches, soon gained him a reputation; and Alexander the Great condescended to visit the philosopher in his tub."

127 Thoreau was referring to the "fruit of the various species of cornels and viburnums, poke, arum, medeola, thorns, etc." [J 5:417].

128 On the previous day Thoreau had come across checkerberries "full grown, but green" [J 5:423].

129 Cremona, in northern Italy, was known for the manufacture of fine violins in the 16th through 18th centuries, particularly those of Antonio Stradivari (ca. 1644–1737) and the Amati family.

**130** Michael Flannery (1800–1900). Sanborn described Flannery as an "industrious Irishman from Kerry . . . who took the prize at the cattle show, and had it taken away from him by his employer, another Concord farmer; which so incensed Thoreau that he collected the sum among his neighbors and paid it to Mike, whom Thoreau ever afterward befriended." The Concord farmer was Abiel Wheeler: cf. 26 March 1857.

**131** Possible allusion to Genesis 19, in which the Lord promises to save Sodom if Abraham can find ten righteous people.

**132** John Goodwin (1803–1860), who was described by Horace Hosmer as "a stout, square built man of medium height, a hunter, trapper, day laborer &c. he had double teeth all round and when moderately full of rum, would take a cracker, and a glass tumbler (such as was used in bar rooms) and take a bite alternately from each." He lived at the intersection of Corner Road and the Back Road.

**133** Probably Jonathan M. Dodd, who lived on Main Street.

**134** Similarly, in *Walden* Thoreau wrote: "The farmer is endeavoring to solve the problem of a livelihood by a formula more complicated than the problem itself. To get his shoe-strings he speculates in herds of cattle" [Wa 32].

*October 12.* To-day I have had the experience of borrowing money for a poor Irishman who wishes to get his family to this country.[130] One will never know his neighbors till he has carried a subscription paper among them. Ah! it reveals many and sad facts to stand in this relation to them. To hear the selfish and cowardly excuses some make,—that *if* they help any they must help the Irishman who lives with them,—and him they are sure never to help! Others, with whom public opinion weighs, will think of it, trusting you never will raise the sum and so they will not be called on again; who give stingily after all. What a satire in the fact that you are much more inclined to call on a certain slighted and so-called crazy woman in moderate circumstances rather than on the president of the bank! But some are generous and save the town from the distinction which threatened it,[131] and *some* even who do not lend, plainly would if they could.

*October 22.* Yesterday, toward night, gave Sophia and Mother a sail as far as the Battle-Ground. One-eyed John Goodwin, the fisherman,[132] was loading into a hand-cart and conveying home the piles of driftwood which of late he had collected with his boat. It was a beautiful evening, and a clear amber sunset lit up all the eastern shores; and that man's employment, so simple and direct,—though he is regarded by most as a vicious character,—whose whole motive was so easy to fathom,—thus to obtain his winter's wood,—charmed me unspeakably. So much do we love actions that are simple. They are all poetic. We, too, would fain be so employed. So unlike the pursuits of most men, so artificial or complicated. Consider how the broker[133] collects his winter's wood, what sport he make of it, what is his boat and hand-cart! Postponing instant life, he makes haste to Boston in the cars, and there deals in stocks, not quite relishing his employment,—and so earns the money with which he buys his fuel.[134] And when, by chance, I meet him about this indirect and complicated business, I am not struck with the beauty of his employment. It does not harmonize with the amber sunset. How much more the former consults his genius, some genius at any rate! Now I should love to get my fuel so, — I have got it so, — but though I may be glad to have it, I do not love to get it in any other way less simple and direct. For if I buy one necessary of life, I cheat myself to some extent, I deprive myself of the pleasure, the inexpressible joy, which is the unfailing reward of satisfying any want of our nature simply and truly.[135]

No *trade* is simple, but artificial and complex. It postpones life and substitutes death. It goes against the grain. If the first generation does not die of it, the third or fourth does. In face of all statistics, I will never believe that it is the descendants of tradesmen who keep the state alive, but of simple yeomen or laborers. This, indeed, statistics say of the city reinforced by the country. The oldest, wisest politician grows not more human so, but is merely a gray wharf rat at last. He makes a habit of disregarding the moral right and wrong for the legal or political, commits a slow suicide, and thinks to recover by retiring on to a farm at last. This simplicity it is, and the vigor it imparts, that enables the simple vagabond, though he does get drunk and is sent to the house of correction, to hold up his head among men.

"If I go to Boston every day and sell tape[136] from morning till night," says the merchant (which we will admit is not a beautiful action), "some time or other I shall be able to buy the best of fuel without stint." Yes, but not the pleasure of picking it up by the riverside, which, I may say, is of more value than the warmth it yields, for it but keeps the vital heat in us that we may repeat such pleasing exercises. It warms us twice, and the first warmth is the most wholesome and memorable, compared with which the other is mere coke.[137] It is

135 Cf. 20 October 1855.
136 Narrow strip of woven fabric, used in sewing, bookbinding, and as string for tying.
137 Solid product of the carbonization of coal, similar to charcoal from wood.

138 In *Walden* Thoreau asked: "What was the meaning of this so steady and self-respecting, this small Herculean labor, I knew not. I came to love my rows, my beans, though so many more than I wanted. They attached me to the earth, and so I got strength like Antæus. But why should I raise them? Only Heaven knows. . . . What shall I learn of beans or beans of me?" [Wa 150].

139 Cf. 28 March 1857: "What noble work is plowing, with the broad and solid earth for material, the ox for fellow-laborer, and the simple but efficient plow for tool!" In an early journal entry on "interesting facts in history" Thoreau wrote: "How cheering is it, after toiling through the darker pages of history,—the heartless and fluctuating crust of human rest and unrest,—to alight on the solid earth where the sun shines, or rest in the checkered shade" [J 1:23–24]. In *The Maine Woods:* "Think of our life in nature, daily to be shown matter, to come in contact with it, rocks, trees, wind on our cheeks! the *solid* earth! the *actual* world! the *common sense! Contact! Contact!*" [W 3:79].

to give no account of my employment to say that I cut wood to keep me from freezing, or cultivate beans to keep me from starving.[138] Oh, no, the greatest value of these labors is received before the wood is teamed home, or the beans are harvested (or winnowed from it). Goodwin stands on the solid earth.[139] The earth looks solider under him, and for such as he no *political* economies, with *their* profit and loss, supply and demand, need ever be written, for they will need to use no policy. As for the complex ways of living, I love them not, however much I practice them. In as many places as possible, I will get my feet down to the earth. There is no secret in his trade, more than in the sun's. It is no mystery how he gets his living; no, not even when he steals it. But there is less double-dealing in his living than in your trade.

Goodwin is a most constant fisherman. He must well know the taste of pickerel by this time. He will fish, I would not venture to say how many days in succession. When I can remember to have seen him fishing almost daily for some time, if it rains, I am surprised on looking out to see him slowly wending his way to the river in his oilcloth coat, with his basket and pole. I saw him the other day fishing in the middle of the stream, the day after I had seen him fishing on the shore, while by a kind of magic I sailed by him; and he said he was catching minnow for bait in the winter. When I was twenty rods off, he held up a pickerel that weighed two and a half pounds, which he had forgotten to show me before, and the next morning, as he afterward told me, he caught one that weighed three pounds. If it is ever necessary to appoint a committee on fish-ponds and pickerel, let him be one of them. Surely he is tenacious of life, hard to scale.

*October 26.* I well remember the time this year when I first heard the dream of the toads. I was laying out house-lots on Little River in Haverhill.[140] We had had some raw, cold and wet weather. But this day was remarkably warm and pleasant, and I had thrown off my outside coat. I was going home to dinner, past a shallow pool, which was green with springing grass, and where a new house was about being erected, when it occurred to me that I heard the dream of the toad. It rang through and filled all the air, though I had not heard it once. And I turned my companion's attention to it, but he did not appear to perceive it as a new sound in the air. Loud and prevailing as it is, most men do not notice it at all. It is to them, perchance, a sort of simmering or seething of all nature. That afternoon the dream of the toads rang through the elms by Little River and affected the thoughts of men, though they were not conscious that they heard it.

How watchful we must be to keep the crystal well that we were made, clear! — that it be not made turbid by our contact with the world, so that it will not reflect objects. What other liberty is there worth having, if we have not freedom and peace in our minds, — if our inmost and most private man is but a sour and turbid pool? Often we are so jarred by chagrins in dealing with the world, that we cannot reflect. Everything beautiful impresses us as sufficient to itself. Many men who have had much intercourse with the world and not borne the trial well affect me as all resistance, all bur and rind, without any gentleman, or tender and innocent core left. They have become hedgehogs.

Ah! the world too much with us,[141] and our whole soul is stained by what it works in, like the dyer's hand.[142] A man had better starve at once than lose his innocence in the process of getting his bread. This is the pool of Bethsaida which must be stilled and become smooth before we can enter to be healed.[143] If within the old man there is not a young man, — within the sophisticated,

**140** Thoreau left on 11 April 1853 for Haverhill, where he surveyed several properties, and returned to Concord on 29 April. He stayed with and was assisted by Moses Emerson (probably Moses Emerson 3rd, listed as age 56 in the 1850 Haverhill census). On 13 April he noted in his journal: "First hear toads (and take off coat), a loud, ringing sound filling the air, which yet few notice" [J 5:110].

**141** Allusion to Wordsworth's sonnet "The World Is Too Much with Us."

**142** Allusion to Shakespeare's Sonnet 111, ll. 6–7: "my nature is subdued / To what it works in, like the dyer's hand."

**143** Allusion to the pool of Bethsaida, or Bethesda, in John 5:4: "For an angel went down at a certain season into the pool, and troubled the water: whosoever then first after the troubling of the water stepped in was made whole of whatsoever disease he had."

144 Allusion to "the devil and his angels" in Matthew 25:41.

145 Thoreau opened his "Natural History of Massachusetts" with: "Books of natural history make the most cheerful winter reading" [W 5:103].

146 James Munroe and Company published *A Week on the Concord and Merrimack Rivers* in May 1849. Although Thoreau did not have to pay the publisher's expenses up front, he did have to guarantee those costs in full if the sales did not cover them. In a letter to Blake of 27 February 1853 Thoreau referred to the work as "that book which I printed" [C 295]. Thoreau's distinction, between a publisher that acts only as a printer and one that publicizes a work and puts into circulation in addition to having it printed, was common. As Emerson wrote in "Spiritual Laws": "Therefore Aristotle said of his works, 'They are published and not published.'" Thoreau wrote to Calvin Greene (1817–1898) in 1856 that his book "had so poor a publisher that it is quite uncertain whether you will find it in any shop" [C 406].

147 Ultimately Thoreau paid $290 for publication.

one unsophisticated,—then he is but one of the devil's angels.[144]

It is surprising how any reminiscence of a different season of the year affects us. When I meet with any such in my Journal, it affects me as poetry, and I appreciate that other season and that particular phenomenon more than at the time. The world so seen is all one spring, and full of beauty. You only need to make a faithful record of an average summer day's experience and summer mood, and read it in the winter,[145] and it will carry you back to more than that summer day alone could show. Only the rarest flavor, the purest melody, of the season thus comes down to us.

When, after feeling dissatisfied with my life, I aspire to something better, am more scrupulous, more reserved and continent, as if expecting somewhat, suddenly I find myself full of life as a nut of meat,—am overflowing with a quiet, genial mirthfulness. I think to myself, I must attend to my diet; I must get up earlier and take a morning walk; I must have done with luxuries and devote myself to my muse. So I dam up my stream, and my waters gather to a head. I am freighted with thought.

*October 28.* For a year or two past, my *publisher,*[146] falsely so called, has been writing from time to time to ask what disposition should be made of the copies of "A Week on the Concord and Merrimack Rivers" still on hand, and at last suggesting that he had use for the room they occupied in his cellar. So I had them all sent to me here, and they have arrived to-day by express, filling the man's wagon,—706 copies out of an edition of 1000 which I bought of Munroe four years ago and have been ever since paying for, and have not quite paid for yet.[147] The wares are sent to me at last, and I have an opportunity to examine my purchase. They are something more substantial than fame, as my back knows, which has borne them up two flights of stairs to a place similar to that to which they trace their origin.[148] Of the remaining two hundred and ninety odd, seventy-five were given away, the rest sold. I have now a library of nearly nine hundred volumes, over seven hundred of which I wrote myself. Is it not well that the author should behold the fruits of his labor? My works are piled up on one side of my chamber half as high as my head, my *opera omnia.* This is authorship; these are the work of my brain. There was just one piece of good luck in the venture. The unbound were tied up by the printer four years ago in stout paper wrappers, and inscribed,—

H. D. Thoreau's
Concord River
50 cops.

So Munroe had only to cross out "River" and write "Mass." and deliver them to the expressman[149] at once. I can see now what I write for, the result of my labors.

Nevertheless, in spite of this result, sitting beside the inert mass of my works, I take up my pen to-night to record what thought or experience I may have had, with as much satisfaction as ever. Indeed, I believe that this result is more inspiring and better for me than if a thousand had bought my wares. It affects my privacy less and leaves me freer.

*November 2.* What is Nature unless there is an eventful human life passing within her?

*November 3.* I make it my business to extract from Nature whatever nutriment she can furnish me, though at the risk of endless iteration. I milk the sky and the earth.

148 Although he began writing the book at Walden Pond, Thoreau worked on it while living in the Emerson house and also in the Thoreau family's Texas house, where he wrote in the attic.
149 Driver of an express wagon who receives and delivers articles.

150 Also called Kalmia Swamp, on the west side of the Sudbury River, just north of Conantum.

*November 7.* This is the time for *our* best walnuts; the smallest, say the last of October. Got a peck and a half shelled. I did not wish to slight any of Nature's gifts. I am partial to the peculiar and wholesome sweetness of a nut, and I think that some time is profitably spent every autumn in gathering even such as our pignuts. Some of them are a very sizable, rich-looking, and palatable fruit. How can we expect to understand Nature unless we accept like children these her smallest gifts, valuing them more as her gifts than for their intrinsic value? I love to get my basket full, however small and comparatively worthless the nut.

*November 9.* P.M. — To Fair Haven Hill by boat with Channing.

We rowed against a very powerful wind, sometimes scarcely making any headway. It was with difficulty often that we moved our paddles through the air for a new stroke. As Channing said, it seemed to blow out of a hole. We had to turn our oars edgewise to it. But we worked our way slowly upward, nevertheless, for we came to feel and hear it blow and see the waves run. There was quite a sea running on the lee shore, — broad black waves with white crests, which made our boat toss very pleasantly.

Landed and walked over Conant's Indian rye-field, and I picked up two good arrowheads. The river with its waves has a very wild look southward, and I see the white caps of the waves in Fair Haven Bay. Went into the woods by Holden Swamp[150] and sat down to hear the wind roar amid the tree-tops. What an incessant straining of the trees! It is a music that wears better than the opera, methinks. This reminds me how the telegraph-wire hummed coarsely in the tempest as we passed under it.

Hitherto it had only rained a little from time to time,

but now it began suddenly in earnest. We hastily rowed across to the firm ground of Fair Haven Hillside, drew up our boat and turned it over in a twinkling on to a clump of alders covered with cat-briars which kept up the lee side, and crawled under it. There we lay half an hour on the damp ground and cat-briars, hardly able to see out to the storm which we heard on our roof, through the thick alder stems, much pleased with the tightness of our roof, which we frequently remarked upon. We took immense satisfaction in the thoroughness of the protection against the rain which it afforded. Remembered that such was the origin of the Numidian architecture[151] and, as some think, of the nave (ship)[152] in Gothic architecture, and if we had had a dry bed beneath us, and an ugly gap under the windward side of the boat through which the wind drew had been stopped, we should have lain there longer. At length, as it threatened to be an all-night storm, we crawled out again and set sail homeward.

It now began to rain harder than ever, and the wind was so strong and gusty, and blew so nearly at right angles with the river, that we found it impossible to keep the stream long at a time with our sail set, sitting on one side till the water came in plentifully, that the side might act as a keel, but were repeatedly driven ashore amid the button-bushes, and then had to work our way to the other side slowly and start again. What with water in the boat and in our clothes, we were now indifferent to wet. At length it began to rain so much harder than before, the great drops seeming to flat down the waves and suppress the wind, and feeling like hail on our hands and faces, that, as we remembered, it had only sprinkled before. By this time of course we were wet quite through and through, and Channing began to inquire and jest about the condition of our money—a singular prudence methought—and buried his wallet in his pocket-

151 Allusion to the Roman historian Sallust's (ca. 86–ca. 34 B.C.E.) *De Catalinae Conjuractione, Belloque Jugurthino, Historiae,* in which Thoreau would have read in the Latin original: "To this day the huts of the Numidian rustics, which they call *mapalia,* are oblong, with curved roofs, as if they were the hulls of ships." The Numidians occupied an ancient country of northwest Africa.
152 "Nave" is derived from the Latin word for ship, *navis.*

**153** Thoreau was elected secretary of the Lyceum in October 1839 and curator in November 1839. In 1840 he was again elected curator and secretary, but declined, retiring from the position in December 1840, although he was again elected curator several more times. As curator in 1843–1844 he had been allowed $109.20 with which to contract speakers. At the end of the season he had spent only $100, and had arranged for twenty-five speakers, including Emerson, Horace Greeley (cf. 1854 note 59), and Theodore Parker (1810–1860). "How much might be done for this town with a hundred dollars!" Thoreau wrote in his journal. "I could provide a select course of lectures for the summer or winter with that sum, which would be an incalculable benefit to every inhabitant" [J 1:487]. At this point, ten years later, when he was again elected curator, Thoreau declined the position.

handkerchief and returned it to his pocket again. He thought that bank-bills would be spoiled. It had never occurred to me if a man got completely wet through how it might affect the bank-bills in his wallet, it is so rare a thing for me to have any there. At length we both took to rowing vigorously to keep ourselves warm, and so got home just after candlelight.

*November 12.* I cannot but regard it as a kindness in those who have the steering of me that, by the want of pecuniary wealth, I have been nailed down to this my native region so long and steadily, and made to study and love this spot of earth more and more. What would signify in comparison a thin and diffused love and knowledge of the whole earth instead, got by wandering? The traveller's is but a barren and comfortless condition.

*November 15.* After having some business dealings with men, I am occasionally chagrined, and feel as if I had done some wrong, and it is hard to forget the ugly circumstance. I see that such intercourse long continued would make me thoroughly prosaic, hard, and coarse. But the longest intercourse with Nature, though in her rudest moods, does not thus harden and make coarse. A hard, insensible man whom we liken to a rock is indeed much harder than a rock. From hard, coarse, insensible men with whom I have no sympathy, I go to commune with the rocks, whose hearts are comparatively soft.

I was the other night elected a curator of our Lyceum, but was obliged to decline, because I did not know where to find good lecturers enough to make a course for the winter.[153] We commonly think that we cannot have a good journal in New England, because we have not enough writers of ability; but we do not suspect likewise that we have not good lecturers enough to make a Lyceum.

*November 20.* I once came near speculating in cranberries. Being put to it to raise the wind[154] to pay for "A Week on the Concord and Merrimack Rivers," and having occasion to go to New York to peddle some pencils which I had made,[155] as I passed through Boston I went to Quincy Market and inquired the price of cranberries. The dealers took me down cellar, asked if I wanted wet or dry, and showed me them. I gave them to understand that I might want an indefinite quantity. It made a slight sensation among them and for aught I know raised the price of the berry for a time. I then visited various New York packets and was told what would be the freight, on deck and in the hold, and one skipper was very anxious for my freight. When I got to New York, I again visited the markets as a purchaser, and "the best of Eastern Cranberries" were offered me by the barrel at a cheaper rate than I could buy them in Boston. I was obliged to manufacture a thousand dollars' worth of pencils and slowly dispose of and finally sacrifice them, in order to pay an assumed debt of a hundred dollars.

What enhances my interest in dew—I am thinking of the summer[156]—is the fact that it is so distinct from rain, formed most abundantly after bright, starlit nights, a product especially of the clear, serene air. The manna of fair weather;[157] the upper side of rain, as the country above the clouds. That nightly rain called dew, which gathers and falls in so low a stratum that our heads tower above it like mountains in an ordinary shower. It only consists with comparatively fair weather above our heads. Those warm volumes of air, forced high up the hillsides in summer nights, are driven thither to drop their dew there, like kine to their yards to be milked; that the moisture they hold may be condensed and so dew formed before morning on the tops of the hills. A writer in *Harper's Magazine* (vol. vii, page 505) says that the mist at evening does not rise, "but gradually forms higher up

154 To obtain ready money by any means.
155 It is uncertain when this peddling expedition took place.
156 Thoreau made many entries during the previous summer noting the dew, such as on 21 July: "Ten minutes before sunset I saw large clear dewdrops at the tips, or half an inch below the tips, of the pontederia leaves" [J 5:324]; and 24 July: "Yesterday a dew-like, gentle summer rain. You scarcely know if you are getting wet" [J 5:327].
157 Manna, which rained from the heavens, was the food God provided the children of Israel in the Sinai desert. According to Exodus 16:21: "Each morning everyone gathered as much as he needed, and when the sun grew hot, it melted away."

**158** Quoted here and below from an unattributed article, "Does the Dew Fall?" in *Harper's New Monthly Magazine* (September 1853), 504–506.

**159** The author of "Does the Dew Fall?" wrote: "You will now understand why it is so dangerous to be out late in the evening, and especially after midnight. Then the dew is forming, and the air is so damp and chilly, that you are almost sure to take cold; for nothing is worse than that cold chilling dampness which pervades the air when dew is forming. On a cloudy night there is far less danger; for the air is then warmer and drier, and dew is not deposited. Dew is, however, always more abundant when a clear and bright morning succeeds to a misty evening, and when dry weather follows rain; so that at such times it is not prudent to venture out until the sun begins to rise, and to warm the air with its morning beams."

**160** Although he never developed this book, the idea did provide the origin for the essay "Autumnal Tints," which Thoreau began in 1857 and first delivered as a lecture in February 1859. It was posthumously published in the *Atlantic Monthly: A Magazine of Literature, Art, and Politics* (October 1862).

**161** The publisher James Munroe also operated as a bookseller with a shop on Washington Street in Boston.

in the air."[158] He calls it the moisture of the air become visible. Says there is most dew in clear nights, because clouds prevent the cooling down of the air; they radiate the heat of the earth back to it; and that a strong wind, by keeping the air in motion, prevents its heat from passing off. Therefore, I proceed, for a plentiful dew it must not only be clear but calm. The above writer says bad conductors of heat have always most dew on them, and that wool or swan's-down is "good for experimenting on the quantity of dew falling,"—weight before and after. Thinks it not safe to walk in clear nights, especially after midnight, when the dew is most abundantly forming; better in cloudy nights, which are drier. Also thinks it not prudent to venture out until the sun begins to rise and warms the air.[159] But methinks this prudence begets a tenderness that will catch more cold at noonday than the opposite hardiness at midnight.

*November 22.* If there is any one with whom we have a quarrel, it is most likely that that one makes some just demand on us which we disappoint.

I was just thinking it would be fine to get a specimen leaf from each changing tree and shrub and plant in autumn, in September and October, when it had got its brightest characteristic color, the intermediate ripeness in its transition from the green to the russet or brown state, outline and copy its color exactly with paint in a book,—a book which should be a memorial of October, be entitled October Hues or Autumnal Tints.[160]

*November 28.* Settled with J. Munroe & Co., and on a new account placed twelve of my books with him on sale.[161] I have paid him directly out of pocket since the book was published two hundred and ninety dollars and taken his receipt for it. This does not include postage on proof-sheets, etc., etc. I have received from other quarters about fifteen dollars. This has been the pecuniary value of the book.

**November 30.** When I returned to town the other night by the Walden road through the meadows from Brister's Hill to the poorhouse, I fell to musing upon the origin of the meanders in the road; for when I look straight before or behind me, my eye met the fences at a short distance, and it appeared that the road, instead of being built in a straight line across the meadows, as one might have expected, pursued a succession of curves like a cow-path. In fact, it was just such a meandering path as an eye of taste requires, and the landscape-gardener consciously aims to make, and the wonder is that a body of laborers left to themselves, without instruments or geometry, and perchance intending to make a straight road,—in short, that circumstances ordinarily,—will so commonly make just such a meandering road as the eye requires. A man advances in his walk somewhat as a river does, meanderingly, and such, too, is the progress of the race. The law that plants the rushes in waving lines along the edge of a pond, and that curves the pond-shore itself, incessantly beats against the straight fences and highways of men and makes them conform to the line of beauty which is most agreeable to the eye at last.

**December 2.** The skeleton which at first sight excites only a shudder in all mortals becomes at last not only a pure but suggestive and pleasing object to science. The more we know of it, the less we associate it with any goblin of our imaginations. The longer we keep it, the less likely it is that any such will come to claim it. We discover that the only spirit which haunts it is a universal intelligence[162] which has created it in harmony with all nature. Science never saw a ghost, nor does it look for any, but it

**162** Comprehension of reason: cf. 1840s note 73.

**163** William Henry Channing (1810–1884), Unitarian minister, Christian socialist, editor of the *Western Messenger,* and contributor to the *Dial* and *Memoirs of Margaret Fuller.* Channing was the cousin of Thoreau's friend William Ellery Channing (cf. 1850 note 25) and nephew of the elder William Ellery Channing, also a Unitarian minister (cf. 1851 note 181).

**164** A method used sometimes by artists and often by Thoreau of bending over and looking at things upside-down: "I look between my legs up the river across Fair Haven" [J 3:333], and "What shall we make of the fact that you have only to stand on your head a moment to be enchanted with the beauty of the landscape?" [J 2:51]. Emerson suggested in *Nature:* "Turn the eyes upside down, by looking at the landscape through your legs, and how agreeable is the picture, though you have seen it any time these twenty years!"

**165** Thoreau was surveying James Potter Brown's (1810–1871) Corner Spring Lot.

**166** Cf. 12 December 1851.

**167** Although he was not a strict vegetarian, Thoreau ate meat only occasionally, usually when it was a matter of convention or practicality. Moncure Conway wrote in his *Autobiography:* "Thoreau ate no meat; he told me his only reason was a feeling of the filthiness of flesh-eating. A bear huntsman he thought was entitled to his steak. He had never attempted to make any general principle on the subject, and later in life ate meat in order not to cause inconvenience to the family."

sees everywhere the traces, and it is itself the agent, of a Universal Intelligence.

*December 8.* I was amused by Emerson's telling me that he drove his own calf out of the yard, as it was coming in with the cow, not knowing it to be his own, a drove going by at the time.

*December 11.* Emerson told me that William Henry Channing[163] conjectured that the landscape looked fairer when we turned our heads, because we beheld it with nerves of the eye unused before.[164] Perhaps this reason is worth more for suggestion than explanation. It occurs to me that the reflection of objects in still water is in a similar manner fairer than the substance, and yet we do not employ unused nerves to behold it. Is it not that we let much more light into our eyes,—which in the usual position are shaded by the brows,—in the first case by turning them more to the sky, and in the case of the reflections by having the sky placed under our feet? *i. e.* in both cases we see terrestrial objects with the sky or heavens for a background or field. Accordingly they are not dark and terrene, but lit and elysian.

*December 22.* Surveying the last three days.[165] They have not yielded much that I am aware of. All I find is old bound-marks, and the slowness and dullness of farmers reconfirmed. They even complain that I walk too fast for them. Their legs have become stiff from toil. This coarse and hurried outdoor work compels me to live grossly or be inattentive to my diet; that is the worst of it. Like work, like diet; that, I find, is the rule.[166] Left to my chosen pursuits, I should never drink tea nor coffee, nor eat meat.[167] The diet of any class or generation is the natural result of its employment and locality. It is remarkable how unprofitable it is for the most part to talk with farmers. They commonly stand on their good behavior and attempt to moralize or philosophize in a serious conversation. Sportsmen and loafers are better company. For society a man must not be too *good* or well-disposed, to spoil his natural disposition. The bad are frequently good enough to let you see how bad they are, but the good as frequently endeavor to get between you and themselves.

I have dined out five times and tea'd once within a week. Four times there was tea on the dinner-table, always meat, but once baked beans, always pie, but no puddings. I suspect tea has taken the place of cider with farmers. I am reminded of Haydon the painter's experience when he went about painting the nobility.[168] I go about to the houses of the farmers and squires in like manner. This is my portrait-painting,—when I would fain be employed on higher subjects. I have offered myself much more earnestly as a lecturer than a surveyor. Yet I do not get any employment as a lecturer; was not invited to lecture once last winter, and only once (without pay) this winter.[169] But I can get surveying enough,[170] which a hundred others in this county can do as well as I, though it is not boasting much to say that a hundred others in New England cannot lecture as well as I on my themes. But they who do not make the highest demand on you shall rue it. It is because they make a low demand on themselves. All the while that they use only your humbler faculties, your higher unemployed faculties, like an invisible cimetar,[171] are cutting them in twain. Woe be to the generation that lets any higher faculty in its midst go unemployed! That is to deny God and know him not,[172] and he, accordingly, will know not of them.

*December 26.* Was overtaken by an Irishman seeking work. I asked him if he could chop wood. He said he was not long in this country; that he could cut one side

**168** Benjamin Robert Haydon (1786–1846), whose autobiography, *Life of Benjamin Robert Haydon, Historical Painter, from His Autobiography and Journals,* published in 1853, Thoreau was reading. Such passages as "Perhaps portrait painting may do me good . . . but I, who paint every thing from Nature, don't want such means," and "I do not despise portrait. . . . I am adapted for something else," may have reminded Thoreau of his own situation in needing to survey and do other labor to support himself. Haydon's position in relation to his patrons may have also resonated with Thoreau. Haydon wrote, "When I know better than others, princes or peers, I show it. When they know better, I bow. They would have me bow in both instances, but I can't, and, what's more, I won't. . . . And so, artists, be humble and discreet." Thoreau wrote to Blake: "Pray read the life of Haydon the painter, if you have not. It is a small revelation for these latter days; a great satisfaction to know that he has lived, though he is now dead" [C 312–313].

**169** On 14 December Thoreau gave a lecture titled "Journey to Moose Head Lake" for the Concord Lyceum. Most recently before that he had given two lectures, "Walking" and "The Wild," at Leydon Hall, Plymouth, on 12 May 1852.

**170** During the same period (May 1852–December 1853) Thoreau was employed as a surveyor thirty times.

**171** Scimitar: a sword with a thin curved blade, known for its sharpness.

**172** Allusion to Peter in Luke 22:57: "And he denied him, saying, Woman, I know him not."

173  Crossing the cut or carve, from the obsolete word *carf* for carve.

174  Here Thoreau added a note: "In an ordinary snow-storm, when snowing fast, Jan 1st '54, I can see E. Wood's house, or about a mile."

175  The snow bunting, which Thoreau called "true winter birds . . . winged snowballs" [W 6:34].

of a tree well enough, but he had not learned to change hands and cut the other without going around it,—what we call crossing the carf.[173] They get very small wages at this season of the year; almost give up the ghost in the effort to keep soul and body together. He left me on the run to find a new master.

*December 29.* We survive, in one sense, in our posterity and in the continuance of our race, but when a race of men, of Indians for instance, becomes extinct, is not this the end of the world for them? Is not the world forever beginning and coming to an end, both to men and races? Suppose we were to foresee that the Saxon race to which we belong would become extinct the present winter,—disappear from the face of the earth,—would it not look to us like the end, the dissolution of the world? Such is the prospect of the Indians.

All day a driving snow-storm, imprisoning most, stopping the cars, blocking up the roads. No school today. I cannot see a house fifty rods off from my window through it;[174] yet in midst of all I see a bird, probably a tree sparrow, partly blown, partly flying, over the house to alight in a field. The snow penetrates through the smallest crevices under doors and side of windows.

P.M.—Tried my snow-shoes. They sink deeper than I expected, and I throw the snow upon my back. When I returned, twenty minutes after, my great tracks were not to be seen. It is the worst snow-storm to bear that I remember. The strong wind from the north blows the snow almost horizontally, and, beside freezing you, almost takes your breath away. The driving snow blinds you, and where you are protected, you can see but little way, it is so thick. Yet in spite, or on account, of all, I see the first flock of arctic snowbirds (*Emberiza nivalis*)[175] near the depot, white and black, with a sharp, whistle-like note. An hour after I discovered half a pint of snow in each pocket of my greatcoat.

What a contrast between the village street now and last summer! The leafy elms then resounding with the warbling vireo, robins, bluebirds, and the fiery hang-bird,[176] etc., to which the villagers, kept indoors by the heat, listen through open lattices. Now it is like a street in Nova Zembla,[177] — if they were to have any there. I wade to the post-office as solitary a traveller as ordinarily in a wood-path in winter. The snow is mid-leg deep, while drifts as high as one's head are heaped against the houses and fences, and here and there range across the street like snowy mountains. You descend from this, relieved, into capacious valleys with a harder bottom, or more fordable. The track of one large sleigh alone is visible, nearly snowed up. There is not a track leading from any door to indicate that the inhabitants have been forth to-day, any more than there is track of any quadruped by the wood-paths. It is all pure untrodden snow, banked up against the houses now at 4 P.M., and no evidence that a villager has been abroad to-day. In one place the drift covers the front-yard fence and stretches thence upward to the top of the front door, shutting all in, and frequently the snow lies banked up three or four feet high against the front doors, and the windows are all snowed up, and there is a drift over each window, and the clapboards are all hoary with it. It is as if the inhabitants were all frozen to death, and now you threaded the desolate streets weeks after that calamity. There is not a sleigh or vehicle of any kind on the Mill-Dam, but one saddled horse on which a farmer has come into town. The cars are nowhere. Yet they are warmer, merrier than ever there within. At the post-office they ask each traveller news of the cars, — "Is there any train up or down?" — or how deep the snow is on a level.

176 Baltimore oriole (*Icterus galbula*).
177 Archipelago in the Arctic Ocean made up of two major islands and many smaller ones.

**178** Leading north from Concord to Lowell. Thoreau was on the railroad tracks beyond Walden.

**179** In 1853 Thoreau was reading Richard Chenevix Trench's *On the Study of Words,* in which the word heathen is traced back to the introduction of Christianity in Germany, where "the wild dwellers on the 'heaths' longest resisted the truth" of the Church. Cf. 30 December 1860.

**180** Cf. 1851 note 24.

**181** Cf. 28 November 1853.

*December 31.* The town and country are now so still, there being no rattle of wagons nor even jingle of sleigh-bells, every tread being as with woolen feet, I hear very distinctly from the railroad causeway the whistle of the locomotive on the Lowell road.[178] For the same reason, in such a day as this the crowing of a cock is heard very far and distinctly. I frequently mistake at first a very distant whistle for the higher tones of the telegraph harp by my side. The telegraph and railroad are closely allied, and it is fit and to be expected that at a little distance their music should be the same. There are a few sounds still which never fail to affect me. The notes of the wood thrush and the sound of a vibrating chord, these affect me as many sounds once did often, and as almost all should. The strains of the æolian harp and of the wood thrush are the truest and loftiest preachers that I know now left on this earth. I know of no missionaries to us heathen[179] comparable to them. They, as it were, lift us up in spite of ourselves. They intoxicate, they charm us. Where was that strain mixed into which this world was dropped but as a lump of sugar to sweeten the draught? I would be drunk, drunk, drunk, dead drunk to this world with it forever. He that hath ears, let him hear.[180] The contact of sound with a human ear whose hearing is pure and unimpaired is coincident with an ecstasy. Sugar is not so sweet to the palate, as sound to the healthy ear; the hearing of it makes men brave.

(How can a poet afford to keep an account with a bookseller?)[181] These things alone remind me of my immortality, which is else a fable. I hear it, and I realize and see clearly what at other times I only dimly remember. I get the value of the earth's extent and the sky's depth. It, as it were, takes me out of my body and gives me the freedom of all bodies and all nature. I leave my body in a trance and accompany the zephyr and the fragrance.

**1854**

AGE 36–37

1 Thoreau added a note here: "But all that we see is the impress of its spirit."

2 On the next day Thoreau tried to "thaw out to life the snow-fleas which yesterday covered the snow like pepper, in a frozen state" [J 6:60]. He tried again on 11 February: "When I breathe on them I find them all alive and ready to skip" [J 6:113].

3 Thoreau had gone to Hayward's Mill Pond, on Second Division Brook, south of Damon's Mills with William Aspinwall Tappan, whom Thoreau met in New York. Tappan married Caroline Sturgis (1818 or 1819–1888), poet, friend of Emerson and Margaret Fuller, and contributor to the *Dial*.

*January 1.* The snow is the great betrayer. It not only shows the tracks of mice, otters, etc., etc., which else we should rarely if ever see, but the tree sparrows are more plainly seen against its white ground, and they in turn are attracted by the dark weeds which it reveals. It also drives the crows and other birds out of the woods to the villages for food. We might expect to find in the snow the footprint of a life superior to our own, of which no zoölogy takes cognizance. Is there no trace of a nobler life than that of an otter or an escaped convict to be looked for in the snow? Shall we suppose that that is the only life that has been abroad in the night? It is only the savage that can see the track of no higher life than an otter. Why do the vast snow plains give us pleasure, the twilight of the bent and half-buried woods? Is not all there consonant with virtue, justice, purity, courage, magnanimity? Are we not cheered by the sight? And does not all this amount to the track of a higher life than the otter's, a life which has not gone by and left a foot print merely,[1] but is there with its beauty, its music, its perfume, its sweetness, to exhilarate and recreate us?

*January 9.* Found many snow-fleas, apparently frozen, on the snow.[2]

Tappan[3] has a singularly elastic step. He will run through the snow, lifting his knees like a child who enjoys the motion. When he slumped once through to water and called my attention to it, with an indescribable

4 Hawthorne's son Julian (1846–1934) recalled in his *Memoirs:* "Once, when I was nearly seven years old, Thoreau came to make a survey of our land, bringing his survey apparatus on his shoulder. I watched the short, dark, unbeautiful man with interest and followed him about, all over the place, never losing sight of a movement and never asking a question or uttering a word. The thing must have lasted a couple of hours; when we got back, Thoreau remarked to my father: 'Good boy! Sharp eyes, and no tongue!' On that basis I was admitted to his friendship; a friendship or comradeship which began in 1852 and was to last until his death in 1862."

5 The following day Thoreau reiterated: "With Tappan, his speech is frequently so frugal and reserved, in monosyllables not fairly uttered clear of his thought, that I doubt if he did not cough merely, or let it pass for such, instead of asking what he said or meant, for fear it might turn out that he coughed merely" [J 6:61].

6 Native American tribe of Canada, formerly inhabiting the area north of the Saint Lawrence River. The week before, on 1 January, Thoreau wrote about Native American languages: "Our orators might learn much from the Indians. They are remarkable for their precision; nothing is left at loose ends. They address more senses than one, so as to preclude misunderstanding" [J 6:45–46].

7 "I have an old account-book," Thoreau wrote in his journal on 27 January 1854. "Its cover is brown paper, on which, amid many marks and scribblings, I find written:—

'Mr. Ephraim Jones
His Wast Book
Anno Domini
1742'

It extends from November 8th, 1742, to June 20th, 1743 (inclusive)" [J 6:77]. Ephraim Jones (1705–1756) was a captain during the Battle of Concord,

flash of his eye, he reminded me forcibly of Hawthorne's little son Julian.[4] He uses the greatest economy in speech of any man I know. Speaks low, beside, and without emphasis; in monosyllables.[5] I cannot guess what the word was for a long time. His language is different from the Algonquin.[6]

*January 10.* I mistook the creaking of a tree in the woods the other day for the scream of a hawk. How numerous the resemblances of the animate to the inanimate!

*January 31.* A hundred years ago, as I learn from Ephraim Jones's ledger,[7] they sold bark in our street. He gives credit for a load. Methinks my genius is coeval with that time. That is no great wildness or *selvaggia*[8] that cannot furnish a load of bark, where the forest has lost its shagginess. This is an attempt to import the wildness into the cities in a thousand shapes. Bark is carried thither by ship and by cartloads. Bark contains the principle of tannin, by which not only the fibre of skins but of men's thoughts is hardened and consolidated. It was then that a voice was given to the dog, and a manly tone to the human voice. Ah! Already I shudder for these degenerate days of the village, when you can not collect a load of bark of good thickness.

We too have our thaws. They come to our January moods, when our ice cracks, and our sluices break loose. Thought that was frozen up under stern experience gushes forth in feeling and expression. There is a freshet which carries away dams of accumulated ice. Our thoughts hide unexpressed, like the buds under their downy or resinous scales; they would hardly keep a partridge from starving. If you would know what are my winter thoughts look for them in the partridge's crop. They are like the laurel buds,—some leaf, some blossom buds,—which, though food for such indigenous creatures, will not expand into leaves and flowers until summer comes.

*February 5.* Shall we not have sympathy with the musk-rat which gnaws its third leg off,[9] not as pitying its sufferings, but, through our kindred mortality, appreciating its majestic pains and its heroic virtue? Are we not made its brothers by fate? For whom are psalms sung and mass said, if not for such worthies as these? When I hear the church organ peal, or feel the trembling tones of the base viol, I see in imagination the musquash[10] gnawing off his leg, I offer a note that his affliction may be sanctified to each and all of us. Prayer and praise fitly follow such exploits. I look round for majestic pains and pleasures.[11] They have our sympathy, both in their joys and in their pains. When I think of the tragedies which are constantly permitted in the course of all animal life, they make the plaintive strain of the universal harp which elevates us above the trivial.[12] When I think of the muskrat gnawing off his leg, it is as the plectrum on the harp or the bow upon the viol, drawing forth a majestic strain or psalm, which immeasurably dignifies our common fate. Even as the worthies of mankind are said to recommend human life by having lived it, so I could not spare the example of the muskrat.

*February 8.* The poets, philosophers, historians, and all writers have always been disposed to praise the life of the farmer and prefer it to that of the citizen. They have been inclined to regard trade and commerce as not merely uncertain modes of getting a living, but as running into the usurious and disreputable. And even at the present day the trader, as carrier or go-between, the speculator, the forestaller, and corporations do not escape a fling. Trade has always been regarded to some extent as a questionable mode of getting a livelihood.

town clerk from 1749 to 1754, and a representative in the General Court of the Massachusetts legislature for the years 1745–1750 and 1753. Thoreau's journal contains four separate entries recording details from and comments on this and two others of Jones's account books: 27 January, 31 January, 5 February (which entry appeared in the "Winter Animals" chapter of *Walden*), and 5 February (P.M.) 1854.

**8** Italian: wild or savage, as in the opening to Dante's *Inferno*: "selva selvaggia" (woodland wild). In "Chesuncook" Thoreau wrote: "Our woods are sylvan, and their inhabitants woodmen and rustics; that is *selvaggia,* and the inhabitants are *salvages*" [W 3:172].

**9** George Melvin (b. 1813), a Concord trapper, told Thoreau: "Oh, the muskrats are the greatest fellows to gnaw their legs off. Why, I caught one once that had just gnawed his third leg off, this being the third time he had been trapped; and he lay dead by the trap, for he could n't run on one leg" [J 1:481].

**10** Muskrat.

**11** Allusion to Wordsworth's "Laodamia" 72: "Calm pleasures there abide—majestic pains."

**12** In the "Sounds" chapter of *Walden* Thoreau wrote: "At a sufficient distance over the woods this sound acquires a certain vibratory hum, as if the pine needles in the horizon were the strings of a harp which it swept. All sound heard at the greatest possible distance produces one and the same effect, a vibration of the universal lyre, just as the intervening atmosphere makes a distant ridge of earth interesting to our eyes by the azure tint it imparts to it. There came to me in this case a melody which the air had strained, and which had conversed with every leaf and needle of the wood, that portion of the sound which the elements had taken up and modulated and echoed from vale to vale. The echo is, to some extent, an original sound, and therein is the magic and charm of it. It is not merely a repetition of what was worth repeating in the bell, but partly the voice of the wood; the same trivial words and notes sung by a wood-nymph" [Wa 119–120]. Cf. sphere music: 1830s note 20.

**13** Channing.

**14** During this period Thoreau sent portions of the fair copy of *Walden* to the printer, receiving proofs back in sections.

But now, by means of railroads and steamboats and telegraphs, the country is denaturalized, the old pious, stable, and unenvied gains of the farmer are liable to all the suspicion which only the merchant's formerly excited. All milk-farms and fruit-farms, etc., are so many markets with their customs in the country.

*February 9.* My ink was frozen last month, and is now pale.

*March 12.* My companion[13] tempts me to certain licenses of speech, *i. e.* to reckless and sweeping expressions which I am wont to regret that I have used. That is, I find that I have used more harsh, extravagant, and cynical expressions concerning mankind and individuals than I intended. I find it difficult to make to him a sufficiently moderate statement. I think it is because I have not his sympathy in my sober and constant view. He asks for a paradox, an eccentric statement, and too often I give it to him.

*March 15.* I am sorry to think that you do not get a man's most effective criticism until you provoke him. Severe truth is expressed with some bitterness.

*March 31.* In criticizing your writing, trust your fine instinct. There are many things which we come very near questioning, but do not question. When I have sent off my manuscripts to the printer,[14] certain objectionable sentences or expressions are sure to obtrude themselves on my attention with force, though I had not consciously suspected them before. My critical instinct then at once breaks the ice and comes to the surface.

*April 5.* These days, when a soft west or southwest wind blows and it is truly warm, and an outside coat is oppressive,—these bring out the butterflies and the frogs, and the marsh hawks which prey on the last. Just so simple is every year. Whatever year it may be, I am surveying, perhaps, in the woods; I have taken off my outside coat, perhaps for the first time, and hung it on a tree; the zephyr is positively agreeable on my cheek; I am thinking what an elysian day it is, and how I seem always to be keeping the flocks of Admetus such days—that is my luck; when I hear a single, short, well-known stertorous croak from some pool half filled with dry leaves. You may see anything now—the buff-edged butterfly and many hawks—along the meadow; and hark! while I was writing down that field note, the shrill peep of the hylodes[15] was borne to me from afar through the woods.

I rode with my employer[16] a dozen miles to-day, keeping a profound silence almost all the way as the most simple and natural course. I treated him simply as if he had bronchitis and could not speak, just as I would a sick man, a crazy man, or an idiot. The disease was only an unconquerable stiffness in a well-meaning and sensible man.

*April 8.* At the Lyceum the other night I felt that the lecturer had chosen a theme too foreign to himself[17] and so failed to interest me as much as formerly. He described things not in or near to his heart, but toward his extremities and superficies.[18] The poet deals with his privatest experience. There was no *central* nor centralizing thought in the lecture.[19]

*April 10.* I bought me a spy-glass some weeks since.[20] I buy but few things, and those not till long after I began to want them, so that when I do get them I am prepared to make a perfect use of them and extract their whole sweet.

15 The piping frog (*Hyla pickeringii*): cf. 1850 note 5.
16 Thoreau was in Carlisle and Concord, where he was surveying for Samuel Hoar (1778–1856). Hoar, Concord's leading citizen, a lawyer, and a former judge on the Massachusetts Supreme Court, was described by Sanborn in a poem as having a "cold demeanor, the warm heart beneath." Emerson wrote: "Nobody cared to speak of thoughts or aspirations to a black-letter lawyer, who only studied to keep men out of prison, and their lands out of attachment."
17 Emerson, who lectured on France (hence Thoreau's pun) at the Concord Lyceum on 5 April 1854.
18 Outer surfaces.
19 This entry became the opening to Thoreau's "Life with Principle" [W 4:455].
20 While in Boston on 13 March 1854 Thoreau purchased a telescoping spyglass for eight dollars. Cf. 24 September 1859: "Some eyes cannot see, even through a spy-glass. I showed my spy-glass to a man whom I met this afternoon, who said that he wanted to see if he could look through it. I tried it carefully on him, but he failed" [J 12:347].

21 Thoreau had been surveying in Lincoln.
22 In Greek mythology, Orpheus's music had supernatural powers and his singing could charm animals and inanimate objects.
23 Relating to Vulcan, Roman god of fire and metalworking.
24 Also known as the book of judgment, a record of human activities held against the day of judgment, as in Revelation 20:12, 15: "And I saw the dead, small and great, stand before God; and the books were opened: and another book was opened, which is the book of life: and the dead were judged out of those things which were written in the books, according to their works. . . . And whosoever was not found written in the book of life was cast into the lake of fire."
25 Cf. 19 April 1854: "I am not interested in mere phenomena, though it were the explosion of a planet, only as it may have lain in the experience of a human being" [J 6:206].

*April 12.* Waited at Lincoln Depot an hour and a half.[21] Heard the telegraph harp. I perceived distinctly that man melts at the sound of music, just like a rock exposed to a furnace heat. They need not have fabled that Orpheus moved the rocks and trees,[22] for there is nothing more insensible than man; he sets the fashion to the rocks, and it is as surprising to see him melted, as when children see their lead begin to flow in a crucible. I observe that it is when I have been intently, and it may be laboriously, at work, and am somewhat listless or abandoned after it, reposing, that the muse visits me, and I see or hear beauty. It is from out the shadow of my toil that I look into the light. The music of the spheres is but another name for the Vulcanic[23] force. May not such a record as this be kept on one page of the Book of Life:[24] "A man was melted to-day."

*May 6.* There is no such thing as pure *objective* observation. Your observation, to be interesting, *i. e.* to be significant, must be *subjective.* The sum of what the writer of whatever class has to report is simply some human experience, whether he be poet or philosopher or man of science. The man of most science is the man most alive, whose life is the greatest event. Senses that take cognizance of outward things merely are of no avail. It matters not where or how far you travel,—the farther commonly the worse,—but how much alive you are. If it is possible to conceive of an event outside to humanity, it is not of the slightest significance, though it were the explosion of a planet.[25] Every important worker will report what life there is in him. It makes no odds into what seeming deserts the poet is born. Though all his neighbors pronounce it a Sahara, it will be a paradise to him; for the desert which we see is the result of the barrenness of our experience. No mere willful activity whatever, whether in writing verses or collecting statistics, will produce true poetry or science. If you are really a sick man, it is indeed to be regretted, for you cannot accomplish so much as if you were well. All that a man has to say or do that can possibly concern mankind, is in some shape or other to tell the story of his love,—to sing; and, if he is fortunate and keeps alive, he will be forever in love. This alone is to be alive to the extremities. It is a pity that this divine creature should ever suffer from cold feet; a still greater pity that the coldness so often reaches to his heart. I look over the report of the doings of a scientific association[26] and am surprised that there is so little life to be reported; I am put off with a parcel of dry technical terms. Anything living is easily and naturally expressed in popular language. I cannot help suspecting that the life of these learned professors has been almost as inhuman and wooden as a rain-gauge or self-registering magnetic machine. They communicate no fact which rises to the temperature of blood-heat. It does n't all amount to one rhyme.

*May 9.* Sat on end of Long Wharf.[27] Was surprised to observe that so many of the men on board the shipping were pure countrymen in dress and habits, and the seaport is no more than a country town to which they come a-trading. I found about the wharves, steering the coasters[28] and unloading the ships, men in farmer's dress. As I watched the various craft successively unfurling their sails and getting to sea, I felt more than for many years inclined to let the wind blow me also to other climes.

*May 10.* In Boston yesterday an ornithologist[29] said significantly, "If you held the bird in your hand—;" but I would rather hold it in my affections.

*May 23.* We soon get through with Nature. She excites an expectation which she cannot satisfy. The merest child

26 Thoreau read the reports of several scientific associations, such as the *Memoirs of the American Academy of Arts and Sciences* and the Smithsonian Institution's *Annual Report of the Board of Regents.*
27 In Boston, built in 1710 and extending more than a thousand feet into the harbor.
28 Ships engaged in trade along a coastline.
29 Probably Henry Bryant (1820–1867) at the Natural History rooms of the Boston Society of Natural History, founded in 1830.

**30** Any of several predominantly red birds, such as the cardinal, tanager, or bullfinch. Edward Jarvis wrote that election days were for the boys in the town "a day of great expectation and exhilaration. They looked forward to it with fondness and yet with anxiety lest the weather should be unfavorable for out-of-door sports. A large part expected to go hunting birds in the woods and fields . . . and early on Election Day they went forth on their cruel and wanton amusement."

**31** In *A Week on the Concord and Merrimack Rivers* Thoreau wrote: "I had seen the red Election-birds brought from their recesses on my comrades' string, and fancied that their plumage would assume stranger and more dazzling colors, like the tints of evening, in proportion as I advanced farther into the darkness and solitude of the forest. Still less have I seen such strong and wilderness tints on any poet's string" [W 1:56–57].

**32** Forested mountain range in New Hampshire.

which has rambled into a copsewood dreams of a wilderness so wild and strange and inexhaustible as Nature can never show him. The red-bird which I saw on my companion's string on election days[30] I thought but the outmost sentinel of the wild, immortal camp,—of the wild and dazzling infantry of the wilderness,—that the deeper woods abounded with redder birds still; but, now that I have threaded all our woods and waded the swamps, I have never yet met with his compeer, still less his wilder kindred.[31] The red-bird which is the last of Nature is but the first of God. The White Mountains,[32] likewise, were smooth mole-hills to my expectation. We *condescend* to climb the crags of earth. It is our weary legs alone that praise them. That forest on whose skirts the red-bird flits is not of earth. I expected a fauna more infinite and various, birds of more dazzling colors and more celestial song. How many springs shall I continue to see the common sucker (*Catostomus Bostoniensis*) floating dead on our river! Will not Nature select her types from a new fount? The vignette of the year. This earth which is spread out like a map around me is but the lining of my inmost soul exposed. In me is the sucker that I see. No wholly extraneous object can compel me to recognize it. I am guilty of suckers. I go about to look at flowers and listen to birds. There was a time when the beauty and the music were all within, and I sat and listened to my thoughts, and there was a song in them. I sat for hours on rocks and wrestled with the melody which possessed me. I sat and listened by the hour to a positive though faint and distant music, not sung by any bird, nor vibrating any earthly harp. When you walked with a joy which knew not its own origin. When you were an organ of which the world was but one poor broken pipe. I lay long on the rocks, foundered like a harp on the seashore, that knows not how it is dealt with. You sat on the earth as on a raft, listening to music that was not of the earth, but which ruled and arranged it. Man *should be* the harp articulate. When your cords were tense.

Think of going abroad out of one's self to hear music,—to Europe or Africa! Instead of so living as to be the lyre which the breath of the morning causes to vibrate with that melody which creates worlds—to sit up late and hear Jane Lind![33]

*May 28.* It would be worth the while to ask ourselves weekly, Is our life innocent enough? Do we live *inhumanely,* toward man or beast, in thought or act? To be serene and successful we must be at one with the universe. The least conscious and needless injury inflicted on any creature is to its extent a suicide. What peace—or life—can a murderer have?

The inhumanity of science concerns me, as when I am tempted to kill a rare snake that I may ascertain its species. I feel that this is not the means of acquiring true knowledge.[34]

*June 16.* There is a fine ripple and sparkle on the pond, seen through the mist.[35] But what signifies the beauty of nature when men are base? We walk to lakes to see our serenity reflected them. When we are not serene, we go not to them. Who can be serene in a country where both rulers and ruled are without principle? The remembrance of the baseness of politicians spoils my walks.[36] My thoughts are murder to the State; I endeavor in vain to observe nature; my thoughts involuntarily go plotting against the State.[37] I trust that all just men will conspire.

*June 17.* Another remarkably hazy day; our view is confined, the horizon near, no mountains; as you look off only four or five miles, you see a succession of dark

[33] Jenny Lind (1820–1887), Swedish soprano known as the Swedish Nightingale, who toured the United States in 1850–1852 under the management of P. T. (Phineas Taylor) Barnum (1810–1891).

[34] During the late 1840s Thoreau occasionally sent specimens to the Swiss-born naturalist Louis Agassiz (1807–1873), who came to the United States in 1846. In 1848 Agassiz became a professor of zoology and geology at Harvard.

[35] Thoreau was on Heywood's Peak, on the north side of Walden Pond.

[36] Allusion to the Kansas-Nebraska Act, which Congress passed on 24 May 1854. It gave the settlers of those territories the right to decide whether to allow slavery, thereby repealing the Missouri Compromise, which had forbidden slavery in the northern part of the Louisiana Purchase.

[37] This passage is in direct response to the Anthony Burns (ca. 1834–1862) case, and with minor variants appeared in "Slavery in Massachusetts" [W 4:407]. Burns, whose situation occupied Thoreau's mind from 29 May through 18 June, was a fugitive slave who was arrested on 24 May 1854. Within days handbills were posted announcing: "A MAN KIDNAPPED! A PUBLIC MEETING AT FANEUIL HALL! WILL BE HELD THIS FRIDAY EVEN'G, May 26th, at 7 o'clock, To secure justice for A MAN CLAIMED AS A SLAVE by a VIRGINIA KIDNAPPER! And NOW IMPRISONED IN BOSTON COURT HOUSE, in defiance of the Laws of Massachusetts, Shall be plunged into the Hell of Virginia Slavery by a Massachusetts Judge of Probate! BOSTON, May 26, 1854." A strong attempt to rescue him by force failed. Burns was convicted on 2 June of being a fugitive slave and was brought to the waterfront, shackled, under the escort of 1,500 Massachusetts militiamen, the entire Boston police force, 145 federal troops with cannon, and 100 special deputies, to be placed on a ship to return him to slavery in Virginia. An estimated crowd of 50,000 lined the streets of Boston to witness the occasion. The later fate of Burns—the purchase of his freedom

within the year, his attending Oberlin College, his service as a Baptist minister—received no mention in Thoreau's writings.

**38** Allusion to the Free Soil Party, a short-lived political party founded in 1848 in to oppose the extension of slavery into territories the United States acquired from Mexico. The party dissolved in 1854.

**39** Personal liberty laws, which allowed for trial by jury for fugitive slaves in many states, were virtually abolished by the Fugitive Slave Act. In reaction Massachusetts and other states passed new personal liberty laws prohibiting the use of state jails for detaining fugitives; providing counsel for alleged fugitives; securing the benefits of *habeas corpus* and trial by jury; forbidding state officials to issue writs or give any assistance to claimants; and imposing heavy fines and imprisonment for the crime of forcibly seizing or representing as a slave any free person with intent to reduce him to slavery.

wooded ridges and vales filled with mist. It is dry, hazy June weather. We are more of the earth, farther from heaven, these days. We live in a grosser element. We are getting deeper into the mists of earth. Even the birds sing with less vigor and vivacity. The season of hope and promise is past; already the season of small fruits has arrived. The Indian marked the midsummer as the season when berries were ripe. We are a little saddened, because we begin to see the interval between our hopes and their fulfillment. The prospect of the heavens is taken away, and we are presented only with a few small berries.

*June 18.* What we want is not mainly to colonize Nebraska with free men, but to colonize Massachusetts with free men,—to be free ourselves. As the enterprise of a few individuals, that is brave and practical; but as the enterprise of the State, it is cowardice and imbecility. What odds where we squat, or how much ground we cover? It is not the soil that we would make free,[38] but men.

As for asking the South to grant us the trial by jury in the case of runaway slaves,[39] it is as if, seeing a righteous man sent to hell, we should run together and petition the devil first to grant him a trial by jury, forgetting that there is another power to be petitioned, that there is another law and other precedents.

*July 3.* What a luxury to bathe now! It is gloriously hot,—the first of this weather. I cannot get wet enough. I must let the water soak into me. When you come out, it is rapidly dried on you or absorbed into your body, and you want to go in again. I begin to inhabit the planet, and see how I may be naturalized at last.

*August 2.* My attic chamber has compelled me to sit below with the family at evening for a month. I feel the necessity of deepening the stream of my life; I must cultivate privacy. It is very dissipating to be with people too much. As Channing says, it takes the edge off a man's thoughts to have been much in society. I cannot spare my moonlight and my mountains for the best of man I am likely to get in exchange.

I am inclined now for a pensive evening walk.

I sat on the Bittern Cliff[40] as the still eve drew on. There was a man on Fair Haven furling his sail and bathing from his boat. A boat on a river whose waters are smoothed, and a man disporting in it! How it harmonizes with the stillness and placidity of the evening! Who knows but he is a poet in his yet obscure but golden youth? Few else go alone in to retired scenes without gun or fishing-rod. He bathes in the middle of the pond while his boat slowly drifts away. As I go up the hill, surrounded by its shadow, while the sun is setting, I am soothed by the delicious stillness of the evening, save that on the hills the wind blows. I was surprised by the sound of my own voice. It is an atmosphere burdensome with thought. For the first time for a month, at least, I am reminded that thought is possible. The din of trivialness is silenced. I float over or through the deeps of silence. It is the first silence I have heard for a month. My life had been a River Platte,[41] tinkling over its sands but useless for all great navigation, but now it suddenly became a fathomless ocean. It shelved off to unimagined depths.

Fields[42] to-day sends me a specimen copy of my "Walden." It is to be published on the 12 *inst.*[43]

***August 5.*** I find that we are now in the midst of the meadow-haying season, and almost every meadow or section of a meadow has its band of half a dozen mow-

40  Also called Tupelo Cliff, on the Sudbury River, a half mile north of Fair Haven Bay.
41  Shallow, nonnavigable 310-mile tributary of the Missouri River.
42  James T. Fields (1817–1881), partner in the Boston publishing firm of Ticknor and Fields.
43  *Walden* was published on 9 August 1854.

44 Thoreau's variant spelling of *craunching,* meaning crunching, more specifically crushing or grinding with the teeth.

ers and rakers, either bending to their manly work with regular and graceful motion or resting in the shade, while the boys are turning the grass to the sun. I passed as many as sixty or a hundred men thus at work to-day. They stick up a twig with the leaves on, on the river's brink, as a guide for the mowers, that they may not exceed the owner's bounds. I hear their scythes cronching[44] the coarse weeds by the river's brink as I row near. The horse or oxen stand near at hand in the shade on the firm land, waiting to draw home a load anon. I see a platoon of three or four mowers, one behind the other, diagonally advancing with regular sweeps across the broad meadow and ever and anon standing to whet their scythes. Or else, having made several bouts, they are resting in the shade on the edge of the firm land. In one place I see one sturdy mower stretched on the ground amid his oxen in the shade of an oak, trying to sleep; or I see one wending far inland with a jug to some well-known spring.

*August 6.* We prefer to sail to-day (Sunday) because there are no haymakers in the meadow.

*August 7.* It is inspiriting at last to hear the wind whistle and moan about my attic, after so much trivial summer weather, and to feel cool in my thin pants.

Do you not feel the fruit of your spring and summer beginning to ripen, to harden its seed within you? Do not your thoughts begin to acquire consistency as well as flavor and ripeness? How can we expect a harvest of thought who have not had a seed-time of character? Already some of my small thoughts—fruit of my spring life—are ripe, like the berries which feed the first broods of birds; and other some are prematurely ripe and bright, like the lower leaves of the herbs which have felt the summer's drought.

Seasons when our mind is like the strings of a harp

which is swept, and we stand and listen. A man may hear strains in his thought far surpassing any oratorio.[45]

*August 9. Wednesday.* — To Boston.
 "Walden" published.[46] Elder-berries. Waxwork yellowing.

*August 13.* I remember only with a pang the past spring and summer thus far. I have not been an early riser. Society seems to have invaded and overrun me. I have drank tea and coffee and made myself cheap and vulgar. My days have been all noontides, without sacred mornings and evenings. I desire to rise early henceforth, to associate with those whose influence is elevating, to have such dreams and waking thoughts that my diet may not be indifferent to me.

*August 16.* At the steam-mill sand-bank[47] was the distinct shadow of our shadows,[48] — first on the water,  then the double one on the bank bottom to bottom, one being upside down, — three in all, — one on water, two on land or bushes.

*September 8.* The grapes would no doubt be riper a week hence, but I am compelled to go now before the vines are stripped. I partly smell them out. I pluck splendid great bunches of the purple ones, with a rich bloom on them and the purple glowing through it like a fire; large red ones, also, with light dots, and some clear green. Sometimes I crawl under low and thick bowers, where they have run over the alders only four or five feet high, and see the grapes hanging from a hollow hemisphere of leaves over my head. At other times I see them dark-purple or black against the silvery undersides of the

**45** "One will lose no music by not attending the oratorios and operas," Thoreau wrote in his journal in 1851 [J 2:379]. "My profession is . . . to attend all the oratorios, the operas, in nature" [J 2:472].
**46** Although this brief entry may indicate a lack of enthusiasm or anticipation, Emerson wrote in a letter on 28 August 1854 that Thoreau was "walking up & down Concord, firm-looking, but in a tremble of great expectation."
**47** On 5 January 1852 Thoreau described the sand-bank from Fair Haven: "Sitting on the Cliffs, I see plainly . . . forty or fifty rods west, on the mainland . . . the still almost raw and shelving edge of the bank, the raw sand-scar" [J 3:176].
**48** Thoreau sailed to Fair Haven with John Lewis Russell (1808–1873), Unitarian minister and professor of botany and horticultural physiology at the Massachusetts Horticultural Society from 1833 until his death.

those woods.) The extreme length was eight feet and two inches. Another cow moose, which I have since measured in those woods with a tape, was just six feet from the tip of the hoof to the shoulders, and eight feet long as she lay" [W 3:126].

**58** The central exhibition hall of the Great Exhibition of Art and Industry, which opened in New York on 14 July 1853.

**59** Horace Greeley (1811–1872), journalist and abolitionist who founded and edited the *New York Tribune.* He was a good friend to Thoreau, serving at times as his agent. The *New York Tribune* carried one of the few reviews of *A Week on the Concord and Merrimack Rivers,* and on 29 March 1854 it published an excerpt from the forthcoming *Walden.*

**60** George Snow, financial editor for the *Tribune.*

**61** Solon Robinson (1803–1880), popular writer on primarily agricultural subjects for the *Cultivator* and one-time head of the agricultural department for the *New York Tribune.*

**62** William Henry Fry (1813–1864), composer and, starting in 1852, music critic for the *Tribune.*

**63** Giulia Grisi (1811–1869), Italian soprano who toured the United States in 1854.

**64** P. T. Barnum's American Museum, on the corner of Broadway and Ann Street in lower Manhattan, which Thoreau visited again on 25 October 1856.

**65** Giraffes.

**66** Thoreau delivered "What Shall It Profit?" at the Railroad Hall, Providence. This lecture became the essay "Life Without Principle."

**67** In December 1853 Emerson wrote in his journal: "The other day, Henry Thoreau was speaking to me about my lecture on the Anglo-American, and regretting that whatever was written for a lecture, or whatever succeeded with the audience was bad, etc. I said, I am ambitious to write something which all can read, like Robinson Crusoe. And when I have written a paper or a book, I see with regret that it is not solid, with a right materialistic treatment, which delights every-

est stood about fifteen feet high at most (twelve or thirteen ordinarily). The body was only about five feet long. Why has it horns, but for ornament? Looked through his diorama, and found the houses all over the world much alike. Greeley appeared to know and be known by everybody; was admitted free to the opera, and we were led by a page to various parts of the house at different times. Saw at Museum some large flakes of cutting arrowhead stone made into a sort of wide cleavers, also a hollow stone tube, probably from mounds.

*December 6.* To Providence to lecture.[66]

I see thick ice and boys skating all the way to Providence, but know not when it froze, I have been so busy writing my lecture; probably the night of the 4th.

After lecturing twice this winter I feel that I am in danger of cheapening myself by trying to become a successful lecturer, *i. e.,* to interest my audiences. I am disappointed to find that most that I am and value myself for is lost, or worse than lost, on my audience. I fail to get even the attention of the mass. I should suit them better if I suited myself less. I feel that the public demand an average man, — average thoughts and manners, — not originality, nor even absolute excellence. You cannot interest them except as you are like them and sympathize with them.[67] I would rather that my audience come to me than that I should go to them, and so they be sifted; *i. e.,* I would rather write books than lectures. That is fine, this coarse. To read to a promiscuous audience who are at your mercy the fine thoughts you solaced yourself with far away is as violent as to fatten geese by cramming,[68] and in this case they do not get fatter.

*December 8.* Winter has come unnoticed by me, I have been so busy writing. This is the life most lead in respect to Nature. How different from my habitual one! It is hasty, coarse, and trivial, as if you were a spindle in a factory. The other is leisurely, fine, and glorious, like a flower. In the first case you are merely getting your living; in the second you live as you go along. You travel only on roads of the proper grade without jar or running off the track, and sweep round the hills by beautiful curves.

Here is the river frozen over in many places, I am not sure whether the fourth night or later, but the skating is hobbly or all hobbled like a coat of mail or thickly bossed shield, apparently sleet frozen in water. Very little smooth ice. How black the water where the river is open when I look from the light, by contrast with the surrounding white, the ice and snow! A black artery here and there concealed under a pellicle of ice.

Went over the fields on the crust to Walden, over side of Bear Garden.[69] Already foxes have left their tracks. How the crust shines afar, the sun now setting! There is a glorious clear sunset sky, soft and delicate and warm even like a pigeon's neck. Why do the mountains never look so fair as from my native fields?

*December 20.* P.M.—Skated to Fair Haven with Channing.

Channing's skates are not the best, and beside he is far from an easy skater, so that, as he said, it was killing work for him. Time and again the perspiration actually dropped from his forehead on to the ice, and it froze in long icicles on his beard. Yet he kept up his spirits and his fun, said he had seen much more suffering than I, etc., etc.

I am surprised to find how fast the dog[70] can run in a straight line on the ice. I am not sure that I can beat him on skates, but I can turn much shorter.

body. Henry objected, of course, and vaunted the better lectures which only reached a few persons."
**68** Cramming, also called gavage, the force-feeding of poultry to fatten them, a practice prized by epicures in ancient Egypt, Greece, and Rome. The liver of a force-fed goose produces *foie gras*.
**69** Hill in Concord, east of the Sudbury River, a half mile directly west of Walden Pond.
**70** Channing owned a Newfoundland dog that would often accompany Thoreau and him on their walks together.

71 Something spurious or counterfeit, as in a Bungtown copper, a New England term for a coin counterfeiting the English copper half-penny, and not legal tender; possibly related to the slang term, bung, for a pickpocket or sharper.

72 Daniel Ricketson (1813–1898), a Quaker from New Bedford, started a correspondence and friendship with Thoreau after reading *Walden* that continued for the rest of Thoreau's life.

73 Thoreau wrote very little at this time. Of the more than 200 poems he wrote in his life, the majority were written by the mid-1840s. By 1854 Thoreau was rarely writing poetry, producing barely half a dozen more before he died. On 19 February 1852 he lamented: "The strains from my muse are as rare nowadays, or of late years, as the notes of birds in the winter,—the faintest occasional tinkling sound, and mostly of the woodpecker kind or the harsh jay or crow. It never melts into a song" [J 3:312]. Cf. 18 February 1852.

*December 21.* What a grovelling appetite for profitless jest and amusement our countrymen have! Next to a good dinner, at least, they love a good joke,—to have their sides tickled, to laugh sociably, as in the East they bathe and are shampooed. Curators of lyceums write to me:—

Dear Sir,—I hear that you have a lecture of some humor. Will you do us the favor to read it before the Bungtown[71] Institute?

*December 26.* At Ricketson's.[72]

I do not remember to have ever seen such a day as this in Concord. There is no snow here (though there has been excellent sleighing at Concord since the 5th), but it is very muddy, the frost coming out of the ground as in spring with us. I went to walk in the woods with Ricketson. It was wonderfully warm and pleasant, and the cockerels crowed just as in a spring day at home. I felt the winter breaking up in me, and if I had been at home I should have tried to write poetry.[73]

## 1855

AGE 37–38

1 John Boynton Hill (1796–1886), with whom Emerson kept a correspondence. Emerson was lecturing in Bangor on 28 and 29 December 1854. Hill and his twin brother, Joseph Bancroft Hill (1796–1864), were both classmates of Emerson.
2 Charts published by the United States Coast Survey, established in 1807 by President Thomas Jefferson to create accurate representations of the nation's coastal waters.
3 The Mill Brook began near the eastern edge of Concord and ran through the center of the village before joining the Concord River.

*January 5.* Emerson told of Mr. Hill, his classmate, of Bangor,[1] who was much interested in my "Walden," but relished it merely as a capital satire and joke, and even thought that the survey and map of the pond were not real, but a caricature of the Coast Surveys.[2]

*January 12.* After a spitting of snow in the forenoon, I see the blue sky here and there, and the sun is coming out. It is still and warm. The earth is two thirds bare. I walk along the Mill Brook below Emerson's,[3] looking into it for some life.

Perhaps what most moves us in winter is some reminiscence of far-off summer. How we leap by the side of the open brooks! What beauty in the running brooks! What life! What society! The cold is merely superficial; it is summer still at the core, far, far within. It is in the cawing of the crow, the crowing of the cock, the warmth of the sun on our backs. I hear faintly the cawing of a crow far, far away, echoing from some unseen wood-side, as if deadened by the spring-like vapor which the sun is drawing from the ground. It mingles with the slight murmur of the village, the sound of children at play, as one stream empties gently into another, and the wild and tame are one. What a delicious sound! It is not merely crow calling to crow, for it speaks to me too. I am part of one great creature with him; if he has voice, I have ears. I can hear when he calls, and have engaged not to shoot nor stone him if he will caw to me each spring. On the one hand,

4 Reference to the method of learning by rote.
5 Quoted from the opening of Psalms 103: "Bless the LORD, O my soul: and all that is within me, bless his holy name. Bless the LORD, O my soul, and forget not all his benefits."

it may be, is the sound of children at school saying their a, b, ab's,[4] on the other, far in the wood-fringed horizon, the cawing of crows from their blessed eternal vacation, out at their long recess, children who have got dismissed! While the vaporous incense goes up from all the fields of the spring—if it were spring. Ah, bless the Lord, O my soul![5] bless him for wildness, for crows that will not alight within gunshot! and bless him for hens, too, that croak and cackle in the yard!

*January 26.* What changes in the aspect of the earth! one day russet hills, and muddy ice, and yellow and greenish pools in the fields; the next all painted white, the fields and woods and roofs laid on thick. The great sloshy pools in the fields, freezing as they dried away, look like bread that has spewed in the baking, the fungi of a night, an acre in extent; but trust not your feet on it, for the under side is not done; there the principle of water still prevails.

*February 5.* I notice my old skate-tracks like this:—

It is better skating to-day than yesterday. This is the sixth day of some kind of skating.

*February 5.* In a journal it is important in a few words to describe the weather, or character of the day, as it affects our feelings. That which was so important at the time cannot be unimportant to remember.

*February 7.* The coldest night for a long, long time was last. Sheets froze stiff about the faces. Cat mewed to have the door opened, but was at first disinclined to go out.

When she came in at nine she smelt of meadow-hay. We all took her up and smelled of her, it was so fragrant. Had cuddled in some barn. People dreaded to go to bed. The ground cracked in the night as if a powder-mill had blown up,[6] and the timbers of the house also. My pail of water was frozen in the morning so that I could not break it. Must leave many buttons unbuttoned, owing to numb fingers. Iron was like fire in the hands. Thermometer at about 7.30 A. M. gone into the bulb, –19° at least. The cold has stopped the clock. Every bearded man in the street is a graybeard. Bread, meat, milk, cheese, etc., etc., all frozen. See the inside of your cellar door all covered and sparkling with frost like Golconda.[7] Pity the poor who have not a large wood-pile.

*February 19.* Many will complain of my lectures[8] that they are transcendental. "Can't understand them." "Would you have us return to the savage state?" etc., etc. A criticism true enough, it may be, from their point of view. But the fact is, the earnest lecturer can speak only to his like, and the adapting of himself to his audience is a mere compliment which he pays them. If you wish to know how I think, you must endeavor to put yourself in my place. If you wish me to speak as if I were you, that is another affair.

*February 21.* A warmth begins to be reflected from the partially dried ground here and there in the sun in sheltered places, very cheering to invalids who have weak lungs, who think they may weather it till summer now. Nature is more genial to them. When the leaves on the forest floor are dried, and begin to rustle under such a sun and wind as these, the news is told to how many myriads of grubs that underlie them! When I perceive this dryness under my feet, I feel as if I had got a new sense,

**6** Cf. 7 January 1853, when the Acton Powder Mills exploded.
**7** A fortress and ruined city in India associated with the diamonds found southeast of, and cut in, the city.
**8** Thoreau had recently delivered his lecture "What Shall It Profit?" on 6 December 1854.

or rather I realize what was incredible to me before, that there is a new life in Nature beginning to awake, that her halls are being swept and prepared for a new occupant. It is whispered through all the aisles of the forest that another spring is approaching. The wood mouse listens at the mouth of his burrow, and the chickadee passes the news along.

*March 8.* This morning I got my boat out of the cellar and turned it up in the yard to let the seams open before I calk it. The blue river, now almost completely open (*i. e.* excepting a little ice in the recesses of the shore and a good deal over the meadows), admonishes me to be swift.

*March 20.* Trying the other day to imitate the honking of geese, I found myself flapping my sides with my elbows, as with wings, and uttering something like the syllables *mow-ack* with a nasal twang and twist in my head; and I produced their note so perfectly in the opinion of the hearers that I thought I might possibly draw a flock down.

*March 29.* As I stand on Heywood's Peak, looking over Walden, more than half its surface already sparkling blue water, I inhale with pleasure the cold but wholesome air like a draught of cold water, contrasting it in my memory with the wind of summer, which I do not thus eagerly swallow. This, which is a chilling wind to my fellow, is decidedly refreshing to me, and I swallow it with eagerness as a panacea. I feel an impulse, also, already, to jump into the half-melted pond. This cold wind is refreshing to my palate, as the warm air of summer is not, methinks. I love to stand there and be blown on as much as a horse in July. A field of ice nearly half as big as the pond has drifted against the eastern shore and crumbled up against it, forming a shining white wall of its fragments.

*May 5.* Looking over my book,[9] I found I had done my errands, and said to myself I would find a crow's nest. (I had heard a crow scold at a passing hawk a quarter of an hour before.) I had hardly taken this resolution when, looking up, I saw a crow wending his way across an interval in the woods towards the highest pines in the swamp, on which he alighted. I directed my steps to them and was soon greeted with an angry *caw,* and, within five minutes from my resolve, I detected a new nest close to the top of the tallest white pine in the swamp. A crow circled cawing about it within gunshot, then over me surveying, and, perching on an oak directly over my head within thirty-five feet, cawed angrily. But suddenly, as if having taken a new resolution, it flitted away, and was joined by its mate and two more, and they went off silently a quarter of a mile or more and lit in a pasture, as if they had nothing to concern them in the wood.

*August 5.* It seems that I used to tie a regular granny's knot in my shoe-strings, and I learned of myself—rediscovered—to tie a true square knot, or what sailors sometimes call a reef-knot.[10] It needed to be as secure as a reef-knot in any gale, to withstand the wringing and twisting I gave it in my walks.

*September 25.* In the evening went to Welch's (?) circus[11] with Channing. Approaching, I perceived the peculiar scent which belongs to such places, a certain sourness in the air, suggesting trodden grass and cigar smoke. The curves of the great tent, at least eight or ten rods in diameter,—the main central curve and wherever it rested on a post,—suggested that the tent was the origin of much of the Oriental architecture, the Arabic perhaps. There was

**9** His notebook: cf. 1858 note 30.
**10** Cf. 25 July 1853.
**11** Rufus Welch's (1800–1855) National Circus, which was in or near Concord on this date, as it traveled from Marlboro on 22 September to Groton on 26 September.

the pagoda in perfection. It is remarkable what graceful attitudes feats of strength and agility seem to require.

***October 18.*** How much beauty in decay! I pick up a white oak leaf, dry and stiff, but yet mingled red and green, October-like, whose pulpy part some insect has eaten beneath, exposing the delicate network of its veins. It is very beautiful held up to the light,—such work as only an insect eye could perform. Yet, perchance, to the vegetable kingdom such a revelation of ribs is as repulsive as the skeleton in the animal kingdom. In each case it is some little gourmand, working for another end, that reveals the wonders of nature. There are countless oak leaves in this condition now, and also with a submarginal line of network exposed.

***October 19.*** I see Mrs. Riordan and her little boy[12] coming out of the woods with their bundles of fagots on their backs. It is surprising what great bundles of wood an Irishwoman will contrive to carry. I confess that though I could carry one I should hardly think of making such a bundle of them. They are first regularly tied up, and then carried on the back by a rope,—somewhat like the Indian women and their straps. There is a strange similarity; and the little boy carries his bundle proportionally large. The sticks about four feet long. They make haste to deposit their loads before I see them, for they do not know how pleasant a sight it is to me. The Irishwoman does the squaw's part in many respects. Riordan also buys the old railroad sleepers[13] at three dollars a hundred, but they are much decayed and full of sand.

***October 20.*** I have collected and split up now quite a pile of driftwood,—rails and riders and stems and stumps of trees,—perhaps half or three quarters of a tree. It is more amusing, not only to collect this with my boat and bring it up from the river on my back, but to split it also, than it would be to speak to a farmer for a load of wood and to saw and split that. Each stick I deal with has a history, and I read it as I am handling it, and, last of all, I remember my adventures in getting it, while it is burning in the winter evening. That is the most interesting part of its history. It has made part of a fence or a bridge, perchance, or has been rooted out of a clearing and bears the marks of fire on it. When I am splitting it, I study the effects of water on it, and, if it is a stump, the curiously winding grain by which it separates into so many prongs,—how to take advantage of its grain and split it most easily. I find that a dry oak stump will split pretty easily in the direction of its diameter, but not at right angles with it or along its circles of growth. I got out some good knees for a boat. Thus one half the value of my wood is enjoyed before it is housed, and the other half is equal to the whole value of an equal quantity of the wood which I buy.

Some of my acquaintances have been wondering why I took all this pains, bringing some nearly three miles by water, and have suggested various reasons for it. I tell them in my despair of making them understand me that it is a profound secret,—which it has proved,—yet I did hint to them that one reason was that I wanted to get it. I take some satisfaction in eating my food, as well as in being nourished by it. I feel well at dinner-time as well as after it. The world will never find out why you don't love to have your bed tucked up for you,—why you will be so perverse. I enjoy more drinking water at a clear spring than out of a goblet at a gentleman's table. I like best the bread which I have baked, the garment which I have made, the shelter which I have constructed, the fuel which I have gathered.

It is always a recommendation to me to know that a man has ever been poor, has been regularly born into this world, knows the language. I require to be assured of certain philosophers that they have once been barefooted, footsore, have eaten a crust because they had nothing better, and know what sweetness resides in it.

*October 23.* Now is the time for chestnuts. A stone cast against the trees shakes them down in showers upon one's head and shoulders. But I cannot excuse myself for using the stone. It is not innocent, it is not just, so to maltreat the tree that feeds us. I am not disturbed by considering that if I thus shorten its life I shall not enjoy its fruit so long, but am prompted to a more innocent course by motives purely of humanity. I sympathize with the tree, yet I heaved a big stone against the trunks like a robber,—not too good to commit murder. I trust that I shall never do it again. These gifts should be accepted, not merely with gentleness, but with a certain humble gratitude. The tree whose fruit we would obtain should not be too rudely shaken even. It is not a time of distress, when a little haste and violence even might be pardoned. It is worse than boorish, it is criminal, to inflict an unnecessary injury on the tree that feeds or shadows us. Old trees are our parents, and our parents' parents, perchance. If you would learn the secrets of Nature, you must practice more humanity than others.[14] The thought that I was robbing myself by injuring the tree did not occur to me, but I was affected as if I had cast a rock at a sentient being,—with a duller sense than my own, it is true, but yet a distant relation. Behold a man cutting down a tree to come at the fruit! What is the moral of such an act?

*November 5.* I hate the present modes of living and getting a living. Farming and shopkeeping and working at a trade or profession are all odious to me. I should relish getting my living in a simple, primitive fashion. The life which society proposes to me to live is so artificial and complex—bolstered up on many weak supports, and sure to topple down at last—that no man surely can ever be inspired to live it, and only "old fogies"[15] ever praise it. At best some think it their duty to live it. I believe in the infinite joy and satisfaction of helping myself and others to the extent of my ability. But what is the use in trying to live simply, raising what you eat, making what you wear, building what you inhabit, burning what you cut or dig, when those to whom you are allied insanely want and will have a thousand other things which neither you nor they can raise and nobody else, perchance, will pay for?

*November 7.* I find it good to be out this still, dark, mizzling afternoon; my walk or voyage is more suggestive and profitable than in bright weather. The view is contracted by the misty rain, the water is perfectly smooth, and the stillness is favorable to refection. I am more open to impressions, more sensitive (not calloused or indurated by sun and wind), as if in a chamber still. My thoughts are concentrated; I am all compact. The solitude is real, too, for the weather keeps other men at home. The mist is like a roof and walls over and around, and I walk with a domestic feeling. The sound of a wagon going over an unseen bridge is louder than ever, and so of other sounds. I am *compelled* to look at near objects. All things have a soothing effect; the very clouds and mists brood over me. My power of observation and contemplation is much increased. My attention does not wander. The world and my life are simplified. What now of Europe and Asia?

*November 9.* Found a good stone jug, small size, floating stopple up.[16] I drew the stopple and smelled, as I expected, molasses and water, or something stronger

15 Old and dull persons, possibly from the Scottish *foggie*, originally an army pensioner or veteran.
16 On the Assabet, near the Leaning Hemlocks.

**17** A mixture of rum or whiskey with molasses and vinegar.

**18** Cf. 20 October 1857 for further thoughts on gathering useful things one finds outdoors.

**19** Reuben Rice (1790–1888), who lived on Walden Street in Concord, owned a farm in Sudbury, and kept bees. The night before this entry Rice had talked with Thoreau about "how hard a head a goat had. When he lived in Roxbury a man asked him to kill a goat for him. He accordingly struck the goat with a hatchet, hard enough, as he supposed, to dash his brains out, but the goat instantly, with a bleat, leaped on to a wall and ran twenty rods on the wall faster than they could on the ground after him, and he saw him as much as a month afterward none the worse for the blow" [J 8:25].

**20** The cutting iron or chisel of a plane.

(black-strap?),[17] which it *had* contained. Probably some meadow-haymakers' jug left in the grass, which the recent rise in the river has floated off. It will do to put with the white pitcher I found and keep flowers in. Thus I get my furniture.

I affect what would commonly be called a mean and miserable way of living. I thoroughly sympathize with all savages and gypsies in so far as they merely assert the original right of man to the production of Nature and a place in her.[18] The Irishman moves into the town, sets up a shanty on the railroad land, and then gleans the dead wood from the neighboring forest, which would never get to market. But the so-called owner forbids it and complains of him as a trespasser. The highest law gives a thing to him who can use it.

*November 17.* It is interesting to me to talk with Rice,[19] he lives so thoroughly and satisfactorily to himself. He has learned that rare art of living, the very elements of which most professors do not know. His life has been not a failure but a success. Seeing me going to sharpen some plane-irons,[20] and hearing me complain of the want of tools, he said that I ought to have a chest of tools. But I said it was not worth the while. I should not use them enough to pay for them. "You would use them more, if you had them," said he. "When I came to do a piece of work I used to find commonly that I wanted a certain tool, and I made it a rule first always to make that tool. I have spent as much as $3000 thus on my tools." Comparatively speaking, his life is a success; not such a failure as most men's. He gets more out of any enterprise than his neighbors, for he helps himself more and hires less. Whatever pleasure there is in it he enjoys. By good sense and calculation he has become rich and has invested his property well, yet practices a fair and neat economy, dwells not in untidy luxury. It costs him less to live, and he gets more out of life, than others. To get his living, or keep it, is not a hasty or disagreeable toil. He works slowly but surely, enjoying the sweet of it. He buys a piece of meadow at a profitable rate, works at it in pleasant weather, he and his son,[21] when they are inclined, goes a-fishing or a-bee-hunting or a-rifle-shooting quite as often, and thus the meadow gets redeemed, and potatoes get planted, perchance, and he is very sure to have a good crop stored in his cellar in the fall, and some to sell. He always has the best of potatoes there. In the same spirit in which he and his son tackle up their Dobbin[22] (he never keeps a fast horse) and go a-spearing or a-fishing through the ice, they also tackle up and go to their Sudbury farm to hoe or harvest a little, and when they return they bring home a load of stumps in their hay-rigging, which impeded their labors, but, perchance, supply them with winter wood. All the woodchucks they shoot or trap in the bean-field are brought home also. And thus their life is a long sport and they know not what hard times arc.

*November 30.* On the 27th, when I made my last voyage for the season,[23] I found a large sound pine log about four feet long floating, and brought it home. Off the larger end I sawed two wheels, about a foot in diameter and seven or eight inches thick, and I fitted to them an axle-tree[24] made of a joist, which also I found in the river, and thus I had a convenient pair of wheels on which to get my boat up and roll it about.[25] The assessors called me into their office this year and said they wished to get an inventory of my property; asked if I had any real estate. No. Any notes at interest or railroad shares? No. Any taxable property? None that I knew of. "I own a boat," I said; and one of them thought that that might come under the head of a pleasure carriage, which is taxable.

21 Edward Rice (1843–1873).
22 Often a working farm horse, although sometimes used to describe a quiet plodding horse.
23 Thoreau went to Jacob Brown Farmer's (1801–1872) by way of the Assabet River and Dodge's, or Dakin's, Brook which, according to Thoreau, ran through his farm [J 5:206].
24 Axle.
25 The boat built by Thoreau and his brother John for their 1839 river excursion was also "provided with wheels in order to be rolled around falls" [W 1:13].

26  Holden Spruce Swamp.

Now that I have wheels to it, it comes nearer to it. I was pleased to get my boat in by this means rather than on a borrowed wheelbarrow. It was fit that the river should furnish the material, and that in my last voyage on it, when the ice reminded me that it was time to put it in winter quarters.

*December 11.* For the first time I wear gloves, but I have not walked *early* this season.

I see no birds, but hear, methinks, one or two tree sparrows. No snow; scarcely any ice to be detected. It is only an aggravated November. I thread the tangle of the spruce swamp, admiring the leafets of the swamp pyrus which had put forth again, now frost-bitten, the great yellow buds of the swamp-pink, the round red buds of the high blueberry, and the fine sharp red ones of the panicled andromeda. Slowly I worm my way amid the snarl, the thicket of black alders and blueberry, etc.; see the forms, apparently, of rabbits at the foot of maples, and catbirds' nests now exposed in the leafless thicket.

Standing there,[26] though in this *bare* November landscape, I am reminded of the incredible phenomenon of small birds in winter. That ere long, amid the cold powdery snow, as it were a fruit of the season, will come twittering a flock of delicate crimson-tinged birds, lesser redpolls, to sport and feed on the seeds and buds now just ripe for them on the sunny side of a wood, shaking down the powdery snow there in their cheerful social feeding, as if it were high midsummer to them. These crimson aerial creatures have wings which would bear them quickly to the regions of summer, but here is all the summer they want. What a rich contrast! tropical colors, crimson breasts, on cold white snow! Such etherealness, such delicacy in their forms, such ripeness in their colors, in this stern and barren season! It is as surprising as if you were to find a brilliant crimson flower which flourished amid snows. They greet the chopper and the hunter in their furs. Their Maker gave them the last touch and launched them forth the day of the Great Snow.[27] He made this bitter imprisoning cold before which man quails, but He made at the same time these warm and glowing creatures to twitter and be at home in it. He said not only, Let there be[28] linnets in winter, but linnets of rich plumage and pleasing twitter, bearing summer in their natures. The snow will be three feet deep, the ice will be two feet thick, and last night, perchance, the mercury sank to thirty degrees below zero. All the fountains of nature seem to be sealed up. The traveller is frozen on his way. But under the edge of yonder birch wood will be a little flock of crimson-breasted lesser redpolls, busily feeding on the seeds of the birch and shaking down the powdery snow! As if a flower were created to be now in bloom, a peach to be now first fully ripe on its stem. I am struck by the perfect confidence and success of nature. There is no question about the existence of these delicate creatures, their adaptedness to their circumstances. There is superadded superfluous paintings and adornments, a crystalline, jewel-like health and soundness, like the colors reflected from ice-crystals.

When some rare northern bird like the pine grosbeak is seen thus far south in the winter, he does not suggest poverty, but dazzles us with his beauty. There is in them a warmth akin to the warmth that melts the icicle. Think of these brilliant, warm-colored, and richly warbling birds, birds of paradise, dainty-footed, downy-clad, in the midst of a New England, a Canadian winter. The woods and fields, now somewhat solitary, being deserted by their more tender summer residents, are now frequented by these rich but delicately tinted and hardy northern immigrants of the air. Here is no imperfection to be suggested. The winter, with its snow and ice, is not an evil to be corrected. It is as it was designed and

27 Possible reference to the "Great Snow" of 17 February 1717 described by Cotton Mather in his *Magnalia Christi Americana,* but more likely a general reference to any large snowstorm, as in Thoreau's journal entry for 28 March 1856.
28 Allusion to the phrase used in the Creation, as in Genesis 1:3, 6, 14: "And God said, Let there be . . ."

**29** Thin flake of dead epidermis shed from the surface of the skin.

**30** Although not a common item as today, the battery was an integral part of the telegraph. Thoreau may have been remembering his experience of 30 July 1855: "Saw the lightning on the telegraph battery and heard the shock about sundown from our window,—an intensely bright white light" [J 7:444].

**31** "All change is a miracle to contemplate; but it is a miracle which is taking place every instant," Thoreau wrote in *Walden* [Wa 11]. Unlike the Unitarians, who believed that the miracles of the Bible were performed as part of a special Providence that was not part of the normal course of nature, the view of the Transcendentalists was that miracles were not relegated to the past. Emerson in his Divinity School Address wrote: "He [Jesus] spoke of miracles; for he felt that man's life was a miracle, and all that man doth, and he knew that this daily miracle shines, as the man is diviner. But the very word Miracle, as pronounced by Christian churches, gives a false impression; it is Monster. It is not one with the blowing clover and the falling rain." Thoreau wrote in his journal of 9 June 1850: "Men talk about Bible miracles because there is no miracle in their lives" [J 2:33].

made to be, for the artist has had leisure to add beauty to use. My acquaintances, angels from the north. I had a vision thus prospectively of these birds as I stood in the swamps. I saw this familiar—too *familiar*—fact at a different angle, and I was charmed and haunted by it. But I could only attain to be thrilled and enchanted, as by the sound of a strain of music dying away. I had seen into paradisaic regions, with their air and sky, and I was no longer wholly or merely a denizen of this vulgar earth. Yet had I hardly a foothold there. I was only sure that I was charmed, and no mistake. It is only necessary to behold thus the least fact or phenomenon, however familiar, from a point a hair's breadth aside from our habitual path or routine, to be overcome, enchanted by its beauty and significance. Only what we have touched and worn is trivial,—our scurf,[29] repetition, tradition, conformity. To perceive freshly, with fresh senses, is to be inspired. Great winter itself looked like a precious gem, reflecting rainbow colors from one angle.

My body is all sentient. As I go here or there, I am tickled by this or that I come in contact with, as if I touched the wires of a battery.[30] I can generally recall— have fresh in my mind—several scratches last received. These I continually recall to mind, reimpress, and harp upon. The age of miracles is each moment thus returned.[31] Now it is wild apples, now river reflections, now a flock of lesser redpolls. In winter, too, resides immortal youth and perennial summer. Its head is not silvered; its cheek is not blanched but has a ruby tinge to it.

If any part of nature excites our pity, it is for ourselves we grieve, for there is eternal health and beauty. We get only transient and partial glimpses of the beauty of the world. Standing at the right angle, we are dazzled by the colors of the rainbow in colorless ice. From the right point of view, every storm and every drop in it is a rainbow. Beauty and music are not mere traits and exceptions. They are the rule and character. It is the exception that we see and hear. Then I try to discover what it was in the vision that charmed and translated me. What if we could daguerreotype[32] our thoughts and feelings! for I am surprised and enchanted often by some quality which I cannot detect. I have seen an attribute of another world and condition of things. It is a wonderful fact that I should be affected, and thus deeply and powerfully, more than by aught else in all my experience, — that this fruit should be borne in me, sprung from a seed finer than the spores of fungi, floated from other atmospheres! finer than the dust caught in the sails of vessels a thousand miles from land! Here the invisible seeds settle, and spring, and bear flowers and fruits of immortal beauty.

*December 23.* I admire those old root fences which have almost entirely disappeared from tidy fields, — white pine roots got out when the neighboring meadow was a swamp, — the monuments of many a revolution. These roots have not penetrated into the ground, but spread over the surface, and, having been cut off four or five feet from the stump, were hauled off and set up on their edges for a fence. The roots are not merely interwoven, but grown together into solid frames, full of loopholes[33] like Gothic windows of various sizes and all shapes, triangular and oval and harp-like, and the slenderer parts are dry and resonant like harp-strings. They are rough and unapproachable, with a hundred snags and horns which bewilder and balk the calculation of the walker who would surmount them. The part of the trees above ground presents no such fantastic forms. Here is one seven paces, or more than a rod, long, six feet high in the middle, and yet only one foot thick, and two men could turn it up, and in this case the roots were six or nine inches thick at the extremities. The roots of pines growing in swamps grow thus in the form of solid frames

**32** Early negativeless form of photograph print on glass plates, invented in the mid-1830s by French photographic pioneer Louis Jacques Mandé Daguerre (1789–1851).
**33** An architectural term for narrow slits used for observation or through which to fire arrows or other small weapons.

34 Not liable to harm or injury.

or rackets, and those of different trees are interwoven with all so that they stand on a very broad foot and stand or fall together to some extent before the blasts, as herds meet the assault of beasts of prey with serried front. You have thus only to dig into the swamp a little way to find your fence,—post, rails, and slats already solidly grown together and of material more durable than any timber. How pleasing a thought that a field should be fenced with the roots of the trees got out in clearing the land a century before! I regret them as mementoes of the primitive forest. The tops of the same trees made into fencing-stuff would have decayed generations ago. These roots are singularly unobnoxious[34] to the effects of moisture.

*December 26.* In a true history or biography, of how little consequence those events of which so much is commonly made! For example, how difficult for a man to remember in what towns or houses he has lived, or when! Yet one of the first steps of his biographer will be to establish these facts, and he will thus give an undue importance to many of them. I find in my Journal that the most important events in my life, if recorded at all, are not dated.

*December 27.* Recalled this evening, with the aid of Mother, the various houses (and towns) in which I have lived and some events of my life.

# 1856

AGE 38–39

*January 10.* I love to wade and flounder through the swamp now,[1] these bitter cold days when the snow lies deep on the ground, and I need travel but little way from the town to get to a Nova Zembla solitude, — to wade through the swamps, all snowed up, untracked by man, into which the fine dry snow is still drifting till it is even with the tops of the water andromeda and half-way up the high blueberry bushes. I penetrate to islets inaccessible in summer, my feet slumping to the sphagnum far out of sight beneath, where the alder berry glows yet and the azalea buds, and perchance a single tree sparrow or chickadee lisps by my side, where there are few tracks even of wild animals; perhaps only a mouse or two have burrowed up by the side of some twig, and hopped away in straight lines on the surface of the light, deep snow, as if too timid to delay, to another hole by the side of another bush; and a few rabbits have run in a path amid the blueberries and alders about the edge of the swamp. This is instead of a Polar Expedition and going after Franklin.[2]

This freezing weather[3] I see the pumps dressed in mats and old clothes or bundled in straw. Fortunate he who has placed his cottage on the south side of some high hill or some dense wood, and not on the middle of the Great Fields, where there is no hill nor tree to shelter it. There the winds have full sweep, and such a day as yesterday the house is but a fence to stay the drifting snow. Such

1 Thoreau noted above this entry: "Remembering the walk of yesterday," when he had walked to Beck Stow's Swamp.
2 Sir John Franklin (1786–1847), English explorer, who was last seen in Baffin Bay. He disappeared in 1847 in the Arctic attempting to find the Northwest Passage, and his remains were not discovered until 1859. Sherard Osborn's (1822–1875) *Stray Leaves from an Artic Journal; or, Eighteen Months in the Polar Regions in Search of Sir John Franklin's Expedition in the Years 1850–51* was published in 1852 and Elisha Kent Kane's *The United States Grinnell Expedition in Search of Sir John Franklin: A Personal Narrative* in 1853.
3 Thoreau noted earlier in this day's entry that "the weather has considerably moderated; −2° at breakfast time (it was −8° at seven last evening); but this has been the coldest night probably. You lie with your feet or legs curled up, waiting for morning, the sheets shining with frost about your mouth. Water left by the stove is frozen thickly, and what you sprinkle in bathing falls on the floor ice. The house plants are all frozen and soon droop and turn black" [J 8:98].

is the piercing wind, no man loiters between his house and barn. The road-track is soon obliterated, and the path which leads round to the back of the house, dug this morning, is filled up again, and you can no longer see the tracks of the master of the house, who only an hour ago took refuge in some half-subterranean apartment there. You know only by an occasional white wreath of smoke from his chimney, which is at once snapped up by the hungry air, that he sits warming his wits there within, studying the almanac to learn how long it is before spring. But his neighbor, who, only half a mile off, has placed his house in the shelter of a wood, is digging out of a drift his pile of roots and stumps, hauled from the swamp, at which he regularly dulls his axe and saw, reducing them to billets that will fit his stove. With comparative safety and even comfort he labors at this mine.

As for the other, the windows give no sign of inhabitants, for they are frosted over as if they were ground glass, and the curtains are down beside. The path is snowed up, and all tracks to and fro. No sound issues from within. It remains only to examine the chimney's nostrils. I look long and sharp at it, and fancy that I see some smoke against the sky there, but this is deceptive, for, as we are accustomed to walk up to an empty fireplace and imagine that we feel some heat from it, so I have convinced myself that I saw smoke issuing from the chimney of a house which had not been inhabited for twenty years. I had so vivid an idea of smoke curling up from a chimney's top that no painter could have matched my imagination. It was as if the spirits of the former inhabitants, revisiting their old haunts, were once more boiling a spiritual kettle below, — a small whitish-bluish cloud, almost instantly dissipated, as if the fire burned with a very clear flame, or else, the postmeridian hours having arrived, it were partially raked up, and the inhabitants were taking their siesta.

*January 20.* In my experience I have found nothing so truly impoverishing as what is called wealth,[4] *i. e.* the command of greater means than you had before possessed, though comparatively few and slight still, for you thus inevitably acquire a more expensive habit of living, and even the very same necessaries and comforts cost you more than they once did. Instead of gaining, you have lost some independence, and if your income should be suddenly lessened, you would find yourself poor, though possessed of the same means which once made you rich. Within the last five years I have had the command of a little more money than in the previous five years, for I have sold some books and some lectures;[5] yet I have not been a whit better fed or clothed or warmed or sheltered, not a whit richer, except that I have been less concerned about my living, but perhaps my life has been the less serious for it, and, to balance it, I feel now that there is a possibility of failure. Who knows but I *may* come upon the town, if, as is likely, the public want no more of my books, or lectures (which last is already the case)?[6] Before, I was much likelier to take the town upon my shoulders. That is, I have lost some of my independence on them, when they would say that I had gained an independence. If you wish to give a man a sense of poverty, give him a thousand dollars. The next hundred dollars he gets will not be worth more than ten that he used to get. Have pity on him; withhold your gifts.

*January 22.* I have attended the felling and, so to speak, the funeral of this old citizen of the town,[7] — I who commonly do not attend funerals,[8] — as it became me to do. I was the chief if not the only mourner there. I have taken the measure of his grandeur; have spoken a few words of eulogy at his grave, remembering the maxim *de mortuis nil nisi bonum*[9] (in this case *magnum*[10]). But there were only the choppers and the passers-by to hear

**4** This is the kind of literary device of which Emerson wrote in his eulogy of Thoreau: "The habit of a realist to find things the reverse of their appearance inclined him to put every statement in a paradox. A certain habit of antagonism defaced his earlier writings, — a trick of rhetoric not quite outgrown in his later, of substituting for the obvious word and thought its diametrical opposite. He praised wild mountains and winter forests for their domestic air, in snow and ice he would find sultriness, and commended the wilderness for resembling Rome and Paris." Cf. also Thoreau's statement in *Walden* that he found no companion "so companionable as solitude" [Wa 131]. Thoreau listed this device as a fault in his journal: "Paradoxes, — saying just the opposite, — a style which may be imitated" [J 7:7].

**5** *Walden* went on sale in August 1854. Since 1850 Thoreau had given twenty-seven lectures, although he was not always remunerated for them. He had also earned money from more than seventy surveying jobs, some menial jobs for Emerson, and the family pencil business.

**6** In 1855 Thoreau had only two speaking engagements (in January and February), producing a stretch from then until this journal entry of nearly a year without giving a lecture.

**7** The Great Davis Elm, under the old Hill Burying Ground (cf. 1857 note 109) on the property of Charles Davis. Thoreau noted: "Davis and the neighbors were much alarmed by the creaking in the late storms, for fear it would fall on their roofs. It stands two or three feet into Davis's yard" [J 8:117]. Thoreau had measured the tree on 2 June 1852, again on 19 January 1854, and a third time on 21 January after it was cut down (a process that took several days). On 26 January he counted its rings and found that the tree was 127 years old.

**8** On 3 August 1852 Thoreau wrote in his journal apropos of funerals: "What remarkable customs still prevail at funerals! The chief mourner, though it may be a maiden who has lost her lover, consents to be made a sort of puppet and is by them put forward to walk behind the corpse in the street, before the eyes of all, at a time which should be sacred to grief; is, beside, compelled, as it were to attend to the coarse and unfeeling, almost inevitably to her impertinent, words of consolation or admonition, so called, of whatever clerical gentleman may be in the neighborhood. Friends and neighbors of the family should bury their dead" [J 4:277].

**9** Latin: Of the dead say nothing but what is good. The first recorded use is found in Diogenes Laërtius's *Lives of the Eminent Philosophers* (3rd century c.e.).

**10** Latin: great, grand.

**11** Allusion to 2 Samuel 1:19: "The beauty of Israel is slain upon thy high places: how are the mighty fallen!"

**12** In Boston, the Massachusetts General Court is the state legislature.

**13** The most ornate of the three classical Greek styles of architectural column and the only containing flowering leaflike designs.

**14** Peter Bulkeley (1583–1659), a founder and the first minister of Concord, and author of *The Gospel-Covenant; or The Covenant of Grace Opened;* Ezra Ripley (1751–1841), minister of the First Parish in Concord, and Emerson's step-grandfather, who helped establish a town school committee, the Concord Lyceum, and the first local Temperance Society, and authored a *History of the Fight at Concord.*

**15** Vertical beam connecting the apex of a triangular truss with the base, and as such, a structural support.

me. Further the town was not represented; the fathers of the town, the selectmen, the clergy were not there. But I have not known a fitter occasion for a sermon of late. Travellers whose journey was for a short time delayed by its prostrate body were forced to pay it some attention and respect, but the axe-boys had climbed upon it like ants, and commenced chipping at it before it had fairly ceased groaning. There was a man already bargaining for some part. How have the mighty fallen![11] Its history extends back over more than half the whole history of the town. Since its kindred could not conveniently attend, I attended. Methinks its fall marks an epoch in the history of the town. It has passed away together with the clergy of the old school and the stage-coach which used to rattle beneath it. Its virtue was that it steadily grew and expanded from year to year to the very last. How much of old Concord falls with it! The town clerk will not chronicle its fall. I will, for it is of greater moment to the town than that of many a human inhabitant would be. Instead of erecting a monument to it, we take all possible pains to obliterate its stump, the only monument of a tree which is commonly allowed to stand. Another link that bound us to the past is broken. How much of old Concord was cut away with it! A few such elms would alone constitute a township. They might claim to send a representative to the General Court[12] to look after their interests, if a fit one could be found, a native American one in a true and worthy sense, with catholic principles. Our town has lost some of its venerableness. No longer will our eyes rest on its massive gray trunk, like a vast Corinthian column[13] by the wayside; no longer shall we walk in the shade of its lofty, spreading dome. It is as if you had laid the axe at the feet of some venerable Buckley or Ripley.[14] You have laid the axe, you have made fast your tackle, to one of the king-posts[15] of the town. I feel the whole building wracked by it. Is it not sacrilege to cut down the tree which has so long looked over Concord beneficently?

*January 24.* A journal is a record of experiences and growth, not a preserve of things well done or said. I am occasionally reminded of a statement which I have made in conversation and immediately forgotten, which would read much better than what I put in my journal. It is a ripe, dry fruit of long-past experience which falls from me easily, without giving pain or pleasure. The charm of the journal must consist in a certain greenness, though freshness, and not in maturity. Here I cannot afford to be remembering what I said or did, my scurf cast off, but what I am and aspire to become.

Reading the hymns of the Rig Veda, translated by Wilson,[16] which consist in a great measure of simple epithets addressed to the firmament, or the dawn, or the winds, which mean more or less as the reader is more or less alert and imaginative, and seeing how widely the various translators have differed,[17] they regarding not the poetry, but the history and philology, dealing with very concise Sanscrit, which must almost always be amplified to be understood, I am sometimes inclined to doubt if the translator has not made something out of nothing,—whether a real idea or sentiment has been thus transmitted to us from so primitive a period. I doubt if learned Germans[18] might not thus edit pebbles from the seashore[19] into hymns of the Rig Veda, and translators translate them accordingly, extracting the meaning which the sea has imparted to them in very primitive times. While the commentators and translators are disputing about the meaning of this word or that, I hear only the resounding of the ancient sea and put into it all the meaning I am possessed of, the deepest murmurs I can recall, for I do not the least care where I get my ideas, or what suggests them.

16 Horace Hayman Wilson's (1786–1860) six-volume *Rig-Veda-Sanhitá: A Collection of Ancient Hindu Hymns* (London: W. H. Allen, 1850–1888).
17 Reference to Rajah Rammohun Roy's (ca. 1772–1833) *Translation of Several Principal Books, Passages, and Texts of the Veds* (London, 1832) or to any of several early French translations, such as Simon Alexandre Langlois's *Rig-véda, or Livres des Hymes* (Paris, 1848–1851), Jules Barthélemy Saint-Hilaire's (1805–1895) *Des Védas* (Paris, 1854), or Félix Nève's (1816–1893) *Études sur les Hymnes du Rig-Vêda* (Paris, 1842).
18 Allusion to the higher criticism—biblical exegesis free from confessional and dogmatic theology, in which the same principles of science and historical method applied to secular works are applied to sacred literature—of German scholars such as Johann Salomo Semler (1725–1791), Johann Gottfried Eichhorn (1752–1827), Ferdinand Christian Baur (1792–1860), and Julius Wellhausen (1844–1918).
19 Possible allusion to Isaac Newton's statement about pebbles on the seashore: cf. 1858 note 62.

**20** Cf. 12 May 1851.

**21** Mary Moody Emerson: cf. 1851 note 174.

**22** Thoreau asked in *Walden:* "Could a greater miracle take place than for us to look through each other's eyes for an instant?" [Wa 10].

**23** Eastern red cedar (*Juniperus virginiana*).

**24** Cf. "The Succession of Forest Trees," in which Thoreau elaborated his theory of seed dispersion. He wrote of the cherry: "Thus, though these seeds are not provided with vegetable wings, Nature has impelled the thrush tribe to take them into their bills and fly away with them; and they are winged in another sense, and more effectually than the seeds of pines, for these are carried even against the wind. The consequence is, that cherry trees grow not only here but there. The same is true of a great many other seeds" [W 5:188].

**25** In 1850 the United States and Great Britain signed the Clayton-Bulwer Treaty, an agreement that both nations were not to colonize or control any Central American republic. The purpose was to prevent one country from building a canal across Central America that the other would not be able to use and thus ensuring that any canal built would be open to all nations on equal terms. In 1856 the United States claimed that Britain was bound to surrender its possessions in British Honduras, the Bay Islands, and the Mosquito Protectorate. Britain declined to accede to this interpretation, but offered to abide by the award of a third party, to which the United States would not agree. At the start of 1856 war seemed probable.

**26** Professional card player, often a cheat, who frequented the Mississippi riverboats.

**27** Thoreau added a note here: "Will it not be thought disreputable at length, as duelling between individuals now is?"

*January 26.* When I took the ether[20] my consciousness amounted to this: I put my finger on myself in order to keep the place, otherwise I should never have returned to this world.

Talking with Miss Mary Emerson[21] this evening, she said, "It was not the fashion to be so original when I was young." She is readier to take my view — look through my eyes for the time[22] — than any young person that I know in the town.

*February 4.* I have often wondered how red cedars[23] could have sprung up in some pastures which I knew to be miles distant from the nearest fruit-bearing cedar, but it now occurs to me that these and barberries, etc., may be planted by the crows, and probably other birds.[24]

*February 27.* The papers are talking about the prospect of a war between England and America.[25] Neither side sees how its country can avoid a long and fratricidal war without sacrificing its honor. Both nations are ready to take a desperate step, to forget the interests of civilization and Christianity and their commercial prosperity and fly at each other's throats. When I see an individual thus beside himself, thus desperate, ready to shoot or be shot, like a blackleg[26] who has little to lose, no serene aims to accomplish, I think he is a candidate for bedlam. What asylum is there for nations to go to? Nations are thus ready to talk of wars and challenge one another,[27] because they are made up to such an extent of poor, low-spirited, despairing men, in whose eyes the chance of shooting somebody else without being shot themselves exceeds their actual good fortune. Who, in fact, will be the first to enlist but the most desperate class, they who have lost all hope? And they may at last infect the rest.

*March 4.* I had two friends. The one offered me friendship on such terms that I could not accept it, without a sense of degradation.[28] He would not meet me on equal terms, but only be to some extent my patron. He would not come to see me, but was hurt if I did not visit him. He would not readily accept a favor, but would gladly confer one. He treated me with ceremony occasionally, though he could be simple and downright sometimes; and from time to time acted a part, treating me as if I were a distinguished stranger; was on stilts, using made words. Our relation was one long tragedy, yet I did not directly speak of it. I do not believe in complaint, nor in explanation. The whole is but too plain, alas, already. We grieve that we do not love each other, that we cannot confide in each other. I could not bring myself to speak, and so recognize an obstacle to our affection.

I had another friend, who, through a slight obtuseness, perchance, did not recognize a fact which the dignity of friendship would by no means allow me to descend so far as to speak of,[29] and yet the inevitable effect of that ignorance was to hold us apart forever.

*March 10.* Think of the art of printing, what miracles it has accomplished! Covered the very waste paper which flutters under our feet like leaves and is almost as cheap, a stuff now commonly put to the most trivial uses, with thought and poetry! The woodchopper reads the wisdom of ages recorded on the paper that holds his dinner, then lights his pipe with it. When we ask for a scrap of paper for the most trivial use, it may have the confessions of Augustine[30] or the sonnets of Shakespeare, and we not observe it. The student kindles his fire, the editor packs his trunk, the sportsman loads his gun,[31] the traveller wraps his dinner, the Irishman papers his shanty, the schoolboy peppers the plastering,[32] the belle pins up her

28 Emerson, who wrote of Thoreau the previous month: "If I knew only Thoreau, I should think cooperation of good men impossible. Must we always talk for victory, and never once for truth, for comfort, and joy? Centrality he has, and penetration, strong understanding, and the higher gifts—the insight of the real or from the real, and the moral rectitude that belongs to it; but all this and all his resources of wit and invention are lost to me in every experiment, year after year, that I make, to hold intercourse with his mind. Always some weary captious paradox to fight you with, and the time and temper wasted."

29 Channing: cf. 12 April 1852.

30 Saint Augustine of Hippo (354–430), theologian and author of *City of God*, whose *Confessions* traced the progression from his sinful youth through his conversion to Catholicism.

31 As a wad used to press the powder and shot close.

32 Chewed and used as a projectile.

**33** On 30 March 1814 the allied armies of England, Russia, Prussia, and Austria marched into Paris. This formally ended the Napoleonic domination of Europe.

hair, with the printed thoughts of men. Surely he who can see so large a portion of earth's surface thus darkened with the record of human thought and experience, and feel no desire to learn to read it, is without curiosity. He who cannot read is worse than deaf and blind, is yet but half alive, is still-born.

*March 11.* When it was proposed to me to go abroad, rub off some rust, and *better my condition* in a worldly sense, I fear lest my life will lose some of its homeliness. If these fields and streams and woods, the phenomena of nature here, and the simple occupations of the inhabitants should cease to interest and inspire me, no culture or wealth would atone for the loss. I fear the dissipation that travelling, going into society, even the best, the enjoyment of intellectual luxuries, imply. If Paris is much in your mind, if it is more and more to you, Concord is less and less, and yet it would be a wretched bargain to accept the proudest Paris in exchange for my native village. At best, Paris could only be a school in which to learn to live here, a stepping-stone to Concord, a school in which to fit for this university. I wish so to live ever as to derive my satisfactions and inspirations from the commonest events, every-day phenomena, so that what my senses hourly perceive, my daily walk, the conversation of my neighbors, may inspire me, and I may dream of no heaven but that which lies about me. A man may acquire a taste for wine or brandy, and so lose his love for water, but should we not pity him?

The sight of a marsh hawk in Concord meadows is worth more to me than the entry of the allies into Paris.[33] In this sense I am not ambitious. I do not wish my native soil to become exhausted and run out through neglect. Only that travelling is good which reveals to me the value of home and enables me to enjoy it better. That man is the richest whose pleasures are the cheapest.

It is strange that men are in such haste to get fame as teachers rather than knowledge as learners.

*March 21.* 10 A.M. It is worth the while to know that there is all this sugar in our woods,[34] much of which might be obtained by using the refuse wood lying about, without damage to the proprietors, who use neither the sugar nor the wood.

Had a dispute with Father about the *use* of my making this sugar when I knew it could be done and might have bought sugar cheaper at Holden's.[35] He said it took me from my studies.[36] I said I made it my study; I felt as if I had been to a university.

*March 23.* I spend a considerable portion of my time observing the habits of the wild animals, my brute neighbors. By their various movements and migrations they fetch the year about to me. Very significant are the flight of geese and the migration of suckers, etc., etc.[37] But when I consider that the nobler animals have been exterminated here,—the cougar, panther, lynx, wolverene, wolf, bear, moose, deer, the beaver, the turkey, etc., etc.,[38]—I cannot but feel as if I lived in a tamed, and, as it were, emasculated country. Would not the motions of those larger and wilder animals have been more significant still? Is it not a maimed and imperfect nature that I am conversant with? As if I were to study a tribe of Indians that had lost all its warriors. Do not the forest and the meadow now lack expression, now that I never see nor think of the moose with a lesser forest on his head in the one, nor of the beaver in the other? When I think what were the various sounds and notes, the migrations and works, and changes of fur and plumage which ushered in the spring and marked the other seasons of the year, I am reminded that this my life in na-

34 Thoreau had gone to his "red maple sugar camp" in Trillium Woods, a quarter mile northwest of his Walden house site, gathering sap that he made into sugar.

35 Walcott and Holden's grocery store in Concord.

36 Thoreau described his father as "wholly unpretending; and there was this peculiarity in his aim, that, though he had pecuniary difficulties to contend with the greater part of his life, he always studied merely how to make a *good* article, pencil or other, (for he practised various arts) and was never satisfied with what he had produced,—nor was he ever in the least disposed to put off a *poor* one for the sake of pecuniary gain;—as if he labored for a higher end" [C 546].

37 Cf. 18 April 1852: "I am serene and satisfied when the birds fly and the fishes swim as in fable, for the moral is not far off; when the migration of the goose is significant and has a moral to it; when the events of the day have a mythological character, and the most trivial is symbolical."

38 Although deer had been hunted nearly to extinction, not all of these animals were completely exterminated in the Concord area in Thoreau's day. Some of them were still sighted in the eastern part of the state, and Thoreau wrote as much in his "Natural History of Massachusetts": "It appears from the Report that there are about forty quadrupeds belonging to the State, and among these one is glad to hear of a few bears, wolves, lynxes, and wildcats" [W 5:114].

**39** Cf. 11 March 1856.

**40** Charles Dunbar (1780–1856), Thoreau's maternal uncle, who discovered a deposit of high-quality graphite in Bristol, New Hampshire, and began what eventually became the Thoreau family pencil business. On 3 April 1856 Thoreau reminisced: "He had a strong head and never got drunk; would drink gin sometimes, but not to excess. Did not use tobacco, except snuff out of another's box sometimes. Was very neat in his person. Was not profane, though vulgar. . . . Uncle Charles used to say that he had n't a single tooth in his head. The fact was they were all double, and I have heard that he lost about all of them by the time he was twenty-one. Ever since I knew him he could swallow his nose" [J 8:246].

**41** Variant of intervale: chiefly a New England term meaning a tract of low-lying land between hills.

ture, this particular round of natural phenomena which I call a year, is lamentably incomplete. I listen to a concert in which so many parts are wanting. The whole civilized country is to some extent turned into a city, and I am that citizen whom I pity.[39] Many of those animal migrations and other phenomena by which the Indians marked the season are no longer to be observed. I seek acquaintance with Nature,—to know her moods and manners. Primitive Nature is the most interesting to me. I take infinite pains to know all the phenomena of the spring, for instance, thinking that I have here the entire poem, and then, to my chagrin, I hear that it is but an imperfect copy that I possess and have read, that my ancestors have torn out many of the first leaves and grandest passages, and mutilated it in many places. I should not like to think that some demigod had come before me and picked out some of the best of the stars. I wish to know an entire heaven and an entire earth. All the great trees and beasts, fishes and fowl are gone. The streams, perchance, are somewhat shrunk.

*March 27.* Uncle Charles[40] died this morning, about midnight, aged seventy-six.

*March 28.* Uncle Charles buried. He was born in February, 1780, the winter of the Great Snow, and he dies in the winter of another great snow,—a life bounded by great snows.

I think to say to my friend, There is but one interval[41] between us. You are on one side of it, I on the other. You know as much about it as I,—how wide, how impassable it is. I will endeavor not to blame you. Do not blame me. There is nothing to be said about it. Recognize the truth, and pass over the intervals that are bridged.

Farewell, my friends, my path inclines to this side the

mountain, yours to that. For a long time you have appeared further and further off to me. I see that you will at length disappear altogether. For a season my path seems lonely without you. The meadows are like barren ground. The memory of me is steadily passing away from you. My path grows narrower and steeper, and the night is approaching. Yet I have faith that, in the definite future, new suns will rise, and new plains expand before me, and I trust that I shall therein encounter pilgrims who bear that same virtue that I recognized in you, who will be that very virtue that was you. I accept the everlasting and salutary law, which was promulgated as much that spring that I first knew you, as this that I seem to lose you.

My former friends, I visit you as one walks amid the columns of a ruined temple. You belong to an era, a civilization and glory, long past. I recognize still your fair proportions, notwithstanding the convulsions which we have felt, and the weeds and jackals that have sprung up around. I come here to be reminded of the past, to read your inscriptions, the hieroglyphics, the sacred writings. We are no longer the representatives[42] of our former selves.

*April 3.* I revive with Nature; her victory is mine.

*April 9.* I go off a little to the right of the railroad, and sit on the edge of that sand-crater near the spring by the railroad. Sitting there on the warm bank, above the broad, shallow, crystalline pool, on the sand, amid russet banks of curled early sedge-grass, showing a little green at base, and dry leaves, I hear one hyla peep faintly several times. This is, then, a degree of warmth sufficient for the hyla. He is the first of his race to awaken to the new year and pierce the solitudes with his voice. He shall wear the medal for this year. You hear him, but you will never find him. He is somewhere down amid the with-

42 Possible allusion to Emerson's *Representative Men.*

ered sedge and alder bushes there by the water's edge, but where? From that quarter his shrill blast sounded, but he is silent, and a kingdom will not buy it again.

The communications from the gods to us are still deep and sweet, indeed, but scanty and transient,—enough only to keep alive the memory of the past. I remarked how many old people died off on the approach of the present spring.[43] It is said that when the sap begins to flow in the trees our diseases become more violent. It is now advancing toward summer apace, and we seem to be reserved to taste its sweetness, but to perform what great deeds? Do we detect the reason why we also did not die on the approach of spring?

*April 22.* Soon after I turned about in Fair Haven Pond, it began to rain hard. The wind was but little south of east and therefore not very favorable for my voyage. I raised my sail and, cowering under my umbrella in the stern, wearing the umbrella like a cap and holding the handle between my knees, I steered and paddled, almost perfectly sheltered from the heavy rain. Yet my legs and arms were a little exposed sometimes, in my endeavors to keep well to windward so as to double certain capes ahead. For the wind occasionally drove me on to the western shore. From time to time, from under my umbrella, I could see the ducks spinning away before me, like great bees. For when they are flying low directly from you, you see hardly anything but their vanishing dark bodies, while the rapidly moving wings or paddles, seen edgewise, are almost invisible. At length, when the river turned more easterly, I was obliged to take down my sail and paddle slowly in the face of the rain, for the most part not seeing my course, with the umbrella slanted before me. But though my progress was slow and laborious, and at length I began to get a little wet, I enjoyed the adventure because it combined to some ex-

43 According to the Concord *Reports of the Selectmen, Overseers of the Poor, and Other Town Officers,* of the 39 persons who died in 1856, 17 were over the age of 50. Of the 35 who died the previous year, 11 were over 50.

tent the advantages of being at home in my chamber and abroad in the storm at the same time.

It is highly important to invent a dress which will enable us to be abroad with impunity in the severest storms. We cannot be said to have fully invented clothing yet. In the meanwhile the rain-water collects in the boat, and you must sit with your feet curled up on a paddle, and you expose yourself in taking down your mast and raising it again at the bridges.

*April 28.* Surveying the Tommy Wheeler farm.[44]

Again, as so many times, I am reminded of the advantage to the poet, and philosopher, and naturalist, and whomsoever, of pursuing from time to time some other business than his chosen one,—seeing with the side of the eye. The poet will so get visions which no deliberate abandonment can secure. The philosopher is so forced to recognize principles which long study might not detect. And the naturalist even will stumble upon some new and unexpected flower or animal.

*April 30.* A fine morning. I hear the first brown thrasher singing within three or four rods of me on the shrubby hillside in front of the Hadley place.[45] I think I had a glimpse of one darting down from a sapling-top into the bushes as I rode by the same place on the morning of the 28th. This, I think, is the very place to hear them early, a dry hillside sloping to the south, covered with young wood and shrub oaks. I am the more attracted to that house as a dwelling-place. To live where you would hear the first brown thrasher! First, perchance, you have a glimpse of one's ferruginous long brown back, instantly lost amid the shrub oaks, and are uncertain if it was a thrasher, or one of the other thrushes; and your uncertainty lasts commonly a day or two, until its rich and varied strain is heard. Surveying[46] seemed a noble

44 A 26-acre plot between the Old Marlboro Road guidepost and Williams Road. Thoreau's note: "I believe it was this morning there was quite a fog."
45 The former Hadley place, north of the Wheeler farm across the railroad tracks, was at this time owned by Joseph Hosmer (cf. 1851 note 180).
46 Thoreau was continuing his survey of the Wheeler farm on this date.

47 Natural spring in Jacob Baker's beech grove on his farm in Lincoln. Cf. 12 July 1857.

48 Figuratively, showing marks of injury or rough usage.

49 German: with a natural slowness. Thoreau may have known the term from Johann Peter Eckermann's (1792–1854) compilation *Gespräche mit Goethe* for 1 October 1828: "Man muß mit der Natur langsam und läßlich verfahren, wenn man ihr etwas abgewinnen will," which Margaret Fuller translated as: "We must go to work slowly and indulgently (*lasslich*) with nature, if we would get any thing from her." As Emerson wrote to Fuller in 1839: "We are strangely impatient of the secular crystallizations of nature in Cavern or in Man, of that which Goethe distinguishes by the grand word *Naturlangsamkeit*," and similarly in "Friendship": "Our impatience is thus sharply rebuked. Bashfulness and apathy are a tough husk, in which a delicate organization is protected from premature ripening. It would be lost if it knew itself before any of the best souls were yet ripe enough to know and own it. Respect the *naturlangsamkeit* which hardens the ruby in a million years, and works in duration in which Alps and Andes come and go as rainbows."

50 Thoreau was visiting Daniel Ricketson in New Bedford from 23 June to 2 July. Martha Simons, sometimes Simon (d. ca. 1859), was a Wampanoag, a member of the Algonquian people of Rhode Island and Massachusetts. In his journal Ricketson wrote: "Made an excursion to the end of Sconticut Neck with my friend Thoreau, in search of marine plants, &c. On our return called to see an old Indian woman by the name of Martha Simonds [sic] living alone in a little dwelling of but one room. It was very interesting to see her, as she is not only a pure blooded Indian, but the last of her tribe, probably the Nemaskets."

51 Unidentified.

employment which brought me within hearing of this bird.

*May 15.* Cleared out the Beech Spring,[47] which is a copious one. So I have done some service, though it was a wet and muddy job. Cleared out a spring while you have been to the wars.[48] Now that warmer days make the traveller thirsty, this becomes an important work.

*May 17.* How plainly we are a part of nature!

*June 10.* A painted tortoise laying her eggs ten feet from the wheel-track on the Marlborough road. She paused at first, but I sat down within two feet, and she soon resumed her work. Had excavated a hollow about five inches wide and six long in the moistened sand, and cautiously, with long intervals, she continued her work, resting always on the same spot her fore feet, and never looking round, her eye shut all but a narrow slit. Whenever I moved, perhaps to brush off a mosquito, she paused. A wagon approached, rumbling afar off, and then there was a pause, till it had passed and long, long after, a tedious, *naturlangsam*[49] pause of the slow-blooded creature, a sacrifice of time such as those animals are up to which slumber half a year and live for centuries.

*June 26.* Heard of, and sought out, the hut of Martha Simons, the only pure-blooded Indian left about New Bedford.[50] She lives alone on the narrowest point of the Neck, near the shore, in sight of New Bedford. Her hut stands some twenty-five rods from the road on a small tract of Indian land, now wholly hers. It was formerly exchanged by a white man for some better land, then occupied by Indians, at Westport, which he wanted. So said a Quaker minister, her neighbor.[51] The squaw was not at home when we first called. It was a little hut not so big as mine.[52] *Vide* sketch by Ricketson, with the bay not far behind it.[53] No garden; only some lettuce amid the thin grass in front, and a great white pile of clam and quahog shells one side. She ere long came in from the seaside, and we called again. We knocked and walked in, and she asked us to sit down. She had half an acre of the real tawny Indian face, broad with high cheekbones, black eyes, and straight hair, originally black but now a little gray, parted in the middle. Her hands were several shades darker than her face. She had a peculiarly vacant expression, perhaps characteristic of the Indian, and answered our questions listlessly, without being interested or implicated, mostly in monosyllables, as if hardly present there. To judge from her physiognomy, she might have been King Philip's[54] own daughter. Yet she could not speak a word of Indian, and knew nothing of her race. Said she had lived with the whites, gone out to service to them when seven years old. Had lived part of her life at Squaw Betty's Neck, Assawampsett Pond.[55] Did she know Sampson's?[56] She 'd ought to; she 'd done work enough there. She said she was sixty years old, but was probably nearer seventy. She sat with her elbows on her knees and her face in her hands and that peculiar vacant stare, perhaps looking out the window between us, not repelling us in the least, but perfectly indifferent to our presence.

She was born on that spot. Her grandfather also lived on the same spot, though not in the same house. He was the last of her race who could speak Indian. She had heard him pray in Indian, but could only understand "Jesus Christ." Her only companion was a miserable tortoise-shell kitten which took no notice of us. She had a stone chimney, a small cooking-stove without fore legs, set up on bricks within it, and a bed covered with dirty bed-clothes. Said she hired out her field as pasture; better for her than to cultivate it. There were two young heifers

52 Thoreau's house at Walden was ten by fifteen feet.

53 Ricketson made two similar sketches, one of which he drew directly into his own journal, and the other (below), a little more detailed, which Thoreau placed into his manuscript journal.

(Sketch reproduced courtesy of the Morgan Library and Museum.)

54 Chief sachem of the Wampanoag (ca. 1639–1676).

55 Sometimes Assawompsett, Assawamsett, or Nemasket Pond, the largest inland freshwater pond in Massachusetts.

56 Sampson's Tavern, a large inn and stage-coach stop between Boston and New Bedford. It first opened in 1798 and was able to feed a hundred people at one sitting and could stable forty horses.

57 Colicroot (*Aletris farinosa*), also called star-grass.

58 Cf. 23 June 1852.

59 Most likely the same minister neighbor mentioned above.

60 Indian corn is said to grow quickly on warm summer nights. This image, repeated in *Walden*, first appeared in Thoreau's journal for 26 February 1840: "Corn grows in the night" [J 1:113]. In "Walking" Thoreau wrote: "I believe in the forest, and in the meadow, and in the night in which the corn grows" [W 5:225].

in it. The question she answered with most interest was, "What do you call that plant?" and I reached her the aletris[57] from my hat. She took it, looked at it a moment, and said, "That's husk-root. It's good to put into bitters for a weak stomach." The last year's light-colored and withered leaves surround the present green star like a husk. This must be the origin of the name. Its root is described as intensely bitter. I ought to have had my hat full of plants.[58]

A conceited old Quaker minister, her neighbor,[59] told me with a sanctified air, "I think that the Indians were human beings; dost thee not think so?" He only convinced me of his doubt and narrowness.

*August 1.* Since July 30th, inclusive, we have had perfect dog-days without interruption. The earth has suddenly become invested with a thick musty mist. The sky has become a mere fungus. A thick blue musty veil of mist is drawn before the sun. The sun has not been visible, except for a moment or two once or twice a day, all this time, nor the stars by night. Moisture reigns. You cannot dry a napkin at the window, nor press flowers without their mildewing. You imbibe so much moisture from the atmosphere that you are not so thirsty, nor is bathing so grateful as a week ago. The burning heat is tempered, but as you lose sight of the sky and imbibe the musty, misty air, you exist as a vegetable, a fungus. Unfortunate those who have not got their hay. I see them wading in overflowed meadows and pitching the black and mouldy swaths about in vain that they may dry. In the meanwhile, vegetation is becoming rank, vines of all kinds are rampant. Squashes and melons *are said* to grow a foot in a night. But weeds grow as fast. The corn unrolls.[60] Berries abound and attain their full size. Once or twice in the day there is an imperfect gleam of yellow sunlight for a moment through some thinner part of the veil, reminding us that we have not seen the sun so long, but no blue sky is revealed. The earth is completely invested with cloudlike wreaths of vapor (yet fear no rain and need no veil), beneath which flies buzz hollowly and torment, and mosquitoes hum and sting as if they were born of such an air.

We have a dense fog every night, which lifts itself but a short distance during the day. At sundown I see it curling up from the river and meadows. However, I love this moisture in its season. I believe it is good to breathe, wholesome as a vapor bath.[61] Toadstools shoot up in the yards and paths.

*August 7.* Heard this forenoon what I thought at first to be children playing on pumpkin stems in the next yard,[62] but it turned out to be the new steam-whistle music, what they call the Calliope (!) in the next town.[63] It sounded still more like the pumpkin stem near at hand, only a good deal louder. Again I mistook it for an instrument in the house or at the door, when it was a quarter of a mile off, from habit locating it by its loudness. At Acton, six miles off, it sounded like some new seraphim[64] in the next house with the blinds closed. All the milkmen and their horses stood still to hear it. The horses stood it remarkably well. It was not so musical as the ordinary whistle.

*August 8.* When I came forth, thinking to empty my boat and go a-meditating along the river,—for the full ditches and drenched grass forbade other routes, except the highway,—and this is one advantage of a boat,—I learned to my chagrin that Father's pig was gone.[65] He had leaped out of the pen some time since his breakfast, but his dinner was untouched. Here was an ugly duty not to be shirked,—a wild shoat[66] that weighed

**61** Thoreau did not believe, as many commonly did, that breathing fog was injurious. He wrote on 7 July 1852: "How wholesome these fogs which some fear! They are cool, medicated vapor baths, mingled by Nature, which bring to our senses all the medical properties of the meadows. The touchstones of health. Sleep with all your windows open, and let the mist embrace you" [J 4:198].
**62** Flutes or whistles made from pumpkin stems. Edward Emerson remembered Thoreau making "pipes of all sorts, of grass, of leaf-stalk of squash and pumpkin, handsome but fragrant flageolets of onion tops, but chiefly of the golden willow-shoot, when the rising sap in spring loosens the bark."
**63** The calliope makes sounds by forcing steam though whistles. It was a new instrument at the time, having been invented the previous year by Joshua C. Stoddard (1814–1902) of Worcester, Massachusetts. It was named after the Greek muse of epic poetry.
**64** Seraphine: a musical instrument invented in the 1830s by John Green of London, similar to the harmonium, of which it was the precursor. The name was used later for any free-standing reed organ.
**65** An anonymous piece, "Reminiscences of Thoreau," published in *Outlook* (2 December 1899), reported a similar escape: "We had finished supper, but were lingring at the table, when the servant threw open the door, exclaiming, with wild excitement, 'Faith! the' pig's out o'th' pin, an' th'way he's tearin' roun' Jege Hoore's flur-bids es enuf ter scare er budy.' Henry and his father at once rushed out in pursuit of the marauder, and the ladies flew to the window to see the fray. Never was practical strategy more in evidence; plotting and counterplotting on both sides, repeated circumvention of well-laid plans. . . . It was truly a triumph of the intellectual over the animal nature, whose brief enjoyment of wild destructive liberty was suddenly ended by the power of superior will. It was remarked at the time how much

mental and physical strength had to be expended to subdue so inferior an animal."

**66** Young pig just after weaning.

**67** Allusion to Carlyle's *Sartor Resartus:* "Most true it is, as a wise man teaches us, that 'Doubt of any sort cannot be removed except by Action.' On which ground too let him who gropes painfully in darkness or uncertain light, and prays vehemently that the dawn may ripen into day, lay this other precept well to heart, which to me was of invaluable service: '*Do the Duty which lies nearest thee,*' which thou knowest to be a Duty!"

but ninety to be tracked, caught, and penned,—an afternoon's work, at least (if I were lucky enough to accomplish it so soon), prepared for me, quite different from what I had anticipated. I felt chagrined, it is true, but I could not ignore the fact nor shirk the duty that lay so near to me. Do the duty that lies nearest to thee.[67] I proposed to Father to sell the pig as he was running (somewhere) to a neighbor who had talked of buying him, making a considerable reduction. But my suggestion was not acted on, and the responsibilities of the case all devolved on me, for I could run faster than Father. Father looked to me, and I ceased to look to the river. Well, let us see if we can track him. Yes, this is the corner where he got out, making a step of his trough. Thanks to the rain, his tracks are quite distinct. Here he went along the edge of the garden over the water and muskmelons, then through the beans and potatoes, and even along the front-yard walk I detect the print of his divided hoof, his two sharp toes (*ungulæ*). It's a wonder we did not see him. And here he passed out under the gate, across the road,—how naked he must have felt!—into a grassy ditch, and whither next? Is it of any use to go hunting him up unless you have devised some mode of catching him when you have found? Of what avail to know where he has been, even where he is? He was so shy the little while we had him, of course he will never come back; he cannot be tempted by a swillpail. Who knows how many miles off he is! Perhaps he has taken the back track and gone to Brighton, or Ohio! At most, probably we shall only have the satisfaction of glimpsing the nimble beast at a distance, from time to time, as he trots swiftly through the green meadows and corn-fields. But, now I speak, what is that I see pacing deliberately up the middle of the street forty rods off? It is *he.* As if to tantalize, to tempt us to waste our afternoon without further hesitation, he thus offers himself. He roots a foot or two and then lies down on his belly in the middle of the street. But think not to catch him a-napping. He has his eyes about, and his ears too. He has already been chased. He gives that wagon a wide berth, and now, seeing me, he turns and trots back down the street. He turns into a front yard. Now if I can only close that gate upon him ninety-nine hundredths of the work is done, but ah! he hears me coming afar off, he foresees the danger, and, with swinish cunning and speed, he scampers out. My neighbor in the street tries to head him; he jumps to this side the road, then to that, before him; but the third time the pig was there first and went by. "Whose is it?" he shouts. "It's ours." He bolts into that neighbor's yard and so across his premises. He has been twice there before, it seems; he knows the road; see what work he has made in his flower-garden! He must be fond of bulbs. Our neighbor picks up one tall flower with its bulb attached, holds it out at arm's length. He is excited about the pig; it is a subject he is interested in. But where is he gone now? The last glimpse I had of him was as he went through the cow-yard; here are his tracks again in this corn-field, but they are lost in the grass. We lose him; we beat the bushes in vain; he may be far away. But hark! I heard a grunt. Nevertheless for half an hour I do not see him that grunted. At last I find fresh tracks along the river, and again lose them. Each neighbor whose garden I traverse tells me some anecdote of losing pigs, or the attempt to drive them, by which I am not encouraged. Once more he crosses our first neighbor's garden and is said to be in the road. But I am not there yet; it is a good way off. At length my eyes rest on him again, after three quarters of an hour's separation. There he trots with the whole road to himself, and now again drops on his belly in a puddle. Now he starts again, seeing me twenty rods off, deliberates, considers which way I want him to go, and goes the other. There was some chance of driving him along the

**68** Fence with patterned openings, such as latticework.

**69** Allusion to Milton's poem "Lycidas" (l. 193): cf. 1850 note 32.

**70** Michael Flannery (cf. 1853 note 130), along with his wife and son.

**71** Allusion to Napoleon I (1769–1821). In his *Representative Men* Emerson quoted Bonaparte on the importance of confidence: "In all battles a moment occurs when the bravest troops, after having made the greatest efforts, feel inclined to run. That terror proceeds from a want of confidence in their own courage, and it only requires a slight opportunity, a pretence, to restore confidence to them. The art is, to give rise to the opportunity and to invent the pretence."

sidewalk, or letting him go rather, till he slipped under our gate again, but of what avail would that be? How corner and catch him who keeps twenty rods off? He never lets the open side of the triangle be less than half a dozen rods wide. There was one place where a narrower street turned off at right angles with the main one, just this side our yard, but I could not drive him past that. Twice he ran up the narrow street, for he knew I did not wish it, but though the main street was broad and open and no traveller in sight, when I tried to drive him past this opening he invariably turned his piggish head toward me, dodged from side to side, and finally ran up the narrow street or down the main one, as if there were a high barrier erected before him. But really he is no more obstinate than I. I cannot but respect his tactics and his independence. He will be he, and I may be I. He is not unreasonable because he thwarts me, but only the more reasonable. He has a strong will. He stands upon his idea. There is a wall across the path not where a man bars the way, but where he is resolved not to travel. Is he not superior to man therein? Once more he glides down the narrow street, deliberates at a corner, chooses wisely for him, and disappears through an openwork fence[68] eastward. He has gone to fresh gardens and pastures new.[69] Other neighbors stand in the doorways but half sympathizing, only observing, "Ugly thing to catch." "You have a job on your hands." I lose sight of him, but hear that he is far ahead in a large field. And there we try to let him alone a while, giving him a wide berth.

At this stage an Irishman[70] was engaged to assist. "I can catch him," says he, with Buonapartean confidence.[71] He thinks him a family Irish pig. His wife is with him, bareheaded, and his little flibbertigibbet of a boy, seven years old. "Here, Johnny, do you run right off there" (at the broadest possible angle with his own course). "Oh, but he can't do anything." "Oh, but I only want him to tell me where he is,—to keep sight of him." Michael soon discovers that he is not an Irish pig, and his wife and Johnny's occupation are soon gone. Ten minutes afterward I am patiently tracking him step by step through a corn-field, a near-sighted man helping me, and then into garden after garden far eastward, and finally into the highway, at the graveyard; but hear and see nothing. One suggests a dog to track him. Father is meanwhile selling him to the blacksmith, who also is trying to get sight of him. After fifteen minutes since he disappeared eastward, I hear that he has been to the river twice far on the north, through the first neighbor's premises. I wend that way. He crosses the street far ahead, Michael behind; he dodges up an avenue. I stand in the gap there, Michael at the other end, and now he tries to corner him. But it is a vain hope to corner him in a yard. I see a carriage-manufactory door open. "Let him go in there, Flannery." For once the pig and I are of one mind; he bolts in, and the door is closed. Now for a rope. It is a large barn, crowded with carriages. The rope is at length obtained; the windows are barred with carriages lest he bolt through. He is resting quietly on his belly in the further corner, thinking unutterable things.

Now the course recommences within narrower limits. Bump, bump, bump he goes, against wheels and shafts. We get no hold yet. He is all ear and eye. Small boys are sent under the carriages to drive him out. He froths at the mouth and deters them. At length he is stuck for an instant between the spokes of a wheel, and I am securely attached to his hind leg. He squeals deafeningly, and is silent. The rope is attached to a hind leg. The door is opened, and the *driving* commences. Roll an egg as well. You may drag him, but you cannot drive him. But he is in the road, and now another thunder-shower greets us. I leave Michael with the rope in one hand and a switch in the other and go home. He seems to be gaining a little

72 Cf. Thoreau's entry of 15 February 1857, "How to Catch a Pig" [J 9:260].

73 Running south of Great Meadows and named for Peter Hutchinson (d. 1881), whom Thoreau described on 12 December 1857: "I saw Peter, the dexterous pig-butcher, busy in two or three places, and in the afternoon I saw him with washed hands and knives in sheath and his leather overalls drawn off, going to his solitary house on the edge of the Great Fields, carrying in the rain a piece of the pork he had slaughtered, with a string put through it. Often he carries home the head, which is less prized, taking his pay thus in kind, and these supplies do not come amiss to his outcast family" [J 9:179–180].

74 The Crimean War (1853–1856), which began as a conflict between Russia and Turkey. Britain and France entered as allies of Turkey in 1854.

westward. But, after long delay, I look out and find that he makes but doubtful progress. A boy is made to face him with a stick, and it is only when the pig springs at him savagely that progress is made homeward. He will be killed before he is driven home. I get a wheelbarrow and go to the rescue. Michael is alarmed. The pig is rabid, snaps at him. We drag him across the barrow, hold him down, and so, at last, get him home.

If a wild shoat like this gets loose, first track him if you can, or otherwise discover where he is. Do not scare him more than you can help. Think of some yard or building or other inclosure that will hold him and, by showing your forces—yet as if uninterested parties—fifteen or twenty rods off, let him of his own accord enter it. Then slightly shut the gate. Now corner and tie him and put him into a cart or barrow.[72]

All progress in driving at last was made by facing and endeavoring to switch him from home. He rushed upon you and made a few feet in the desired direction. When I approached with the barrow he advanced to meet it with determination.

So I get home at dark, wet through and supperless, covered with mud and wheel-grease, without any rare flowers.

*August 12.* An arrowhead in Peter's Path.[73] How many times I have found an arrowhead by that path, as if that had been an Indian trail! Perchance it was, for some of the paths we travel are much older than we think, especially some which the colored race in our midst still use, for they are nearest to the Indian trails.

*August 28.* June, July, and August, the tortoise eggs are hatching a few inches beneath the surface in sandy fields. You tell of active labors, of works of art, and wars the past summer;[74] meanwhile the tortoise eggs underlie this turmoil. What events have transpired on the lit and airy surface three inches above them! Sumner knocked down;[75] Kansas living an age of suspense.[76] Think what is a summer to them! How many worthy men have died and had their funeral sermons preached since I saw the mother turtle bury her eggs here![77] They contained an undeveloped liquid then, they are now turtles. June, July, and August, — the livelong summer, — what are they with their heats and fevers but sufficient to hatch a tortoise in. Be not in haste; mind your private affairs. Consider the turtle.[78] A whole summer — June, July, and August — is not too good nor too much to hatch a turtle in. Perchance you have worried yourself, despaired of the world, meditated the end of life, and all things seemed rushing to destruction; but nature has steadily and serenely advanced with a turtle's pace. The young turtle spends its infancy within its shell. It gets experience and learns the ways of the world through that wall. While it rests warily on the edge of its hole, rash schemes are undertaken by men and fail. Has not the tortoise also learned the true value of time? You go to India and back, and the turtle eggs in your field are still unhatched. French empires rise or fall, but the turtle is developed only so fast. What's a summer? Time for a turtle's eggs to hatch. So is the turtle developed, fitted to endure, for he outlives twenty French dynasties. One turtle knows several Napoleons. They have seen no berries, had no cares, yet has not the great world existed for them as much as for you?

*August 30.* I have come out this afternoon a-cranberrying, chiefly to gather some of the small cranberry, *Vaccinium Oxycoccus,* which Emerson says is the common cranberry of the north of Europe.[79] This was a small object, yet not to be postponed, on account of imminent frosts, *i. e.,* if I would know this year the flavor of the European cranberry as compared with our larger kind. I thought

**75** Charles Sumner (1811–1874), Massachusetts senator, who on 22 May 1856 was attacked by Preston S. Brooks (1819–1857), a congressman from South Carolina. *Harper's New Monthly Magazine* (July 1856) reported: "The debates in Congress upon the affairs of Kansas have taken a wide range, and have been marked by great personal asperity. In the Senate, on the 20th of May, Mr. Sumner, of Massachusetts, concluded a long and elaborate speech, in which he commented with great asperity upon the course pursued by Mr. Butler, of South Carolina, and others who had taken a prominent part on the opposite side. This drew forth sharp retorts from Messrs. Mason and Douglas, and a severe rejoinder from Mr. Sumner. On the morning of the 22d, after the adjournment of the Senate, while Mr. Sumner was seated at his desk, he was accosted by Mr. Preston S. Brooks, a nephew of Mr. Butler, and Member of the House from South Carolina, who said that Mr. Sumner had libeled the State of South Carolina, and his (Mr. Brooks's) aged relative, and that he had come to chastise him; following the words by repeated blows from a cane, by which Mr. Sumner was prostrated and so severely injured that for some days his condition was extremely critical. Mr. Brooks proceeded to a magistrate, surrendered himself, and was released on bail. On the following morning committees were appointed by both Houses to investigate the matter."

**76** Regarding its fate as a free or slave state as a result of the Kansas-Nebraska Act, a law passed by Congress in 1854 that created two new territories, Kansas and Nebraska. This law effectively repealed the Missouri Compromise, which had prohibited slavery in these territories, thus outraging abolitionists, leading to the collapse of the Whig Party and the rise of the Republican Party, and bringing the nation one step closer to civil war.

**77** Cf. 10 June 1856.

**78** Possible echo of the phrases in the Bible: "Consider the ravens" (Luke 12:24) and "Consider the lilies" (Luke 12:27).

**79** Allusion to George B. Emerson's *A Report on*

the Trees and Shrubs Growing Naturally in the Forests of Massachusetts, which lists a species of the
European cranberry: "It is the common cranberry
of the north of Europe, where it grows in turfy,
mossy bogs, particularly on mountains."

**80** Beck Stow's Swamp, sometimes called Becky
Stow's Swamp, south of Bedford Road before
it meets Old Bedford Road. One of Thoreau's
favorite places, of which he wrote: "Beck Stow's
swamp! What an incredible spot to think of in
town or city! When life looks sandy and barren,
is reduced to its lowest terms, we have no appetite, and it has no flavor, then let me visit such a
swamp as this, deep and impenetrable, where the
earth quakes for a rod around you at every step,
with its open water where the swallows skim and
twitter, its meadow and cotton-grass, its dense
patches of dwarf andromeda, now brownish-
green, with clumps of blueberry bushes, its
spruces and its verdurous border of woods im-
bowering it on every side" [J 4:231].

**81** Pro-slavery Missouri residents who, in the
1850s, entered the territory of Kansas seeking to
intimidate the anti-slavery people through violence.

I should like to have a dish of this sauce on the table at
Thanksgiving of my own gathering. I could hardly make
up my mind to come this way, it seemed so poor an object to spend the afternoon on. I kept foreseeing a lame
conclusion,—how I should cross the Great Fields, look
into Beck Stow's,[80] and then retrace my steps no richer
than before. In fact, I expected little of this walk, yet it
did pass through the side of my mind that somehow, on
this very account (my small expectation), it would turn
out well, as also the advantage of having some purpose,
however small, to be accomplished,—of letting your
deliberate wisdom and foresight in the house to some
extent direct and control your steps. If you would really
take a position outside the street and daily life of men,
you must have deliberately planned your course, you
must have business which is not your neighbors' business, which they cannot understand. For only absorbing
employment prevails, succeeds, takes up space, occupies
territory, determines the future of individuals and states,
drives Kansas out of your head, and actually and permanently occupies the only desirable and free Kansas
against all border ruffians.[81] The attitude of resistance is
one of weakness, inasmuch as it only faces an enemy; it
has its back to all that is truly attractive. You shall have
your affairs, I will have mine. You will spend this afternoon in setting up your neighbor's stove, and be paid for
it; I will spend it in gathering the few berries of the *Vaccinium Oxycoccus* which Nature produces here, before it
is too late, and *be paid for it also* after another fashion. I
have always reaped unexpected and incalculable advantages from carrying out at last, however tardily, any little
enterprise which my genius suggested to me long ago
as a thing to be done,—some step to be taken, however
slight, out of the usual course.

How many schools I have thought of which I might
go to but did not go to! expecting foolishly that some

greater advantage or schooling would come to me! It is these comparatively cheap and private expeditions that substantiate our existence and batten[82] our lives, as, where a vine touches the earth in its undulating course, it puts forth roots and thickens its stock. Our employment generally is tinkering, mending the old worn-out teapot of society. Our stock in trade is solder. Better for me, says my genius, to go cranberrying this afternoon for the *Vaccinium Oxycoccus* in Gowing's Swamp,[83] to get but a pocketful and learn its peculiar flavor, aye, and the flavor of Gowing's Swamp and of *life* in New England, than to go consul to Liverpool[84] and get I don't know how many thousand dollars for it, with no such flavor. Many of our days should be spent, not in vain expectations and lying on our oars, but in carrying out deliberately and faithfully the hundred little purposes which every man's genius must have suggested to him. Let not your life be wholly without an object, though it be only to ascertain the flavor of a cranberry, for it will not be only the quality of an insignificant berry that you will have tasted, but the flavor of your life to that extent, and it will be such a sauce as no wealth can buy.

Both a conscious and an unconscious life are good. Neither is good exclusively, for both have the same source. The wisely conscious life springs out of an unconscious suggestion. I have found my account in travelling in having prepared beforehand a list of questions which I would get answered, not trusting to my interest at the moment, and can then travel with the most profit. Indeed, it is by obeying the suggestions of a higher light within you that you escape from yourself and, in the transit, as it were see with the unworn sides of your eye, travel totally new paths. What is that pretended life that does not take up a claim, that does not occupy ground, that cannot build a causeway to its objects, that sits on a bank looking over a bog, singing its desires?

**82** Thrive or prosper at the expense of another.
**83** A quarter mile northwest of the corner of Old Bedford Road and the Boston–Lexington Road.
**84** In 1853 President Franklin Pierce (1804–1869; president, 1853–1857) appointed Nathaniel Hawthorne as consul in Liverpool, a position he held until October 1857.

85 Unidentified.

However, it was not with such blasting expectations as these that I entered the swamp. I saw bags of cranberries, just gathered and tied up, on the banks of Beck Stow's Swamp. They must have been raked out of the water, now so high, before they should rot. I left my shoes and stockings on the bank far off and waded bare-legged through rigid andromeda and other bushes a long way, to the soft open sphagnous centre of the swamp.

I waded quite round the swamp for an hour, my bare feet in the cold water beneath, and it was a relief to place them on the warmer surface of the sphagnum. I filled one pocket with each variety, but sometimes, being confused, crossed hands and put them into the wrong pocket.

I enjoyed this cranberrying very much, notwithstanding the wet and cold, and the swamp seemed to be yielding its crop to me alone, for there are none else to pluck it or to value it. I told the proprietor[85] once that they grew here, but he, learning that they were not abundant enough to be gathered for the market, has probably never thought of them since. I am the only person in the township who regards them or knows of them, and I do not regard them in the light of their pecuniary value. I have no doubt I felt richer wading there with my two pockets full, treading on wonders at every step, than any farmer going to market with a hundred bushels which he has raked, or hired to be raked. I got further and further away from the town every moment, and my good genius seemed to have smiled on me, leading me hither, and then the sun suddenly came out clear and bright, but it did not warm my feet. I would gladly share my gains, take one, or twenty, into partnership and get this swamp with them, but I do not know an individual whom this berry cheers and nourishes as it does me. When I exhibit it to them I perceive that they take but a momentary interest in it and commonly dismiss it from their thoughts with the consideration that it cannot be profitably cultivated. You could not get a pint at one haul of a rake, and Slocum[86] would not give you much for them. But I love it the better partly for that reason even. I fill a basket with them and keep it several days by my side. If anybody else—any farmer, at least—should spend an hour thus wading about here in this secluded swamp, barelegged, intent on the sphagnum, filling his pocket only, with no rake in his hand and no bag or bushel on the bank, he would be pronounced insane and have a guardian put over him; but if he'll spend his time skimming and watering his milk and selling his small potatoes for large ones, or generally in skinning flints,[87] he will probably be made guardian of somebody else.[88]

I seemed to have reached a new world, so wild a place that the very huckleberries grew hairy and were inedible. I feel as if I were in Rupert's Land,[89] and a slight cool but agreeable shudder comes over me, as if equally far away from human society. What's the need of visiting far-off mountains and bogs, if a half-hour's walk will carry me into such wildness and novelty? But why should not as wild plants grow here as in Berkshire,[90] as in Labrador? Is Nature so easily tamed? Is she not as primitive and vigorous here as anywhere? How does this particular acre of secluded, unfrequented, useless (?) quaking bog differ from an acre in Labrador? Has any white man ever settled on it? Does any now frequent it? Not even the Indian comes here now. I see that there are some square rods within twenty miles of Boston just as wild and primitive and unfrequented as a square rod in Labrador, as unaltered by man. Here grows the hairy huckleberry as it did in Squaw Sachem's day and a thousand years before, and concerns me perchance more than it did her. I have no doubt that for a moment I experience

86 Possibly the Slocum of New Bedford whom Thoreau had recently met. On 26 June 1856 he wrote: "Talked with a farmer by name of Slocum, hoeing on the Neck, a rather dull and countrified fellow for our neighborhood" [J 8:389–390].
87 A term at least as old as the 18th century, used to describe an act of great effort for small gain.
88 Similarly, Thoreau wrote in "Life Without Principle" from a 17 June 1853 journal passage: "If a man walk in the woods for love of them half of each day, he is in danger of being regarded as a loafer; but if he spends his whole day as a speculator, shearing off those woods and making earth bald before her time, he is esteemed an industrious and enterprising citizen" [W 4:457].
89 Former district of Canada, originally owned by the Hudson's Bay Company and named after Prince Rupert (1619–1682), first governor of the company.
90 Westernmost county in Massachusetts.

91 Allusion to the axiom "They that dance must pay the fiddler."
92 Jenny Lind: cf. 1854 note 33.

exactly the same sensations as if I were alone in a bog in Rupert's Land, and it saves me the trouble of going there; for what in any case makes the difference between being here and being there but many such little differences of flavor and roughness put together? Rupert's Land is recognized as much by one sense as another. I felt a shock, a thrill, an agreeable surprise in one instant, for, no doubt, all the possible inferences were at once drawn, with a rush, in my mind,—I could be in Rupert's Land and supping at home within the hour! This beat the railroad. I recovered from my surprise without danger to my sanity, and permanently annexed Rupert's Land. That wild hairy huckleberry, inedible as it was, was equal to a domain secured to me and reaching to the South Sea. That was an unexpected harvest. I hope you have gathered as much, neighbor, from your corn and potato fields. I have got in my huckleberries. I shall be ready for Thanksgiving. It is in vain to dream of a wildness distant from ourselves. There is none such. It is the bog in our brain and bowels, the primitive vigor of Nature in us, that inspires that dream. I shall never find in the wilds of Labrador any greater wildness than in some recess in Concord, *i. e.* than I import into it. A little more manhood or virtue will make the surface of the globe anywhere thrillingly novel and wild. That alone will provide and pay the fiddler;[91] it will convert the district road into an untrodden cranberry bog, for it restores all things to their original primitive flourishing and promising state.

A cold white horizon sky in the north, forerunner of the fall of the year. I go to bed and dream of cranberry-pickers far in the cold north. With windows partly closed, with continent concentrated thoughts, I dream. I get my new experiences still, not at the opera listening to the Swedish Nightingale,[92] but at Beck Stow's Swamp listening to the native wood thrush.

Wading in the cold swamp braces me. I was invigorated, though I tasted not a berry.

Better it is to go a-cranberrying than to go a-huckleberrying. For that is cold and bracing, leading your thoughts beyond the earth, and you do not surfeit on crude or terrene berries. It feeds your spirit, now in the season of white twilights, when frosts are apprehended, when edible berries are mostly gone.

Those small gray sparrow-egg cranberries lay so prettily in the recesses of the sphagnum, I could wade for hours in the cold water gazing at them, with a swarm of mosquitoes hovering about my bare legs,—but at each step the friendly sphagnum in which I sank protected my legs like a buckler,—not a crevice by which my foes could enter.

I see that all is not garden and cultivated field and crops, that there are square rods in Middlesex County as purely primitive and wild as they were a thousand years ago, which have escaped the plow and the axe and the scythe and the cranberry-rake, little oases of wildness in the desert of our civilization, wild as a square rod on the moon, supposing it to be uninhabited. I believe almost in the personality of such planetary matter, feel something akin to reverence for it, can even worship it as terrene, titanic matter extant in my day. We are so different we admire each other, we healthily attract one another. I love it as a maiden. These spots are meteoric, aerolitic, and such matter has in all ages been worshipped. Aye, when we are lifted out of the slime and film of our habitual life, we see the whole globe to be an aerolite, and reverence it as such, and make pilgrimages to it, far off as it is. How happens it that we reverence the stones which fall from another planet, and not the stones which belong to this,—another globe, not this,—heaven, and not

**93** Used here as a generic name for a farmer.
**94** Allusion to the sacred stone in the Kaaba in the great mosque in Mecca, the birthplace of Muhammad and the holiest city of Islam. According to Sir Richard Burton's (1821–1890) *Personal Narrative of a Pilgrimage to El-Madinah and Meccah:* "Moslems agree that it was originally white, and became black by reason of men's sins. It appeared to me a common aerolite covered with a thick slaggy coating, glossy and pitch-like, worn and polished."
**95** Channing: cf. 25 July 1851.

earth? Are not the stones in Hodge's[93] wall as good as the aerolite at Mecca?[94] Is not our broad back-door-stone as good as any corner-stone in heaven?

It would imply the regeneration of mankind, if they were to become elevated enough to truly worship stocks and stones. It is the sentiment of fear and slavery and habit which makes a heathenish idolatry. Such idolaters abound in all countries, and heathen cross the seas to re-form heathen, dead to bury the dead, and all go down to the pit together. If I could, I would worship the parings of my nails. If he who makes two blades of grass grow where one grew before is a benefactor, he who discovers two gods where there was only known the one (and such a one!) before is a still greater benefactor. I would fain improve every opportunity to wonder and worship, as a sunflower welcomes the light. The more thrilling, wonderful, divine objects I behold in a day, the more expanded and immortal I become. If a stone appeals to me and elevates me, tells me how many miles I have come, how many remain to travel,—and the more, the better,—reveals the future to me in some measure, it is a matter of private rejoicing. If it did the same service to all, it might well be a matter of public rejoicing.

*August 31.* There sits one[95] by the shore who wishes to go with me, but I cannot think of it. I must be fancy-free. There is no such mote in the sky as a man who is not perfectly transparent to you,—who has any opacity. I would rather attend to him earnestly for half an hour, on shore or elsewhere, and then dismiss him. He thinks I could merely take him into my boat and then not mind him. He does not realize that I should by the same act take him into my mind, where there is no room for him, and my bark would surely founder in such a voyage as I was contemplating. I know very well that I should never reach that expansion of the river I have in my mind, with him aboard with his broad terrene qualities. He would sink my bark (not to another sea)[96] and never know it. I could better carry a heaped load of meadow mud and sit on the thole-pins. There would be more room for me, and I should reach that expansion of the river nevertheless.

I could better afford to take him into bed with me, for then I might, perhaps, abandon him in my dreams. Ah! you are a heavy fellow, but I am well disposed. If you could go without going, then you might go. There's the captain's stateroom, empty to be sure, and you say you could go in the steerage. I know very well that only your baggage would be dropped in the steerage, while you would settle right down into that other snug recess. Why, I am *going,* not staying. I have come on purpose to sail, to paddle away from such as you, and you have waylaid me at the shore. You have chosen to make your assault at the moment of embarkation. Why, if I thought you were steadily gazing after me a mile off, I could not endure it. It is because I trust that I shall ere long depart from your thoughts, and so you from mine, that I am encouraged to set sail at all. I make haste to put several meanders and some hills between us. This Company is obliged to make a distinction between dead freight[97] and passengers. I will take almost any amount of freight for you cheerfully,—anything, my dear sir, but yourself.

Some are so inconsiderate as to ask to walk or sail with me regularly every day—I have known such—and think that, because there will be six inches or a foot between our bodies, we shall not interfere! These things are settled by fate. The good ship sails—when she is ready. For freight or passage apply to—?? Ask my friend where. What is getting into a man's carriage when it is full, compared with putting your foot in his mouth and popping right into his mind without considering whether it is occupied or not? If I remember aright, it was only on

[96] Allusion to Channing's poem "A Poet's Hope," which ends: "If my bark sinks, 't is to another sea." This quotation was also used as the final line in Emerson's "Montaigne, or the Skeptic."

[97] That part of a cargo which does not belong to, and is not counted in, the freight, and when the cargo is delivered is not to be reckoned.

Cf. 5 January 1860. Thoreau expressed this concept many times, as in his 19 May 1859 letter to Mary Brown: "In the long run, we find what we expect" [C 551]. This echoes Matthew 7:7 and Luke 11:9: "Seek and ye shall find; knock and it shall be opened to you."

condition *that you were asked* that you were to go with a man one mile or twain. Suppose a man asks, not you to go with him, but to go with you! Often, I would rather undertake to shoulder a barrel of pork and carry it a mile than take into my company a man. It would not be so heavy a weight upon my mind. I could put it down and only feel my *back* ache for it.

*September 2.* A few pigeons were seen a fortnight ago. I have noticed none in all walks, but George Minott, whose mind runs on them so much, but whose age and infirmities confine him to his wood-shed on the hillside, saw a small flock a fortnight ago. I rarely pass at any season of the year but he asks if I have seen any pigeons. One man's mind running on pigeons, he will sit thus in the midst of a village, many of whose inhabitants never see nor dream of a pigeon except in the pot, and where even naturalists do not observe them, and he, looking out with expectation and faith from morning till night, will surely see them.

I think we may detect that some sort of preparation and faint expectation preceded every discovery we have made.[98] We blunder into no discovery but it will appear that we have prayed and disciplined ourselves for it. Some years ago I sought for Indian hemp (*Apocynum cannabinum*) hereabouts in vain, and concluded that it did not grow here. A month or two ago I read again, as many times before, that its blossoms were very small, scarcely a third as large as those of the common species, and for some unaccountable reason this distinction kept recurring to me, and I regarded the size of the flowers I saw, though I did not believe that it grew here; and in a day or two my eyes fell on it, aye, in three different places, and different varieties of it. Also, a short time ago, I was satisfied that there was but one kind of sunflower (*divaricatus*) indigenous here. Hearing that one had found another kind, it occurred to me that I had seen a taller one than usual lately, but not so distinctly did I remember this as to name it to him or even fully remember it myself. (I rather remembered it afterward.) But within that hour my genius conducted me to where I had seen the tall plants, and it was the other man's new kind. The next day I found a third kind, miles from there, and, a few days after, a fourth in another direction.

It commonly chances that I make my most interesting botanical discoveries when I am in a thrilled and expectant mood, perhaps wading in some remote swamp where I have just found something novel and feel more than usually remote from the town. Or some rare plant which for some reason has occupied a strangely prominent place in my thoughts for some time will present itself. My expectation ripens to discovery. I am prepared for strange things.

I feel this difference between great poetry and small: that in the one, the sense outruns and overflows the words; in the other, the words the sense.

**September 15.** Sophia says, bringing company into my sanctum,[99] by way of apology, that I regard the dust on my furniture like the bloom on fruits, not to be swept off.[100]

**October 1.** I do not perceive the poetic and dramatic capabilities of an anecdote or story which is told me, its significance, till some time afterwards. One of the qualities of a pregnant fact is that it does not surprise us, and we only perceive afterward how interesting it is, and then must know all the particulars. We do not enjoy poetry fully unless we know it to be poetry.

**99** Allusion to the *sanctum sanctorum* (Latin: holy of holies), the innermost shrine of a tabernacle or temple, and thus an inviolably private place.
**100** When Thoreau was living at Walden he had "three pieces of limestone on my desk, but I was terrified to find that they required to be dusted daily, when the furniture of my mind was all undusted still, and threw them out the window in disgust" [Wa 35].

**101** George Everett lived on Lincoln Road, a quarter mile south of the Cambridge Turnpike.

**102** Emerson noted in his journal at the beginning of May 1857 that Thoreau "had found, he said, lately a fungus which was a perfect Phallus." He later noted in 1865: "I have since seen this very undesirable neighbor under my study window." (Thoreau's sketch reproduced courtesy of the Morgan Library and Museum.)

**103** Thoreau's note, referring to the work of John Claudius Loudon (1783–1843): "This is very similar to if not the same with that represented in Loudon's *Encyclopædia* and called '*Phallus impudicus,* Stinking Morel, very fetid.'"

***October 5.*** It is well to find your employment and amusement in simple and homely things. These wear best and yield most. I think I would rather watch the motions of these cows in their pasture for a day, which I now see all headed one way and slowly advancing,—watch them and project their course carefully on a chart, and report all their behavior faithfully,—than wander to Europe or Asia and watch other motions there; for it is only ourselves that we report in either case, and perchance we shall report a more restless and worthless self in the latter case than in the first.

***October 16.*** Found amid the sphagnum on the dry bank on the south side of the Turnpike, just below Everett's meadow,[101] a rare and remarkable fungus, such as I have heard of but never seen before.

The whole height six and three quarters inches, two thirds of it being buried in the sphagnum. It may be divided into three parts, pileus, stem, and base,—or scrotum, for it is a perfect phallus.[102] One of those fungi named *impudicus,* I think.[103] In all respects a most disgusting object, yet very suggestive. It is hollow from top to bottom, the form of the hollow answering to that of the outside. The color of the outside white excepting the pileus, which is olive-colored and somewhat coarsely corrugated, with an oblong mouth at tip about one eighth of an inch long, or, measuring the white lips, half an inch. This cap is thin and white within, about one and three eighths inches high by one and a half wide. The stem (bare portion) is three inches long (tapering more rapidly than in the drawing), horizontally viewed of an oval form.

Longest diameter at base one and a half inches, at top (on edge of pileus) fifteen sixteenths of an inch. Short diameters in both cases about two thirds as much. It is a delicate white cylinder of a finely honeycombed and crispy material about three sixteenths of an inch thick, or more, the whole very straight and regular. The base, or scrotum, is of an irregular bag form, about one inch by two in the extremes, consisting of a thick trembling gelatinous mass surrounding the bottom of the stem and covered with a tough white skin of a darker tint than the stem. The whole plant rather frail and trembling. There was at first a very thin delicate white collar (or *volva*?)[104] about the base of the stem above the scrotum. It was as offensive to the eye as to the scent, the cap rapidly melting and defiling what it touched with a fetid, olivaceous, semiliquid matter. In an hour or two the plant scented the whole house wherever placed, so that it could not be endured. I was afraid to sleep in my chamber where it had lain until the room had been well ventilated. It smelled like a dead rat in the ceiling, in all the ceilings of the house. Pray, what was Nature thinking of when she made this? She almost puts herself on a level with those who draw in privies. The cap had at first a smooth and almost dry surface, of a sort of olive slate-color, but the next day this colored surface all melted out, leaving deep corrugations or gills—rather honeycomb-like cells— with a white bottom.

*October 18.* Men commonly exaggerate the theme. Some themes they think are significant and others insignificant. I feel that my life is very homely, my pleasures very cheap. Joy and sorrow, success and failure, grandeur and meanness, and indeed most words in the English language do not mean for me what they do for my neighbors. I see that my neighbors look with compassion on me, that they think it is a mean and unfortunate destiny

104 Cuplike structure around the base of the stalk of certain fungi.

105 Jean Thoreau (1754–1801), who was born on the Isle of Jersey, coming to America in 1773.
106 The American Revolution.
107 Cruising in a privateer, a nongovernmental armed vessel privately owned and commissioned for the purpose of harassing and attacking commercial or war ships of an enemy nation. The governmental commission distinguished the privateer from a pirate ship.
108 Levi Melcher (1773–1847), later a merchant, related to Franklin Sanborn through Sanborn's mother's family, the Leavitts.

which makes me to walk in these fields and woods so much and sail on this river alone. But so long as I find here the only real elysium, I cannot hesitate in my choice. My work is writing, and I do not hesitate, though I know that no subject is too trivial for me, tried by ordinary standards; for, ye fools, the theme is nothing, the life is everything. All that interests the reader is the depth and intensity of the life excited. We touch our subject but by a point which has no breadth, but the pyramid of our experience, or our interest in it, rests on us by a broader or narrower base. That is, man is all in all, Nature nothing, but as she draws him out and reflects him. Give me simple, cheap, and homely themes.

*October 21.* Father told me about his father[105] the other night,—that he remembers his father used to breakfast before the family at one time, on account of his business, and he with him. His father used to eat the under crusts of biscuits, and he the upper. His father died in 1801, aged forty-seven. When the war[106] came on, he was apprentice or journeyman to a cooper who employed many hands. He called them together, and told them that on account of the war his business was ruined and he had no more work for them. So, my father thinks, his father went privateering.[107] Yet he remembers his telling him of his being employed digging at some defenses, when a cannon-ball came and sprinkled the sand all over them.

After the war he went into business as a merchant, commencing with a single hogshead of sugar. His shop was on Long Wharf. He was a short man, a little taller than my father, stout and very strong for his size. Levi Melcher,[108] a powerful man, who was his clerk or tender, used to tell my father that he did not believe he was so strong a man as his father was. He would never give in to him in handling a hogshead of molasses,—setting it on its head, or the like.

*December 1.* I love and could embrace the shrub oak with its scanty garment of leaves rising above the snow, lowly whispering to me, akin to winter thoughts, and sunsets, and to all virtue. Covert which the hare and the partridge seek, and I too seek. What cousin of mine is the shrub oak? How can any man suffer long? For a sense of want is a prayer, and all prayers are answered. Rigid as iron, clean as the atmosphere, hardy as virtue, innocent and sweet as a maiden is the shrub oak. In proportion as I know and love it, I am natural and sound as a partridge.

*December 2.* Got in my boat, which before I had got out and turned up on the bank. It made me sweat to wheel it home through the snow, I am so unused to work of late.

As for the sensuality in Whitman's "Leaves of Grass," I do not so much wish that it was not written, as that men and women were so pure that they could read it without harm.[109]

*December 3.* Mizzles and rains all day, making sloshy walking which sends us all to the shoemaker's. Bought me a pair of cowhide boots, to be prepared for winter walks.[110] The shoemaker[111] praised them because they were made a year ago. I feel like an armed man now. The man who has bought his boots feels like him who has got in his winter's wood. There they stand beside me in the chamber, expectant, dreaming of far woods and wood-paths, of frost-bound or sloshy roads, or of being bound with skate-straps and clogged with ice-dust.

For years my appetite was so strong that I fed—I browsed—on the pine forest's edge seen against the winter horizon. How cheap my diet still! Dry sand that has fallen in railroad cuts and slid on the snow beneath

**109** Walt Whitman's (1819–1892) *Leaves of Grass* was published in July 1855, a copy of which was sent by Whitman to Emerson, who shared it with Thoreau and others. On 10 November 1856 Thoreau and Bronson Alcott visited Whitman in New York. Whitman told Horace Traubel (1858–1919): "Thoreau, in Brooklyn, the first time he came to see me, referred to my critics as 'reprobates.' I asked him: 'would you apply so severe a word to them?' He was surprised: 'Do you regard that as a severe word? Reprobates? What they really deserve is something infinitely stronger, more caustic: I thought I was letting them off easy.'"

**110** On 12 February 1854 Thoreau described his different boots: "It becomes quite a study how a man will shoe himself for a winter. For outdoor life in winter, I use three kinds of shoes or boots: first and chiefly, for the ordinary dry snows or bare ground, cowhide boots; secondly, for shallow thaws, half-shoe depth, and spring weather, light boots and india-rubbers; third, for the worst sloshy weather, about a week in the year, india-rubber boots" [J 6:114–115].

**111** Hastings (cf. 4 December 1856), with whom Thoreau sometimes went bee hunting.

112  Vyasa, sometimes called Vedavyasa, is known as the literary incarnation of Krishna because he is reported to have imparted the Vedic wisdom to the world by compiling the *Vedas*, the *Puranas*, the *Vedanta-sutra* and the *Mahabharata*. In *A Week on the Concord and Merrimack Rivers* Thoreau wrote: "I would say to the readers of Scriptures, if they wish for a good book, read the Bhagvat-Geeta, an episode to the Mahabharat, said to have been written by Kreeshna Dwypayen Veias" [W 1:147–148].

113  Locals with whom Thoreau often conversed: George Minott (cf. 1851 note 142); Reuben Rice (cf. 1855 note 19); George Melvin (cf. 1854 note 9); John Goodwin (cf. 1853 note 132); and Puffer, unidentified further, but whose suicide Thoreau mentioned on 19 November 1858 [J 11:335].

114  Thoreau told several anecdotes about the Thoreau family's Maltese cat in his journals, as on 1 February 1856: "Our kitten Min, two-thirds grown, was playing with Sophia's broom this morning, as she was sweeping the parlor, when she suddenly went into a fit, dashed round the room, and, the door being opened, rushed up two flights of stairs and leaped from the attic window to the ice and snow by the side of the door-step,—a descent of a little more than twenty feet,—passed round the house and was lost. But she made her appearance again about noon, at the window, quite well and sound in every joint, even playful and frisky" [J 8:158].

115  Unidentified.

is a condiment to my walk. I ranged about like a gray moose, looking at the spiring tops of the trees, and fed my imagination on them,—far-away, ideal trees not disturbed by the axe of the wood-cutter, nearer and nearer fringes and eyelashes of my eye. Where was the sap, the fruit, the value of the forest for me, but in that line where it was relieved against the sky? That was my wood-lot; that was my lot in the woods. The silvery needles of the pines straining the light.

How I love the simple, reserved countrymen, my neighbors, who mind their own business and let me alone, who never waylaid nor shot at me, to my knowledge, when I crossed their fields, though each one has a gun in his house! For nearly twoscore years I have known, at a distance, these long-suffering men, whom I never spoke to, who never spoke to me, and now feel a certain tenderness for them, as if this long probation were but the prelude to an eternal friendship. What a long trial we have withstood, and how much more admirable we are to each other, perchance, than if we had been bedfellows! I am not only grateful because Veias,[112] and Homer, and Christ, and Shakespeare have lived, but I am grateful for Minott, and Rice, and Melvin, and Goodwin, and Puffer even.[113] I see Melvin all alone filling his sphere, in russet suit, which no other could fill or suggest. He takes up as much room in nature as the most famous.

*December 4.* Sophia says that just before I came home Min[114] caught a mouse and was playing with it in the yard. It had got away from her once or twice, and she had caught it again; and now it was stealing off again, as she lay complacently watching it with her paws tucked under her, when her friend Riordan's[115] stout but solitary cock stepped up inquisitively, looked down at it with one eye, turning his head, then picked it up by the tail and gave it two or three whacks on the ground, and giving it a dexterous toss into the air, caught it in its open mouth, and it went head foremost and alive down his capacious throat in the twinkling of an eye, never again to be seen in this world, Min, all the while, with paws comfortably tucked under her, looking on unconcerned. What matters it one mouse more or less to her? The cock walked off amid the currant bushes, stretched his neck up, and gulped once or twice, and the deed was accomplished, and then he crowed lustily in celebration of the exploit. It might be set down among the *gesta* (if not *digesta*) *Gallorum*.[116] There were several human witnesses. It is a question whether Min ever understood where that mouse went to. Min sits composedly sentinel, with paws tucked under her, a good part of her days at present, by some ridiculous little hole, the possible entryway of a mouse. She has a habit of stretching or sharpening her claws on all smooth hair-bottomed chairs and sofas, greatly to my mother's vexation.

When I bought my boots yesterday, Hastings[117] ran over his usual rigmarole. Had he any stout old-fashioned cowhide boots? Yes, he thought he could suit me. "There's something that 'll turn water about as well as anything. Billings[118] had a pair just like them the other day, and he said they kept his feet as dry as a bone. But what 's more than that, they were made above a year ago upon honor. They are just the thing, you may depend on it. I had an eye to you when I was making them." "But they are too soft and thin for me. I want them to be thick and stand out from my foot." "Well, there is another pair, maybe a little thicker. I'll tell you what it is, these were made of dry hide."

Both were warranted single leather and not split. I

**116** Thoreau's title is an echo of the *Gesta Romanorum*, a medieval collection of Latin stories, "Deeds of the Romans," and would translate as "Deeds of the French," but Thoreau punned on the meaning of gallorum as the genitive plural noun for a domestic cock, thus "Deeds of the Cocks" with a further pun on *digesta*, Latin for a collection of writings under a certain head, as related to the English word to digest, or eat.
**117** Jonas Hastings (1805–1873).
**118** Unidentified.

**119** On 1 September 1859 he wrote of another experience with a shoemaker: "Bought a pair of shoes the other day, and, observing that as usual they were only wooden-pegged at the toes, I required the seller to put in an extra row of iron pegs there while I waited for them. So he called to his boy to bring those zinc pegs, but I insisted on iron pegs and no zinc ones. He gave me considerable advice on the subject of shoes, but I suggested that even the wearer of shoes, of whom I was one, had an opportunity to learn some of their qualities. I have learned to respect my own opinion in this matter. As I do not use blacking and the seller often throws in a box of blacking when I buy a pair of shoes, they accumulate on my hands" [J 12:311].
**120** Jacob Bigelow's (1786–1879) *Florula Bostoniensis: A Collection of Plants of Boston and Its Vicinity* (Boston: Hilliard Gray, Little and Wilkins, 1829).
**121** Cf. 23 June 1852.
**122** Relating to flowerless and seedless plants that reproduce by means of spores: ferns, mosses, algae, fungi.

took the last. But after wearing them round this cold day I found that the little snow which rested on them and melted wet the upper leather through like paper and wet my feet, and I told Hastings of it, that he might have an offset to Billings's experience. "Well, you can't expect a new pair of boots to turn water at first. I tell the farmers that the time to buy boots is at midsummer, or when they are hoeing their potatoes, and the pores have a chance to get filled with dirt."[119]

My first botany, as I remember, was Bigelow's "Plants of Boston and Vicinity,"[120] which I began to use about twenty years ago, looking chiefly for the popular names and the short references to the localities of plants, even without any regard to the plant. I also learned the names of many, but without using any system, and forgot them soon. I was not inclined to pluck flowers; preferred to leave them where they were, liked them best there. I was never in the least interested in plants in the house. But from year to year we look at Nature with new eyes. About half a dozen years ago I found myself again attending to plants with more method, looking out the name of each one and remembering it. I began to bring them home in my hat, a straw one with a scaffold lining to it, which I called my botany-box.[121] I never used any other, and when some whom I visited were evidently surprised at its dilapidated look, as I deposited it on their front entry table, I assured them it was not so much my hat as my botany-box. I remember gazing with interest at the swamps about those days and wondering if I could ever attain to such familiarity with plants that I should know the species of every twig and leaf in them, that I should be acquainted with every plant (excepting grasses and cryptogamous[122] ones), summer and winter, that I saw. Though I knew most of the flowers, and there were not in any particular swamp more than half a dozen shrubs that I did not know, yet these made it seem like a maze to me, of a thousand strange species, and I even thought of commencing at one end and looking it faithfully and laboriously through till I knew it all. I little thought that in a year or two I should have attained to that knowledge without all that labor. Still I never studied botany, and do not to-day systematically, the most natural system is still so artificial. I wanted to know my neighbors, if possible, — to get a little nearer to them. I soon found myself observing when plants first blossomed and leafed, and I followed it up early and late, far and near, several years in succession, running to different sides of the town and into the neighboring towns, often between twenty and thirty miles in a day. I often visited a particular plant four or five miles distant, half a dozen times within a fortnight, that I might know exactly when it opened, beside attending to a great many others in different directions and some of them equally distant, at the same time. At the same time I had an eye for birds and whatever else might offer.

*December 5.* My themes shall not be far-fetched. I will tell of homely every-day phenomena and adventures. Friends! Society! It seems to me that I have an abundance of it, there is so much that I rejoice and sympathize with, and men, too, that I never speak to but only know and think of. What you call bareness and poverty is to me simplicity.[123] God could not be unkind to me if he should try. I love the winter, with its imprisonment and its cold, for it compels the prisoner to try new fields and resources. I love to have the river closed up for a season and a pause put to my boating, to be obliged to get my boat in. I shall launch it again in the spring with so much more pleasure. This is an advantage in point of

**123** On 8 February 1857 Thoreau wrote: "By poverty, *i. e.* simplicity of life and fewness of incidents, I am solidified and crystallized, as a vapor or liquid by cold. It is a singular concentration of strength and energy and flavor. . . . You think that I am impoverishing myself by withdrawing from men, but in my solitude I have woven for myself a silken web or *chrysalis,* and, nymph-like, shall ere long burst forth a more perfect creature, fitted for a higher society. By simplicity, commonly called poverty, my life is concentrated and so becomes organized, or a κόσμος, which before was inorganic and lumpish" [J 9:246–247].

**124** From the 16th-century phrase "in the nick," the now obsolete word nick meaning "the critical moment," or from tallies marked with nicks or notches. Shakespeare referred to "the prick of noon" (*Romeo and Juliet*, 2.3.100), an allusion to the custom of pricking tallies with a pin. If a man entered chapel just before the doors closed, he would be just in time to get nicked or pricked, and would therefore enter at the nick, or prick, of time.

**125** Later known as Baker Bridge, in Lincoln, about which on 3 December Thoreau had noted: "A man killed at the fatal Lincoln Bridge died in the village the other night" [J 9:151]. In the 19th century, "kill" was sometimes used to mean "strike down" but not necessarily to deprive of life.

**126** Brakemen had to manually set the brakes, which were situated on the tops of the railway cars. Despite the use of the telltale—several pieces of rope hung from a metal frame, designed to gently hit the brakeman as a warning of an approaching low hazard—thousands of railroad workmen were killed or injured annually.

**127** Allusion to Shakespeare's *A Midsummer Night's Dream* (2.1.249): "I know a bank where the wild thyme blows."

**128** Allusion to the English ballad "The Dragon of Wantley," which Thoreau read in Thomas Percy's (1729–1811) *Reliques of Ancient English Poetry*.

**129** Originally a group from the Caribbean Islands that dried and smoked flesh or fish and hunted wild cattle and swine for skins, but later, as in the term buccaneer, a pirate.

**130** Echo of Cain's reply in Genesis 4:9: "And the Lord said unto Cain, Where is Abel thy brother? And he said, I know not. Am I my brother's keeper?"

abstinence and moderation compared with the seaside boating, where the boat ever lies on the shore. I love best to have each thing in its season only, and enjoy doing without it at all other times. It is the greatest of all advantages to enjoy no advantage at all. I find it invariably true, the poorer I am, the richer I am. What you consider my disadvantage, I consider my advantage. While you are pleased to get knowledge and culture in many ways, I am delighted to think that I am getting rid of them. I have never got over my surprise that I should have been born into the most estimable place in all the world, and in the very nick of time,[124] too.

*December 10.* Yesterday I walked under the murderous Lincoln Bridge,[125] where at least ten men have been swept dead from the cars within as many years.[126] I looked to see if their heads had indented the bridge, if there were sturdy blows given as well as received, and if their brains lay about. But I could see neither the one nor the other. The bridge is quite uninjured, even, and straight, not even the paint worn off or discolored. The ground is clean, the snow spotless, and the place looks as innocent as a bank whereon the wild thyme grows.[127] It does its work in an artistic manner. We have another bridge of exactly the same character on the other side of the town, which has killed one, at least, to my knowledge. Surely the approaches to our town are well guarded. These are our modern Dragons of Wantley.[128] Boucaniers[129] of the Fitchburg Railroad, they lie in wait at the narrow passes and decimate the employees. The Company has signed a bond to give up one employee at this pass annually. The Vermont mother commits her son to their charge, and when she asks for him again, the Directors say: "I am not your son's keeper.[130] Go look beneath the ribs of the Lincoln Bridge." It is a monster which would not have minded Perseus with his Medusa's head.[131] If he could be held back only four feet from where he now crouches, all travellers might pass in safety and laugh him to scorn. This would require but a little resolution in our legislature, but it is preferred to pay tribute still. I felt a curiosity to see this famous bridge, naturally far greater than my curiosity to see the gallows on which Smith was hung,[132] which was burned in the old courthouse,[133] for the exploits of this bridge are ten times as memorable. Here they are killed without priest, and the bridge, unlike the gallows, is a fixture. Besides, the gallows bears an ill name, and I think deservedly. No doubt it has hung many an innocent man, but this Lincoln Bridge, long as it has been in our midst and busy as it has been, no legislature, nobody, indeed, has ever seriously complained of, unless it was some bereaved mother, who was naturally prejudiced against it. To my surprise, I found no difficulty in getting a sight of it. It stands right out in broad daylight in the midst of the fields. No sentinels, no spiked fence, no crowd about it, and you have to pay no fee for looking at it. It is perfectly simple and easy to construct, and does its work silently. The days of the gallows are numbered. The next time this county has a Smith to dispose of, they have only to hire him out to the Fitchburg Railroad Company. Let the priest accompany him to the freight-train, pray with him, and take leave of him there. Another advantage I have hinted at, an advantage to the morals of the community, that, strange as it may seem, no crowd ever assembles at this spot; there are no morbidly curious persons, no hardened reprobates, no masculine women, no anatomists there.

Does it not make life more serious? I feel as if these were stirring times, as good as the days of the Crusaders, the Northmen, or the Boucaniers.[134]

**131** In Greek mythology, Perseus was the hero who killed Medusa, the Gorgon whose look could turn a person to stone. With the help of winged shoes, a magical sword, and a polished shield, Perseus swooped down on Medusa from the air, used the shield as a mirror so that he wasn't looking at her directly, and cut off her head.
**132** Samuel Smith (1745–1799) was hanged in Concord on 26 December 1799 for the crime of burglary. Ezra Ripley delivered the execution sermon.
**133** In 1849.
**134** Piratical adventurers, chiefly French and British, who combined to make depredations on the Spanish in America in the second half of the 17th century, so called because the French were driven from their business of bucaning—salting and smoking meat to preserve it—on the island of Hispaniola by the Spanish authorities.

135 Established or fixed, and called by the congregation to be their minister, as opposed to occasional or interim.

*December 17.* A farmer once asked me what shrub oaks were made for, not knowing any use they served. But I can tell him that they do me good. They are my parish ministers, regularly settled.[135] They never did any man harm that I know.

Now you have the foliage of summer painted in brown. Go through the shrub oaks. All growth has ceased; no greenness meets the eye, except what there may be in the bark of this shrub. The green leaves are all turned to brown, quite dry and sapless. The little buds are sleeping at the base of the slender shrunken petioles. Who observed when they passed from green to brown? I do not remember the transition; it was very gradual. But these leaves still have a kind of life in them. They are exceedingly beautiful in their withered state. If they hang on, it is like the perseverance of the saints. Their colors are as wholesome, their forms as perfect, as ever. Now that the crowd and bustle of summer is passed, I have leisure to admire them. Their figures never weary my eye. Look at the few broad scallops in their sides. When was that pattern first cut? With what a free stroke the curve was struck! With how little, yet just enough, variety in their forms! Look at the fine bristles which arm each pointed lobe, as perfect now as when the wild bee hummed about them, or the chewink scratched beneath them. What pleasing and harmonious colors within and without, above and below! The smooth, delicately brown-tanned upper surface, acorn-color, the very pale (some silvery or ashy) ribbed under side. How poetically, how like saints or innocent and beneficent beings, they give up the ghost! How spiritual! Though they have lost their sap, they have not given up the ghost. Rarely touched by work or insect, they are as fair as ever. These are the forms of some: —

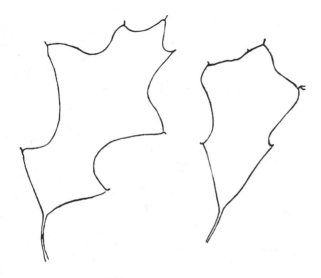

**136** Thoreau delivered his lecture "Walking, or The Wild" in the Congregationalist Church in Amherst, New Hampshire, on 18 December. On 31 December 1856 he wrote to Blake: "My writing has not taken the shape of lectures, and therefore I should be obliged to read one of three or four old lectures, the best of which I have read to some of your auditors before. I carried that one which I call 'Walking, or the Wild,' to Amherst, N.H., the evening of that cold Thursday, and I am to read another at Fitchburg, February 3. I am simply their hired man. This will probably be the extent of my lecturing hereabouts" [C 461].

When was it ordained that this leaf should turn brown in the fall?

*December 18.* At my lecture,[136] the audience attended to me closely, and I was satisfied; that is all I ask or expect generally. Not one spoke to me afterward, nor needed they. I have no doubt that they liked it, in the main, though few of them would have dared say so, provided they were conscious of it. Generally, if I can only get the ears of an audience, I do not care whether they say they like my lecture or not. I think I know as well as they can tell. At any rate, it is none of my business, and it would be impertinent for me to inquire. The stupidity of most of these country towns, not to include the cities, is in its innocence infantile. Lectured in basement (vestry) of the orthodox church, and I trust helped to undermine it.

*December 19.* Withered leaves! this is our frugal winter diet, instead of the juicy salads of spring and summer. I

**137** Thoreau's lecture "Autumnal Tints" was first delivered on 22 February 1859 in Worcester.

**138** The picturesque school of landscape architecture, which was distinguished by wild ruggedness, irregularity, and textural variety, in imitation of the wild and uncultivated aspects of untrained nature, promoted in the late 18th century by several writers but most prominently by William Gilpin (1724–1804) in *Remarks on Forest Scenery and Other Woodland Views, Relative Chiefly to Picturesque Beauty* (1791) and *Three Essays: On Picturesque Beauty; On Picturesque Travel; and on Sketching Landscape* (1792).

**139** Eskimo, a native inhabitant of northern Canada, Alaska, Greenland, and eastern Siberia.

**140** Bugleweed or water horehound (*Lycopus americanus*), which has a slight minty scent.

**141** The Moluccas, an eastern Indonesian island group, center for the Dutch spice monopoly begun in the 17th century, from which they became known as the Spice Islands.

**142** Small bottle filled with a preparation, usually smelling salts, sniffed as a restorative or stimulant.

**143** Anointing oil, as in the fragrant ointment of myrrh, cinnamon, and calamus in Exodus 30:25: "an oil of holy ointment, an ointment compound after the art of the apothecary: it shall be an holy anointing oil."

**144** Cf. "Solitude" in *Walden:* "I never found the companion that was so companionable as solitude" [Wa 131].

think I could write a lecture on "Dry Leaves,"[137] carrying a specimen of each kind that hangs on in the winter into the lecture-room as the heads of my discourse. They have long hung to some extent in vain, and have not found their poet yet. The pine has been sung, but not, to my knowledge, the shrub oak. Most think it is useless. How glad I am that it serves no vulgar use! It is never seen on the woodman's cart. The citizen who has just bought a sprout-land on which shrub oaks alone come up only curses it. But it serves a higher use than they know. Shrub oak! how true its name! Think first what a family it belongs to. The oak, the king of trees, is its own brother, only of ampler dimensions. The oaks, so famous for grandeur and picturesqueness,[138] so prized for strength by the builder, for knees or for beams; and this is the oak of smaller size, the Esquimau[139] of oaks, the shrub oak! The oaken shrub! I value it first for the noble family it belongs to. It is not like brittle sumach or venomous dogwood, which you must beware how you touch, but wholesome to the touch, though rough; not producing any festering sores, only honest scratches and rents.

*December 24.* I do not take snuff. In my winter walks, I stoop and bruise between my thumb and finger the dry whorls of the lycopus, or water horehound,[140] just rising above the snow, stripping them off, and smell that. That is as near as I come to the Spice Islands.[141] That is my smelling-bottle,[142] my ointment.[143]

*December 28.* I thrive best on solitude. If I have had a companion only one day in a week, unless it were one or two I could name, I find that the value of the week to me has been seriously affected.[144] It dissipates my days, and often it takes me another week to get over it. As the

Esquimaux of Smith's Strait in North Greenland laughed when Kane warned them of their utter extermination,[145] cut off as they were by ice on all sides from their race, unless they attempted in season to cross the glacier southward, so do I laugh when you tell me of the danger of impoverishing myself by isolation. It is here that the walrus and the seal, and the white bear, and the eider ducks and auks on which I batten, most abound.

*December 29.* We must go out and re-ally ourselves to Nature every day. We must make root, send out some little fibre at least, even every winter day. I am sensible that I am imbibing health when I open my mouth to the wind. Staying in the house breeds a sort of insanity always. Every house is in this sense a hospital.[146] A night and a forenoon is as much confinement to those wards as I can stand. I am aware that I recover some sanity which I had lost almost the instant that I come abroad.

*December 30.* What an evidence it is, after all, of civilization, or of a capacity for improvement, that savages like our Indians, who in their protracted wars stealthily slay men, women, and children without mercy, with delight, who delight to burn, torture, and devour one another, proving themselves more inhuman in these respects even than beasts,—what a wonderful evidence it is, I say, of their capacity for improvement that even they can enter into the most formal compact or treaty of peace, burying the hatchet, etc., etc., and treating with each other with as much consideration as the most enlightened states. You would say that they had a genius for diplomacy as well as for war. Consider that Iroquois, torturing his captive, roasting him before a slow fire, biting off the fingers of him alive, and finally eating the heart of him dead, betraying not the slightest evidence of humanity;[147] and

145 Elisha Kent Kane (cf. 1854 note 56), although the specific incident Thoreau referred to has not been identified. Esquimaux was a common spelling for the plural of Eskimo.

146 In the sense of an institution or establishment for dispensing hospitality or care for the needy or an asylum for shelter or maintenance, as in the term foundling hospital.

147 Allusion to such narratives as Christophe Regnaut's "A Veritable Account of the Martyrdom and Blessed Death of Father Jean de Breboeuf and of Father Gabriel L'Alemant, in New France, in the Country of the Hurons, by the Iroquois, Enemies of the Faith": "They put on him a belt of bark, full of pitch and resin, and set fire to it, which roasted his whole body. . . . To prevent him from speaking more, they cut off his tongue, and both his upper and lower lips. After that, they set themselves to strip the flesh from his legs, thighs, and arms, to the very bone; and then put it to roast before his eyes, in order to eat it. . . . Another one of those barbarians, seeing that the good Father would soon die, made an opening in the upper part of his chest, and tore out his heart, which he roasted and ate." And to Isaac Jogues's (1607–1646) *Novum Belgium*: "Two of them then dragged me back to where I had been before, and scarcely had I begun to breathe, when some other, attacking me, tore out, by biting, almost all my nails, and crunched my two fore-fingers with their teeth, giving me intense pain."

now behold him in the council-chamber, where he meets the representatives of the hostile nation to treat of peace, conducting with such perfect dignity and decorum, betraying such a sense of justness. These savages are equal to us civilized men in their treaties, and, I fear, not essentially worse in their wars.

# 1857

AGE 39–40

1 Thoreau had been surveying Davis Elwell's farm, also known as the Lee Farm, near Naw-shawtuct Hill on 30–31 December 1856 and 1 and 4 January 1857.

*January 4.* After spending four or five days surveying and drawing a plan incessantly,[1] I especially feel the necessity of putting myself in communication with nature again, to recover my tone, to withdraw out of the wearying and unprofitable world of affairs. The things I have been doing have but a fleeting and accidental importance, however much men are immersed in them, and yield very little valuable fruit. I would fain have been wading through the woods and fields and conversing with the sane snow. Having waded in the very shallowest stream of time, I would now bathe my temples in eternity. I wish again to participate in the serenity of nature, to share the happiness of the river and the woods. I thus from time to time break off my connection with eternal truths and go with the shallow stream of human affairs, grinding at the mill of the Philistines; but when my task is done, with never-failing confidence I devote myself to the infinite again. It would be sweet to deal with men more, I can imagine, but where dwell they? Not in the fields which I traverse.

*January 7.* There is nothing so sanative, so poetic, as a walk in the woods and fields even now, when I meet none abroad for pleasure. Nothing so inspires me and excites such serene and profitable thought. The objects are elevating. In the street and in society I am almost invariably cheap and dissipated, my life is unspeakably mean. No amount of gold or respectability would in the

2 Allusion to the short-lived Town and Country Club formed by Alcott in 1849, of which Thoreau attended the first meeting. Alcott explained that the club's aim was a "diffusion of the Ideas and tendencies proper to the nineteenth century; and to concert measures, if deemed desirable, for promoting the ends of good fellowship."

3 The Concord Farmers' Club, established in 1852, as a medium in which local farmers could share knowledge and exchange ideas.

least redeem it,—dining with the Governor or a member of Congress!! But alone in distant woods or fields, in unpretending sprout-lands or pastures tracked by rabbits, even in a bleak and, to most, cheerless day, like this, when a villager would be thinking of his inn, I come to myself, I once more feel myself grandly related, and that cold and solitude are friends of mine. I suppose that this value, in my case, is equivalent to what others get by churchgoing and prayer. I come to my solitary woodland walk as the homesick go home. I thus dispose of the superfluous and see things as they are, grand and beautiful. I have told many that I walk every day about half the daylight, but I think they do not believe it. I wish to get the Concord, the Massachusetts, the America, out of my head and be sane a part of every day. If there are missionaries for the heathen, why not send them to me? I wish to know something; I wish to be made better. I wish to forget, a considerable part of every day, all mean, narrow, trivial men (and this requires usually to forego and forget all personal relations so long), and therefore I come out to these solitudes, where the problem of existence is simplified. I get away a mile or two from the town into the stillness and solitude of nature, with rocks, trees, weeds, snow about me. I enter some glade in the woods, perchance, where a few weeds and dry leaves alone lift themselves above the surface of the snow, and it is as if I had come to an open window. I see out and around myself. Our *skylights* are thus far away from the ordinary resorts of men. I am not satisfied with ordinary windows. I must have a true *skylight*. My true skylight is on the outside of the village. I am not thus expanded, recreated, enlightened, when I meet a company of men. It chances that the sociable, the town and country,[2] or the farmers' club[3] does not prove a skylight to me. I do not invariably find myself translated under those circumstances. They bore me. The man I meet with is not often so instructive as the silence he breaks. This stillness, solitude, wildness of nature is a kind of thoroughwort, or boneset,[4] to my intellect. This is what I go out to seek. It is as if I always met in those places some grand, serene, immortal, infinitely encouraging, though invisible, companion, and walked with him. There at last my nerves are steadied, my senses and my mind do their office. I am aware that most of my neighbors would think it a hardship to be compelled to linger here one hour, especially this bleak day, and yet I receive this sweet and ineffable compensation for it. It is the most agreeable thing I do. Truly, my coins are uncurrent with them.

*January 11.* For some years past I have partially offered myself as a lecturer; have been advertised as such several years.[5] Yet I have had but two or three invitations to lecture in a year, and some years none at all. I congratulate myself on having been permitted to stay at home thus, I am so much richer for it. I do not see what I should have got of much value, but money, by going about, but I do see what I should have lost. It seems to me that I have a longer and more liberal lease of life thus. I cannot afford to be telling my experience, especially to those who perhaps will take no interest in it. I wish to be getting experience. You might as well recommend to a bear to leave his hollow tree and run about all winter scratching at all the hollow trees in the woods. He would be leaner in the spring than if he had stayed at home and sucked his claws. As for the lecture-goers, it is none of their business what I think. I perceive that most make a great account of their relations, more or less personal and direct, to many men, coming before them as lecturers, writers, or public men. But all this is impertinent and unprofitable to me. I never yet recognized, nor was recognized by, a crowd of men. I was never assured of their existence, nor they of mine.

**4** *Eupatorium perfoliatum:* a perennial herb used in a tonic for treating colds, fever, and ague, and to restore normal temperature.
**5** As in the list of "names and post office address of those hitherto widely invited as Lecturers, for the convenience of those who are now making out their lists and addressing invitations" in the 20 September 1854 issue of the *New York Tribune.*

7 Cf. *Walden:* "The mass of men lead lives of quiet desperation" [Wa 7].
8 Emerson was away on a lecture tour taking him to New York, Ohio, and Illinois, having left Concord on 8 January.
9 Emerson's son Edward.

❧

I demand of my companion some evidence that he has travelled further than the sources of the Nile,[6] that he has seen something, that he has been *out of town, out of the house.* Not that he can tell a good story, but that he can keep a good silence. Has he attended to a silence more significant than any story? Did he ever get out of the road which all men and fools travel? You call yourself a great traveller, perhaps, but can you get beyond the influence of a certain class of ideas?

*January 15.* What is there in music that it should so stir our deeps? We are all ordinarily in a state of desperation;[7] such is our life; ofttimes it drives us to suicide. To how many, perhaps to most, life is barely tolerable, and if it were not for the fear of death or of dying, what a multitude would immediately commit suicide! But let us hear a strain of music, we are at once advertised of a life which no man had told us of, which no preacher preaches. Suppose I try to describe faithfully the prospect which a strain of music exhibits to me. The field of my life becomes a boundless plain, glorious to tread, with no death nor disappointment at the end of it. All meanness and trivialness disappear. I become adequate to any deed. No particulars survive this expansion; persons do not survive it. In the light of this strain there is no thou nor I. We are actually lifted above ourselves.

*January 20.* At Emerson's this evening,[8] at about 6 P.M., I was called out to see Eddy's[9] cave in the snow. It was a hole about two and a half feet wide and six feet long, into a drift, a little winding, and he had got a lamp at the inner extremity. I observed, as I approached in a course at right angles with the length of the cave, that the mouth of the cave was lit as if the light were close to it, so that I did not suspect its depth. Indeed, the light of this lamp was remarkably reflected and distributed. The snowy walls were one universal reflector with countless facets. I think that one lamp would light sufficiently a hall built of this material. The snow about the mouth of the cave within had the yellow color of the flame to one approaching, as if the lamp were close to it. We afterward buried the lamp in a little crypt in this snow-drift and walled it in, and found that its light was visible, even in this *twilight,* through fifteen inches' thickness of snow. The snow was all aglow with it. If it had been darker, probably it would have been visible through a much greater thickness. But, what was most surprising to me, when Eddy crawled into the extremity of his cave and shouted at the top of his voice, it sounded ridiculously faint, as if he were a quarter of a mile off, and at first I could not believe that he spoke loud, but we all of us crawled in by turns, and though our heads were only six feet from those outside, our loudest shouting only amused and surprised them. Apparently the porous snow drank up all the sound. The voice was, in fact, muffled by the surrounding snow walls, and I saw that we might lie in that hole screaming for assistance in vain, while travellers were passing along twenty feet distant. It had the effect of ventriloquism. So you only need make a snow house in your yard and pass an hour in it, to realize a good deal of Esquimau life.[10]

*February 4.* I sometimes hear a prominent but dull-witted worthy man say, or hear that he has said, rarely, that if it were not for his firm belief in "an overruling power," or a "perfect Being," etc., etc. But such poverty-stricken expressions only convince me of his habitual doubt and that he is surprised into a transient belief. Such a man's expression of faith, moving solemnly in the traditional furrow, and casting out all free-thinking and living souls with the rusty mould-board of his compas-

**10** Ellen Tucker Emerson (1839–1909) wrote to her father on 22 January 1857: "Mr Thoreau was here night before last and Eddy illuminated his snow cave and called out to us; we couldn't hear what he said though we were close at the mouth of the cave and Mr Thoreau said 'Speak louder' so Eddy spoke again and we could hear some very feeble words. Then Mr Thoreau told him to holla as loud as he could, but we heard only very weak squeaks. The Mr Thoreau was very surprised, as he said he could hardly believe Eddy was calling loud, and he went in himself and shouted and it sounded as if someone was in trouble over the brook near Mr Stow's. And Edie went in and peeped and that sounded very feeble. Mr Thoreau thought the snow sucked up the sound. Then he said he should like to see how transparent snow was, and we dug into the snow-drift a hole with one side 4 inches thick and one 14 and about 6 inches from the top, then we put the lamp in and walled it up with a block of snow eight inches thick, through the four inches one could see to read, through fourteen the lamp shone bright and shining like a lantern—a Norwegian would think it was a Troll-mount. Mr Thoreau was quite delighted and so we all were with our experiments."

11 Allusion to the marble quay in Lisbon, Portugal, on which people gathered for safety during the earthquake of 1 November 1755 and subsequently perished. On the centennial of the calamity *Harper's Magazine* (November 1855) carried a piece, "An Earthquake or Two," in which was written: "The quay itself has sunk to unknown depths, and neither any fragment thereof, nor any trace of the thousands who had sought refuge on its surface is ever seen again."

12 Thin or weak ice that bends when a person walks across it, or the game in which children attempt to get across thin ice by running or skating, the object being to bend the ice without breaking it. The term has many variants, such as "kiddly-benders," "kettle-benders," and "tickly-benders."

13 1 February 1857.

sion or contempt, thinking that he has Moses and all the prophets in his wake, discourages and saddens me as an expression of his narrow and barren want of faith. I see that the infidels and skeptics have formed themselves into churches and weekly gather together at the ringing of a bell.

Sometimes when, in conversation or a lecture, I have been grasping at, or even standing and reclining upon, the serene and everlasting truths that underlie and support our vacillating life, I have seen my auditors standing on their *terra firma,* the quaking earth, crowded together on their Lisbon Quay,[11] and compassionately or timidly watching my motions as if they were the antics of a rope-dancer or mountebank pretending to walk on air; or here and there one creeping out upon an overhanging but cracking bough, unwilling to drop to the adamantine floor beneath, or perchance even venturing out a step or two, as if it were a dangerous kittly-bender,[12] timorously sounding as he goes. So the other day,[13] as I stood on Walden, drinking at a puddle on the ice, which was probably two feet thick, and thinking how lucky I was that I had not got to cut through all that thickness, I was amused to see an Irish laborer on the railroad, who had come down to drink, timidly tiptoeing toward me in his cowhide boots, lifting them nearly two feet at each step and fairly trembling with fear, as if the ice were already bending beneath his ponderous body and he were about to be engulfed. "Why, my man," I called out to him, "this ice will bear a loaded train, half a dozen locomotives side by side, a whole herd of oxen," suggesting whatever would be a weighty argument with him. And so at last he fairly straightened up and quenched his thirst. It was very ludicrous to me, who was thinking, by chance, what a labor it would be to get at the water with an axe there and that I was lucky to find some on the surface.

So, when I have been resting and quenching my thirst on the eternal plains of truth, where rests the base of those beautiful columns that sustain the heavens, I have been amused to see a traveller who had long confined himself to the quaking shore, which was all covered with the traces of the deluge, come timidly tiptoeing toward me, trembling in every limb.

I see the crowd of materialists gathered together on their Lisbon Quay for safety, thinking it a *terra firma.*

Though the farmer has been all winter teaming wood along the river, the timid citizen that buys it, but who has not stepped out of the road, thinks it all kittly-benders there and warns his boys not to go near it.

*February 6.* Winckelmann says in his "History of Ancient Art," vol. i, page 95: "I am now past forty, and therefore at an age when one can no longer sport freely with life. I perceive, also, that a certain delicate spirit begins to evaporate, with which I raised myself, by powerful soarings, to the contemplation of the beautiful."[14]

*February 8.* Again and again I congratulate myself on my so-called poverty. I was almost disappointed yesterday to find thirty dollars in my desk which I did not know that I possessed, though now I should be sorry to lose it.

In the society of many men, or in the midst of what is called success, I find my life of no account, and my spirits rapidly fall. I would rather be the barrenest pasture lying fallow than cursed with the compliments of kings, than be the sulphurous and accursed desert where Babylon once stood.[15] But when I have only a rustling oak leaf, or the faint metallic cheep of a tree sparrow, for variety in my winter walk, my life becomes continent and sweet as the kernel of a nut. I would rather hear a single shrub oak leaf at the end of a wintry glade rustle of

**14** Quoted from Johann Joachim Winckelmann's (1717–1768) *The History of Ancient Art.* Thoreau would turn forty in five months.
**15** Ancient city in Mesopotamia, located on the Euphrates River.

**16** In medieval chivalry, the order of the garter was created in 1348 by Edward III of England; the star (*Ordre de l'Étoile*) was created in 1351 by Jean II of France.

**17** Cf. 28 March 1856.

**18** Plural of genius: cf. 1830s note 58.

its own accord at my approach, than receive a shipload of stars and garters[16] from the strange kings and peoples of the earth.

And now another friendship is ended.[17] I do not know what has made my friend doubt me, but I know that in love there is no mistake, and that every estrangement is well founded. But my destiny is not narrowed, but if possible the broader for it. The heavens withdraw and arch themselves higher. I am sensible not only of a moral, but even a grand physical pain, such as gods may feel, about my head and breast, a certain ache and fullness. This rending of a tie, it is not my work nor thine. It is no accident that we mind; it is only the awards of fate that are affecting. I know of no æons, or periods, no life and death, but these meetings and separations. My life is like a stream that is suddenly dammed and has no outlet; but it rises the higher up the hills that shut it in, and will become a deep and silent lake. Certainly there is no event comparable for grandeur with the eternal separation—if we may conceive it so—from a being that we have known. I become in a degree sensible of the meaning of finite and infinite. What a grand significance the word "never" acquires! With one with whom we have walked on high ground we cannot deal on any lower ground ever after. We have tried for so many years to put each other to this immortal use, and have failed. Undoubtedly our good genii[18] have mutually found the material unsuitable. We have hitherto paid each other the highest possible compliment; we have recognized each other constantly as divine, have afforded each other that opportunity to live that no other wealth or kindness can afford. And now, for some reason inappreciable by us, it has become necessary for us to withhold this mutual aid. Perchance there is none beside who knows us for a god, and none whom we know for such. Each man and woman is a veritable god or goddess, but to the mass of their fellows disguised. There is only one in each case who sees through the disguise. That one who does not stand so near to any man as to see the divinity in him is truly alone. I am perfectly sad at parting from you. I could better have the earth taken away from under my feet, than the thought of you from my mind. One while I think that some great injury has been done, with which you are implicated, again that you are no party to it. I fear that there may be incessant tragedies, that one may treat his fellow as a god but receive somewhat less regard from him. I now almost for the first time *fear* this. Yet I believe that in the long run there is no such inequality.

*February 15.* I have just been reading the account of Dr. Ball's sufferings on the White Mountains.[19] Of course, I do not wonder that he was lost. I should say: Never undertake to ascend a mountain or thread a wilderness where there is any danger of being lost, without taking thick clothing, partly india-rubber, if not a tent or material for one; the best map to be had and a compass; salt pork and hard-bread and salt; fish-hooks and lines; a good jack-knife, at least, if not a hatchet, and perhaps a gun; matches in a vial stopped water-tight; some strings and paper. Do not take a dozen steps which you could not with tolerable accuracy protract on a chart. I never do otherwise. Indeed, you must have been living all your life in some such methodical and assured fashion, though in the midst of cities, else you will be lost in spite of all this preparation.

*February 19.* A man cannot be said to succeed in this life who does not satisfy one friend.

19  Dr. Benjamin Lincoln Ball's (1820–1860) *Three Days on the White Mountains, Being the Perilous Adventure of Dr. B. L. Ball on Mount Washington, During October 25, 26, and 27, 1855* (Boston: N. Noyes, 1856). Toward the end of his account Ball wrote: "To recapitulate, then, in brief, my exposure on the Mountains without food, shelter or fire, with snow and ice only for drink, was about *sixty hours;* and I had been without sleep for upwards of *eighty hours*—of which one night was spent at the Camp House, and two in the snow, subjected to a furious storm and intense cold, with the sole protection of an umbrella."

**20** Possible allusion to Matthew 18:9: "And if thine eye offend thee, pluck it out, and cast it from thee."

**21** Allusion to Chang and Eng Bunker (1811–1874), conjoined twins from Siam made famous in America and Europe when they traveled on exhibit starting in 1829. Although Thoreau's comment anticipated their actual death, false rumors of their death had circulated prior to 1857. The *Scientific American* of 20 July 1850 reported that the "Paris Journal des Debats announces the death, in England, of the famous Siamese Twins."

**22** Possible allusion to Emerson's "Friendship," in which he wrote: "Better be a nettle in the side of your friend than his echo."

**23** Corner Spring Woods, near Corner Spring.

**24** Abiel Heywood Wheeler (1807–1896), Concord farmer.

*February 20.* What is hope, what is expectation, but a seed-time whose harvest cannot fail, an irresistible expedition of the mind, at length to be victorious?

*February 23.* I have not yet known a friendship to cease, I think. I fear I have experienced its decaying. Morning, noon, and night, I suffer a physical pain, an aching of the breast which unfits me for my tasks. It is perhaps most intense at evening.

If the teeth ache they can be pulled. If the heart aches, what then? Shall we pluck it out?[20]

Must friends then expect the fate of those Oriental twins, — that one shall at last bear about the corpse of the other, by that same ligature that bound him to a living companion?[21]

*February 24.* If I should make the least concession, my friend would spurn me. I am obeying his law as well as my own.[22]

Those whom we can love, we can hate; to others we are indifferent.

*March 26.* As I come out of the Spring Woods[23] I see Abiel Wheeler[24] planting peas and covering them up on his warm sandy hillside, in the hollow next the woods. It is a novel sight, that of the farmer distributing manure with a shovel in the fields and planting again. The earth looks warm and genial again. The sight of the earliest planting with carts in the field so lately occupied with snow is suggestive of the genialness of Nature. I could almost lie down in the furrow and be warmed into her life and growth.

*March 28.* When I witness the first plowing and planting, I acquire a long-lost confidence in the earth,—that it will nourish the seed that is committed to its bosom. I am surprised to be reminded that there is warmth in it. We have not only warmer skies, then, but a warmer earth. The frost is out of it, and we may safely commit these seeds to it in some places. Yesterday I walked with Farmer[25] beside his team and saw one furrow turned quite round his field. What noble work is plowing, with the broad and solid earth for material, the ox for fellow-laborer, and the simple but efficient plow for tool! Work that is not done in any shop, in a cramped position, work that tells, that concerns all men, which the sun shines and the rain falls on, and the birds sing over! You turn over the whole vegetable mould, expose how many grubs, and put a new aspect on the face of the earth. It comes pretty near to making a world. Redeeming a swamp does, at any rate. A good plowman is a *terrae filius.*[26] The plowman, we all know, whistles as he drives his team afield.[27]

Often I can give the truest and most interesting account of any adventure I have had after years have elapsed,[28] for then I am not confused, only the most significant facts surviving in my memory. Indeed, all that continues to interest me after such a lapse of time is sure to be pertinent, and I may safely record all that I remember.

*March 31.* A very pleasant day. Spent a part of it in the garden preparing to set out fruit trees. It is agreeable once more to put a spade into the warm mould. The victory is ours at last, for we remain and take possession of the field. In this climate, in which we do not commonly bury our dead in the winter on account of the frozen

25 Jacob Farmer: cf. 1855 note 23.
26 Latin: son of the earth.
27 Allusion to Milton's "L'Allegro": "While the ploughman near at hand, / Whistles o'er the furrowed land . . ."
28 As he wrote to H. G. O. Blake later this year: "Let me suggest a theme for you: to state to yourself precisely and completely what that walk over the mountains amounted to for you. . . . Don't suppose that you can tell it precisely the first dozen times you try, but at 'em again, especially when, after a sufficient pause, you suspect that you are touching the heart or summit of the matter, reiterate your blows there, and account for the mountain to yourself. Not that the story need be long, but it will take a long while to make it short. It did not take very long to get over the mountain, you thought; but have you got over it indeed? . . . Going up there and being blown on is nothing. We never do much climbing while we are there, but we eat our luncheon, etc., very much as at home. It is after we get home that we really go over the mountain, if ever. What did the mountain say? What did the mountain do?" [C 498]. Cf. 11 November 1851.

29 Although not every winter produced conditions in which the ground was too frozen to allow interment, most New England cemeteries, such as Mount Auburn in Cambridge, had receiving tombs in which casketed bodies could be held until the ground was thawed enough to allow burial.

30 Thoreau was in New Bedford, visiting Daniel Ricketson from 1 April to 15 April. He first heard of Kate Brady (1837–1930) and her sister in September 1855 from Ricketson, who "said that they were particularly bright girls and lovers of nature; had read my 'Walden'" [J 7:467]. Kate and her sister had both worked in the Ricketson house.

31 Ultimately she married a whaler named Francis C. Eldredge (1828–1890) by whom she had two daughters and who she survived by forty years, never remarrying.

32 Squin's Brook in New Bedford, of which Daniel Ricketson wrote in his *History of New Bedford* that the Acushnet River takes its rise "near the south shores of two of the beautiful Middleborough ponds, Apponequet or Long Pond, and Aquitticaset, in a richly wooded dell, about ten miles from New Bedford, and for some distance on its course is known by the humble name of 'Squin's Brook,' so called from Watuspaquin, a noted Sachem of the Nemasket or Middleborough Indians."

ground,[29] and find ourselves exposed on a hard bleak crust, the coming out of the frost and the first turning up of the soil with a spade or plow is an event of importance.

*April 23.* I saw at Ricketson's a young woman, Miss Kate Brady,[30] twenty years old, her father an Irishman, a worthless fellow, her mother a smart Yankee. The daughter formerly did sewing, but now keeps school for a livelihood. She was born at the Brady house, I think in Freetown, where she lived till twelve years old and helped her father in the field. There she rode horse to plow and was knocked off the horse by apple tree boughs, kept sheep, caught fish, etc., etc. I never heard a girl or woman express so strong a love for nature. She purposes to return to that lonely ruin, and dwell there alone, since her mother and sister will not accompany her; says that she knows all about farming and keeping sheep and spinning and weaving, though it would puzzle her to shingle the old house. There she thinks she can "live free."[31] I was pleased to hear of her plans, because they were quite cheerful and original, not professedly reformatory, but growing out of her love for "Squin's Brook and the Middleborough ponds."[32] A strong love for outward nature is singularly rare among both men and women. The scenery immediately about her homestead is quite ordinary, yet she appreciates and can use that part of the universe as no other being can. Her own sex, so tamely bred, only jeer at her for entertaining such an idea, but she has a strong head and a love for good reading, which may carry her through. I would by no means discourage, nor yet particularly encourage her, for I would have her so strong as to succeed in spite of all ordinary discouragements.

It is very rare that I hear one express a strong and imperishable attachment to a particular scenery, or to the whole of nature,—I mean such as will control their whole lives and characters. Such seem to have a true home in nature, a hearth in the fields and woods, whatever tenement may be burned. The soil and climate is warm to them. They alone are naturalized, but most are tender and callow creatures that wear a house as their outmost shell and must get their lives insured when they step abroad from it. They are lathed and plastered in from all natural influences, and their delicate lives are a long battle with the dyspepsia. The others are fairly rooted in the soil, and are the noblest plant it bears, more hardy and natural than sorrel. The dead earth seems animated at the prospect of their coming, as if proud to be trodden on by them. It recognizes its lord. Children of the Golden Age. Hospitals and almshouses are not their destiny. When I hear of such an attachment in a reasonable, a divine, creature to a particular portion of the earth, it seems as if then first the earth succeeded and rejoiced, as if it had been made and existed only for such a use. These various soils and reaches which the farmer plods over, which the traveller glances at and the geologist dryly describes, then first flower and bear their fruit. Does he chiefly own the land who coldly uses it and gets corn and potatoes out of it, or he who loves it and gets inspiration from it? How rarely a man's love for nature becomes a ruling principle with him, like a youth's affection for a maiden, but more enduring! All nature is my bride. That nature which to one is a stark and ghastly solitude is a sweet, tender, and genial society to another.

*April 26.* A great part of our troubles are literally domestic or originate in the house and from living indoors. I could write an essay to be entitled "Out of Doors,"—undertake a crusade against houses.[33] What a different thing Christianity preached to the house-bred and to a party who lived out of doors! Also a sermon is needed on

33 Thoreau wrote later in "Walking": "I think that I cannot preserve my health and spirits, unless I spend four hours a day at least—and it is commonly more than that—sauntering through the woods and over the hills and fields, absolutely free from all worldly engagements. . . . I, who cannot stay in my chamber for a single day without acquiring some rust, and when sometimes I have stolen forth for a walk at the eleventh hour, or four o'clock in the afternoon, too late to redeem the day, when the shades of night were already beginning to be mingled with the daylight, have felt as if I had committed some sin to be atoned for,—I confess that I am astonished at the power of endurance, to say nothing of the moral insensibility, of my neighbors who confine themselves to shops and offices the whole day for weeks and months, aye, and years almost together. . . . How womankind, who are confined to the house still more than men, stand it I do not know; but I have ground to suspect that most of them do not *stand* it at all" [W 5:207–209].

**34** Allusion to the tribute money from the Hebrews for Rome demanded by King Herod (73–4 B.C.E.).

**35** Anyone who willfully causes destruction, from the Vandals, a Germanic tribe that sacked Rome in 455 and plundered the spoils of the Temple in Jerusalem brought to Rome by Titus.

**36** Sanborn described Ricketson's shanty as "a retreat he built near his country house, for solitary musing, or the companionship of his books and his pen." When Ricketson first wrote to Thoreau on 12 April 1854 it was his temporary home while his house was being repaired: "I love a quiet, peaceful, rural retirement, but it was not my fate to realize this until a little past thirty years of age; since then I have been a sort of rustic. Genteel, perhaps, rustic. Not so very genteel, you might reply, if you saw the place where I am writing. It is a rough board shanty 12 x 14, three miles from New Bedford, in a quiet and secluded spot—here for the present I eat and sleep, read, write, receive visitors, etc."

**37** When Ricketson visited Concord in the following month, Emerson wrote in his journal on 25 May 1857 that he "expressed some sad views of life & religion. A thunderstorm is a terror to him, and his theism was judaical."

**38** Arthur (1835–1912) and Walton (1839–1923).

economy of fuel. What right has my neighbor to burn ten cords of wood, when I burn only one? Thus robbing our half-naked town of this precious covering. Is he so much colder than I? It is expensive to maintain him in our midst. If some earn the salt of their porridge, are we certain that they earn the fuel of their kitchen and parlor? One man makes a little of the driftwood of the river or of the dead and refuse (unmarketable!) wood of the forest suffice, and Nature rejoices in him. Another, Herod-like,[34] requires ten cords of the best of young white oak or hickory, and he is commonly esteemed a virtuous man. He who burns the most wood on his hearth is the least warmed by the sight of it growing. Leave the trim wood-lots to widows and orphan girls. Let men tread gently through nature. Let us religiously burn stumps and worship in groves, while Christian vandals[35] lay waste the forest temples to build miles of meeting-houses and horse-sheds and feed their box stoves.

*April 27.* Ricketson frequents his shanty[36] by day and evening as much as his house, but does not sleep there, partly on account of his fear of lightning, which he cannot overcome.[37] His timidity in this respect amounts to an idiosyncrasy. I was awaked there in a thunder-storm at midnight by Ricketson rushing about the house, calling to his sons[38] to come down out of the attic where they slept and bolting in to leave a light in my room. His fear of death is equally singular. The thought of it troubles him more perhaps than anything else. He says that he knows nothing about another life, he would like to stay here always. He does not know what to think of the Creator that made the lightning and established death.

*May 3.* All well men and women who are not restrained by superstitious custom come abroad this morning by land or water, and such as have boats launch them and put forth in search of adventure.[39] Others, less free or, it may be, less fortunate, take their station on bridges, watching the rush of water through them and the motions of the departing voyagers, and listening to the notes of blackbirds from over the smooth water. They see a swimming snake, or a muskrat dive,—airing and sunning themselves there until the first bell rings.

Up and down the town, men and boys that are under subjection are polishing their shoes and brushing their go-to-meeting clothes. I, a descendant of Northmen who worshipped Thor,[40] spend my time worshipping neither Thor nor Christ; a descendant of Northmen who sacrificed men and horses, sacrifice neither men nor horses. I care not for Thor nor for the Jews. I sympathize not today with those who go to church in newest clothes and sit quietly in straight-backed pews. I sympathize rather with the boy who has none to look after him, who borrows a boat and paddle and in common clothes sets out to explore these temporary vernal lakes. I meet such a boy paddling along under a sunny bank, with bare feet and his pants rolled up above his knees, ready to leap into the water at a moment's warning. Better for him to read "Robinson Crusoe" than Baxter's "Saints' Rest."[41]

*May 8.* Within a week I have had made a pair of corduroy pants, which cost when done $1.60. They are of that peculiar clay-color, reflecting the light from portions of their surface. They have this advantage, that, beside being very strong, they will look about as well three months hence as now,—or as ill, some would say. Most of my friends are disturbed by my wearing them.[42] I can get four or five pairs for what one ordinary pair would cost in Boston, and each of the former will last two or three times as long under the same circumstances. The tailor said that the stuff was not made in this country; that it was worn by the Irish at home, and now they would not look at it,

**39** This was a Sunday morning. In *A Week on the Concord and Merrimack Rivers* Thoreau wrote: "I was once reproved by a minister who was driving a poor beast to some meeting-house horse-sheds among the hills of New Hampshire, because I was bending my steps to a mountaintop on the Sabbath. . . . He declared that I was 'breaking the Lord's fourth commandment,' and proceeded to enumerate, in a sepulchral tone, the disasters which had befallen him whenever he had done any ordinary work on the Sabbath. He really thought that a god was on the watch to trip up those men who followed any secular work on this day, and did not see that it was the evil conscience of the workers that did it. The country is full of this superstition" [W 1:76–77].

**40** In Norse mythology, the god of thunder. Thoreau wrote metaphorically, not genealogically, here, while punning on the accented first syllable of his surname. His paternal ancestors were French by way of the Isle of Jersey, and his maternal ancestors Scottish.

**41** *The Saints' Everlasting Rest; or, A Treatise of the Blessed State of the Saints in Their Enjoyment of God in Glory* by the Puritan evangelist Richard Baxter (1615–1691). In the introductory chapter Baxter wrote: "The saints' rest is the most happy state of a Christian; or, it is *the perfect endless enjoyment of God by the perfected saints, according to the measure of their capacity, to which their souls arrive at death, and both soul and body most fully after the resurrection and final judgment.*"

**42** Sanborn wrote, concerning Thoreau's sartorial habits, that he "dresses very plainly, wears his collar turned over, like Mr. Emerson, and often an old dress-coat, broad in the skirts, and by no means a fit," and most often wore "a kind of corduroy."

**43** In *Walden* Thoreau wrote of his neighbors living "mean and sneaking lives . . . always on the limits" [Wa 5–6]. Concord resident Edward Jarvis (1803–1884) recorded:

> Under the old law many poor debtors were brought to jail to remain there at least for a month or until they were willing to take the poor debtors' oath before a magistrate, or to "swear out." But the law allowed them to have "the liberty of the yard" by giving sureties that they would not transgress the prescribed limits. This was technically called "the liberty of the yard." Perhaps originally it only included the prison yard, but this privilege was extended. . . . This was in order that the debtors might obtain opportunity to work and support themselves. There were generally ten to twenty of these debtors, a few confined in prison, but most of them "out on the limits" as it was termed.

but others would not wear it, durable and cheap as it is, because it is worn by the Irish.

*May 12.* When I consider how many species of willow have been planted along the railroad causeway within ten years, of which no one knows the history, and not one in Concord beside myself can tell the name of one, so that it is quite a discovery to identify a single one in a year, and yet within this period the seeds of all these kinds have been conveyed from some other locality to this, I am reminded how much is going on that man wots not of.

I ordinarily plod along a sort of whitewashed prison entry, subject to some indifferent or even grovelling mood. I do not distinctly realize my destiny. I have turned down my light to the merest glimmer and am doing some task which I have set myself. I take incredibly narrow views, live on the limits,[43] and have no recollection of absolute truth. Mushroom institutions hedge me in. But suddenly, in some fortunate moment, the voice of eternal wisdom reaches me, even in the strain of the sparrow, and liberates me, whets and clarifies my senses, makes me a competent witness.

*May 20.* How suddenly, after all, pines seem to shoot up and fill the pastures! I wonder that the farmers do not earlier encourage their growth. To-day, perchance, as I go through some run-out pasture, I observe many young white pines dotting the field, where last year I had noticed only blackberry vines; but I see that many are already destroyed or injured by the cows which have dived into them to scratch their heads or for sport (such is their habit; they break off the leading shoot and bend down the others of different evergreens), or perchance where the farmer has been mowing them down, and I think the owner would rather have a pasture here than a wood-lot. A year or two later, as I pass through the same field, I am surprised to find myself in a flourishing young wood-lot, from which the cows are now carefully fenced out, though there are many open spaces, and I perceive how much further advanced it would have been if the farmer had been more provident and had begun to abet nature a few years earlier. It is surprising by what leaps—two or three feet in a season—the pines stretch toward the sky, affording shelter also to various hardwoods which plant themselves in their midst.

*May 29.* As I stand on the rocks,[44] examining the blossoms of some forward black oaks which close overhang it, I think I hear the sound of flies against my hat. No, it is scattered raindrops, though the sky is perfectly clear above me, and the cloud from which they come is yet far on one side. I see through the tree-tops the thin vanguard of the storm scaling the celestial ramparts, like eager light infantry, or cavalry with spears advanced. But from the west a great, still, ash-colored cloud comes on. The drops fall thicker, and I seek a shelter under the Cliffs. I stand under a large projecting portion of the Cliff, where there is ample space above and around, and I can move about as perfectly protected as under a shed. To be sure, fragments of rock look as if they would fall, but I see no marks of recent ruin about me.

Soon I hear the low all-pervading hum of an approaching hummingbird circling above the rock, which afterward I mistake several times for the gruff voices of men approaching, unlike as these sounds are in some respects, and I perceive the resemblance even when I know better. Now I am sure it is a hummingbird, and now that it is two farmers approaching. But presently the hum becomes more sharp and thrilling, and the little fellow suddenly perches on an ash twig within a rod of me, and

**44** On Lee's Cliff.

45  Fair Haven Bay.
46  A cavity or chamber.

plumes himself while the rain is fairly beginning. He is quite out of proportion to the size of his perch. It does not acknowledge his weight.

I sit at my ease and look out from under my lichen-clad rocky roof, half-way up the Cliff, under freshly leafing ash and hickory trees on to the pond,[45] while the rain is falling faster and faster, and I am rather glad of the rain, which affords me this experience. The rain has compelled me to find the cosiest and most homelike part of all the Cliff. The surface of the pond, though the rain dimples it all alike and I perceive no wind, is still divided into irregular darker and lighter spaces, with distinct boundaries, as it were *watered* all over. Even now that it rains very hard and the surface is all darkened, the boundaries of those spaces are not quite obliterated. The countless drops seem to spring again from its surface like stalagmites.

A mosquito, sole living inhabitant of this antrum,[46] settles on my hand.

It lights up a little, and the drops fall thinly again, and the birds begin to sing, but now I see a new shower coming up from the southwest, and the wind seems to have changed somewhat. Already I had heard the low mutterings of its thunder—for this is a thunder-shower—in the midst of the last. It seems to have shifted its quarters merely to attack me on a more exposed side of my castle. Two foes appear where I had expected none. But who can calculate the tactics of the storm? It is a first regular summer thunder-shower, preceded by a rush of wind, and I begin to doubt if my quarters will prove a sufficient shelter. I am fairly besieged and know not when I shall escape. I hear the still roar of the rushing storm at a distance, though no trees are seen to wave. And now the forked flashes descending to the earth succeed rapidly to the hollow roars above, and down comes the deluging rain. I hear the alarmed notes of birds flying to a shelter. The air at length is cool and chilly, the atmosphere is darkened, and I have forgotten the smooth pond and its reflections. The rock feels cold to my body, as if it were a different season of the year. I almost repent of having lingered here; think how far I should have got if I had started homeward. But then what a condition I should have been in! Who knows but the lightning will strike this cliff and topple the rocks down on me? The crashing thunder sounds like the overhauling of lumber on heaven's loft. And now, at last, after an hour of steady confinement, the clouds grow thin again, and the birds begin to sing. They make haste to conclude the day with their regular evening songs (before the rain is fairly over) according to the program. The pe-pe[47] on some pine tree top was heard almost in the midst of the storm. One or two bullfrogs trump. They care not how wet it is. Again I hear the still rushing, all-pervading roar of the withdrawing storm, when it is at least half a mile off, wholly beyond the pond, though no trees are seen to wave. It is simply the sound of the countless drops falling on the leaves and the ground. You were not aware what a sound the rain made. Several times I attempt to leave my shelter, but return to it. My first stepping abroad seems but a signal for the rain to commence again. Not till after an hour and a half do I escape.

*May 30.* Perhaps I could write meditations under a rock in a shower.

When first I had sheltered myself under the rock, I began at once to look out on the pond with new eyes, as from my house. I was at Lee's Cliff as I had never been there before, had taken up my residence there, as it were. Ordinarily we make haste away from all opportunities to be where we have instinctively endeavored to get. When the storm was over where I was, and only

**47** Olive-sided flycatcher (*Nuttallornis borealis*), of which Thoreau wrote on 6 June 1857: "I see a pe-pe. . . . Regularly, at short intervals, it utters its monotonous note like *till-till-till*, or *pe-pe-pe*" [J 9:408].

**48** Charles Dibdin's "Poor Tom Bowling, or The Sailor's Epitaph"—sometimes spelled "Tom Bowline"—was Thoreau's favorite song. Edward Emerson, on recalling Thoreau singing it, wrote: "To this day that song, heard long years ago, rings clear and moving to me." Sanborn thought Thoreau sang it as "a reminiscence of his brother John, so early lost and so dearly loved. The voice was unpracticed and rather harsh, but the sentiment made the song interesting."

a few thin drops were falling around me, I plainly saw the rear of the rain withdrawing over the Lincoln woods south of the pond, and, above all, heard the grand rushing sound made by the rain falling on the freshly green forest, a very different sound when thus heard at a distance from what it is when we are in the midst of it. In the latter case we are soothed by a gentle pattering and do not suspect the noise which a rainstorm makes. This Cliff thus became my house. I inhabited it. When, at length, it cleared up, it was unexpectedly early and light, and even the sun came out and shone warm on my back as I went home. Large puddles occupied the cart-paths and rose above the grass in the fields.

In the midst of the shower, though it was not raining very hard, a black and white creeper came and inspected the limbs of a tree before my rock, in his usual zigzag, prying way, head downward often, and when it thundered loudest, heeded it not. Birds appear to be but little incommoded by the rain. Yet they do not often sing in it.

The blue sky is never more celestial to our eyes than when it is first seen here and there between the clouds at the end of a storm,—a sign of speedy fair weather. I saw clear blue patches for twenty minutes or more in the southwest before I could leave my covert, for still I saw successive fine showers falling between me and the thick glaucous white pine beneath.

I think that such a projection as this, or a cave, is the only effectual protection that nature affords us against the storm.

I sang "Tom Bowling"[48] there in the midst of the rain, and the dampness seemed to be favorable to my voice. There was a slight rainbow on my way home.

***June 3.*** I have several friends and acquaintances who are very good companions in the house or for an afternoon walk, but whom I cannot make up my mind to make a longer excursion with; for I discover, all at once, that they are too gentlemanly in manners, dress, and all their habits. I see in my mind's eye that they wear black coats, considerable starched linen, glossy hats and shoes, and it is out of the question. It is a great disadvantage for a traveller to be a gentleman of this kind; he is so ill-treated, only a prey to landlords. It would be too much of a circumstance to enter a strange town or house with such a companion. You could not travel incognito; you might get into the papers. You should travel as a common man. If such a one were to set out to make a walking-journey, he would betray himself at every step. Every one would see that he was trying an experiment, as plainly as they see that a lame man is lame by his limping. The natives would bow to him, other gentlemen would invite him to ride, conductors would warn him that this was the second-class car, and many would take him for a clergyman; and so he would be continually pestered and balked and run upon. You would not see the natives at all. Instead of going in quietly at the back door and sitting by the kitchen fire, you would be shown into a cold parlor, there to confront a fireboard, and excite a commotion in a whole family. The women would scatter at your approach, and their husbands and sons would go right up to hunt up their black coats,—for they all have them; they are as cheap as dirt. You would go trailing your limbs along the highways, mere bait for corpulent innholders, as a pickerel's leg is trolled along a stream,[49] and your part of the profits would be the frog's. No, you must be a common man, or at least travel as one, and then nobody will know that you are there or have been there. I would not undertake a simple pedestrian excursion with one of these, because to enter a village, or a hotel, or a private house, with such a one, would be too great a circumstance, would create too great a stir. You

[49] The leg of a pickerel frog (*Rana palustris*), a common eastern North American meadow frog with squarish dark spots on the back, was used for bait. It was so named because it was often used by anglers fishing for pickerel.

50 In botany, the scurf is an outer covering that resembles scales or bran, while the liber is the inner bark of plants, lying next to the wood.
51 Ankle-high shoes.

could only go half as far with the same means, for the price of board and lodgings would rise everywhere; so much you have to pay for wearing that kind of coat. Not that the difference is in the coat at all, for the character of the scurf is determined by that of the true liber[50] beneath. Innkeepers, stablers, conductors, clergymen, know a true wayfaring man at first sight and let him alone. It is of no use to shove your gaiter shoes[51] a mile further than usual. Sometimes it is mere shiftlessness or want of originality,—the clothes wear them; sometimes it is egotism, that cannot afford to be treated like a common man,—they wear the clothes. They wish to be at least fully appreciated by every stage-driver and schoolboy. They would like well enough to see a new place, perhaps, but then they would like to be regarded as important public personages. They would consider it a misfortune if their names were left out of the published list of passengers because they came in the steerage,—an obscurity from which they might never emerge.

*June 6.* This is June, the month of grass and leaves. The deciduous trees are investing the evergreens and revealing how dark they are. Already the aspens are trembling again, and a new summer is offered me. I feel a little fluttered in my thoughts, as if I might be too late. Each season is but an infinitesimal point. It no sooner comes than it is gone. It has no duration. It simply gives a tone and hue to my thought. Each annual phenomenon is a reminiscence and prompting. Our thoughts and sentiments answer to the revolutions of the seasons, as two cog-wheels fit into each other. We are conversant with only one point of contact at a time, from which we receive a prompting and impulse and instantly pass to a new season or point of contact. A year is made up of a certain series and number of sensations and thoughts which have their language in nature. Now I am ice, now

I am sorrel. Each experience reduces itself to a mood of the mind. I see a man grafting, for instance. What this imports chiefly is not apples to the owner or bread to the grafter, but a certain mood or train of thought to my mind. That is what this grafting is to me. Whether it is anything at all, even apples or bread, to anybody else, I cannot swear, for it would be worse than swearing *through glass.* For I only see those other facts as through a glass darkly.[52]

*June 16.* Stopped on the northwest edge of Yarmouth[53] and inquired of the ticket-master the way to Friends Village in the southeast part of the town.[54] He never heard of it. A stage-driver said it was five miles, and both directed me first northerly a quarter of a mile to the main street and then down that easterly some two miles before I turned off; and when I declared it must be nearer to go across lots, the driver said he would rather go round than get over the fences. Thus it is commonly; the landlords and stage-drivers are bent on making you walk the whole length of their main street first, wherever you are going. They know no road but such as is fit for a coach and four. I looked despairingly at this straggling village whose street I must run the gantlet of,[55] —so much time and distance lost. Nevertheless, I turned off earlier than they directed, and found that, as usual, I might have taken a shorter route across the fields and avoided the town altogether.

With my chart and compass I can generally find a shorter way than the inhabitants can tell me. I stop at a depot a little one side of a village and ask the way to some place I am bound to. The landlords and stage-drivers would fain persuade me to go first down on to the main street and follow that a piece; and when I show them a shorter way on the map, which leaves their village on one side, they shrug their shoulders, and say they

52 Allusion to I Corinthians 13:12: "For now we see through a glass, darkly, but then face to face."
53 While on his fourth Cape Cod excursion (12–22 June).
54 In 1713 a reservation in South Yarmouth was set aside for the use of the Native Americans. By 1763, most of the Native American population had been killed by the smallpox epidemic. The town of Yarmouth set aside a few acres of what was known as Indian Town for the last remaining native, Thomas Greenough, and ordered that the remaining lands be sold. The Quakers bought much of this land along Bass River and it soon became known as the Quaker, or Friends, Village.
55 To run the gantlet (sometimes, run the gauntlet) is to be exposed to danger, criticism, or other adversity. Dating from the early 17th century, it referred to a form of military punishment where a man ran between two rows of soldiers or sailors who struck him with sticks or knotted ropes, but also to a Native American form of humiliation and torture that Thoreau would have been aware of from such sources as John Warner Barber's (1798–1885) *Historical Collections, Being a General Collection of Interesting Facts, Traditions, Biographical Sketches, Anecdotes, &c.*: "The gauntlet consisted of two files of Indians, of both sexes and of all ages, containing all that could be mustered in the village; and the unhappy prisoners were obliged to run between them, when they were scoffed at and beaten by each one as they passed, and were sometimes marks at which the younger Indians threw their hatchets. This cruel custom was often practised by many of the tribes, and not unfrequently the poor prisoner sunk beneath it."

In "The Village" chapter of *Walden* Thoreau wrote: "I observed that the vitals of the village were the grocery, the bar-room, the post-office, and the bank; and, as a necessary part of the machinery, they kept a bell, a big gun, and a fire-engine, at convenient places; and the houses were so arranged as to make the most of mankind, in lanes and fronting one another, so that every traveller had to run the gantlet, and every

man, woman, and child might get a lick at him"
[Wa 163].
**56** A light two-wheeled vehicle, drawn by a single
horse, for one person.
**57** Coach driver, but also a hunter who keeps to
the road rather than going across country.
**58** Cf. 14 November 1839: "There is nowhere
any apology for despondency. Always there is life
which, rightly lived, implies a divine satisfaction."
**59** In Provincetown. While on his first excursion
to Cape Cod in October 1849, Thoreau stayed
at "Fuller's Hotel, passing by the Pilgrim House
as too high for us (we learned afterward that we
need not have been so particular)" [W 4:251].

would rather go round than get over the fences. I have
found the compass and chart safer guides than the inhabitants, though the latter universally abuse the maps. I
do not love to go through a village street any more than a
cottage yard. I feel that I am there only by sufferance; but
I love to go by the villages by my own road, seeing them
from one side, as I do theoretically. When I go through a
village, my legs ache at the prospect of the hard gravelled
walk. I go by the tavern with its porch full of gazers, and
meet a miss taking a walk or the doctor in his sulky,[56]
and for half an hour I feel as strange as if I were in a
town in China; but soon I am at home in the wide world
again, and my feet rebound from the yielding turf.

*June 17.* At a retired house where I inquired the road to
Brewster, a woman told me that if I wanted to go to Brewster I had come a good deal out of my way, and yet she
did not know where I had come from, and I was certainly
taking the right course to keep in the way. But they presume that a traveller inquiring the way wishes to be anywhere but where he is. They take me for a roadster,[57] and
do not know where *my* way is. They take it for granted
that my way is a direct one from village to village.

I go along the settled road, where the houses are interspersed with woods, in an unaccountably desponding
mood, but when I come out upon a bare and solitary
heath am at once exhilarated. This is a common experience in my travelling. I plod along, thinking what a miserable world this is and what miserable fellows we that
inhabit it, wondering what it is tempts men to live in it;
but anon I leave the towns behind and am lost in some
boundless heath, and life becomes gradually more tolerable, if not even glorious.[58]

*June 21.* At the Pilgrim House,[59] though it was not
crowded, they put me into a small attic chamber which

had two double beds in it, and only one window, high in a corner, twenty and a half inches by twenty-five and a half, in the alcove when it was swung open, and it required a chair to look out conveniently. Fortunately it was not a cold night and the window could be kept open, though at the risk of being visited by the cats, which appear to swarm on the roofs of Provincetown like the mosquitoes on the summits of its hills. I have spent four memorable nights there in as many different years,[60] and have added considerable thereby to my knowledge of the natural history of the cat and the bedbug. Sleep was out of the question. A night in one of the attics of Provincetown! to say nothing of what is to be learned in entomology. It would be worth the while to send a professor there, one who was also skilled in entomology. Such is your *Pilgerruhe* or Pilgrims'-Rest.[61] Every now and then one of these animals on its travels leaped from a neighboring roof on to mine, with such a noise as if a six-pounder[62] had fallen within two feet of my head, — the discharge of a catapult, — a twelve-pounder[63] discharged by a catapult, — and then followed such a scrambling as banished sleep for a long season, while I watched lest they came in at the open window. A kind of foretaste, methought, of the infernal regions.[64] I did n't wonder they gave quitclaim deeds[65] of their land here. My experience is that you fare best at private houses. The barroom may be defined a place to spit.

*July 12.* It would be worth the while, methinks, to make a map of the town with all the good springs on it, indicating whether they were cool, perennial, copious, pleasantly located, etc. The farmer is wont to celebrate the virtues of some one on his own farm above all others. Some cool rills in the meadows should be remembered also, for some such in deep, cold, grassy meadows are as cold as springs. I have sometimes drank warm or foul

60  This was Thoreau's fourth and final trip to Provincetown. He wrote of his first three visits in *Cape Cod*: "Wishing to get a better view than I had yet had of the ocean, which, we are told, covers more than two thirds of the globe, but of which a man who lives a few miles inland may never see any trace, more than of another world, I made a visit to Cape Cod in October, 1849, another the succeeding June, and another to Truro in July, 1855; the first and last time with a single companion, the second time alone. I have spent, in all, about three weeks on the Cape" [W 4:3].

61  Pilgerruh (German: Pilgrim's rest): the first European-American settlement in the Cuyahoga Valley in Ohio, founded by three Moravian missionaries in 1786.

62  A six-pound cannonball.

63  A twelve-pound cannonball.

64  Allusion to Dante's *Inferno* (Canto 3): "These miscreants, who never were alive, / Were naked, and were stung exceedingly / By gadflies and by hornets that were there."

65  Document transferring title or claim to another party.

water, not knowing such cold streams were at hand. By many a spring I know where to look for the dipper or glass which some mower has left. When a spring has been allowed to fill up, to be muddied by cattle, or, being exposed to the sun by cutting down the trees and bushes, to dry up, it affects me sadly, like an institution going to decay. Sometimes I see, on one side the tub,—the tub overhung with various wild plants and flowers, its edge almost completely concealed even from the searching eye,—the white sand freshly cast up where the spring is bubbling in. Often I sit patiently by the spring I have cleaned out and deepened with my hands,[66] and see the foul water rapidly dissipated like a curling vapor and giving place to the cool and clear. Sometimes I can look a yard or more into a crevice under a rock, toward the sources of a spring in a hillside, and see it come cool and copious with incessant murmuring down to the light. There are few more refreshing sights in hot weather.

*July 13.* I sometimes awake in the night and think of friendship and its possibilities, a new life and revelation to me, which perhaps I had not experienced for many months. Such transient thoughts have been my nearest approach to realization of it, thoughts which I know of no one to communicate to. I suddenly erect myself in my thoughts, or find myself erected, infinite degrees above the possibility of ordinary endeavors, and see for what grand stakes the game of life may be played. Men, with their indiscriminate attentions and ceremonious good-will, offer you trivial baits, which do not tempt; they are not serious enough either for success or failure. I wake up in the night to these higher levels of life, as to a day that begins to dawn, as if my intervening life had been a long night. I catch an echo of the great strain of Friendship played somewhere, and feel compensated for months and years of commonplace. I rise into a diviner atmosphere, in which simply to exist and breathe is a triumph, and my thoughts inevitably tend toward the grand and infinite, as aeronauts[67] report that there is ever an upper current hereabouts which sets toward the ocean. If they rise high enough they go out to sea, and behold the vessels seemingly in mid-air like themselves. It is as if I were serenaded, and the highest and truest compliments were paid me. The universe gives me three cheers.

Friendship is the fruit which the year should bear; it lends its fragrance to the flowers, and it is in vain if we get only a large crop of apples without it. This experience makes us unavailable for the ordinary courtesy and intercourse of men. We can only recognize them when they rise to that level and realize our dream.

*July 14.* Set fire to the carburetted hydrogen[68] from the sawdust shoal with matches, and heard it flash. It must be an interesting sight by night.

*September 28.* I see that Elijah Wood[69] has sent a couple of Irishmen, with axe and bush-whack, to cut off the natural hedges of sumach, Roxbury waxwork, grapes, etc., which have sprung up by the walls on this hill farm, in order that his cows may get a little more green. And they have cut down two or three of the very rare celtis trees,[70] not found anywhere else in town. The Lord deliver us from these vandalic proprietors! The botanist and lover of nature has, perchance, discovered some rare tree which has sprung up by a farmer's wall-side to adorn and bless it, sole representative of its kind in these parts. Strangers send for a seed or a sprig from a distance, but, walking there again, he finds that the farmer has sent a raw Irishman, a hireling just arrived on these shores, who was never there before,—and, we trust, will never be let loose there again,—who knows not whether he is hack-

67  Balloonists.
68  Gaseous compound, primarily methane, which occurs in coal mines (where it is known as firedamp) and about stagnant pools, such as the sawdust shoal. Thoreau wrote on 28 February 1856 while visiting Warren Miles's mill: "What a smell as of gun-wash when he raised the gate! He calls it the sulphur from the pond. It must be the carburetted hydrogen gas from the bottom of the pond under the ice. It powerfully scents the whole mill. A powerful smelling-bottle" [J 8:190].
69  Elijah Wood, Jr. (1816–1882), lived on Sudbury Road just north of the railroad tracks. On 14 May 1853 Thoreau noted that Wood had "added a pair of ugly wings to his house, bare of trees and painted white, particularly conspicuous from the river" [J 5:152].
70  The hackberry, or nettle, tree (*Celtis occidentalis*).

71 Fabulous poisonous tree that Carlyle referred to in *Past and Present* as "deadly Unwisdom overshadowing all things." Erasmus Darwin (1731–1802) called it "the hydra-tree of death" in his poem *The Loves of the Plants*.

72 The tree of knowledge of good and evil, which grew next to the tree of life in the garden of Eden. In Genesis 3:1–6 the serpent tempted Eve to eat the fruit of this tree, of which God said: "Ye shall not eat of it, neither shall ye touch it, lest ye die."

73 Scythe with a short, or stub, blade 12 inches long.

74 Allusion to Exodus 14:13: "For the Egyptian whom ye have seen today, ye shall see them again no more for ever."

75 A German mercenary in the British army fighting in America during the Revolutionary War.

76 When Thoreau presented his "The Succession of Forest Trees" before the Middlesex Agricultural Society at the Middlesex Cattle Show and Ploughing Match on 20 September 1860, he began: "Every man is entitled to come to Cattleshow, even a transcendentalist" [W 5:184].

77 The journal at this point contains several passages relating to Thoreau's July 1847 excursion to Maine, much of which was used in *The Maine Woods*. This passage, not used there, is apropos the phosphorescent wood in "The Allegash and East Branch": "Getting up some time after midnight to collect the scattered brands together, while my companions were sound asleep, I observed, partly in the fire, which had ceased to blaze, a perfectly regular elliptical ring of light, about five inches in its shortest diameter, six or seven in its longer, and from one eighth to one quarter of an inch wide. It was fully as bright as the fire, but not reddish or scarlet, like a coal, but a white and slumbering light, like the glow-worm's. I could tell it from the fire only by its whiteness. I saw at once that it must be phosphorescent wood, which I had so often heard of, but never chanced to see" [W 3:198–199].

ing at the upas tree[71] or the Tree of Knowledge,[72] with axe and stub-scythe[73] to exterminate it, and he will know it no more forever.[74] What is trespassing? This Hessian,[75] the day after he was landed, was whirled twenty miles into the interior to do this deed of vandalism on our favorite hedge. I would as soon admit a living mud turtle into my herbarium. If some are prosecuted for abusing children, others deserve to be prosecuted for maltreating the face of nature committed to their care.

*September 29.* All sorts of men come to Cattle-Show. I see one with a blue hat.[76]

*September 30.* Consider what actual phenomena await us. To say nothing of life, which may be rare and difficult to detect, and death, which is startling enough, we cannot begin to conceive of anything so surprising and thrilling but that something more surprising may be actually presented to us.[77]

*October 4.* While I lived in the woods I did various jobs about the town,—some fence-building, painting, gardening, carpentering, etc., etc. One day a man came from the east edge of the town and said that he wanted to get me to brick up a fireplace, etc., etc., for him. I told him that I was not a mason, but he knew that I had built my own house entirely and would not take no for an answer. So I went.

It was three miles off, and I walked back and forth each day, arriving early and working as late as if I were living there. The man was gone away most of the time, but had left some sand dug up in his cow-yard for me to make mortar with. I bricked up a fireplace, papered a chamber, but my principal work was whitewashing ceilings. Some were so dirty that many coats would not conceal the dirt. In the kitchen I finally resorted to yellow-wash to cover the dirt. I took my meals there, sitting down with my employer (when he got home) and his hired men. I remember the awful condition of the sink, at which I washed one day, and when I came to look at what was called the towel I passed it by and wiped my hands on the air, and thereafter I resorted to the pump. I worked there hard three days, charging only a dollar a day.

About the same time I also contracted to build a wood-shed of no mean size, for, I think, exactly six dollars, and cleared about half of it by a close calculation and swift working. The tenant wanted me to throw in a gutter and latch, but I carried off the board that was left and gave him no latch but a button. It stands yet, — behind the Kettle house.[78] I broke up Johnny Kettle's old "trow,"[79] in which he kneaded his bread, for material. Going home with what nails were left in a flour bucket on my arm, in a rain, I was about getting into a hay-rigging, when my umbrella frightened the horse, and he kicked at me over the fills,[80] smashed the bucket on my arm, and stretched me on my back; but while I lay on my back, his leg being caught over the shaft, I got up, to see him sprawling on the other side. This accident, the sudden bending of my body backwards, sprained my stomach so that I did not get quite strong there for several years, but had to give up some fence-building and other work which I had undertaken from time to time.

*October 6.* I have just read Ruskin's "Modern Painters."[81] I am disappointed in not finding it a more out-of-door book, for I have heard that such was its character, but its title might have warned me. He does not describe Nature as Nature, but as Turner[82] painted her, and though the work betrays that he has given a close attention to Nature, it appears to have been with an artist's and critic's design. How much is written about Nature

**78** Old Kettell Place on Virginia Road, belonging at the time to Isaac Watts, across from the house in which Thoreau was born. On 9 November 1850 Thoreau reminisced about this place "where twenty-five years ago I played horse in the paths of a thick wood and roasted apples and potatoes in an old pigeon-place and gathered fruit at the pie-apple tree" [J 2:88].
**79** Variant of trough.
**80** Variant of thills, the two shafts extending from the body of a cart or carriage on either side of the last horse and by which the carriage is supported in a horizontal position.
**81** John Ruskin's (1819–1900) *Modern Painters,* about which Thoreau wrote Blake on 16 November 1857: "Have you ever read Ruskin's books? If not, I would recommend you to try the second and third volumes (not parts) of his 'Modern Painters.' I am now reading the fourth, and have read most of his other books lately. They are singularly good and encouraging, though not without crudeness and bigotry. The themes in the volumes referred to are Infinity, Beauty, Imagination, Love of Nature, etc., — all treated in a very living manner. I am rather surprised by them. It is remarkable that these things should be said with reference to painting chiefly, rather than literature. The 'Seven Lamps of Architecture,' too, is made of good stuff; but, as I remember, there is too much about art in it for me and the Hottentots. We want to know about matters and things in general. Our house is as yet a hut" [C 497].
**82** Joseph Mallord William Turner (1775–1851), British landscape artist.

as somebody has portrayed her, how little about Nature as she is, and chiefly concerns us, *i. e.* how much prose, how little poetry!

***October 7.*** I do not know how to entertain one who can't take long walks. The first thing that suggests itself is to get a horse to draw them, and that brings us at once into contact with stablers and dirty harness, and I do not get over my ride for a long time. I give up my forenoon to them and get along pretty well, the very elasticity of the air and promise of the day abetting me, but they are as heavy as dumplings by mid-afternoon. If they can't walk, why won't they take an honest nap and let me go in the afternoon? But, come two o'clock, they alarm me by an evident disposition to sit. In the midst of the most glorious Indian-summer afternoon, there they sit, breaking your chairs and wearing out the house, with their backs to the light, taking no note of the lapse of time.

As I sat on the high bank at the east end of Walden this afternoon, at five o'clock, I saw, by a peculiar intention or dividing of the eye, a very striking subaqueous rainbow-like phenomenon. A passer-by might, perhaps would, have noticed that the bright-tinted shrubs about the high shore on the sunny side were reflected from the water; but, unless on the alert for such effects, he would have failed to perceive the full beauty of the phenomenon. Unless you look for reflections, you commonly will not find them. Those brilliant shrubs, which were from three to a dozen feet in height, were all reflected, dimly so far as the details of leaves, etc., were concerned, but brightly as to color, and, of course, in the order in which they stood, — scarlet, yellow, green, etc.; but, there being a slight ripple on the surface, these reflections were not true to their height though true to their breadth, but were extended downward with mathematical perpendicularity, three or four times too far, forming sharp pyramids of the several colors, gradually reduced to mere dusky points. The effect of this prolongation of the reflection was a very pleasing softening and blending of the colors, especially when a small bush of one bright tint stood directly before another of a contrary and equally bright tint. It was just as if you were to brush firmly aside with your hand or a brush a fresh line of paint of various colors, or so many lumps of friable[83] colored powders. There was, accordingly, a sort of belt, as wide as the whole height of the hill, extending downward along the whole north or sunny side of the pond, composed of exceedingly short and narrow inverted pyramids of the most brilliant colors intermixed. I have seen, indeed, similar inverted pyramids in the old drawings of tattooing about the waists of the aborigines of this country. Walden, too, like an Indian maiden, wears this broad rainbow-like belt of brilliant-colored points or cones round her waist in October. The color seems to be reflected and re-reflected from ripple to ripple, losing brightness each time by the softest possible gradation, and tapering toward the beholder, since he occupies a mere point of view. This is one of the prettiest effects of the autumnal change.

*October 9.* It has come to this,—that the lover of art is one, and the lover of nature another, though true art is but the expression of our love of nature. It is monstrous when one cares but little about trees but much about Corinthian columns, and yet this is exceedingly common.

*October 12.* This was what those scamps did in California.[84] The trees were so grand and venerable that they could not afford to let them grow a hair's breadth bigger, or live a moment longer to reproach themselves. They were so big that they resolved they should never be bigger. They were so venerable that they cut them right

83 Easily broken into small fragments or reduced to powder.

84 The sequoia or "big trees" of California were first discovered, or at least publicized, in 1852 by Augustus Dowd. In 1853 the first tree Dowd saw, called the "Discovery Tree," was cut down, the bark of which was displayed in the Union Club, New York. In 1854 another tree, known as "The Mother of the Forest," was stripped of its bark to a height of 116 feet. The bark was reassembled for exhibition at the Crystal Palace, New York, in 1855, and later in London.

85 The panic, sometimes called the revulsion, of 1857 began on 24 August 1857 with the closing of the New York branch of the Ohio Life Insurance and Trust Company. Before the end of the year nearly 5,000 businesses closed.
86 Thoreau's note: "You cannot break them. If you should slump, 't is to a finer sand." This is an echo of Channing's poem "A Poet's Hope," which ends: "If my bark sinks, 't is to another sea."
87 Stock exchange, with a possible reference specifically to the New York Stock Exchange (originated in 1792 with the Buttonwood Agreement) or the Boston Stock Exchange (founded in 1834).
88 A private bank in Boston, organized in 1818, that operated the first note-clearing system in the United States.
89 Pun: faith and confidence as well as something held by one party for the benefit of the other.
90 Allusion to such works as Foote's *The Universal Counterfeit Bank Note Detector at Sight* with its engraved "Universal Counterfeit Detector," Bicknell's *Counterfeit Detector and Bank Note List,* or Clark's *New-England Bank Note List and Counterfeit Bill Detector.*

down. It was not for the sake of the wood; it was only because they were very grand and venerable.

*October 14.* P.M. — To White Pond.

Another, the tenth of these memorable days. We have had some fog the last two or three nights, and this forenoon it was slow to disperse, dog-day-like, but this afternoon it is warmer even than yesterday. I should like it better if it were not so warm. I am glad to reach the shade of Hubbard's Grove; the coolness is refreshing. It is indeed a golden autumn. These ten days are enough to make the reputation of any climate. A tradition of these days might be handed down to posterity. They deserve a notice in history, in the history of Concord. All kinds of crudities have a chance to get ripe this year. Was there ever such an autumn? And yet there was never such a panic and hard times in the commercial world. The merchants and banks are suspending and failing all the country over,[85] but not the sand-banks, solid and warm, and streaked with bloody blackberry vines. You may run upon them as much as you please,[86] — even as the crickets do, and find their account in it. They are the stockholders in these banks, and I hear them creaking their content. You may see them on change[87] any warmer hour. In these banks, too, and such as these, are my funds deposited, a fund of health and enjoyment. Their (the crickets) prosperity and happiness and, I trust, mine do not depend on whether the New York banks suspend or no. We do not rely on such slender security as the thin paper of the Suffolk Bank.[88] To put your trust[89] in such a bank is to be swallowed up and undergo suffocation. Invest, I say, in these country banks. Let your capital be simplicity and contentment. Withered goldenrod (*Solidago nemoralis*) is no failure, like a broken bank, and yet in its most golden season nobody counterfeits it. Nature needs no counterfeit-detector.[90] I have no compassion for, nor sympathy with, this miserable state of things. Banks built of granite, after some Grecian or Roman style, with their porticoes and their safes of iron, are not so permanent, and cannot give me so good security for capital invested in them, as the heads of withered hardhack in the meadow. I do not suspect the solvency of these. I know who is their president and cashier.

I take all these walks to every point of the compass, and it is always harvest-time with me. I am always gathering my crop from these woods and fields and waters, and no man is in my way or interferes with me. My crop is not their crop. To-day I see them gathering in their beans and corn, and they are a spectacle to me, but are soon out of my sight. I am not gathering beans and corn. Do they think there are no fruits but such as these? I am a reaper; I am not a gleaner. I go reaping, cutting as broad a swath as I can, and bundling and stacking up and carrying it off from field to field, and no man knows nor cares. My crop is not sorghum[91] nor Davis seedlings.[92] There are other crops than these, whose seed is not distributed by the Patent Office.[93] I go abroad over the land each day to get the best I can find, and that is never carted off even to the last day of November, and I do not go as a gleaner.

Looking now toward the north side of the pond, I perceive that the reflection of the hillside seen from an opposite hill is not so broad as the hillside itself appears, owing to the different angle at which it is seen. The reflection exhibits such an aspect of the hill, *apparently,* as you would get if your eye were placed at that part of the surface of the pond where the reflection seems to be. In this instance, too, then, Nature avoids repeating herself. Not even reflections in still water are like their substances as seen by us. This, too, accounts for my seeing portions of the sky through the trees in reflections often when

**91** A canelike grass cultivated as grain and forage or as a source of syrup.

**92** A species of potato.

**93** In 1839 Congress invested $1,000 in the Congressional Seed Distribution Program, administered by the U.S. Patent Office, to increase the amount of free seeds mailed to anyone requesting them.

none appear in the substance. Is the reflection of a hillside, however, such an aspect of it as can be obtained by the eye directed to the hill itself from any single point of view? It plainly is not such a view as the eye would get looking upward from the immediate base of the hill or water's edge, for there the first rank of bushes on the lower part of the hill would conceal the upper. The reflection of the top appears to be such a view of it as I should get with my eye at the water's edge above the edge of the reflection; but would the lower part of the hill also appear from this point as it does in the reflection? Should I see as much of the under sides of the leaves there? If not, then the reflection is never a true copy or repetition of its substance, but a new composition, and this may be the source of its novelty and attractiveness, and of this nature, too, may be the charm of an echo. I doubt if you can ever get Nature to repeat herself exactly.

*October 15.* Concord Bank has suspended.

*October 19.* Mr. Sanborn[94] tells me that he looked off from Wachusett last night, and that he saw the shadow of the mountain gradually extend itself eastward not only over the earth but finally *on to the sky* in the horizon. Thought it extended as much as two diameters of the moon on to the sky, in a small cone. This was like the spectre of the Brocken.[95]

*October 20.* I had gone but little way on the old Carlisle road when I saw Brooks Clark,[96] who is now about eighty and bent like a bow, hastening along the road, barefooted, as usual, with an axe in his hand; was in haste perhaps on account of the cold wind on his bare feet. It is he who took the *Centinel*[97] so long. When he got up to me, I saw that besides the axe in one hand, he had his shoes in the other, filled with knurly apples and a dead robin. He stopped and talked with me a few moments; said that we had had a noble autumn and might now expect some cold weather. I asked if he had found the robin dead. No, he said, he found it with its wing broken and killed it. He also added that he had found some apples in the woods, and as he had n't anything to carry them in, he put 'em in his shoes. They were queer-looking trays to carry fruit in. How many he got in along toward the toes, I don't know. I noticed, too, that his pockets were stuffed with them. His old tattered frock coat was hanging in strips about the skirts, as were his pantaloons about his naked feet. He appeared to have been out on a scout this gusty afternoon, to see what he could find, as the youngest boy might. It pleased me to see this cheery old man, with such a feeble hold on life, bent almost double, thus enjoying the evening of his days. Far be it from me to call it avarice or penury, this childlike delight in finding something in the woods or fields and carrying it home in the October evening, as a trophy to be added to his winter's store. Oh, no; he was happy to be Nature's pensioner still, and bird-like to pick up his living. Better his robin than your turkey, his shoes full of apples than your barrels full; they will be sweeter and suggest a better tale. He can afford to tell how he got them, and we to listen. There is an old wife, too, at home, to share them and hear how they were obtained. Like an old squirrel shuffling to his hole with a nut. Far less pleasing to me the loaded wain, more suggestive of avarice and of spiritual penury.

This old man's cheeriness was worth a thousand of the church's sacraments and *memento mori*'s.[98] It was better than a prayerful mood. It proves to me old age as tolerable, as happy, as infancy. I was glad of an occasion to suspect that this afternoon he had not been at "work" but living somewhat after my own fashion (though he did not explain the axe),—had been out to see what na-

**98** Latin: literally, remember to die, i.e., a reminder of death.

**99** Cf. 22 April 1841.

**100** Margaret Fuller wrote similarly in her essay "Goethe" in the July 1841 issue of the *Dial:* "Writing is worthless except as the record of life. . . . His book should be only an indication of himself."

**101** Thoreau walked to and around Flint's Pond by way of his old bean field and Goose Pond.

**102** Conflation of Robinson Crusoe, the hero of Daniel Defoe's (1660–1731) novel *Robinson Crusoe* (1790), who was shipwrecked on an unnamed island and saw footprints in the sand, and Alexander Selkirk (1676–1721), who was abandoned on Juan Fernandez Island, and whose story was Defoe's inspiration. Thoreau made the same conflation on 21 July 1851: "I see the track of a bare human foot in the dusty road, the toes and muscles all faithfully imprinted. Such a sight is so rare that it affects me with surprise, as the footprint on the shore of Juan Fernandez did Crusoe" [J 2:328].

**103** Pun on the characters found in cuneiform writing, so called from each letter being formed by marks or elements resembling an arrowhead or a wedge.

ture had for him, and now was hastening home to a burrow he knew, where he could warm his old feet. If he had been a young man, he would probably have thrown away his apples and put on his shoes when he saw me coming, for shame. But old age is manlier; it has learned to live, makes fewer apologies, like infancy. This seems a very manly man. I have known him within a few years building stone wall by himself, barefooted.

*October 21.* Is not the poet bound to write his own biography?[99] Is there any other work for him but a good journal? We do not wish to know how his imaginary hero, but how he, the actual hero, lived from day to day.[100]

*October 22.* There is scarcely a square rod of sand exposed, in this neighborhood,[101] but you may find on it the stone arrowheads of an extinct race. Far back as that time seems when men went armed with bows and pointed stones here, yet so numerous are the signs of it. The finer particles of sand are blown away and the arrow-point remains. The race is as clean gone—from here—as this sand is clean swept by the wind. Such are our antiquities. These were our predecessors. Why, then, make so great ado about the Roman and the Greek, and neglect the Indian? We need not wander off with boys in our imaginations to Juan Fernandez, to wonder at footprints in the sand there.[102] Here is a print still more significant at our doors, the print of a race that has preceded  us, and this the little symbol that Nature has transmitted to us. Yes, *this* arrowheaded character[103] is probably more ancient than any other, and to my mind it has not been deciphered. Men should not go to New Zealand to write or think of Greece and Rome, nor more to New England. New earths, new themes expect us. Celebrate not the Garden of Eden, but your own.

What a perfect chest the chestnut is packed in! I now hold a green bur in my hand which, round, must have been two and a quarter inches in diameter, from which three plump nuts have been extracted. It has a straight, stout stem three sixteenths of an inch in diameter, set on strongly and abruptly. It has gaped in four segments or quarters, revealing the thickness of its walls, from five eighths to three quarters of an inch. With such wonderful care Nature has secluded and defended these nuts, as if they were her most precious fruits, while diamonds are left to take care of themselves. First it bristles all over with sharp green prickles, some nearly half an inch long, like a hedgehog rolled into a ball; these rest on a thick, stiff, bark-like rind, one sixteenth to one eighth of an inch thick, which, again, is most daintily lined with a kind of silvery fur or velvet plush one sixteenth of an inch thick, even rising in a ridge between the nuts, like the lining of a casket in which the most precious commodities are kept.[104] I see the brown-spotted white cavities where the bases of the nuts have rested and sucked up nourishment from the stem. The little stars on the top of the nuts are but shorter and feebler spines which mingle with the rest. They stand up close together, three or more, erecting their tiny weapons, as an infant in the brawny arms of its nurse might put out its own tiny hands, to fend off the aggressor. There is no waste room. The chest is packed quite full; half-developed nuts are the waste paper used in the packing, to fill the vacancies. At last Frost comes to unlock this chest; it alone holds the true key. Its lids straightway gape open, and the October air rushes in, dries the ripe nuts, and then with a ruder gust shakes them all out in a rattling shower down upon the withered leaves.

104 Jewell casket: a small chest or box for jewels or other precious objects.

*October 24.* I find my account in this long-continued monotonous labor of picking chestnuts all the afternoon, brushing the leaves aside without looking up, absorbed in that, and forgetting better things awhile. My eye is educated to discover anything on the ground, as chestnuts, etc. It is probably wholesomer to look at the ground much than at the heavens. As I go stooping and brushing the leaves aside by the hour, I am not thinking of chestnuts merely, but I find myself humming a thought of more significance. This occupation affords a certain broad pause and opportunity to start again afterward, — turn over a new leaf.

*October 26.* These regular phenomena of the seasons get at last to be — they were *at first,* of course — simply and plainly phenomena or phases of my life. The seasons and all their changes are in me. I see not a dead eel or floating snake, or a gull, but it rounds my life and is like a line or accent in its poem. Almost I believe the Concord would not rise and overflow its banks again, were I not here. After a while I learn what my moods and seasons are. I would have nothing subtracted. I can imagine nothing added. My moods are thus periodical, not two days in my year alike. The perfect correspondence of Nature to man, so that he is at home in her!

*October 27.* The real facts of a poet's life would be of more value to us than any work of his art. I mean that the very scheme and form of his poetry (so called) is adopted at a sacrifice of vital truth and poetry. Shakespeare has left us his fancies and imaginings, but the truth of his life, with its becoming circumstances, we know nothing about. The writer is reported, the liver not at all. Shakespeare's house! how hollow it is! No man can conceive of Shakespeare in that house. But we want the basis of fact, of an actual life, to complete our Shakespeare, as much as a statue wants its pedestal. A poet's life with this broad actual basis would be as superior to Shakespeare's as a lichen, with its base or thallus, is superior in the order of being to a fungus.

The Littleton Giant[105] brought us a load of coal within the week. He appears deformed and weakly, though naturally well formed. He does not nearly stand up straight. His knees knock together; they touch when he is standing most upright, and so reduce his height at least three inches. He is also very round-shouldered and stooping, probably from the habit of crouching to conceal his height. He wears a low hat for the same purpose. The tallest man looks like a boy beside him. He has a seat to his wagon made on purpose for him. He habitually stops before all doors. You wonder what his horses think of him,—that a strange horse is not afraid of him. His voice is deep and full, but mild, for he is quite modest and retiring,—really a worthy man, 't is said. Pity he could n't have been undertaken by a committee in season and put through, like the boy Safford,[106] been well developed bodily and also mentally, taught to hold up his head and not mind people's eyes or remarks. It is remarkable that the giants have never correspondingly great hearts.

***October 29.*** There are some things of which I cannot at once tell whether I have dreamed them or they are real; as if they were just, perchance, establishing, or else losing, a real basis in my world. This is especially the case in the early morning hours, when there is a gradual transition from dreams to waking thoughts, from illusions to actualities, as from darkness, or perchance moon and star light, to sunlight. Dreams are real, as is the light of the stars and moon, and theirs is said to be a *dreamy* light. Such early morning thoughts as I speak of occupy a de-

105 Henry Dix Kimball (1829–1882), a man over seven feet tall who had uncommon physical strength. In his journal of 17 January 1852 Thoreau wrote that Kimball was "a monstrous man and dwarfed all whom he stood by, so that I didn't know whether he was large or they were small. . . . It troubled him that he was so large, for people looked at him. There is at once something monstrous, in the bad sense, suggested by the sight of such a man. Great size is inhuman" [J 3:202–203].
106 Truman Henry Safford (1836–1901), a mathematical prodigy who in 1846 was taken under the care of Harvard, from where he graduated in 1854.

107  Thoreau wrote to H. G. O. Blake on 16 November 1857: "I keep a mountain anchored off eastward a little way, which I ascend in my dreams both awake and asleep. Its broad base spreads over a village or two, which do not know it; neither does it know them, nor do I when I ascend it. I can see its general outline as plainly now in my mind as that of Wachusett. I do not invent in the least, but state exactly what I see. I find that I go up it when I am light-footed and earnest. It ever smokes like an altar with its sacrifice. I am not aware that a single villager frequents it or knows of it. I keep this mountain to ride instead of a horse" [C 498].

batable ground between dreams and waking thoughts. They are a sort of permanent dream in my mind. At least, until we have for some time changed our position from prostrate to erect, and commenced or faced some of the duties of the day, we cannot tell what we have dreamed from what we have actually experienced.

This morning, for instance, for the twentieth time at least, I thought of that mountain in the easterly part of our town (where no high hill actually is) which once or twice I had ascended, and often allowed my thoughts alone to climb.[107] I now contemplate it in my mind as a familiar thought which I have surely had for many years from time to time, but whether anything could have reminded me of it in the middle of yesterday, whether I ever before remembered it in broad daylight, I doubt. I can now eke out the vision I had of it this morning with my old and yesterday forgotten dreams.

My way up used to lie through a dark and unfrequented wood at its base, — I cannot now tell exactly, it was so long ago, under what circumstances I first ascended, only that I shuddered as I went along (I have an indistinct remembrance of having been out overnight alone), — and then I steadily ascended along a rocky ridge half clad with stinted trees, where wild beasts haunted, till I lost myself quite in the upper air and clouds, seeming to pass an imaginary line which separates a hill, mere earth heaped up, from a mountain, into a superterranean grandeur and sublimity. What distinguishes that summit above the earthy line, is that it is unhandselled, awful, grand. It can never become familiar; you are lost the moment you set foot there. You know no path, but wander, thrilled, over the bare and pathless rock, as if it were solidified air and cloud. That rocky, misty summit, secreted in the clouds, was far more thrillingly awful and sublime than the crater of a volcano spouting fire.

This is a business we can partly understand. The perfect mountain height is already thoroughly purified. It is as if you trod with awe the face of a god turned up, unwittingly but helplessly, yielding to the laws of gravity. And are there not such mountains, east or west, from which you may look down on Concord in your thought, and on all the world? In dreams I am shown this height from time to time, and I seem to have asked my fellow once to climb there with me, and yet I am constrained to believe that I never actually ascended it. It chances, now I think of it,[108] that it rises in my mind where lies the Burying-Hill.[109] You might go through its gate to enter that dark wood,[110] but that hill and its graves are so concealed and obliterated by the awful mountain that I never thought of them as underlying it. Might not the graveyards of the just always be hills, ways by which we ascend and overlook the plain?

But my old way down was different, and, indeed, this was another way up, though I never so ascended. I came out, as I descended, breathing the thicker air. I came out the belt of wood into a familiar pasture, and along down by a wall. Often, as I go along the low side of this pasture, I let my thoughts ascend toward the mount, gradually entering the stinted wood (Nature subdued) and the thinner air, and drape themselves with mists. There are ever two ways up: one is through the dark wood, the other through the sunny pasture. That is, I reach and discover the mountain only through the dark wood, but I see to my surprise, when I look off between the mists from its summit, how it is ever adjacent to my native fields, nay, imminent over them, and accessible through a sunny pasture. Why is it that in the lives of men we hear more of the dark wood than of the sunny pasture?

A hard-featured god reposing, whose breath hangs about his forehead.

Though the pleasure of ascending the mountain is

**108** Thoreau's note: "Now *first think of it,* at this stage of my description, which makes it the more singularly symbolical. The interlineations on the last page were made before this." The interlineations are the words "only that I shuddered as I went along (I have an indistinct remembrance of having been out overnight alone)" in the previous paragraph.

**109** Hill Burying Ground, the oldest cemetery in Concord, adjacent to the Unitarian (First) Church.

**110** Allusion to the opening canto of Dante's *Inferno*: "In the middle of the journey of our life, I found myself in a dark wood; for the straight way was lost." Thoreau's note: "Perchance that was the grave."

111 Objects commonly associated with the pilgrim.
112 Thread used to guide a person out of a labyrinth, from Greek mythology, in which Theseus was able to kill the Minotaur within the labyrinth and escape, using the clew, a thread to follow, given him by Ariadne.

largely mixed with awe, my thoughts are purified and sublimed by it, as if I had been translated.

I see that men may be well-mannered or conventionally polite toward men, but skeptical toward God.

Forever in my dream and in my morning
        thought,
    Eastward a mount ascends;
But when in the sunbeam its hard outline is
        sought,
    It all dissolves and ends.
The woods that way are gates; the pastures too
        slope up
    To an unearthly ground;
But when I ask my mates to take the staff and
        cup,[111]
    It can no more be found.
Perhaps I have no shoes fit for the lofty soil
    Where my thoughts graze,
No properly spun clues,[112] nor well-strained mid-
        day oil,
    Or must I mend my ways?
It is a promised land which I have not yet earned.
    I have not made beginning
With consecrated hand, nor have I ever learned
    To lay the underpinning.
The mountain sinks by day, as do my lofty
        thoughts,
    Because I'm not high-minded.
If I could think alway above these hills and warts,
    I should see it, though blinded.
It is a spiral path within the pilgrim's soul
    Leads to this mountain's brow;
Commencing at his hearth he climbs up to this
        goal
    He knows not when nor how.

We see mankind generally either (from ignorance or avarice) toiling too hard and becoming mere machines in order to acquire wealth, or perhaps inheriting it or getting it by other accident, having recourse, for relaxation after excessive toil or as a mere relief to their idle ennui, to artificial amusements, rarely elevating and often debasing. I think that men generally are mistaken with regard to amusements. Every one who deserves to be regarded as higher than the brute may be supposed to have an earnest purpose, to accomplish which is the object of his existence, and this is at once his work and his supremest pleasure; and for diversion and relaxation, for suggestion and education and strength, there is offered the never-failing amusement of getting a living,—never-failing, I mean, when temperately indulged in. I know of no such amusement,—so wholesome and in every sense profitable,—for instance, as to spend an hour or two in a day picking some berries or other fruits which will be food for the winter, or collecting driftwood from the river for fuel, or cultivating the few beans or potatoes which I want. Theatres and operas, which intoxicate for a season, are as nothing compared to these pursuits. And so it is with all the true arts of life. Farming and building and manufacturing and sailing are the greatest and wholesomest amusements that were ever invented (for God invented them), and I suppose that the farmers and mechanics know it, only I think they indulge to excess generally, and so what was meant for a joy becomes the sweat of the brow.[113] Gambling, horse-racing, loafing, and rowdyism generally, after all tempt but few. The mass are tempted by those other amusements, of farming, etc. It is a great amusement, and more profitable than I could have invented, to go and spend an afternoon hour picking cranberries. By these various pursuits your experience becomes singularly complete and rounded. The novelty and significance of such pursuits are remarkable. Such is

113 Allusion to Genesis 3:19: "In the sweat of thy face shalt thou eat bread, till thou return unto the ground."

114 Herbaceous plants with medicinal properties.
115 Lucius Quinctius Cincinnatus (ca. 519–438
B.C.E.), Roman statesman regarded as a model of
simple virtue. Twice called to assume the dictator-
ship of Rome, he each time retired to his farm.

the path by which we climb to the heights of our being; and compare the poetry which such simple pursuits have inspired with the unreadable volumes which have been written about art.

Who is the most profitable companion? He who has been picking cranberries and chopping wood, or he who has been attending the opera all his days? I find when I have been building a fence or surveying a farm, or even collecting simples,[114] that these were the true paths to perception and enjoyment. My being seems to have put forth new roots and to be more strongly planted. This is the true way to crack the nut of happiness. If, as a poet or naturalist, you wish to explore a given neighborhood, go and live in it, *i. e.* get your living in it. Fish in its streams, hunt in its forests, gather fuel from its water, its woods, cultivate the ground, and pluck the wild fruits, etc., etc. This will be the surest and speediest way to those perceptions you covet. No amusement has worn better than farming. It tempts men just as strongly to-day as in the day of Cincinnatus.[115] Healthily and properly pursued, it is not a whit more grave than huckleberrying, and if it takes any airs on itself as superior there's something wrong about it.

I have aspired to practice in succession all the honest arts of life, that I may gather all their fruits.

*October 31.* If you are afflicted with melancholy at this season, go to the swamp and see the brave spears of skunk-cabbage buds already advanced toward a new year.

*November 5.* I think that the man of science makes this mistake, and the mass of mankind along with him: that you should coolly give your chief attention to the phenomenon which excites you as something independent on you, and not as it is related to you. The important fact is its effect on me.[116] He thinks that I have no business to see anything else but just what he defines the rainbow to be, but I care not whether my vision of truth is a waking thought or dream remembered, whether it is seen in the light or in the dark. It is the subject of the vision, the truth alone, that concerns me. The philosopher for whom rainbows, etc., can be explained away never saw them. With regard to such objects, I find that it is not they themselves (with which the men of science deal) that concern me; the point of interest is somewhere *between* me and them (*i. e.* the objects).[117]

*November 20.* In books, that which is most generally interesting is what comes home to the most cherished private experience of the greatest number. It is not the book of him who has travelled the farthest over the surface of the globe, but of him who has lived the deepest and been the most at home. If an equal emotion is excited by a familiar homely phenomenon as by the Pyramids, there is no advantage in seeing the Pyramids. It is on the whole better, as it is simpler, to use the common language. We require that the reporter be very permanently planted before the facts which he observes, not a mere passer-by; hence the facts cannot be too homely. A man is worth most to himself and to others, whether as an observer, or poet, or neighbor, or friend, where he is most himself, most contented and at home. There his life is the most intense and he loses the fewest moments. Familiar and surrounding objects are the best symbols and illustrations of his life. If a man who has had deep experiences should endeavor to describe them in a book of travels, it would be to use the language of a wandering tribe instead of a universal language. The poet has made the best roots in his native soil of any man, and is the hardest to transplant. The man who is often thinking that it is better to be somewhere else than where he

**116** Cf. 18 February 1841: "I do not judge men by anything they can do. Their greatest deed is the impression they make on me."
**117** Cf. 27 September 1852: "I see the very peak,—there can be no mistake,—but how much I do not see that is between me and it!"

**118** Cf. 1857 note 84.

**119** Thomas Robert Malthus (1766–1834), who, in his *Essay on the Principles of Population* (1798), posited the theory that population growth, which was growing geometrically, would exceed subsistence, which was growing arithmetically.

**120** Possible allusion to such works as Adam Smith's (1723–1790) *The Wealth of Nations*— "Every species of animals naturally multiplies in proportion to the means of their subsistence, and no species can ever multiply beyond it"—or Jonathan Swift's satire "A Modest Proposal."

**121** Allusion, which Thoreau had just used nine days before in a letter to Blake with the same play on words, to John 9:4: "the night cometh, when no man can work."

**122** Unidentified.

is excommunicates himself. If a man is rich and strong anywhere, it must be on his native soil. Here I have been these forty years learning the language of these fields that I may the better express myself. If I should travel to the prairies, I should much less understand them, and my past life would serve me but ill to describe them. Many a weed here stands for more of life to me than the big trees of California[118] would if I should go there. We only need travel enough to give our intellects an airing. In spite of Malthus[119] and the rest,[120] there will be plenty of room in this world, if every man will mind his own business. I have not heard of any planet running against another yet.

*November 25.* This is November of the hardest kind,— bare frozen ground covered with pale-brown or straw-colored herbage, a strong, cold, cutting northwest wind which makes me seek to cover my ears, a perfectly clear and cloudless sky. The cattle in the fields have a cold, shrunken, shaggy look, their hair standing out every way, as if with electricity, like the cat's. Ditches and pools are fast skimming over, and a few slate-colored snowbirds, with thick, shuffling twitter, and fine-chipping tree sparrows flit from bush to bush in the otherwise deserted pastures. This month taxes a walker's resources more than any. For my part, I should sooner think of going into quarters in November than in the winter. If you do feel any fire at this season out of doors, you may depend upon it, it is your own. It is but a short time, these afternoons, before the night cometh, in which no man can walk.[121] If you delay to start till three o'clock, there will be hardly time left for a long and rich adventure,—to get fairly out of town Novembers. Eat heart,[122]—is that the name of it? Not only the fingers cease to do their office, but there is often a benumbing of the faculties generally. You can hardly screw up your courage to take a walk when all is thus tightly locked or frozen up and so little is to be seen in field or wood. I am inclined to take to the swamps or woods as the warmest place, and the former are still the openest. Nature has herself become like the few fruits which she still affords, a very thick-shelled nut with a shrunken meat within. If I find anything to excite or warm my thoughts abroad, it is an agreeable disappointment, for I am obliged to go abroad willfully and against my inclinations at first. The prospect looks so barren, so many springs are frozen up, not a flower perchance and but few birds left, not a companion abroad in all these fields for me, I am slow to go forth. I seem to anticipate a fruitless walk. I think to myself hesitatingly, Shall I go there, or there, or there? and cannot make up my mind to any route, all seem so unpromising, mere surface walking and fronting the cold wind, so that I have to force myself to it often and at random. But then I am often unexpectedly compensated, and the thinnest yellow light of November is more warming and exhilarating than any wine they tell of; and then the mite which November contributes becomes equal in value to the bounty of July. I may meet with something which interests me, and immediately it is as warm as in July, as if it were the south instead of the northwest wind that blowed.

I do not know if I am singular when I say that I believe there is no man with whom I can associate who will not, comparatively speaking, spoil my afternoon. That society or encounter may at last yield a fruit which I am not aware of, but I cannot help suspecting that I should have spent those hours more profitably alone.

*December 8.* Staples[123] says he came to Concord some twenty-four years ago a poor boy with a dollar and three cents in his pocket, and he spent the three cents for drink at Bigelow's tavern, and now he's worth "twenty hundred

**123** Sam Staples (d. 1895), who, in his capacity as tax collector and jailer, arrested Thoreau in July 1846. Cf. "Resistance to Civil Government." Thoreau remained on good terms with Staples, who was sometimes employed by Thoreau to assist in his surveying work. On 6 July 1851 Thoreau wrote: "There is some advantage in being the humblest, cheapest, least dignified man in the village, so that the very stable boys shall damn you. Methinks I enjoy that advantage to an unusual extent. There is many a coarsely well-meaning fellow, who knows only the skin of me, who addresses me familiarly by my Christian name. I get the whole good of him and lose nothing myself. There is 'Sam,' the jailer,—whom I never call Sam, however,—who exclaimed last evening: 'Thoreau, are you going up the street pretty soon? Well, just take a couple of these handbills along and drop one in at Hoar's Piazza and one at Holbrook's, and I'll do as much for you another time.' I am not above being used, aye abused, sometimes" [J 2:285–286].

**124** The woven edge on cloth that prevents fraying.

dollars clear." He remembers many who inherited wealth whom he can buy out to-day. I told him that he had done better than I in a pecuniary respect, for I had only earned my living. "Well," said he, "that's all I've done, and I don't know as I've got much better clothes than you." I was particularly poorly clad then, in the woods; my hat, pants, boots, rubbers, and gloves would not have brought four-pence, and I told the Irishman that it was n't everybody could afford to have a fringe round his legs, as I had, my corduroys not preserving a selvage.[124]

Staples said there was one thing he liked. "What is that?" "An honest man." If he lent a man money, and when it became due he came and asked for more time because he could not pay, he excused him, but if, after it had become due, he went to the man, and he then made the same excuse, he lost all confidence in him.

*December 13.* In sickness and barrenness it is encouraging to believe that our life is dammed and is coming to a head, so that there seems to be no loss, for what is lost in time is gained in power. All at once, unaccountably, as we are walking in the woods or sitting in our chamber, after a worthless fortnight, we cease to feel mean and barren.

# 1858

AGE 40–41

1 In December 1857 Thoreau had thirteen surveying jobs, many of which were woodlots.

*January 1.* I have lately been surveying the Walden woods
so extensively and minutely that I now see it mapped in
my mind's eye—as, indeed, on paper—as so many men's
wood-lots,[1] and am aware when I walk there that I am
at a given moment passing from such a one's wood-lot
to such another's. I fear this particular dry knowledge
may affect my imagination and fancy, that it will not be
easy to see so much wildness and native vigor there as
formerly. No thicket will seem so unexplored now that I
know that a stake and stones may be found in it.

*January 23.* Who can doubt that men are by a certain
fate what they are, contending with unseen and unimagined difficulties, or encouraged and aided by equally
mysterious auspicious circumstances? Who can doubt
this essential and innate difference between man and
man, when he considers a whole race, like the Indian,
inevitably and resignedly passing away in spite of our
efforts to Christianize and educate them? Individuals
accept their fate and live according to it, as the Indian
does. Everybody notices that the Indian retains his habits
wonderfully,—is still the same man that the discoverers
found. The fact is, the history of the white man is a history of improvement, that of the red man a history of
fixed habits of stagnation.

To insure health, a man's relation to Nature must
come very near to a personal one; he must be conscious
of a friendliness in her; when human friends fail or die,

she must stand in the gap to him. I cannot conceive of any life which deserves the name, unless there is a certain tender relation to Nature. This it is which makes winter warm, and supplies society in the desert and wilderness. Unless Nature sympathizes with and speaks to us, as it were, the most fertile and blooming regions are barren and dreary.

*January 25.* The creditor is servant to his debtor, especially if he is about paying his due. I am amused to see what airs men take upon themselves when they have money to pay me. No matter how long they have deferred it, they imagine that they are my benefactors or patrons, and send me word graciously that *if I will come to their houses* they will pay me, when it is their business to come to me.

*January 26.* When it rains it is like an April shower. The brook is quite open, and there is no snow on the banks or fields. From time to time I see a trout glance, and sometimes, in an adjoining ditch, quite a school of other fishes, but I see no tortoises. In a ditch I see very light-colored and pretty large lizards moving about, and I suspect I may even have heard a frog drop into the water once or twice. I like to sit still under my umbrella and meditate in the woods in this warm rain.

How protean is life! One may eat and drink and sleep and digest, and do the ordinary duties of a man, and have no excuse for sending for a doctor, and yet he may have reason to doubt if he is as truly alive or his life is as valuable and divine as that of an oyster. He may be the very best citizen in the town, and yet it shall occur to him to prick himself with a pin to see if he is alive. It is wonderful how quiet, harmless, and ineffective a living creature may be. No more energy may it have than a fungus that lifts the bark of a decaying tree.

*January 27.* Time never passes so quickly and unaccountably as when I am engaged in composition, *i. e.* in writing down my thoughts. Clocks seem to have been put forward.

*March 2.* The last new journal[2] thinks that it is very liberal, nay, bold, but it dares not publish a child's thought on important subjects, such as life and death and good books. It requires the sanction of the divines just as surely as the tamest journal does. If it had been published at the time of the famous dispute between Christ and the doctors,[3] it would have published only the opinions of the doctors and suppressed Christ's. There is no need of a law to check the license of the press. It is law enough, and more than enough, to itself. Virtually, the community have come together and agreed what things shall be uttered, have agreed on a platform and to excommunicate him who departs from it, and not one in a thousand dares utter anything else. There are plenty of journals brave enough to say what they think about the government, this being a free one; but I know of none, widely circulated or well conducted, that dares say what it thinks about the Sunday or the Bible. They have been bribed to keep dark. They are in the service of hypocrisy.

*March 5.* We read the English poets; we study botany and zoölogy and geology, lean and dry as they are; and it is rare that we get a new suggestion. It is ebb-tide with the scientific reports, Professor——[4] in the chair. We would fain know something more about these animals and stones and trees around us. We are ready to skin the

**2** The *Atlantic Monthly,* the first issue of which was published in November 1857. Its first editor was James Russell Lowell (1819–1891).
**3** Allusion to Luke 2:46–50: "And it came to pass, that after three days they found him in the temple, sitting in the midst of the doctors, both hearing them, and asking them questions. And all that heard him were astonished at his understanding and answers. And when they saw him, they were amazed: and his mother said unto him, Son, why has thou thus dealt with us? Behold, thy father and I have sought thee sorrowing. And he said unto them, How is it that ye sought me? Wist ye not that I must be about my Father's business? And they understood not the saying which he spake unto them." Cf. 1858 note 47.
**4** Thoreau used dashes in place of a name in the journal manuscript.

5 Latin: tree of life; a member Of the cyprus family.

6 Reference to the "Dictionary of the Abnaki Language" compiled by Father Sébastian Rasles, sometimes Rasle, Rale, or Ralle (1652–1724). Rasles was a missionary to the Abenaki Indians from 1694 to 1724, and was killed during a raid on their village by the British. His dictionary was not published until 1833 in the *Memoirs of the American Academy of Arts and Sciences*. Thoreau may also be referring in part to the "Chippeway Indian, a Doctor Mung-somebody" [J 10:291] that he had gone to hear on this date.

7 Allusion to William Wood (fl. 1629–1635?), who wrote in his *New England's Prospects, Being a True, Lively, and Experimental Description of that Part of America Commonly Called New-England* (spelling modernized): "Concerning Lions, I will not say that I ever saw any myself, but some affirm that they have seen a Lion at *Cape-Anne,* which is not above ten leagues from *Boston:* Some likewise being lost in the woods, have heard such terrible roarings, as have made them much aghast; which must be either devils or Lions; there being no other creatures which use to roar, saving Bears."

8 Rasles's Abenaki dictionary had three columns of entries for "Canot" [canoe]: "mon canot . . . canot de bois . . . Petits planches de cédre p'r faire &c. . . . Le bois qui est au bout en dedans, qui est debout" [my canoe . . . dug-out . . . small cedar planks to make etc. . . . wood that is thin at the end, that is upright].

animals alive to come at them. Our scientific names convey a very partial information only; they suggest certain thoughts only. It does not occur to me that there are other names for most of these objects, given by a people who stood between me and them, who had better senses than our race. How little I know of that *arbor-vitæ*[5] when I have learned only what science can tell me! It is but a word. It is not a *tree of life.* But there are twenty words for the tree and its different parts which the Indian gave,[6] which are not in our botanies, which imply a more practical and vital science. He used it every day. He was well acquainted with its wood, and its bark, and its leaves. No science does more than arrange what knowledge we have of any class of objects. But, generally speaking, how much more conversant was the Indian with any wild animal or plant than we are, and in his language is implied all that intimacy, as much as ours is expressed in our language. How many words in his language about a moose, or birch bark, and the like! The Indian stood nearer to wild nature than we. The wildest and noblest quadrupeds, even the largest fresh-water fishes, some of the wildest and noblest birds and the fairest flowers have actually receded as *we* advanced, and we have but the most distant knowledge of them. A rumor has come down to us that the skin of a lion was seen and his roar heard here by an early settler.[7] But there was a race here that slept on his skin. It was a new light when my guide gave me Indian names for things for which I had only scientific ones before. In proportion as I understood the language, I saw them from a new point of view.

A dictionary of the Indian language reveals another and wholly new life to us. Look at the word "canoe," and see what a story it tells of outdoor life, with the names of all its parts and modes of using it,[8] as our words describing the different parts and seats of a coach,—with the difference in practical knowledge between him who rides and him who walks; or at the word "wigwam,"[9] and see how close it brings you to the ground; or "Indian corn,"[10] and see which race was most familiar with it. It reveals to me a life within a life, or rather a life without a life, as it were threading the woods between our towns still, and yet we can never tread in its trail. The Indian's earthly life was as far off from us as heaven is.

*April 19.* Spend the day hunting for my boat, which was stolen.

*April 30.* Frogs, etc., are perfect thermometers.[11]

*May 6.* The thinker, he who is serene and self-possessed, is the brave, not the desperate soldier. He who can deal with his thoughts as a material, building them into poems in which future generations will delight, he is the man of the greatest and rarest vigor, not sturdy diggers and lusty polygamists. He is the man of energy, in whom subtle and poetic thoughts are bred. Common men can enjoy partially; they can go a-fishing rainy days; they can *read* poems perchance, but they have not the vigor to beget poems. They can enjoy feebly, but they cannot create. Men talk of freedom! How many are free to think? free from fear, from perturbation, from prejudice? Nine hundred and ninety-nine in a thousand are perfect slaves. How many can exercise the highest human faculties? He is the man truly—courageous, wise, ingenious—who can use his thoughts and ecstasies as the material of fair and durable creations. One man shall derive from the fisherman's story more than the fisher has got who tells it. The mass of men do not know how to cultivate the fields they traverse. The mass glean only a scanty pittance where the thinker reaps an abundant harvest. What is all your building, if you do not build with thoughts? No exercise implies more real manhood and vigor than join-

9 Rasles had two columns of entries for "Cabane, maison" [cabin, house]: "grande . . . petite . . . ronde . . . ronde par le haut . . . logette pour le bois de chauffage [big . . . little . . . round . . . round above . . . small cabin for firewood].
10 Rasles had two columns of entries describing several varieties of corn: "Blé d'Inde . . . blé entire qui n'est pas pile . . . blanc . . . rouge . . . noir . . . jaune" [Indian corn . . . whole corn that isn't stacked . . . white . . . red . . . black . . . yellow].
11 Cf. 24 March 1859.

12 In Greek mythology, Hercules, son of Zeus, in order to be released from his servitude to Eurystheus, had to complete twelve seemingly impossible labors or tasks.

13 Thoreau met H. G. O. Blake in Fitchburg. They traveled together to Mount Monadnock in New Hampshire, camping two nights, and then walked to the depot in Winchendon, Massachusetts, from where they traveled home separately.

14 Thoreau's question mark. The allusion is unidentified.

15 Possibly for the virtues described in John Gerard's *Herball, or Generall Historie of Plantes* (1597), which lists garlic as "an enemie to all cold poisons, and to the bitings of venemous beasts."

16 Nickname of Robert Paterson (1715–1801), who wandered through Scotland cleaning and repairing gravestones of the Covenanters. The antiquary in Sir Walter Scott's (1771–1832) *Old Mortality* is based on Paterson.

ing thought to thought. How few men can tell what they have thought! I hardly know half a dozen who are not too lazy for this. They cannot get over some difficulty, and therefore they are on the long way round. You conquer fate by thought. If you think the fatal thought of men and institutions, you need never pull the trigger. The consequences of thinking inevitably follow. There is no more Herculean task[12] than to think a thought about this life and then get it expressed.

*June 2.* 8:30 A. M. — Start for Monadnock.[13]

Notwithstanding the newspaper and egg-shell left by visitors, these parts of nature are still peculiarly unhandselled and untracked. The natural terraces of rock are the steps of this temple, and it is the same whether it rises above the desert or a New England village. Even the inscribed rocks are as solemn as most ancient gravestones, and nature reclaims them with bog and lichens. They reminded me of the grave and pass of Ben Waddi (?).[14] These sculptors seemed to me to court such alliance with the grave as they who put their names over tombstones along the highway. One, who was probably a blacksmith, had sculptured the emblems of his craft, an anvil and hammer, beneath his name. Apparently a part of the regular outfit of mountain-climbers is a hammer and cold-chisel, and perhaps they allow themselves a supply of garlic also.[15] Certainly you could not hire a stonecutter to do so much engraving for less than several thousand dollars. But no Old Mortality[16] will ever be caught renewing these epitaphs. It reminds what kinds of steeps do climb the false pretenders to fame, whose chief exploit is the carriage of the tools with which to inscribe their names. For speaking epitaphs they are, and the mere name is a sufficient revelation of the character. They are all of one trade, — stonecutters, defacers of mountain-tops. "Charles & Lizzie!" Charles carried the sledge-hammer, and Lizzie the cold-chisel. Some have carried up a paint-pot, and painted their names on the rocks.

We returned to our camp and got our tea in our sunken yard. While one went for water to the spring, the other kindled a fire. The whole rocky part of the mountain, except the extreme summit, is strewn with the relics of spruce trees,[17] a dozen or fifteen feet long, and long since dead and bleached, so that there is plenty of dry fuel at hand. We sat out on the brink of the rocky plateau near our camp, taking our tea in the twilight, and found it quite dry and warm there, though you would not have thought of sitting out at evening in the surrounding valleys. It was evidently warmer and drier there than below. I have often perceived the warm air high on the sides of hills late into the night, while the valleys were filled with a cold damp night air, as with water, and here the air was warmer and drier the greater part of the night. We perceived no dew there this or the next night. This was our parlor and supper-room; in another direction was our wash-room. The chewink sang before night, and this, as I have before observed, is a very common bird on mountain-tops. It seems to love a cool atmosphere, and sometimes lingers quite late with us. And the wood thrush, indefinitely far or near, a little more distant and unseen, as great poets are. Early in the evening the nighthawks were heard to spark and boom over these bare gray rocks, and such was our serenade at first as we lay on our spruce bed. We were left alone with the nighthawks. These withdrawn bare rocks must be a very suitable place for them to lay their eggs, and their dry and unmusical, yet supramundane and spirit-like, voices and sounds gave fit expression to this rocky mountain solitude. It struck the very key-note of the stern, gray, barren solitude. It was a thrumming of the mountain's rocky chords; strains

17  From lumbering.

18 In Greek mythology, the vacant, unfathomable space and confusion from which all things earthly and divine arose.

from the music of Chaos,[18] such as were heard when the earth was rent and these rocks heaved up. Thus they went sparking and booming, while we were courting the first access of sleep, and I could imagine their dainty limping flight, circling over the kindred rock, with a spot of white quartz in their wings. No sound could be more in harmony with that scenery. Though common below, it seemed peculiarly proper here. But ere long the nighthawks were stilled, and we heard only the sound of our companion's breathing or of a bug in our spruce roof. I thought I heard once faintly the barking of a dog far down under the mountain, and my companion thought he heard a bullfrog.

A little after 1 A.M., I woke and found that the moon had risen, and heard some little bird near by sing a short strain of welcome to it, somewhat song-sparrow-like. But every sound is a little strange there, as if you were in Labrador. Before dawn the nighthawks commenced their sounds again, and these sounds were as good as a clock to us, telling how the night got on.

*June 4.* It is remarkable how, as you are leaving a mountain and looking back at it from time to time, it gradually gathers up its slopes and spurs to itself into a regular whole, and makes a new and total impression. The lofty beaked promontory which, when you were on the summit, appeared so far off and almost equal to it, seen now against the latter, scarcely deepens the tinge of bluish, misty gray on its side. The mountain has several spurs or ridges, bare and rocky, running from it, with a considerable depression between the central peak and them; *i. e.,* they attain their greatest height half a mile or more from the central apex. There is such a spur, for instance, running off southward about a mile. When we looked back from four or five miles distant on the south, this, which had appeared like an independent summit, was almost totally lost to our view against the general misty gray of the side of the principal summit. We should not have suspected its existence if we had not just come from it, and though the mountain ranges northeasterly and southwesterly, or not far from north and south, and is much the longest in that direction, it now presented a pretty regular pyramidal outline with a broad base, as if it were broadest east and west. That is, when you are on the mountain, the different peaks and ridges appear more independent; indeed, there is a bewildering variety of ridge and valley and peak, but when you have withdrawn a few miles, you are surprised at the more or less pyramidal outline of the mountain and that the lower spurs and peaks are all subordinated to the central and principal one. The summit appears to rise and the surrounding peaks to subside, though some new prominences appear. Even at this short distance the mountain has lost most of its rough and jagged outline, considerable ravines are smoothed over, and large boulders which you must go a long way round make no impression on the eye, being swallowed up in the air.

*July 2.* What a relief and expansion of my thoughts when I come out from that inland position by the graveyard to this broad river's shore![19] This vista was incredible there. Suddenly I see a broad reach of blue beneath, with its curves and headlands, liberating me from the more terrene earth. What a difference it makes whether I spend my four hours' nooning[20] between the hills by yonder roadside, or on the brink of this fair river, within a quarter of a mile of that! Here the earth is fluid to my thought, the sky is reflected from beneath, and around yonder cape is the highway to other continents. This current allies me to all the world. Be careful to sit in an elevating and inspiring place. There my thoughts were confined and trivial, and I hid myself from the gaze of travellers.

**19** Thoreau was on an excursion to the White Mountains with Edward Hoar, leaving on either 1 or 2 July in a private carriage, and returning on 19 July. They were accompanied by Blake and Theophilus Brown (1811–1879). During this excursion they visited the cemetery in Old Dunstable (now Nashua, New Hampshire), which Thoreau described in *A Week on the Concord and Merrimack Rivers:* "It is a wild and antiquated looking graveyard, overgrown with bushes, on the highroad, about a quarter of a mile from and overlooking the Merrimack, with a deserted mill-stream bounding it on one side, where lie the earthly remains of the ancient inhabitants of Dunstable" [W 1:176–177].
**20** Resting at noon during the hottest part of the day.

**21** Allusion to the Fourth of July, or Independence Day.
**22** Massachusetts became a state on 6 February 1788; New Hampshire followed four months later, on 21 June.

Here they are expanded and elevated, and I am charmed by the beautiful river-reach. It is equal to a different season and country and creates a different mood. As you travel northward from Concord, probably the reaches of the Merrimack River, looking up or down them from the bank, will be the first inspiring sight. There is something in the scenery of a broad river equivalent to culture and civilization. Its channel conducts our thoughts as well as bodies to classic and famous ports, and allies us to all that is fair and great. I like to remember that at the end of half a day's walk I can stand on the bank of the Merrimack. It is just wide enough to interrupt the land and lead my eye and thoughts down its channel to the sea. A river is superior to a lake in its liberating influence. It has motion and indefinite length. A river touching the back of a town is like a wing, it may be unused as yet, but ready to waft it over the world. With its rapid current it is a slightly fluttering wing. River towns are winged towns.

*July 4.* It is far more independent[21] to travel on foot. You have to sacrifice so much to the horse. You cannot choose the most agreeable places in which to spend the noon, commanding the finest views, because commonly there is no water there, or you cannot get there with your horse. New Hampshire being a more hilly and newer state than Massachusetts,[22] it is very difficult to find a suitable place to camp near the road, affording water, a good prospect, and retirement. We several times rode on as much as ten miles with a tired horse, looking in vain for such a spot, and then almost invariably camped in some low, unpleasant spot. There are very few, scarcely any, lanes, or even paths and bars along the road. Having got beyond the range of the chestnut, the few bars that might be taken down are long and heavy planks or slabs, intended to confine sheep, and there is no passable road behind. And beside, when you have chosen a place one must stay behind to watch your effects, while the other looks about. I frequently envied the independence of the walker, who can spend the midday hours and take his lunch in the most agreeable spot on his route. The only alternative is to spend your noon at some trivial inn, pestered by flies and tavern loungers.

*July 8.* The fog was very bewildering.[23] You would think that the rock you steered for was some large boulder twenty rods off, or perchance it looked like the brow of a distant spur, but a dozen steps would take you to it, and it would suddenly have sunk into the ground. I discovered this illusion. I said to my companions, "You see that boulder of a peculiar form, slanting over another. Well, that is in our course. How large do you think it is, and how far?" To my surprise, one answered three rods, but the other said nine. I guessed four, and we all thought it about eight feet high. We could not see beyond it, and it looked like the highest part of a ridge before us. At the end of twenty-one paces or three and a half rods, I stepped upon it, — less than two feet high, — and I could not have distinguished it from the hundred similar ones around it, if I had not kept my eye on it all the while.

It is unwise for one to ramble over these mountains at any time, unless he is prepared to move with as much certainty as if he were solving a geometrical problem.[24] A cloud may at any moment settle around him, and unless he has a compass and knows which way to go, he will be lost at once. One lost on the summit of these mountains should remember that if he will travel due east or west eight or nine miles, or commonly much less, he will strike a public road. Or whatever direction he might take, the average distance would not be more than eight miles and the extreme distance twenty. Follow some water-course running easterly or westerly. If the weather were severe

**23** Thoreau was headed toward Tuckerman's Ravine.
**24** Thoreau probably had in mind Benjamin Ball's being lost for three days in the White Mountains: cf. 15 February 1857.

**25** In August 1857 James Russell Lowell went on a deer hunt in the Adirondacks. The following year Lowell and William James Stillman (1828–1901) invited fellow members of the Saturday Club, a group of writers and scholars who met for monthly dinners in Boston at the Parker House, to form the Adirondack Club. In August, Lowell and Stillman, along with Emerson, Louis Agassiz, and others, went on a hunting and camping excursion. Longfellow and Thoreau declined. Emerson's poem "The Adirondacs" described their party as:

> Ten scholars, wonted to lie warm and soft
> In well-hung chambers daintily bestowed,
> Lie here on hemlock-boughs, like Sacs and
>     Sioux,
> And greet unanimous the joyful change.

**26** Lack of confidence in Emerson's hunting ability went beyond Concord. Stillman wrote: "I did my best to enroll Longfellow in the party, but, though he was for a moment hesitating, I think the fact that Emerson was going with a gun settled him in the determination to decline. 'Is it true that Emerson is going to take a gun?' he asked me; and when I said that he had finally decided to do so, he ejaculated, 'Then somebody will be shot!' and would talk no more of going."

on the summit, so as to prevent searching for the summit houses or the path, I should at once take a westward course from the southern part of the range or an eastward one from the northern part. To travel there with security, a person must know his bearings at every step, be it fair weather or foul. An ordinary rock in a fog, being in the apparent horizon, is exaggerated to, perhaps, at least ten times its size and distance. You will think you have gone further than you have to get to it.

*July 19.* It is surprising how much more bewildering is a mountain-top than a level area of the same extent. Its ridges and shelves and ravines add greatly to its apparent extent and diversity. You may be separated from your party by only stepping a rod or two out of the path. We turned off three or four rods to the pond on our way up Lafayette, knowing that Hoar was behind, but so we lost him for three quarters of an hour and did not see him again till we reached the summit. One walking a few rods more to the right or left is not seen over the ridge of the summit, and, other things being equal, this is truer the nearer you are to the apex.

If you take one side of a rock, and your companion another, it is enough to separate you sometimes for the rest of the ascent.

*August 6.* Emerson is gone to the Adirondack country with a hunting party.[25] Eddy says he has carried a double-barrelled gun, one side for shot, the other for ball, for Lowell killed a bear there last year. But the story on the Mill-Dam is that he has taken a gun which throws shot from one end and ball from the other![26]

I think that I speak impartially when I say that I have never met with a stream so suitable for boating and botanizing as the Concord, and fortunately nobody knows it. I know of reaches which a single country-seat would spoil beyond remedy, but there has not been any important change here since I can remember. The willows slumber along its shore, piled in light but low masses, even like the cumuli clouds above. We pass haymakers in every meadow, who may think that we are idlers. But Nature takes care that every nook and crevice is explored by some one. While they look after the open meadows, we farm the tract between the river's brinks and behold the shores from that side. We, too, are harvesting an annual crop with our eyes, and think you Nature is not glad to display her beauty to us?

*August 9.* It is surprising to what extent the world is ruled by cliques. They who constitute, or at least lead, New England or New York society, in the eyes of the world, are but a clique, a few "men of the age" and of the town, who work best in the harness provided for them. The institutions of almost all kinds are thus of a sectarian or party character. Newspapers, magazines, colleges, and all forms of government and religion express the superficial activity of a few, the mass either conforming or not attending. The newspapers have just got over that eating-fullness or dropsy which takes place with the annual commencements and addresses before the Philomathean or Alpha Beta Gamma societies.[27] Neither they who make these addresses nor they who attend to them are representative of the latest age. The boys think that these annual recurrences are part and parcel of the annual revolution of the system. There are also regattas and fireworks and "surprise parties" and horse-shows. So that I am glad when I see or hear of a man anywhere who does not know of these things nor recognizes these particular fuglers.[28]

It is surprising what a tissue of trifles and crudities make the daily news. For one event of interest there are

27 The Boston Philomathean Society, formed in 1836, was probably patterned after the New York organization of the same name founded in 1832 to encourage debate, oratory, and composition. Alpha Beta Gamma refers to the collegiate fraternal societies usually designated by Greek letters. The first such society was Phi Beta Kappa, founded in 1776 at the College of William and Mary, Williamsburg, Virginia.
28 Fuglemen: expert and well-drilled soldiers who take the front in a military company as an example or model.

**29** The first successful (albeit briefly so) telegraph cable between America and Europe, resting on the ocean floor, was completed in 1858. It was followed by a permanent cable in 1866.

**30** Thoreau's practice was to make field notes, or minutes, which he later transcribed into his journal.

nine hundred and ninety-nine insignificant, but about the same stress is laid on the last as on the first. The newspapers have just told me that the transatlantic telegraph-cable is laid.[29] That is important, but they instantly proceed to inform me how the news was received in every larger town in the United States,—how many guns they fired, or how high they jumped,—in New York, and Milwaukee, and Sheboygan; and the boys and girls, old and young, at the corners of the streets are reading it all with glistening eyes, down to the very last scrap, not omitting what they did at New Rochelle and Evansville. And all the speeches are reported, and some think of collecting them into a volume!!!

You say that you have travelled far and wide. How many men have you seen that did not belong to any sect, or party, or clique? Did you go further than letters of introduction would avail?

*August 11.* Now is our rainy season. It has rained half the days for ten days past. Instead of dog-day clouds and mists, we have a rainy season. You must walk armed with an umbrella. It is wettest in the woods, where the air has had no chance to dry the bushes at all.

*August 12.* When I came down-stairs this morning, it raining hard and steadily, I found an Irishman sitting with his coat on his arm in the kitchen, waiting to see me. He wanted to inquire what I thought the weather would be to-day! I sometimes ask my aunt, and she consults the almanac. So we shirk the responsibility.

*August 18.* Having left my note-book[30] at home, I strip off a piece of birch bark for paper. It begins at once to curl up, yellow side out, but I hold that side to the sun, and as soon as it is dry it gives me no more trouble.

*August 23.* Emerson says that he and Agassiz and Company broke some dozens of ale-bottles, one after another, with their bullets, in the Adirondack country,[31] using them for marks! It sounds rather Cockneyish.[32] He says that he shot a peetweet for Agassiz, and this, I think he said, was the first game he ever bagged. He carried a double-barrelled gun,—rifle and shotgun,—which he bought for the purpose, which he says received much commendation,—all parties thought it a very pretty piece. Think of Emerson shooting a peetweet (with shot) for Agassiz, and cracking an ale-bottle (after emptying it) with his rifle at six rods! They cut several pounds of lead out of the tree.

*September 9.* How differently the poet and the naturalist look at objects! A man sees only what concerns him. A botanist absorbed in the pursuit of grasses does not distinguish the grandest pasture oaks. He as it were tramples down oaks unwittingly in his walk.

*October 1.* The cat sleeps on her head! What does this portend?

*October 10.* Genius is inspired by its own works; it is hermaphroditic.

*October 12.* This town has made a law recently against cattle going at large, and assigned a penalty of five dollars.[33] I am troubled by an Irish neighbor's cow and horse, and have threatened to have them put in the pound. But a lawyer tells me that these town laws are hard to put through, there are so many quibbles. He never knew the complainant to get his case if the defendant were a-mind to contend. However, the cattle were kept out several days, till a Sunday came, and then they were all in my

**31** Cf. 6 August 1858.
**32** From the Middle English, *cocknei:* a city dweller or pampered child.
**33** Town of Concord bylaw, "in relation to the pasturing of cattle &c. approved July 27th, AD 1858," which states: "No person shall be allowed to pasture any cattle or other animals upon any of the streets or ways in said town, either with or without a keeper, except within the limits of such street or way adjoining his own premises. And all persons violating the provisions of these bylaws shall be punished by a fine of five dollars for each offense: to be recovered by a complaint before any Justice of the Peace within the County of Middlesex, and any and all fines so recovered shall enure to the benefit of the poor in said town."

34 Barrett's Saw and Grist Mill.

35 On 3 December 1858 Thoreau wrote, "I improve every opportunity to go into a grist-mill, any excuse to see its cobweb-tapestry. I put questions to the miller as an excuse for staying, while my eye rests delighted on the cobwebs above his head and perchance on his hat" [J 11:363].

36 Samuel Barrett (1812–1872).

37 On Poplar Hill, north of Sleepy Hollow.

38 Cf. 1860 note 30.

grounds again, as I heard, but all my neighbors tell me that I cannot have them impounded on that day. Indeed, I observe that very many of my neighbors do *for this reason* regularly turn their cattle loose on Sundays.

*October 19.* P.M. — Ride to Sam Barrett's mill.[34]

Am pleased again to see the cobweb drapery of the mill.[35] Each fine line hanging in festoons from the timbers overhead and on the sides, and on the discarded machinery lying about, is covered and greatly enlarged by a coating of meal, by which its curve is revealed, like the twigs under their ridges of snow in winter. It is like the tassels and tapestry of counterpane and dimity in a lady's bedchamber, and I pray that the cobwebs may not have been brushed away from the mills which I visit. It is as if I were aboard a man-of-war, and this were the fine "rigging" of the mill, the sails being taken in. All things in the mill wear the same livery or drapery, down to the miller's hat and coat. I knew Barrett[36] forty rods off in the cranberry meadow by the meal on his hat.

*November 1.* We are not wont to see our dooryard as a part of the earth's surface. The gardener does not perceive that some ridge or mound in his garden or lawn is related to yonder hill or the still more distant mountain in the horizon, is, perchance, a humble spur of the last. We are wont to look on the earth still as a sort of chaos, formless and lumpish. I notice from this height[37] that the curving moraine forming the west side of Sleepy Hollow[38] is one of several arms or fingers which stretch away from the hill range that runs down the north side of the Boston road, turning northward at the Court-House; that this finger-like moraine is continued northward by itself almost to the river, and points plainly enough to Ponkawtasset Hill on the other side, even if the Poplar Hill range itself did not indicate this connection; and so the sloping cemetery lots on the west of Sleepy Hollow are related to the distant Ponkawtasset. The smooth-shaven knoll in the lawn, on which the children swing, is, perchance, only a spur of some mountains of the moon,[39] which no traveller has ever reached,[40] heaved up by the same impulse.

As the afternoons grow shorter, and the early evening drives us home to complete our chores, we are reminded of the shortness of life, and become more pensive, at least in this twilight of the year. We are prompted to make haste and finish our work before the night comes. I leaned over a rail in the twilight on the Walden road, waiting for the evening mail to be distributed, when such thoughts visited me. I seemed to recognize the November evening as a familiar thing come round again, and yet I could hardly tell whether I had ever known it or only divined it. The November twilights just begun! It appeared like a part of a panorama at which I sat spectator, a part with which I was perfectly familiar just coming into view, and I foresaw how it would look and roll along, and prepared to be pleased.[41] Just such a piece of art merely, though infinitely sweet and grand, did it appear to me, and just as little were any active duties required of me. We are independent on all that we see.

Think of the consummate folly of attempting to go away from *here!* When the constant endeavor should be to get nearer and nearer *here.* Here are all the friends I ever had or shall have, and as friendly as ever. Why, I never had any quarrel with a friend but it was just as sweet as unanimity could be. I do not think we budge an inch forward or backward in relation to our friends. How many things can you go away from? They see the comet from the northwest coast just as plainly as we do, and the same stars through its tail. Take the shortest way

**39** The popular name for the Ruwenzori Mountains of Central Africa, bordering Uganda and Zaire, deriving from Ptolemy (2nd century c.e.), who believed them to be the source of the Nile River.

**40** Possible reference to James Bruce's (1730–1794) *Travels to Discover the Source of the Nile, in the Years 1768, 1769, 1770, 1771, 1772, and 1773,* published in 1790, or to the earlier account, *A Voyage to the Mountains of the Moon Under the Equator, or, Parnassus Reform'd: Being the Apotheosis of Sir Samuel Garth,* published in *Miscellanea Aurea: or, The Golden Medley* in 1720, which proved to be travel romances in the manner of Sir Thomas Mandeville (cf. 1840s note 18).

**41** Allusion to such panoramic depictions as John Banvard's (1815–1891) painting of the Mississippi River, which was stretched between two rollers that were slowly turned to give the appearance of viewing the entire river from the deck of a steamboat, or to Samuel B. Stockwell's (1813–1854) "Colossal Moving Panorama of the Upper and Lower Mississippi Rivers."

42 Small sticks of wood used primarily for fire-wood.

43 Hero of the Trojan War, represented in the *Iliad* as a gigantic man, slow of thought and speech, but quick in battle and always showing courage.

round and stay at home. A man dwells in his native valley like a corolla in its calyx, like an acorn in its cup. *Here,* of course, is all that you love, all that you expect, all that you are. Here is your bride elect, as close to you as she can be got. Here is all the best and all the worst you can imagine. What more do you want? Bear hereaway then! Foolish people imagine that what they imagine is somewhere else. That stuff is not made in any factory but their own.

*November 3.* By fall I mean literally the falling of the leaves, though some mean by it the changing or the acquisition of a brighter color. This I call the autumnal tint, the ripening to the fall.

*November 4.* On the 1st, when I stood on Poplar Hill, I saw a man, far off by the edge of the river, splitting billets[42] off a stump. Suspecting who it was, I took out my glass, and beheld Goodwin, the one-eyed Ajax,[43] in his short blue frock, short and square-bodied, as broad as for his height he can afford to be, getting his winter's wood; for this is one of the phenomena of the season. As surely as the ants which he disturbs go into winter quarters in the stump when the weather becomes cool, so does Goodwin revisit the stumpy shores with his axe. As usual, his powder-flask peeped out from a pocket on his breast, his gun was slanted over a stump near by, and his boat lay a little further along. He had been at work laying wall still further off, and now, near the end of the day, betook himself to those pursuits which he loved better still. It would be no amusement to me to see a gentleman buy his winter wood. It is to see Goodwin get his. I helped him tip over a stump or two. He said that the owner of the land had given him leave to get them out, but it seemed to me a condescension for him to ask any man's leave to grub up these stumps. The stumps to those who can use them, I say, — to those who will split them. He might as well ask leave of the farmer to shoot the musquash and the meadow-hen, or I might as well ask leave to look at the landscape. Near by were large hollows in the ground, now grassed over, where he had got out white oak stumps in previous years. But, strange to say, the town does not like to have him get his fuel in this way. They would rather the stumps would rot in the ground, or be floated down-stream to the sea. They have almost without dissent agreed on a different mode of living, with their division of labor. They would have him stick to laying wall, and buy corded wood for his fuel, as they do. He has drawn up an old bridge sleeper and cut his name in it for security, and now he gets into his boat and pushes off in the twilight, saying he will go and see what Mr. Musquash is about.

*November 8.* Each phase of nature, while not invisible, is yet not too distinct and obtrusive. It is there to be found when we look for it, but not demanding our attention. It is like a silent but sympathizing companion in whose company we retain most of the advantages of solitude, with whom we can walk and talk, or be silent, naturally, without the necessity of talking in a strain foreign to the place.

I know of but one or two persons with whom I can afford to walk.[44] With most the walk degenerates into a mere vigorous use of your legs, ludicrously purposeless, while you are discussing some mighty argument, each one having his say, spoiling each other's day, worrying one another with conversation, hustling one another with our conversation. I know of no use in the walking part in this case, except that we may seem to be getting on together toward some goal; but of course we keep our original distance all the way. Jumping every wall and ditch with vigor in the vain hope of shaking your

**44** In "Walking" this became: "I have met with but one or two persons in the course of my life who understood the art of Walking, that is, of taking walks, — who had a genius, so to speak, for *sauntering*" [W 5:205].

companion off. Trying to kill two birds with one stone, though they sit at opposite points of the compass, to see nature and do the honors to one who does not.

*November 9.* It is of no use to plow deeper than the soil is, unless you mean to follow up that mode of cultivation persistently, manuring highly and carting on muck at each plowing,—making a soil, in short. Yet many a man likes to tackle mighty themes, like immortality, but in his discourse he turns up nothing but yellow sand, under which what little fertile and available surface soil he may have is quite buried and lost. He should teach frugality rather,—how to postpone the fatal hour,—should plant a crop of beans. He might have raised enough of these to make a deacon of him, though never a preacher. Many a man runs his plow so deep in heavy or stony soil that it sticks fast in the furrow. It is a great art in the writer to improve from day to day just that soil and fertility which he has, to harvest that crop which his life yields, whatever it may be, not be straining as if to reach apples or oranges when he yields only ground-nuts. He should be digging, not soaring. Just as earnest as your life is, so deep is your soil. If strong and deep, you will sow wheat and raise bread of life in it.

*November 16.* Preaching? Lecturing? Who are ye that ask for these things? What do ye want to hear, ye puling infants? A trumpet-sound that would train you up to mankind, or a nurse's lullaby? The preachers and lecturers deal with men of straw, as they are men of straw themselves. Why, a free-spoken man, of sound lungs, cannot draw a long breath without causing your rotten institutions to come toppling down by the vacuum he makes. Your church is a baby-house made of blocks, and so of the state. It would be a relief to breathe one's self occasionally among men. If there were any magnanimity in us, any grandeur of soul, anything but sects and parties undertaking to patronize God and keep the mind within bounds, how often we might encourage and provoke one another by a free expression! I will not consent to walk with my mouth muzzled, not till I am rabid, until there is danger that I shall bite the unoffending and that my bite will produce hydrophobia.

Freedom of speech! It hath not entered into your hearts to conceive what those words mean. It is not leave given me by your sect to say this or that; it is when leave is given to your sect to withdraw. The church, the state, the school, the magazine, think they are liberal and free! It is the freedom of a prison-yard. I ask only that one fourth part of my honest thoughts be spoken aloud. What is it you tolerate, you church to-day? Not truth, but a lifelong hypocrisy. Let us have institutions framed not out of our rottenness, but out of our soundness. This factitious piety is like stale gingerbread. I would like to suggest what a pack of fools and cowards we mankind are. They want me to agree not to breathe too hard in the neighborhood of their paper castles. If I should draw a long breath in the neighborhood of these institutions, their weak and flabby sides would fall out, for my own inspiration would exhaust the air about them. The church! it is eminently the timid institution, and the heads and pillars of it are constitutionally and by principle the greatest cowards in the community. The voice that goes up from the monthly concerts is not so brave and so cheering as that which rises from the frog-ponds of the land. The best "preachers," so called, are an effeminate class; their bravest thoughts wear petticoats. If they have any manhood they are sure to forsake the ministry, though they were to turn their attention to baseball.[45] Look at your editors of popular magazines. I have dealt with two or three the most liberal of them. They are afraid to print a whole sentence, a *round* sentence, a

45 Probably the early form of baseball known as the Massachusetts Game or Town Ball.

**46** Earlier this year Thoreau submitted "Chesuncook" to the *Atlantic Monthly*. The editor, James Russell Lowell, expurgated a sentence about the pine tree: "It is as immortal as I am, and perchance will go to as high a heaven, there to tower above me still." Thoreau was outraged at the liberties taken by the editor, writing him a letter on 22 June 1858, in which he stated: "The editor has, in this case, no more right to omit a sentiment than to insert one, or put words into my mouth. . . . I am not willing to be associated in any way, unnecessarily, with parties who will confess themselves so bigoted & timid as this implies. I could excuse a man who was afraid of an uplifted fist, but if one manifests fear at the utterance of a sincere thought, I must think that his life is a kind of nightmare continued into broad daylight" [C 515–516].

**47** Variantly in "Life Without Principle": "There is not a popular magazine in this country that would dare print a child's thought on important subjects without comment. It must be submitted to the D.D.'s [Doctors of Divinity]" [W 4:469].

**48** Allusion to 2 Peter 3–4: "Knowing this first, that there shall come in the last days scoffers, walking after their own lusts, And saying, Where is the promise of his coming?"

free-spoken sentence.[46] They want to get thirty thousand subscribers, and they will do anything to get them. They consult the D.D.'s and all the letters of the alphabet before printing a sentence.[47] I have been into many of these cowardly New England towns where they *profess* Christianity,—invited to speak, perchance,—where they were trembling in their shoes at the thought of the things you might say, as if they knew their weak side,—that they were weak on all sides. The devil they have covenanted with is a timid devil. If they would let their sores alone they might heal, and they could to the wars again like men; but instead of that they get together in meeting-house cellars, rip off the bandages and poultice them with sermons.

One of our New England towns is sealed up hermetically like a molasses-hogshead,—such is its sweet Christianity,—only a little of the sweet trickling out at the cracks enough to daub you. The few more liberal-minded or indifferent inhabitants are the flies that buzz about it. It is Christianity bunged up. I see awful eyes looking out through a bull's-eye at the bung-hole. It is doubtful if they can fellowship with me.

The further you go up country, I think the worse it is, the more benighted they are. On the one side you will find a barroom which holds the "Scoffers,"[48] so called, on the other a vestry where is a monthly concert of prayer. There is just as little to cheer you in one of these companies as the other. It may be often the truth and righteousness of the barroom that saves the town. There is nothing to redeem the bigotry and moral cowardice of New-Englanders in my eyes. You may find a cape which runs six miles into the sea that has not a man of moral courage upon it. What is called faith is an immense prejudice. Like the Hindoos and Russians and Sandwich-Islanders (that were), they are the creatures of an institution. They do not think; they adhere like oysters to what their fathers and grandfathers adhered to. How often is it that the shoemaker, by thinking over his last, can think as valuable a thought as he makes a valuable shoe?

I have been into the town, being invited to speak to the inhabitants, not valuing, not having read even, the Assembly's Catechism,[49] and I try to stimulate them by reporting the best of my experience. I see the craven priest looking round for a hole to escape at, alarmed because it was he that invited me thither, and an awful silence pervades the audience. They think they will never get me there again. But the seed has not all fallen in stony and shallow ground.

It is no compliment to be invited to lecture before the rich Institutes and Lyceums. The settled lecturers are as tame as the settled ministers. The audiences do not want to hear any prophets; they do not wish to be stimulated and instructed, but entertained. They, their wives and daughters, go to the Lyceum to suck a sugarplum. The little of medicine they get is disguised with sugar. It is never the reformer they hear there, but a faint and timid echo of him only. They seek a passtime merely. Their greatest guns[50] and sons of thunder[51] are only wooden guns and great-grandsons of thunder, who give them smooth words well pronounced from manuscripts well punctuated,—they who have stolen the little fire they have from prophets whom the audience would quake to hear. They ask for orators that will entertain them and leave them where they found them. The most successful lecturing on Washington, or what-not, is an awful scratching of backs to the tune, it may be, of fifty thousand dollars. Sluggards that want to have a lullaby sung to them! Such manikins[52] as I have described are they, alas, who have made the greatest stir (and what a shallow stir) in the church and Lyceum, and in Congress. They

**49** Allusion to, probably, the shorter and more popular of the two catechisms (the Larger and Shorter) established by the Westminster Assembly, which first convened on 1 July.

**50** Cannons, but also something noisy and blustery, from British naval slang of the late 18th century meaning a violent gale.

**51** Declamatory and vociferous orators, from association with the apostles James and John in Mark 3:17: "And James the son of Zebedee, and John the brother of James; and he surnamed them Boanerges, which is, The sons of thunder."

**52** Term for small persons, although Thoreau may also have had in mind the artist's small wooden clay figure.

**53** The Lowell Institute, in Boston, named after John Lowell, Jr. (1799–1838), who in 1836 granted an endowment for the creation of public lectures to benefit the citizens of Boston.

**54** The defining statements of Anglican doctrine, defined by the Church of England in 1571.

**55** Cf. 1858 note 27.

**56** Latin: in the same state.

**57** Cf. 1852 note 42.

**58** On the Assabet River, approximately a half mile from its confluence with the Concord and Sudbury Rivers.

want a medicine that will not interfere with their daily meals.

There is the Lowell Institute[53] with its restrictions, requiring a certain faith in the lecturers. How can any free-thinking man accept its terms? It is as if you were to resolve that you would not eat oysters that were not of a particular faith,—that, for instance, did not believe the Thirty-Nine Articles,[54]—for the faith that is in an oyster is just as valuable as the faith referred to in Mr. Lowell's will. These popular lecturers, our preachers, and magazines are for women and children *in the bad sense*.

The curators have on their lists the names of the men who came before the Philomathean Institute[55] in the next large town and did no harm; left things *in statu quo*,[56] so that all slept the better for it; only confirmed the audience in their previous badness; spoke a good word for God; gave the clergy, that heavy set, a lift; told the youngsters to be good boys. A man may have a good deal to say who has not any desk[57] to thump on, who does not thunder in bad air.

They want all of a man but his truth and independence and manhood.

One who spoke to their condition would of course make them wince, and they would retaliate, *i. e.* kick him out, or stop their ears.

*November 17.* Leaving my boat, I walk through the low wood west of Dove Rock,[58] toward the scarlet oak. The very sunlight on the pale-brown bleached fields is an interesting object these cold days. I naturally look toward it as to a wood-fire. Not only different objects are presented to our attention at different seasons of the year, but we are in a frame of body and of mind to appreciate different objects at different seasons. I see one thing when it is cold and another when it is warm.

Looking toward the sun now when an hour high,

there being many small alders and birches between me and it for half a dozen rods, the light reflected from their twigs has the appearance of an immense cobweb with closely concentric lines, of which I see about one fourth, on account of the upward curve of the twigs on each side, and the light not being reflected to me at all from one side of the trees directly in front of me. The light is thus very pleasantly diffused.

We are interested at this season by the manifold ways in which the light is reflected to us. Ascending a little knoll covered with sweet-fern, shortly after, the sun appearing but a point above the sweet-fern, its light was reflected from a dense mass of the bare downy twigs of this plant in a surprising manner which would not be believed if described. It was quite like the sunlight reflected from grass and weeds covered with hoar frost. Yet in an ordinary light these are but dark or dusky looking twigs with scarcely a noticeable downiness. Yet as I saw it, there was a perfect halo of light resting on the knoll as I moved to right or left. A myriad of surfaces are now prepared to reflect the light. This is one of the hundred silvery lights of November. The setting sun, too, is reflected from windows more brightly than at any other season. "November Lights" would be a theme for me.

*November 28.* I cannot now walk without leaving a track behind me; that is one peculiarity of winter walking. Anybody may follow my trail. I have walked, perhaps, a particular wild path along some swamp-side all summer, and thought to myself, I am the only villager that ever comes here. But I go out shortly after the first snow has fallen, and lo, here is the track of a sportsman and his dog in my secluded path, and probably he preceded me in the summer as well. Yet my hour is not his, and I may never meet him!

**59** Thoreau had observed the bream several days before, on 26 and 27 November, and brought some of them home, remarking: "They are exceedingly pretty seen floating dead on their sides in a bowl of water, with all their fins spread out" [J 11:348].

**60** In *Walden* Thoreau wrote, "When I was four years old, as I well remember, I was brought from Boston to this my native town, through these very woods and this field, to the pond. It is one of the oldest scenes stamped on my memory" [Wa 151]. In a journal entry from August 1845, however, he noted that he first visited Walden Pond "Twenty-three years since, when I was 5 years old" [J 1:380].

**61** According to Lemuel Shattuck's *History of the Town of Concord* (1835): "Tahattawan (sometimes written Tahattwants, Attawan, Attawance, and Ahatawance) was a sagamore, or 'sachem of the blood, or chief of the royal line,' of Musketaquid, . . . a worthy upright Indian." He was the sachem living near what is now Concord when English settlers arrived in 1635. In his journal of 15 February 1857 Thoreau made the following notes from his reading in Shattuck: "Shattuck says that the principal sachem of our Indians, Tahattawan, lived 'near Nahshawtuck hill' . . . and he describes Squaw Sachem and John Tahattawan, son of Tahattawan, as Musketaquid Indians" [J 9:255].

***November 30.*** I cannot but see still in my mind's eye those little striped breams poised in Walden's glaucous water.[59] They balance all the rest of the world in my estimation at present, for this is the bream that I have just found, and for the time I neglect all its brethren and am ready to kill the fatted calf on its account. For more than two centuries have men fished here and have not distinguished this permanent settler of the township. It is not like a new bird, a transient visitor that may not be seen again for years, but there it dwells and has dwelt permanently, who can tell how long? When my eyes first rested on Walden[60] the striped bream was poised in it, though I did not see it, and when Tahatawan[61] paddled his canoe there. How wild it makes the pond and the township to find a new fish in it! America renews her youth here. But in my account of this bream I cannot go a hair's breadth beyond the mere statement that it exists,—the miracle of its existence, my contemporary and neighbor, yet so different from me! I can only poise my thought there by its side and try to think like a bream for a moment. I can only think of precious jewels, of music, poetry, beauty, and the mystery of life. I only see the bream in its orbit, as I see a star, but I care not to measure its distance or weight. The bream, appreciated, floats in the pond as the centre of the system, another image of God. Its life no man can explain more than he can his own. I want you to perceive the mystery of the bream. I have a contemporary in Walden. It has fins where I have legs and arms. I have a friend among the fishes, at least a new acquaintance. Its character will interest me, I trust, not its clothes and anatomy. I do not want it to eat. Acquaintance with it is to make my life more rich and eventful. It is as if a poet or an anchorite had moved into the town, whom I can see from time to time and think of yet oftener. Perhaps there are a thousand of these striped bream which no one had thought of in that pond,—not their mere impressions in stone, but in the full tide of the bream life.

Though science may sometimes compare herself to a child picking up pebbles on the seashore,[62] that is a rare mood with her; ordinarily her practical belief is that it is only a few pebbles which are *not* known, weighed and measured. A new species of fish signifies hardly more than a new name. See what is contributed in the scientific reports. One counts the fin-rays, another measures the intestines, a third daguerreotypes a scale, etc., etc.; otherwise there's nothing to be said. As if all but this were done, and these were very rich and generous contributions to science. Her votaries may be seen wandering along the shore of the ocean of truth, with their backs to that ocean, ready to seize on the shells which are cast up. You would say that the scientific bodies were terribly put to it for objects and subjects. A dead specimen of an animal, if it is only well preserved in alcohol, is just as good for science as a living one preserved in its native element.

What is the amount of my discovery to me? It is not that I have got one in a bottle, that it has got a name in a book, but that I have a little fishy friend in the pond. How was it when the youth first discovered fishes? Was it the number of their fin-rays or their arrangement, or the place of the fish in some system that made the boy dream of them? Is it these things that interest mankind in the fish, the inhabitant of the water? No, but a faint recognition of a living contemporary, a provoking mystery. One boy thinks of fishes and goes a-fishing from the same motive that his brother searches the poets for rare lines. It is the poetry of fishes which is their chief use; their flesh is their lowest use. The beauty of the fish, that is what it is best worth the while to measure. Its place in our systems is of comparatively little importance. Generally the boy loses some of his perception and his interest

**62** Allusion to Isaac Newton (1642–1727), who said, as recorded in Sir David Brewster's (1781–1868) *The Life of Sir Isaac Newton:* "I do not know what I may appear to the world; but to myself I seem to have been only like a boy playing on the sea-shore, and diverting myself by now and then finding a smoother pebble or a prettier shell than ordinary, while the great ocean of truth lay all undiscovered before me."

**63** Ironically, Thoreau made a note referencing this entry a few days later, 3 December, in which he measured and described four bream [J 11:363]. As early as 1851 Thoreau was concerned about becoming too scientific in his appreciation of nature, writing in his journal: "I fear that the character of my knowledge is from year to year becoming more distinct and scientific; that, in exchange for views as wide as heaven's scope, I am being narrowed down to the field of the microscope. I see details, not wholes nor the shadow of the whole" [J 2:406].

**64** Thoreau was skating to Israel Rice's (1788–1872) property on the Sudbury River.

in the fish; he degenerates into a fisherman or an ichthyologist.[63]

*December 27.* Talk of fate! How little one can know what is fated to another!—what he can do and what he can not do! I doubt whether one can give or receive any very pertinent advice. In all important crises one can only consult his genius. Though he were the most shiftless and craziest of mortals, if he still recognizes that he has any genius to consult, none may presume to go between him and it. They, methinks, are poor stuff and creatures of a miserable fate who can be advised and persuaded in very important steps. Show me a man who consults his genius, and you have shown me a man who cannot be advised. You may know what a thing costs or is worth to you; you can never know what it costs or is worth to me. All the community may scream because one man is born who will not do as it does, who will not conform because conformity to him is death,—he is so constituted. They know nothing about his case; they are fools when they presume to advise him. The man of genius knows what he is aiming at; nobody else knows. And he alone knows when something comes between him and his object. In the course of generations, however, men will excuse you for not doing as they do, if you will bring enough to pass in your own way.

*December 29.* I think more of skates than of the horse or locomotive as annihilators of distance,[64] for while I am getting along with the speed of the horse, I have at the same time the satisfaction of the horse and his rider, and far more adventure and variety than if I were riding. We never cease to be surprised when we observe how swiftly the skater glides along. Just compare him with one walking or running. The walker is but a snail in comparison, and the runner gives up the contest after a few rods. The skater can afford to follow all the windings of a stream, and yet soon leaves far behind and out of sight the walker who cuts across. Distance is hardly an obstacle to him. I observe that my ordinary track is like this:

the strokes being seven to ten feet long. The new stroke is eighteen or twenty inches one side of the old. The briskest walkers appear to be stationary to the skater. The skater has wings, *talaria,* to his feet. Moreover, you have such perfect control of your feet that you can take advantage of the narrowest and most winding and sloping bridge of ice in order to pass between the button-bushes and the open stream or under a bridge on a narrow shelf, where the walker cannot go at all. You can glide securely within an inch of destruction on this the most slippery of surfaces, more securely than you could walk there, perhaps, on any other material. You can pursue swiftly the most intricate and winding path, even leaping obstacles which suddenly present themselves.

**1** Nathan B. Stow's (1822–1901) woodlot west of the Deep Cut.

**2** Daniel Webster (cf. 1851 note 2), known for his oratorical skills.

**3** Samuel Kirkham's (1797–1843) *English Grammar in Familiar Lectures: Accompanied by a Compendium Embracing a New and Systematick Order of Parsing, a New System of Punctuation, Exercises in False Syntax, and a Key to the Exercises Designed for the Use of School and Private Learners.*

*1859*

AGE 41–42

*January 2.* P.M. — To Cliffs and Walden.

Going up the hill through Stow's young oak woodland,[1] I listen to the sharp, dry rustle of the withered oak leaves. This is the voice of the wood now. It would be comparatively still and more dreary here in other respects, if it were not for these leaves that hold on. It sounds like the roar of the sea, and is enlivening and inspiriting like that, suggesting how all the land is seacoast to the aerial ocean. It is the sound of the surf, the rut of an unseen ocean, billows of air breaking on the forest like water on itself or on sand and rocks. It rises and falls, wells and dies away, with agreeable alternation as the sea surf does. Perhaps the landsman can foretell a storm by it. It is remarkable how universal these grand murmurs are, these backgrounds of sound, — the surf, the wind in the forest, waterfalls, etc., — which yet to the ear and in their origin are essentially one voice, the earth-voice, the breathing or snoring of the creature. The earth is our ship, and this is the sound of the wind in her rigging as we sail. Just as the inhabitant of Cape Cod hears the surf ever breaking on its shores, so we countrymen hear this kindred surf on the leaves of the forest.

When I hear the hypercritical quarrelling about grammar and style, the position of the particles, etc., etc., stretching or contracting every speaker to certain rules of theirs, — Mr. Webster,[2] perhaps, not having spoken according to Mr. Kirkham's rule,[3] — I see that they forget that the first requisite and rule is that expression shall be vital and natural, as much as the voice of a brute or an interjection: first of all, mother tongue; and last of all, artificial or father tongue.[4] Essentially your truest poetic sentence is as free and lawless as a lamb's bleat. The grammarian is often one who can neither cry nor laugh, yet thinks that he can express human emotions. So the posture-masters[5] tell you how you shall walk,—turning your toes out, perhaps, excessively,—but so the beautiful walkers are not made.

*January 18.* Every one, no doubt, has looked with delight, holding his face low, at that beautiful frostwork which so frequently in winter mornings is seen bristling about the throat of every breathing-hole in the earth's surface. In this case the fog, the earth's breath made visible,[6] was in such abundance that it invested all our vales and hills, and the frostwork, accordingly, instead of being confined to the chinks and crannies of the earth, covered the mightiest trees, so that we, walking beneath them, had the same wonderful prospect and environment that an insect would have in the former case. We, going along our roads, had such a prospect as an insect would have making its way through a chink in the earth which was bristling with hoar frost.

That glaze! I know what it was by my own experience; it was the frozen breath of the earth upon its beard.

Take the most rigid tree, the whole effect is peculiarly soft and spirit-like, for there is no marked edge or outline. How could you draw the outline of these snowy fingers seen against the fog, without exaggeration? There is no more a boundary-line or circumference that can be drawn, than a diameter. Hardly could the New England farmer drive to market under these trees without feeling that his sense of beauty was addressed. He would be

**4** On 3 February 1860 Thoreau wrote: "When I read some of the rules for speaking and writing the English language correctly,—as that a sentence must never end with a particle,—and perceive how implicitly even the learned obey it, I think—

Any fool can make a rule
And every fool will mind it" [J 13:125].

**5** Teachers or practitioners of artificial postures of the body.
**6** Cf. 20 November 1853.

**7** Neither the miller nor the farmer is identified.

aware that the phenomenon called beauty was become visible, if one were at leisure or had had the right culture to appreciate it. A miller with whom I rode actually remarked on the beauty of the trees; and a farmer[7] told me in all sincerity that, having occasion to go into Walden Woods in his sleigh, he thought he never saw anything so beautiful in all his life, and if there had been men there who knew how to write about it, it would have been a great occasion for them.

Many times I thought that if the particular tree, commonly an elm, under which I was walking or riding were the only one like it in the country, it would be worth a journey across the continent to see it. Indeed, I have no doubt that such journeys would be undertaken on hearing a true account of it. But, instead of being confined to a single tree, this wonder was as cheap and common as the air itself. Every man's woodlot was a miracle and surprise to him, and for those who could not go so far there were the trees in the street and the weeds in the yard. It was much like (in effect) that snow that lodges on the fine dead twigs on the lower part of a pine wood, resting there in the twilight commonly only till it has done snowing and the wind arises. But in this case it did not rest *on* the twig, but grew out from it horizontally, and it was not confined to the lowest twigs, but covered the whole forest and every surface.

Looking down the street, you might say that the scene differed from the ordinary one as frosted cake differs from plain bread. In some moods you might suspect that it was the work of enchantment. Some magician had put your village into a crucible and it had crystallized thus. The weeping willow, with its thickened twigs, seemed more precise and regularly curved than ever, and as still as if it were carved of alabaster. The maples, with their few long shoots, were rather set and still. It was remarkable that when the fog was a little thinner, so that you could see the pine woods a mile or more off, they were a distinct dark blue. If any tree is set and stiff, it was now more stiff, if airy and graceful, it was now more graceful. The birches especially were a great ornament.

*January 28.* When you have been deprived of your usual quantity of sleep for several nights,[8] you sleep much more soundly for it, and wake up suddenly like a bullet that strikes a wall.

*February 3.* Five minutes before 3 P.M., Father died.[9]

After a sickness of some two years, going down-town in pleasant weather, doing a little business from time to time, hoeing a little in the garden, etc., Father took to his chamber January 13th, and did not come down again. Most of the time previously he had coughed and expectorated a great deal. Latterly he did not cough, but continued to raise. He continued to sit up in his chamber till within a week before he died. He sat up for a little while on the Sunday four days before he died. Generally he was very silent for many months. He was quite conscious to the last, and his death was so easy that we should not have been aware that he was dying, though we were sitting around his bed, if we had not watched very closely.[10]

I have touched a body which was flexible and warm, yet tenantless,—warmed by what fire? When the spirit that animated some matter has left it, who else, what else, can animate it?

How enduring are our bodies, after all! The forms of our brothers and sisters, our parents and children and wives, lie still in the hills and fields round about us, not

**8** At this time Thoreau was administering to the needs of his dying father. Edward Emerson recalled in his *Henry Thoreau as Remembered by a Young Friend:* "After his father's death his mother said, 'But for this I should never have seen the tender side of Henry,' who had nursed him with loving care."

**9** In his manuscript journal this sentence was given an entire page to itself.

**10** On 12 February 1859 Thoreau wrote to Daniel Ricketson: "I sent you the notice of my Father's death as much because you knew him, as because you know me. I can hardly realize that he is dead. He had been sick about two years, and at last declined rather rapidly though steadily. Till within a week or ten days before he died, he was hoping to see another spring; but he then discovered that this was a vain expectation, and thinking that he was dying he took his leave of us several times within a week before his departure. Once or twice he expressed a slight impatience at the delay. He was quite conscious to the last, and his death was so easy, that though we had all been sitting around the bed for an hour or more, expecting that event, as we had sat before, he was gone at last almost before we were aware of it" [C 546].

11 Cf. 28 January 1859.

to mention those of our remoter ancestors, and the matter which composed the body of our first human father still exists under another name.

When in sickness the body is emaciated, and the expression of the face in various ways is changed, you perceive unexpected resemblances to other members of the same family; as if within the same family there was a greater general similarity in the framework of the face than in its filling up and clothing.

As far as I know, Father, when he died, was not only one of the oldest men in the middle of Concord, but the one perhaps best acquainted with the inhabitants, and the local, social, and street history of the middle of the town, for the last fifty years. He belonged in a peculiar sense to the village street; loved to sit in the shops or at the post-office and read the daily papers. I think that he remembered more about the worthies (and unworthies) of Concord village forty years ago, both from dealing as a trader and from familiar intercourse with them, than any one else. Our other neighbors, now living or very recently dead, have either come to the town more recently than he, or have lived more aloof from the mass of the inhabitants.

I perceive that we partially die ourselves through sympathy at the death of each of our friends or near relatives. Each such experience is an assault on our vital force. It becomes a source of wonder that they who have lost many friends still live. After long watching around the sick-bed of a friend, we, too, partially give up the ghost with him, and are the less to be identified with this state of things.[11]

The writer must to some extent inspire himself. Most of his sentences may at first lie dead in his essay, but when all are arranged, some life and color will be reflected on them from the mature and successful lines; they will appear to pulsate with fresh life, and he will be enabled to eke out their slumbering sense, and make them worthy of their neighborhood. In his first essay on a given theme, he produces scarcely more than a frame and groundwork for his sentiment and poetry. Each clear thought that he attains to draws in its train many divided thoughts or perceptions. The writer has much to do even to create a theme for himself. Most that is first written on any subject is a mere groping after it, mere rubble-stone and foundation. It is only when many observations of different periods have been brought together that he begins to grasp his subject and can make one pertinent and just observation.

*February 5.* When we have experienced many disappointments, such as the loss of friends, the notes of birds cease to affect us as they did.

*February 13.* Sometimes in our prosaic moods, life appears to us but a certain number more of days like those which we have lived, to be cheered not by more friends and friendship but probably fewer and less. As, perchance, we anticipate the end of this day before it is done, close the shutters, and with a cheerless resignation commence the barren evening whose fruitless end we clearly see, we despondingly think that all of life that is left is only this experience repeated a certain number of times. And so it would be, if it were not for the faculty of imagination.

*February 25.* Measure your health by your sympathy with morning and spring. If there is no response in you to the awakening of nature,—if the prospect of an early

**12** Light, open, two-wheeled carriage drawn by two horses abreast.

morning walk does not banish sleep, if the warble of the first bluebird does not thrill you, — know that the morning and spring of your life are past. Thus may you feel your pulse.

*March 3.* Talk about reading! — a good reader! It depends on how he is heard. There may be elocution and pronunciation (recitation, say) to satiety, but there can be no good reading unless there is good hearing also. It takes two at least for this game, as for love, and they must coöperate. The lecturer will read best those parts of his lecture which are best heard. Sometimes, it is true, the faith and spirits of the reader may run a little ahead and draw after the good hearing, and at other times the good hearing runs ahead and draws on the good reading. The reader and the hearer are a team not to be harnessed tandem, the poor wheel horse supporting the burden of the shafts, while the leader runs pretty much at will, while the lecture lies passive in the painted curricle[12] behind. I saw some men unloading molasses-hogsheads from a truck at a depot the other day, rolling them up an inclined plane. The truckman stood behind and shoved, after putting a couple of ropes one round each end of the hogshead, while two men standing in the depot steadily pulled at the ropes. The first man was the lecturer, the last was the audience. It is the duty of the lecturer to team his hogshead of sweets to the depot, or Lyceum, place the horse, arrange the ropes, and shove; and it is the duty of the audience to take hold of the ropes and pull with all their might. The lecturer who tries to read his essay without being abetted by a good hearing is in the predicament of a teamster who is engaged in the Sisyphean labor of rolling a molasses-hogshead up an inclined plane alone, while the freight-master and his men stand indifferent with their hands in their pockets.

I have seen many such a hogshead which had rolled off the horse and gone to smash, with all its sweets wasted on the ground between the truckman and the freight-house,—and the freight-masters thought that the loss was not theirs.

Read well! Did you ever know a full well that did not yield of its refreshing waters to those who put their hands to the windlass or the well-sweep? Did you ever suck cider through a straw? Did you ever know the cider to push out of the straw when you were not sucking,—unless it chanced to be in a complete ferment? An audience will draw out of a lecture, or enable a lecturer to read, only such parts of his lecture as they like. A lecture is like a barrel half full of some palatable liquor. You may tap it at various levels,—in the sweet liquor or in the froth or in fixed air above. If it is pronounced good, it is partly to the credit of the hearers; if bad, it is partly their fault. Sometimes a lazy audience refuses to coöperate and pull on the ropes with a will, simply because the hogshead is full and therefore heavy, when if it were empty, or had only a little sugar adhering to it, they would whisk it up the slope in a jiffy. The lecturer, therefore, desires of his audience a long pull, a strong pull, and all pull together. I have seen a sturdy truckman, or lecturer, who had nearly broken his back with shoving his lecture up such an inclined plane while the audience were laughing at him, at length, as with a last effort, set it a-rolling in amid the audience and upon their toes, scattering them like sheep and making them cry out with pain, while he drove proudly away. Rarely it is a very heavy freight of such hogsheads stored in a vessel's hold that is to be lifted out and deposited on the public wharf, and this is accomplished only after many a hearty pull all together and a good deal of heave-yo-ing.[13]

13 Thoreau was probably comparing the different responses he got from his lecture "Autumnal Tints" on 22 February and on 2 March in Concord, of which Ellen Emerson wrote her sister, Edith (1841–1929): "Last night Mr Thoreau lectured a grand lecture on Autumnal Tints. Father and Mother, Mr Sanborn and Eddy were equally delighted. It was funny and Father said there were constant spontaneous bursts of laughter and Mr Thoreau was applauded."

***March 6.*** There is a very picturesque large black oak on the Bee-Tree Ridge,[14] of this form: —

***March 7.*** The mystery of the life of plants is kindred with that of our own lives, and the physiologist must not presume to explain their growth according to mechanical laws, or as he might explain some machinery of his own making. We must not expect to probe with our fingers the sanctuary of any life, whether animal or vegetable. If we do, we shall discover nothing but surface still. The ultimate expression or fruit of any created thing is a fine effluence which only the most ingenuous worshipper perceives at a reverent distance from its surface even. The cause and the effect are equally evanescent and intangible, and the former must be investigated in the same spirit and with the same reverence with which the latter is perceived. Science is often like the grub which, though it may have nestled in the germ of a fruit, has merely blighted or consumed it and never truly tasted it. Only that intellect makes any progress toward conceiving of the essence which at the same time perceives the effluence. The rude and ignorant finger is probing in the rind still, for in this case, too, the angles of incidence and excidence are equal,[15] and the essence is as far on the other side of the surface, or matter, as reverence detains the worshipper on this, and only reverence can find out this angle instinctively. Shall we presume to alter the angle at which God chooses to be worshipped?

There is no ripeness which is not, so to speak, something ultimate in itself, and not merely a perfected means to a higher end. In order to be ripe it must serve a transcendent use. The ripeness of a leaf, being perfected, leaves the tree at that point and never returns to it. It has nothing to do with any other fruit which the tree may bear, and only the genius of the poet can pluck it.

The fruit of a tree is neither in the seed nor the timber,—the full-grown tree,—but it is simply the highest use to which it can be put.

*March 24.* Now, when the leaves get to be dry and rustle under your feet, dried by the March winds, the peculiar dry note, *wurrk wurrk wur-r-r-k wurk* of the wood frog is heard faintly by ears on the alert, borne up from some unseen pool in a woodland hollow which is open to the influences of the sun. It is a singular sound for awakening Nature to make, associated with the first warmer days, when you sit in some sheltered place in the woods amid the dried leaves. How moderate on her first awakening, how little demonstrative! You may sit half an hour before you will hear another. You doubt if the season will be long enough for such Oriental and luxurious slowness. But they get on, nevertheless, and by to-morrow, or in a day or two, they croak louder and more frequently. Can you ever be sure that you have heard the very first wood frog in the township croak? Ah! how weather-wise must he be! There is no guessing at the weather with him. He makes the weather in his degree; he encourages it to be mild. The weather, what is it but the temperament of the earth? and he is wholly of the earth, sensitive as its skin in which he lives and of which he is a part. His life relaxes with the thawing ground. He pitches and tunes his voice to chord[16] with the rustling leaves which the March wind has dried. Long before the frost is quite out, he feels the influence of the spring rains and the warmer days. His is the very voice of the weather. He rises and falls like quicksilver in the thermometer. You do not perceive the spring so surely in the actions of men, their

**16** Bring into consonance, harmony, or accord.

lives are so artificial. They may make more fire or less in their parlors, and their feelings accordingly are not good thermometers. The frog far away in the wood, that burns no coal nor wood, perceives more surely the general and universal changes.

*March 28.* It is now high time to look for arrowheads, etc. I spend many hours every spring gathering the crop which the melting snow and rain have washed bare. When, at length, some island in the meadow or some sandy field elsewhere has been plowed, perhaps for rye, in the fall, I take note of it, and do not fail to repair thither as soon as the earth begins to be dry in the spring. If the spot chances never to have been cultivated before, I am the first to gather a crop from it. The farmer little thinks that another reaps a harvest which is the fruit of his toil. As much ground is turned up in a day by the plow as Indian implements could not have turned over in a month, and my eyes rest on the evidences of an aboriginal life which passed here a thousand years ago perchance. Especially if the knolls in the meadows are washed by a freshet where they have been plowed the previous fall, the soil will be taken away lower down and the stones left,—the arrowheads, etc., and soapstone pottery amid them,—somewhat as gold is washed in a dish or tom. I landed on two spots this afternoon and picked up a dozen arrowheads. It is one of the regular pursuits of the spring. As much as sportsmen go in pursuit of ducks, and gunners of musquash, and scholars of rare books, and travellers of adventures, and poets of ideas, and all men of money, I go in search of arrowheads when the proper season comes round again. So I help myself to live worthily, and loving my life as I should. It is a good collyrium to look on the bare earth,—to pore over it so much, getting strength to all your senses, like Antæus.[17] If I did not find arrowheads, I might, perchance, begin to pick up crockery and fragments of pipes,—the relics of a more recent man. Indeed, you can hardly name a more innocent or wholesome entertainment. As I am thus engaged, I hear the rumble of the bowling-alley's thunder, which has begun again in the village. It comes before the earliest natural thunder. But what its lightning is, and what atmospheres it purifies, I do not know. Or I might collect the various bones which I come across. They would make a museum that would delight some Owen[18] at last, and what a text they might furnish me for a course of lectures on human life or the like! I might spend my days collecting the fragments of pipes until I found enough, after all my search, to compose one perfect pipe when laid together.

I have not decided whether I had better publish my experience in searching for arrowheads in three volumes, with plates and an index, or try to compress it into one.[19] These durable implements seem to have been suggested to the Indian mechanic with a view to my entertainment in a succeeding period. After all the labor expended on it, the bolt may have been shot but once perchance, and the shaft which was devoted to it decayed, and there lay the arrowhead, sinking into the ground, awaiting me. They lie all over the hills with like expectation, and in due time the husbandman is sent, and, tempted by the promise of corn or rye, he plows the land and turns them up to my view. Many as I have found, methinks the last one gives me about the same delight that the first did. Some time or other, you would say, it had rained arrowheads, for they lie all over the surface of America. You may have your peculiar tastes. Certain localities in your town may seem from association unattractive and uninhabitable to you. You may wonder that the land bears any money value there, and pity some poor fellow who is said to

**17**  In Greek mythology, a giant who became stronger whenever he touched the earth, his mother. He was defeated by Hercules, who raised him so that he no longer made contact with the earth, and squeezed him to death. In *Walden* Thoreau wrote that his beans "attached me to the earth, and so I got strength like Antæus" [Wa 150].

**18**  Richard Owen (1804–1892), who, when appointed superintendent of the British Museum's Natural History Department in 1856, began a campaign to create a new and separate natural history museum.

**19**  Thoreau had collected approximately 900 Native American artifacts. On 22 August 1860, after finding some Indian pottery, he wrote: "Indeed, I never find a remarkable Indian relic—and I find a good many—but I have first divined its existence, and planned the discovery of it" [J 14:59–60]. Whether he was seriously intending to compile a work specifically on arrowheads is unclear. Although Thoreau began compiling notebooks of his readings on Native Americans in 1850, his final intentions for this material are unspecified and indeterminate.

**20** Allusion to the Greek hero Jason, who, arriving in Colchis, had to perform certain tasks in order to claim the Golden Fleece, one being to sow a field with the teeth of a dragon. The teeth grew into soldiers that Jason then had to defeat.
**21** Pun on the stone, or pit, inside some fruit.
**22** Exposed to sight.
**23** Thoreau may have had in mind the Peruvian mummies that Samuel George Morton (cf. 1852 note 86) described in *Crania Americana* as "charged with desiccated vermin" [J 4:228].
**24** Jehojakin, also known as Mantatuket or Mantatukwet, a Christian Indian of Natick who testified in 1684 that he had once "lived within the bounds of that place which is now called Concord . . . and that he was present at a bargain made at the house of Mr. Peter Bulkeley (now Capt. Timothy Wheeler's) between Mr. Simon Willard, Mr. John Jones, Mr. Spencer, and several others, in behalfe of the Englishmen who were settling upon the said town of Concord, and Squaw Sachem, Tahattawan, and Nimrod, Indians, which said Indians (according to their particular rights and interest) then sold a tract of land containing six miles square (the said house being accounted about the centre) to the said English for a place to settle a town in." Mantatuket Rock, or Point, where the Sudbury and Concord Rivers meet, was named for him.

survive in that neighborhood. But plow up a new field there, and you will find the omnipresent arrow-points strewn over it, and it will appear that the red man, with other tastes and associations, lived there too. No matter how far from the modern road or meeting-house, no matter how near. They lie in the meeting-house cellar, and they lie in the distant cow-pasture. And some collections which were made a century ago by the curious like myself have been dispersed again, and they are still as good as new. You cannot tell the third-hand ones (for they are all second-hand) from the others, such is their persistent out-of-door durability; for they were chiefly made to be lost. They are sown, like a grain that is slow to germinate, broadcast over the earth. Like the dragon's teeth which bore a crop of soldiers,[20] these bear crops of philosophers and poets, and the same seed is just as good to plant again. It is a stone fruit.[21] Each one yields me a thought. I come nearer to the maker of it than if I found his bones. His bones would not prove any wit that wielded them, such as this work of his bones does. It is humanity inscribed on the face of the earth, patent[22] to my eyes as soon as the snow goes off, not hidden away in some crypt or grave or under a pyramid. No disgusting mummy,[23] but a clean stone, the best symbol or letter that could have been transmitted to me.

*The Red Man, his mark*

At every step I see it, and I can easily supply the "Tahatawan" or "Mantatuket"[24] that might have been written if he had had a clerk. It is no single inscription on a particular rock, but a footprint—rather a mind-print—left everywhere, and altogether illegible. No vandals, however vandalic in their disposition, can be so industrious as to destroy them.

Time will soon destroy the works of famous painters and sculptors, but the Indian arrowhead will balk his efforts and Eternity will have to come to his aid. They are not fossil bones, but, as it were, fossil thoughts, forever reminding me of the mind that shaped them. I would fain know that I am treading in the tracks of human game,—that I am on the trail of mind,—and these little reminders never fail to set me right. When I see these signs I know that the subtle spirits that made them are not far off, into whatever form transmuted. What if you do plow and hoe amid them, and swear that not one stone shall be left upon another?[25] They are only the less like to break in that case. When you turn up one layer you bury another so much the more securely. They are at peace with rust. This arrow-headed character[26] promises to outlast all others. The larger pestles and axes may, perchance, grow scarce and be broken, but the arrowhead shall, perhaps, never cease to wing its way through the ages to eternity. It was originally winged for but a short flight, but it still, to my mind's eye, wings its way through the ages, bearing a message from the hand that shot it. Myriads of arrow-points lie sleeping in the skin of the revolving earth, while meteors revolve in space. The footprint, the mind-print of the oldest men. When some Vandal chieftain has razed to the earth the British Museum,[27] and, perchance, the winged bulls from Nineveh shall have lost most if not all of their features, the arrowheads which the museum contains will, perhaps, find themselves at home again in familiar dust, and resume their shining in new springs upon the bared surface of the earth then, to be picked up for the thousandth time by the shepherd or savage that may be wandering there, and once more suggest their story to him.

*April 3.* Men's minds run so much on work and money that the mass instantly associate all literary labor with a

**25** Allusion to Matthew 24:2 (and variants at Mark 13:2 and Luke 21:6): "And Jesus said unto them, See ye not all these things? verily I say unto you, There shall not be left here one stone upon another, that shall not be thrown down."
**26** Cf. 1857 note 103.
**27** The British Museum, which was established by act of Parliament in 1753 and opened in 1759 as a national repository for treasures in science and art, contained the results of Layard's archeological digs at Nineveh: cf. 1851 note 40.

28 From Romans 6:23: "For the wages of sin is death; but the gift of God is eternal life through Jesus Christ our Lord."
29 Extant records show that Thoreau lectured outside Concord at least once during all but one year of the previous decade. In only one year did he lecture more in Concord than out.
30 In 1843 (cf. 1840s note 78).

pecuniary reward. They are mainly curious to know how much money the lecturer or author gets for his work. They think that the naturalist takes so much pains to collect plants or animals because he is paid for it. An Irishman who saw me in the fields making a minute in my note-book took it for granted that I was casting up my wages and actually inquired what they came to, as if he had never dreamed of any other use for writing. I might have quoted to him that the wages of sin is death,[28] as the most pertinent answer. "What do you get for lecturing now?" I am occasionally asked. It is the more amusing since I only lecture about once a year out of my native town, often not at all;[29] so that I might as well, if my objects were merely pecuniary, give up the business. Once, when I was walking on Staten Island,[30] looking about me as usual, a man who saw me would not believe me when I told him that I was indeed from New England but was not looking at that region with a pecuniary view,—a view to speculation; and he offered me a handsome bonus if I would sell his farm for him.

*April 8.* What a pitiful business is the fur trade, which has been pursued now for so many ages, for so many years by famous companies which enjoy a profitable monopoly and control a large portion of the earth's surface, unweariedly pursuing and ferreting out small animals by the aid of all the loafing class tempted by rum and money, that you may rob some little fellow-creature of its coat to adorn or thicken your own, that you may get a fashionable covering in which to hide your head, or a suitable robe in which to dispense justice to your fellow-men! Regarded from the philosopher's point of view, it is precisely on a level with rag and bone picking in the streets of the cities. The Indian led a more respectable life before he was tempted to debase himself so much by the white man. Think how many musquash and weasel skins the Hudson's Bay Company[31] pile up annually in their warehouses, leaving the bare red carcasses on the banks of the streams throughout all British America,[32]—and this it is, chiefly, which makes it *British* America. It is the place where Great Britain goes a-mousing. We have heard much of the wonderful intelligence of the beaver, but that regard for the beaver is all a pretense, and we would give more for a beaver hat than to preserve the intelligence of the whole race of beavers.

When we see men and boys spend their time shooting and trapping musquash and mink, we cannot but have a poorer opinion of them, unless we thought meanly of them before. Yet the world is imposed on by the fame of the Hudson's Bay and Northwest Fur Companies,[33] who are only so many partners more or less in the same sort of business, with thousands of just such loafing men and boys in their service to abet them. On the one side is the Hudson's Bay Company, on the other the company of scavengers who clear the sewers of Paris of their vermin. There is a good excuse for smoking out or poisoning rats which infest the house, but when they are as far off as Hudson's Bay, I think that we had better let them alone. To such an extent do time and distance, and our imaginations, consecrate at last not only the most ordinary but even vilest pursuits. The efforts of legislation from time to time to stem the torrent are significant as showing that there is some sense and conscience left, but they are insignificant in their effects. We will fine Abner[34] if he shoots a singing bird, but encourage the army of Abners that compose the Hudson's Bay Company.

*April 15.* The bay-wing[35] now sings—the first I have been able to hear—both about the Texas house[36] and the fields this side of Hayden's,[37] both of them similar dry and open pastures. I heard it just before noon, when the sun began to come out, and at 3 P.M., singing loud

**31**  Fur-trading company founded in 1670.
**32**  Canada.
**33**  The North West Company was formed in 1783, and merged with the Hudson's Bay Company in 1821.
**34**  A common name.
**35**  Vesper sparrow (*Pooecetes gramineus*), which Thoreau also called by the names grass-bird, grass-finch, and white-in-tail.
**36**  The Thoreau family home from 1845 to 1850, so named for its location west of the railroad depot, in an area of town called "Texas" because of its distance from the mill-dam. Thoreau and his father built the house in September 1844 on a three-quarter-acre plot. The Thoreaus continued to own the house, renting it out after moving to the Yellow house on Main Street.
**37**  Approximately two miles north of Well Meadow.

and clear and incessantly. It sings with a pleasing deliberation, contrasting with the spring vivacity of the song sparrow, whose song many would confound it with. It comes to revive with its song the dry uplands and pastures and grass-fields about the skirts of villages. Only think how finely our life is furnished in all its details,— sweet wild birds provided to fill its interstices with song! It is provided that while we are employed in our corporeal, or intellectual, or other, exercises we shall be lulled and amused or cheered by the singing of birds. When the laborer rests on his spade to-day, the sun having just come out, he is not left wholly to the mercy of his thoughts, nature is not a mere void to him, but he can hardly fail to hear the pleasing and encouraging notes of some newly arrived bird. The strain of the grass finch is very likely to fall on his ear and convince him, whether he is conscious of it or not, that the world is beautiful and life a fair enterprise to engage in. It will make him calm and contented. If you yield for a moment to the impressions of sense, you hear some bird giving expression to its happiness in a pleasant strain. We are provided with singing birds and with ears to hear them. What an institution that! Nor are we obliged to catch and cage them, nor to be bird-fanciers in the common sense. Whether a man's work be hard or easy, whether he be happy or unhappy, a bird is appointed to sing to a man while he is at his work.

*April 24.* There is a season for everything,[38] and we do not notice a given phenomenon except at that season, if, indeed, it can be called the same phenomenon at any other season. There is a time to watch the ripples on Ripple Lake,[39] to look for arrowheads, to study the rocks and lichens, a time to walk on sandy deserts; and the observer of nature must improve these seasons as much as the farmer his. So boys fly kites and play ball or hawkie[40] at particular times all over the State. A wise man will know what game to play to-day, and play it. We must not be governed by rigid rules, as by the almanac, but let the season rule us. The moods and thoughts of man are revolving just as steadily and incessantly as nature's. Nothing must be postponed. Take time by the forelock. Now or never! You must live in the present, launch yourself on every wave, find your eternity in each moment. Fools stand on their island opportunities and look toward another land. There is no other land; there is no other life but this, or the like of this. Where the good husbandman is, there is the good soil. Take any other course, and life will be a succession of regrets. Let us see vessels sailing prosperously before the wind, and not simply stranded barks. There is no world for the penitent and regretful.

Dr. Bartlett[41] asked me what I found that was new these days, if I was still looking after the beautiful. I told him yes, and that I wished to hire two or three good observers.

*May 1.* We accuse savages of worshipping only the bad spirit, or devil, though they may distinguish both a good and a bad; but they regard only that one which they fear and worship the devil only. We too are savages in this, doing precisely the same thing. This occurred to me yesterday as I sat in the woods admiring the beauty of the blue butterfly. We are not chiefly interested in birds and insects, for example, as they are ornamental to the earth and cheering to man, but we spare the lives of the former only on condition that they eat more grubs than they do cherries, and the only account of the insects which the State encourages is of the "Insects *Injurious to Vegetation.*"[42] We too admit both a good and a bad spirit, but we worship chiefly the bad spirit, whom we

40  Field hockey.
41  Dr. Josiah Bartlett (1796–1878), physician in Concord for 57 years.
42  *A Report on the Insects of Massachusetts, Injurious to Vegetation* (1841), by Thaddeus William Harris (1795–1856), which Thoreau reviewed as part of his essay "Natural History of Massachusetts." Harris was the librarian of Harvard from 1831 to 1856 and lectured on natural history there from 1837 to 1842. Thoreau often appealed to him for help with questions of natural history.

**43** Asa Fitch's (1809–1878) *Reports on the Noxious, Beneficial, and Other Insects of New York,* 4 vols. (Albany: C. van Benthuysen, 1856–1867), first published as a series of 14 reports in *Transactions of the New York State Agricultural Society.*

**44** To appraise a gift, from the practice of evaluating the age of a horse by looking at its teeth.

**45** One of several references in Thoreau's writings to the Romantic notion that children stood closer to God than adults, as found in William Wordsworth's "Ode: Intimations of Immortality" (ll. 66–76):

> Heaven lies about us in our infancy!
> Shades of the prison-house begin to close
>     Upon the growing Boy,
> But He beholds the light, and whence it flows,
>     He sees it in his joy;
> The Youth, who daily farther from the east
>     Must travel, still is Nature's Priest,
>     And by the vision splendid
>     Is on his way attended;
> At length the Man perceives it die away,
> And fade into the light of common day.

**46** Allusion to Genesis, in which, after viewing his work during the days of Creation, "God saw that it was good."

**47** Probably the peninsula of Nahant, in Essex County, northeast of Boston, a popular beach area lined with summer cottages.

**48** Allusion to the Golden Rule, found in the New Testament—Matthew 5:44, 7:12, and Luke 6:31 ("And as ye would that men should do to you, do ye also to them likewise")—as well as in the Talmud, the Koran, the Analects of Confucius, and other religious and philosophical writings.

fear. We do not think first of the good but of the harm things will do us.

The catechism says that the chief end of man is to glorify God and enjoy him forever, which of course is applicable mainly to God as seen in his works. Yet the only account of its beautiful insects,—butterflies, etc.— which God has made and set before us which the State ever thinks of spending any money on is the account of those which are injurious to vegetation! This is the way we glorify God and enjoy him forever. Come out here and behold a thousand painted butterflies and other beautiful insects which people the air, then go to the libraries and see what kind of prayer and glorification of God is there recorded. Massachusetts has published her report on "Insects Injurious to Vegetation," and our neighbor the "Noxious Insects of New York."[43] We have attended to the evil and said nothing about the good. This is looking a gift horse in the mouth[44] with a vengeance. Children are attracted by the beauty of butterflies, but their parents and legislators deem it an idle pursuit. The parents remind me of the devil, but the children of God.[45] Though God may have pronounced his work good,[46] we ask, "Is it not poisonous?"

Science is inhuman. Things seen with a microscope begin to be insignificant. So described, they are as monstrous as if they should be magnified a thousand diameters. Suppose I should see and describe men and houses and trees and birds as if they were a thousand times larger than they are! With our prying instruments we disturb the balance and harmony of nature.

*July 11.* I hear that Mr. and Mrs. Such-a-one are "going to the beach"[47] for six weeks. What a failure and defeat this suggests their lives to be! Here they live, perchance, the rest of the year, trying to do as they would be done by[48] and to exercise charity of all kinds, and now at last, the parents not having realized their aspirations in the married state, and the misses now begun to be old maids without having found any match at all, succumb and slope to the beach for six weeks. Yet, so far from being felt to be a proof of failure in the lives of these Christians, it is thought to be the culminating-point of their activity. At length their season of activity is arrived, and they go to the beach, they energetically keep cool. They bathe daily and are blown on by the sea-breeze. This keeps their courage up for the labors of the year. This recess which the Sabbath-school teachers take! What if they were to abide, instead, with the caravan of sweltering pilgrims making their way over this Sahara to their Mecca?[49]

We hear at length that Miss Such-a-one, now well advanced in years, has at length shut up house and gone to the beach. Man servant and maid servant went long ago to prepare the way for her,—to get the bottles of all kinds ready. She has fought the good fight[50] here until at length no shield nor pretense will serve, and now she has gone to the beach, and have not her principles gone with her? She has flitted to Swallow Cave,[51] where, perchance, no duties lurk.

Ah, shall we not go to the beach after another fashion some of us one day? Think of the numbers who are imbeached by this time! How they flutter like devil's-needles[52] and butterflies commingled along our pontederia'd shores![53]

They have gone and left an empty house. The silver is cached, as prairie travellers leave behind provisions which they expect to return to. But the rent of the last house goes on nevertheless, and is to be added to the board at the great watering-place. So is it with every domicil we rent; the rent never ceases, but enlarges from year to year. They have gone to the beach to get a few pebbles, which help digestion[54] for the rest of the year.

49 The birthplace of Muhammad and thus sacred as a pilgrimage site for Muslims, but also used generally to mean a place that attracts many visitors.

50 Allusion to either 1 Timothy 6:12 ("Fight the good fight of faith, lay hold on eternal life, whereunto thou art also called") or 2 Timothy 4:7 ("I have fought a good fight, I have finished my course, I have kept the faith").

51 More often Swallow's Cave, in Nahant: a 70-foot cave or grotto in which Indians hid during King Philip's War in 1675.

52 Regional name (New England, western and upper-northern U.S.) for the dragonfly.

53 The shores of shallow waters of eastern North America were abundant in pickerel weed, the common name for *Pontederia cordata*, a freshwater plant having heart-shaped leaves and spikes of violet-blue flowers. On 28 September 1851 Thoreau wrote of the "pontederia, which apparently makes the mass of the weeds by the side of the river" [J 3:32–33], and on 12 July 1860 described it as "the only broad and thick leaf that rises above the water" [J 13:398].

54 Allusion to seed-eating birds that swallow small stones or gravel to enhance digestion.

**55** The melons Thoreau grew were celebrated each autumn in his annual melon party. Edward Emerson wrote in *Henry Thoreau Remembered by a Young Man:* "He especially loved to raise melons. I once went to a melon-party at his mother's with various people, young and old, where his work had furnished the handsome and fragrant pink or salmon fruit on which alone we were regaled; and he, the gardener, came in to help entertain the guests."

**56** Querl: a coil or twist.

*August 27.* All our life, *i. e.* the living part of it, is a persistent dreaming awake. The boy does not camp in his father's yard. That would not be adventurous enough, there are too many sights and sounds to disturb the illusion; so he marches off twenty or thirty miles and there pitches his tent, where stranger inhabitants are tamely sleeping in their beds just like his father at home, and camps in *their* yard, perchance. But then he dreams uninterruptedly that he is anywhere but where he is.

There are various ways in which you can tell if a watermelon is ripe.[55] If you have had your eye on the patch much from the first, and so know which formed first, you may presume that these will ripen soonest; or else you may incline to those which lie nearest the centre of the hill or root, as the oldest. Next the dull dead color and want of bloom are as good signs as any. Some look green and livid and have a very fog or mildew of bloom on them, like a fungus. These are as green as a leek through and through, and you'll find yourself in a pickle if you open one. Others have a dead dark greenness, the circulations being less rapid in their cuticles and their blooming period passed, and these you may safely bet on. If the vine is quite green and lively, the death of the quirl[56] at the root of the stem is almost a sure sign. For fear we should not discover it before, this is placed for a sign that there is redness and ripeness (if not mealiness) within. Of two otherwise similar, take that which yields the lowest tone when struck with your knuckles, *i. e.,* which is hollowest. The old or ripe ones sing base; the young, tenor or falsetto. Some use the violent method of pressing to hear if they crack within, but this is not to be allowed. Above all no tapping on the vine is to be tolerated, suggestive of a greediness which defeats its own purpose. It is very childish. One man told me that he could n't raise melons because his children would cut them all up. I thought that he convicted himself out of his own mouth,[57] and was not fit to be the ruler of a country according to Confucius' standard,[58] that at any rate he could not raise children in the way they should go. I once saw one of his boys astride of my earliest watermelon, which grew near a broken paling, and brandishing a case-knife over it, but I instantly blowed him off with my voice from a neighboring window before serious damage was done, and made such an ado about it as convinced him that he was not in his father's dominions, at any rate. This melon, though it lost some of its bloom then, grew to be a remarkably large and sweet one, though it bore to the last a triangular scar of the tap which the thief had designed on it.

*August 28.* I hear that some of the villagers were aroused from their sleep before light by the groans or bellowings of a bullock which an unskillful butcher was slaughtering at the slaughter-house.[59] What morning or Memnonian[60] music was that to ring through the quiet village? What did that clarion sing of? What a comment on our village life! Song of the dying bullock! But no doubt those who heard it inquired, as usual, of the butcher the next day, "What have you got to-day?" "Sirloin, good beefsteak, rattleran,"[61] etc.

*August 29.* I hear in the street this morning a goldfinch sing part of a sweet strain.

It is so cool a morning that for the first time I move into the entry to sit in the sun. But in this cooler weather I feel as if the fruit of my summer were hardening and maturing a little, acquiring color and flavor like the corn and other fruits in the field. When the very earliest ripe grapes begin to be scented in the cool nights, then, too,

**57** Possible allusion to Job 9:20: "If I justify myself, mine own mouth shall condemn me: if I say, I am perfect, it shall also prove me perverse," or Job 15:6: "Thine own mouth condemneth thee."
**58** Allusion to the precept found in Confucius (ca. 551–478 B.C.E.), *The Great Learning*, which Thoreau translated from the French translation in Jean-Pierre-Guillaume Pauthier's (1801–1873) *Confucius et Mencius* as: "Conduct yourself suitably toward the persons of your family, then you will be able to instruct and to direct a nation of men" [C 446].
**59** Thoreau wrote in an early journal entry: "In the midst of our village, as in most villages, there is a slaughter-house, and throughout the summer months, day and night, to the distance of half a mile, which embraces the greater part of the village, the air [is] filled with such scents as we instinctively avoid in a woodland walk; and doubtless, if our senses were once purified and educated by a simpler and truer life, we should not consent to live in such a neighborhood" [J 1:480–481].
**60** Associated with Memnon, a king of Ethiopia, son of Aurora and Tithonus, who was slain by Achilles in the Trojan War. According to Lemprière's *Bibliotheca Classica:* "The Æthiopians or Egyptians, over whom Memnon reigned, erected a celebrated statue to the honour of their monarch. This statue had the wonderful property of uttering a melodious sound every day, at sun-raising, like that which is heard at the breaking of the string of a harp when it is wound up. This was effected by the rays of the sun when they fell upon it."
**61** Sometimes rattle-ran, also called plate-piece: the lower or under half of the fore quarter of beef, used for corning.

**62**  Put a new nib, the point, onto a pen.

**63**  The first fruits of the season were considered the best and so were often consecrated. As stipulated in Exodus 23:19, the first fruits of the ground were offered unto God by biblical injunction: "Bring the best of the first-fruits of your soil to the house of the Lord your God."

**64**  Probably John Le Grosse, sometimes Legross (b. 1789), for whom Thoreau surveyed on 11, 12, and 17 January 1852, and who brought Thoreau "a quantity of red huckleberries" on 1 August 1853 [J 5:352].

**65**  Thoreau wrote on 25 August 1859, referring to the forthcoming muster: "The prospect is that Concord will not be herself that week. I fear it will be more like Discord. Thank fortune, the camps will be nearly 2 miles west of us; yet the *scamps* will be 'all over the lot.' The very anticipation of this muster has greatly increased the amount of travel past our house, for a month; & now, at last, whole houses have begun to roll that way" [C 555–556].

**66**  As there were several stores in Concord at this time, the specific store and storekeeper cannot be unidentified.

**67**  Nathaniel Prentice Banks (1816–1894; governor, 1858–1861).

the first cooler airs of autumn begin to waft my sweetness on the desert airs of summer. Now, too, poets nib their pens afresh.[62] I scent their first-fruits[63] in the cool evening air of the year. By the coolness the experience of the summer is condensed and matured, whether our fruits be pumpkins or grapes. Man, too, ripens with the grapes and apples.

*September 2.* I once did some surveying for a man who remarked, *but not till the job was done,* that he did not know when he should pay me.[64] I did not pay much heed to this, though it was unusual, supposing that he meant to pay me some time or other. But after a while he sent to me a quart of red huckleberries, and this I thought was ominous and he distinguished me altogether too much by this gift, since I was not his particular friend. I saw it was the first installment, which would go a great way toward being the last. In course of years he paid a part of the debt in money, and that is the last I have heard of it.

*September 8.* The 7th, 8th, and 9th, the State muster is held here.[65] The only observation I have to make is that Concord is fuller of dust and more uninhabitable than I ever knew it to be before. Not only the walls, fences, and houses are thickly covered with dust, but the fields and meadows and bushes; and the pads in the river for half a mile from the village are white with it. From a mile or two distant you see a cloud of dust over the town and extending thence to the muster-field. I went to the store the other day to buy a bolt for our front door, for, as I told the storekeeper,[66] the Governor[67] was coming here. "Aye," said he, "and the Legislature too." "Then I will take two bolts," said I. He said that there had been a steady demand for bolts and locks of late, for our protectors were coming. The surface of the roads for three to six inches in depth is a light and dry powder like ashes.

*September 14.* Like the fruits, when cooler weather and frosts arrive, we too are braced and ripened. When we shift from the shady to the sunny side of the house, and sit there in an extra coat for warmth, our green and leafy and pulpy thoughts acquire color and flavor, and perchance a sweet nuttiness at last, worth your cracking. Now all things suggest fruit and the harvest, and flowers look *late,* and for some time the sound of the flail has been heard in the barns.[68]

*September 16.* I am invited to take some party of ladies or gentlemen on an excursion,—to walk or sail, or the like,—but by all kinds of evasions I omit it, and am thought to be rude and unaccommodating therefore. They do not consider that the wood-path and the boat are my studio, where I maintain a sacred solitude and cannot admit promiscuous company. I will see them occasionally in an evening or at the table, however. They do not think of taking a child away from its school to go a-huckleberrying with them.[69] Why should not I, then, have my school and school hours to be respected? Ask me for a certain number of dollars if you will, but do not ask me for my afternoons.

*September 18.* Dr. Bartlett handed me a paper to-day, desiring me to subscribe for a statue to Horace Mann.[70] I declined, and said that I thought a man ought not any more to take up room in the world after he was dead. We shall lose one advantage of a man's dying if we are to have a statue of him forthwith. This is probably meant to be an opposition statue to that of Webster.[71] At this rate they will crowd the streets with them. A man will

**68** Often an autumn or winter sound, as in "A Winter Walk": "The imprisoning drifts increase the sense of comfort which the house affords, and in the coldest days we are content to sit over the hearth and see the sky through the chimney-top, enjoying the quiet and serene life that may be had in a warm corner by the chimney-side, or feeling our pulse by listening to the low of cattle in the street, or the sound of the flail in distant barns all the long afternoon" [W 5:182]. On 13 September 1858 he wrote: "From many a barn these days I hear the sound of the flail. For how many generations this sound will continue to be heard here! At least until they discover a new way of separating the chaff from the wheat" [J 11:158].

**69** In his incomplete lecture "Huckleberries," Thoreau wrote: "I well remember with what a sense of freedom and spirit of adventure I used to take my way across the fields with my pail, some years later, toward some distant hill or swamp, when dismissed for all day, and I would not now exchange such an expansion of all my being for all the learning in the world. Liberation and enlargement—such is the fruit which all culture aims to secure. I suddenly knew more about my books than if I had never ceased studying them. I found myself in a schoolroom where I could not fail to see and hear things worth seeing and hearing—where I could not help getting my lesson—for my lesson came to me. Such experience often repeated, was the chief encouragement to go to the Academy and study a book at last" [H 27–28].

**70** Horace Mann (1796–1859) established the first public school in the United States in nearby Lexington in 1839. As secretary of the nation's first state board of education from 1837 to 1848 Mann advocated for commonly controlled nonreligious schools attended by all people regardless of race, class, or sex, as an equalizer of educational opportunities.

**71** By Hiram Powers (1805–1873) and installed at the Massachusetts State House in 1859.

have to add a clause to his will, "No statue to be made of me." It is very offensive to my imagination to see the dying stiffen into statues at this rate. We should wait till their bones begin to crumble—and then avoid too near a likeness to the living.

*September 24.* A man must attend to Nature closely for many years to know when, as well as where, to look for his objects, since he must always anticipate her a little. Young men have not learned the phases of Nature; they do not know what constitutes a year, or that one year is like another. I would know when in the year to expect certain thoughts and moods, as the sportsman knows when to look for plover.

*October 3.* Looking from the hog-pasture over the valley of Spencer Brook[72] westward, we see the smoke rising from a huge chimney above a gray roof amid the woods, at a distance, where some family is preparing its evening meal. There are few more agreeable sights than this to the pedestrian traveller. No cloud is fairer to him than that little bluish one which issues from the chimney. It suggests all of domestic felicity beneath. There beneath, we suppose, that life is lived of which we have only dreamed. In our minds we clothe each unseen inhabitant with all the success, with all the serenity, which we can conceive of. If old, we imagine him serene; if young, hopeful. Nothing can exceed the perfect peace which reigns there. We have only to see a gray roof with its plume of smoke curling up amid the trees to have this faith. There we suspect no coarse haste or bustle, but serene labors which proceed at the same pace with the declining day. *There* is no hireling in the barn nor in the kitchen. Why does any distant prospect ever charm us? Because we instantly and inevitably imagine a life to be lived there such as is not lived elsewhere, or where we are. We presume that success is the rule. We forever carry a perfect sampler in our minds. Why are distant valleys, why lakes, why mountains in the horizon, ever fair to us? Because we realize for a moment that they may be the home of man, and that man's life may be in harmony with them. Shall I say that we thus forever delude ourselves? We do not suspect that *that* farmer goes to the depot with his milk. *There* the milk is not watered. We are constrained to imagine a life in harmony with the scenery and the hour. The sky and clouds, and the earth itself, with their beauty forever preach to us, saying, Such an abode we offer you, to such and such a life we encourage you. *There* is not haggard poverty and harassing debt. There is not intemperance, moroseness, meanness, or vulgarity. Men go about sketching, painting landscapes, or writing verses which celebrate man's opportunities. To go into an actual farmer's family at evening, see the tired laborers come in from their day's work thinking of their wages, the sluttish[73] help in the kitchen and sink-room,[74] the indifferent stolidity and patient misery which only the spirits of the youngest children rise above,—that suggests one train of thoughts. To look down on that roof from a distance in an October evening, when its smoke is ascending peacefully to join the kindred clouds above,— that suggests a different train of thoughts. We think that we see these fair abodes and are elated beyond all speech, when we see only our own roofs, perchance. We are ever busy hiring house and lands and peopling them in our imaginations. *There* is no beauty in the sky, but in the eye that sees it. Health, high spirits, serenity, these are the great landscape-painters. Turners, Claudes, Rembrandts[75] are nothing to them. We never see any beauty but as the garment of some virtue. Men love to walk in those picture-galleries still, because they have not quite forgotten their early dreams. When I see only the roof of a house above the woods and do not know whose it is, I

73 Careless of dress and neatness; slovenly.
74 Room containing a wooden sink from which water was carried outside through a drainpipe.
75 Joseph Mallord William Turner, Claude Lorrain (1600–1682), and Rembrandt van Rijn (1606–1669).

**76** Cf. 1851 note 69.

**77** To bear the charges or burden of holding or having, as here, to hold a mortgage.

**78** Allusion to the Faust legend, most well known through Goethe's *Faust* and Christopher Marlowe's (1564–1593) *The Tragical History of Doctor Faustus*, wherein Faust signs away his soul to the devil in exchange for knowledge.

**79** Similarly, Thoreau wrote in an early journal entry on the way to approach God: "It is only by forgetting yourself that you draw near to him" [J 2:3].

presume that one of the worthies of the world dwells beneath it, and for a season I am exhilarated at the thought. I would fain sketch it that others may share my pleasure. But commonly, if I see or know the occupant, I am affected as by the sight of the almshouse or hospital.

Consider the infinite promise of a man, so that the sight of his roof at a distance suggests an idyll or pastoral, or of his grave an Elegy in a Country Churchyard.[76] How all poets have idealized the farmer's life! What graceful figures and unworldly characters they have assigned to them! Serene as the sky, emulating nature with their calm and peaceful lives. As I come by a farmer's to-day, the house of one who died some two years ago, I see the decrepit form of one whom he had engaged to "carry through,"[77] taking his property at a venture, feebly tying up a bundle of fagots with his knee on it, though time is fast loosening the bundle that he is. When I look down on that roof I am not reminded of the mortgage which the village bank has on that property,—that that family long since sold itself to the devil and wrote the deed with their blood.[78] I am not reminded that the old man I see in the yard is one who has lived beyond his calculated time, whom the young one is merely "carrying through" in fulfillment of his contract; that the man at the pump is watering the milk. I am not reminded of the idiot that sits by the kitchen fire.

*October 4.* It is only when we forget all our learning that we begin to know.[79] I do not get nearer by a hair's breadth to any natural object so long as I presume that I have an introduction to it from some learned man. To conceive of it with a total apprehension I must for the thousandth time approach it as something totally strange. If you would make acquaintance with the ferns you must forget your botany. You must get rid of what is commonly called *knowledge* of them. Not a single scientific term or distinction is the least to the purpose, for you would fain perceive something, and you must approach the object totally unprejudiced. You must be aware that *no thing* is what you have taken it to be. In what book is this world and its beauty described? Who has plotted the steps toward the discovery of beauty? You have got to be in a different state from common. Your greatest success will be simply to perceive that such things are, and you will have no communication to make to the Royal Society.[80] If it were required to know the position of the fruit-dots or the character of the indusium,[81] nothing could be easier than to ascertain it; but if it is required that you be affected by ferns, that they amount to anything, signify anything, to you, that they be another sacred scripture and revelation to you, helping to redeem your life, this end is not so surely accomplished. In the one case, you take a sentence and analyze it, you decide if it is printed in large primer or small pica;[82] if it is long or short, simple or compound, and how many clauses it is composed of; if the i's are all dotted, or some for variety without dots; what the color and composition of the ink and the paper; and it is considered a fair or mediocre sentence accordingly, and you assign its place among the sentences you have seen and kept specimens of. But as for the meaning of the sentence, that is as completely overlooked as if it had none. This is the Chinese, the Aristotelean, method.[83] But if you should ever perceive the meaning you would disregard all the rest. So far science goes, and it punctually leaves off there, — tells you finally where it is to be found and its synonyms, and rests from its labors.

*October 15.* Each town should have a park, or rather a primitive forest, of five hundred or a thousand acres, where a stick should never be cut for fuel, a common

**80** The Royal Society was first incorporated in 1662 as the Royal Society of London for Improving Natural Knowledge, having been founded in 1660 by a group of natural philosophers who had been meeting since the mid-1640s to promote scientific discussion.

**81** On ferns, a thin membrane covering immature spore clusters, which are also known as fruit dots.

**82** Type sizes: great primer being 18 points, and small pica 12 points.

**83** On descriptive or scientific methods that are, like Aristotle's definition of art, "the work without the wood" [W 1:386], cf. 13 October 1860: "In a sense you have got nothing new thus, for every object that we see mechanically is mechanically daguerreotyped on our eyes, but a true description growing out of the perception and appreciation of it is itself a new fact, never to be daguerreotyped, indicating the highest quality of the plant, — its relation to man, — of far more importance than any merely medicinal quality that it may possess, or be thought to-day to possess."

84 Land set aside for the use and benefit of the ministers of a town.

85 Also called Lily Bay: on the west side of the Sudbury River, approximately a quarter mile south of the railroad.

possession forever, for instruction and recreation. We hear of cow-commons and ministerial lots,[84] but we want *men*-commons and lay lots, inalienable forever. Let us keep the New World *new,* preserve all the advantages of living in the country. There is meadow and pasture and wood-lot for the town's poor. Why not a forest and huckleberry-field for the town's rich? All Walden Wood might have been preserved for our park forever, with Walden in its midst, and the Easterbrooks Country, an unoccupied area of some four square miles, might have been our huckleberry-field. If any owners of these tracts are about to leave the world without natural heirs who need or deserve to be specially remembered, they will do wisely to abandon their possession to all, and not will them to some individual who perhaps has enough already. As some give to Harvard College or another institution, why might not another give a forest or huckleberry-field to Concord? A town is an institution which deserves to be remembered. We boast of our system of education, but why stop at schoolmasters and schoolhouses? We are all schoolmasters, and our schoolhouse is the universe. To attend chiefly to the desk or schoolhouse while we neglect the scenery in which it is placed is absurd. If we do not look out we shall find our fine schoolhouse standing in a cow-yard at last.

*October 16.* When I get to Willow Bay[85] I see the new musquash-houses erected, conspicuous on the now nearly leafless shores. To me this is an important and suggestive sight, as, perchance, in some countries new haystacks in the yards; as to the Esquimaux the erection of winter houses. I remember this phenomenon annually for thirty years. A more constant phenomenon here than the new haystacks in the yard, for they were erected here probably before man dwelt here and may still be erected here when man has departed. For thirty years I have annually observed, about this time or earlier, the freshly erected winter lodges of the musquash along the riverside, reminding us that, if we have no gypsies, we have a more indigenous race of furry, quadrupedal men maintaining their ground in our midst still. This may not be an annual phenomenon to you. It may not be in the Greenwich almanac or ephemeris,[86] but it has an important place in my Kalendar.[87] So surely as the sun appears to be in Libra or Scorpio, I see the conical winter lodges of the musquash rising above the withered pontederia and flags. There will be some reference to it, by way of parable or otherwise, in *my* New Testament. Surely, it is a defect in our Bible that it is not truly ours, but a Hebrew Bible. The most pertinent illustrations for us are to be drawn, not from Egypt or Babylonia, but from New England.

Talk about learning our *letters* and being *literate!* Why, the roots of *letters* are *things.* Natural objects and phenomena are the original symbols or types which express our thoughts and feelings,[88] and yet American scholars, having little or no root in the soil, commonly strive with all their might to confine themselves to the imported symbols alone. All the true growth and experience, the living speech, they would fain reject as "Americanisms."[89] It is the old error, which the church, the state, the school ever commit, choosing darkness rather than light, holding fast to the old and to tradition. A more intimate knowledge, a deeper experience, will surely originate a word. When I really know that our river pursues a serpentine course to the Merrimack, shall I continue to describe it by referring to some other river no older than itself which is like it, and call it a *meander?* It is no more *meandering* than the Meander[90] is *musketaquidding.*[91] As well sing of the nightingale here

**86** *The Nautical Almanac and Astronomical Ephemeris* first published by Astronomer Royal of England in 1767, or its American equivalent, *The American Ephemeris and Nautical Almanac,* first published by the U.S. Naval Observatory in 1852.
**87** A calendar of nature (cf. 1851 note 20), so named after John Evelyn's *Kalendarium Hortense: or, Gard'ners Almanac.* Cf. 4 December 1856 on Thoreau's efforts to track "when plants first blossomed and leafed."
**88** In *Nature* Emerson wrote: "Language is a third use which Nature subserves to man. Nature is the vehicle, and in a simple, double, and threefold degree. 1. Words are signs of natural facts. 2. Particular natural facts are symbols of particular spiritual facts. 3. Nature is the symbol of spirit."
**89** Probable reference to John Russell Bartlett's (1805–1886) *Dictionary of Americanisms,* published in 1848.
**90** A winding river in Asia Minor (now the river Mendere), compared to the Minoan labyrinth in Ovid's (43 B.C.E.–17 C.E.) *Metamorphoses* (8:213–221):

> He confounds his worke with sodaine stops
>     and stayes,
> And with the great uncertaintie of sundrie
>     winding wayes
> Leades in and out, and to and fro, at divers
>     doores astray.
> And as with trickling streame the Brooke
>     Maeander seemes to play
> In Phrygia, and with doubtfull race runnes
>     counter to and fro,
> And meeting with himselfe doth looke If all his
>     streame or no
> Come after, and retiring *eft* cleane backward to
>     his spring
> And marching eft to open Sea as streight as
>     any string,
> Indenteth with reversed streame.

**91** Cf. 1840s note 50.

**92** A recurring period of time used as a larger unit in reckoning events, such as the 28-year solar cycle, the 19-year lunar cycle, or the 15-year cycle of tax assessment called the Roman Indiction.

**93** A day or period of religious celebration or feasting, occurring on a specific day of the week succeeding a certain day of the month or phase of the moon.

**94** An annual forty-day period of fasting and penitence, beginning with Ash Wednesday and continuing till Easter, observed from very early times in the Christian church in commemoration of the forty-day fast of Jesus (Matthew 4:2).

**95** British royal appointment established by Charles II (1630–1685), initially to study the stars as a method toward perfecting the art of navigation.

as the Meander. What if there were a tariff on words, on language, for the encouragement of home manufactures? Have we not the genius to coin our own? Let the schoolmaster distinguish the true from the counterfeit.

They go on publishing the "chronological cycles"[92] and "movable festivals of the Church"[93] and the like from mere habit, but how insignificant are these compared with the annual phenomena of your life, which fall within your experience! The signs of the zodiac are not nearly of that significance to me that the sight of a dead sucker in the spring is. That is the occasion for an *immovable festival* in my church. Another kind of Lent[94] then begins in my thoughts than you wot of. I am satisfied then to live on fish alone for a season.

Men attach a false importance to celestial phenomena as compared with terrestrial, as if it were more respectable and elevating to watch your neighbors than to mind your own affairs. The nodes of the stars are not the knots we have to untie. The phenomena of our year are one thing, those of the almanac another. For October, for instance, instead of making the sun enter the sign of the scorpion, I would much sooner make him enter a musquash-house. Astronomy is a fashionable study, patronized by princes, but not fungi. "Royal Astronomer."[95] The snapping turtle, too, must find a place among the constellations, though it may have to supplant some doubtful characters already there. If there is no place for him overhead, he can serve us bravely underneath, supporting the earth.

*October 17.* What I put into my pocket, whether berry or apple, generally has to keep company with an arrowhead or two. I hear the latter chinking against a key as I walk. These are the perennial crop of Concord fields. If they were sure it would pay, we should see farmers raking the fields for them.

*October 18.* Why can we not oftener refresh one another with original thoughts? If the fragrance of the dicksonia fern is so grateful and suggestive to us,[96] how much more refreshing and encouraging—re-creating—would be fresh and fragrant thoughts communicated to us fresh from a man's experience and life! I want none of his pity, nor sympathy, in the common sense, but that he should emit and communicate to me his essential fragrance, that he should not be forever repenting and going to church (when not otherwise sinning), but, as it were, going a-huckleberrying in the fields of thought, and enrich all the world with his visions and his joys.

Why do you flee so soon, sir, to the theatres, lecture-rooms, and museums of the city? If you will stay here awhile I will promise you strange sights. You shall walk on water;[97] all these brooks and rivers and ponds shall be your highway. You shall see the whole earth covered a foot or more deep with purest white crystals, in which you slump or over which you glide, and all the trees and stubble glittering in icy armor.

*October 19.*[98] The brutish, thick-skinned herd, who do not know a *man* by sympathy, make haste home from their ballot-boxes and churches to their Castles of Indolence,[99] perchance to cherish their valor there with some nursery talk of knights and dragons. A whole nation will for ages cling to the memory of its Arthur,[100] or other imaginary hero, who perhaps never assailed its peculiar institution or sin, and, being imaginary, never failed, when they are themselves the very freebooters and craven knights whom he routed, while they forget their real heroes.

I have seen no hearty approbation for this man in any Abolition journal; as if it were not consistent with their policy to express it, or maybe they did not feel it. And as

96  On 24 September 1859 Thoreau wrote: "To my senses the dicksonia fern has the most wild and primitive fragrance, quite unalloyed and untamable, such as no human institutions give out,—the early morning fragrance of the world, antediluvian, strength and hope imparting. They who scent it can never faint" [J 12:349].

97  Allusion to Matthew 14:28–29: "And Peter answered him and said, Lord, if it be thou, bid me come unto thee on the water. And he said, Come. And when Peter was come down out of the ship, he walked on the water, to go to Jesus."

98  Thoreau's notes on John Brown (1800–1859) begin on this date. He used most of them in "A Plea for John Brown," the first public statement in support of Brown, which he delivered in Concord on 30 October and repeated in Boston on 1 November. Brown was captured on 18 October following his raid two days earlier on the federal arsenal at Harper's Ferry, Virginia. There were erroneous newspaper accounts that Brown had been killed at the time of his capture.

99  Allusion to James Thomson's (1700–1748) allegorical poem *The Castle of Indolence.*

100  Legendary king of the Britons who organized the Knights of the Round Table at Camelot.

**101** Thoreau praised the *New York Tribune* on 30 January 1852 for such an action: "It is an encouraging bit of news, when I read in the *Weekly Tribune,* appended to an article on 'The Liquor Groceries' which had appeared in the Daily . . . that the worst of those establishments had refused to receive the *Tribune,* being offended by its disclosures" [J 3:250].

**102** Thoreau wrote a few days later, on 17 November: "I have been so absorbed of late in Captain Brown's fate as to be surprised whenever I detected the old routine running still,—met persons going about their affairs indifferent. It appeared strange to me that the little dipper should be still diving in the river as of yore; and this suggested that this grebe might be diving here when Concord shall be no more. Any affecting human event may blind our eyes to natural objects" [J 12:447–448].

for the herd of newspapers, I do not chance to know one in the country that will deliberately print anything that will ultimately and permanently reduce the number of its subscribers.[101] They do not believe it would be *expedient.* If we do not say pleasant things, they argue, nobody will attend to us. And so they are like some auctioneers, who sing an obscene song in order to draw a crowd around them.

If Christ should appear on earth he would on all hands be denounced as a mistaken, misguided man, insane and crazed.

*October 21.* I do not complain of any tactics that are effective of good, whether one wields the quill or the sword, but I shall not think him mistaken who quickest succeeds to liberate the slave. I will judge of the tactics by the fruits.

*November 12.* I do not know how to distinguish between our waking life and a dream. Are we not always living the life that we imagine we are? Fear creates danger, and courage dispels it.

There was a remarkable sunset, I think the 25th of October. The sunset sky reached quite from west to east, and it was the most varied in its forms and colors of any that I remember to have seen. At one time the clouds were most softly and delicately rippled, like the ripplemarks on sand. But it was hard for me to see its beauty then, when my mind was filled with Captain Brown.[102] So great a wrong as his fate implied overshadowed all beauty in the world.

*Nov. 26.* P.M. I find, sometimes, after I have been lotting off a large wood-lot for auction, that I have been cutting new paths to walk in. I cut lines an inch or two long in arbitrary directions,[103] in and around some dense wood-lot which perhaps is not crossed once a month by any mortal, nor has been for thirty or fifty years, and thus I open to myself new works,—enough in a lot of forty acres to occupy me for an afternoon. A forty-acre wood-lot which otherwise would not detain a walker more than half an hour, being thus opened and carved out, will entertain him for half a day.

In this case there was a cultivated field here[104] some thirty years ago, but, the wood being suffered to spring up, from being open and revealed this part of the earth became a covert and concealed place. Excepting an occasional hunter who crossed it maybe once in several months, nobody has walked there, nobody has pene-trated its recesses. The walker habitually goes round it, or follows the single cart-path that winds through it. Woods, both the primitive and those which are suffered to spring up in cultivated fields, thus preserve the mys-tery of nature. How private and sacred a place a grove thus becomes!—merely because its denseness excludes man. It is worth the while to have these thickets on vari-ous sides of the town, where the rabbit lurks and the jay builds its nest.

*November 28.* P.M. To Ebby Hubbard's[105] Wood.

Goodwin[106] tells me that Therien,[107] who lives in a shanty of his own building and alone in Lincoln, uses for a drink only checkerberry-tea.[108] (Goodwin also called it "ivory-leaf.") Is it not singular that probably only one *tea*-drinker in this neighborhood should use for his bev-erage a plant which grows here? Therien, really drinking his checkerberry-tea from motives of simplicity or econ-omy and saying nothing about it, deserves well of his country. As he does now, we may all do at last.

103 An inch on his survey or plan.
104 The Colburn Farm, between Sudbury Road and Clamshell Hill, approximately a half mile south of the railroad tracks on the west bank of the Sudbury River.
105 Ebenezer Hubbard (1782–1871).
106 John Goodwin: cf. 1853 note 132.
107 Alek Therien (1812–1885), the Canadian woodchopper Thoreau described in the "Visitors" chapter of *Walden:* "He interested me because he was so quiet and solitary and so happy withal; a well of good humor and contentment which over-flowed at his eyes. His mirth was without alloy. . . . He was so simply and naturally humble—if he can be called humble who never aspires—that humility was no distinct quality in him, nor could he conceive of it. . . . I loved to sound him on the various reforms of the day, and he never failed to look at them in the most simple and practical light. He had never heard of such things before. Could he do without factories? I asked. He had worn the home-made Vermont gray, he said, and that was good. Could he dispense with tea and coffee? Did this country afford any beverage beside water? He had soaked hemlock leaves in water and drank it, and thought that was better than water in warm weather" [Wa 141–143]. Ac-cording to Edward Emerson the name Therien, despite its French origin, was pronounced as if it were English: Thē´rĭ-ĕn.
108 Thoreau had tried checkerberry tea on 30 July 1857 in Maine: "Asking for a new kind of tea, he made us some, pretty good, of the checker-berry (*Gaultheria procumbens*), which covered the ground, dropping a little bunch of it tied up with cedar bark into the kettle" [W 3:301].

109 Concord farmer who lived on Sudbury Road.
110 Wood chips from an area where wood has been chopped.

There is scarcely a wood of sufficient size and density left now for an owl to haunt in, and if I hear one hoot I may be sure where he is.

Goodwin is cutting out a few cords of dead wood in the midst of Ebby Hubbard's old lot. This has been Hubbard's practice for thirty years or more, and so, it would seem, they are all dead before he gets to them.

Saw Abel Brooks[109] there with a half-bushel basket on his arm. He was picking up chips[110] on his and neighboring lots; had got about two quarts of old and blackened pine chips, and with these was returning home at dusk more than a mile. Such a petty quantity as you would hardly have gone to the end of your yard for, and yet he said that he had got more than two cords of them at home, which he had collected thus and sometimes with a wheelbarrow. He had thus spent an hour or two and walked two or three miles in a cool November evening to pick up two quarts of pine chips scattered through the woods. He evidently takes real satisfaction in collecting his fuel, perhaps gets more heat of all kinds out of it than any man in town. He is not reduced to taking a walk for exercise as some are. It is one thing to *own* a wood-lot as he does who perambulates its bounds almost daily, so as to have worn a path about it, and another to own one as many another does who hardly knows where it is. Evidently the quantity of chips in his basket is not essential; it is the chippy idea which he pursues. It is to him an unaccountably pleasing occupation. And no doubt he loves to see his pile grow at home.

Think how variously men spend the same hour in the same village! The lawyer sits talking with his client in the twilight; the trader is weighing sugar and salt; while Abel Brooks is hastening home from the woods with his basket half full of chips. I think I should prefer to be with Brooks. He was literally as smiling as a basket of chips. A basket of chips, therefore, must have been regarded as a singularly pleasing (if not pleased) object.

*December 3.* Rode with a man[111] this forenoon who said that if he did not clean his teeth when he got up, it made him sick all the rest of the day, but he had found by late experience that when he had not cleaned his teeth for several days they cleaned themselves. I assured him that such was the general rule,—that when from any cause we were prevented from doing what we had commonly thought indispensable for us to do, things *cleaned* or took care of themselves.

X was betrayed by his eyes, which had a glaring film over them and no serene depth into which you could look. Inquired particularly the way to Emerson's and the distance, and when I told him, said he knew it as well as if he saw it. Wished to turn and proceed to his house. Told me one or two things which he asked me not to tell Sanborn.[112] Said, "I know I am insane,"—and I knew it too. Also called it "nervous excitement." At length, when I made a certain remark, he said, "I don't know but *you* are Emerson; are you? You look somewhat like him." He said as much two or three times, and added once, "But then Emerson would n't lie." Finally put his questions to me, of Fate, etc., etc., as if I *were* Emerson. Getting to the woods, I remarked upon them, and he mentioned my name, but never to the end suspected who his companion was. Then "proceeded to business,"—"since the time was short,"—and put to me the questions he was going to put to Emerson. His insanity exhibited itself chiefly by his incessant excited talk, scarcely allowing me to interrupt him, but once or twice apologizing for his behavior. What he said was for the most part connected and sensible enough.

When I hear of John Brown and his wife weeping at length,[113] it is as if the rocks sweated.

111 At the time of this entry Thoreau was unaware that his companion (called "X" in the next paragraph) was Francis Jackson Merriam (1837–1865), one of John Brown's men escaping to Canada. Sanborn recounted the story in the *Harvard Register* (April 1881): "Francis Jackson Merriam, of Boston, who had joined Brown's band in Maryland a few weeks before, had escaped with Owen Brown, and, after a little rest in Canada, had come back to Boston to raise another expedition against the slave-holders. He was quite unfit to lead or even join in such an affair, being weak in body and almost distracted in mind; and I insisted that he should return at once to Canada . . . and he finally, before I left him, agreed to go back that night, by a train on the Fitchburg Railroad. But by accident he took another train which ran no farther than Concord, and early in the evening repaired to my house there, and was received by my sister in my absence. A reward of several thousand dollars had been offered for his arrest, and it was unsafe, even in Massachusetts, for him to be seen. Nor did I think it well to see him again, lest I should be questioned about him. I therefore obtained from Mr. Emerson the loan of his horse and covered wagon, to be ready at sunrise next morning; then went to Mr. Thoreau who lived near me, and asked him to drive the wagon from Mr. Emerson's to my house, take in a Mr. Lockwood (the name by which Merriam was then called,) and see that he was put on board the next train for Canada, at the South Acton station, four miles away. Thoreau readily consented, and early the next morning walked to Mr. Emerson's, found the horse harnessed, drove him to my door, and took in Merriam, under the name of 'Lockwood,' neither of them knowing who the other really was. Merriam was in a flighty state of mind, and though he had agreed to go back to Canada, and knew his own life depended on it, could not keep to that purpose. He insisted to Mr. Thoreau that he must see Mr. Emerson . . . and flung himself out of the wagon. What measures my friend took to get his passenger in again he never told me,

but I suspect some judicious force was used, accompanied by the grave, persuasive speech which was natural to Thoreau. At any rate, he drove on, brought his man in due season to South Acton, saw him on board the Canada train, returned the wagon to Mr. Emerson, (who knew nothing of its use, though suspecting it, and glad to promote such escapes,) and reported to me that 'Mr. Lockwood had taken passage for Montreal,' where he safely arrived the next day."

112  Sanborn was one of the Secret Six, a small group of Northern abolitionists offering financial support to Brown before his raid.

113  It is unclear where Thoreau got his information on Brown and his wife weeping. There were no published accounts of John and Mary Brown's final meeting at the time of Thoreau's journal entry, but it was described several days later, in the Staunton (Va.) *Spectator* of 6 December 1859, as "not a very affecting one. . . . On first meeting they kissed and affectionately embraced, and Mrs. Brown shed a few tears, but immediately checked her feelings.—They stood embraced and she sobbing for nearly five minutes, and he was apparently unable to speak. The prisoner only gave way for a moment and was soon calm and collected, and remained firm throughout the interview. At the close they shook hands but did not embrace, and as they parted he said, 'God bless you and the children.' Mrs. Brown replied, 'God have mercy on you,' and continued calm until she left the room, when she remained in tears a few moments and then prepared to depart." Although he may have heard an embellished account through Sanborn, who was in contact with the Brown family, there is no extant documentation to support this.

114  Unidentified.

*December 5.* Returning from the post-office at early candle-light, I noticed for the first time this season the peculiar effect of lights in offices and shops seen over the snowy streets, suggesting how withdrawn and inward the life in the former, how exposed and outward in the latter.

*December 8.* How is it that what is actually present and transpiring is commonly perceived by the common sense and understanding only, is bare and bald, without halo or the blue enamel of intervening air? But let it be past or to come, and it is at once idealized. As the man dead is spiritualized, so the fact remembered is idealized. It is a deed ripe and with the bloom on it. It is not simply the understanding now, but the imagination, that takes cognizance of it. The imagination requires a long range. It is the faculty of the poet to see present things as if, in this sense, also past and future, as if distant or universally significant. We do not know poets, heroes, and saints for our contemporaries, but we locate them in some far-off vale, and, the greater and better, the further off we are accustomed to consider them. We believe in spirits, we believe in beauty, but not now and here. They have their abode in the remote past or in the future.

*December 12.* There is a certain Irish woodchopper[114] who, when I come across him at his work in the woods in the winter, never fails to ask me what time it is, as if he were in haste to take his dinner-pail and go home. This is not as it should be. Every man, and the woodchopper among the rest, should love his work as much as the poet does his. All good political arrangements proceed on this supposition. If labor mainly, or to any considerable degree, serves the purpose of a police, to keep men out of mischief, it indicates a rottenness at the foundation of our community.

❧

I am inclined to think of late that as much depends on the state of the bowels as of the stars. As are your bowels, so are the stars.

*December 13.* My first true winter walk is perhaps that which I take on the river, or where I cannot go in the summer. It is the walk peculiar to winter, and now first I take it. I see that the fox too has already taken the same walk before me, just along the edge of the button-bushes, where not even he can go in the summer. We both turn our steps hither at the same time.

But how long can a man be in a mood to watch the heavens? That melon-rind arrangement,[115] so very common, is perhaps a confirmation of Wise the balloonist's statement that at a certain height there is a current of air moving from west to east.[116] Hence we so commonly see the clouds arranged in parallel columns in that direction.

What a spectacle the subtle vapors that have their habitation in the sky present these winter days! You have not only ever-varying forms of a given type of cloud, but various types at different heights or hours. It is a scene, for variety, for beauty and grandeur, out of all proportion to the attention it gets. Who watched the forms of the clouds over this part of the earth a thousand years ago? Who watches them to-day?

Now that the river is frozen we have a sky under our feet also.

*December 15.* Philosophy is a Greek word by good rights,[117] and it stands almost for a Greek thing. Yet some rumor of it has reached the commonest mind. Martial Miles,[118] who came to collect his wood bill to-day, said, when I objected to the small size of his wood, that it

**115** Cf. 21 December 1851: "To-night, as so many nights within the year, the clouds arrange themselves in the east at sunset in long converging bars, according to the simple tactics of the sky. It is the melon-rind jig. It would serve for a permanent description of the sunset. Such is the morning and such the evening, converging bars inclose the day at each end as within a melon rind, and the morning and evening are one day" [J 3:148].
**116** In *A System of Aeronautics, Comprehending Its Earliest Investigations, and Modern Practice and Art* (1850), John Wise wrote: "It is now beyond a doubt, in my mind established, *that a current from west to east in the atmosphere is constantly in motion* within the height of 12,000 feet above the ocean."
**117** From the Greek *philosophia,* from *philosophos,* lover of wisdom.
**118** Marshall Miles (1820–1890), farmer, also referred to in Thoreau's poem "The Old Marlborough Road": "Where sometimes Martial Miles / Singly files" [W 5:214].

**119** John Gerard (1545–1612), *Herball, or Generall Historie of Plantes*, first published in 1597. Thoreau's note: "*Vide* extracts from preface made in October, 1859." These extracts, research for his later unfinished natural history writings, were not transcribed into his journal.

**120** Boston bookseller and publisher owned by Charles Coffin Little (1799–1869) and James Brown (1800–1855), who formed a partnership in 1837.

was necessary to split wood fine in order to cure it well, that he had found that wood that was more than four inches in diameter would not dry, and moreover a good deal depended on the manner in which it was corded up in the woods. He piled his high and tightly. If this were not well done the stakes would spread and the wood lie loosely, and so the rain and snow find their way into it. And he added, "I have handled a good deal of wood, and I think that I understand the *philosophy* of it."

*December 16.* To Cambridge, where I read in Gerard's Herbal.[119] His admirable though quaint descriptions are, to my mind, greatly superior to the modern more scientific ones. He describes not according to rule but to his natural delight in the plants. He brings them vividly before you, as one who has seen and delighted in them. It is almost as good as to see the plants themselves. It suggests that we cannot too often get rid of the barren assumption that is in our science. His leaves are leaves; his flowers, flowers; his fruit, fruit. They are green and colored and fragrant. It is a man's knowledge added to a child's delight. Modern botanical descriptions approach ever nearer to the dryness of an algebraic formula, as if $x + y$ were = to a love-letter. It is the keen joy and discrimination of the child who has just seen a flower for the first time and comes running in with it to its friends. How much better to describe your object in fresh English words rather than in these conventional Latinisms! He has really seen, and smelt, and tasted, and reports his sensations.

Bought a book at Little & Brown's,[120] paying a ninepence more on a volume than it was offered me for elsewhere. The customer thus pays for the more elegant style of the store.

*December 19.* When a man is young and his constitution and body have not acquired firmness, *i. e.,* before

he has arrived at middle age, he is not an assured inhabitant of the earth, and his compensation is that he
is not quite earthy, there is something peculiarly tender
and divine about him. His sentiments and his weakness,
nay, his very sickness and the greater uncertainty of his
fate, seem to ally him to a noble race of beings, to whom
he in part belongs, or with whom he is in communication. The young man is a demigod; the grown man,
alas! is commonly a mere mortal. He is but half here, he
knows not the men of this world, the powers that be.
They know him not. Prompted by the reminiscence of
that other sphere from which he so lately arrived, his actions are unintelligible to his seniors. He bathes in light.
He is interesting as a stranger from another sphere. He
really thinks and talks about a larger sphere of existence
than this world. It takes him forty years to accommodate
himself to the carapax[121] of this world. This is the age
of poetry. Afterward he may be the president of a bank,
and go the way of all flesh.[122] But a man of settled views,
whose thoughts are few and hardened like his bones, is
truly mortal, and his only resource is to say his prayers.

***December 25.*** How different are men and women, *e. g.*
in respect to the adornment of their heads! Do you ever
see an old or jammed bonnet on the head of a woman
at a public meeting? But look at any assembly of men
with their hats on; how large a proportion of the hats
will be old, weather-beaten, and indented, but I think so
much the more picturesque and interesting! One farmer
rides by my door in a hat which it does me good to see,
there is so much character in it,—so much independence
to begin with, and then affection for his old friends,
etc., etc. I should not wonder if there were lichens on
it. Think of painting a hero in a bran-new[123] hat! The
chief recommendation of the Kossuth hat[124] is that it
looks old to start with, and almost as good as new to end

121 Carapace: the protective shell of a tortoise,
turtle, crab, or other crustaceous animal.
122 Allusion to 1 Kings 2:2 as translated in the
Douay-Rheims edition of the Bible: "I am going
the way of all flesh: take thou courage, and shew
thyself a man," although more commonly translated as "the way of all the earth." The phrase
was popularized in John Webster (ca. 1580–1634)
and Thomas Dekker's (1570–1632) *Westward Hoe*
(2.2): "I saw him now going the way of all flesh,"
although here it meant toward the kitchen.
123 More properly, brand new, although commonly spelled "bran new" in the 19th century,
from the 16th-century usage meaning fresh or
new from the fire.
124 Hat named after Lajos Kossuth (1802–1894),
Hungarian patriot who worked, unsuccessfully,
to achieve Hungarian independence from Austria
in the 1840s. *Scientific American* reported on 27
December 1851: "Since Kossuth came to New
York, the Kossuth hat has become quite fashionable. This is a low crowned hat with a small
black ostrich feather stuck at one side. . . . These
are made of felted wool, and allow gas to pass
from the head to escape freely. . . . Oldish people
of a sedate turn, although they would prefer the
'Kossuth hat,' do not like to adopt it just yet, from
a prudential fear of being conspicuous." The hat
was promoted by the New York merchant John
Nicholas Genin (1819–1878).

**125** Probable allusion to Alcott, "one of the last of the philosophers" [Wa 259].

**126** A popular phrase, particularly in London, of which Dickens wrote in *Household Words* (28 July 1855): "Who does not remember the curious cry 'What a shocking bad hat'?" Charles Mackay wrote in *Memoirs of Extraordinary Popular Delusions and the Madness of Crowds* (1852): "'*What a shocking bad hat!*' was the phrase that was next in vogue. No sooner had it become universal, than thousands of idle but sharp eyes were on the watch for the passenger whose hat showed any signs, however slight, of ancient service. Immediately the cry arose, and, like the war-whoop of the Indians, was repeated by a hundred discordant throats."

**127** Intellectual or literary woman, from the literary parties held in London around 1750 by three society ladies and later called the Blue Stocking Society. The name came from their custom of wearing casual rather than formal dress; when dressing informally, men at the time wore blue (actually gray worsted) stockings, rather than black silk. By the 19th century the term had become pejorative.

with. Indeed, it is generally conceded that a man does not look the worse for a somewhat dilapidated hat. But go to a lyceum and look at the bonnets and various other headgear of the women and girls,—who, by the way, keep their hats on, it being too dangerous and expensive to take them off!! Why, every one looks as fragile as a butterfly's wings, having just come out of a bandbox,—as it will go into a bandbox again when the lyceum is over. Men wear their hats for use; women theirs for ornament. I have seen the greatest philosopher[125] in the town with what the traders would call "a shocking bad hat"[126] on, but the woman whose bonnet does not come up to the mark is at best a "bluestocking."[127] The man is not particularly proud of his beaver and musquash, but the woman flaunts her ostrich and sable in your face.

***December 31.*** How vain to try to teach youth, or anybody, truths! They can only learn them after their own fashion, and when they get ready. I do not mean by this to condemn our system of education, but to show what it amounts to.

I think it will be found that he who speaks with most authority on a given subject is not ignorant of what has been said by his predecessors. He will take his place in a regular order, and substantially add his own knowledge to the knowledge of previous generations.

A man may be old and infirm. What, then, are the thoughts he thinks? what the life he lives? They and it are, like himself, infirm. But a man may be young, athletic, active, beautiful. Then, too, his thoughts will be like his person. They will wander in a living and beautiful world. If you are well, then how brave you are! How you hope! You are conversant with joy! A man thinks as well through his legs and arms as his brain. We exaggerate the importance and exclusiveness of the headquarters. Do you suppose they were a race of consumptives and dyspeptics who invented Grecian mythology and poetry? The poet's words are, "You would almost say the body thought!"[128] I quite say it. I trust we have a good body then.

128 Allusion to John Donne's (1572–1631) "The Second Anniversarie. Of the Progres of the Soule" (243–247):

> we understood
> Her by the sight, her pure and eloquent blood
> Spoke in her cheekes, and so distinctly
>     wrought,
> That one might almost say, her body thought,
> Shee, shee, thus richly, & largely hous'd, is
>     gone.

This poem was also quoted, in part, in Emerson's essay, "Love."

**1** Cf. 2 September 1856: "I think we may detect that some sort of preparation and faint expectation preceded every discovery we have made."
**2** Allusion to section 14 of book 6 of Aristotle's *The History of Animals*. On 26 December 1859 Thoreau wrote about Aristotle's work: "Aristotle, being almost if not quite the first to write systematically on animals, gives them, of course, only popular names, such as the hunters, fowlers, fishers, and farmers of his day used. He used no scientific terms. But he, having the priority and having, as it were, created science and given it its laws, those popular Greek names, even when the animal to which they were applied cannot be identified, have been in great part preserved and make those learned far-fetched and commonly unintelligible names of genera to-day, *e. g.* Ὀλοθούριον, etc., etc. His History of Animals has thus become a very storehouse of scientific nomenclature" [J 13:55].
**3** Rufus Merriam, sometimes Meriam (1801–1870), lived on Boston Road just past Old Bedford Road.

## 1860

AGE 42–43

*January 5.* A man receives only what he is ready to receive,[1] whether physically or intellectually or morally, as animals conceive at certain seasons their kind only. We hear and apprehend only what we already half know. If there is something which does not concern me, which is out of my line, which by experience or by genius my attention is not drawn to, however novel and remarkable it may be, if it is spoken, we hear it not, if it is written, we read it not, or if we read it, it does not detain us. Every man thus *tracks himself* through life, in all his hearing and reading and observation and travelling. His observations make a chain. The phenomenon or fact that cannot in any wise be linked with the rest which he has observed, he does not observe. By and by we may be ready to receive what we cannot receive now. I find, for example, in Aristotle something about the spawning, etc., of the pout and perch,[2] because I know something about it already and have my attention aroused; but I do not discover till very late that he has made other equally important observations on the spawning of other fishes, because I am not interested in those fishes.

*January 9.* I hear that Rufus Merriam,[3] a rich old farmer who lives in a large house, with a male housekeeper and no other family, gets up at three or four o'clock these winter mornings and milks seventeen cows regularly. When asked why he works so hard he answers that the poor are obliged to work hard. Only think, what a creature of fate he is, this old Jotun,[4] milking his seventeen cows though the thermometer goes down to −25°, and not knowing why he does it,—draining sixty-eight cows' teats in the dark of the coldest morning! Think how helpless a rich man who can only do as he has done, and as his neighbors do, one or all of them! What an account he will have to give of himself! He spent some time in a world, alternately cold and warm, and every winter morning, with lantern in hand, when the frost goblins were playing their tricks, he resolutely accomplished his task and milked his seventeen cows, while the man housekeeper prepared his breakfast! If this were original with him, he would be a hero to be celebrated in history. Think how tenaciously every man does his deed, of some kind or other, though it be idleness! He is rich, dependent on nobody, and nobody is dependent on him; has as good health as the average, at least, can do as he pleases, as we say. Yet he gravely rises every morning by candle-light, dons his cowhide boots and his frock, takes his lantern and wends to the barn and milks his seventeen cows, milking with one hand while he warms the other against the cow or his person. This is but the beginning of his day, and his Augean stable work.[5] So serious is the life he lives.

*January 25.* In keeping a journal of one's walks and thoughts it seems to be worth the while to record those phenomena which are most interesting to us at the time. Such is the weather. It makes a material difference whether it is foul or fair, affecting surely our mood and thoughts. Then there are various degrees and kinds of foulness and fairness. It may be cloudless, or there may be sailing clouds which threaten no storm, or it may be partially overcast. On the other hand it may rain, or snow, or hail, with various degrees of intensity. It may be a transient thunder-storm, or a shower, or a flurry of

4 In Norse mythology, one of a race of giants.
5 In Greek mythology, the fifth of Hercules' twelve labors was to clean the Augean stables in one day. The stalls, home to three thousand oxen, had not been cleaned for many years. He accomplished this labor by redirecting the course of two rivers through the stables. In *Walden* Thoreau used this image as a symbol of insurmountable, or unending, labor: "How many a poor immortal soul have I met well nigh crushed and smothered under its load, creeping down the road of life, pushing before it a barn seventy-five feet by forty, its Augean stables never cleansed, and one hundred acres of land, tillage, mowing, pasture, and wood-lot!" [Wa 3].

6 Sometimes, pan: a hard, impenetrable layer of soil.

snow, or it may be a prolonged storm of rain or snow. Or the sky may be overcast or rain-threatening. So with regard to temperature. It may be warm or cold. Above 40° is warm for winter. One day, at 38 even, I walk dry and it is good sleighing; the next day it may have risen to 48, and the snow is rapidly changed to slosh. It may be calm or windy. The finest winter day is a cold but clear and glittering one. There is a remarkable life in the air then, and birds and other creatures appear to feel it, to be excited and invigorated by it. Also warm and melting days in winter are inspiring, though less characteristic.

I will call the weather fair, if it does not threaten rain or snow or hail; foul, if it rains or snows or hails, or is so overcast that we expect one or the other from hour to hour. To-day it is fair, though the sky is slightly overcast, but there are *sailing* clouds in the southwest.

*January 27.* When you think that your walk is profitless and a failure, and you can hardly persuade yourself not to return, it is on the point of being a success, for then you are in that subdued and knocking mood to which Nature never fails to open.

*February 13.* Always you have to contend with the stupidity of men. It is like a stiff soil, a hard-pan.[6] If you go deeper than usual, you are sure to meet with a pan made harder even by the superficial cultivation. The stupid you have always with you. Men are more obedient at first to words than ideas. They mind names more than things. Read to them a lecture on "Education," naming that subject, and they will think that they have heard something important, but call it "Transcendentalism," and they will think it moonshine. Or halve your lecture, and put a psalm at the beginning and a prayer at the end of it and read it from a pulpit, and they will pronounce it good without thinking.

*February 17.* We cannot spare the very lively and lifelike descriptions of some of the old naturalists. They sympathize with the creatures which they describe. Edward Topsell in his translation of Conrad Gesner, in 1607, called "The History of Four-footed Beasts,"[7] says of the antelopes that "they are bred in India and Syria, near the river Euphrates," and then—which enables you to realize the living creature and its habitat—he adds, "and delight much to drink of the cold water thereof." The beasts which most modern naturalists describe do not *delight* in anything, and their water is neither hot nor cold. Reading the above makes you want to go and drink of the Euphrates yourself, if it is warm weather. I do not know how much of his spirit he owes to Gesner, but he proceeds in his translation to say that "they have horns growing forth of the crown of their head, which are very long and sharp; so that Alexander affirmed they pierced through the shields of his soldiers, and fought with them very irefully: at which time his company slew as he travelled to India, eight thousand five hundred and fifty, which great slaughter may be the occasion why they are so rare and seldom seen to this day."

Now here *something* is described at any rate; it is a real account, whether of a real animal or not. You can plainly see the horns which "grew forth" from their crowns, and how well that word "irefully" describes a beast's fighting! And then for the number which Alexander's men slew "as he travelled to India,"—and what a travelling was that, my hearers![8]—eight thousand five hundred and fifty, just the number you would have guessed after the thousands were given, and an easy one to remember too. He goes on to say that "their horns are great and made like a saw, and they with them can cut asunder the branches of osier or small trees, whereby it cometh to pass that many times their necks are taken in the twists of the falling boughs, whereat the beast with repining cry, bewrayeth himself

**7** Edward Topsell's (d. 1638) *History of Four-Footed Beasts,* based on Konrad Gesner's (1516–1565) *Historiae Animalium.* All quotations are from the first entry, "The Antalope," with minor variants.
**8** Cf. 1850 note 29.

**9** The illustration of an antelope from Topsell's *History of Four-Footed Beasts:*

The *ANTALOPE.*

**10** From Latin: a current of air, wind, or breath, the vital principle, life, soul.

to the hunters, and so is taken." The artist too has done his part equally well, for you are presented with a drawing of the beast with serrated horns, the tail of a lion, a cheek tooth (canine?) as big as a boar's, a stout front, and an exceedingly "ireful" look, as if he were facing all Alexander's army.[9]

Though some beasts are described in this book which have no existence as I can learn but in the imagination of the writers, they really have an existence there, which is saying not a little, for most of our modern authors have not imagined the actual beasts which they presume to describe.

They had an adequate idea of the wildness of beasts and of men, and in their descriptions and drawings they did not always fail when they *surpassed* nature.

*February 18.* I think that the most important requisite in describing an animal, is to be sure and give its character and spirit, for in that you have, without error, the sum and effect of all its parts, known and unknown. You must tell what it is to man. Surely the most important part of an animal is its *anima,*[10] its vital spirit, on which is based its character and all the peculiarities by which it most concerns us. Yet most scientific books which treat of animals leave this out altogether, and what they describe are as it were phenomena of dead matter. What is most interesting in a dog, for example, is his attachment to his master, his intelligence, courage, and the like, and not his anatomical structure or even many habits which affect us less.

If you have undertaken to write the biography of an animal, you will have to present to us the living creature, *i. e.,* a result which no man can understand, but only in his degree report the impression made on him.

Science in many departments of natural history does

not pretend to go beyond the shell; *i. e.,* it does not get to animated nature at all. A history of animated nature must itself be animated.

***February 23.*** A fact stated barely is dry. It must be the vehicle of some humanity in order to interest us. It is like giving a man a stone when he asks you for bread. Ultimately the moral is all in all, and we do not mind it if inferior truth is sacrificed to superior, as when the moralist fables and makes animals speak and act like men. It must be warm, moist, incarnated,—have been breathed on at least. A man has not seen a thing who has not felt it.

***March 3.*** When I read Topsell's account of the ichneumon eating his way out of the crocodile,[11] I think that, though it be not true in fact, it is very true in fancy, and it is no small gift to be able to give it so good a setting-forth. What a pity that our modern naturalists cannot tell their truths with half this zest and spirit!

***March 5.*** The old naturalists were so sensitive and sympathetic to nature that they could be surprised by the ordinary events of life. It was an incessant miracle to them, and therefore gorgons and flying dragons were not incredible to them. The greatest and saddest defect is not credulity, but our habitual forgetfulness that our science is ignorance.

***March 26.*** I had a suit once in which, methinks, I could glide across the fields unperceived half a mile in front of a farmer's windows. It was such a skillful mixture of browns, dark and light properly proportioned, with even some threads of green in it by chance. It was of loose texture and about the color of a pasture with patches of withered sweet-fern and lechea. I trusted a good deal to my invisibility in it when going across lots, and many a

11 Topsell's *History of Four-Footed Beasts* told of the ichneumon, a type of mongoose, which "entreth into the belly of the crocodile" and, "sitting close upon the liver of the Crocodile, and feeding full sweetly upon his intrails, until at last being satisfied, eateth out her own passage through the belly of her hoast."

12 Pedestrians.

13 Ankle-high shoes with elastic gussets in the sides.

14 Unidentified.

15 For Thoreau's description of his hat as a botany box, cf. 4 December 1856.

16 Coarse, undyed cloth made of homespun wool.

17 On 3 April federal marshals came to Concord to arrest Sanborn in regard to his connection with John Brown. A struggle ensued during which the marshals were driven off by a combination of physical and legal means. Sanborn, armed with a revolver, spent the night in the home of George Prescott. Thoreau elected to stay at Sanborn's house to protect Sanborn's sister, Sarah, in case the marshals returned.

time I was aware that to it I owed the near approach of wild animals.

No doubt my dusty and tawny cowhides surprise the street walkers[12] who wear patent-leather or Congress shoes,[13] but they do not consider how absurd such shoes would be in my vocation, to thread the woods and swamps in. Why should I wear *Congress* who walk alone, and not where there is any congress of my kind?

Channing was saying, properly enough, the other day, as we were making our way through a dense patch of shrub oak: "I suppose that those villagers think that we wear these old and worn hats with holes all along the corners for oddity, but Coombs,[14] the musquash hunter and partridge and rabbit snarer, knows better. He understands us. He knows that a new and square-cornered hat would be spoiled in one excursion through the shrub oaks."

The walker and naturalist does not wear a hat, or a shoe, or a coat, to be looked at, but for other uses.[15] When a citizen comes to take a walk with me I commonly find that he is lame,—disabled by his shoeing. He is sure to wet his feet, tear his coat, and jam his hat, and the superior qualities of my boots, coat, and hat appear. I once went into the woods with a party for a fortnight. I wore my old and common clothes, which were of Vermont gray.[16] They wore, no doubt, the best they had for such an occasion,—of a fashionable color and quality. I thought that they were a little ashamed of me while we were in the towns. They all tore their clothes badly but myself, and I, who, it chanced, was the only one provided with needles and thread, enabled them to mend them. When we came out of the woods I was the best dressed of any of them.

*April 4.* Lodged at Sanborn's last night after his *rescue,* he being away.[17]

*May 2.* A crowd of men seem to generate vermin even of the human kind. In great towns there is degradation undreamed of elsewhere,—gamblers, dog-killers, rag-pickers. Some live by robbery or by luck. There was the Concord muster (of last September).[18] I see still a well-dressed man carefully and methodically searching for money on the muster-fields, far off across the river. I turn my glass upon him and notice how he proceeds. (I saw them searching there in the fall till the snow came.) He walks regularly and slowly back and forth over the ground where the soldiers had their tents,—still marked by the straw,—with his head prone, and poking in the straw with a stick, now and then turning back or aside to examine something more closely. He is dressed, methinks, better than an average man whom you meet in the streets. How can he pay for his board thus? He dreams of finding a few coppers, or perchance a half-dime,[19] which have fallen from the soldiers' pockets, and no doubt he *will* find something of the kind, having dreamed of it,— having knocked, this door will be opened to him.[20]

*May 4.* When the locomotive was first introduced into Concord,[21] the cows and horses ran in terror to the other sides of their pastures as it passed along, and I suppose that the fishes in the river manifested equal alarm at first; but I notice (to-day, the 11th of May)[22] that a pickerel by Derby's Bridge,[23] poised in a smooth bay, did not stir perceptibly when the train passed over the neighboring bridge and the locomotive screamed remarkably loud. The fishes have, no doubt, got used to the sound.

*May 13.* Hear the *pebbly* notes of the frog.

*July 12.* The best way to drink, especially at a shallow spring, or one so sunken below the surface as to be difficult to reach, is through a tube. You can commonly find

**18** On 7–9 September 1859.
**19** A five-cent silver coin, which was replaced in 1866 by the copper and nickel coin popularly called a nickel.
**20** Allusion to Matthew 7:7–8 and Luke 11:9–10: "Knock, and it shall be opened unto you: For every one that asketh receiveth; and he that seeketh findeth; and to him that knocketh it shall be opened."
**21** In 1844.
**22** As he did here, Thoreau sometimes added to or continued an entry at a later date.
**23** Just south of where the railroad crosses the Assabet River.

24 On 30 April 1860 Thoreau wrote: "Surveying Emerson's wood-lot to see how much was burned near the end of March, I find that what I anticipated is exactly true,—that the fire did not burn hard on the northern slopes, there being then frost in the ground, and where the bank was very steep, say at angle of forty-five degrees, which was the case with more than a quarter of an acre, it did not run down at all, though no man hindered it" [J 13:268].

growing near a spring a hollow reed or weed of some kind suitable for this purpose, such as rue or touch-me-not or water saxifrage, or you can carry one in your pocket.

*July 20.* Emerson's lot that was burnt,[24] between the railroad and the pond, has been cut off within the last three months, and I notice that the oak sprouts have commonly met with a check after growing one or two feet, and small reddish leafets have again put forth at the extremity within a week or so, as in the spring. Some of the oak sprouts are five to six feet high already.

On his hill near by, where the wood was cut about two years ago, this second growth of the oaks, especially white oaks, is much more obvious, and commenced longer ago. The shoots of this year are generally about two feet long, but the first foot consists of large dark-green leaves which expanded early, before the shoot met with a check. This is surmounted by another foot of smaller yellowish-green leaves. This is very generally the case, and produces a marked contrast. Dark-green bushes surmounted by a light or yellowish-green growth.

Sometimes, in the first-mentioned sprout-land, you see where the first shoot withered, as if frost-bitten at the end, and often only some large buds have formed there as yet. Many of these sprouts, the rankest of them, are fated to fall, being but slightly joined to the stump, riddled by ants there; and others are already prostrated.

*July 23.* I saw the other day where the lightning on the 12th or 13th had struck the telegraph-posts at Walden Pond. It had shattered five posts in succession, they being a dozen rods apart, spoiling them entirely; though all of them *stood* but one, yet they were a mere wrack of splinters through which you could look. It had omitted a great many more posts and struck half a dozen more at a great distance from these on each side. The furthest

I noticed was near by the second mile-post, the nearest midway the causeway. And at the same time there was a smart shock, an explosion, at the operating office at the depot, two miles off from the furthest point. I should think, speaking from memory, that the posts struck were the oldest and dampest, or most rotten. At one or two posts it had plainly entered the ground and plowed toward the railroad-track, slightly injuring it. It struck a pitch pine standing within four or five feet of the wire, leaving a white seam down one side of it, also two large oaks a little further off. This was where the telegraph ran parallel to, and a few feet only from, a wood. It also struck a small oak on the opposite side of the track. The lightning struck for two miles (!!) at least.

***August 9.*** There were a great many visitors to the summit,[25] both by the south and north, *i. e.* the Jaffrey and Dublin paths, but they did not turn off from the beaten track. One noon, when I was on the top, I counted forty men, women, and children around me, and more were constantly arriving while others were going. Certainly more than one hundred ascended in a day. When you got within thirty rods you saw them seated in a row along the gray parapets, like the inhabitants of a castle on a gala-day; and when you behold Monadnock's blue summit fifty miles off in the horizon, you may imagine it covered with men, women, and children in dresses of all colors, like an observatory on a muster-field. They appeared to be chiefly mechanics and farmers' boys and girls from the neighboring towns. The young men sat in rows with their legs dangling over the precipice, squinting through spy-glasses and shouting and hallooing to each new party that issued from the woods below. Some were playing cards; others were trying to see their house or their neighbor's. Children were running about and playing as usual. Indeed, this peak in pleasant weather is

**25** At Mount Monadnock, where Thoreau was making his fourth and final excursion, leaving Concord on 4 August and returning on 9 August. He was accompanied by Ellery Channing.

the most trivial place in New England. There are probably more arrivals daily than at any of the White Mountain houses. Several were busily engraving their names on the rocks with cold-chisels, whose incessant clink you heard, and they had but little leisure to look off. The mountain was not free of them from sunrise to sunset, though most of them left about 5 P.M. At almost any hour of the day they were seen wending their way single file in various garb up or down the shelving rocks of the peak. These figures on the summit, seen in relief against the sky (from our camp), looked taller than life. I saw some that camped there, by moonlight, one night. On Sunday, twenty or thirty, at least, in addition to the visitors to the peak, came up to pick blueberries, and we heard on all sides the rattling of dishes and their frequent calls to each other.

They who simply climb to the peak of Monadnock have seen but little of the mountain. I came not to look *off from* it, but to look *at* it. The view of the pinnacle itself from the plateau below surpasses any view which you get from the summit. It is indispensable to see the top itself and the sierra of its outline from one side. The great charm is not to look off from a height but to walk over this novel and wonderful rocky surface. Moreover, if you would enjoy the prospect, it is, methinks, most interesting when you look from the edge of the plateau immediately down into the valleys, or where the edge of the lichen-clad rocks, only two or three rods from you, is seen as the lower frame of a picture of green fields, lakes, and woods, suggesting a more stupendous precipice than exists. There are much more surprising effects of this nature along the edge of the plateau than on the summit. It is remarkable what haste the visitors make to get to the top of the mountain and then look away from it.

*August 22.* When I used to pick the berries for dinner on the East Quarter[26] hills I did not eat one till I had done, for going a-berrying implies more things than eating the berries. They at home got only the pudding: I got the forenoon out of doors, and the appetite for the pudding.

It is true, as is said, that we have as good a right to make berries private property as to make grass and trees such; but what I chiefly regret is the, in effect, dog-in-the-manger result, for at the same time that we exclude mankind from gathering berries in our field, we exclude them from gathering health and happiness and inspiration and a hundred other far finer and nobler fruits than berries, which yet we shall not gather ourselves there, nor even carry to market. We strike only one more blow at a simple and wholesome relation to nature. As long as the berries are free to all comers they are beautiful, though they may be few and small, but tell me that is a blueberry swamp which somebody has hired, and I shall not want even to look at it. In laying claim for the first time to the spontaneous fruit of our pastures we are, accordingly, aware of a little meanness inevitably, and the gay berry party whom we turn away naturally look down on and despise us. If it were left to the berries to say who should have them, is it not likely that they would prefer to be gathered by the party of children in the hay-rigging, who have come to have a good time merely?

I do not see clearly that these successive losses are ever quite made up to us. This is one of the taxes which we pay for having a railroad. Almost all our improvements, so called, tend to convert the country into the town.

This suggests what origin and foundation many of our laws and institutions have, and I do not say this by way of complaining of this particular custom. Not that I love Cæsar less, but Rome more.[27]

26 East of the Concord River and bordered by Bedford and Lincoln.
27 Allusion to Shakespeare's *Julius Caesar* (3.2.20–21): "not that I loved Caesar less, but that I loved Rome more."

**28** Although there is no indication in his journal, on this day Thoreau delivered his lecture "The Succession of Forest Trees" before the Middlesex Agricultural Society at the Middlesex Cattle Show and Ploughing Match. The essay was printed in the *New York Weekly Tribune* (6 October 1860) and *Transactions of the Middlesex Agricultural Society for the Year 1860.*

**29** Thoreau expanded this paragraph for his unfinished "Huckleberries" as: "I have observed that many English naturalists have a pitiful habit of speaking of their proper pursuit as a sort of trifling or waste of time—a mere interruption to more important employments and 'severer studies'—for which they must ask pardon of the reader. As if they would have you believe that all the rest of their lives was consecrated to some truly great and serious enterprise. But it happens that we never hear more of this, as we certainly should, if it were only some great public or philanthropic service, and therefore conclude that they have been engaged in the heroic and magnanimous enterprise of feeding, clothing, housing and warming themselves and their dependents, the chief value of all which was that it enabled them to pursue just these studies of which they speak so slightingly. The 'severer study' they refer to was keeping their accounts. Comparatively speaking—what they call their graver pursuits and severer studies was the real trifling and misspense of life—and were they such fools as not to know it? It is, in effect at least, mere cant. All mankind have depended on them for this intellectual food" [H 4].

**30** Sleepy Hollow Cemetery, at the dedication of which in September 1855 Emerson said: "This spot for twenty years has borne the name of *Sleepy Hollow.* Its seclusion from the village in its immediate neighborhood had made it to all the inhabitants an easy retreat on a Sabbath day, or a summer twilight, and it was inevitably chosen by them when the design of a new cemetery was broached, if it did not suggest the design, as the fit place for their final repose. In all the multitudes

*September 1.* We are so accustomed to see another forest spring up immediately as a matter of course, whether from the stump or from the seed, when a forest is cut down, never troubling about the succession, that we hardly associate the seed with the tree, and do not anticipate the time when this regular succession will cease and we shall be obliged to plant, as they do in all old countries. The planters of Europe must have a very different, a much correcter, notion of the value of the seed of forest trees than we. To speak generally, they know that the forest trees spring from seeds, as we do of apples and pears, but we know only that they come out of the earth.

*September 20.* Cattle-Show.[28]
Rainy in forenoon.

*October 7.* Many people have a foolish way of talking about small things, and apologize for themselves or another having attended to a small thing, having neglected their ordinary business and amused or instructed themselves by attending to a small thing; when, if the truth were known, their ordinary business was the small thing, and almost their whole lives were misspent, but they were such fools as not to know it.[29]

*October 10.* In August, '55, I levelled for the artificial pond at Sleepy Hollow.[30] They dug gradually for three or four years and completed the pond last year, '59. It is now about a dozen rods long by five or six wide and two or three deep, and is supplied by copious springs in the meadow. There is a long ditch leading into it, in which no water now flows, nor has since winter at least, and a short ditch leading out of it into the brook. It is about sixty rods from the very source of the brook. Well, in this pond thus dug in the midst of a meadow a year or two ago and supplied by springs in the meadow, I find to-day several small patches of the large yellow and the kalmiana lily already established. Thus in the midst of death we are in life.[31]

P.M.—Went to a fire—or smoke—at Mrs. Hoar's. There is a slight blaze and more smoke. Two or three hundred men rush to the house, cut large holes in the roof, throw many hogsheads of water into it,—when a few pails full well directed would suffice,—and then they run off again, leaving your attic three inches deep with water, which is rapidly descending through the ceiling to the basement and spoiling all that can be spoiled, while a torrent is running down the stairways. They were very forward to put out the fire, but they take no pains to put out the water, which does far more damage. The first was amusement; the last would be mere work and utility. Why is there not a little machine invented to throw the water out of a house?

They are hopelessly cockneys[32] everywhere who learn to swim with a machine.[33] They take neither disease nor health, nay, nor life itself, the natural way. I see dumbbells in the minister's study, and some of their dumbness gets into his sermons. Some travellers carry them round the world in their carpetbags. Can he be said to travel who requires still this exercise? A party of school-children had a picnic at the Easterbrooks Country[34] the other day, and they carried bags of beans from their gymnasium to exercise with there. I cannot be interested in these extremely artificial amusements. The traveller is no longer a wayfarer, with his staff and pack and dusty coat. He is not a pilgrim, but he travels in a saloon,[35] and carries dumb-bells to exercise with in the intervals of his journey.

*October 11.* The season is as favorable for pears as for apples. Emerson's garden is strewn with them.[36] They

of woodlands and hillsides, which within a few years have been laid out with a similar design, I have not known one so fitly named. *Sleepy Hollow.*"

**31** Inversion of the phrase found in the *Book of Common Prayer:* "In the midst of life we are in death."

**32** Cf. 1858 note 32.

**33** A mechanical aid for learning to swim—used on land, not in the water—on which one is supported by upright padded posts and straps on pulleys to learn the strokes.

**34** A large tract in the north of Concord about which Thoreau wrote on 10 June 1853: "What shall this great wild tract over which we strolled be called? Many farmers have pastures there, and wood-lots, and orchards. It consists mainly of rocky pastures. . . . Ponkawtasset bounds it on the south. There are a few frog-ponds and one old mill-pond within it, and Bateman's Pond on its edge. What shall the whole be called? The old Carlisle road, which runs through the middle of it, is bordered on each side with wild apple pastures. . . . These orchards are very extensive, and yet many of these apple trees, growing as forest trees, bear good crops of apples. It is a paradise for walkers in the fall. There are also boundless huckleberry pastures as well as many blueberry swamps. Shall we call it the Easterbrooks Country? It would make a princely estate in Europe, yet it is owned by farmers, who live by the labor of their hands and do not esteem it much" [J 5:239–240].

**35** Saloon car: a drawing-room car on a railroad train.

**36** Edward Emerson wrote about his father's pears in *Emerson in Concord* that his gardening was confined "to pruning his trees and picking up pears and apples. . . . [He] groaned to see the September gale rudely throw down his treasures before the 'Cattle-show' Exhibition, and always sent thither specimens from his garden. One day after this exhibition a party of gentlemen visited his orchard. . . . He smiled with modest pride at having his little orchard thus honored, but the Hon. S—— D——, the chairman, said, 'Mr. Emerson, the committee have called to see the soil which produces such poor specimens of such fine varieties.' . . . In his journal he answers some caviller who has said, 'Your pears cost you more than mine which I buy.' 'Yes, they are costly, but we all have expensive vices. You play at billiards, I at pear-trees.' . . . The orchard throve and in time became a source of profit, but pears and apples were to him more than so many barrels of sweet and perfumed pulp to eat or sell."

**37**  American eating apple cultivated by Loammi Baldwin (1740–1807) after discovering the apple in Wilmington, Massachusetts.

**38**  Parlor.

**39**  Louise Bonne de Jersey, sometimes called Bonne Louise d'Avranches: a late-18th-century variety of pear cultivated in France.

are not so handsome as apples,—are of more earthy and homely colors,—yet they are of a wholesome color enough. Many, inclining to a rough russet or even ferruginous, both to touch (rusty) and eye, look as if they were proof against frost. After all, the few varieties of wild pears here have more color and are handsomer than the many celebrated varieties that are cultivated. The cultivated are commonly of so dull a color that it is hard to distinguish them from the leaves, and if there are but two or three left you do not see them revealing themselves distinctly at a distance amid the leaves, as apples do, but I see that the gatherer has overlooked half a dozen large ones on this small tree, which were concealed by their perfect resemblance to the leaves,—a yellowish green, spotted with darker-green rust or fungi (?). Yet some have a fair cheek, and, generally, in their form they are true pendants, as if shaped expressly to hang from the trees.

They are a more aristocratic fruit. How much more attention they get from the proprietor! The hired man gathers the apples and barrels them. The proprietor plucks the pears at odd hours for a pastime, and his daughter wraps them each in its paper. They are, perchance, put up in the midst of a barrel of Baldwins[37] as if something more precious than these. They are spread on the floor of the best room.[38] They are a gift to the most distinguished guest. Judges and ex-judges and honorables are connoisseurs of pears, and discourse of them at length between sessions. I hold in my hand a Bonne Louise[39] which is covered with minute brown specks or dots one twelfth to one sixteenth of an inch apart, largest and most developed on the sunny side, quite regular and handsome, as if they were the termination or operculum of pores which had burst in the very thin pellicle of the fruit, producing a slight roughness to the touch. Each of these little ruptures, so to call them, is in form a perfect star with five rays; so that, if the apple is higher-colored, reflecting the sun, on the duller surface of this pear the whole firmament with its stars shines forth. They whisper of the happy stars under whose influence they have grown and matured. It is not the case with all of them, but only the more perfect specimens.

Pears, it is truly said, are less poetic than apples.[40] They have neither the beauty nor the fragrance of apples, but their excellence is in their flavor, which speaks to a grosser sense. They are *glouts-morceaux*.[41] Hence, while children dream of apples, ex-judges realize pears. They are named after emperors and kings and queens and dukes and duchesses. I fear I shall have to wait till we get to pears with American names, which a republican can swallow.

*October 13.* The scientific differs from the poetic or lively description somewhat as the photographs, which we so weary of viewing, from paintings and sketches, though this comparison is too favorable to science. All science is only a makeshift, a means to an end which is never attained. After all, the truest description, and that by which another living man can most readily recognize a flower, is the unmeasured and eloquent one which the sight of it inspires. No scientific description will supply the want of this, though you should count and measure and analyze every atom that seems to compose it.

Surely poetry and eloquence are a more universal language than that Latin which is confessedly dead. In science, I should say, all description is postponed till we know the whole, but then science itself will be cast aside. But unconsidered expressions of our delight which any natural object draws from us are something complete and final in themselves, since all nature is to be regarded as it concerns man; and who knows how near to absolute truth such unconscious affirmations may come? Which

40 According to a version of this sentence published in *Wild Fruits,* Emerson "says his children complain that they cannot introduce them so well into verse" [Thoreau, *Wild Fruits,* 127].
41 Glou, or Glout, Morceau, an 18th-century pear originally called Beurre d'Hardenpont, after the Belgian priest Abbé Nicolas Hardenpont of Mons (1705–1774).

42 Probable allusion to Rensselaer Polytechnic Institute in Troy, New York, the oldest technological institution in the United States, founded in 1824, or to the Polytechnic University of New York, founded in 1854.

are the truest, the sublime conceptions of Hebrew poets and *seers,* or the guarded statements of modern geologists, which we must modify or unlearn so fast?

As they who were present early at the discovery of gold in California, and observed the sudden fall in its value, have most truly described that state of things, so it is commonly the old naturalists who first received American plants that describe them best. A scientific description is such as you would get if you should send out the scholars of the polytechnic school[42] with all sorts of metres made and patented to take the measures for you of any natural object. In a sense you have got nothing new thus, for every object that we see mechanically is mechanically daguerreotyped on our eyes, but a true description growing out of the perception and appreciation of it is itself a new fact, never to be daguerreotyped, indicating the highest quality of the plant,—its relation to man,—of far more importance than any merely medicinal quality that it may possess, or be thought to-day to possess. There is a certainty and permanence about this kind of observation, too, that does not belong to the other, for every flower and weed has its day in the medical pharmacopœia, but the beauty of flowers is perennial in the taste of men.

Truly this is a world of vain delights. We think that men have a substratum of common sense but sometimes are peculiarly frivolous. But consider what a value is seriously and permanently attached to gold and so-called precious stones almost universally. Day and night, summer and winter, sick or well, in war and in peace, men speak of and believe in gold as a great treasure. By a thousand comparisons they prove their devotion to it. If wise men or true philosophers bore any considerable proportion to the whole number of men, gold would be treated with no such distinction. Men seriously and, if possible, religiously believe in and worship gold. They hope to earn golden opinions, to celebrate their golden wedding.[43] They dream of the golden age. Now it is not its intrinsic beauty or value, but its rarity and arbitrarily attached value, that distinguishes gold. You would think it was the reign of shams.

The one description interests those chiefly who have not seen the thing; the other chiefly interests those who have seen it and are most familiar with it, and brings it home to the reader. We like to read a good description of no thing so well as of that which we already know the best, as our friend, or ourselves even. In proportion as we get and are near to our object, we do without the measured or scientific account, which is like the measure they take, or the description they write, of a man when he leaves his country, and insert in his passport for the use of the detective police of other countries. The men of science merely look at the object with sinister eye, to see if it corresponds with the passport, and merely visé[44] or make some trifling additional mark on its passport and let it go; but the real acquaintances and friends which it may have in foreign parts do not ask to see nor think of its passport.

Gerard[45] has not only heard of and seen and raised a plant, but felt and smelled and tasted it, applying all his senses to it. You are not distracted from the thing to the system or arrangement. In the true natural order the order or system is not insisted on. Each is first, and each last. That which presents itself to us this moment occupies the whole of the present and rests on the very topmost point of the sphere, under the zenith. The species and individuals of all the natural kingdoms ask our attention and admiration in a round robin.[46] We make straight lines, putting a captain at their head and a lieutenant at their tails, with sergeants and corporals all along the line and a flourish of trumpets near the beginning, insisting on a particular uniformity where Nature has

43 Fiftieth wedding anniversary.
44 To examine and endorse, as to put a visa on a passport.
45 John Gerard: cf. 1859 note 119.
46 A written paper, as a petition, memorial, or remonstrance, bearing a number of signatures arranged in a circular or concentric form, whereby the order of signing is concealed.

**47** Squaring a circle, also known as quadrature, is an insoluble problem, both arithmetically and geometrically, despite such books as James Smith's (1805–1872) *The Problem of Squaring the Circle Solved; or, The True Circumference and Area of the Circle Discovered,* published in 1859.

made curves to which belongs their own sphere-music. It is indispensable for us to square her circles,[47] and we offer our rewards to him who will do it.

*October 16.* Our wood-lots, of course, have a history, and we may often recover it for a hundred years back, though we *do* not. A small pine lot may be a side of such an oval, or a half, or a square in the inside with all the curving sides cut off by fences. Yet if we attended more to the history of our lots we should manage them more wisely.

*October 18.* What shall we say to that management that halts between two courses,—does neither this nor that, but botches both? I see many a pasture on which the pitch or white pines are spreading, where the bush-whack is from time to time used with a show of vigor, and I despair of my trees,—I say mine, for the farmer evidently does not mean they shall be his,—and yet this questionable work is so poorly done that those very fields grow steadily greener and more forest-like from year to year in spite of cows and bush-whack, till at length the farmer gives up the contest from sheer weariness, and finds himself the owner of a wood-lot. Now whether wood-lots or pastures are most profitable for him I will not undertake to say, but I am certain that a wood-lot and pasture combined is not profitable.

We find ourselves in a world that is already planted, but is also still being planted as at first. We say of some plants that they grow in wet places and of others that they grow in desert places. The truth is that their seeds are scattered almost everywhere, but here only do they succeed.

*October 31.* I do not state the facts exactly in the order in which they were observed, but select out of very numerous observations extended over a series of years the most important ones, and describe them in their natural order.[48]

So far as our noblest hardwood forests are concerned, the animals, especially squirrels and jays, are our greatest and almost only benefactors. It is to them that we owe this gift. It is not in vain that the squirrels live in or about every forest tree, or hollow log, and every wall and heap of stones.

*November 5.* I am struck by the fact that the more slowly trees grow at first, the sounder they are at the core, and I think that the same is true of human beings. We do not wish to see children precocious, making great strides in their early years like sprouts, producing a soft and perishable timber, but better if they expand slowly at first, as if contending with difficulties, and so are solidified and perfected. Such trees continue to expand with nearly equal rapidity to an extreme old age.

*November 10.* How little there is on an ordinary map! How little, I mean, that concerns the walker and the lover of nature. Between those lines indicating roads is a plain blank space in the form of a square or triangle or polygon or segment of a circle, and there is naught to distinguish this from another area of similar size and form. Yet the one may be covered, in fact, with a primitive oak wood, like that of Boxboro,[49] waving and creaking in the wind, such as may make the reputation of a county, while the other is a stretching plain with scarcely a tree on it. The waving woods, the dells and glades and green banks and smiling fields, the huge boulders, etc., etc., are not on the map, nor to be inferred from the map.

That grand old oak wood is just the most remarkable and memorable thing in Boxboro, and yet if there is a history of this town written anywhere, the history

**48** For more on Thoreau's writing process, cf. 3 February 1859.
**49** Thoreau wrote on 23 October 1860 that Anthony Wright described this as "a noted large and so-called primitive wood, Inches Wood, between the Harvard turnpike and Stow, sometimes called Stow Woods, in Boxboro and Stow" [J 14:167].

50 Acton was first settled as part of Concord, and was incorporated as a town in 1735.

or even mention of this is probably altogether omitted, while that of the first (and may be last) parish is enlarged on.

What sort of cultivation, or civilization and improvement, is ours to boast of, if it turns out that, as in this instance, unhandselled nature is worth more even by our modes of valuation than our improvements are,—if we leave the land poorer than we found it? Is it good economy, to try it by the lowest standards, to cut down all our forests, if a forest will pay into the town treasury a greater tax than the farms which may supplant it,—if the oaks by steadily growing according to their nature leave our improvements in the rear?

How little we insist on truly grand and beautiful natural features! How many have ever heard of the Boxboro oak woods? How many have ever explored them? I have lived so long in this neighborhood and but just heard of this noble forest,—probably as fine an oak wood as there is in New England, only eight miles west of me.

*November 17.* How they do things in West Acton.[50] As we were walking through West Acton the other afternoon, a few rods only west of the centre, on the main road, the Harvard turnpike, we saw a rock larger than a man could lift, lying in the road, exactly in the wheel-track, and were puzzled to tell how it came there, but supposed it had slipped off a drag,—yet we noticed that it was peculiarly black. Returning the same way in the twilight, when we had got within four or five rods of this very spot, looking up, we saw a man in the field, three or four rods on one side of that spot, running off as fast as he could. By the time he had got out of sight over the hill it occurred to us that he was blasting rocks and had just touched one off; so, at the eleventh hour, we turned about and ran the other way, and when we had gone a few rods, off went two blasts, but fortunately none of the rocks struck us. Some time after we had passed we saw the men returning. They looked out for themselves, but for nobody else. This is the way they do things in West Acton. We now understood that the big stone was blackened by powder.

*November 22.* It is glorious to consider how independent man is of all enervating luxuries; and the poorer he is in respect to them, the richer he is. Summer is gone with all its infinite wealth, and still nature is genial to man. Though he no longer bathes in the stream, or reclines on the bank, or plucks berries on the hills, still he beholds the same inaccessible beauty around him. What though he has no juice of the grape stored up for him in cellars; the air itself is wine of an older vintage, and far more sanely exhilarating, than any cellar affords. It is ever some gouty senior and not a blithe child that drinks, or cares for, that so famous wine.

Though so many phenomena which we lately admired have now vanished, others are more remarkable and interesting than before. The smokes from distant chimneys, not only greater because more fire is required, but more distinct in the cooler atmosphere, are a very pleasing sight, and conduct our thoughts quickly to the roof and hearth and family beneath, revealing the homes of men.

*November 23.* Most of us are still related to our native fields as the navigator to undiscovered islands in the sea. We can any autumn discover a new fruit there which will surprise us by its beauty or sweetness. So long as I saw one or two kinds of berries in my walks whose names I did not know, the proportion of the unknown seemed indefinitely if not infinitely great.

Famous fruits imported from the tropics and sold in our markets—as oranges, lemons, pineapples, and ba-

**51** The Concord Social Circle was organized in 1782 "to strengthen the social affections, and disseminate useful communications among its members." Their usual refreshment was an array of apples, nuts, and raisins, sometimes cake, and cider or chocolate for drink. Emerson was a member from 1839 until his death, and wrote of the club: "Much of the best society I have ever known is a club in Concord called the Social Circle, consisting of twenty-five of our citizens, doctor, lawyer, farmer, trader, miller, mechanic, etc., solidest of men, who yield the solidest of gossip." Thoreau was not a member.

**52** David Porter (1780–1843), American naval officer in the War of 1812. He also cruised in the Pacific, warring on British commercial vessels, and in 1813 took formal possession of Nuku Hiva, one of the Marquesas Islands, an act that was not recognized by the United States. In 1814 his ship was blockaded by British ships in the harbor of Valparaiso, Chile. Porter escaped to sea, but a squall disabled his ship, forcing him back to the coast. He was attacked by two British warships and after a hard-fought battle was forced to surrender. While in the West Indies in 1824 on an expedition for suppressing piracy, Porter forced the officials of the town of Foxardo (Fajardo), Puerto Rico, to apologize for jailing an officer from his fleet. The government did not sanction Porter's act, and he was court-martialed and suspended for six months.

**53** Cuthbert William Johnson's (1798–1878) *The Farmer's and Planters Encyclopaedia of Rural Affairs* states: "The Valparaiso squash, the seeds of which were brought from the Pacific by the late Commodore Porter, is a splendid vegetable, without any neck, in shape and size somewhat resembling a long watermelon, flattened, and of a rich citron or orange colour."

nanas—do not concern me so much as many an unnoticed wild berry whose beauty annually lends a new charm to some wild walk, or which I have found to be palatable to an outdoor taste.

The tropical fruits are for those who dwell within the tropics; their fairest and sweetest parts cannot be exported nor imported. Brought here, they chiefly concern those whose walks are through the market-place. It is not the orange of Cuba, but the checkerberry of the neighboring pasture, that most delights the eye and the palate of the New England child. What if the Concord Social Club,[51] instead of eating oranges from Havana, should spend an hour in admiring the beauty of some wild berry from their own fields which they never attended to before? It is not the foreignness or size or nutritive qualities of a fruit that determine its absolute value.

It is not those far-fetched fruits which the speculator imports that concerns us chiefly, but rather those which you have fetched yourself in your basket from some far hill or swamp, journeying all the long afternoon in the hold of a basket, consigned to your friends at home, the first of the season.

We cultivate imported shrubs in our front yards for the beauty of their berries, when yet more beautiful berries grow unregarded by us in the surrounding fields.

As some beautiful or palatable fruit is perhaps the noblest gift of nature to man, so is a fruit with which a man has in some measure identified himself by cultivating or collecting it one of the most suitable presents to a friend. It was some compensation for Commodore Porter,[52] who may have introduced some cannon-balls and bombshells into ports where they were not wanted, to have introduced the Valparaiso squash into the United States.[53] I think that this eclipses his military glory.

As I sail the unexplored sea of Concord, many a dell

and swamp and wooded hill is my Ceram and Amboyna.[54]

*November 25.* How often you make a man richer in spirit in proportion as you rob him of earthly luxuries and comforts!

*November 26.* The value of these wild fruits is not in the mere possession or eating of them, but in the sight or enjoyment of them. The very derivation of the word "fruit" would suggest this. It is from the Latin *fructus,* meaning that which is *used* or *enjoyed.* If it were not so, then going a-berrying and going to market would be nearly synonymous expressions. Of course it is the spirit in which you do a thing which makes it interesting, whether it is sweeping a room or pulling turnips. Peaches are unquestionably a very beautiful and palatable fruit, but the gathering of them for the market is not nearly so interesting as the gathering of huckleberries for your own use.

A man fits out a ship at a great expense and sends it to the West Indies with a crew of men and boys, and after six months or a year it comes back with a load of pineapples. Now, if no more gets accomplished than the speculator commonly aims at,—if it simply turns out what is called a successful venture,—I am less interested in this expedition than in some child's first excursion a-huckleberrying, in which it is introduced into a new world, experiences a new development, though it brings home only a gill[55] of huckleberries in its basket. I know that the newspapers and the politicians declare otherwise, but they do not alter the fact. Then, I think that the fruit of the latter expedition was finer than that of the former. It was a more fruitful expedition. The value of any experience is measured, of course, not by the amount of money, but the amount of development

[54] Islands in the Moluccas (or Spice Islands) of Indonesia.

[55] Unit of measurement equal to four ounces.

56 Echo of Thoreau's statement in *Walden* that "the cost of a thing is the amount of what I will call life which is required to be exchanged for it, immediately or in the long run" [Wa 30].

we get out of it.[56] If a New England boy's dealings with oranges and pineapples have had more to do with his development than picking huckleberries or pulling turnips have, then he rightly and naturally thinks more of the former; otherwise not.

Do not think that the fruits of New England are mean and insignificant, while those of some foreign land are noble and memorable. Our own, whatever they may be, are far more important to us than any others can be. They educate us, and fit us to live in New England. Better for us is the wild strawberry than the pineapple, the wild apple than the orange, the hazelnut or pignut than the cocoanut or almond, and not on account of their flavor merely, but the part they play in our education.

*November 28.* The mass of men are very easily imposed on. They have their runways in which they always travel, and are sure to fall into any pit or box trap set therein. Whatever a great many grown-up boys are seriously engaged in is considered great and good, and, as such, is sure of the recognition of the churchman and statesman. What, for instance, are the blue juniper berries in the pasture, which the cowboy remembers so far as they are beautiful merely, to church or state? Mere trifles which deserve and get no protection. As an object of beauty, though significant to all who really live in the country, they do not receive the protection of any community. Anybody may grub up all that exist. But as an article of commerce they command the attention of the civilized world.

*November 29.* If a man has spent all his days about some business, by which he has merely got to be rich, as it is called, *i. e.,* has got much money, many houses and barns and wood-lots, then his life has been a failure, I think; but if he has been trying to better his condition in a higher sense than this, has been trying to invent something, to be somebody,—*i. e.,* to invent and get a patent for himself,—so that all may see his originality, though he should never get above board,—and great inventors, you know, commonly die poor,—I shall think him comparatively successful.

You would say that some men had been tempted to live in this world at all only by the offer of a bounty by the general government—a bounty on living—to any one who will consent to be *out* at this era of the world, the object of the governors being to create a nursery for their navy. I told such a man the other day that I had got a Canada lynx here in Concord,[57] and his instant question was, "Have you got the reward for him?" What reward? Why, the ten dollars which the State offers.[58] As long as I saw him he neither said nor thought anything about the lynx, but only about this reward. "Yes," said he, "this State offers ten dollars reward." You might have inferred that ten dollars was something rarer in his neighborhood than a lynx even, and he was anxious to see it on that account. I have thought that a lynx was a bright-eyed, four-legged, furry beast of the cat kind, very *current,* indeed, though its natural gait is by leaps. But he knew it to be a draught drawn by the cashier of the wildcat bank[59] on the State treasury, payable at sight. Then I reflected that the first money was of leather, or a whole creature (whence *pecunia,* from *pecus,* a herd),[60] and, since leather was at first furry, I easily understood the connection between a lynx and ten dollars, and found that all money was traceable right back to the original wildcat bank. But the fact was that, instead of receiving ten dollars for the lynx which I had got, I had

**57** John Quincy Adams (b. 1826; not the president) on 9 September 1860 killed a Canada lynx, which Thoreau described extensively on 11 and 13 September [J 14:78–85]. The next day Thoreau cut off a foreleg, which he boiled so he could study the bone.

**58** The town, not the state, offered a bounty for killing noxious animals, according to an 1838 repeal of the 1836 Revised Statutes of Massachusetts, chapter 54, section 1, which had allowed for a state bounty for animals including wolf, bear, wildcat, and fox. The General Statutes for 1860, chapter 18, section 10, gave towns the right to vote for the sums awarded.

**59** Bank that issued notes without adequate security, particularly the unsound and risky banks chartered under state law that flourished and failed, causing panics, during the period of unregulated state banking from 1816 to 1863.

**60** *Pecunia* (Latin: money) is derived from the *pecus* (cattle). In *Walden,* when Thoreau asked Alek Therien "if he could do without money, he showed the convenience of money in such a way as to suggest and coincide with the most philosophical accounts of the origin of this institution, and the very derivation of the word *pecunia.* If an ox were his property, and he wished to get needles and thread at the store, he thought it would be inconvenient and impossible soon to go on mortgaging some portion of the creature each time to that amount" [Wa 143–144].

61 The Emancipation Act of 1833 abolished forced servitude in all British lands, including Canada. For Thoreau, however, slavery extended beyond actual physical bondage. In "Life Without Principle" he wrote that freedom "cannot be freedom in a merely political sense" and that a person can be "still the slave of an economical and moral tyrant" [W 4:476].

62 Cf. 1853 note 179.

63 Latin: of or for a nation, from which the word ethnic is derived. In ecclesiastical and some other writers, ethnic was used for gentile or heathen, as in Ben Jonson's *The Staple of News:* "No certain *species* sure! A kind of *mule!* / That's half an *Ethnick,* half a *Christian!*" Also in Milton's *The Reformation in England:* "And the people of God redeem'd, and wash'd with Christ's blood, and dignify'd with so many glorious titles of Saints, and sons in the Gospel, are now no better reputed than impure ethnicks, and lay dogs."

paid away some dollars in order to get him. So, you see, I was away back in a gray antiquity behind the institution of money,—further than history goes.

We hear a good deal said about moonshine by so-called practical people, and the next day, perchance, we hear of their failure, they having been dealing in fancy stocks; but there really never is any moonshine of this kind in the practice of poets and philosophers; there never are any hard times or failures with them, for they deal with permanent values.

*December 4.* Talk about slavery! It is not the peculiar institution of the South. It exists wherever men are bought and sold, wherever a man allows himself to be made a mere thing or a tool, and surrenders his inalienable rights of reason and conscience. Indeed, this slavery is more complete than that which enslaves the body alone. It exists in the Northern States, and I am reminded by what I find in the newspapers that it exists in Canada.[61] I never yet met with, or heard of, a judge who was not a slave of this kind, and so the finest and most unfailing weapon of injustice. He fetches a slightly higher price than the black man only because he is a more valuable slave.

*December 30.* As in old times they who dwelt on the heath remote from towns were backward to adopt the doctrines which prevailed there, and were therefore called heathen[62] in a bad sense, so we dwellers in the huckleberry pastures, which are our heath lands, are slow to adopt the notions of large towns and cities and may perchance be nicknamed huckleberry people. But the worst of it is that the emissaries of the towns care more for our berries than for our salvation.

In those days the very race had got a bad name, and *ethnicus*[63] was only another name for heathen.

## 1861

AGE 43–44

1 Inches Wood: cf. 1860 note 49.
2 Thoreau noted in his journal of 10 November 1860: "Most think that Inches Wood was worth more twenty or thirty years ago,—that the oaks are now decayed within. Some have suggested that it would be much for the benefit of Boxboro to have it cut off and made into farms, but Boxboro people answer no, that they get a good deal more in taxes from it now than they would then" [J 14:228].

*January 3.* What are the natural features which make a township handsome? A river, with its waterfalls and meadows, a lake, a hill, a cliff or individual rocks, a forest, and ancient trees standing singly. Such things are beautiful; they have a high use which dollars and cents never represent. If the inhabitants of a town were wise, they would seek to preserve these things, though at a considerable expense; for such things educate far more than any hired teachers or preachers, or any at present recognized system of school education. I do not think him fit to be the founder of a state or even of a town who does not foresee the use of these things, but legislates chiefly for oxen, as it were.

Far the handsomest thing I saw in Boxboro was its noble oak wood.[1] I doubt if there is a finer one in Massachusetts. Let her keep it a century longer, and men will make pilgrimages to it from all parts of the country; and yet it would be very like the rest of New England if Boxboro were ashamed of that woodland.

I have since heard, however, that she is contented to have that forest stand instead of the houses and farms that might supplant it, because the land pays a much larger tax to the town now than it would then.[2]

I said to myself, if the history of this town is written, the chief stress is probably laid on its parish and there is not a word about this forest in it.

It would be worth the while if in each town there were a committee appointed to see that the beauty of the town

**3** In "Ktaadn" Thoreau wrote: "The tops of mountains are among the unfinished parts of the globe, whither it is a slight insult to the gods to climb and pry into their secrets, and try their effect on our humanity. Only daring and insolent men, perchance, go there. Simple races, as savages, do not climb mountains,—their tops are sacred and mysterious tracts never visited by them" [W 3:71–72].
**4** On 31 May 1832 the state sold a 25,000-acre tract of land including the summit of Mount Washington to Jacob Sargent and others, becoming known as Sargent's Purchase. In 1853 the Jackson Iron Manufacturing Company bought this land. Another tract north of Sargent's Purchase was sold to Henry B. Wells of Brookline, Massachusetts. Ownership and land rights were contested, resulting in three New Hampshire Supreme Court cases (ca. 1858) involving Wells and Jackson Iron. These cases were not resolved finally until after this entry.

received no detriment. If we have the largest boulder in the county, then it should not belong to an individual, nor be made into door-steps.

As in many countries precious metals belong to the crown, so here more precious natural objects of rare beauty should belong to the public.

Not only the channel but one or both banks of every river should be a public highway. The only use of a river is not to float on it.

Think of a mountain-top in the township—even to the minds of the Indians a sacred place[3]—only accessible through private grounds! a temple, as it were, which you cannot enter except by trespassing and at the risk of letting out or letting in somebody's cattle! in fact the temple itself in this case private property and standing in a man's cow-yard,—for such is commonly the case!

New Hampshire courts have lately been deciding—as if it was for them to decide—whether the top of Mt. Washington belonged to A or to B; and, it being decided in favor of B, as I hear, he went up one winter with the proper officer and took formal possession of it.[4] But I think that the top of Mt. Washington should not be private property; it should be left unappropriated for modesty and reverence's sake, or if only to suggest that earth has higher uses than we put her to. I know it is a mere figure of speech to talk about temples nowadays, when men recognize none, and, indeed, associate the word with heathenism.

It is true we as yet take liberties and go across lots, and steal, or "hook," a good many things, but we naturally take fewer and fewer liberties every year, as we meet with more resistance. In old countries, as England, going across lots is out of the question. You must walk in some beaten path or other, though it may be a narrow one. We are tending to the same state of things here, when practically a few will have grounds of their own, but most will have none to walk over but what the few allow them.

Thus we behave like oxen in a flower-garden. The true fruit of Nature can only be plucked with a delicate hand not bribed by any earthly reward, and a fluttering heart. No hired man can help us to gather this crop.

How few ever get beyond feeding, clothing, sheltering, and warming themselves in this world, and begin to treat themselves as human beings,—as intellectual and moral beings! Most seem not to see any further,—not to see over the ridge-pole of their barns,—or to be exhausted and accomplish nothing more than a full barn, though it may be accompanied by an empty head. They venture a little, run some risks, when it is a question of a larger crop of corn or potatoes; but they are commonly timid and count their coppers, when the question is whether their children shall be educated. He who has the reputation of being the thriftiest farmer and making the best bargains is really the most thriftless and makes the worst. It is safest to invest in knowledge, for the probability is that you can carry that with you wherever you go.

But most men, it seems to me, do not care for Nature and would sell their share in all her beauty, as long as they may live, for a stated sum—many for a glass of rum. Thank God, men cannot as yet fly, and lay waste the sky as well as the earth! We are safe on that side for the present. It is for the very reason that some do not care for those things that we need to continue to protect all from the vandalism of a few.

We cut down the few old oaks which witnessed the transfer of the township from the Indian to the white man, and commence our museum with a cartridge-box taken from a British soldier in 1775![5]

He pauses at the end of his four or five thousand dollars, and then only fears that he has not got enough to

**5**  Reference to the museum established in Concord by Cummings Elothan Davis (1816–1896), who began collecting Americana in the 1850s. It was Thoreau who gave Davis the Revolutionary War cartridge box. On 15 September 1860 Thoreau visited the museum's collection: "Looked at Mr. Davis's museum. Miss Lydia Hosmer (the surviving maiden lady) has given him some relics which belonged to her (the Hosmer) family. A small lead or pewter sun-dial, which she told him was brought over by her ancestors and which has the date 1626 scratched on it. Also some *stone* weights in an ancient linen bag, said to have been brought from England. They were oval stones or pebbles from the shore,—or *might* have been picked up at Walden. There was a pound, a half-pound, a quarter, a two-ounce, and several one-ounce weights, now all rather dark and ancient to look at, like the bag. This was to me the most interesting relic in his collection. I love to see anything that implies a simpler mode of life and greater nearness to the earth" [J 14:87–88]. Davis's museum ultimately became the Concord Museum, although much about its early history is unclear.

**6** Alcott mentioned in his journal of 15 December that Thoreau had "a severe cold on him." On 22 March 1861 Thoreau wrote to Ricketson: "To tell the truth, I am not on the alert for the signs of Spring, not having had any winter yet. I took a severe cold about the 3 of Dec. which at length resulted in a kind of bronchitis, so that I have been confined to the house ever since, excepting a very few experimental trips to the P.O. in some particularly mild noons" [C 609].

**7** Here, as elsewhere, Thoreau used his journal to write drafts of his lectures, in this case for a talk on huckleberries he did not live to complete.

carry him through,—that is, merely to pay for what he will eat and wear and burn and for his lodging for the rest of his life. But, pray, what does he stay here for? Suicide would be cheaper. Indeed, it would be nobler to found some good institution with the money and then cut your throat. If such is the whole upshot of their living, I think that it would be most profitable for all such to be carried or put through by being discharged from the mouth of a cannon as fast as they attained to years of such discretion.

As boys are sometimes required to show an excuse for being absent from school, so it seems to me that men should show some excuse for being here. Move along; you may come upon the town, sir.

I noticed a week or two ago that one of my white pines, some six feet high with a thick top, was bent under a great burden of very moist snow, almost to the point of breaking, so that an ounce more of weight would surely have broken it. As I was confined to the house by sickness,[6] and the tree had already been four or five days in that position, I despaired of its ever recovering itself; but, greatly to my surprise, when, a few days after, the snow had melted off, I saw the tree almost perfectly upright again.

It is evident that trees will bear to be bent by this cause and at this season much more than by the hand of man. Probably the less harm is done in the first place by the weight being so gradually applied, and perhaps the tree is better able to bear it at this season of the year.

*January 11.* I presume that every one of my audience[7] knows what a huckleberry is,—has seen a huckleberry, gathered a huckleberry, and, finally, has tasted a huckleberry,—and, that being the case, I think that I need offer no apology if I make huckleberries my theme this evening.

What more encouraging sight at the end of a long ramble than the endless successive patches of green bushes,—perhaps in some rocky pasture,—fairly blackened with the profusion of fresh and glossy berries?

There are so many of these berries in their season that most do not perceive that birds and quadrupeds make any use of them, since they are not felt to rob us; yet they are more important to them than to us. We do not notice the robin when it plucks a berry, as when it visits our favorite cherry tree, and the fox pays his visits to the field when we are not there.

*January 14.* It is the discovery of science that stupendous changes in the earth's surface, such as are referred to the Deluge, for instance, are the result of causes still in operation, which have been at work for an incalculable period.[8] There has not been a sudden re-formation, or, as it were, new creation of the world, but a steady progress according to existing laws. The same is true in detail also. It is a vulgar prejudice that some plants are "spontaneously generated,"[9] but science knows that they come from seeds, *i. e.* are the result of causes still in operation, however slow and unobserved. It is a common saying that "little strokes fall great oaks,"[10] and it does not imply much wisdom in him who originated it. The sound of the axe invites our attention to such a catastrophe; we can easily count each stroke as it is given, and all the neighborhood is informed by a loud crash when the deed is consummated. But such, too, is the rise of the oak; little strokes of a different kind and often repeated raise great oaks, but scarcely a traveller hears these or turns aside to converse with Nature, who is dealing them the while.

Nature is slow but sure;[11] she works no faster than need be; she is the tortoise that wins the race by her perseverance; she knows that seeds have many other uses

**8** Allusion to the theories of Charles Lyell (1797–1875), British geologist and author of *Principles of Geology.* Lyell advanced the work of James Hutton (1726–1797), a Scottish geologist, whose book *The Theory of the Earth* posited that the earth was formed by slow, naturally occurring processes over a long span of time. The work of these two modern geologists represented a major shift from theology (as in the Noachian Deluge) to science.

**9** Abiogenesis: the hypothesis that life can spontaneously come into being from nonliving materials, an idea that originated with Aristotle and was supported by many natural philosophers and scientists, including Louis Agassiz. In "Succession of Forest Trees" Thoreau wrote: "As for the heavy seeds and nuts which are not furnished with wings, the notion is still a very common one that, when the trees which bear these spring up where none of their kind were noticed before, they have come from seeds or other principles spontaneously generated there in an unusual manner, or which have lain dormant in the soil for centuries, or perhaps been called into activity by the heat of a burning. I do not believe these assertions, and I will state some of the ways in which, according to my observation, such forests are planted and raised" [W 5:187].

**10** Although it did not originate with Benjamin Franklin, this, like many other axioms, became popular through his *Poor Richard's Almanack.* Franklin's adage was an adaptation of John Lyly's (ca. 1554–1606) "The soft droppes of rain perce the hard marble; many strokes overthrow the tallest oaks."

**11** Allusion to the moral of the fable of the tortoise and the hare, as told by Aesop (ca. 620–560 B.C.E.) and Jean de la Fontaine (1621–1695).

**12**  Herodotus (5th century B.C.E.), Roman historian and author of a group of works now known as *The Histories*. Bede (672–735 C.E.), monk at the Northumbrian monastery of Saint Peter and author of *Historia Eccelesiastica Gentis Anglorum* (The Ecclesiastical History of the English People).

than to reproduce their kind. In raising oaks and pines, she works with a leisureliness and security answering to the age and strength of the trees. If every acorn of this year's crop is destroyed, never fear! she has more years to come. It is not necessary that a pine or an oak should bear fruit every year, as it is that a pea-vine should. So, botanically, the greatest changes in the landscape are produced more gradually than we expected. If Nature has a pine or an oak wood to produce, she manifests no haste about it.

*March 8.* I just heard peculiar faint sounds made by the air escaping from a stick which I had just put into my stove. It sounded to my ear exactly like the peeping of the hylodes in a distant pool, a cool and breezy spring evening, — as if it were designed to remind me of that season.

*March 18.* You can't read any genuine history — as that of Herodotus or the Venerable Bede[12] — without perceiving that our interest depends not on the subject but on the man, — on the manner in which he treats the subject and the importance he gives it. A feeble writer and without genius must have what he thinks a great theme, which we are already interested in through the accounts of others, but a genius — a Shakespeare, for instance — would make the history of his parish more interesting than another's history of the world.

Wherever men have lived there is a story to be told, and it depends chiefly on the story-teller or historian whether that is interesting or not. You are simply a witness on the stand to tell what you know about your neighbors and neighborhood. Your account of foreign parts which you have never seen should by good rights be less interesting.

*March 22.* When we consider how soon some plants which spread rapidly, by seeds or roots, would cover an area equal to the surface of the globe, how soon some species of trees, as the white willow, for instance, would equal in mass the earth itself, if all their seeds became full-grown trees, how soon some fishes would fill the ocean if all their ova became full-grown fishes, we are tempted to say that every organism, whether animal or vegetable, is contending for the possession of the planet, and, if any one were sufficiently favored, supposing it still possible to grow, as at first, it would at length convert the entire mass of the globe into its own substance.[13] Nature opposes to this many obstacles, as climate, myriads of brute and also human foes, and of competitors which may preoccupy the ground. Each suggests an immense and wonderful greediness and tenacity of life (I speak of the species, not individual), as if bent on taking entire possession of the globe wherever the climate and soil will permit. And each prevails as much as it does, because of the ample preparations it has made for the contest, — it has secured a myriad chances, — because it never depends on spontaneous generation to save it.

A writer in the *Tribune* speaks of cherries as one of the trees which come up numerously when the forest is cut or burned, though not known there before.[14] This may be true because there was no one knowing in these matters in that neighborhood. But I assert that it *was* there before, nevertheless; just as the little oaks are in the pine woods, but never grow up to trees till the pines are cleared off. Scarcely any plant is more sure to come up in a sprout-land here than the wild black cherry, and yet, though only a few inches high at the end of the first year after the cutting, it is commonly several years old, having maintained a feeble growth there so long. There is where the birds have dropped the stones, and it is doubtful if

13 Thoreau's note: "*Vide* Pliny on man's mission to keep down weeds."
14 E. G. Waters, former postmaster of Coventryville, New York, who wrote in a letter to the *New York Tribune* published on 23 March 1861: "Birch is not the only timber that follows the clearing and burning of land. Wild Cherry, Poplar, and other trees, will grow where they were never known to grow before, seed or no seed."

those dropped in pastures and open land are as likely to germinate. Yet the former rarely if ever get to be trees.

Of course natural successions are taking place where a swamp is gradually filling up with sphagnum and bushes and at length trees, *i. e.,* where the soil is changing.

Botanists talk about the possibility and impossibility of plants being naturalized here or there. But what plants have not been naturalized? Of course only those which grow to-day exactly where the original plant of the species was created. It is true we do not know whether one or many plants of a given kind were originally created, but I think it is the most reasonable and simple to suppose that only one was, — to suppose as little departure as possible from the existing order of things. They commenced to spread themselves at once and by whatever means they possessed as far as they could, and they are still doing so. Many were common to Europe and America at the period of the discovery of the latter country, and I have no doubt that they had naturalized themselves in one or the other country. This is more philosophical than to suppose that they were independently created in each.

I suppose that most have seen — at any rate I can show them — English cherry trees, so called, coming up not uncommonly in our woods and under favorable circumstances becoming full-grown trees. Now I think that they will not pretend that they came up there in the same manner before this country was discovered by the whites. But, if cherry trees come up by spontaneous generation, why should they not have sprung up there in that way a thousand years ago as well as now?

If the pine seed is spontaneously generated, why is it not so produced in the Old World as well as in America? I have no doubt that it can be raised from the seed in corresponding situations there, and that it will seem to spring up just as mysteriously there as it does here. Yet, if it will grow so *after* the seed has been carried thither, why should it not before, if the seed is unnecessary to its production?

The above-mentioned cherry trees come up, though they are comparatively few, just like the red cherry, and, no doubt, the same persons would consider them as spontaneously generated. But why did Nature defer raising that species here by spontaneous generation, until we had raised it from the stones?

It is evident that Nature's designs would not be accomplished if seeds, having been matured, were simply dropped and so planted directly beneath their parent stems, as many will always be in any case. The next consideration with her, then, after determining to create a seed, must have been how to get it transported, though to never so little distance,—the width of the plant, or less, will often be sufficient,—even as the eagle drives her young at last from the neighborhood of her eyrie,—for their own good, since there is not food enough there for all,—without depending on botanists, patent offices,[15] and seedsmen.[16] It is not enough to have matured a seed which will reproduce its kind under favorable conditions, but she must also secure it those favorable conditions. Nature has left nothing to the mercy of man. She has taken care that a sufficient number of every kind of seeds, from a cocoanut to those which are invisible, shall be transported and planted in a suitable place.

A seed, which is a plant or tree in embryo, which has the principle of growth, of life, in it, is more important in my eyes, and in the economy of Nature, than the diamond of Kohinoor.[17]

When we hear of an excellent fruit or a beautiful flower, the first question is if any man has got the seeds in his pocket; but men's pockets are only one of the means of conveyances which Nature has provided.

**15**  Cf. 1857 note 93.

**16**  A dealer in, or one who sows, seeds.

**17**  A 186-carat diamond from India, also known as the "mountain of light." In 1850 the East India Company presented it to Queen Victoria, who had it recut to 108.93 carats. In *Walden* Thoreau wrote of White Pond and Walden Pond: "If they were permanently congealed, and small enough to be clutched, they would, perchance, be carried off by slaves, like precious stones, to adorn the heads of emperors; but being liquid, and ample, and secured to us and our successors forever, we disregard them, and run after the diamond of Kohinoor" [Wa 192–193].

**18** On this date Thoreau began his journey west for his health, accompanied by Horace Mann, Jr. (1844–1868), son of the educator Horace Mann (cf. 1859 note 70) and nephew of Elizabeth Peabody and Sophia Peabody Hawthorne (1811–1871), and a gifted naturalist. Thoreau returned unimproved in the second week of July. He explained to Ricketson on 15 August 1861: "I was away in the far North-West, in search of health. My cold turned to bronchitis which made me a close prisoner almost up to the moment of my starting on that journey, early in May. As I had an incessant cough, my doctor told me that I must 'clear out'—to the West Indies or elsewhere, so I selected Minnesota. I returned a few weeks ago, after a good deal of steady travelling, considerably, yet not essentially better, my cough still continuing. If I do not mend very quickly I shall be obliged to go to another climate again very soon" [C 625]. Although on 19 December 1861 Sophia Thoreau wrote Ricketson that she was "hoping for a short winter and early spring, that the invalid may again be out of doors," in January Alcott was writing: "You have not been informed of Henry's condition this winter, and will be sorry to hear that he grows feebler day by day, and is evidently failing and fading from our sight" [W 6:396–397]. Thoreau died on 6 May 1862.

**19** Many of Thoreau's final journal entries are undated.

**20** Unidentified.

**21** On 4 August 1860 Thoreau wrote: "Choosing a place where the spruce was thick in this sunken rock yard, I cut out with a little hatchet a space for a camp in their midst, leaving two stout ones six feet apart to rest my ridge-pole on, and such limbs of these as would best form the gable ends. I then cut four spruces as rafters for the gable ends, leaving the stub ends of the branches to rest the cross-beams or girders on, of which there were two or three to each slope; and I made the roof very steep. Then cut an abundance of large flat spruce limbs, four or five feet long, and laid them on, shingle-fashion, beginning at the ground

*May 12.* SET OUT FOR MINNESOTA *via* Worcester.[18]

*After July 9.*[19] It is amusing to observe how a kitten regards the attic, kitchen, or shed where it was bred as its castle to resort to in time of danger. It loves best to sleep on some elevated place, as a shelf or chair, and for many months does not venture far from the back door where it first saw the light. Two rods is a great range for it, but so far it is tempted, when the dew is off, by the motions of grasshoppers and crickets and other such small game, sufficiently novel and surprising to it. They frequently have a wheezing cough, which some refer to grasshoppers' wings across their windpipes. The kitten has been eating grasshoppers.

If some member of the household with whom they are familiar—their mistress or master—goes forth into the garden, they are then encouraged to take a wider range, and for a short season explore the more distant bean and cabbage rows, or, if several of the family go forth at once,—as it were a reconnaissance in force,—the kitten does a transient scout duty outside, but yet on the slightest alarm they are seen bounding back with great leaps over the grass toward the castle, where they stand panting on the door-step, with their small lower jaws fallen, until they fill up with courage again. A cat looks down with complacency on the strange dog from the corn-barn window.

*After October 5.* Young Macey,[20] who has been camping on Monadnock this summer, tells me that he found one of my spruce huts made last year in August,[21] and that as many as eighteen, reshingling it, had camped in it while he was there.

Four little kittens just born; lay like stuffed skins of kittens in a heap, with pink feet; so flimsy and helpless they lie, yet blind, without any stiffness or ability to stand.

At three weeks old the kitten begins to walk in a staggering and creeping manner and even to play a little with its mother, and, if you put your ear close, you may hear it purr. It is remarkable that it will not wander far from the dark corner where the cat has left it, but will instinctively find its way back to it, probably by the sense of touch, and will rest nowhere else. Also it is careful not to venture too near the edge of a precipice, and its claws are ever extended to save itself in such places. It washes itself somewhat, and assumes many of the attitudes of an old cat at this age. By the disproportionate size of its feet and head and legs now it reminds you of a lion.

I saw it scratch its ear to-day, probably for the first time; yet it lifted one of its hind legs and scratched its ear as effectually as an old cat does. So this is instinctive, and you may say that, when a kitten's ear first itches, Providence comes to the rescue and lifts its hind leg for it. You would say that this little creature was as perfectly protected by its instinct in its infancy as an old man can be by his wisdom. I observed when she first noticed the figures on the carpet, and also put up her paws to touch or play with surfaces a foot off. By the same instinct that they find the mother's teat before they can see they scratch their ears and guard against falling.

*3 November.* After a violent easterly storm in the night, which clears up at noon (November 3, 1861), I notice that the surface of the railroad causeway, composed of gravel, is singularly marked, as if stratified like some slate rocks, on their edges, so that I can tell within a small fraction of a degree from what quarter the rain came. These lines, as it were of stratification, are perfectly parallel, and straight as a ruler, diagonally across the flat surface of the

and covering the stub ends. This made a foundation for two or three similar layers of smaller twigs. Then made a bed of the same, closed up the ends somewhat, and all was done. All these twigs and boughs, of course, were dripping wet, and we were wet through up to our middles. But we made a good fire at the door, and in an hour or two were completely dried" [J 14:10].

causeway for its whole length. Behind each little pebble, as a protecting boulder, an eighth or a tenth of an inch in diameter, extends northwest a ridge of sand an inch or more, which it has protected from being washed away, while the heavy drops driven almost horizontally have washed out a furrow on each side, and on all sides are these ridges, half an inch apart and perfectly parallel.

All this is perfectly distinct to an observant eye, and yet could easily pass unnoticed by most. Thus each wind is self-registering.

# Choice of Copy Text and Editorial Emendations

The purpose of this book is to provide a fully annotated reading text of selections from Thoreau's journal. The copy text for most of these selections is the 14-volume standard edition, *The Journal of Henry D. Thoreau,* edited by Bradford Torrey and Francis H. Allen (Boston: Houghton Mifflin, 1906). The exceptions are three groups of entries that do not appear in the 1906 edition; the copy text used for these is as follows:

- for 1 November 1840 and 20 January 1841, Henry D. Thoreau, *Consciousness in Concord: The Text of Thoreau's Hitherto "Lost Journal," 1840–1841* (Boston: Houghton Mifflin, 1958);
- for 1843, Thoreau's manuscript journal (MS Am 278.5), published by permission of the Houghton Library, Harvard University;
- for 1848 through 28 February 1850, Thoreau's manuscript journal (HM13182), published by permission of the Huntington Library, San Marino, California.

For consistency, these passages have been silently edited to correspond with the editorial policies used in the 1906 edition.

A space between entries under the same date indicates either a change of subject or the omission, without ellipses, of intervening material. All ellipses and parentheses in the text are authorial, not editorial. The only exception is the bracketed editorial ellipsis in the 16 April 1852 entry, where a space would have interrupted the flow of the passage.

Certain typographical features of the 1906 edition, such as the formatting of dates and the spacing after titles, have not been retained and have been silently regularized.

The text of the 1906 edition has been emended where any of the following circumstances apply:

- The headings Thoreau gave to many early journal passages (in 1837–1839) have been silently excised.
- Inconsistencies in spelling or word division have been regularized.
- The 1906 editors' use of [sic] has been replaced with a less intrusive editorial note, as listed below. Where Thoreau's word choice was correct and the editors' use of [sic] may be considered erroneous or unnecessary, it has been removed without further note.
- Where the 1906 editors' bracketed insertions have been deemed unnecessary, they have been silently removed. Where their bracketed insertions have been adopted, the brackets have been silently removed and the emendation noted below.
- Initials and abbreviations have been silently expanded for ease of reading.
- Names that were replaced with dashes by the 1906 editors have been restored and noted below.
- Undated entries have been dated as precisely as possible: for example, After January 21, After July 9.

The following are the specific minor changes that have been made; these are identified by page number in this edition, followed by line number.

| | | | |
|---|---|---|---|
| 11:17 | *with* inserted (from the 1906 edition) | 117:14 | *to* inserted (1906 edition) |
| 20:13 | *to* inserted (1906 edition) | 130:36 | *were* inserted (1906 edition) |
| 25:32 | *to* inserted (1906 edition) | 132:31 | *of* inserted (1906 edition) |
| 30:35 | *I* inserted (1906 edition) | 133:13 | *what* inserted (1906 edition) |
| 37:20 | *ever* corrected to *never* as in manuscript journal | 138:16–17 | *friends for* corrected to *friends, or* as in manuscript journal |
| 38:26 | *than* inserted | 139:1 | *him* inserted (1906 edition) |
| 39:14 | period inserted at end of text to replace semicolon, which separates the continuation of the paragraph not included here | 150:10 | *a* inserted (1906 edition) |
| | | 150:12 | *a* inserted (1906 edition) |
| | | 151:15 | *the* inserted (1906 edition) |
| | | 151:21 | *to* inserted (1906 edition) |
| | | 151:23 | *be* inserted (1906 edition) |
| 54:31 | *elate* corrected to *elated* as in manuscript journal | 153:22 | *song* corrected to *sound* as in manuscript journal |
| 55:3 | *and* inserted as in manuscript journal | 155:2 | dashes corrected to *Minot* as in manuscript journal |
| 63:17 | *us* inserted (1906 edition) | 159:20 | comma deleted from *loom, in* as in manuscript journal |
| 64:15 | punctuation emended, semicolon moved outside quotation mark | 160:23 | *be* inserted (1906 edition) |
| 67:19 | *whom* inserted (1906 edition) | 163:12 | *beef's* corrected to *beeve's* as in manuscript journal |
| 69:18–19 | *flamelike* emended to *flame-like* | | |
| 70:18 | *was* inserted (1906 edition) | 163:32 | *truth* corrected to *truths* as in manuscript journal |
| 71:6 | *to-day* (hyphenated) corrected to *to day* (two words) as in manuscript journal | 164:2 | *I am* inserted (1906 edition) |
| | | 164:22–23 | *papillaceous feelers* corrected to *papillary-feelers* as in manuscript journal, the intent of Thoreau's interlineation *[nilous]* being unclear |
| 72:33 | *so much* inserted (1906 edition) | | |
| 74:30 | *at* inserted (1906 edition) | | |
| 76:23 | *I* inserted (1906 edition) | | |
| 78:35 | *rather* inserted (1906 edition) | | |
| 81:34 | *a* inserted (1906 edition) | 165:3 | *are* inserted (1906 edition) |
| 83:12 | *would* inserted (1906 edition) | 166:1 | *me* inserted (1906 edition) |
| 84:22 | *the* inserted (1906 edition) | 172:10 | *that* inserted (1906 edition) |
| 86:13 | *are* inserted (1906 edition) | 173:12 | *the* inserted (1906 edition) |
| 98:36 | *be* inserted (1906 edition) | 173:17 | *the* corrected to *thee* as in manuscript journal |
| 104:32 | *it* inserted (1906 edition) | | |
| 106:16 | *like* inserted (1906 edition) | 176:9 | *of miles* inserted (1906 edition) |

| 181:26 | *most* corrected to *moist*, as in manuscript journal; comma added | 284:18 | *them* inserted (1906 edition) |
| | | 284:34 | *it* inserted (1906 edition) |
| 182:22 | *passed* corrected to *poured* as in manuscript journal | 285:11 | *am* inserted (1906 edition) |
| | | 288:32 | *Melchier* emended to *Melcher* |
| 188:22 | *of* inserted (1906 edition) | 291:27 | *day* inserted (1906 ed) |
| 190:15 | *chiefly* corrected to *wholly* following note in the 1906 edition: "'Chiefly' is crossed out in pencil and 'wholly' substituted." | 294:33 | *him, again* emended to *him again,* |
| | | 312:23 | *Squire's* corrected to *Squin's* (I gratefully acknowledge the generosity of Bob Maker for sharing his identification of the original mistranscription) |
| 190:15, 32 | dashes corrected to *Wright* as in manuscript journal | | |
| 194:17 | *to* inserted (1906 edition) | 314:8 | *wood* inserted (1906 edition) |
| 196:25 | dashes corrected to *Conant* as in manuscript journal | 319:15 | *pepe* emended to *pe-pe* |
| | | 329:17 | *flower* emended to *flour* |
| 209:15 | *which* inserted (1906 edition) | 336:25 | *need* inserted (1906 edition) |
| 215:7 | *to* inserted (1906 edition) | 346:33 | *town. November Eatheart,* emended to *town Novembers. Eat heart,* (based on manuscript journal; Thoreau's intention here is unclear) |
| 216:21 | *it* inserted (1906 edition) | | |
| 221:36 | *getting a livelihood* is followed by lengthy quotations in Latin by Cato and Varro with translations by Thoreau, omitted here | | |
| | | 358:27 | *State* corrected to *state,* as in manuscript journal |
| 228:3 | *are* inserted (1906 edition) | 368:2 | *the* inserted (1906 edition) |
| 235:30 | *had* inserted (1906 edition) | 372:31 | *it* inserted (1906 edition) |
| 237:9 | *of* inserted (1906 edition) | 376:11 | *her* emended to *it* for consistency with Thoreau's use of the impersonal pronoun when writing about Genius |
| 237:28 | *springlike* corrected to *spring-like* as in manuscript journal | | |
| 243:1 | *it* inserted (1906 edition) | | |
| 254:23 | *the* inserted (1906 edition); *is* inserted (1906 edition) | 380:12 | *be* inserted (1906 edition) |
| | | 395:20 | *him* inserted (1906 edition) |
| 262:2 | *a* inserted (1906 edition) | 399:11 | *it* inserted (1906 edition) |
| 265:12 | *am* inserted (1906 edition) | 400:25 | *Concord* inserted (1906 edition) |
| 268:17 | *become* inserted (1906 edition) | 411:5 | *works:* the 1906 transcription is retained although Thoreau may have intended to write *walks* here |
| 271:19 | *he* inserted (1906 edition) | | |
| 271:34 | *off* inserted (1906 edition) | | |
| 278:30 | *to* Inserted (1906 edition) | 414:21 | *are* inserted (1906 edition) |
| 284:15 | *he* inserted (1906 edition) | 420:31 | *R.* expanded to *Rufus*; *M——* cor- |

|       | rected to Merriam from the manu- | 434:31 | *of an inch* inserted (1906 edition) |
|-------|----------------------------------|--------|--------------------------------------|
|       | script journal                   | 436:15 | *of* inserted (1906 edition)         |
| 423:30 | *an* inserted (1906 edition)    | 437:18 | *it* inserted (1906 edition)         |
| 427:22 | *the* inserted (1906 edition)   | 447:30 | *it* inserted (1906 edition)         |
| 433:14 | *fire* inserted (1906 edition)  | 448:35 | *be* inserted (1906 edition)         |
| 433:27 | *day* inserted (1906 edition)   | 457:15 | *of* inserted (1906 edition)         |

# Bibliography

*I think it will be found that he who speaks with most authority on a given subject is not ignorant of what has been said by his predecessors. He will take his place in a regular order, and substantially add his own knowledge to the knowledge of previous generations.* — *Thoreau in his journal, 31 December 1859*

Aesop. *The Fable of Aesop and Others, with design on wood by Thomas Bewick.* Newcastle: Printed by E. Walter for T. Bewick, 1818.

*Aesthetic Papers.* Edited by Elizabeth P. Peabody. Boston: The Editor; New York: G. P. Putnam, 1849.

Alcott, Amos Bronson. *The Journals of Bronson Alcott.* Selected and edited by Odell Shepard. Boston: Little, Brown, 1938.

———. *The Letters of A. Bronson Alcott.* Edited by Richard L. Herrnstadt. Ames: Iowa State University Press, 1969.

Alcott, Louisa May. "Thoreau's Flute." *Atlantic Monthly,* September 1863.

Alcott, William Andrus. *Young Man's Guide.* Boston: Lilly, Wait, Colman, and Holden, 1833.

Ammer, Christine. *The American Heritage Dictionary of Idioms.* Boston: Houghton Mifflin, 1997.

Angelo, Ray. *Botanical Index to the Journal of Henry David Thoreau.* Salt Lake City: Peregrine Smith, 1984.

Bailey, Nathan. *A New Universal Etymological English Dictionary.* London: Printed for T. Osborne and J. Snipton, 1755.

Ball, Benjamin Lincoln. *Three Days on the White Mountains, Being the Perilous Adventure of Dr. B. L. Ball on Mount Washington, During October 25, 26, and 27, 1855.* Boston: N. Noyes, 1856.

Barber, John Warner. *Historical Collections, Being a General Collection of Interesting Facts, Traditions, Biographical Sketches, Anecdotes, &c., Relating to the History and Antiquities of Every Town in Massachusetts, with Geographical Descriptions.* Worcester: Dorr, Howland, 1841.

Bartram, William. *Travels Through North and South Carolina, Georgia, East and West Florida, the Cherokee Country, the Extensive Territories of the Muscogulges, or Creek Confederacy, and the Country of the Cherokees.* Philadelphia: Printed by James and Johnson, 1791.

Bigelow, Jacob. *American Medical Botany.* Boston: Cummings and Hilliard, 1817–1820.

Borst, Raymond. *The Thoreau Log: A Documentary Life of Henry David Thoreau, 1817–1862.* New York: G. K. Hall, 1992.

Botkin, Benjamin Albert, ed. *A Treasury of American Folklore: Stories, Ballads, and Traditions of the People.* New York: Crown, 1944.

Brewster, David. *The Life of Sir Isaac Newton.* New York: J. and J. Harper, 1831.

Brown, Mary Hosmer. *Memories of Concord.* Boston: Four Seas, 1926.

Browne, Thomas. *Works, Including His Life and Correspondence.* London: W. Pickering, 1835–1836.

Buel, Jesse. *The Farmer's Companion; or, Essays on the Principles and Practice of American Husbandry.* Boston: Marsh, Capen, Lyon, and Webb, 1840.

Burke, Edmund. *The Works of the Right Honourable Edmund Burke.* London: F. and C. Rivington, 1801.

Burton, Richard F. *Personal Narrative of a Pilgrimage to El-Madinah and Meccah.* New York: Putnam, 1856.

Cameron, Kenneth Walter. *The Massachusetts Lyceum During the American Renaissance.* Hartford: Transcendental Books, 1969.

Canby, Henry Seidel. *Thoreau.* Boston: Houghton Mifflin, 1939.

Carlyle, Thomas. *Past and Present.* Boston: C. C. Little and J. Brown, 1843.

———. *Sartor Resartus: The Life and Opinions of Herr Teufelsdröckh in Three Books.* Introduction and notes by Rodger L. Tarr; text established by Mark Engel and Rodger L. Tarr. Berkeley: University of California Press, 2000.

Cervantes, Miguel de. *History of the Renowned Don Quixote de la Mancha.* From the Spanish, translated by several hands. London: Printed for D. Midwinter, 1743.

Chalmers, Alexander, ed. *The Works of the English Poets, from Chaucer to Cowper.* London: J. Johnson, 1810.

Channing, William Ellery (the Elder). *The Works of William E. Channing, D.D.* Boston: American Unitarian Association, 1901.

Channing, William Ellery II. *The Collected Poems of William Ellery Channing the Younger, 1817–1901.* Facsimile reproductions with an introduction by Walter Harding. Gainesville, Fla.: Scholars' Facsimiles and Reprints, 1967.

———. Notebooks and Journals. Houghton Library, Harvard University.

———. *Thoreau, the Poet-Naturalist: With Memorial Verses.* New edition, enlarged and edited by F. B. Sanborn. Boston: C. E. Goodspeed, 1902.

Chaucer, Geoffrey. *The Canterbury Tales of Chaucer.* With an essay of his language and versification, an introductory discourse, notes, and a glossary by Tho. Tyrwhitt. London: W. Pickering, 1830.

Christie, John Aldrich. *Thoreau as World Traveler.* New York: Columbia University Press, 1965.

Christy, Arthur. *The Orient in American Transcendentalism: A Study of Emerson, Thoreau, and Alcott.* New York: Columbia University Press, 1932.

Collections of the Massachusetts Historical Society for the Year 1794. Boston: The Society, 1794.

Collier, J. Payne. *Old Ballads from Early Printed Copies of the Utmost Rarity.* London: Printed for The Percy Society by C. Richards, 1840.

Collison, Gary. *Shadrach Minkins: From Fugitive Slave to Citizen.* Cambridge: Harvard University Press, 1997.

Commager, Henry Steele. *Theodore Parker.* Boston: Little, Brown, 1936.

*Concord, Massachusetts: Births, Marriages, and Deaths, 1635–1850.* Concord: Printed by the Town, 1895.

Conway, Moncure Daniel. "Thoreau." *Eclectic Magazine,* August 1866; reprinted from *Fraser's Magazine.*

Curtis, George William. *Early Letters of George Wm. Curtis to John S. Dwight: Brook Farm and Concord.* Edited by George Willis Cooke. New York: Harper and Brothers, 1898.

Dante Alighieri. *Divine Comedy: The Inferno.* A literal prose translation, with the text of the original collated from the best editions, and explanatory notes, by John A. Carlyle. New York: Harper and Brothers, 1849.

Dean, Bradley P. "Thoreau and Horace Greeley Exchange Letters on the 'Spontaneous Generation of Plants.'" *New England Quarterly,* December 1993.

Dean, Bradley P., and Ronald Wesley Hoag. "Thoreau's Lectures Before Walden: An Annotated Calendar." *Studies in the American Renaissance 1995.*

———. "Thoreau's Lectures After Walden: An Annotated Calendar." *Studies in the American Renaissance 1996.*

*The Dial: A Magazine for Literature, Philosophy, and Religion.* Boston: Weeks, Jordan, 1840–1844; reprinted, New York: Russell and Russell, 1961.

Dibdin, Charles. *The Songs, Chronologically Arranged: With Notes, Historical, Biographical, and Critical.* London: G. H. Davidson, 1848.

"Does the Dew Fall?" *Harper's New Monthly Magazine,* September 1853, 504–506.

Dykes, Oswald. *English Proverbs.* London: Printed by H. Meere, 1709.

Emerson, Edward. *The Centennial of the Social Circle in Concord: March 21, 1882.* Cambridge: Riverside, 1882.

———. *Emerson in Concord: A Memoir Written for the "Social Circle" in Concord, Massachusetts.* Boston: Houghton Mifflin, 1889.

———. *Henry Thoreau as Remembered by a Young Friend.* Boston: Houghton Mifflin, 1917.

Emerson, Ellen Tucker. *The Letters of Ellen Tucker Emerson.* Edited by Edith E. W. Gregg; foreword by Gay Wilson Allen. Kent, Ohio: Kent State University Press, 1982.

Emerson, George B. *A Report on the Trees and Shrubs Growing Naturally in the Forests of Massachusetts.* Boston: Dutton and Wentworth, 1846.

Emerson, Ralph Waldo. *The Collected Works of Ralph Waldo Emerson.* Cambridge: Harvard University Press, 1971–.

———. *The Complete Works of Ralph Waldo Emerson.* Centenary edition. Boston: Houghton Mifflin, 1903.

———. *The Correspondence of Emerson and Carlyle.* Edited by Joseph Slater. New York: Columbia University Press, 1964.

———. *Early Lectures of Ralph Waldo Emerson.* Edited by Stephen E. Whicher and Robert E. Spiller. Cambridge: Harvard University Press, 1959–1972.

———. *The Journals and Miscellaneous Notebooks of Ralph Waldo Emerson.* Edited by William H. Gilman et al. Cambridge: Harvard University Press, 1960–1982.

———. *Journals of Ralph Waldo Emerson.* Edited by Edward Waldo Emerson and Waldo Emerson Forbes. Cambridge: Riverside, 1909–1914.

———. *The Letters of Ralph Waldo Emerson.* Edited by Ralph L. Rusk and Eleanor Tilton. New York: Columbia University Press, 1939–1995.

———. *Nature; Addresses, and Lectures.* Boston: James Munroe, 1849.

Euler, Leonard. *Elements of Algebra.* Translated from the French by John Hewlett. London: Longman, Orme, 1840.

Evelyn, John. *Sylva; or, A Discourse of Forest-Trees and the Propagation of Timber in His Majesties Dominions . . . Terra, a Philosophical Essay of Earth . . . Also, Kalendarium Hortense, or, The Gard'ners Almanac.* London: Printed for John Martyn, printer to the Royal Society, 1679.

Fink, Steven. *Prophet in the Market-Place.* Princeton: Princeton University Press, 1992.

Fleck, Richard. *Henry Thoreau and John Muir Among the Indians.* Hamden, Conn.: Archon, 1985.

Fuller, Margaret. *Memoirs of Margaret Fuller Ossoli.* Edited by R. W. Emerson, W. H. Channing, and J. F. Clarke. Boston: Phillips, Sampson, 1852.

———. *Summer on the Lakes in 1843.* Introduction by Susan Belasco Smith. Urbana: University of Illinois Press, 1991.

Garcin de Tassy, Joseph Héliodore. *Histoire de la Littérature Hindoui.* Paris: Oriental Translation Committee of Great Britain and Ireland, 1839–1847.

Gerard, John. *Herball, or Generall Historie of Plantes.* New York: Dover, 1975, reprint of the 1633 edition printed by A. Islip, J. Norton, and R. Whitakers, London.

Goethe, Johann Wolfgang von. *Conversations with Goethe in the Last Years of His Life.* Translated by S. M. Fuller. Boston: Hilliard, Gray, 1839.

———. *Gespräche mit Goethe in den Letzten Jahren seines Lebens, 1823–1832.* Compiled by Johann Peter Eckermann. Leipzig: F. A. Brockhaus, 1837–1848.

———. *Werke: Vollstandige Ausgabe Letzer Hand.* Stuttgart and Tübingen: J. G. Cotta, 1828–1833.

Gross, Robert. *Books and Libraries in Thoreau's Concord: Two Essays.* Worcester: American Antiquarian Society, 1988.

Grover, Kathryn, and Janine V. da Silva. *Historic Resource Study: Boston African American National Historic Site,* 31 December 2002 (http://www.cr.nps.gov/history/online_books/bost/hrs.pdf).

Guyot, Arnold Henry. *The Earth and Man: Lectures on Comparative Physical Geography, in Its Relation to the History of Mankind.* Boston: Gould and Lincoln, 1851.

Haddock, John A. "The Perils of Aerial Navigation." *Watertown Reformer,* 5 October 1859.

Harding, Walter. *The Days of Henry Thoreau.* Enlarged and corrected edition. New York: Dover, 1982.

*Harivansa, ou Histoire de la Famille de Hari, Ouvrage Formant un Appendice du Mahabharata, et Traduit sur l'Original Sanscrit.* Translated by Simon Alexandre Langlois. Paris: Printed for the Oriental Translation Fund of Great Britain and Ireland, 1834–1835.

Harlan, Richard. *Fauna Americana, Being a Description of the Mammiferous Animals Inhabiting North America.* Philadelphia: A. Finley, 1825.

Hawthorne, Julian. *The Memoirs of Julian Hawthorne.* Edited by Edith Garrigues Hawthorne. New York: Macmillan, 1938.

Hawthorne, Nathaniel. *The American Notebooks.* Edited by Claude M. Simpson. Columbus: Ohio State University Press, 1972.

Haydon, Benjamin Robert. *Life of Benjamin Robert Haydon, Historical Painter, from His Autobiography and Journals.* Edited by Tom Taylor. New York: Harper and Brothers, 1853.

*The Heetōpadēs of Veeshnoo-Sarmā, in a Series of Connected Fables, Interspersed with Moral, Prudential, and Political Maxims.* Bath: R. Cruttwell, 1787.

Henry, Alexander. *Travels and Adventures in Canada and the Indian Territories Between the Years 1760 and 1776.* New York: I. Riley, 1809.

Hitchcock, Edward. *Report on the Geology, Mineralogy, Botany, and Zoology of Massachusetts: Made and Published by Order of the Government of that State.* Amherst: Press of J. S. and C. Adams, 1833.

Hoar, George F. *Autobiography of Seventy Years.* New York: C. Scribner's Sons, 1903.

Homer. *The Iliad of Homer.* Translated by Alexander Pope. Baltimore: Philip H. Nicklin, Fielding Lucas, Jun. and Samuel Jeffries, 1812.

Hosmer, Horace. *Remembrances of Concord and the Thoreaus: Letters of Horace Hosmer to Dr. S. A. Jones.* Edited by George Hendrick. Urbana: University of Illinois Press, 1977.

Howarth, William L. *The Book of Concord: Thoreau's Life as a Writer.* New York: Viking, 1982.

———. *The Literary Manuscripts of Henry David Thoreau.* Columbus: Ohio State University Press, 1974.

Hudspeth, Robert N. *Ellery Channing.* New York: Twayne, 1973.

Jarvis, Edward. *Traditions and Reminiscences of Concord, Massachusetts, 1779–1878.* Edited by Sarah Chapin; introduction by Robert A. Gross. Amherst: University of Massachusetts Press, 1993.

Johnson, Linck C. *Thoreau's Complex Weave: The Writing of A Week on the Concord and Merrimack Rivers, with the Text of the First Draft.* Charlottesville: Published for the Bibliographical Society of the University of Virginia, by the University Press of Virginia, 1986.

Jones, Samuel Arthur. *Thoreau: A Glimpse.* Concord: A. Lane, The Erudite Press, 1903.

Kane, Elisha Kent. *The United States Grinnell Expedition in Search of Sir John Franklin: A Personal Narrative.* New York: Harper and Brothers, 1853.

Krutch, Joseph Wood. *Henry David Thoreau.* New York: W. Sloane, 1948.

Laing, Samuel. *Journal of a Residence in Norway During the Years 1834, 1835, & 1836, Made with a View to Enquire into the Moral and Political Economy of that Country, and the Condition of its Inhabitants.* London: Printed for Longman, Orme, Brown, Green, and Longmans, 1837.

Lemprière, John. *Bibliotheca Classica; or, A Dictionary of All the Principal Names and Terms Relating to the Geography, Topography, History, Literature, and Mythology of Antiquity and of the Ancients: With a Chronological Table.* Revised and corrected by Lorenzo L. Da Ponte and John D. Ogilby. New York: W. E. Dean, 1837.

McGill, Frederick T., Jr. *Channing of Concord: A Life of William Ellery Channing II.* New Brunswick: Rutgers University Press, 1967.

Mackay, Charles. *Memoirs of Extraordinary Popular Delusions and the Madness of Crowds.* London: Office of the National Illustrated Library, 1852.

Mahābhārata: Bhagvat-gēētā, or Dialogues of Kreeshna and Arjoon. Translated by Charles Wilkin. London, 1785.

Meltzer, Milton, and Walter Harding. *A Thoreau Profile.* New York: Crowell, 1962.

*A Memorial of Daniel Webster, from the City of Boston.* Boston: Little, Brown, 1853.

Michaux, François André. *The North American Sylva, or A Description of the Forest Trees of the United States, Canada, and Nova Scotia.* Paris: Printed by C. d'Hautel, 1818–1819.

Miller, Perry, ed. *The Transcendentalists: An Anthology.* Cambridge: Harvard University Press, 1950.

Mott, Wes, ed. *Biographical Dictionary of Transcendentalism.* Westport, Conn.: Greenwood, 1996.

———. *Encyclopedia of Transcendentalism.* Westport, Conn.: Greenwood, 1996.

Myerson, Joel, ed. *Transcendentalism: A Reader.* New York: Oxford University Press, 2001.

Ovid. *The Fifteen Books of Ovid's Metamorphoses.* Translated by Arthur Golding. London: W. Seres, 1567.

Paul, Sherman. *The Shores of America: Thoreau's Inward Exploration.* Urbana: University of Illinois Press, 1958.

Pauthier, Jean-Pierre-Guillaume. *Confucius et Mencius: Les Quatre Livres de Philosophie Moral et Politique de la Chine.* Paris: Bibliothèque-Charpentier, 1841.

Percy, Thomas. *Reliques of Ancient English Poetry, or A Collection of Old Ballads.* Philadelphia: James E. Moore, 1823.

Poirier, Richard. *A World Elsewhere: The Place of Style in American Literature.* New York: Oxford University Press, 1966.

Rasles, Father Sébastian. "Dictionary of the Abnaki Language." *Memoirs of the American Academy of Arts and Sciences.* Boston: The Academy, 1833.

Regnaut, Cristophe. "A Veritable Account of the Martyrdom and Blessed Death of Father Jean de Breboeuf and of Father Gabriel L'Alemant, in New France, in the Country of the Hurons, by the Iroquois, Enemies of the Faith." In *Relations de ce qui s'est Passé en la Nouvelle France, et l'Années 1633–1672,* Paris, 1633–1672.

"Reminiscences of Thoreau." *Outlook,* 2 December 1899.

*Reports of the Selectmen and Other Officers of the Town of Concord.* Concord: The Town, 1847–.

Richardson, Robert D., Jr. *Emerson: The Mind on Fire.* Berkeley: University of California Press, 1995.

———. *Henry Thoreau: A Life of the Mind.* Berkeley: University of California Press, 1986.

Ricketson, Anna, ed. *Daniel Ricketson and His Friends: Letters, Poems, Sketches, etc.* Boston: Houghton Mifflin, 1902.

Ricketson, Daniel. *The History of New Bedford, Bristol County, Massachusetts: Including a History of the Old Township of Dartmouth and the Present Townships of Westport, Dartmouth, and Fairhaven, from Their Settlement to the Present Time.* New Bedford: The Author, 1858.

Roy, Rajah Rammohun. *Translation of Several Principal Books, Passages, and Texts of the Veds and of Some Controversial Works of Brahmunical Theology.* London, 1832.

Rusk, Ralph L. *The Life of Ralph Waldo Emerson.* New York: C. Scribner's Sons, 1949.

Sallust. *De Catalinæ Conjuractione, Belloque Jugurthino, Historiæ.* Boston: Hilliard, Gray, 1833.

Salt, Henry S. *Life of Henry David Thoreau.* Edited by George Hendrick, Willene Hendrick, and Fritz Oehlschlaeger. Urbana: University of Illinois Press, 1993.

Sanborn, Franklin Benjamin. *The Life of Henry David Thoreau: Including Many Essays Hitherto Unpublished, and Some Account of His Family and Friends.* Boston: Houghton Mifflin, 1917.

———. *Recollections of Seventy Years.* Boston: Gorham, 1909.

———. "An Unpublished Concord Journal." *Century Magazine,* April 1922.

———. "Thoreau." *Harvard Register,* April 1881.

Sattelmeyer, Robert. *Thoreau's Reading: A Study in Intellec-*

*tual History with Bibliographical Catalogue.* Princeton: Princeton University Press, 1988.

Sayre, Robert. *Thoreau and the American Indian.* Princeton: Princeton University Press, 1977.

Scudder, Townsend. *Concord: American Town.* Boston: Little, Brown, 1947.

Seybold, Ethel Thoreau. *Thoreau: The Quest and the Classics.* New Haven: Yale University Press, 1951.

Shakespeare, William. *The Dramatic Works of William Shakespeare, Accurately Printed from the Text of the Corrected Copy Left by the Late George Steevens, Esq.* Hartford: Andrus and Judd, 1833.

———. *The Norton Shakespeare.* Stephen Greenblatt, general editor. New York: W. W. Norton, 1997.

Shattuck, Lemuel. *A History of the Town of Concord, Middlesex County, Massachusetts: From Its Earliest Settlement to 1832; and of the Adjoining Towns, Bedford, Acton, Lincoln, and Carlisle; Containing Various Notices of County and State History not Before Published.* Boston, 1835.

Shea, John G. "The Jogues Papers." *Collections of the New-York Historical Society,* 1857.

Shepard, Odell. *Pedlar's Progress: The Life of Bronson Alcott.* Boston: Little, Brown, 1937.

Stöver, Dietrich Johann Heinrich. *The Life of Sir Charles Linnaeus.* Translated by Joseph Trapp. London: B. and J. White, 1794.

Stowell, Robert F. *A Thoreau Gazetteer.* Edited by William L. Howarth. Princeton: Princeton University Press, 1970.

*Studies in the American Renaissance.* Edited by Joel Myerson. Charlottesville: University Press of Virginia, 1977–1996.

Sturluson, Snorri. *The Heimskringla; or, Chronicle of the Kings of Norway.* Translated by Samuel Laing. London: Longman, Brown, Green, and Longmans, 1844.

Thoreau, Henry D. *Collected Poems of Henry Thoreau.* Enlarged edition. Edited by Carl Bode. Baltimore: Johns Hopkins Press, 1965.

———. *Consciousness in Concord: The Text of Thoreau's Hitherto "Lost Journal," 1840–1841.* Together with notes and a commentary by Perry Miller. Boston: Houghton Mifflin, 1958.

———. *The Correspondence of Henry David Thoreau.* Edited by Walter Harding and Carl Bode. New York: New York University Press, 1958.

———. *Early Essays and Miscellanies.* Edited by Joseph J. Moldenhauer and Edwin Moser, with Alexander Kern. Princeton: Princeton University Pres, 1975.

———. *Faith in a Seed: The Dispersion of Seeds and Other Late Natural History Writings.* Edited by Bradley P. Dean. Washington, D.C.: Island Press/Shearwater Books, 1993.

———. *Huckleberries.* Edited, with an introduction, by Leo Stoller. Iowa City: Windhover Press of the University of Iowa, 1970.

———. *Journal.* Edited by John C. Broderick et al. Princeton: Princeton University Press, 1981–.

———. *The Journal of Henry Thoreau.* Edited by Bradford Torrey and Francis H. Allen. Boston: Houghton Mifflin, 1906.

———. *The Service.* Edited by F. B. Sanborn. Boston: Charles E. Goodspeed, 1902.

———. *Thoreau: Two Fragments from the Journals.* Edited, with a preface, by Alexander C. Kern. Iowa City: Windhover Press of the University of Iowa, 1968.

———. *Thoreau on Birds.* Compiled and with commentary by Helen Cruickshank; foreword by Roger Tory Peterson. New York: McGraw-Hill, 1964.

———. *Thoreau's Fact Book in the Harry Elkins Widener Collection.* Hartford: Transcendental Books, 1966.

———. *Thoreau's Literary Notebook in the Library of Congress.* Edited by K. W. Cameron. Hartford: Transcendental Books, 1964.

———. *Walden: A Fully Annotated Edition.* Edited by Jeffrey S. Cramer. New Haven: Yale University Press, 2004.

———. *Wild Fruits: Thoreau's Rediscovered Last Manuscript.* Edited and introduced by Bradley P. Dean. New York: W. W. Norton, 1999.

————. *The Writings of Henry D. Thoreau*. Walden edition. Boston: Houghton Mifflin, 1906.

*Thoreau Society Bulletin*. Geneseo, N.Y.: Thoreau Society, 1941–.

Todd, Mabel Loomis. *The Thoreau Family Two Generations Ago*. Berkeley Heights, N.J.: Printed for the Thoreau Society by the Oriole Press, 1958.

Topsell, Edward. *The History of Four-Footed Beasts and Serpents and Insects*. New York: Da Capo, 1967, reprint of the 1658 edition.

*Transactions of the Agricultural Societies in the State of Massachusetts, for 1851*. Boston: Dutton and Wentworth, 1847–1852.

Traubel, Horace. *With Walt Whitman in Camden*. New York: Rowman and Littlefield, 1961.

*Treasury of New England Folklore: Stories, Ballads, and Traditions of the Yankee People*. Edited by B. A. Botkin. New York: Crown, 1947.

Trench, Richard Chenevix. *The Study of Words*. New York: Redfield, 1852.

Turner, Sharon. *The History of the Anglo-Saxons from the Earliest Period to the Norman Conquest*. London: Longman, Brown, Green, and Longmans, 1852.

Van Doren, Mark. *Henry David Thoreau: A Study*. Boston: Houghton Mifflin, 1916.

Walker, John. *A Critical Pronouncing Dictionary, and Expositor of the English Language*. New York: Collins and Hannay, 1823.

Wheeler, Ruth. *Concord: Climate of Freedom*. Concord: Concord Antiquarian Society, 1967.

————. *Our American Mile: Concord's Battle Road, the Nation's Most Significant Historic Site*. Concord: Published for the Concord Antiquarian Society, 1957.

White, Gilbert. *The Natural History of Selborne, with Observations on Various Parts of Nature*. London: H. G. Bohn, 1851.

Wilkinson, John James Garth. *The Human Body and Its Connexion with Man*. London: Chapman and Hall, 1851.

Willey, Benjamin Glazier. *Incidents in White Mountain History*. Boston: N. Noyes, 1856.

Wise, John. *A System of Aeronautics, Comprehending Its Earliest Investigations, and Modern Practice and Art*. Philadelphia: J. A. Speel, 1850.

Wordsworth, William. *The Complete Poetical Works of William Wordsworth Together with a Description of the Lakes in the North of England*. Edited by Henry Reed. Boston: James Munroe, 1837.

# Index

Association for the Advancement of Science, 180

astrology, 176

astronomers and astronomy, 74–75, 86, 89, 110, 122, 175–176, 232, 407–408

atheism, 96

*Atlantic Monthly*, 28, 212, 351, 370

attic, 1, 11, 72, 192, 228, 230, 324–325, 456

Augean stables, 421

Augustine, Saint, 259

Aurora (Roman mythology), 78

autobiography. *See* biography

autumn, 22, 30–31, 34–36, 60, 101, 147, 165, 199, 208, 332, 335, 398, 400, 441

autumnal tints, 170, 297

"Autumnal Tints" (Thoreau), 158, 212, 298, 385

awe, 151, 341–342

azalea, 188, 248, 253

Babylon, 18, 74, 307, 407

Bailey, Nathan, 174

Baker, Jacob, 266

Ball, Benjamin Lincoln, 309, 359

barberry, 258

Barnum, P. T., 227; Barnum's American Museum, 233–234

Barrett, Samuel, 364

Bartlett, Josiah, 395, 401

Bartram, William, 86

baseball, 369

bathing, 40, 82–83, 146, 154–155, 157, 187, 228–229, 232, 236, 253, 268–269, 397, 441; boys bathing in river, 144

Baxter, Richard, 315

beans, 204, 270, 330, 333, 343, 368, 389; baked, 215; bean-bags, 433

Bear Garden Hill, 235

beauty, 22, 32, 34, 36, 97, 144–145, 153, 158, 166, 169, 186, 188, 206, 213, 219, 224, 226–227, 232, 237, 250–251, 330, 361, 374–375, 379–380, 395–396, 403, 405, 410, 414–415, 435–437, 441–442, 444, 447–449; in decay, 242

Beck Stow's Swamp, 253–254, 276, 278–281

Bede (the Venerable Bede), 452

Bedford (Mass.), 100, 193, 237, 431

Beech Spring (Lincoln), 266

bees and bee hunting, 247, 264

Bee-Tree Ridge (Concord), 386

bells, 81, 112, 306, 315, 323; alarm, 53; cow, 45–46, 193

berries, 77, 201, 281, 408, 431–432, 441–443, 446, 451; picking, 343. *See also names of specific berries*

*Bhagavad-Gita,* 290

Bible, 47, 103, 250, 351, 407; Acts, 98; Corinthians, 323; Deuteronomy, 98; Job, 6, 399; Ecclesiastes, 78, 93, 394; Exodus, 211, 298, 328, 400; Genesis, 5, 43, 60, 101, 202, 249, 294, 328, 343, 396; Hebrews, 41, 43; Isaiah, 113, 173, 188; James, 9; John, 80, 98, 139, 182, 205, 346; Jonah, 190; Kings, 192, 417; Luke, 32, 69, 79, 215, 275, 284, 351, 391, 396, 427; Mark, 78, 172, 173, 371, 391; Matthew, 22, 23, 40, 79, 90, 98, 183, 206, 284, 310, 391, 396, 408, 409, 427; Peter, 114, 370; Proverbs, 68; Psalms, 43, 52, 173, 186, 238; Revelation, 125, 224; Romans, 392; Samuel, 256; Thessalonians, 98; Timothy, 397. *See also* scriptures

Bigelow, Jacob, 292

bilberry, 16

Billerica Dam, 91

biography, 27, 252, 336

Canada, 103–104, 121, 220, 279, 298, 393, 413–414, 446; Thoreau visits, 168

Cape Cod, 57, 59, 323–325, 378

*Cape Cod* (Thoreau), 58, 325

Caracalla, 157

carbureted hydrogen, Thoreau ignites, 327

Carlyle, Thomas, 3–4, 33, 96, 168, 270, 328

carpentry, 138

catbird, 248

Catechism: larger, 371; shorter, 119, 371, 396

cats, 105, 139, 238–239, 290, 325, 346, 363, 456–457; Min, 290–291

cattle Show, Middlesex, 5, 202, 328, 432–433

caves, 146, 397; Edward Emerson's snow cave, 304–305

cedar, 258, 411

cellars and cellar-hole, 23, 27, 48–49, 62, 150, 181, 211, 239–240, 247, 370, 390, 441

celtis, 327

Cervantes, Miguel de, 20

Chaldean shepherds, 175

Chalmers, Thomas, 184–185

Channing, (William) Ellery (the younger), 50, 81, 85, 105, 111–112, 121, 138, 146, 152, 168, 185, 187, 189, 194, 199, 208–209, 222, 229, 235, 241, 259, 282, 386, 426, 429; as lecturer, 130–131. Works: "A Poet's Hope," 283, 332; *Thoreau, the Poet-Naturalist,* 112

Channing, William Ellery (the elder), 115

Channing, William Henry, 215

Chaos (Greek mythology), 356

character, 17, 19, 21, 24–25, 87, 103, 202, 230

charity, 23, 130, 396

chastity, 65, 132–133, 139, 152

"Chastity and Sensuality" (Thoreau), 65

checkerberry, 140–141, 411, 442

cherry tree, 258, 451, 453–455

chestnuts, 244, 337–338, 358

"Chesuncook" (Thoreau), 118, 221, 233, 370

chewink, 49, 296, 355

chickadee, 10, 114, 240, 253

childhood and children, 33, 44–47, 52, 76–77, 81, 84–85, 100, 105, 116, 146, 156, 159, 165, 186, 192, 195, 208, 219, 224–225, 237–238, 269, 299, 328, 335, 351, 365, 372, 375, 381, 396, 398–399, 401, 403, 416, 429, 431, 433, 435, 439, 441–443, 449–450. *See also* innocence; purity

China and Chinese empire, 16, 324, 405; foot-binding in, 48; infanticide, 85

Chinook, 48

Christianity, 29, 43, 48, 102, 177, 250, 258, 313–314, 349, 370, 397

Cicero, 29

Cincinnatus, Lucius Quinctius, 344

"Civil Disobedience" ("Resistance to Civil Government," Thoreau), 15, 29, 184, 347

civilization, 7, 27, 74, 151, 153, 184, 258, 262–263, 281, 299–300, 358, 440, 444

Clark, John Brooks, 334

Claude Lorrain, 403

Cliffs, the (Walden Woods), 8, 12, 28, 100, 131, 162, 171, 231, 378; in the rain, 317–319

"Cliffs" (poem), 8

cliques, 361

clothing, 129–130, 156, 189, 190, 193, 255, 265, 309, 315, 322, 348, 382, 426, 449

coarseness, 41, 138–139

cock. *See* rooster

coffee, 78, 214

cold, life-threatening, 450

Coleridge, Samuel Taylor, 189

Collins, William, 198
Comet Seeker (telescope), 176
common sense, 13–14, 40, 67, 71, 83, 100, 112, 160, 394, 409, 414, 436
compensation, 10, 19, 303
Conant, Ebenezer, 148, 196–197
Conantum (Walden Woods), 107, 146–148, 157, 162, 197, 208
Concord (Mass.), 26, 29, 45, 58, 87, 99–100, 103–104, 116, 128, 136, 154, 169, 173–174, 192, 236, 256–257, 260, 280, 302, 316, 332, 341, 347, 382, 400, 406, 408, 427, 442, 445
Concord Farmers' Club, 179
*Concord Freeman* (journal), 52, 179
Concord Lyceum, 5, 104, 130, 210, 223, 256; Thoreau lectures at, 20, 215
Concord River, 26, 52, 65–66, 91, 144, 153, 192, 237, 338, 360, 390, 407, 431
Concord Social Circle, 442
Concord Social Library, 178
Concord Town Library, 178
conformity, 213, 376
Confucius, 396, 399
Congress (U.S.), 63, 302, 371
Congressional Seed Distribution Program, 333
conscience. *See* higher laws
Constitution, U.S., not the highest law, 29
consumption. *See* health
contemplation, 66, 96, 127, 245, 307, 319
Conway, Moncure Daniel (on Thoreau), 103, 195, 214
Cook, James, 16
Coombs (musquash hunter), 426
courage and bravery, 26, 103, 159, 164, 219, 228, 346–347, 351, 353, 369, 397, 410, 418, 424, 456; moral, 370. *See also* fear

cramming, 234–235
cranberries, 50, 144, 211, 275–282, 343–344; speculating in, 211
crickets, 9, 12, 70–71, 73, 75, 82, 87–89, 92, 107, 146, 165, 332, 456
Crimean War, 274
crow, 22, 219, 237–238, 241, 258
Crystal Palace, 111, 233, 331
cuckoo, 148
cuttlefish, 164

daguerreotyping, 251, 375, 436
Dana, Richard Henry, 126, 157
Dante Alighieri, 125, 221, 325, 341
Davis, Charles, 255
Davis, Cummings, 449
death and dying, 30–32, 58–60, 124, 177, 255–256, 294–295, 304, 381–382, 392, 401–402, 433
decay, 37, 136, 177, 242, 326
Deep Cut (railroad), 73, 76, 99–100, 101, 174
Defoe, Daniel: *Robinson Crusoe,* 15, 234, 315, 336
deliberation, 39, 81, 91, 265, 276–277, 394
despair and desperation, 35, 37, 94, 258, 275, 304
devil, 23, 26, 80, 172, 195–196, 228, 370, 395–396, 404; devil's angels, 206
*Dial, The,* 124, 160, 336
Diana (Roman mythology), 177, 199
Dibdin, Charles, 43; "Poor Tom Bowling," 320
Dickens, Charles, 86, 418
diet, 10, 40, 93, 116, 206, 214, 231, 289, 297
"different drummer," 17, 78, 79, 85
Diogenes, 123, 125
dipper, theft of Thoreau's, 125

Greeley, Horace, 210, 233–234

Greylock, Mount (Saddleback), 152

Grisi, Giulia, 234

grosbeak, 249

ground-nut, 362

guilt, 20, 52–53, 226

gum-c bird, 81

guns, 229, 238, 241, 247, 259, 290, 309, 360, 363, 366. *See also* hunters and hunting

Hannibal, 18

Hanno, 16

hardhack, 81, 333

Hari, 33, 43, 48

*Harivansa,* 33

harmony, 106, 152, 188, 201, 213, 356, 396, 403

Harvard College (Cambridge), 5, 6, 126, 196, 227, 339, 363, 395, 406; library, 48, 116

Hastings, Jonas, 289, 291–292

hasty pudding, 60–61, 129

hat, as botany-box, 145–146, 292

hawks, 197, 220, 241, 260; marsh-hawk, 35, 223; night-hawk, 162, 355–356

Hawthorne, Julian, 220

Hawthorne, Nathaniel, 35, 81, 277

Haydon, Benjamin Robert, 215

health, 16, 18, 25, 30, 42, 94, 170, 269, 299, 313, 349, 383–384, 403, 431. *See also* bronchitis; sickness

heaven, 4, 22–23, 28, 38, 41, 59, 65, 67–68, 72, 79–80, 82, 89, 93, 98, 100, 102, 107, 119, 126, 135, 153, 176, 228, 260, 262, 281–282, 353

Hebrews, 47, 98, 186, 315, 407, 436

Hemans, Felicia Dorothea, 1

hemlock, 245

hen, 12, 56, 187

Hercules (Greek mythology), 354, 389, 421

Herodotus, 452

heroes and heroism, 2, 8, 15–17, 28, 103, 134, 336, 409, 414, 417, 421, 432; heroic age, 193; heroic virtue of a muskrat, 221

Hesiod, 73

Heywood's Peak, 227, 240

hickory, 314, 318

higher laws, 29, 180–181, 446

Hill, John Boynton, 237

Hill Burying Ground (Concord), 255, 341

Hinduism, 40, 43, 47–48, 64, 257, 370. *See also* Hindu scriptures by name

Hipparchus, 110

history, 3, 27, 37, 40, 62, 65, 73, 104, 188, 204, 243, 252, 257, 316, 332, 349, 382, 421, 425, 438–440, 446–447, 449, 452

Hoar, Edward S., 52, 357

Hoar, Samuel (Squire), 223

hockey, field, 395

Holbrook's Coffee-House, 113, 347

Holden Spruce Swamp, 208, 248

Homer, 39, 134, 290; *Iliad,* 8, 65–66, 94, 141; *Odyssey,* 8, 134

homesickness, 121, 302

horehound, 298

horn, farmer's, 154

horses, 315, 330, 339–340, 358, 363, 376, 384, 427; gift horse, 396; racing, 343; Thoreau kicked by, 329

Hosmer, Edmund, Sr., 154

Hosmer, Horace, 202

Hosmer, Joseph, 114, 265

Hosmer, Lydia, 449

Hostilius, Tullus, 81

houses, 6, 27, 83, 112, 129, 165, 182, 199, 233–234, 252, 265, 299, 304, 313–314,

pilgrim's cup, 46

pine, 10, 44, 105, 118, 131, 177, 185, 241, 247, 249, 289–290, 298, 316–317, 380–381, 412, 438, 452–454; fat, 171; pitch, 56, 104, 171, 429, 438; white, 118, 185, 241, 251, 316, 320, 438, 450; yellow (pumpkin pine), 87, 185–186

pineapples, 441, 443–444

place, sense of, 312–313

plants. *See names of specific plants*

Plato, 5, 29, 82, 181

Pliny the Elder, 453

plover, 402

poets and poetry, 11–13, 34–35, 37–38, 72, 82, 84–85, 89–91, 101, 104, 110, 113, 123, 135–136, 144, 176, 186, 189, 195, 198, 221, 223–225, 236, 257, 265, 285, 330, 336, 338–339, 343–346, 363, 383, 387, 414, 417, 419, 435–436; commonplace book for, 135; Emerson on, 123

poll tax, 15

Polo, Marco, 16, 86

Ponkawtasset Hill (Concord), 146, 364–365

pontederia, 211, 397, 407

Pope, Alexander, translation of *Iliad*, 8, 65–66

Poplar Hill (Concord), 364, 366

Porter, David, 442

post-office, 100, 172, 217, 323, 382, 414

potatoes, 6, 16, 37, 247, 270, 279–280, 292, 313, 333, 343, 449

Potter, Jonas, 80

pout, 36, 50–51, 156, 420

poverty, 255, 293, 307, 403

prairies, 177, 346, 397

Pratt's Powder Mills, 172–173, 239

preachers and preaching, 26, 218, 304, 313, 368–370, 372, 447

present, 1, 13, 62, 76, 170, 395, 414. *See also* future; past

privacy, 17, 160, 207, 229

progress, 2, 3, 32, 59, 79, 87, 129, 135, 166, 213, 386, 451

property, 19, 122, 154, 168, 247, 404, 431, 445, 448

Proteus (Greek mythology), 16, 142

publishers, 206–207

pumpkins, 37, 269, 400

Pythagoras, 4

purity, 34, 65, 78, 85, 133, 138–139, 195, 219. *See also* innocence

quail, 81

Quakers, 266, 268, 323

rabbits, 192, 248, 253, 302, 411

railroads, 7, 49–50, 55, 59, 95, 103, 162, 170, 173, 176, 218, 222, 232, 247, 263, 280, 289–290, 294–295, 306, 316, 376, 427, 431, 457; sleepers, 242, 367; workers, 39, 294–295, 306. *See also* Deep Cut

rain, rainstorms, 10, 13, 16, 118, 128, 159, 198, 199, 204, 208–209, 211, 245, 264–265, 269, 289, 317–320, 350, 362, 387, 388, 421–422, 432, 457; "sobbing" rain, 144; "unspeakable" rain, 141

rainbow, 159, 165, 250, 266, 320, 330–331, 344

Rainers (musical group), 21

Rans des Vaches, 193

Rasles, Sébastian, 352–353

raspberry, 169

Ray, Heman, 55

readers and reading, 24, 25, 33, 37–38, 76, 86, 91, 111, 112, 117, 128, 131, 134–135, 184, 206, 257, 259–260, 288, 289, 315,

surveying, 81, 116, 179, 180, 193, 214–215, 223, 255, 265–266, 301, 344, 347, 349, 400, 428

swallow, 80

Swallow Cave (Nahant, Mass.), 397

swamp-pink. *See* azalea

swamps, 16, 29, 42, 49, 58–60, 105, 168, 226, 241, 251–252, 285, 292–293, 311, 344, 347, 373, 401, 426, 431, 442–443, 454; Beck Stow's Swamp, 253–254, 276, 278–281; Dismal Swamp, 58–60; Gowing's Swamp, 277–278; Holden Spruce Swamp, 208, 248

sweet-fern, 373, 425

Swift, Jonathan, 16, 63, 346

Tahatawan, 374, 390

tailor, 315

talent, 24, 90, 97, 130

Tappan, William Aspinwall, 219–220

Tartary, steppes of, 16

taxes and taxation, 15, 25, 80–81, 136, 247–248, 431, 440, 447

tea, 6, 78, 154, 198, 214, 215, 231, 355, 411

teeth, 9, 66

telegraph, 218, 222, 250, 362; posts struck by lightning, 428–429; transatlantic, 362

telegraph harp, 2, 99–100, 101, 170, 208, 218, 224

telescopes, 74, 75, 122, 169, 176, 232. *See also* spyglass

temperance, 111, 165, 190, 403; intemperance, 201

thaw, 219, 387; personal, 10, 220

"Thaw, The" (poem), 10

Therien, Alek, 411, 445

Thermopylae, 24

thieves, 125, 193, 353

thimble-berry, 81

"Thomas Carlyle and His Works" (Thoreau), 4

Thor (Norse mythology), 315

Thoreau, Cynthia D. (mother), 35, 138, 202–203, 252, 291, 398

Thoreau, Helen (sister), 35, 42

Thoreau, Henry David

—books: *Cape Cod,* 58, 325; *Walden,* 17, 23–24, 39–41, 47, 50–51, 78–79, 81–82, 91, 99–100, 103, 108, 125–127, 139, 143, 154, 159, 171, 176, 183, 185–186, 189, 190, 202, 204, 221–222, 229, 231, 234, 236–237, 250, 255, 258, 268, 285, 298, 304, 312, 316, 323–324, 389, 411, 421, 444–445, 455; *Week on the Concord and Merrimack Rivers,* 2, 4, 8, 10, 12–13, 17, 19, 26, 27, 29–31, 34, 42, 47–48, 51, 58, 72–73, 126, 152, 155, 170, 182, 206–207, 211, 226, 234, 290, 315, 357

—correspondence: from, 3, 24–25, 31–33, 67, 71–72, 74, 113, 180, 201, 206, 215, 261, 284, 297, 311, 329, 340, 370, 381, 399–400, 450, 456; to, 6, 42–43

—essays: "Autumnal Tints," 158, 212; "Chastity and Sensuality," 65; "Chesuncook," 118, 221, 233, 370; "Civil Disobedience" ("Resistance to Civil Government"), 15, 29, 184, 347; "Ktaadn," 14, 64, 152, 175, 448; "Laws of Menu," 124; "Life Without Principle," 24, 57, 100, 143, 186, 234, 279, 370, 446; "Natural History of Massachusetts," 46, 108, 206, 261, 395; "Paradise (to be) Regained," 64; "Service," 17, 115; "Slavery in Massachusetts," 29, 64, 227; "Succession of Forest Trees," 258, 328, 432, 451; "Thomas Carlyle and His Works," 4; "Walking," 14,

Thoreau, Henry David (continued)
27, 43, 59, 80, 83, 232, 234, 268, 313, 367;
"Winter Walk," 401; "Yankee in Canada," 166
—journal, 1, 16, 22, 32–33, 60, 62, 109, 113,
125, 127, 128–129, 138, 157, 193, 206, 238,
252, 257, 267, 328, 336, 381, 421–422, 432,
450, 456
—lectures: "Autumnal Tints," 298, 385;
"Huckleberries," 77, 401, 432, 450;
"Journey to Moose Head Lake," 215;
"Society," 5–7; "Succession of Forest
Trees," 432; "Walking," 215, 297; "What
Shall It Profit?" 234, 239; "Wild," 215,
232; "Wild Apples," 5
—notebooks: commonplace, 154, 160;
field, 22, 111, 241; Indian, 389
—poems: "Any fool can make a rule," 379;
"Cliffs," 8; "Forever in my dream," 342;
"Love," 10; "Man, man is the devil," 172;
"Old Marlborough Road," 415; "Thaw,"
10; "Wachusett," 27–28
Thoreau, Jane (aunt), 184–185
Thoreau, Jean (grandfather), 288
Thoreau, John, Sr. (father), 28, 31, 261,
269–273, 288, 381–382, 393
Thoreau, John, Jr. (brother), 28, 30, 31, 103
Thoreau, Maria (aunt), 184–185
Thoreau, Sophia (sister), 35, 65, 74, 107,
128, 202–203, 285, 290, 456
thought, 57, 65, 80–81, 83–84, 91, 99, 107,
127–128, 138, 160, 167, 180, 193, 226–227,
245, 285, 322, 326–327, 340–342, 347,
351, 357, 374, 408
thrasher, brown, 265–266
thrush, 258, 265; wood-thrush (hermit
thrush), 49, 153–154, 192–193, 218, 280,
355

thunder, 273, 314, 318–320, 389, 421
thunderbolt. *See* lightning
Titans (Greek mythology), 150
toads, 70, 124, 148, 204–205
"Tom Bowling" (song), 43, 320
Topsell, Edward, 423–425
tortoise, 266, 267, 274–275, 350, 451
Town and Country Club, 302
township, natural features of, 184, 256, 278,
447
tracks and tracking, 95, 118, 177, 216–217,
219, 235, 253–254, 270–274, 373, 391, 420
trade, 203–204, 221, 244, 354, 392
transcendence, 40, 65, 120, 136, 137, 387
Transcendentalism and Transcendentalists,
33, 67, 181, 239, 250, 328, 422
trappers and trapping, 111, 221, 247, 393,
444
travel and travelers, 3, 26, 39, 59, 62, 65–
66, 68, 71, 73, 79–81, 84, 86, 89, 95, 100,
121–122, 133, 135, 168–169, 175, 180, 181,
183–184, 210, 217, 224, 235, 249, 253, 256,
259–260, 266, 272, 274, 277, 282, 295,
304–305, 307, 313, 321, 324, 345–346,
357–360, 362, 365, 388, 397, 402, 420,
423, 433, 444, 451
Tree of Knowledge, 328
trees, 27, 29, 50, 57, 80, 87, 102, 106, 124,
131–132, 134, 144, 147–148, 151, 177, 208,
242, 244, 251–252, 262, 264, 290, 302–
303, 311, 318, 322, 326, 331, 340, 351, 373,
379–380, 396, 402, 409, 423, 431, 438–
439, 447, 450, 452–454. *See also names of
specific trees*
Trench, Richard Chenevix, 218; on "rivals,"
174; on "wild," 179
Trojan War, 8, 366, 399
tropes, 186

Wright, H. C., 190–191

writers and writing, 3, 25, 30, 33, 42, 72–73, 91–92, 96, 111–112, 117, 127, 161, 207, 222, 224–225, 234, 236, 288, 293, 311, 336, 351, 353, 370, 376, 379, 392, 403, 439; Emerson's criticism of Thoreau's writing, 255. *See also* books; readers and reading

"Yankee in Canada, A" (Thoreau), 166

Zeus (Greek mythology), 150, 201, 354. *See also* Jove (Roman mythology)